24
15
31
17
7
9
18
23
16
8
14
3
6
4
12
36
32
5
22
2
35
10
33
11
1
13

Book 9 (9)	Book 10 (15, 14, 13)	Book 11 (16)	Book 11 (17)	Book 11 (18)	Book 12 (22, 21, 20, 19)	Book 13 (23)	Book 13 (24)
1920	1926	1938	1940	1942	1942	1944	1945

Volume 4 (35, 34)	Volume 5 (35, 34, 32)	Volume 6 (36)
2003	2003	2004

The Secret History

1. Genesis
2. The Castle of the Djinns
3. The Grail of Montségur
4. The Keys of Saint Peter
5. 1666
6. The Eagle and the Sphinx
7. Our Lady of the Shadows
8. Seven Pillars of Wisdom
9. The Thule Society
10. The Black Stone
11. Arcane 17
12. Lucky Point
13. Twilight of the Gods
14. The Watchers

Arcane Major

1. Pandora
2. The Yellow King
3. Cuba Libré!
4. J.F.K.
5. Lady Luck

Arcanes

1. The Phantom Baron
2. The Lady of Prague
3. The Karadine File
4. The Circle of Patmos, Part I
5. The Circle of Patmos, Part II
6. Bunker 73

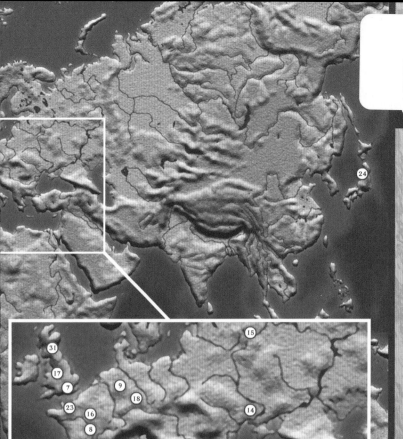

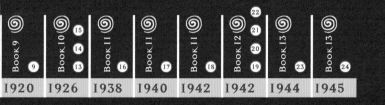

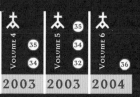

THE SECRET HISTORY

OMNIBUS

VOLUME TWO: *From 1918 to 1945*

THE CHALICE
DYO

THE LANCE
REKA

THE SWORD
AKER

THE SHIELD
ERLIN

THE FIFTH
WILLIAM

Written by **Jean-Pierre Pécau**
Illustrated by **Igor Kordey**
Colors by **Chris Chuckry**

Runestone Designed by **Fred Blanchard**
Cover by **Manchu & Olivier Vatine**
Translated by **Edward Gauvin**
Designed and Lettered by **Scott Newman**
Edited by **Rebecca Taylor**

Published by Archaia

Archaia Entertainment LLC
1680 Vine Street, Suite 912
Los Angeles, California, 90028, USA
www.archaia.com

Originally published in France by Delcourt

THE SECRET HISTORY OMNIBUS: VOLUME TWO

March 2011

FIRST PRINTING

10 9 8 7 6 5 4 3 2 1

ISBN: 1-932386-91-2

ISBN 13: 978-1-932386-91-2

ARCHAIA™   Printed in Korea.

Book Eight

Seven Pillars of Wisdom

1918 A.D.

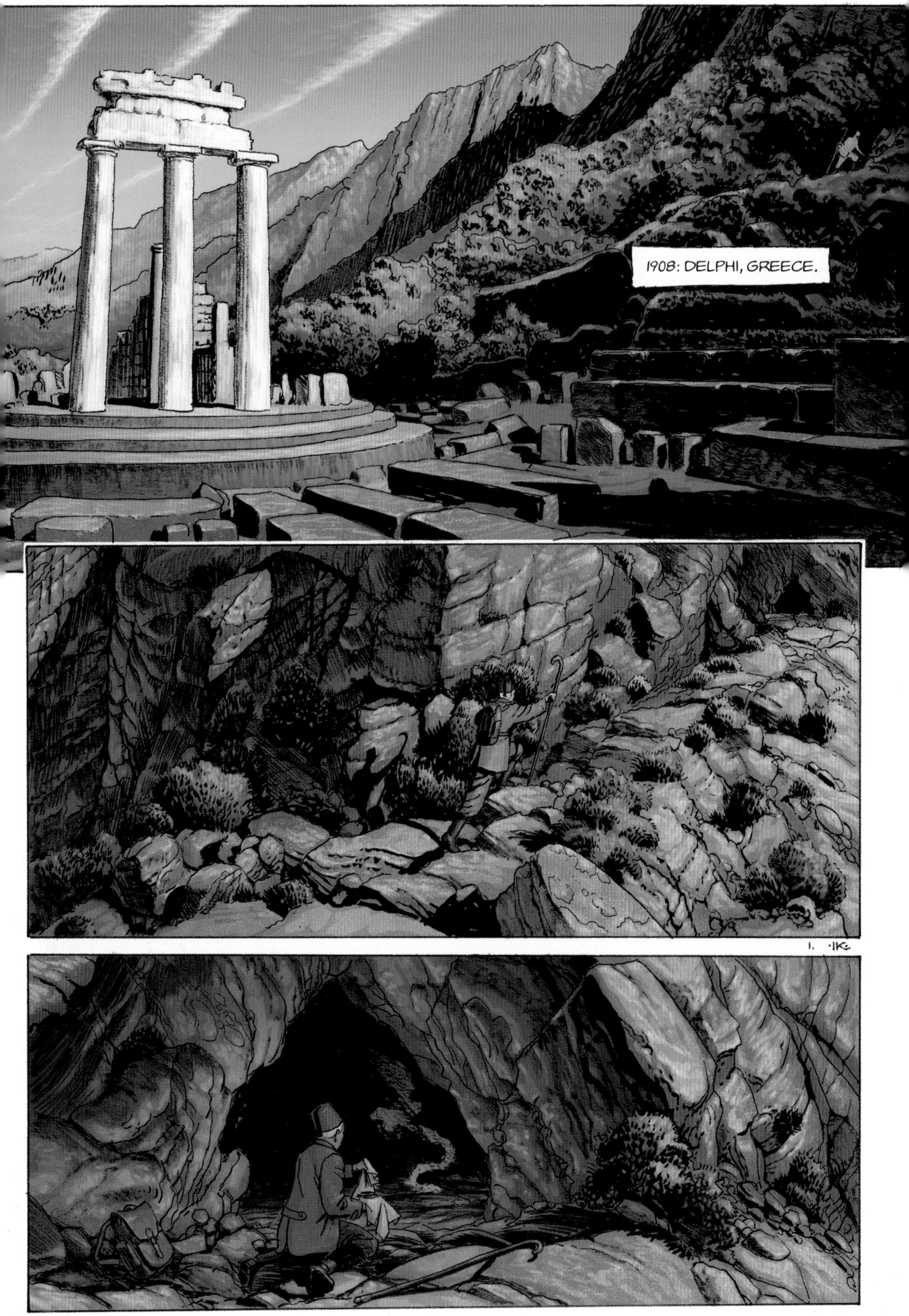
1908: DELPHI, GREECE.

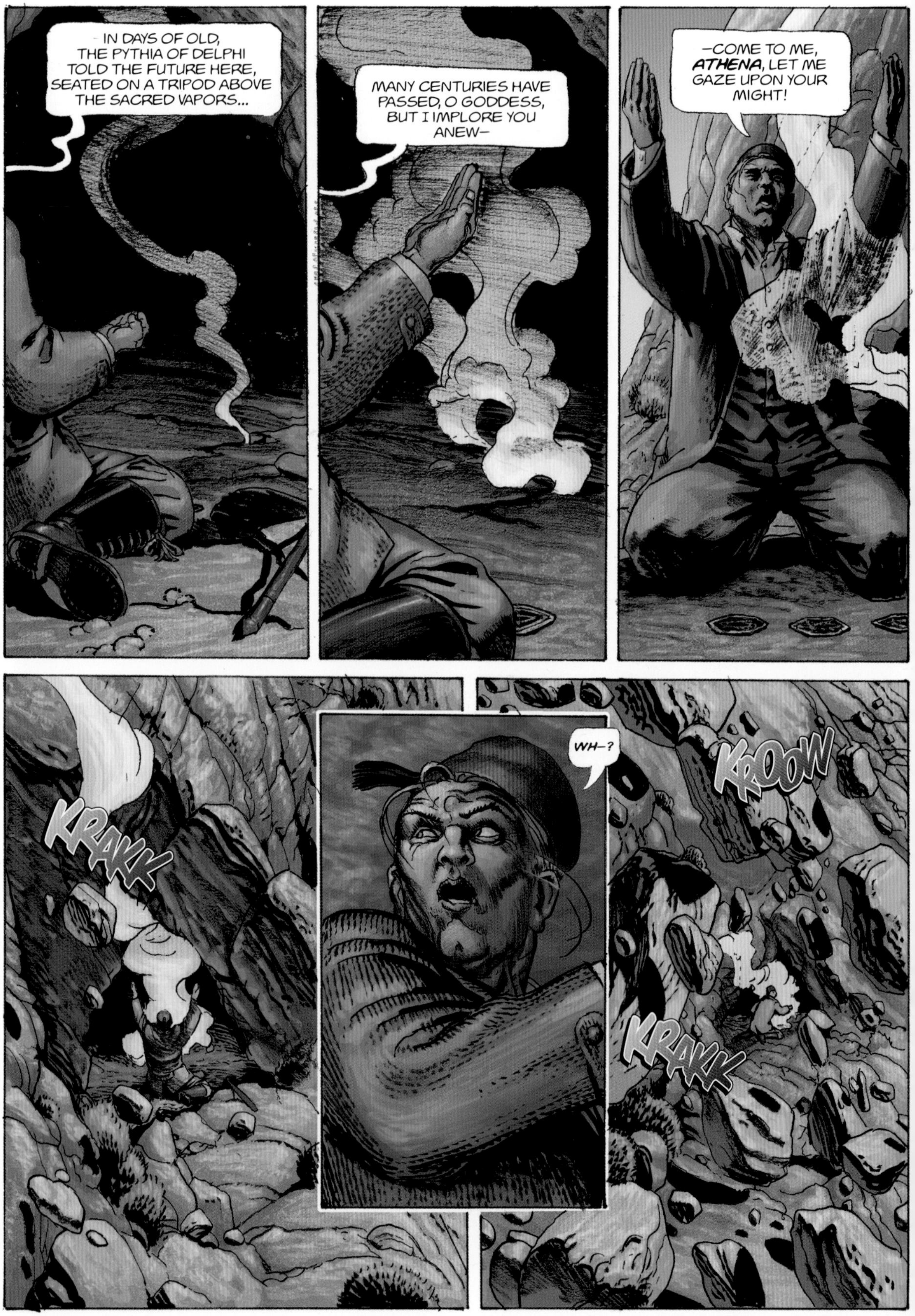
- IN DAYS OF OLD, THE PYTHIA OF DELPHI TOLD THE FUTURE HERE, SEATED ON A TRIPOD ABOVE THE SACRED VAPORS...
MANY CENTURIES HAVE PASSED, O GODDESS, BUT I IMPLORE YOU ANEW-
-COME TO ME, ATHENA, LET ME GAZE UPON YOUR MIGHT!
KRAKK
WH-?
KROOW
KRAKK

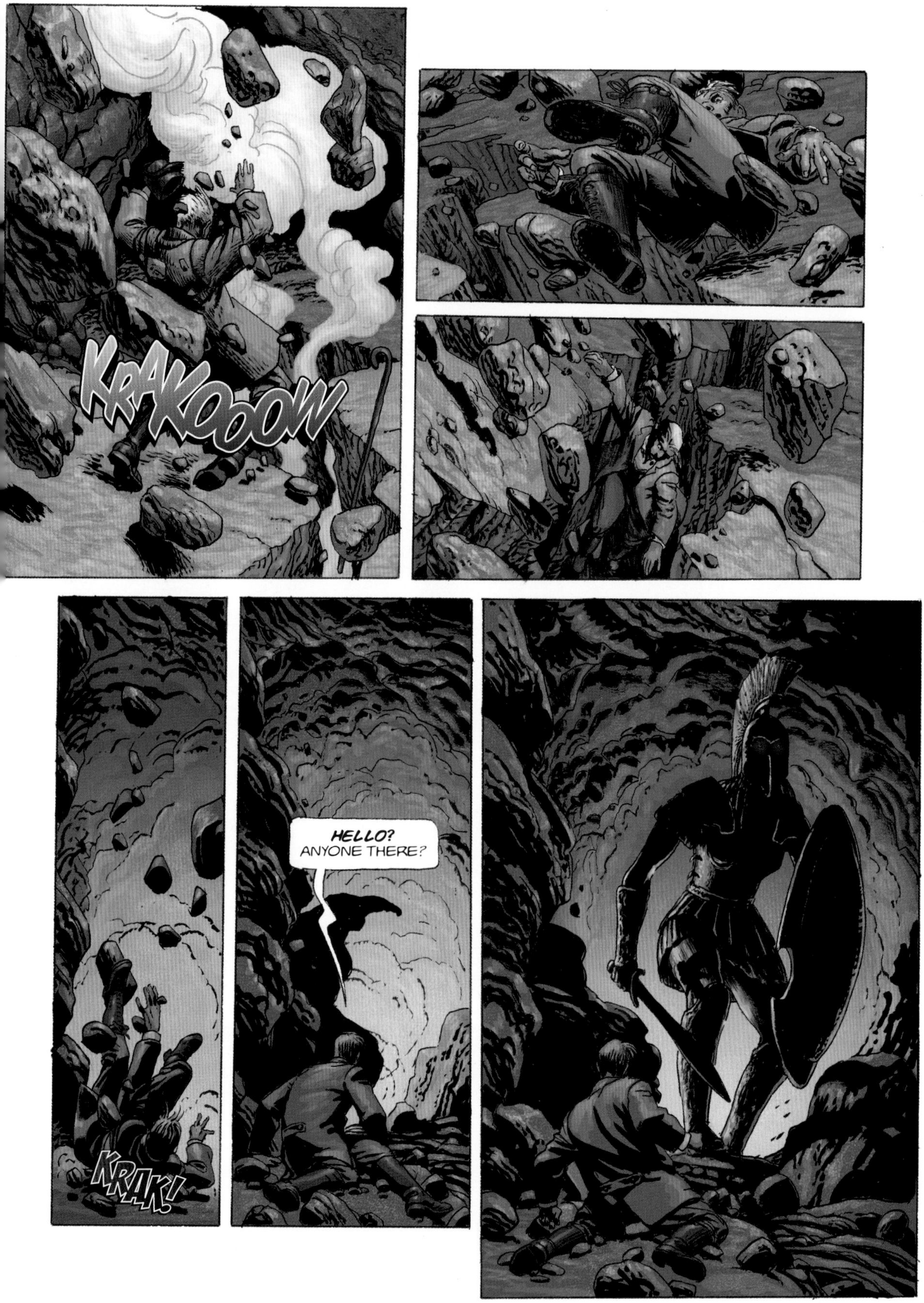
KRAKOOOW
KRAK!
HELLO? ANYONE THERE?

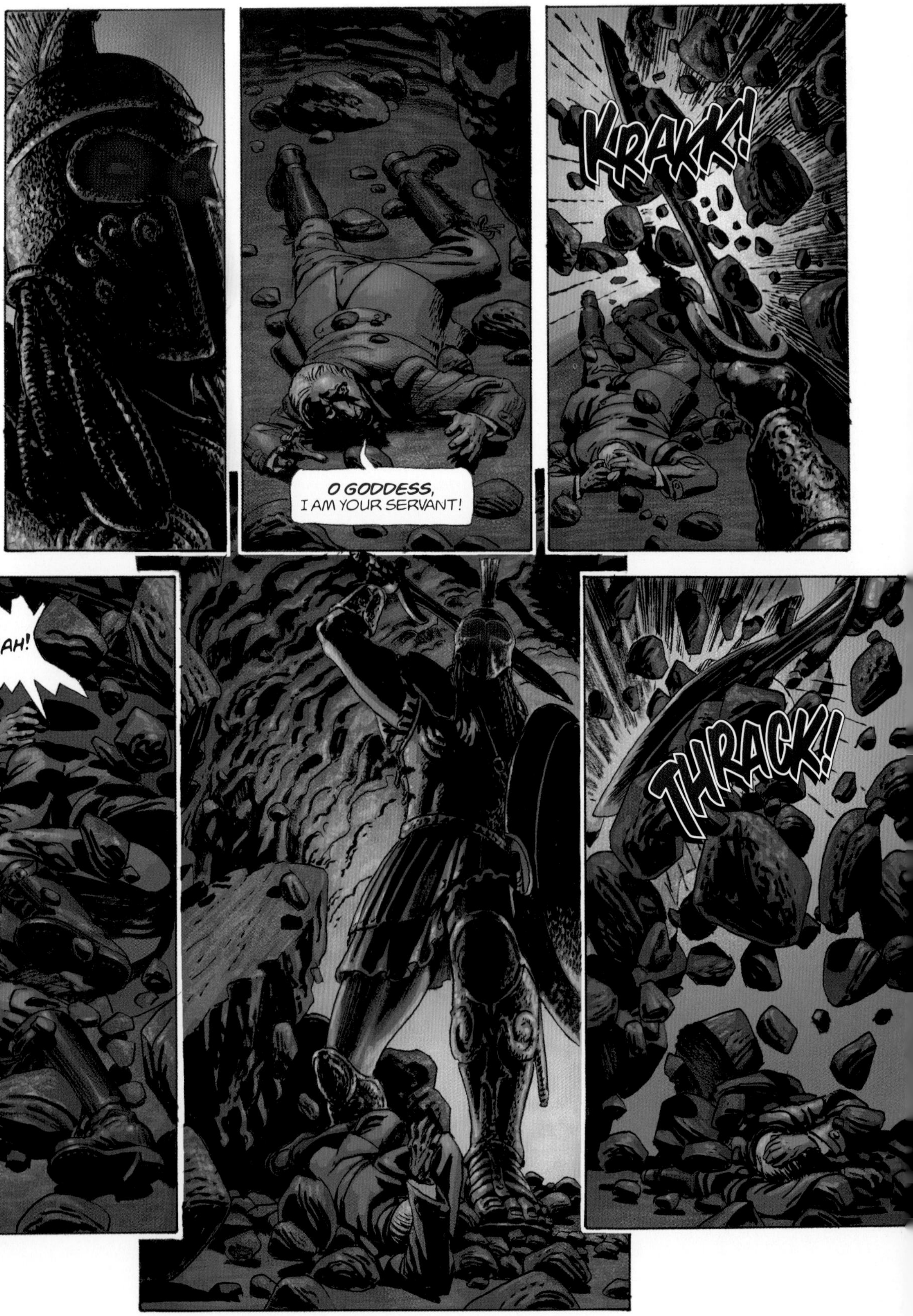
O GODDESS,
I AM YOUR SERVANT!
KRAKK!
AAAH!
THRACK!

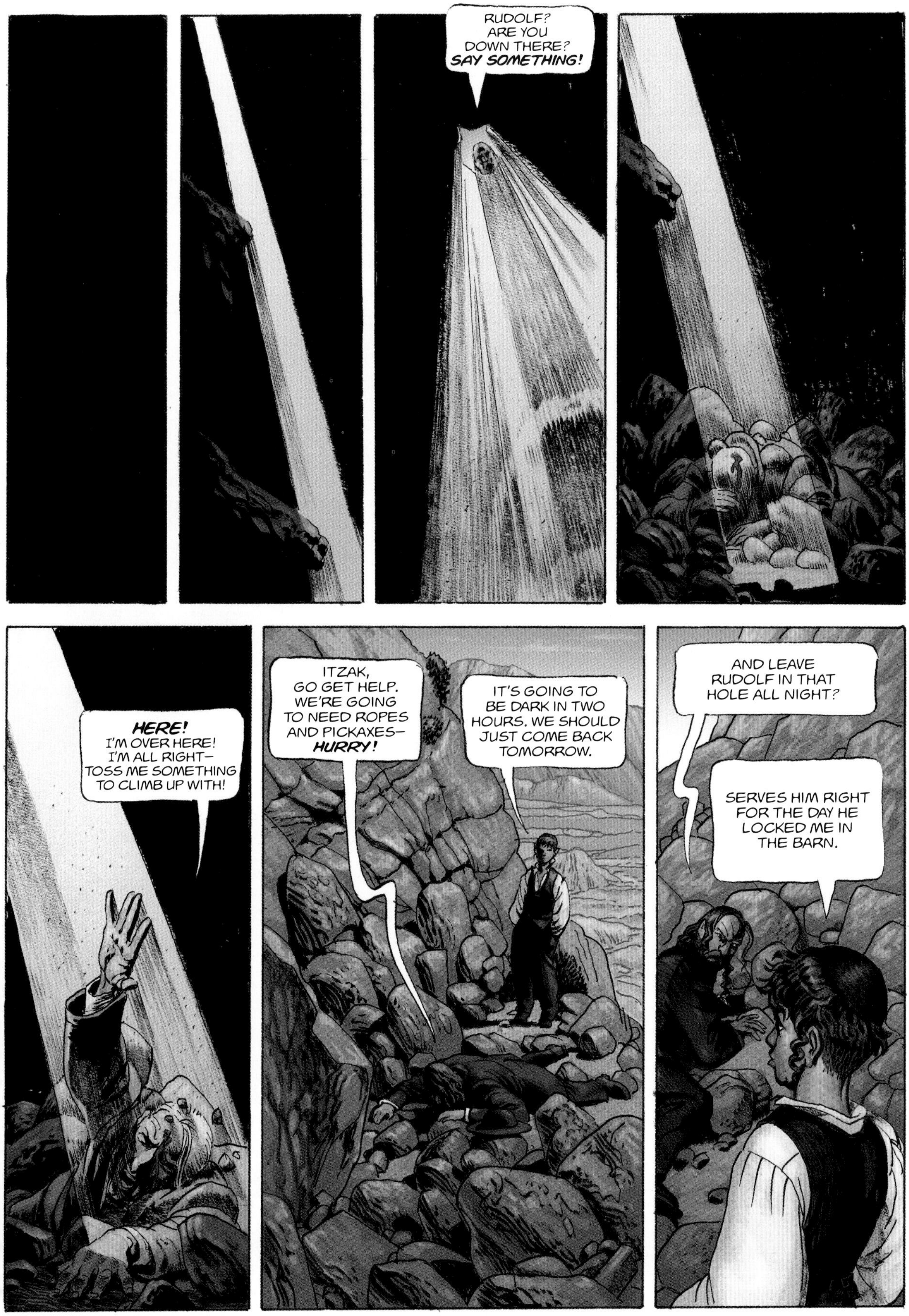
RUDOLF? ARE YOU DOWN THERE? SAY SOMETHING!
HERE! I'M OVER HERE! I'M ALL RIGHT– TOSS ME SOMETHING TO CLIMB UP WITH!
ITZAK, GO GET HELP. WE'RE GOING TO NEED ROPES AND PICKAXES– HURRY!
IT'S GOING TO BE DARK IN TWO HOURS. WE SHOULD JUST COME BACK TOMORROW.
AND LEAVE RUDOLF IN THAT HOLE ALL NIGHT?
SERVES HIM RIGHT FOR THE DAY HE LOCKED ME IN THE BARN.

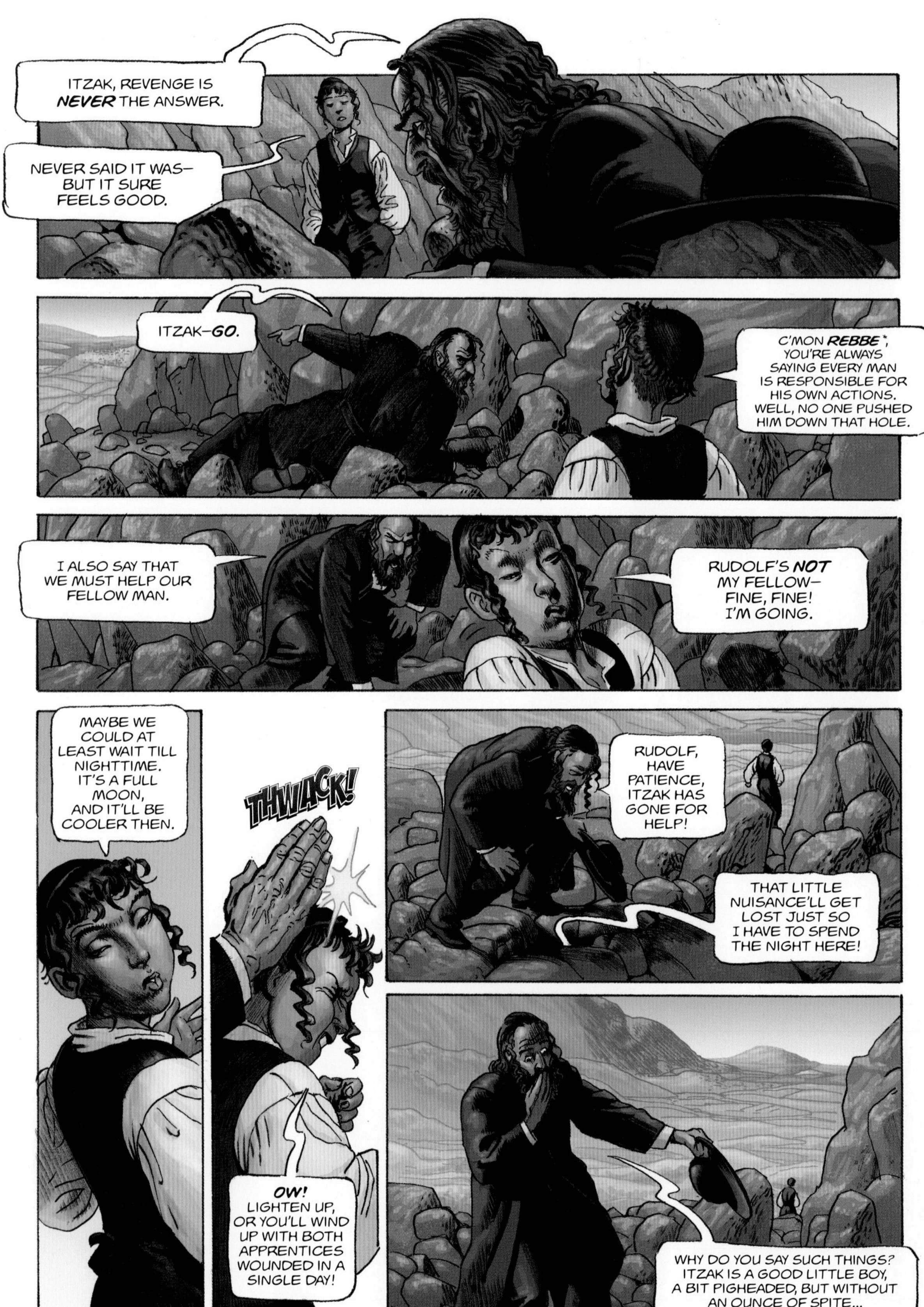
ITZAK, REVENGE IS NEVER THE ANSWER.
NEVER SAID IT WAS— BUT IT SURE FEELS GOOD.
ITZAK—GO.
C'MON REBBE*, YOU'RE ALWAYS SAYING EVERY MAN IS RESPONSIBLE FOR HIS OWN ACTIONS. WELL, NO ONE PUSHED HIM DOWN THAT HOLE.
I ALSO SAY THAT WE MUST HELP OUR FELLOW MAN.
RUDOLF'S NOT MY FELLOW— FINE, FINE! I'M GOING.
MAYBE WE COULD AT LEAST WAIT TILL NIGHTTIME. IT'S A FULL MOON, AND IT'LL BE COOLER THEN.
THWACK!
OW! LIGHTEN UP, OR YOU'LL WIND UP WITH BOTH APPRENTICES WOUNDED IN A SINGLE DAY!
RUDOLF, HAVE PATIENCE, ITZAK HAS GONE FOR HELP!
THAT LITTLE NUISANCE'LL GET LOST JUST SO I HAVE TO SPEND THE NIGHT HERE!
WHY DO YOU SAY SUCH THINGS? ITZAK IS A GOOD LITTLE BOY, A BIT PIGHEADED, BUT WITHOUT AN OUNCE OF SPITE... DID YOU HAPPEN TO OVERHEAR OUR CONVERSATION?

* REBBE: HASIDIC MASTER, TEACHER OF THE KABBALAH.

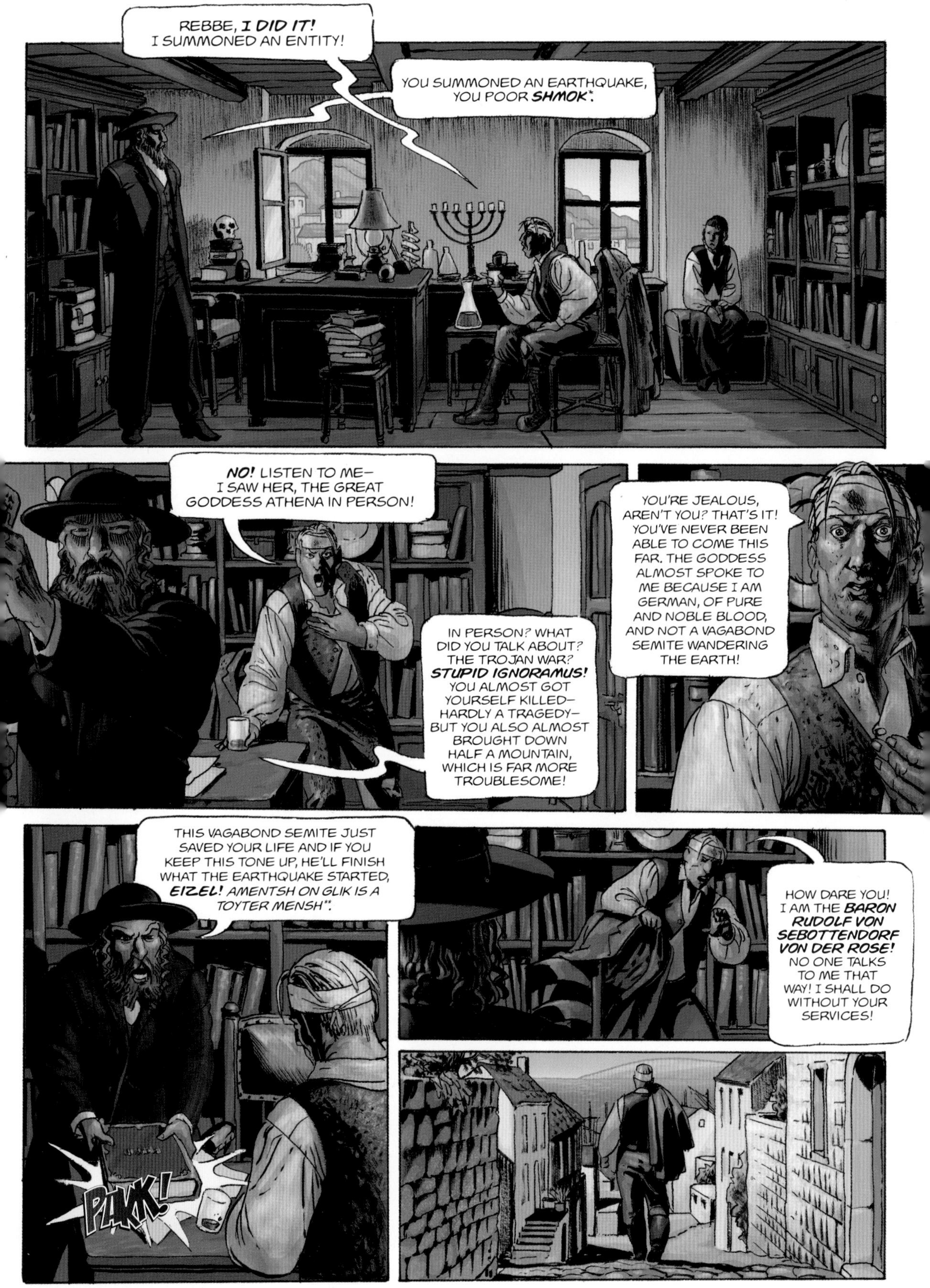
REBBE, I DID IT! I SUMMONED AN ENTITY!
YOU SUMMONED AN EARTHQUAKE, YOU POOR SHMOK*.
NO! LISTEN TO ME— I SAW HER, THE GREAT GODDESS ATHENA IN PERSON!
IN PERSON? WHAT DID YOU TALK ABOUT? THE TROJAN WAR? STUPID IGNORAMUS! YOU ALMOST GOT YOURSELF KILLED— HARDLY A TRAGEDY— BUT YOU ALSO ALMOST BROUGHT DOWN HALF A MOUNTAIN, WHICH IS FAR MORE TROUBLESOME!
YOU'RE JEALOUS, AREN'T YOU? THAT'S IT! YOU'VE NEVER BEEN ABLE TO COME THIS FAR. THE GODDESS ALMOST SPOKE TO ME BECAUSE I AM GERMAN, OF PURE AND NOBLE BLOOD, AND NOT A VAGABOND SEMITE WANDERING THE EARTH!
THIS VAGABOND SEMITE JUST SAVED YOUR LIFE AND IF YOU KEEP THIS TONE UP, HE'LL FINISH WHAT THE EARTHQUAKE STARTED, EIZEL! AMENTSH ON GLIK IS A TOYTER MENSH**.
PAKK!
HOW DARE YOU! I AM THE BARON RUDOLF VON SEBOTTENDORF VON DER ROSE! NO ONE TALKS TO ME THAT WAY! I SHALL DO WITHOUT YOUR SERVICES!

* SHMOK: IMBECILE.
** EIZEL, ETC.: "ASS! AN UNLUCKY MAN IS A DEAD MAN!"

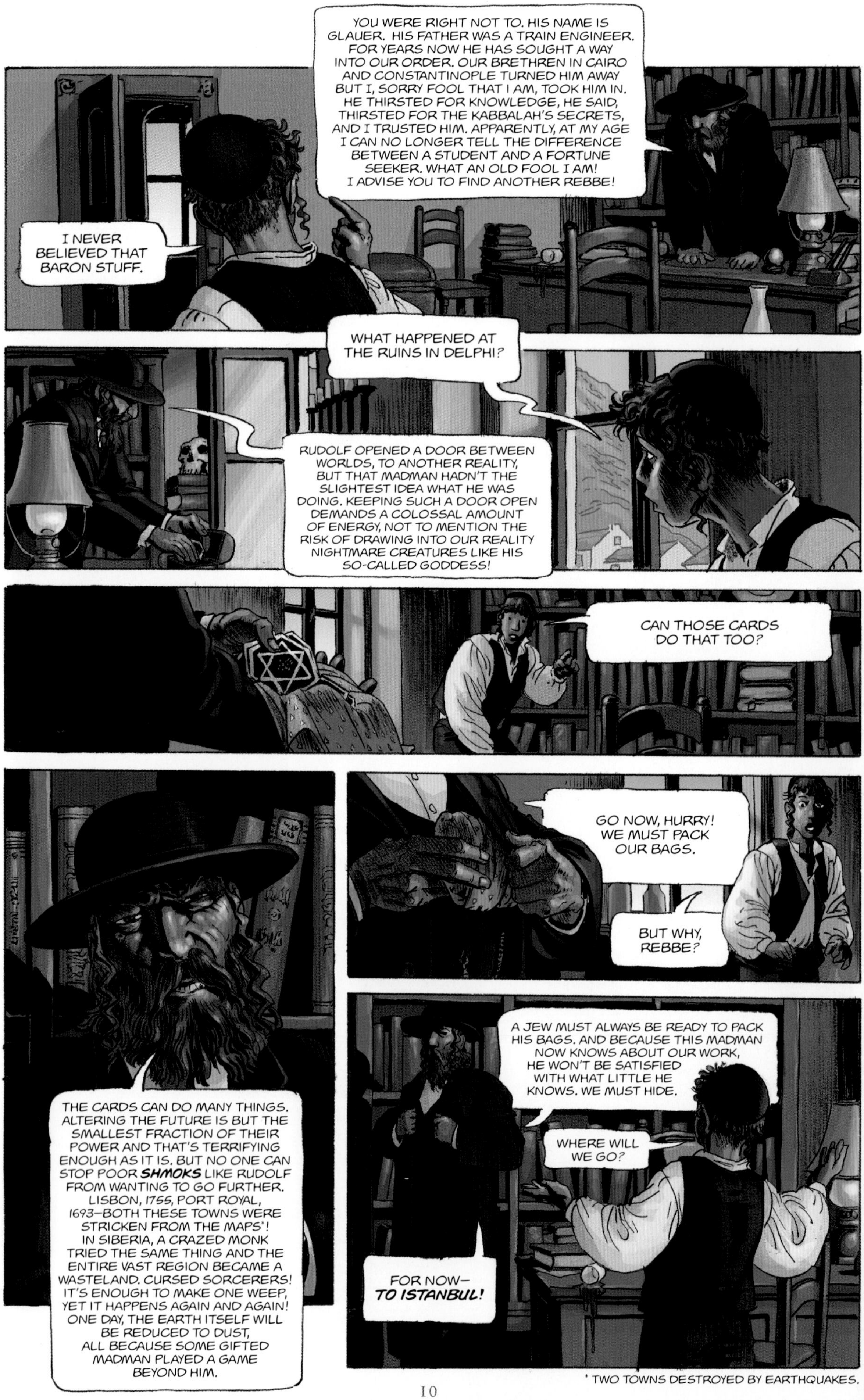

YOU WERE RIGHT NOT TO. HIS NAME IS GLAUER. HIS FATHER WAS A TRAIN ENGINEER. FOR YEARS NOW HE HAS SOUGHT A WAY INTO OUR ORDER. OUR BRETHREN IN CAIRO AND CONSTANTINOPLE TURNED HIM AWAY BUT I, SORRY FOOL THAT I AM, TOOK HIM IN. HE THIRSTED FOR KNOWLEDGE, HE SAID, THIRSTED FOR THE KABBALAH'S SECRETS, AND I TRUSTED HIM. APPARENTLY, AT MY AGE I CAN NO LONGER TELL THE DIFFERENCE BETWEEN A STUDENT AND A FORTUNE SEEKER. WHAT AN OLD FOOL I AM! I ADVISE YOU TO FIND ANOTHER REBBE!
I NEVER BELIEVED THAT BARON STUFF.
WHAT HAPPENED AT THE RUINS IN DELPHI?
RUDOLF OPENED A DOOR BETWEEN WORLDS, TO ANOTHER REALITY, BUT THAT MADMAN HADN'T THE SLIGHTEST IDEA WHAT HE WAS DOING. KEEPING SUCH A DOOR OPEN DEMANDS A COLOSSAL AMOUNT OF ENERGY, NOT TO MENTION THE RISK OF DRAWING INTO OUR REALITY NIGHTMARE CREATURES LIKE HIS SO-CALLED GODDESS!
CAN THOSE CARDS DO THAT TOO?
THE CARDS CAN DO MANY THINGS. ALTERING THE FUTURE IS BUT THE SMALLEST FRACTION OF THEIR POWER AND THAT'S TERRIFYING ENOUGH AS IT IS. BUT NO ONE CAN STOP POOR **SHMOKS** LIKE RUDOLF FROM WANTING TO GO FURTHER. LISBON, 1755, PORT ROYAL, 1693—BOTH THESE TOWNS WERE STRICKEN FROM THE MAPS*! IN SIBERIA, A CRAZED MONK TRIED THE SAME THING AND THE ENTIRE VAST REGION BECAME A WASTELAND. CURSED SORCERERS! IT'S ENOUGH TO MAKE ONE WEEP, YET IT HAPPENS AGAIN AND AGAIN! ONE DAY, THE EARTH ITSELF WILL BE REDUCED TO DUST, ALL BECAUSE SOME GIFTED MADMAN PLAYED A GAME BEYOND HIM.
GO NOW, HURRY! WE MUST PACK OUR BAGS.
BUT WHY, REBBE?
A JEW MUST ALWAYS BE READY TO PACK HIS BAGS. AND BECAUSE THIS MADMAN NOW KNOWS ABOUT OUR WORK, HE WON'T BE SATISFIED WITH WHAT LITTLE HE KNOWS. WE MUST HIDE.
WHERE WILL WE GO?
FOR NOW— **TO ISTANBUL!**

* TWO TOWNS DESTROYED BY EARTHQUAKES.

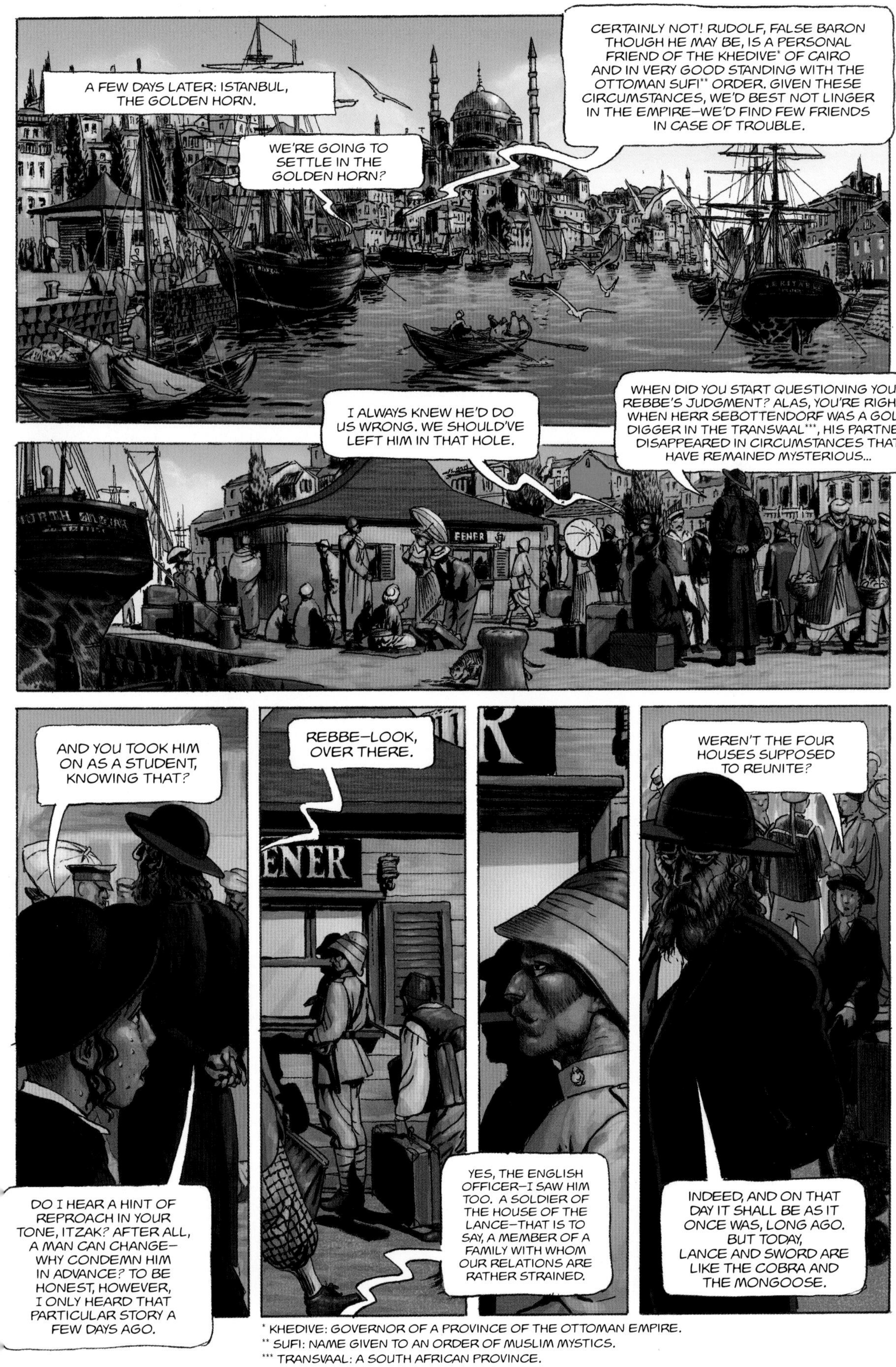
A FEW DAYS LATER: ISTANBUL, THE GOLDEN HORN.
WE'RE GOING TO SETTLE IN THE GOLDEN HORN?
CERTAINLY NOT! RUDOLF, FALSE BARON THOUGH HE MAY BE, IS A PERSONAL FRIEND OF THE KHEDIVE* OF CAIRO AND IN VERY GOOD STANDING WITH THE OTTOMAN SUFI** ORDER. GIVEN THESE CIRCUMSTANCES, WE'D BEST NOT LINGER IN THE EMPIRE–WE'D FIND FEW FRIENDS IN CASE OF TROUBLE.
I ALWAYS KNEW HE'D DO US WRONG. WE SHOULD'VE LEFT HIM IN THAT HOLE.
WHEN DID YOU START QUESTIONING YOUR REBBE'S JUDGMENT? ALAS, YOU'RE RIGHT– WHEN HERR SEBOTTENDORF WAS A GOLD DIGGER IN THE TRANSVAAL***, HIS PARTNER DISAPPEARED IN CIRCUMSTANCES THAT HAVE REMAINED MYSTERIOUS...
FENER
AND YOU TOOK HIM ON AS A STUDENT, KNOWING THAT?
DO I HEAR A HINT OF REPROACH IN YOUR TONE, ITZAK? AFTER ALL, A MAN CAN CHANGE– WHY CONDEMN HIM IN ADVANCE? TO BE HONEST, HOWEVER, I ONLY HEARD THAT PARTICULAR STORY A FEW DAYS AGO.
REBBE–LOOK, OVER THERE.
ENER
YES, THE ENGLISH OFFICER–I SAW HIM TOO. A SOLDIER OF THE HOUSE OF THE LANCE–THAT IS TO SAY, A MEMBER OF A FAMILY WITH WHOM OUR RELATIONS ARE RATHER STRAINED.
WEREN'T THE FOUR HOUSES SUPPOSED TO REUNITE?
INDEED, AND ON THAT DAY IT SHALL BE AS IT ONCE WAS, LONG AGO. BUT TODAY, LANCE AND SWORD ARE LIKE THE COBRA AND THE MONGOOSE.

* KHEDIVE: GOVERNOR OF A PROVINCE OF THE OTTOMAN EMPIRE.
** SUFI: NAME GIVEN TO AN ORDER OF MUSLIM MYSTICS.
*** TRANSVAAL: A SOUTH AFRICAN PROVINCE.

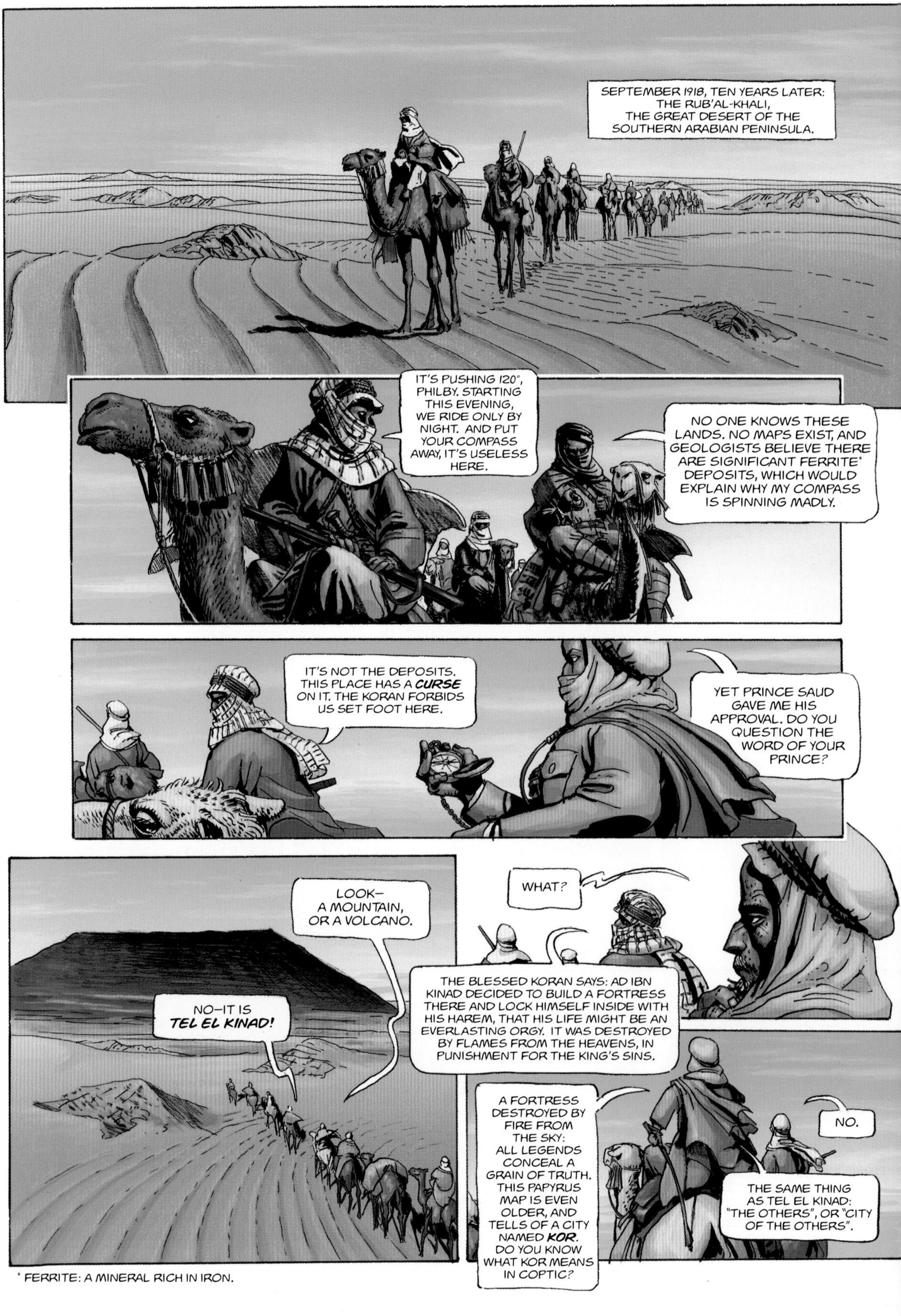
SEPTEMBER 1918, TEN YEARS LATER: THE RUB'AL-KHALI, THE GREAT DESERT OF THE SOUTHERN ARABIAN PENINSULA.
IT'S PUSHING 120°, PHILBY. STARTING THIS EVENING, WE RIDE ONLY BY NIGHT. AND PUT YOUR COMPASS AWAY, IT'S USELESS HERE.
NO ONE KNOWS THESE LANDS. NO MAPS EXIST, AND GEOLOGISTS BELIEVE THERE ARE SIGNIFICANT FERRITE* DEPOSITS, WHICH WOULD EXPLAIN WHY MY COMPASS IS SPINNING MADLY.
IT'S NOT THE DEPOSITS. THIS PLACE HAS A CURSE ON IT. THE KORAN FORBIDS US SET FOOT HERE.
YET PRINCE SAUD GAVE ME HIS APPROVAL. DO YOU QUESTION THE WORD OF YOUR PRINCE?
LOOK— A MOUNTAIN, OR A VOLCANO.
NO—IT IS TEL EL KINAD!
WHAT?
THE BLESSED KORAN SAYS: AD IBN KINAD DECIDED TO BUILD A FORTRESS THERE AND LOCK HIMSELF INSIDE WITH HIS HAREM, THAT HIS LIFE MIGHT BE AN EVERLASTING ORGY. IT WAS DESTROYED BY FLAMES FROM THE HEAVENS, IN PUNISHMENT FOR THE KING'S SINS.
A FORTRESS DESTROYED BY FIRE FROM THE SKY: ALL LEGENDS CONCEAL A GRAIN OF TRUTH. THIS PAPYRUS MAP IS EVEN OLDER, AND TELLS OF A CITY NAMED KOR. DO YOU KNOW WHAT KOR MEANS IN COPTIC?
NO.
THE SAME THING AS TEL EL KINAD: "THE OTHERS", OR "CITY OF THE OTHERS".

* FERRITE: A MINERAL RICH IN IRON.

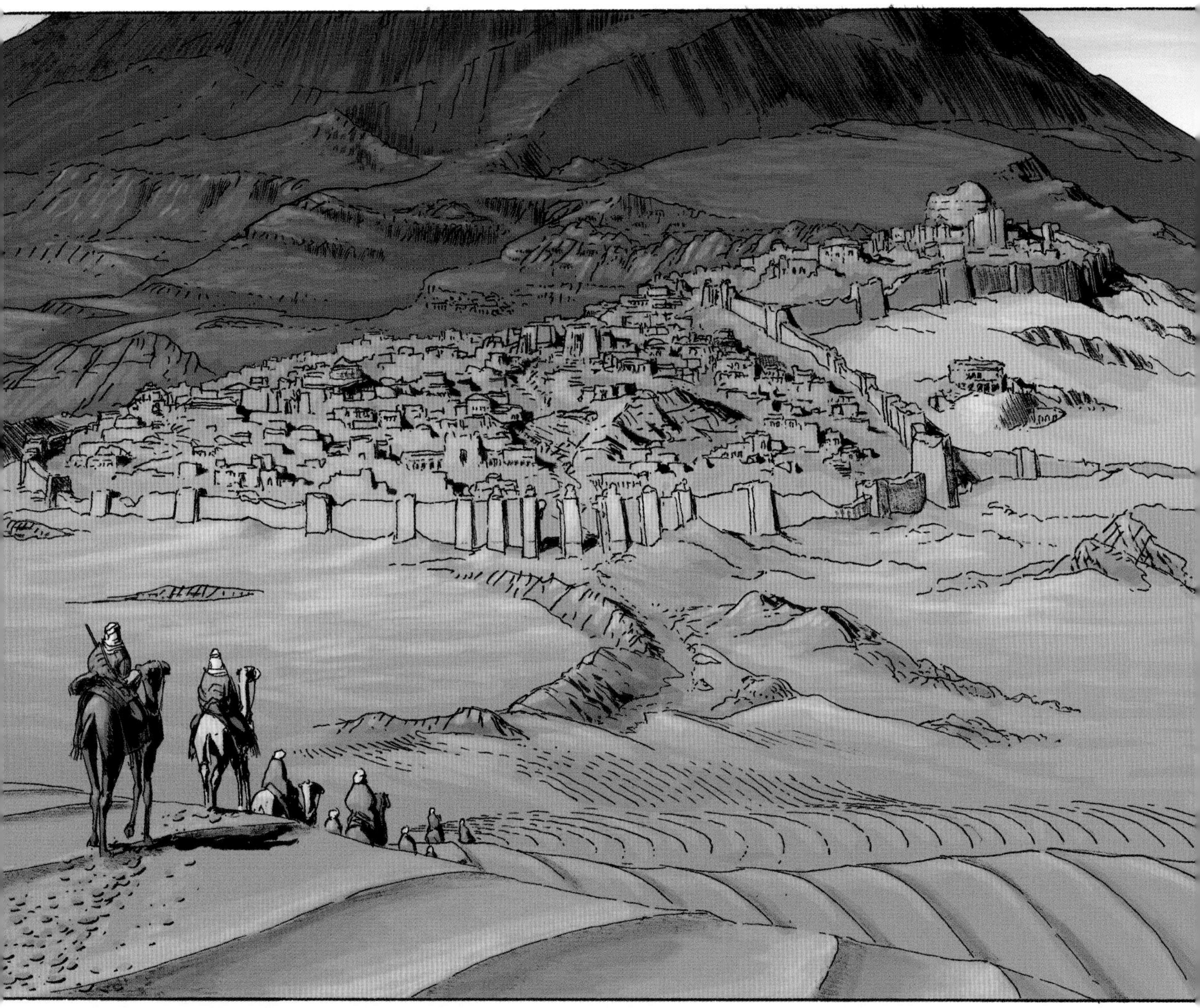

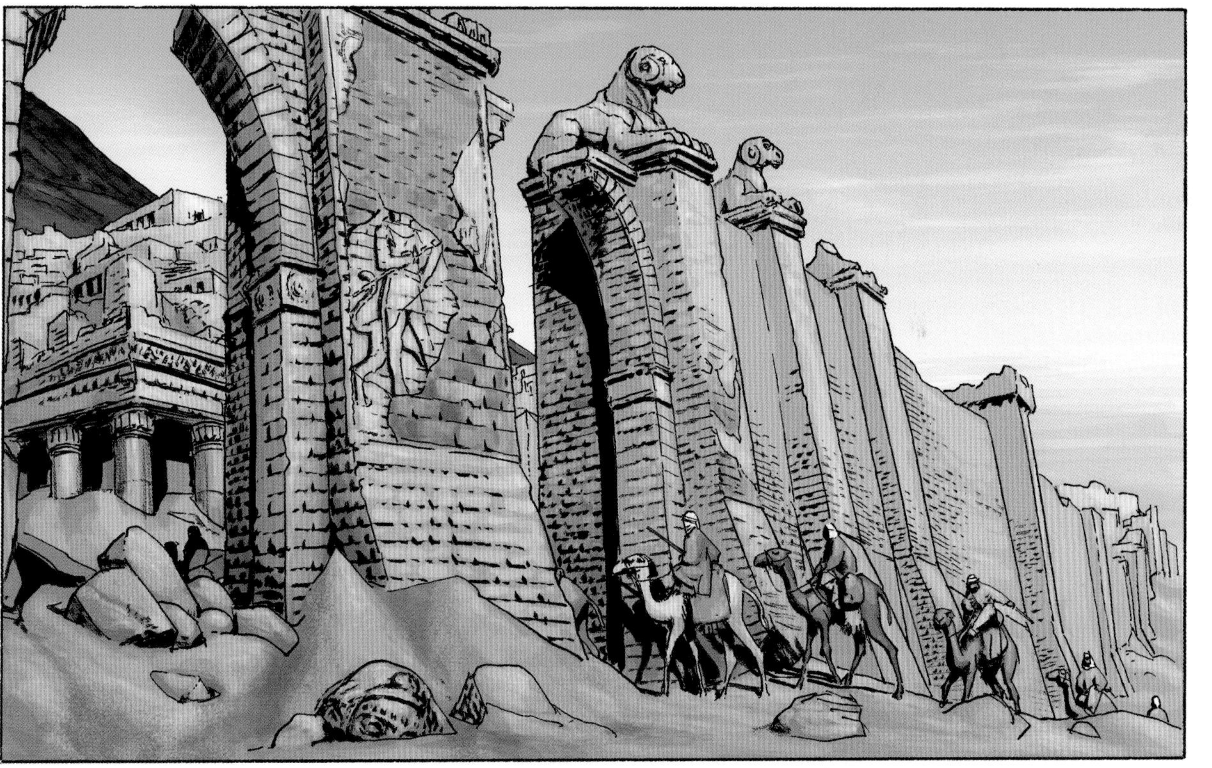

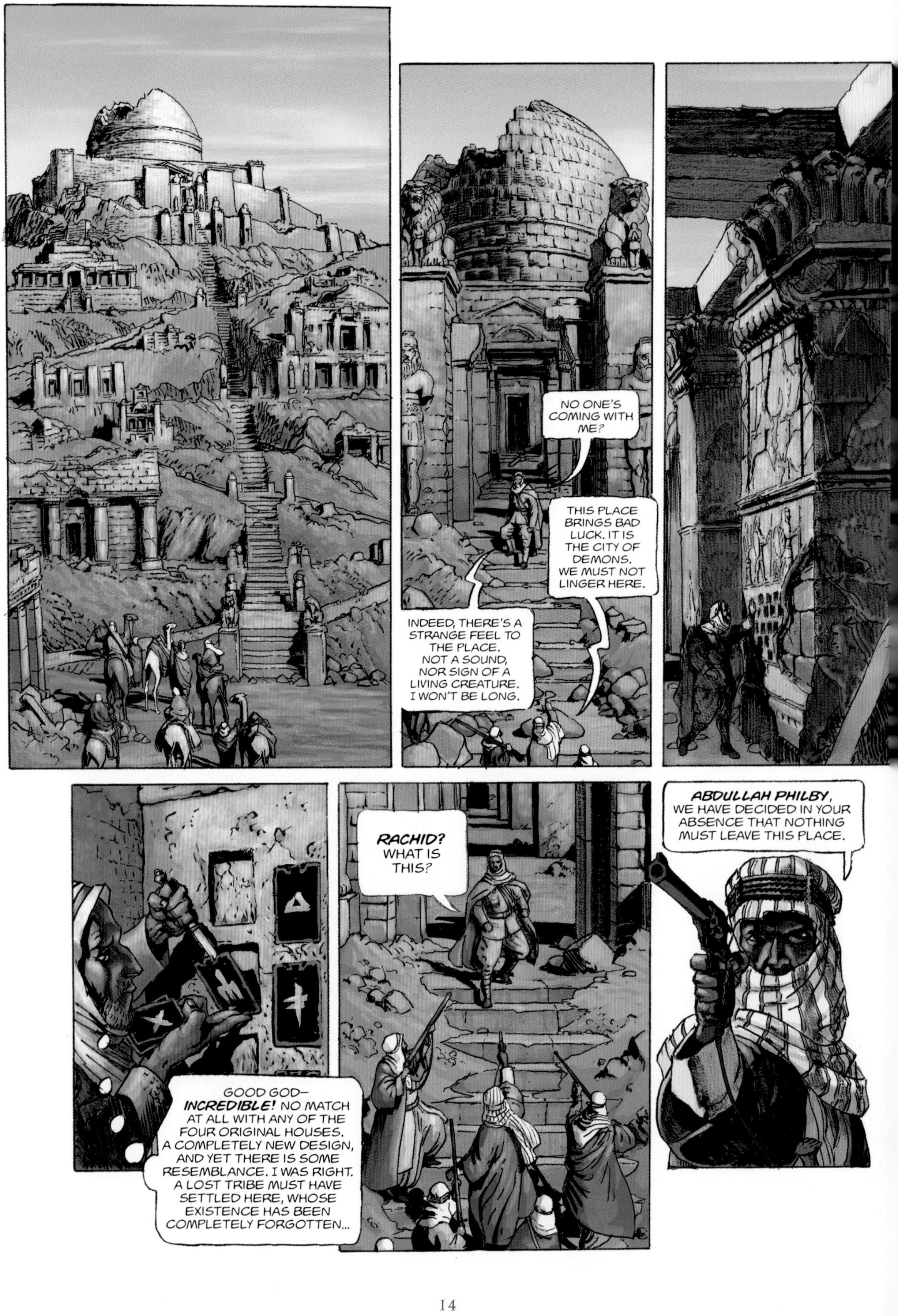

NO ONE'S COMING WITH ME?
THIS PLACE BRINGS BAD LUCK. IT IS THE CITY OF DEMONS. WE MUST NOT LINGER HERE.
INDEED, THERE'S A STRANGE FEEL TO THE PLACE. NOT A SOUND, NOR SIGN OF A LIVING CREATURE. I WON'T BE LONG.
GOOD GOD— INCREDIBLE! NO MATCH AT ALL WITH ANY OF THE FOUR ORIGINAL HOUSES. A COMPLETELY NEW DESIGN, AND YET THERE IS SOME RESEMBLANCE. I WAS RIGHT. A LOST TRIBE MUST HAVE SETTLED HERE, WHOSE EXISTENCE HAS BEEN COMPLETELY FORGOTTEN...
RACHID? WHAT IS THIS?
ABDULLAH PHILBY, WE HAVE DECIDED IN YOUR ABSENCE THAT NOTHING MUST LEAVE THIS PLACE.

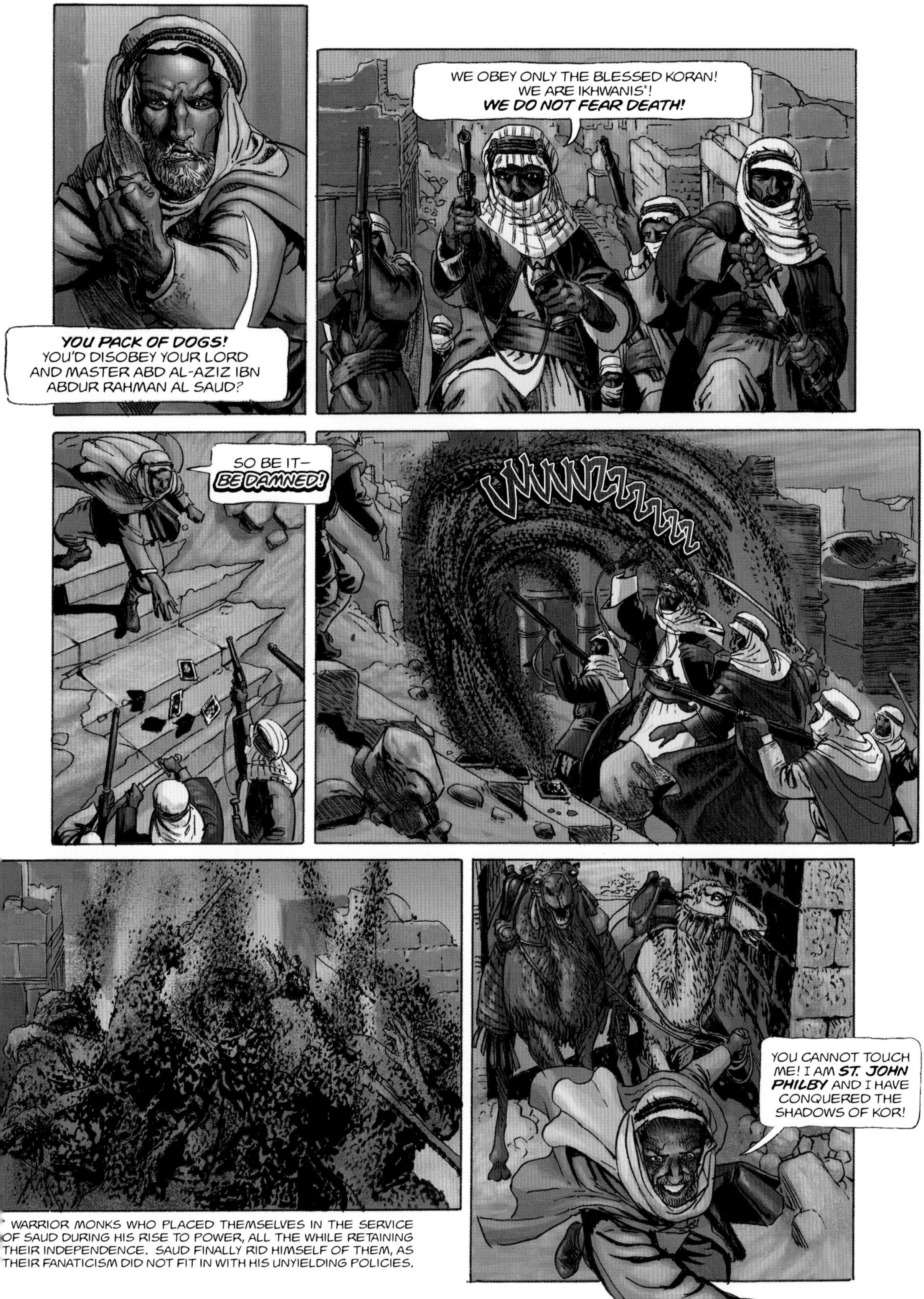
YOU PACK OF DOGS! YOU'D DISOBEY YOUR LORD AND MASTER ABD AL-AZIZ IBN ABDUR RAHMAN AL SAUD?
WE OBEY ONLY THE BLESSED KORAN! WE ARE IKHWANIS*! WE DO NOT FEAR DEATH!
SO BE IT— BE DAMNED!
YOU CANNOT TOUCH ME! I AM ST. JOHN PHILBY AND I HAVE CONQUERED THE SHADOWS OF KOR!

* WARRIOR MONKS WHO PLACED THEMSELVES IN THE SERVICE OF SAUD DURING HIS RISE TO POWER, ALL THE WHILE RETAINING THEIR INDEPENDENCE. SAUD FINALLY RID HIMSELF OF THEM, AS THEIR FANATICISM DID NOT FIT IN WITH HIS UNYIELDING POLICIES.

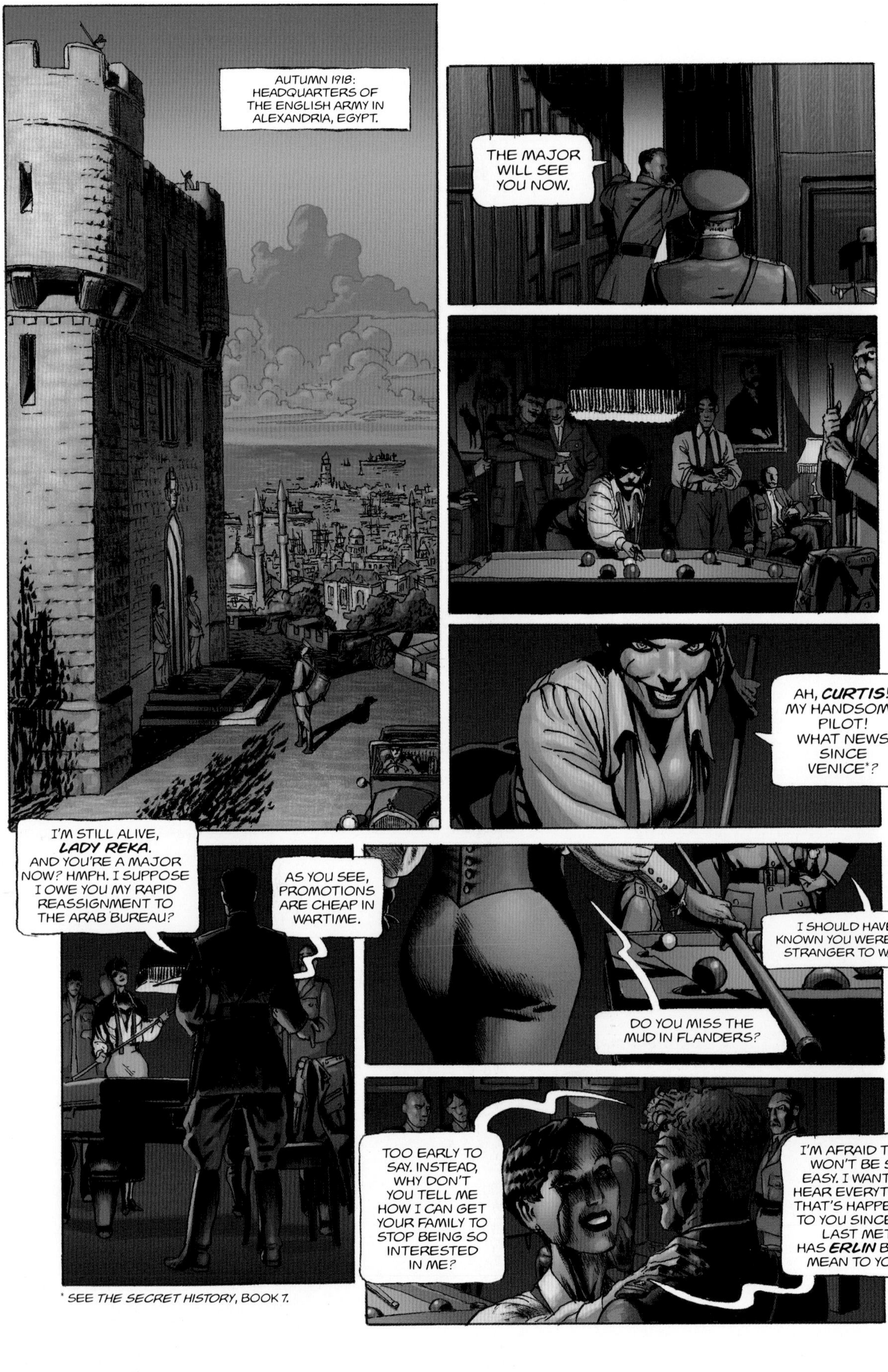
AUTUMN 1918: HEADQUARTERS OF THE ENGLISH ARMY IN ALEXANDRIA, EGYPT.
THE MAJOR WILL SEE YOU NOW.
AH, CURTIS! MY HANDSOME PILOT! WHAT NEWS SINCE VENICE*?
I'M STILL ALIVE, LADY REKA. AND YOU'RE A MAJOR NOW? HMPH. I SUPPOSE I OWE YOU MY RAPID REASSIGNMENT TO THE ARAB BUREAU?
AS YOU SEE, PROMOTIONS ARE CHEAP IN WARTIME.
I SHOULD HAVE KNOWN YOU WERE NO STRANGER TO WAR.
DO YOU MISS THE MUD IN FLANDERS?
TOO EARLY TO SAY. INSTEAD, WHY DON'T YOU TELL ME HOW I CAN GET YOUR FAMILY TO STOP BEING SO INTERESTED IN ME?
I'M AFRAID THAT WON'T BE SO EASY. I WANT TO HEAR EVERYTHING THAT'S HAPPENED TO YOU SINCE WE LAST MET. HAS ERLIN BEEN MEAN TO YOU?

* SEE *THE SECRET HISTORY*, BOOK 7.

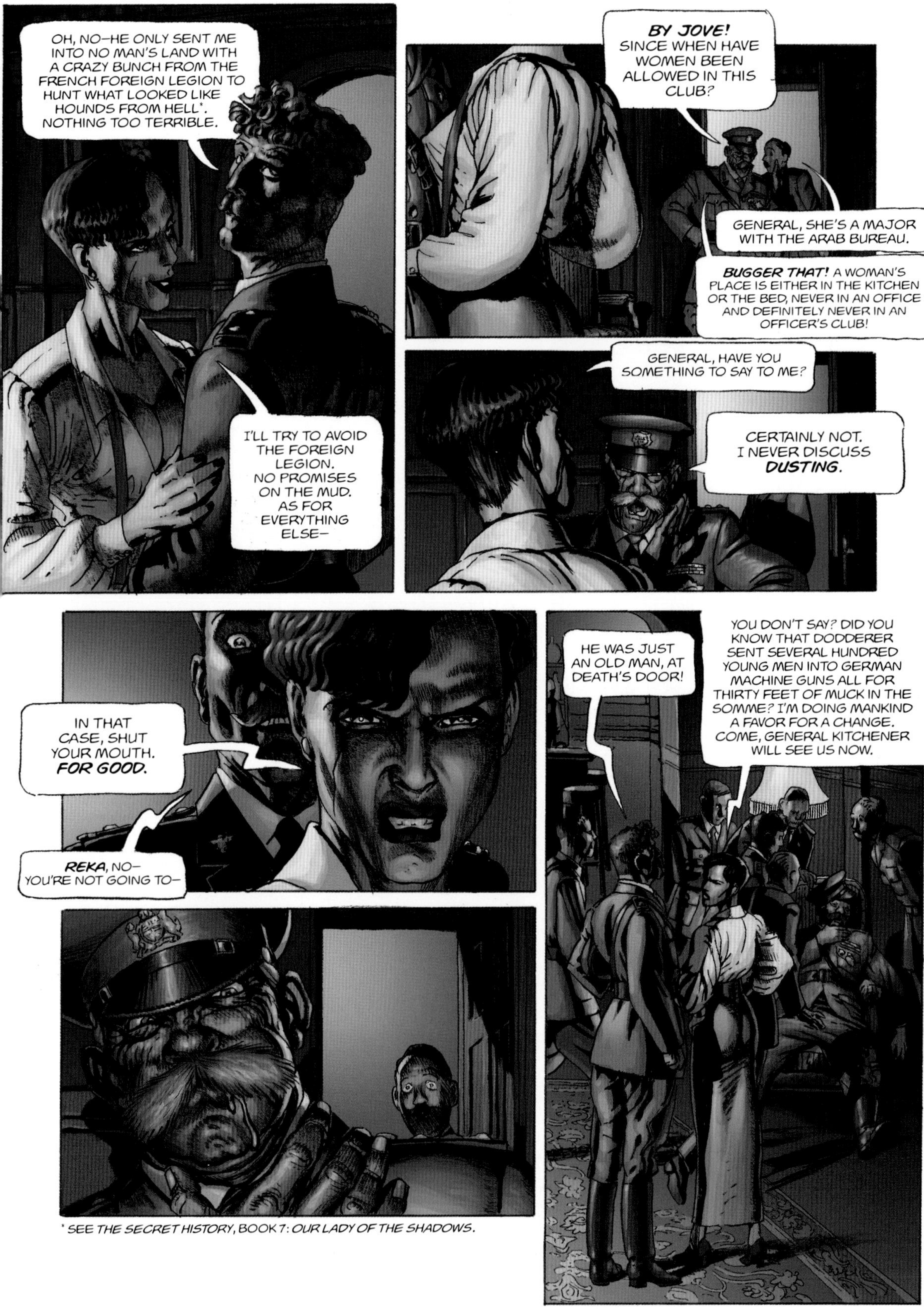
OH, NO—HE ONLY SENT ME INTO NO MAN'S LAND WITH A CRAZY BUNCH FROM THE FRENCH FOREIGN LEGION TO HUNT WHAT LOOKED LIKE HOUNDS FROM HELL*. NOTHING TOO TERRIBLE.
I'LL TRY TO AVOID THE FOREIGN LEGION. NO PROMISES ON THE MUD. AS FOR EVERYTHING ELSE—
BY JOVE! SINCE WHEN HAVE WOMEN BEEN ALLOWED IN THIS CLUB?
GENERAL, SHE'S A MAJOR WITH THE ARAB BUREAU.
BUGGER THAT! A WOMAN'S PLACE IS EITHER IN THE KITCHEN OR THE BED, NEVER IN AN OFFICE AND DEFINITELY NEVER IN AN OFFICER'S CLUB!
GENERAL, HAVE YOU SOMETHING TO SAY TO ME?
CERTAINLY NOT. I NEVER DISCUSS DUSTING.
IN THAT CASE, SHUT YOUR MOUTH. FOR GOOD.
REKA, NO— YOU'RE NOT GOING TO—
HE WAS JUST AN OLD MAN, AT DEATH'S DOOR!
YOU DON'T SAY? DID YOU KNOW THAT DODDERER SENT SEVERAL HUNDRED YOUNG MEN INTO GERMAN MACHINE GUNS ALL FOR THIRTY FEET OF MUCK IN THE SOMME? I'M DOING MANKIND A FAVOR FOR A CHANGE. COME, GENERAL KITCHENER WILL SEE US NOW.

* SEE *THE SECRET HISTORY*, BOOK 7: *OUR LADY OF THE SHADOWS*.

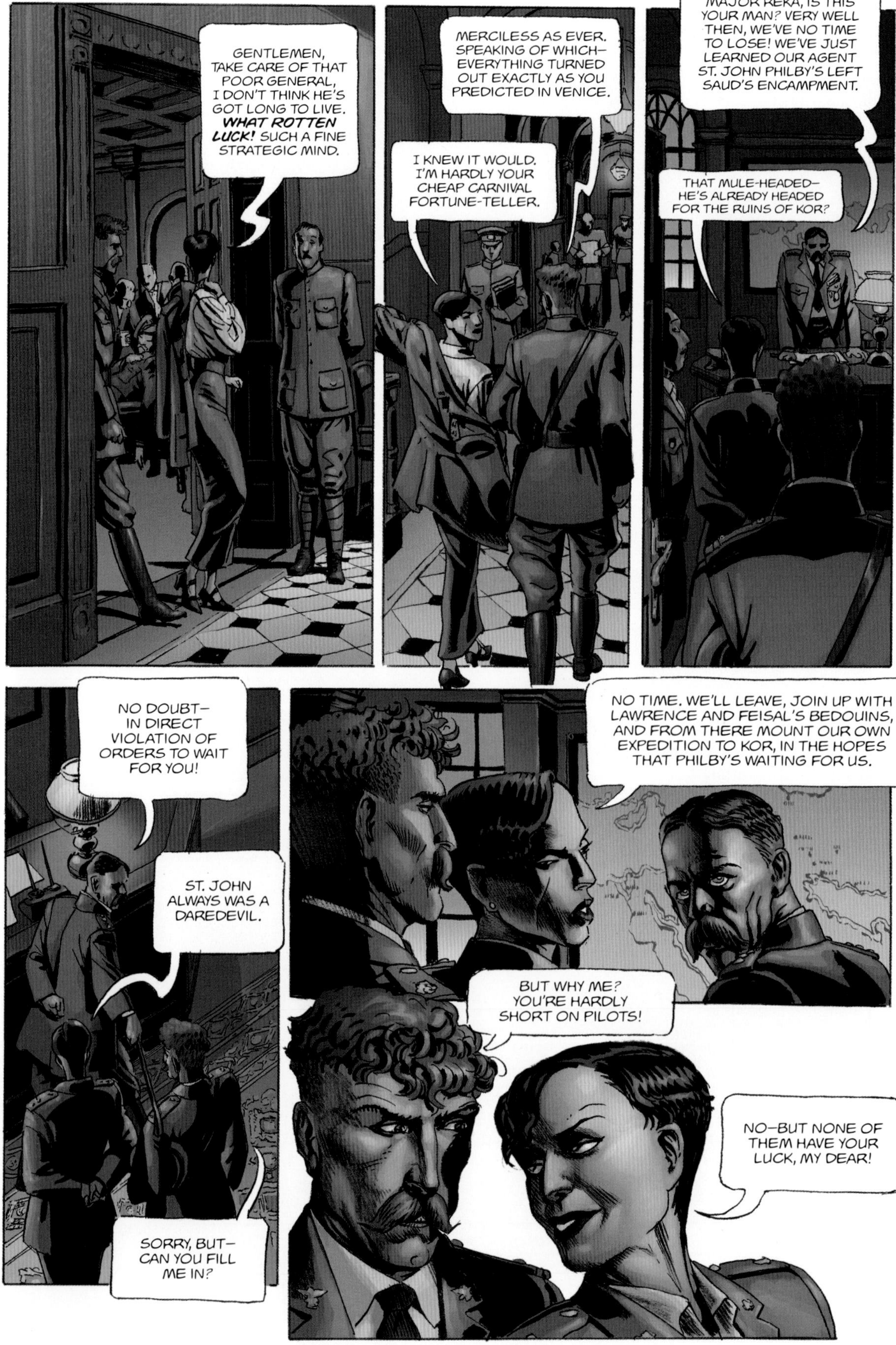
GENTLEMEN, TAKE CARE OF THAT POOR GENERAL, I DON'T THINK HE'S GOT LONG TO LIVE. WHAT ROTTEN LUCK! SUCH A FINE STRATEGIC MIND.
MERCILESS AS EVER. SPEAKING OF WHICH—EVERYTHING TURNED OUT EXACTLY AS YOU PREDICTED IN VENICE.
I KNEW IT WOULD. I'M HARDLY YOUR CHEAP CARNIVAL FORTUNE-TELLER.
MAJOR REKA, IS THIS YOUR MAN? VERY WELL THEN, WE'VE NO TIME TO LOSE! WE'VE JUST LEARNED OUR AGENT ST. JOHN PHILBY'S LEFT SAUD'S ENCAMPMENT.
THAT MULE-HEADED—HE'S ALREADY HEADED FOR THE RUINS OF KOR?
NO DOUBT—IN DIRECT VIOLATION OF ORDERS TO WAIT FOR YOU!
ST. JOHN ALWAYS WAS A DAREDEVIL.
SORRY, BUT—CAN YOU FILL ME IN?
NO TIME. WE'LL LEAVE, JOIN UP WITH LAWRENCE AND FEISAL'S BEDOUINS, AND FROM THERE MOUNT OUR OWN EXPEDITION TO KOR, IN THE HOPES THAT PHILBY'S WAITING FOR US.
BUT WHY ME? YOU'RE HARDLY SHORT ON PILOTS!
NO—BUT NONE OF THEM HAVE YOUR LUCK, MY DEAR!

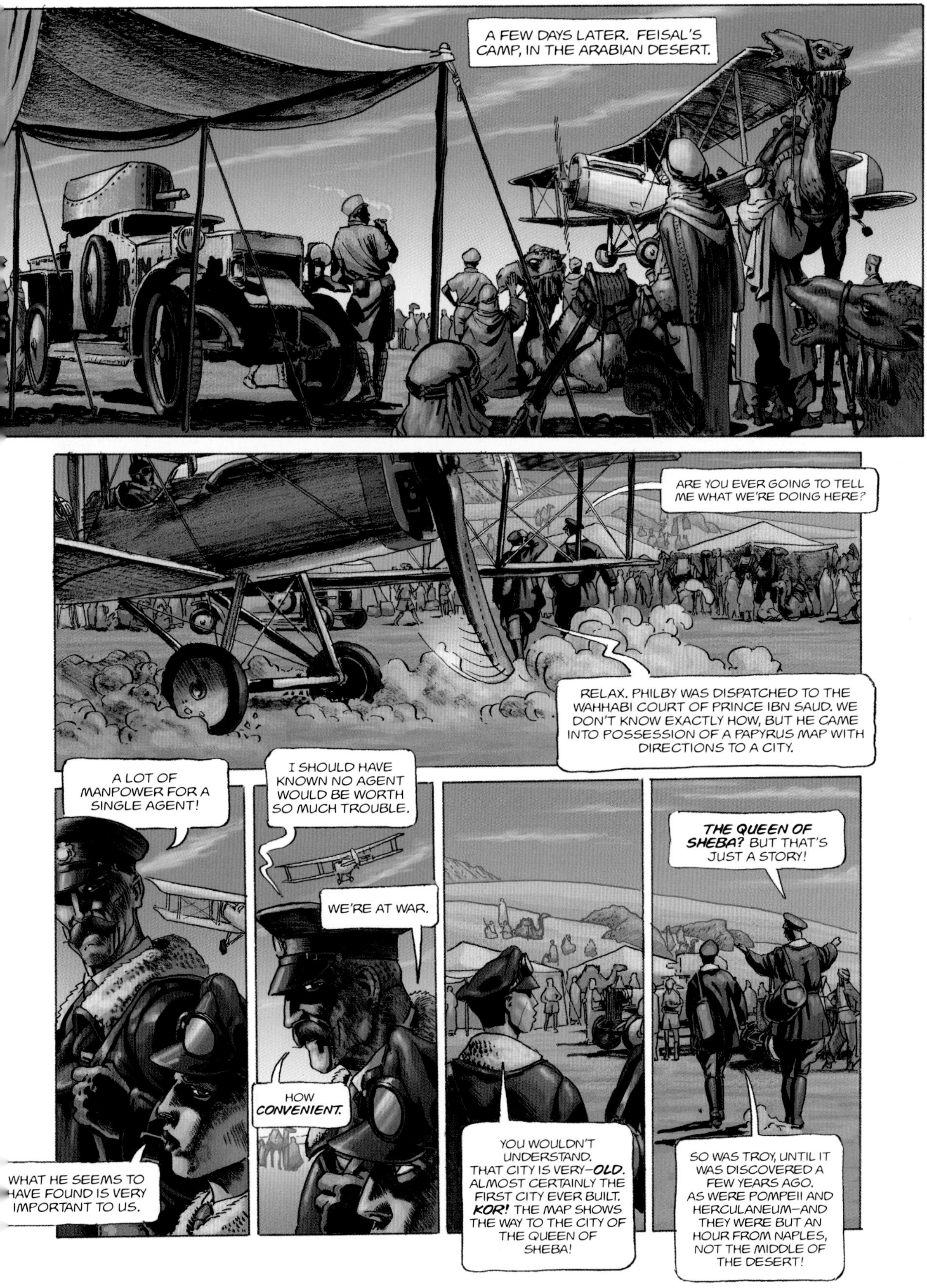
A FEW DAYS LATER. FEISAL'S CAMP, IN THE ARABIAN DESERT.
ARE YOU EVER GOING TO TELL ME WHAT WE'RE DOING HERE?
RELAX. PHILBY WAS DISPATCHED TO THE WAHHABI COURT OF PRINCE IBN SAUD. WE DON'T KNOW EXACTLY HOW, BUT HE CAME INTO POSSESSION OF A PAPYRUS MAP WITH DIRECTIONS TO A CITY.
A LOT OF MANPOWER FOR A SINGLE AGENT!
WHAT HE SEEMS TO HAVE FOUND IS VERY IMPORTANT TO US.
I SHOULD HAVE KNOWN NO AGENT WOULD BE WORTH SO MUCH TROUBLE.
WE'RE AT WAR.
HOW CONVENIENT.
YOU WOULDN'T UNDERSTAND. THAT CITY IS VERY—OLD. ALMOST CERTAINLY THE FIRST CITY EVER BUILT. KOR! THE MAP SHOWS THE WAY TO THE CITY OF THE QUEEN OF SHEBA!
THE QUEEN OF SHEBA? BUT THAT'S JUST A STORY!
SO WAS TROY, UNTIL IT WAS DISCOVERED A FEW YEARS AGO. AS WERE POMPEII AND HERCULANEUM—AND THEY WERE BUT AN HOUR FROM NAPLES, NOT THE MIDDLE OF THE DESERT!

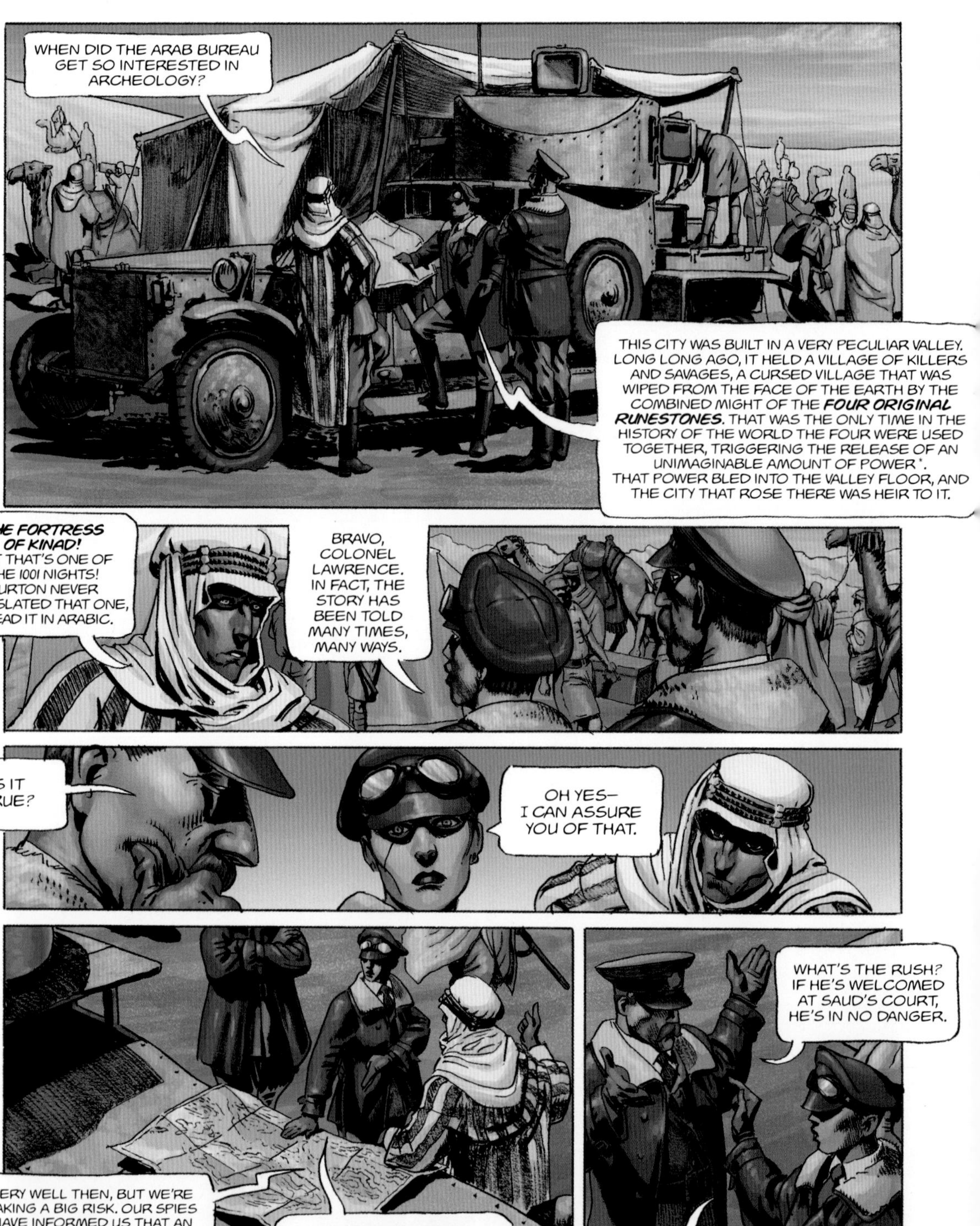
WHEN DID THE ARAB BUREAU GET SO INTERESTED IN ARCHEOLOGY?
THIS CITY WAS BUILT IN A VERY PECULIAR VALLEY. LONG LONG AGO, IT HELD A VILLAGE OF KILLERS AND SAVAGES, A CURSED VILLAGE THAT WAS WIPED FROM THE FACE OF THE EARTH BY THE COMBINED MIGHT OF THE FOUR ORIGINAL RUNESTONES. THAT WAS THE ONLY TIME IN THE HISTORY OF THE WORLD THE FOUR WERE USED TOGETHER, TRIGGERING THE RELEASE OF AN UNIMAGINABLE AMOUNT OF POWER*. THAT POWER BLED INTO THE VALLEY FLOOR, AND THE CITY THAT ROSE THERE WAS HEIR TO IT.
THE FORTRESS OF KINAD! BUT THAT'S ONE OF THE 1001 NIGHTS! BURTON NEVER TRANSLATED THAT ONE, I READ IT IN ARABIC.
BRAVO, COLONEL LAWRENCE. IN FACT, THE STORY HAS BEEN TOLD MANY TIMES, MANY WAYS.
IS IT TRUE?
OH YES— I CAN ASSURE YOU OF THAT.
VERY WELL THEN, BUT WE'RE TAKING A BIG RISK. OUR SPIES HAVE INFORMED US THAT AN ARMORED GERMAN TRAIN IS HEADED OUR WAY. WE MAY FIND OURSELVES TRAPPED BETWEEN IT AND SAUD'S MEN.
AN ARMORED TRAIN, YOU SAY? QUICKLY—WE HAVEN'T A MINUTE TO LOSE! I DON'T KNOW HOW THE GERMANS GOT WIND OF THIS FIND, BUT ONE THING IS CERTAIN: THEY WANT PHILBY!
WHAT'S THE RUSH? IF HE'S WELCOMED AT SAUD'S COURT, HE'S IN NO DANGER.
IT'S NOT SAUD WE MUST FEAR, BUT THE ARMORED TRAIN— THE SAME ONE FROM VENICE**!

* SEE *THE SECRET HISTORY*, BOOK 1.
** SEE *THE SECRET HISTORY*, BOOK 7.

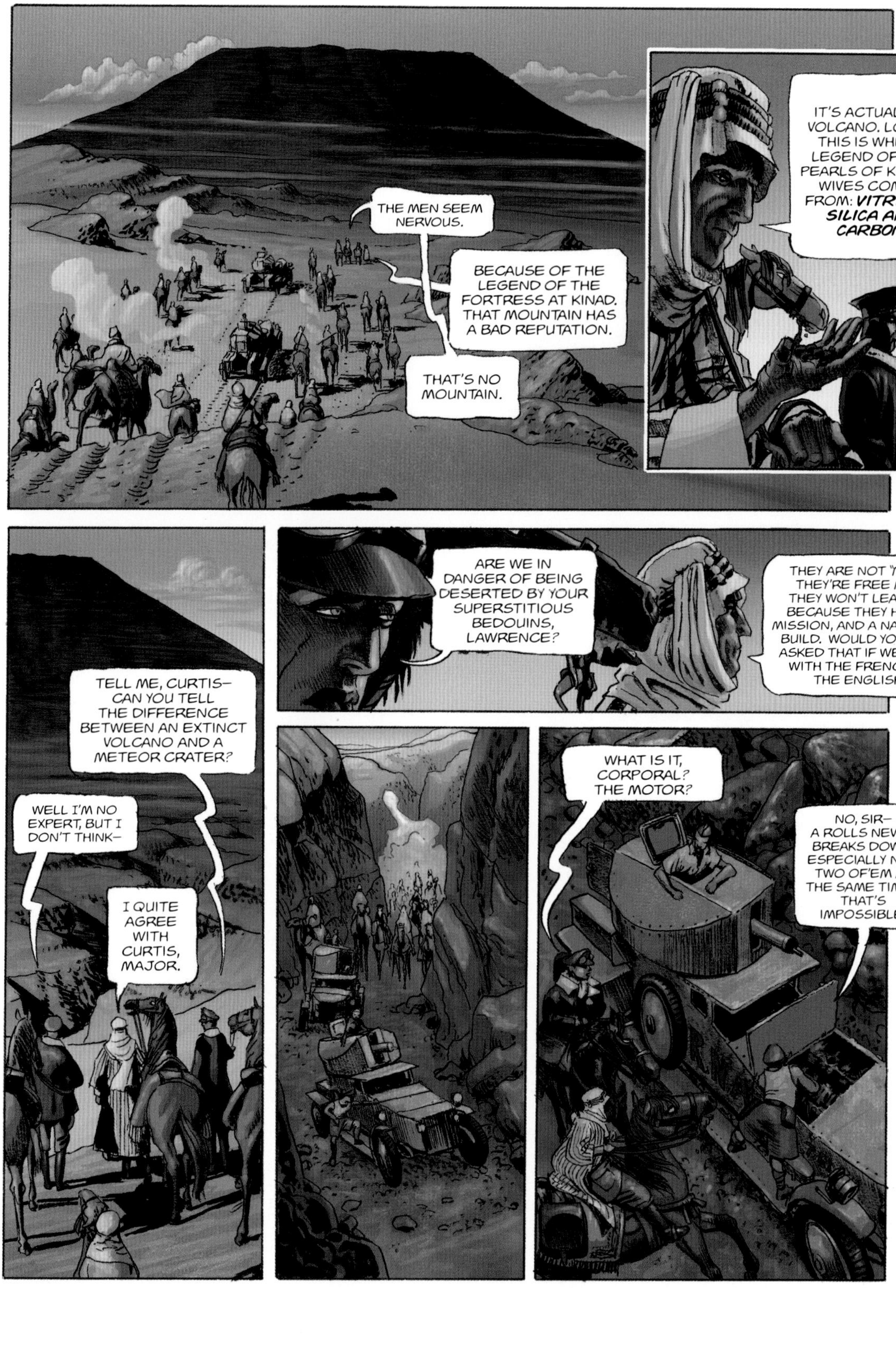
THE MEN SEEM NERVOUS.
BECAUSE OF THE LEGEND OF THE FORTRESS AT KINAD. THAT MOUNTAIN HAS A BAD REPUTATION.
THAT'S NO MOUNTAIN.
IT'S ACTUALLY A VOLCANO. LOOK— THIS IS WHERE LEGEND OF THE PEARLS OF KINAD'S WIVES COMES FROM: VITRIFIED SILICA AND CARBON.
TELL ME, CURTIS— CAN YOU TELL THE DIFFERENCE BETWEEN AN EXTINCT VOLCANO AND A METEOR CRATER?
WELL I'M NO EXPERT, BUT I DON'T THINK—
I QUITE AGREE WITH CURTIS, MAJOR.
ARE WE IN DANGER OF BEING DESERTED BY YOUR SUPERSTITIOUS BEDOUINS, LAWRENCE?
THEY ARE NOT "MINE", THEY'RE FREE MEN. THEY WON'T LEAVE US BECAUSE THEY HAVE A MISSION, AND A NATION TO BUILD. WOULD YOU HAVE ASKED THAT IF WE RODE WITH THE FRENCH OR THE ENGLISH?
WHAT IS IT, CORPORAL? THE MOTOR?
NO, SIR— A ROLLS NEVER BREAKS DOWN. ESPECIALLY NOT TWO OF'EM AT THE SAME TIME— THAT'S IMPOSSIBLE.

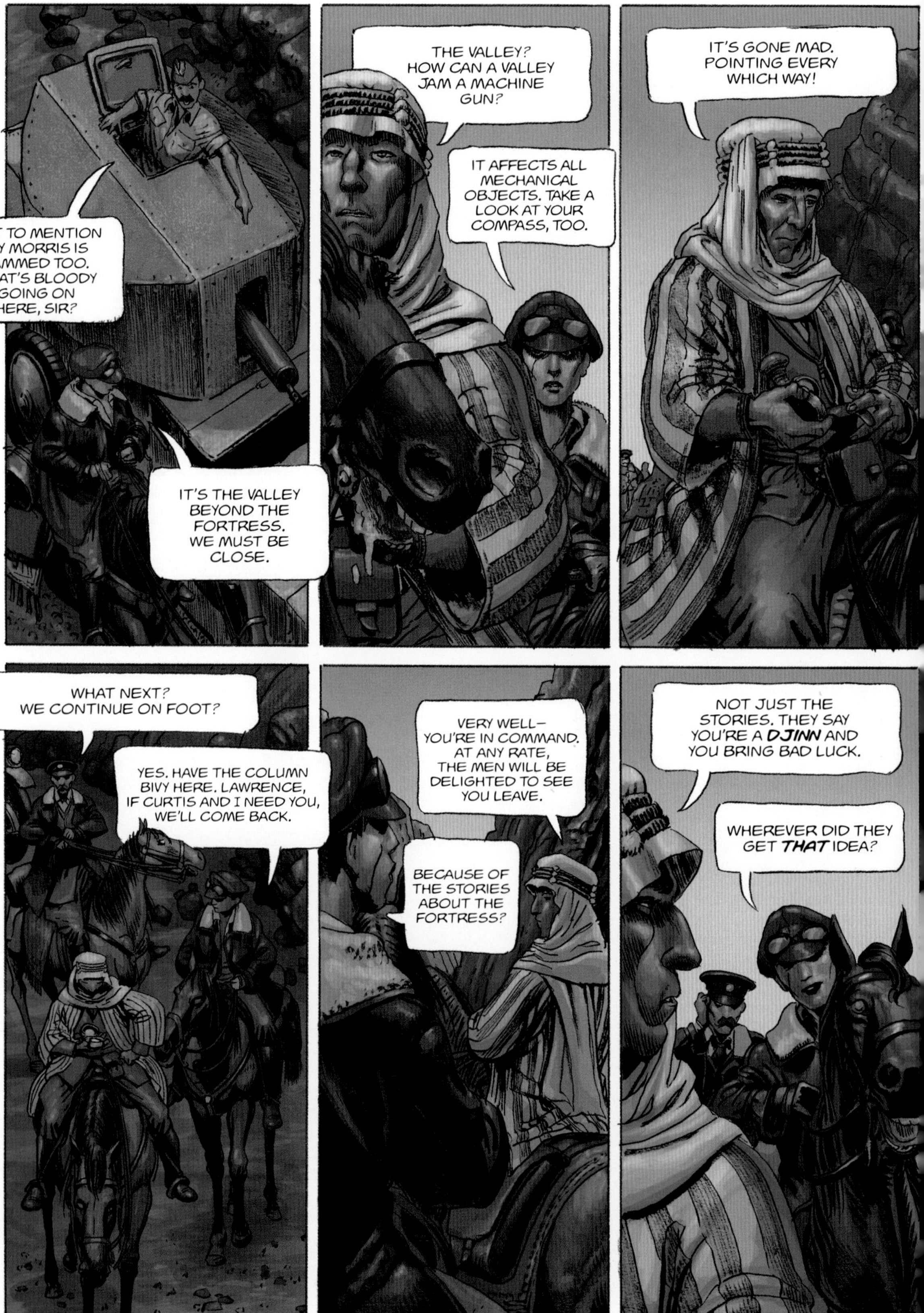
NOT TO MENTION MY MORRIS IS JAMMED TOO. WHAT'S BLOODY GOING ON HERE, SIR?
IT'S THE VALLEY BEYOND THE FORTRESS. WE MUST BE CLOSE.
THE VALLEY? HOW CAN A VALLEY JAM A MACHINE GUN?
IT AFFECTS ALL MECHANICAL OBJECTS. TAKE A LOOK AT YOUR COMPASS, TOO.
IT'S GONE MAD. POINTING EVERY WHICH WAY!
WHAT NEXT? WE CONTINUE ON FOOT?
YES. HAVE THE COLUMN BIVY HERE. LAWRENCE, IF CURTIS AND I NEED YOU, WE'LL COME BACK.
VERY WELL— YOU'RE IN COMMAND. AT ANY RATE, THE MEN WILL BE DELIGHTED TO SEE YOU LEAVE.
BECAUSE OF THE STORIES ABOUT THE FORTRESS?
NOT JUST THE STORIES. THEY SAY YOU'RE A ***DJINN*** AND YOU BRING BAD LUCK.
WHEREVER DID THEY GET ***THAT*** IDEA?

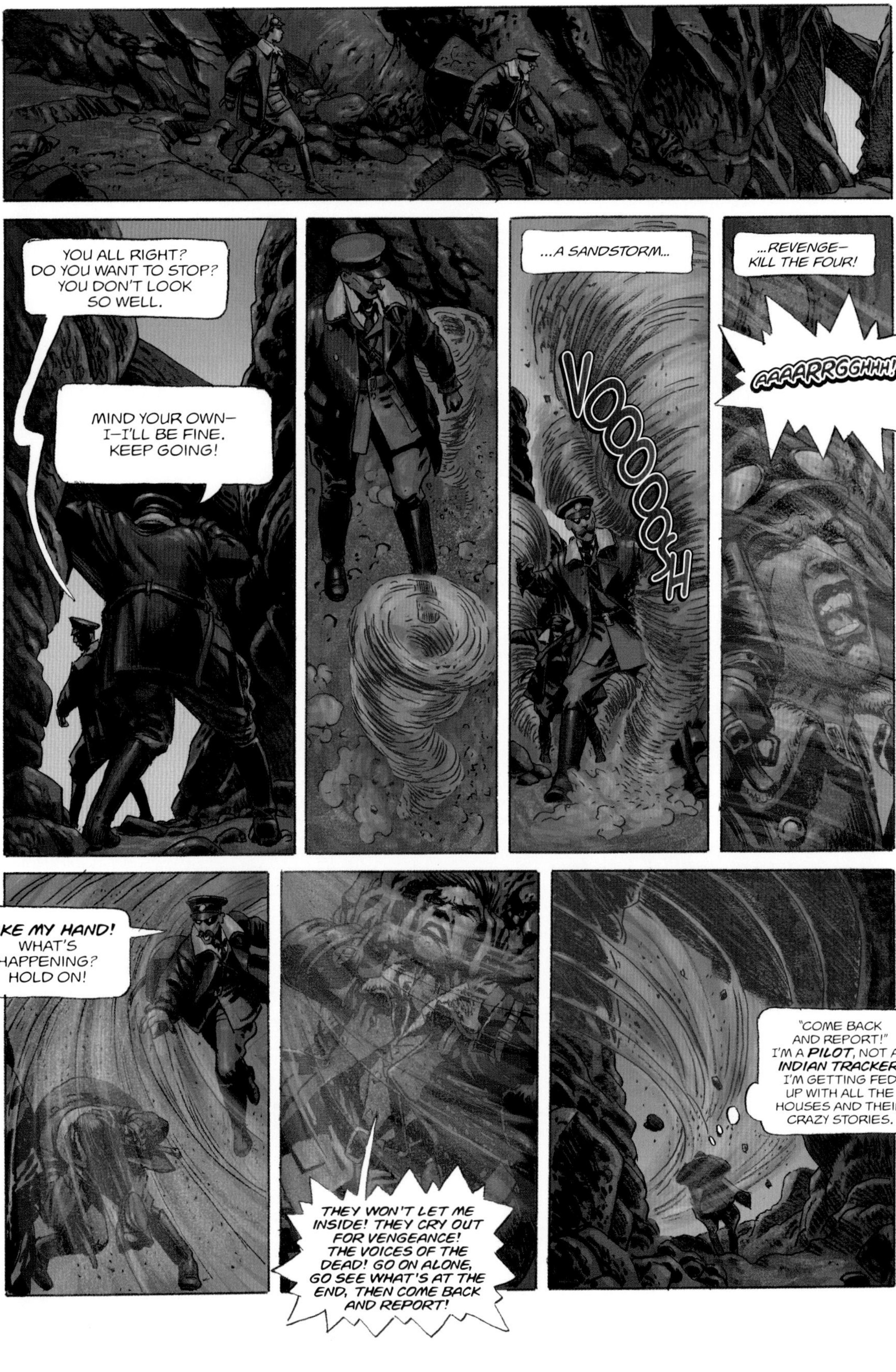
YOU ALL RIGHT? DO YOU WANT TO STOP? YOU DON'T LOOK SO WELL.
MIND YOUR OWN— I—I'LL BE FINE. KEEP GOING!
...A SANDSTORM...
VOOOOOOH
...REVENGE— KILL THE FOUR!
AAAARRGGHHH!
TAKE MY HAND! WHAT'S HAPPENING? HOLD ON!
THEY WON'T LET ME INSIDE! THEY CRY OUT FOR VENGEANCE! THE VOICES OF THE DEAD! GO ON ALONE, GO SEE WHAT'S AT THE END, THEN COME BACK AND REPORT!
"COME BACK AND REPORT!" I'M A PILOT, NOT AN INDIAN TRACKER. I'M GETTING FED UP WITH ALL THE HOUSES AND THEIR CRAZY STORIES.

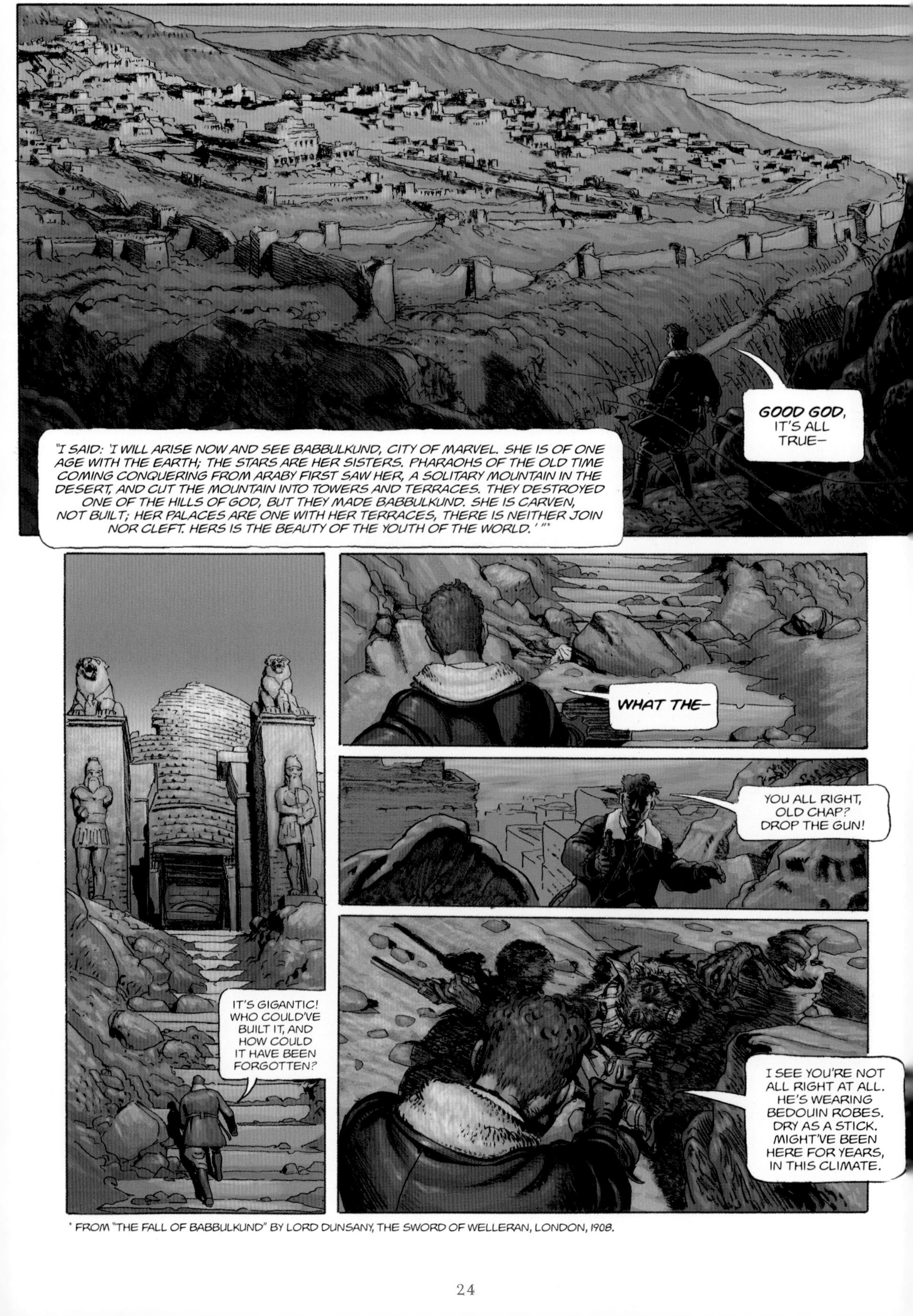
"I SAID: 'I WILL ARISE NOW AND SEE BABBULKUND, CITY OF MARVEL. SHE IS OF ONE AGE WITH THE EARTH; THE STARS ARE HER SISTERS. PHARAOHS OF THE OLD TIME COMING CONQUERING FROM ARABY FIRST SAW HER, A SOLITARY MOUNTAIN IN THE DESERT, AND CUT THE MOUNTAIN INTO TOWERS AND TERRACES. THEY DESTROYED ONE OF THE HILLS OF GOD, BUT THEY MADE BABBULKUND. SHE IS CARVEN, NOT BUILT; HER PALACES ARE ONE WITH HER TERRACES, THERE IS NEITHER JOIN NOR CLEFT. HERS IS THE BEAUTY OF THE YOUTH OF THE WORLD.' "*
GOOD GOD, IT'S ALL TRUE–
IT'S GIGANTIC! WHO COULD'VE BUILT IT, AND HOW COULD IT HAVE BEEN FORGOTTEN?
WHAT THE–
YOU ALL RIGHT, OLD CHAP? DROP THE GUN!
I SEE YOU'RE NOT ALL RIGHT AT ALL. HE'S WEARING BEDOUIN ROBES. DRY AS A STICK. MIGHT'VE BEEN HERE FOR YEARS, IN THIS CLIMATE.

* FROM "THE FALL OF BABBULKUND" BY LORD DUNSANY, THE SWORD OF WELLERAN, LONDON, 1908.

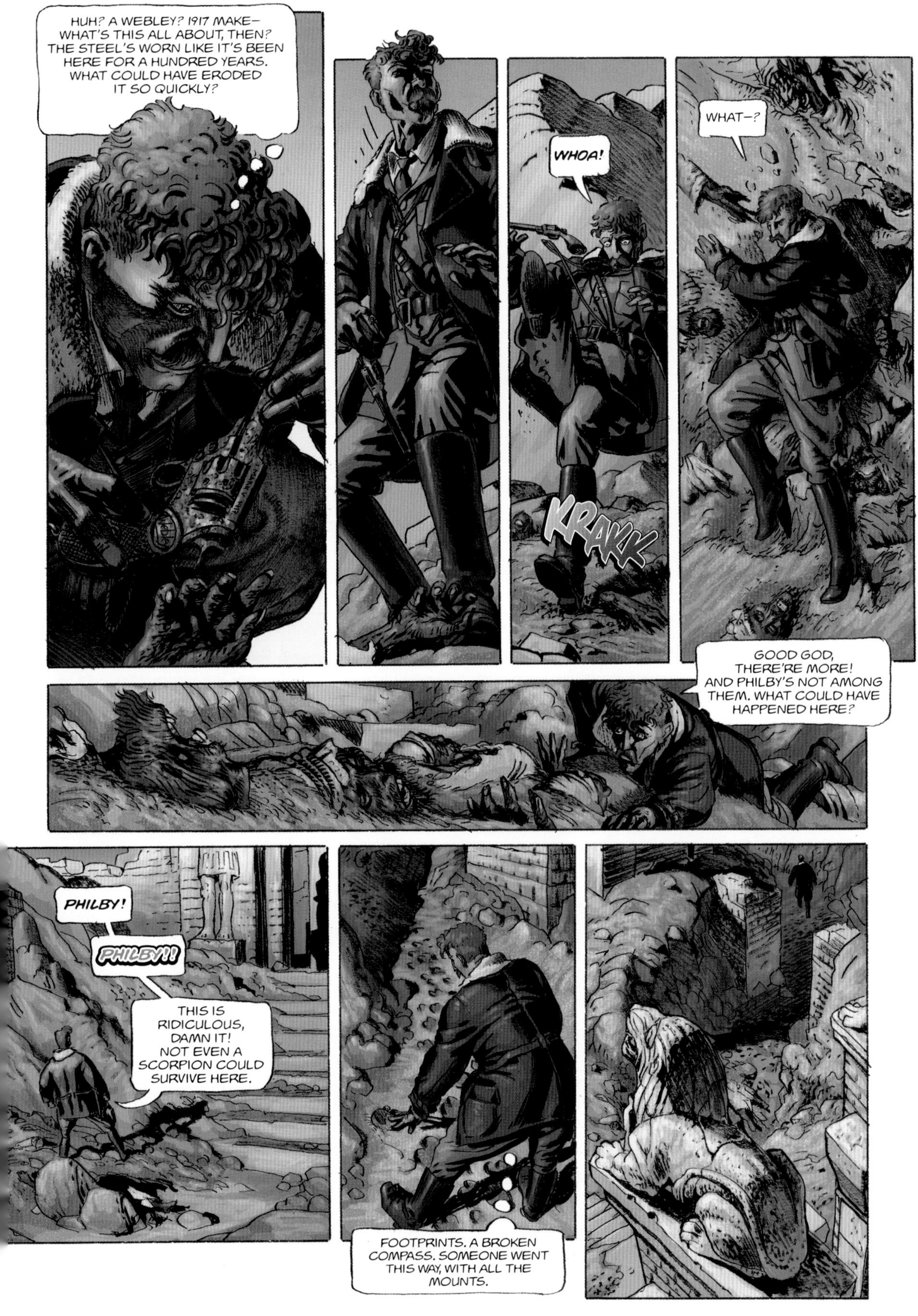
HUH? A WEBLEY? 1917 MAKE— WHAT'S THIS ALL ABOUT, THEN? THE STEEL'S WORN LIKE IT'S BEEN HERE FOR A HUNDRED YEARS. WHAT COULD HAVE ERODED IT SO QUICKLY?
WHOA!
KRAKK
WHAT—?
GOOD GOD, THERE'RE MORE! AND PHILBY'S NOT AMONG THEM. WHAT COULD HAVE HAPPENED HERE?
PHILBY!
PHILBY!!
THIS IS RIDICULOUS, DAMN IT! NOT EVEN A SCORPION COULD SURVIVE HERE.
FOOTPRINTS. A BROKEN COMPASS. SOMEONE WENT THIS WAY, WITH ALL THE MOUNTS.

CURTIS!
IS EVERYTHING ALL RIGHT?
WHAT TOOK YOU
SO LONG?
WHAT DID YOU FIND?

SO LONG?
IT'S BEEN LESS
THAN THREE HOURS.

TRY THREE
DAYS!
I'VE BEEN
WAITING FOR
YOU THREE
DAYS!

I DON'T
UNDERSTAND...
THERE IS A CITY
DOWN THERE,
IN RUINS.
I DON'T KNOW
MY WAY AROUND
ARCHITECTURE
OR ARCHEOLOGY,
BUT I'VE NEVER
SEEN THE LIKE.
NO KNOWN HUMAN
CIVILIZATION COULD
HAVE BUILT IT.

SO... IT IS INDEED THE
VALLEY OF THE CLAN WE
DESTROYED*. IT MUST
HOUSE TREMENDOUS
POWER.

NO TRACE
OF PHILBY?

NO, EXCEPT A FEW BEDOUIN BODIES
DECADES OLD. THE STRANGEST
PART WAS, THEY WERE CARRYING
PISTOLS OF THE LATEST MAKE.
WHICH WOULD SEEM IMPOSSIBLE.

UNLESS TIME
DOESN'T FLOW
THE SAME WAY IN
THAT VALLEY...

I DIDN'T FIND
THEIR CAMELS,
BUT THERE WERE
FOOTPRINTS
LEADING NORTH.

* SEE THE PROLOGUE TO *THE SECRET
HISTORY, BOOK I: GENESIS.*

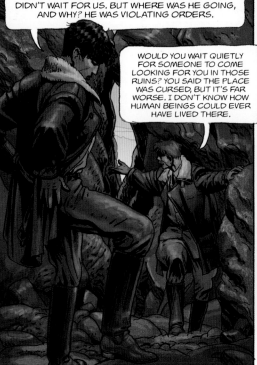

WHICH WOULD LEAD ONE TO PRESUME PHILBY
DIDN'T WAIT FOR US. BUT WHERE WAS HE GOING,
AND WHY? HE WAS VIOLATING ORDERS.

WOULD YOU WAIT QUIETLY
FOR SOMEONE TO COME
LOOKING FOR YOU IN THOSE
RUINS? YOU SAID THE PLACE
WAS CURSED, BUT IT'S FAR
WORSE. I DON'T KNOW HOW
HUMAN BEINGS COULD EVER
HAVE LIVED THERE.

WHO SAID
ANYTHING ABOUT
HUMAN BEINGS?

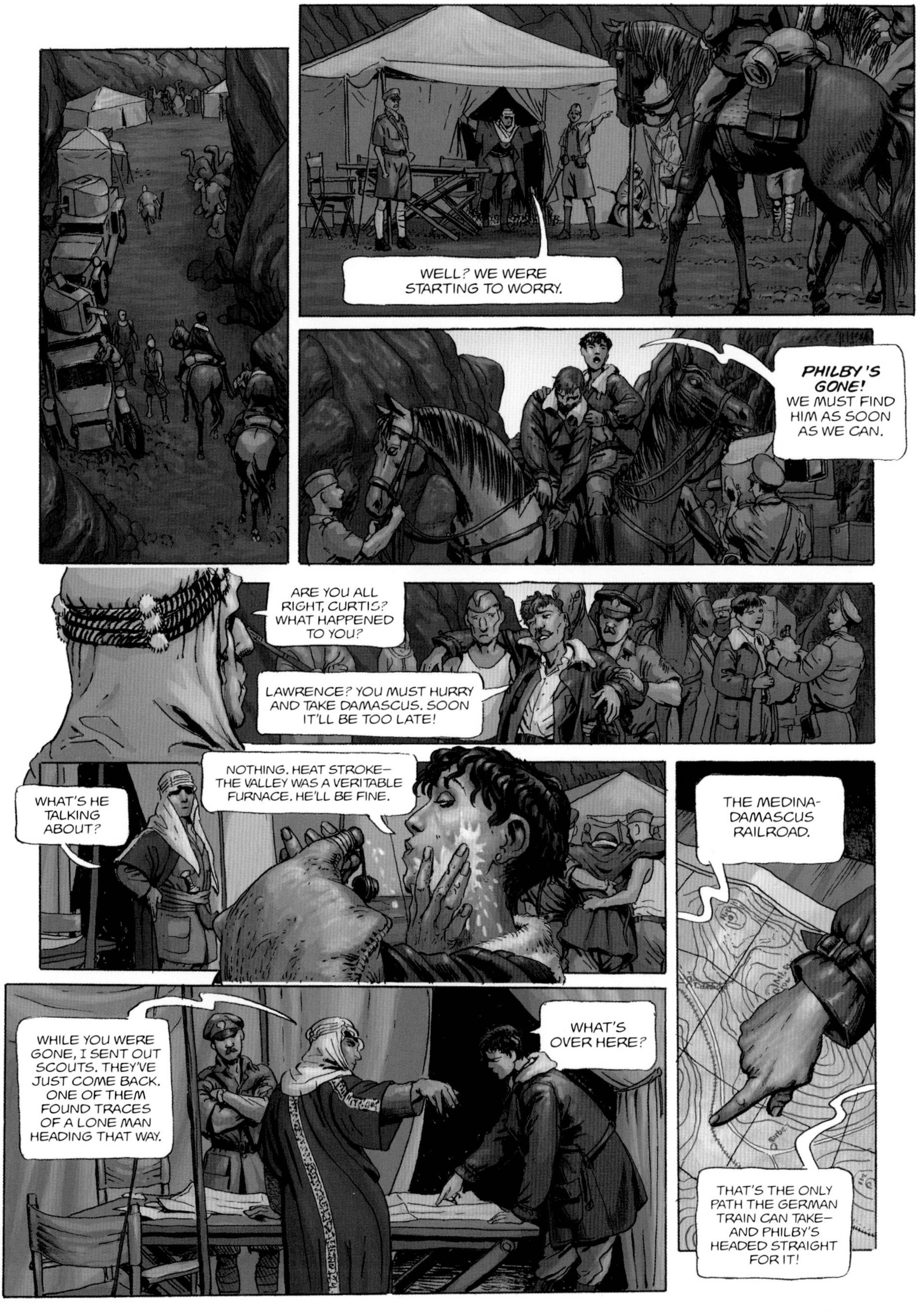
WELL? WE WERE STARTING TO WORRY.
PHILBY'S GONE! WE MUST FIND HIM AS SOON AS WE CAN.
ARE YOU ALL RIGHT, CURTIS? WHAT HAPPENED TO YOU?
LAWRENCE? YOU MUST HURRY AND TAKE DAMASCUS. SOON IT'LL BE TOO LATE!
WHAT'S HE TALKING ABOUT?
NOTHING. HEAT STROKE— THE VALLEY WAS A VERITABLE FURNACE. HE'LL BE FINE.
THE MEDINA-DAMASCUS RAILROAD.
WHILE YOU WERE GONE, I SENT OUT SCOUTS. THEY'VE JUST COME BACK. ONE OF THEM FOUND TRACES OF A LONE MAN HEADING THAT WAY.
WHAT'S OVER HERE?
THAT'S THE ONLY PATH THE GERMAN TRAIN CAN TAKE— AND PHILBY'S HEADED STRAIGHT FOR IT!

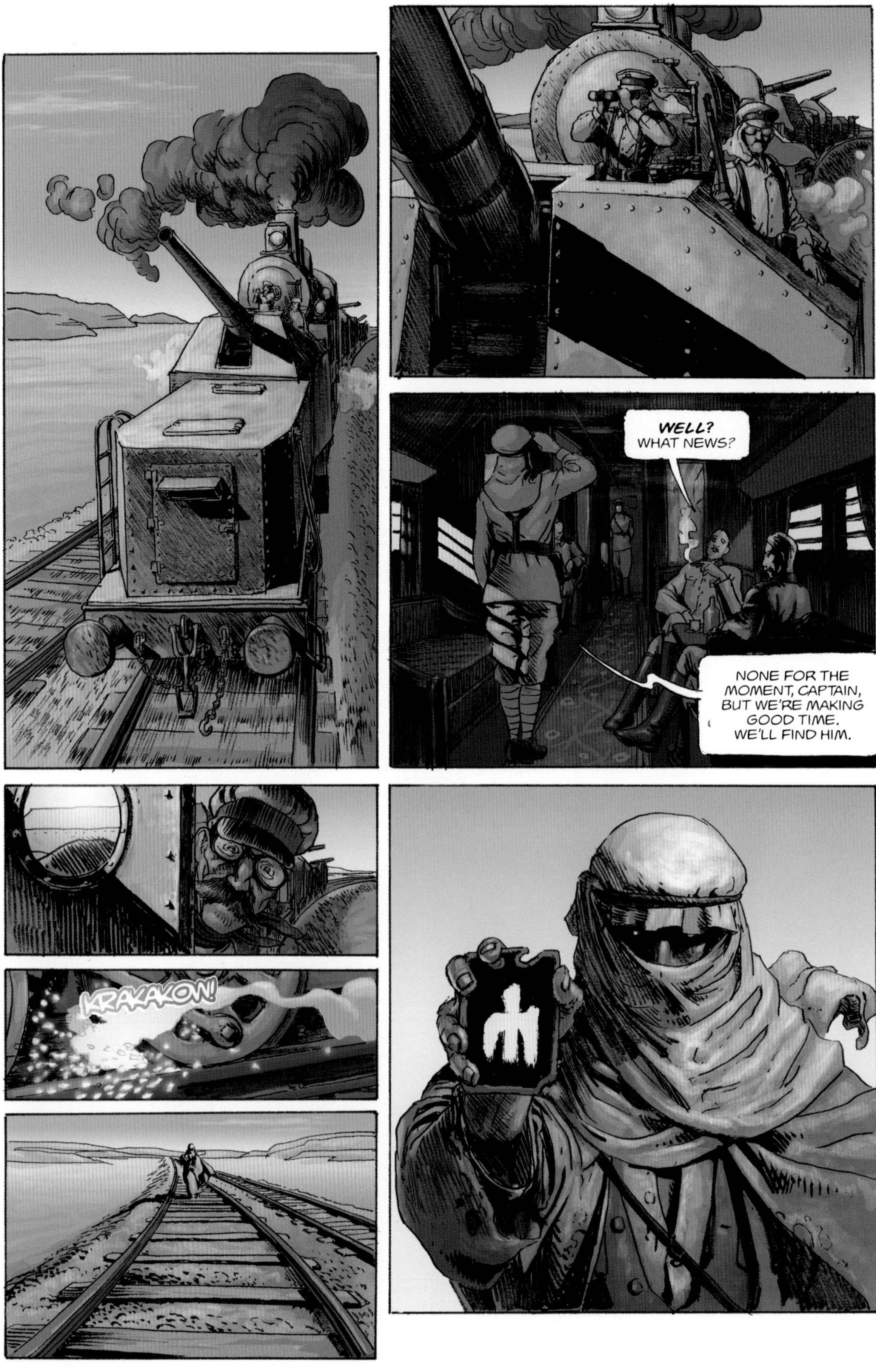
WELL? WHAT NEWS?
NONE FOR THE MOMENT, CAPTAIN, BUT WE'RE MAKING GOOD TIME. WE'LL FIND HIM.
KRAKAKON!

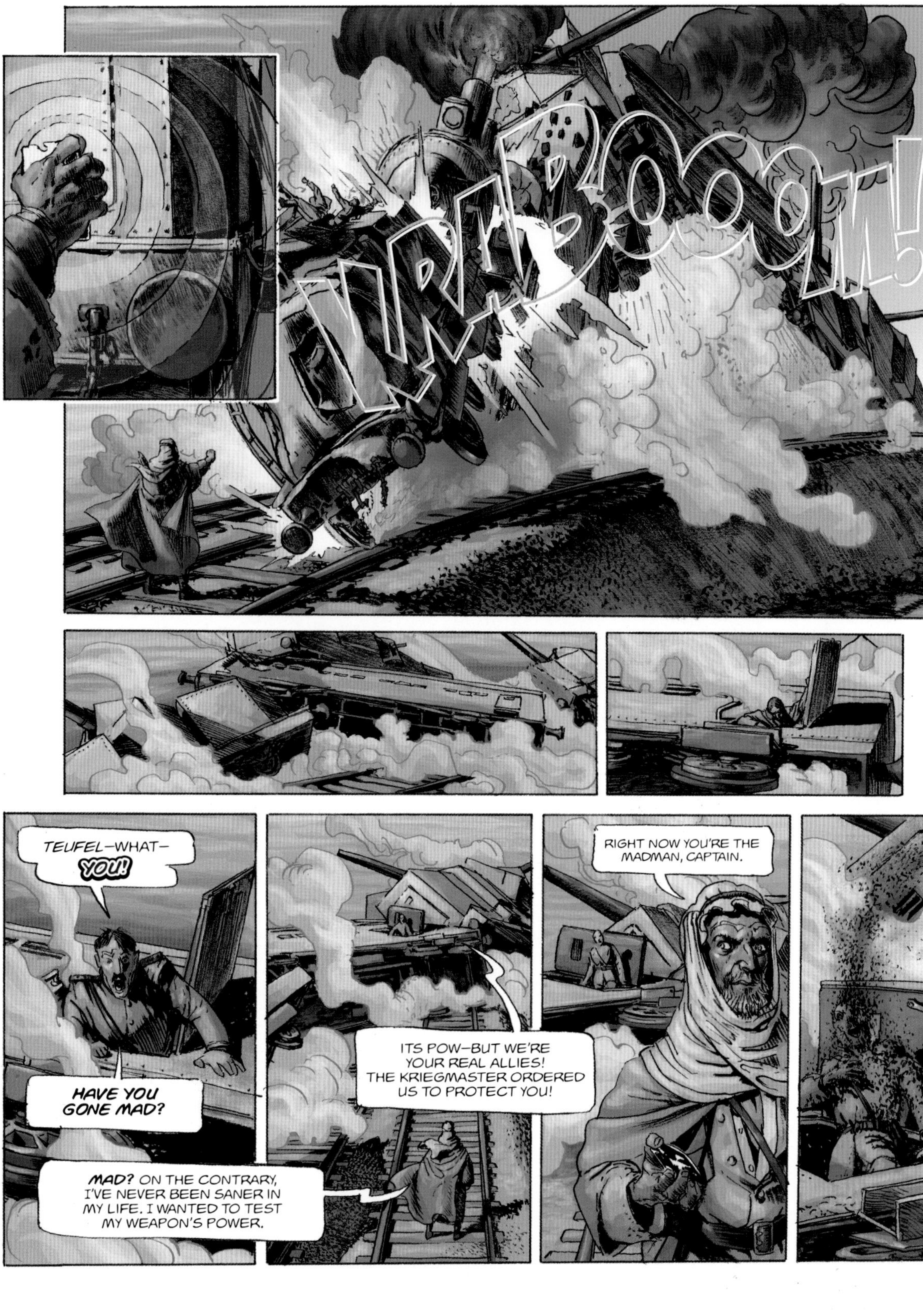
VRABOOOM!
TEUFEL—WHAT—
YOU!
HAVE YOU GONE MAD?
MAD? ON THE CONTRARY, I'VE NEVER BEEN SANER IN MY LIFE. I WANTED TO TEST MY WEAPON'S POWER.
ITS POW—BUT WE'RE YOUR REAL ALLIES! THE KRIEGMASTER ORDERED US TO PROTECT YOU!
RIGHT NOW YOU'RE THE MADMAN, CAPTAIN.

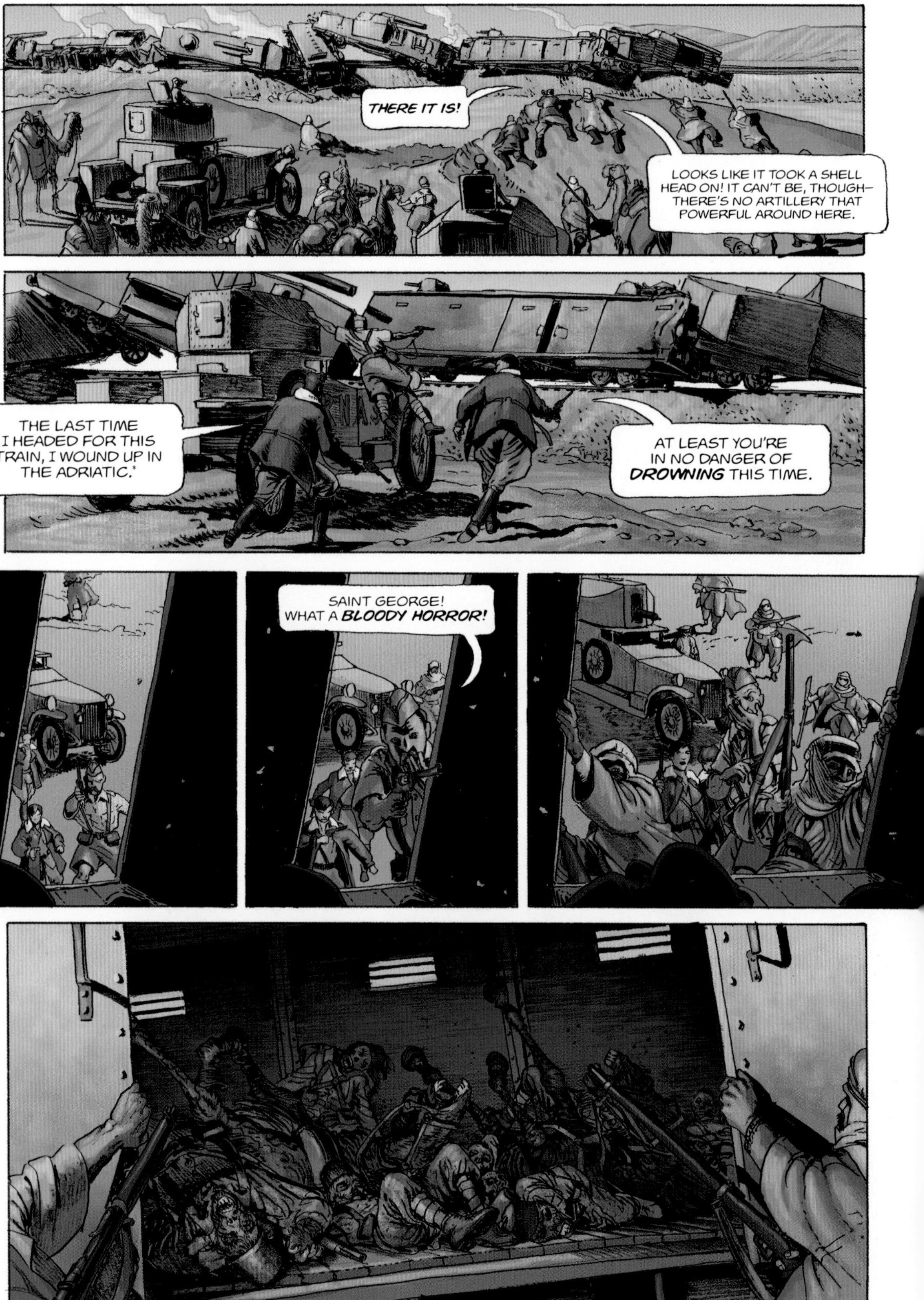
THERE IT IS!
LOOKS LIKE IT TOOK A SHELL HEAD ON! IT CAN'T BE, THOUGH— THERE'S NO ARTILLERY THAT POWERFUL AROUND HERE.
THE LAST TIME I HEADED FOR THIS TRAIN, I WOUND UP IN THE ADRIATIC.*
AT LEAST YOU'RE IN NO DANGER OF DROWNING THIS TIME.
SAINT GEORGE! WHAT A BLOODY HORROR!

* SEE *THE SECRET HISTORY*, BOOK 7: *OUR LADY OF THE SHADOWS*.

SAME ALL OVER— NO SURVIVORS. ONE GIANT GRAVE.

I'VE NEVER SEEN THE LIKE!

THEY LOOK LIKE THE DEAD BEDOUINS I SAW AT KOR!

INTERESTING...

CORPORAL, TELL THE BEDOUINS TO STAY BACK. THEY MUST NOT TAKE ANYTHING. FIND SOME PETROL, AND BURN IT ALL.

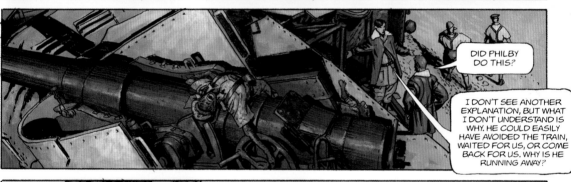

DID PHILBY DO THIS?

I DON'T SEE ANOTHER EXPLANATION, BUT WHAT I DON'T UNDERSTAND IS WHY. HE COULD EASILY HAVE AVOIDED THE TRAIN, WAITED FOR US, OR COME BACK FOR US. WHY IS HE RUNNING AWAY?

HE MUST BE A FORMIDABLE PLAYER.

NO, NOT REALLY. AT LEAST, NOT BEFORE FINDING *SOMETHING* AT KOR THAT CHANGED HIM. NO PLAYER COULD DO SUCH A THING, ONLY AN ARCHON. WHERE ELSE COULD PHILBY HAVE FOUND A SET OF SUCH POWER, IF NOT IN THE RUINS OF KOR?

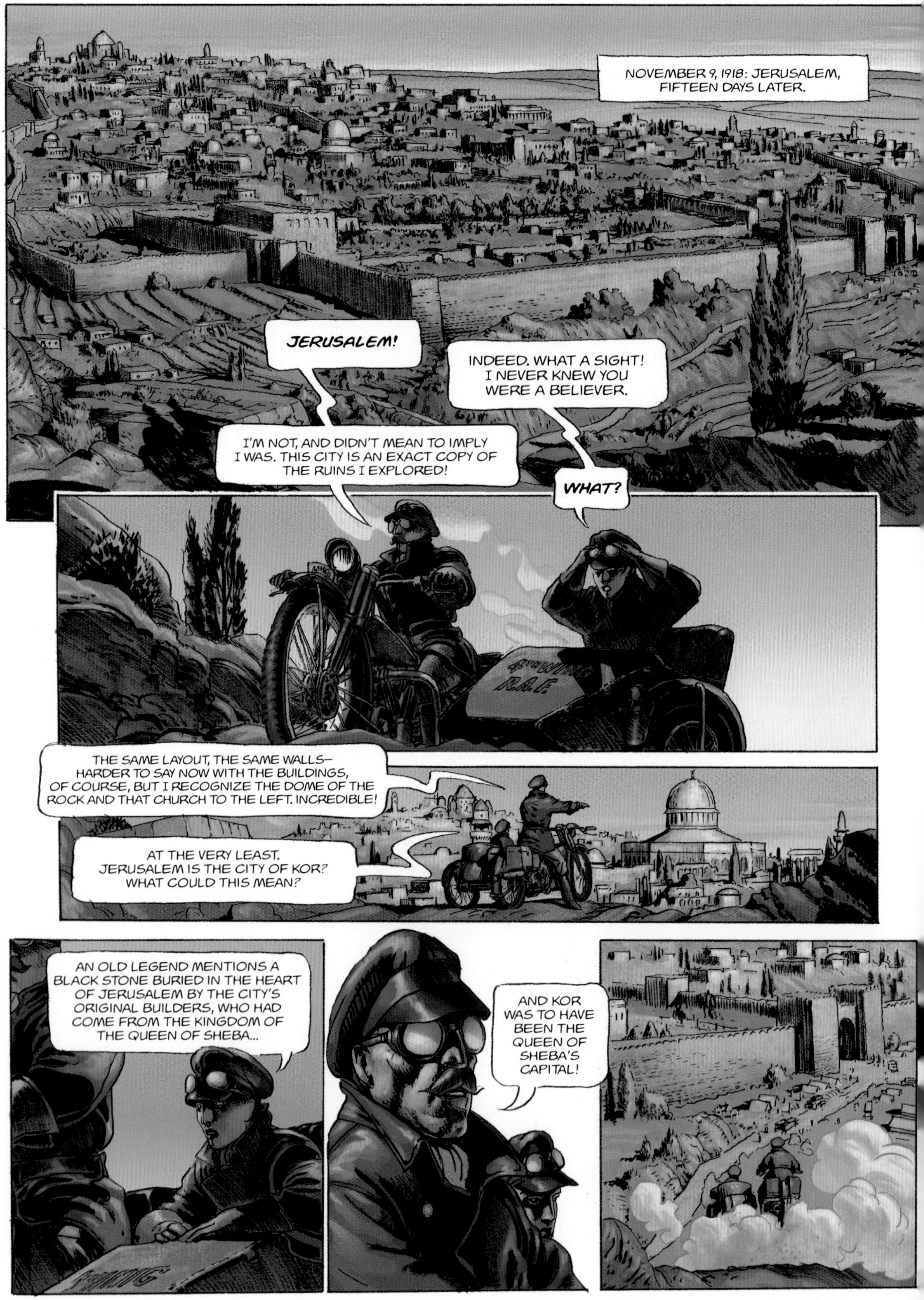
NOVEMBER 9, 1918: JERUSALEM, FIFTEEN DAYS LATER.
JERUSALEM!
INDEED. WHAT A SIGHT! I NEVER KNEW YOU WERE A BELIEVER.
I'M NOT, AND DIDN'T MEAN TO IMPLY I WAS. THIS CITY IS AN EXACT COPY OF THE RUINS I EXPLORED!
WHAT?
R.A.F.
THE SAME LAYOUT, THE SAME WALLS— HARDER TO SAY NOW WITH THE BUILDINGS, OF COURSE, BUT I RECOGNIZE THE DOME OF THE ROCK AND THAT CHURCH TO THE LEFT. INCREDIBLE!
AT THE VERY LEAST. JERUSALEM IS THE CITY OF KOR? WHAT COULD THIS MEAN?
AN OLD LEGEND MENTIONS A BLACK STONE BURIED IN THE HEART OF JERUSALEM BY THE CITY'S ORIGINAL BUILDERS, WHO HAD COME FROM THE KINGDOM OF THE QUEEN OF SHEBA...
AND KOR WAS TO HAVE BEEN THE QUEEN OF SHEBA'S CAPITAL!

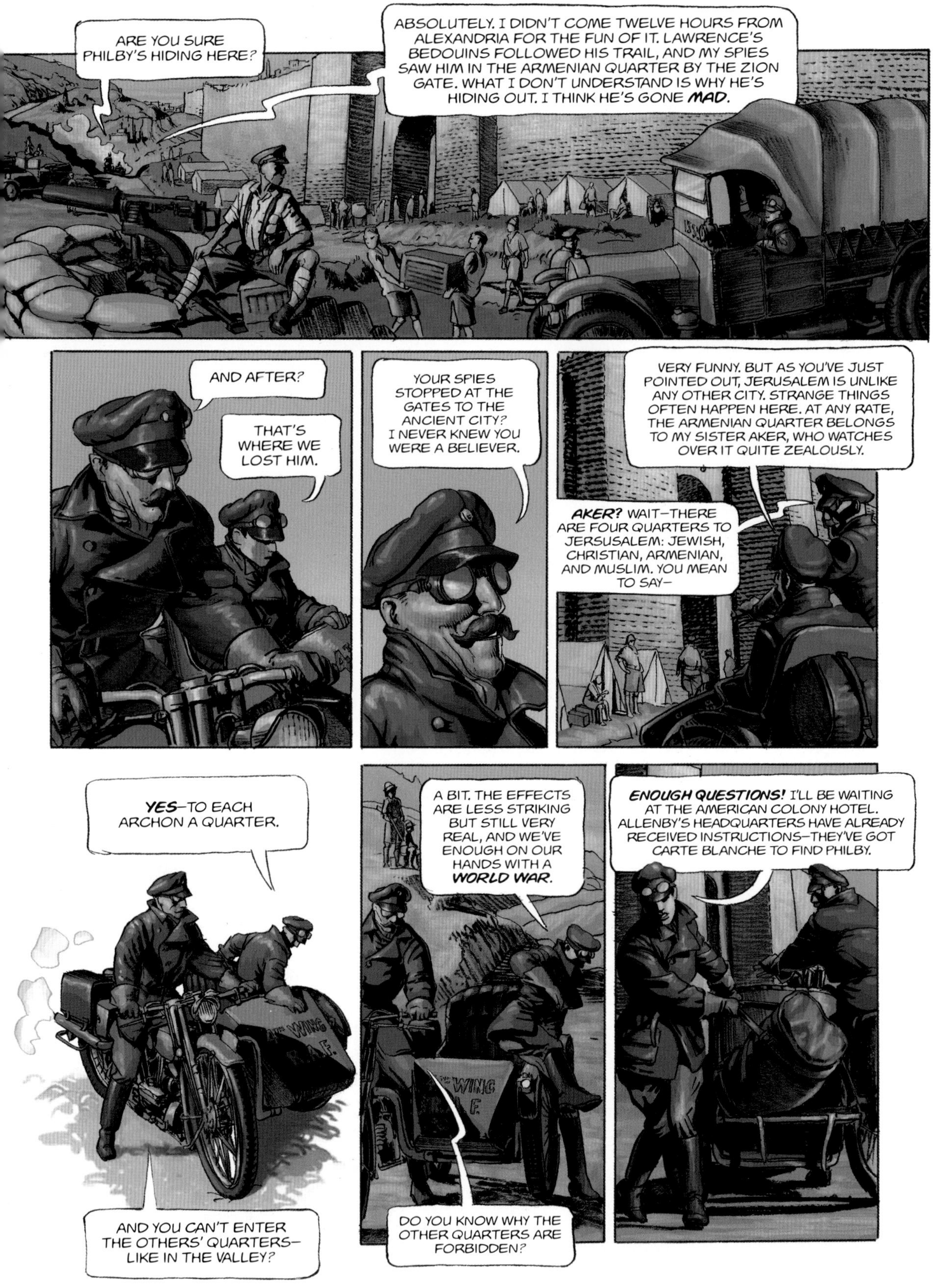

ARE YOU SURE PHILBY'S HIDING HERE?
ABSOLUTELY. I DIDN'T COME TWELVE HOURS FROM ALEXANDRIA FOR THE FUN OF IT. LAWRENCE'S BEDOUINS FOLLOWED HIS TRAIL, AND MY SPIES SAW HIM IN THE ARMENIAN QUARTER BY THE ZION GATE. WHAT I DON'T UNDERSTAND IS WHY HE'S HIDING OUT. I THINK HE'S GONE MAD.
AND AFTER?
THAT'S WHERE WE LOST HIM.
YOUR SPIES STOPPED AT THE GATES TO THE ANCIENT CITY? I NEVER KNEW YOU WERE A BELIEVER.
VERY FUNNY. BUT AS YOU'VE JUST POINTED OUT, JERUSALEM IS UNLIKE ANY OTHER CITY. STRANGE THINGS OFTEN HAPPEN HERE. AT ANY RATE, THE ARMENIAN QUARTER BELONGS TO MY SISTER AKER, WHO WATCHES OVER IT QUITE ZEALOUSLY.
AKER? WAIT—THERE ARE FOUR QUARTERS TO JERSUSALEM: JEWISH, CHRISTIAN, ARMENIAN, AND MUSLIM. YOU MEAN TO SAY—
YES—TO EACH ARCHON A QUARTER.
AND YOU CAN'T ENTER THE OTHERS' QUARTERS—LIKE IN THE VALLEY?
A BIT. THE EFFECTS ARE LESS STRIKING BUT STILL VERY REAL, AND WE'VE ENOUGH ON OUR HANDS WITH A WORLD WAR.
DO YOU KNOW WHY THE OTHER QUARTERS ARE FORBIDDEN?
ENOUGH QUESTIONS! I'LL BE WAITING AT THE AMERICAN COLONY HOTEL. ALLENBY'S HEADQUARTERS HAVE ALREADY RECEIVED INSTRUCTIONS—THEY'VE GOT CARTE BLANCHE TO FIND PHILBY.

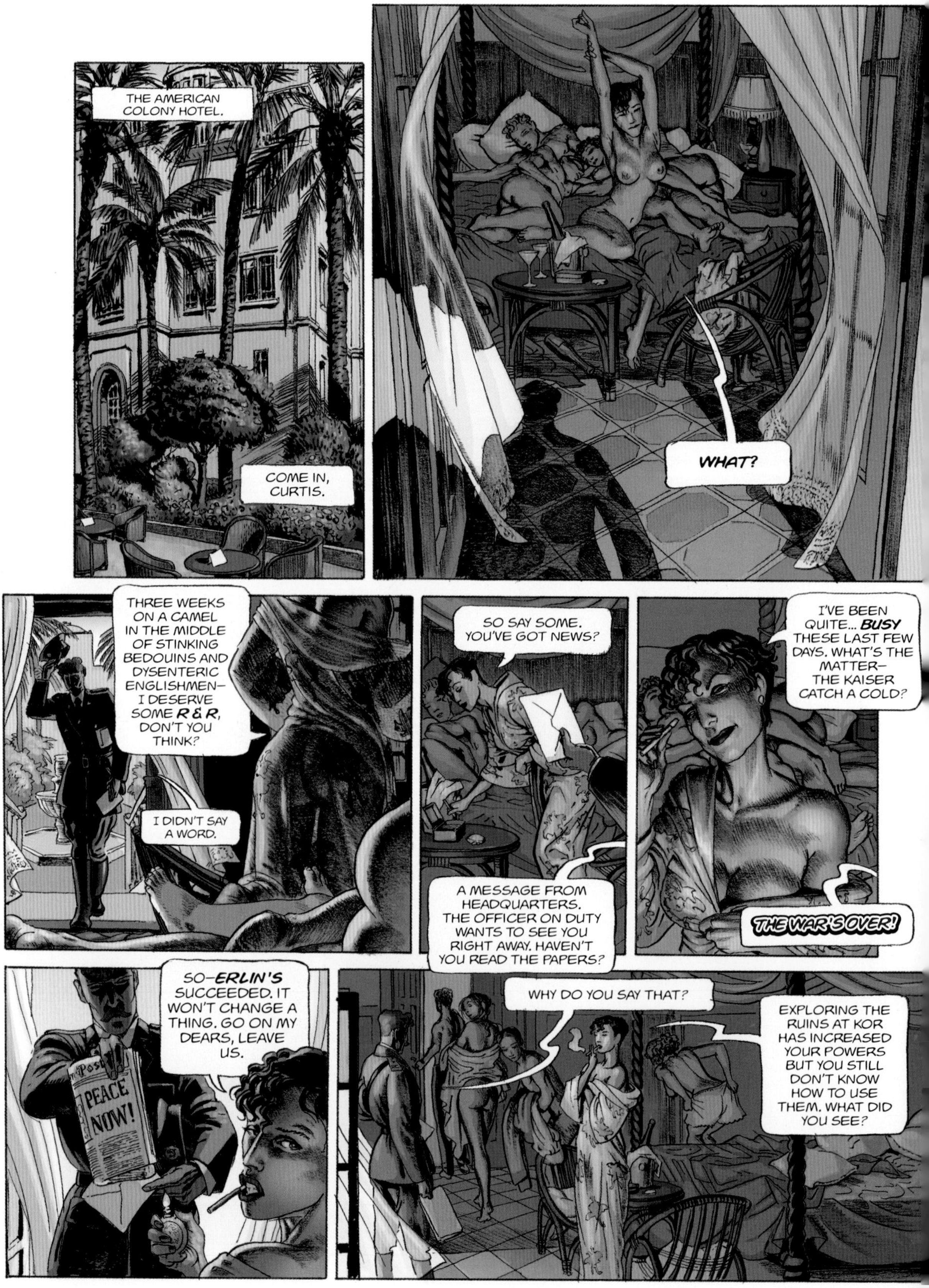
THE AMERICAN COLONY HOTEL.
COME IN, CURTIS.
WHAT?
THREE WEEKS ON A CAMEL IN THE MIDDLE OF STINKING BEDOUINS AND DYSENTERIC ENGLISHMEN— I DESERVE SOME R & R, DON'T YOU THINK?
I DIDN'T SAY A WORD.
SO SAY SOME. YOU'VE GOT NEWS?
A MESSAGE FROM HEADQUARTERS. THE OFFICER ON DUTY WANTS TO SEE YOU RIGHT AWAY. HAVEN'T YOU READ THE PAPERS?
I'VE BEEN QUITE... BUSY THESE LAST FEW DAYS. WHAT'S THE MATTER— THE KAISER CATCH A COLD?
THE WAR'S OVER!
PEACE NOW!
SO—ERLIN'S SUCCEEDED. IT WON'T CHANGE A THING. GO ON MY DEARS, LEAVE US.
WHY DO YOU SAY THAT?
EXPLORING THE RUINS AT KOR HAS INCREASED YOUR POWERS BUT YOU STILL DON'T KNOW HOW TO USE THEM. WHAT DID YOU SEE?

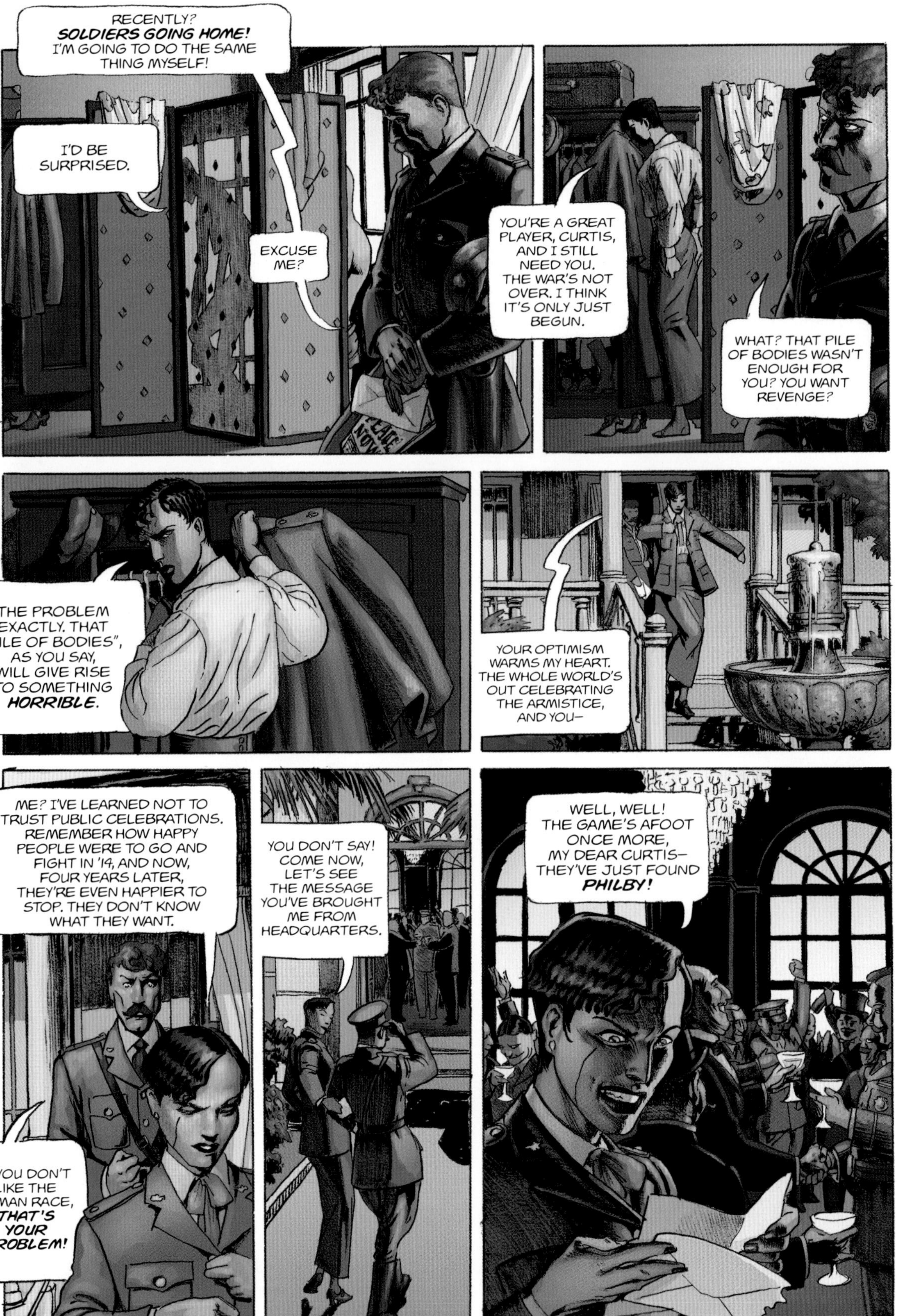
RECENTLY? **SOLDIERS GOING HOME!** I'M GOING TO DO THE SAME THING MYSELF!
I'D BE SURPRISED.
EXCUSE ME?
YOU'RE A GREAT PLAYER, CURTIS, AND I STILL NEED YOU. THE WAR'S NOT OVER. I THINK IT'S ONLY JUST BEGUN.
WHAT? THAT PILE OF BODIES WASN'T ENOUGH FOR YOU? YOU WANT REVENGE?
THE PROBLEM EXACTLY. THAT "PILE OF BODIES", AS YOU SAY, WILL GIVE RISE TO SOMETHING ***HORRIBLE***.
YOUR OPTIMISM WARMS MY HEART. THE WHOLE WORLD'S OUT CELEBRATING THE ARMISTICE, AND YOU–
ME? I'VE LEARNED NOT TO TRUST PUBLIC CELEBRATIONS. REMEMBER HOW HAPPY PEOPLE WERE TO GO AND FIGHT IN '14, AND NOW, FOUR YEARS LATER, THEY'RE EVEN HAPPIER TO STOP. THEY DON'T KNOW WHAT THEY WANT.
IF YOU DON'T LIKE THE HUMAN RACE, ***THAT'S YOUR PROBLEM!***
YOU DON'T SAY! COME NOW, LET'S SEE THE MESSAGE YOU'VE BROUGHT ME FROM HEADQUARTERS.
WELL, WELL! THE GAME'S AFOOT ONCE MORE, MY DEAR CURTIS– THEY'VE JUST FOUND ***PHILBY!***

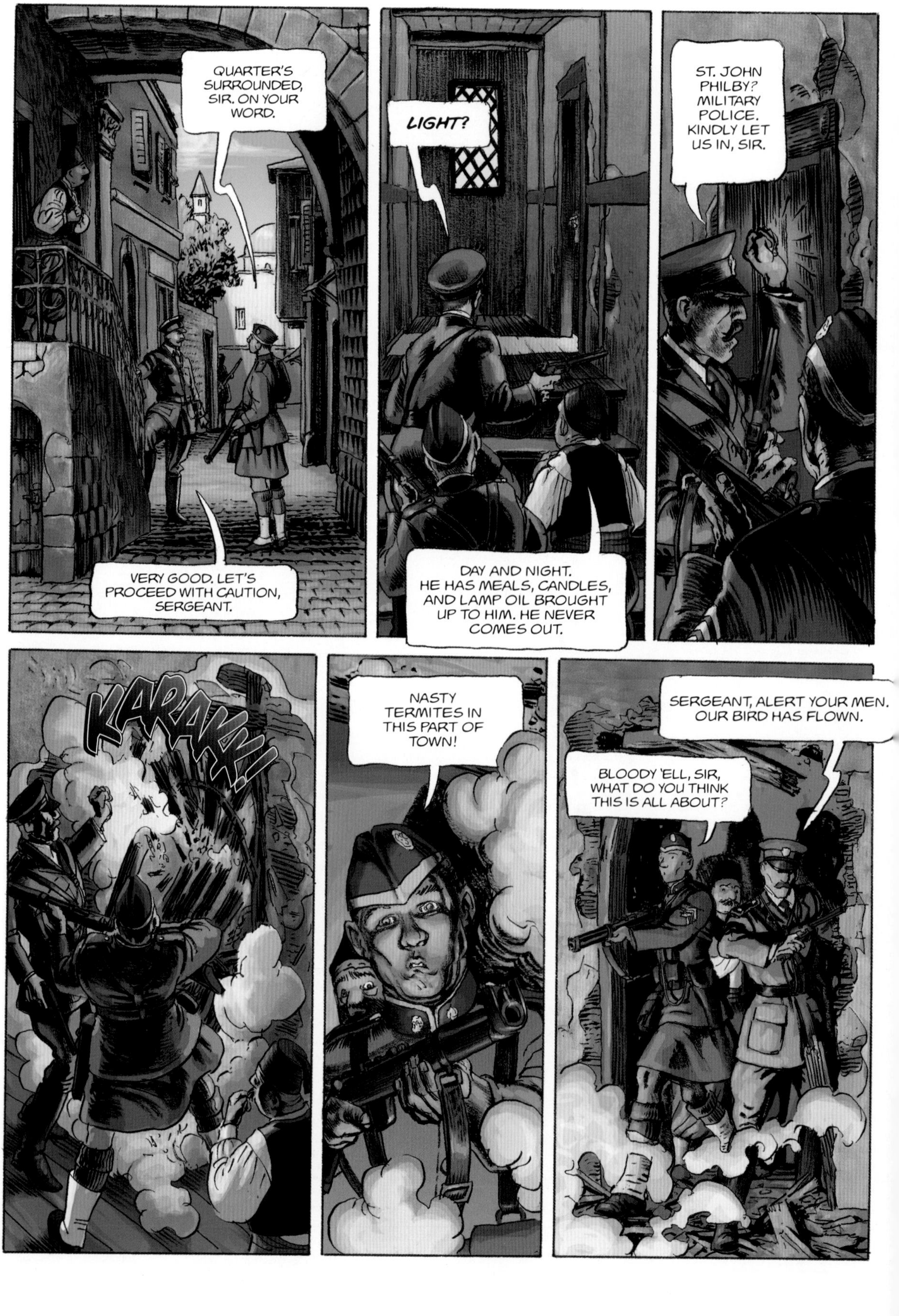
QUARTER'S SURROUNDED, SIR. ON YOUR WORD.
VERY GOOD. LET'S PROCEED WITH CAUTION, SERGEANT.
LIGHT?
DAY AND NIGHT. HE HAS MEALS, CANDLES, AND LAMP OIL BROUGHT UP TO HIM. HE NEVER COMES OUT.
ST. JOHN PHILBY? MILITARY POLICE. KINDLY LET US IN, SIR.
KARAKK!
NASTY TERMITES IN THIS PART OF TOWN!
SERGEANT, ALERT YOUR MEN. OUR BIRD HAS FLOWN.
BLOODY 'ELL, SIR, WHAT DO YOU THINK THIS IS ALL ABOUT?

NOT THE SLIGHTEST, OLD CHAP.

I— AAAAAAH!

KRAKOOOW

EVERYTHING ALL RIGHT, SIR?

I'M FINE, SERGEANT. SET UP A BARRIER AND CALL THE ENGINEER CORPS. I WON'T HAVE US ACCUSED OF TEARING DOWN THE ANCIENT CITY.

MARKINGS, YOU SAY? WHAT KIND OF MARKINGS?

NO, I DON'T THINK SO. ACCORDING TO THE ENGINEERS, THE WALLS WERE ABOUT TO COLLAPSE, AS THOUGH THEY'D BEEN THROUGH AN EARTHQUAKE.

NO EARTHQUAKES HAVE BEEN REPORTED IN THIS AREA FOR YEARS!

PHILBY WAS THERE FOR OVER A MONTH!

LIKE ON THE RUNESTONES. THERE WERE HUNDREDS ON THE WALLS. *A WARD?*

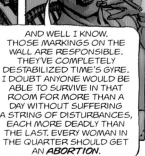

AND WELL I KNOW. THOSE MARKINGS ON THE WALL ARE RESPONSIBLE. THEY'VE COMPLETELY DESTABILIZED TIME'S GYRE. I DOUBT ANYONE WOULD BE ABLE TO SURVIVE IN THAT ROOM FOR MORE THAN A DAY WITHOUT SUFFERING A STRING OF DISTURBANCES, EACH MORE DEADLY THAN THE LAST. EVERY WOMAN IN THE QUARTER SHOULD GET AN *ABORTION*.

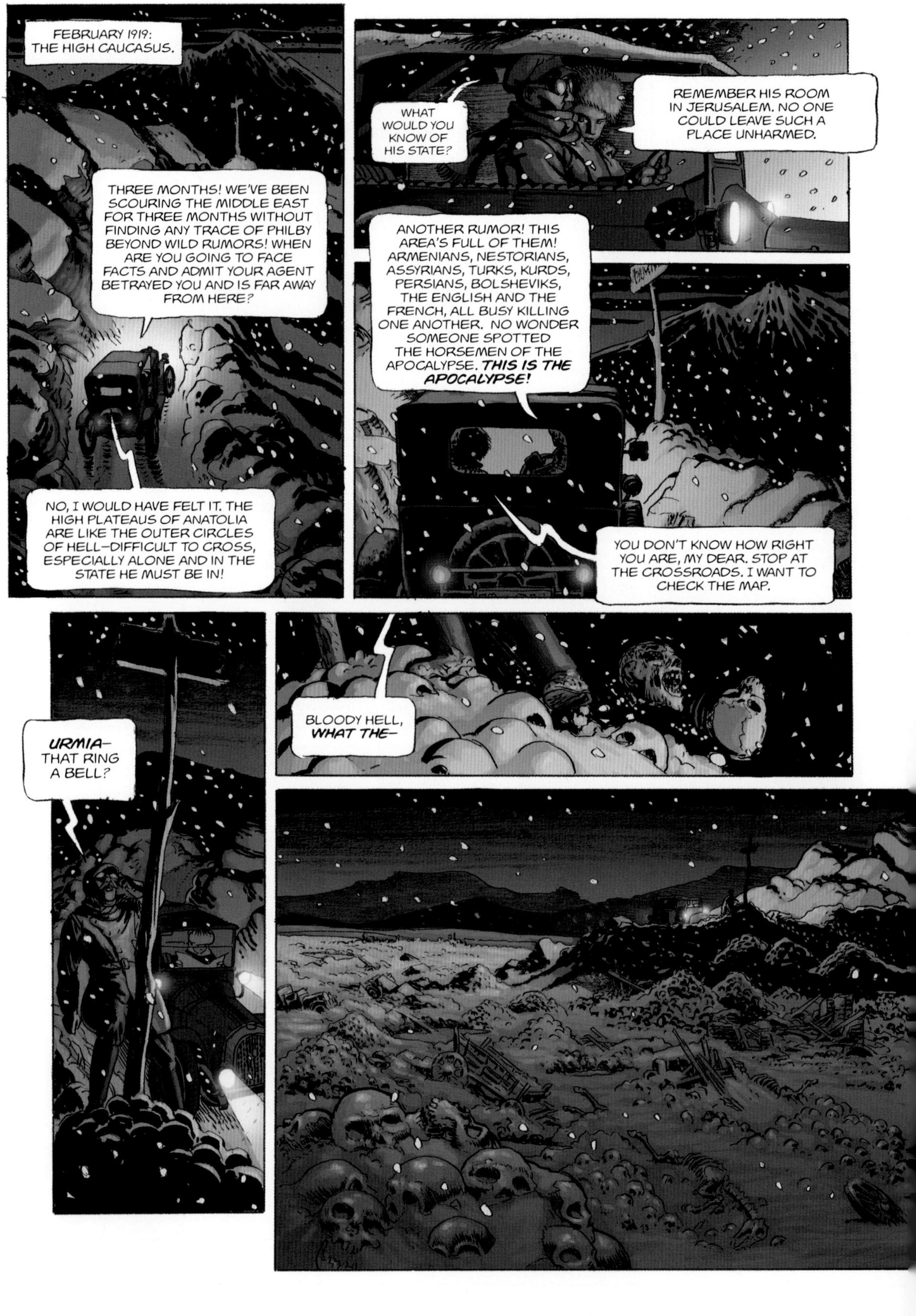
FEBRUARY 1919: THE HIGH CAUCASUS.
THREE MONTHS! WE'VE BEEN SCOURING THE MIDDLE EAST FOR THREE MONTHS WITHOUT FINDING ANY TRACE OF PHILBY BEYOND WILD RUMORS! WHEN ARE YOU GOING TO FACE FACTS AND ADMIT YOUR AGENT BETRAYED YOU AND IS FAR AWAY FROM HERE?
NO, I WOULD HAVE FELT IT. THE HIGH PLATEAUS OF ANATOLIA ARE LIKE THE OUTER CIRCLES OF HELL—DIFFICULT TO CROSS, ESPECIALLY ALONE AND IN THE STATE HE MUST BE IN!
WHAT WOULD YOU KNOW OF HIS STATE?
REMEMBER HIS ROOM IN JERUSALEM. NO ONE COULD LEAVE SUCH A PLACE UNHARMED.
ANOTHER RUMOR! THIS AREA'S FULL OF THEM! ARMENIANS, NESTORIANS, ASSYRIANS, TURKS, KURDS, PERSIANS, BOLSHEVIKS, THE ENGLISH AND THE FRENCH, ALL BUSY KILLING ONE ANOTHER. NO WONDER SOMEONE SPOTTED THE HORSEMEN OF THE APOCALYPSE. THIS IS THE APOCALYPSE!
YOU DON'T KNOW HOW RIGHT YOU ARE, MY DEAR. STOP AT THE CROSSROADS. I WANT TO CHECK THE MAP.
URMIA— THAT RING A BELL?
BLOODY HELL, WHAT THE—

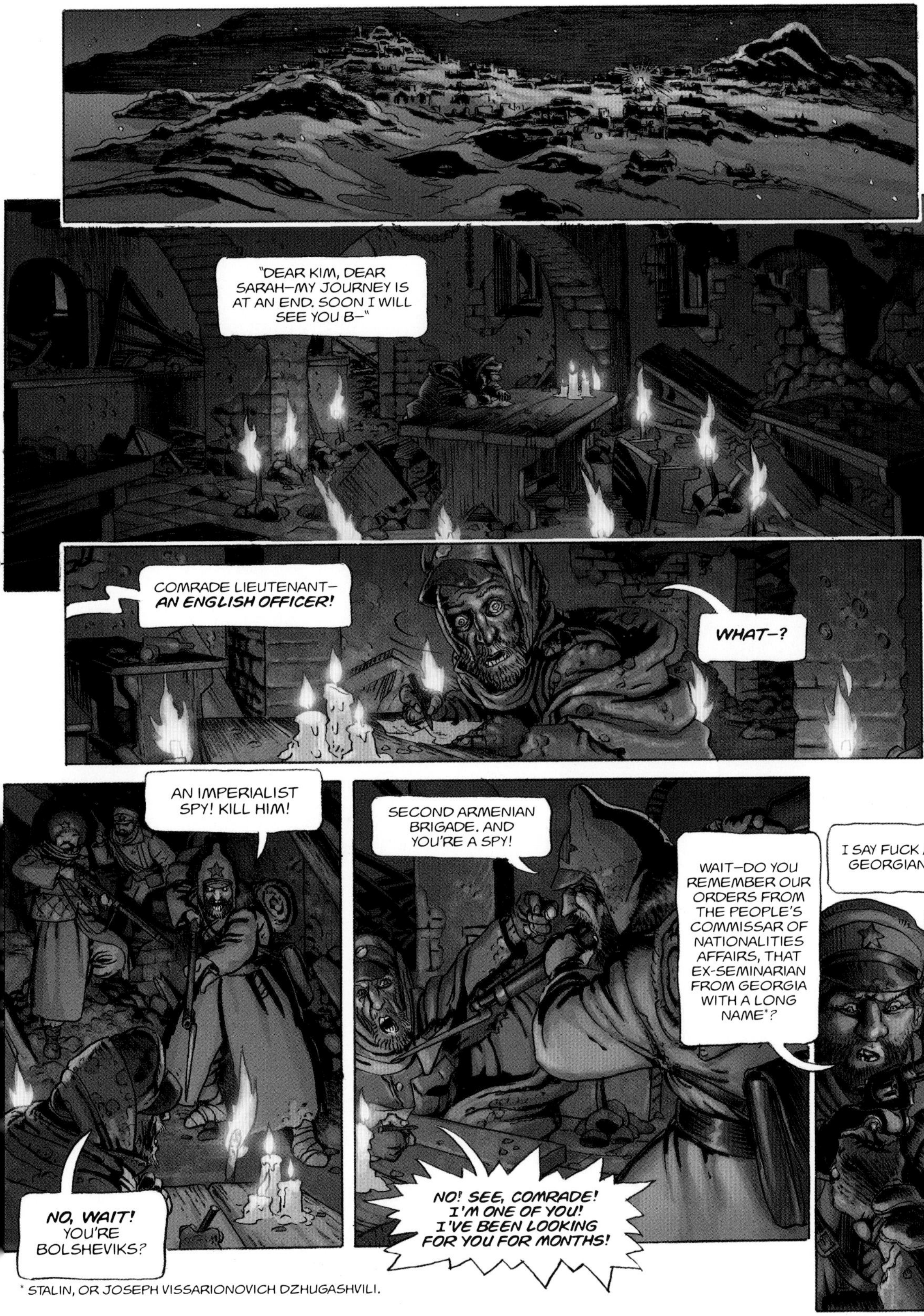
"DEAR KIM, DEAR SARAH—MY JOURNEY IS AT AN END. SOON I WILL SEE YOU B—"
COMRADE LIEUTENANT— AN ENGLISH OFFICER!
WHAT—?
AN IMPERIALIST SPY! KILL HIM!
NO, WAIT! YOU'RE BOLSHEVIKS?
SECOND ARMENIAN BRIGADE. AND YOU'RE A SPY!
NO! SEE, COMRADE! I'M ONE OF YOU! I'VE BEEN LOOKING FOR YOU FOR MONTHS!
WAIT—DO YOU REMEMBER OUR ORDERS FROM THE PEOPLE'S COMMISSAR OF NATIONALITIES AFFAIRS, THAT EX-SEMINARIAN FROM GEORGIA WITH A LONG NAME*?
I SAY FUCK ALL GEORGIANS!

* STALIN, OR JOSEPH VISSARIONOVICH DZHUGASHVILI.

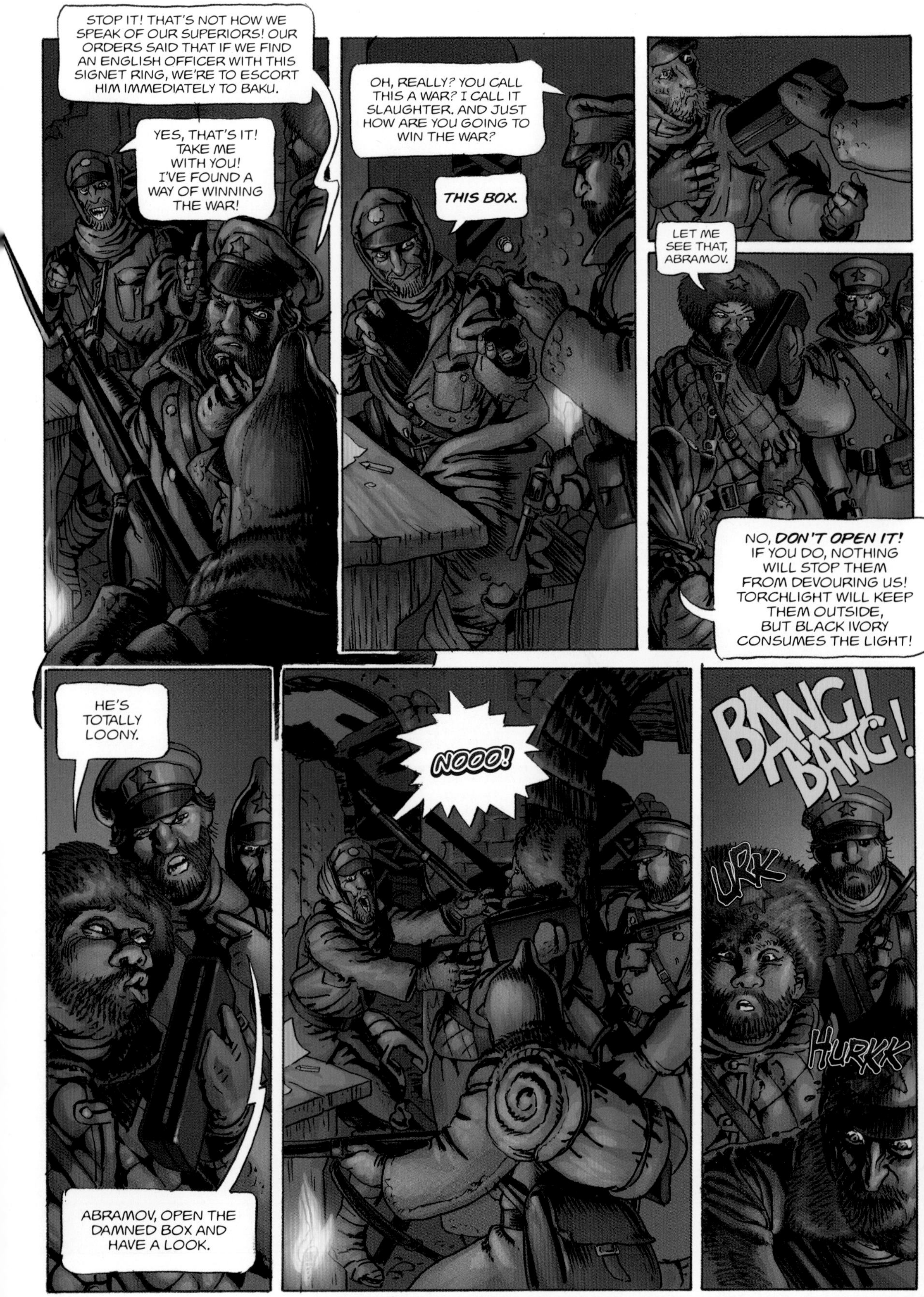
STOP IT! THAT'S NOT HOW WE SPEAK OF OUR SUPERIORS! OUR ORDERS SAID THAT IF WE FIND AN ENGLISH OFFICER WITH THIS SIGNET RING, WE'RE TO ESCORT HIM IMMEDIATELY TO BAKU.
YES, THAT'S IT! TAKE ME WITH YOU! I'VE FOUND A WAY OF WINNING THE WAR!
OH, REALLY? YOU CALL THIS A WAR? I CALL IT SLAUGHTER. AND JUST HOW ARE YOU GOING TO WIN THE WAR?
THIS BOX.
LET ME SEE THAT, ABRAMOV.
NO, DON'T OPEN IT! IF YOU DO, NOTHING WILL STOP THEM FROM DEVOURING US! TORCHLIGHT WILL KEEP THEM OUTSIDE, BUT BLACK IVORY CONSUMES THE LIGHT!
HE'S TOTALLY LOONY.
ABRAMOV, OPEN THE DAMNED BOX AND HAVE A LOOK.
NOOO!
BANG! BANG!
URK
HURKK

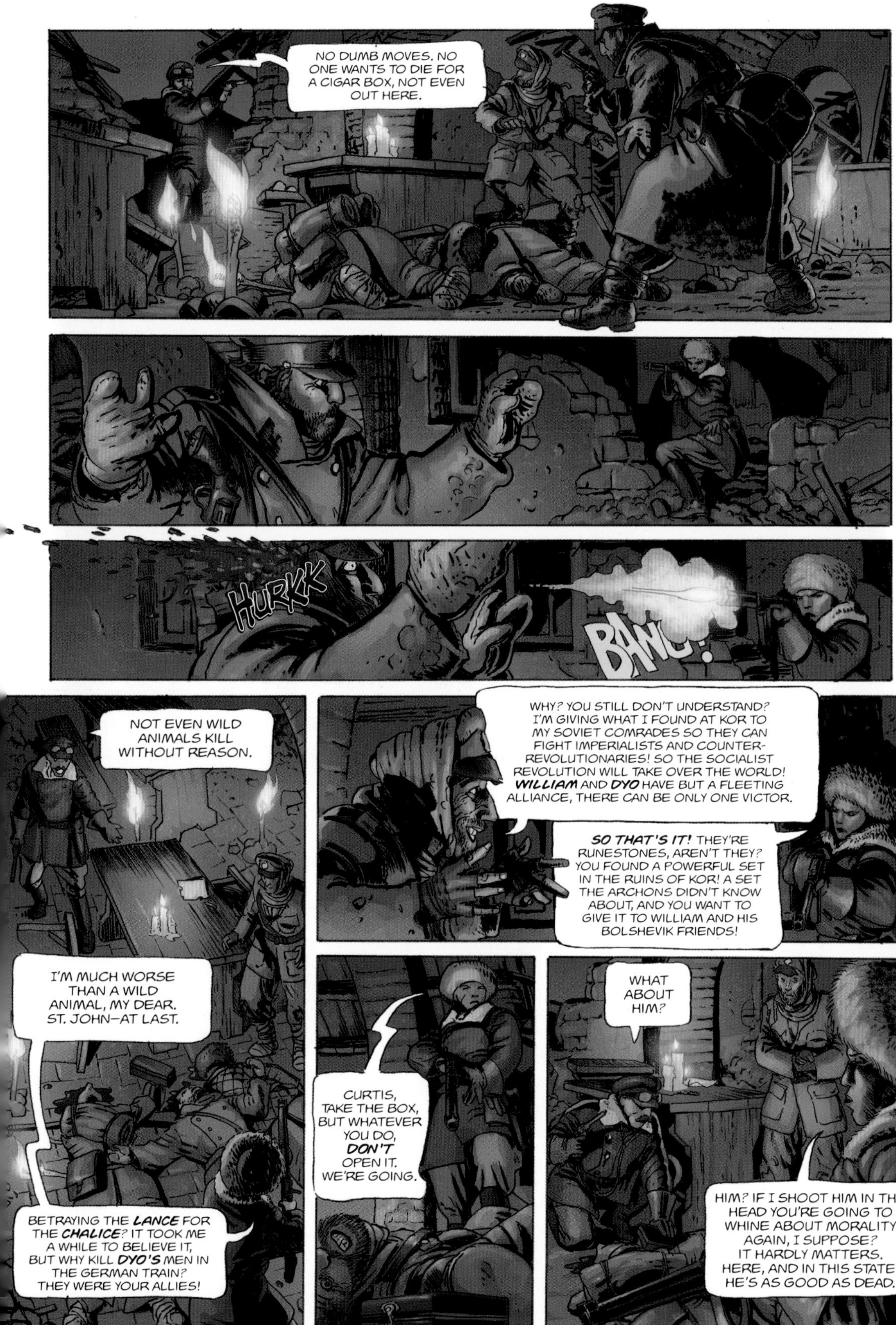
NO DUMB MOVES. NO ONE WANTS TO DIE FOR A CIGAR BOX, NOT EVEN OUT HERE.
HURKK
BANG!
NOT EVEN WILD ANIMALS KILL WITHOUT REASON.
I'M MUCH WORSE THAN A WILD ANIMAL, MY DEAR. ST. JOHN—AT LAST.
BETRAYING THE LANCE FOR THE CHALICE? IT TOOK ME A WHILE TO BELIEVE IT, BUT WHY KILL DYO'S MEN IN THE GERMAN TRAIN? THEY WERE YOUR ALLIES!
WHY? YOU STILL DON'T UNDERSTAND? I'M GIVING WHAT I FOUND AT KOR TO MY SOVIET COMRADES SO THEY CAN FIGHT IMPERIALISTS AND COUNTER-REVOLUTIONARIES! SO THE SOCIALIST REVOLUTION WILL TAKE OVER THE WORLD! WILLIAM AND DYO HAVE BUT A FLEETING ALLIANCE, THERE CAN BE ONLY ONE VICTOR.
SO THAT'S IT! THEY'RE RUNESTONES, AREN'T THEY? YOU FOUND A POWERFUL SET IN THE RUINS OF KOR! A SET THE ARCHONS DIDN'T KNOW ABOUT, AND YOU WANT TO GIVE IT TO WILLIAM AND HIS BOLSHEVIK FRIENDS!
CURTIS, TAKE THE BOX, BUT WHATEVER YOU DO, DON'T OPEN IT. WE'RE GOING.
WHAT ABOUT HIM?
HIM? IF I SHOOT HIM IN THE HEAD YOU'RE GOING TO WHINE ABOUT MORALITY AGAIN, I SUPPOSE? IT HARDLY MATTERS. HERE, AND IN THIS STATE, HE'S AS GOOD AS DEAD.

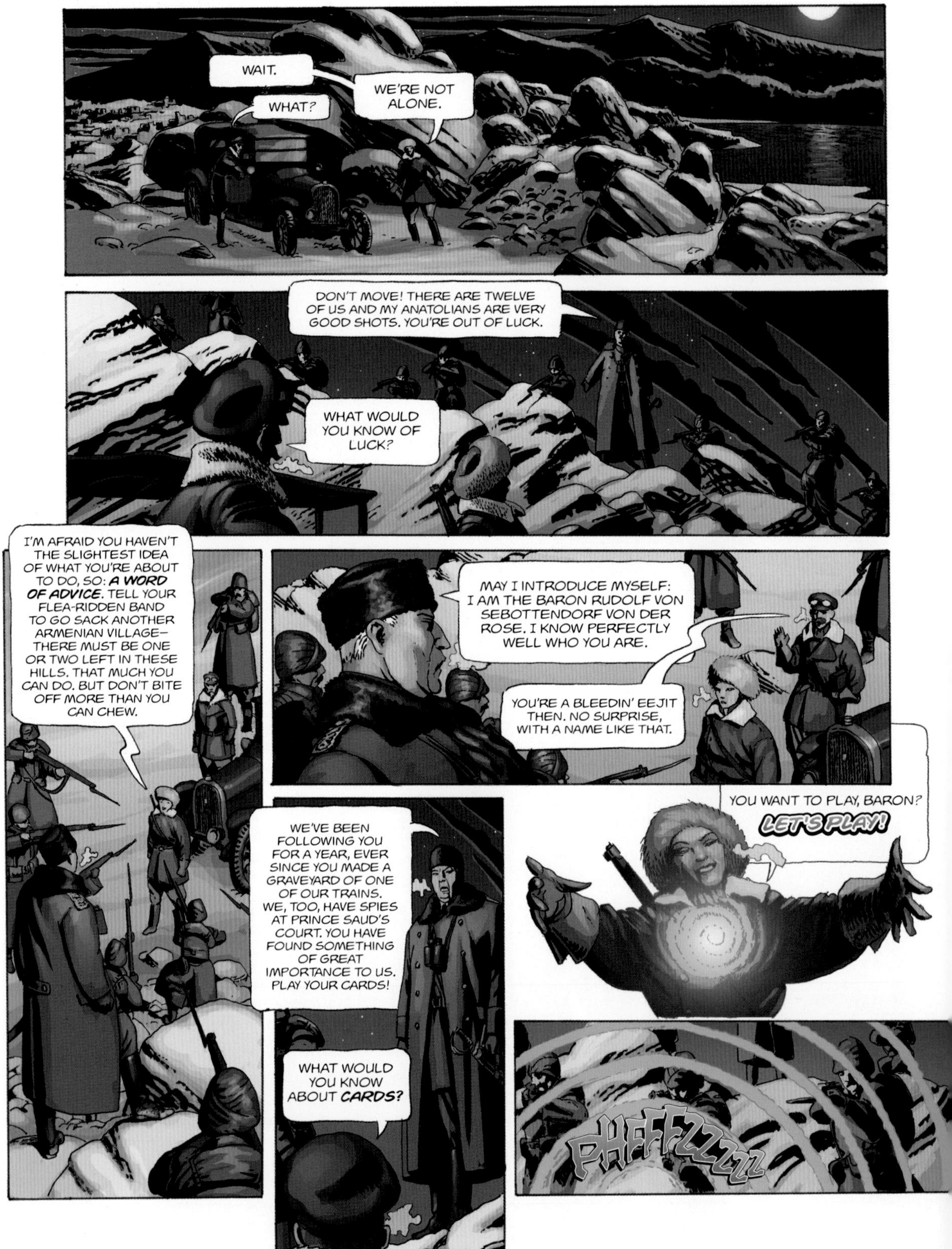
WAIT.
WHAT?
WE'RE NOT ALONE.
DON'T MOVE! THERE ARE TWELVE OF US AND MY ANATOLIANS ARE VERY GOOD SHOTS. YOU'RE OUT OF LUCK.
WHAT WOULD YOU KNOW OF LUCK?
I'M AFRAID YOU HAVEN'T THE SLIGHTEST IDEA OF WHAT YOU'RE ABOUT TO DO, SO: A WORD OF ADVICE. TELL YOUR FLEA-RIDDEN BAND TO GO SACK ANOTHER ARMENIAN VILLAGE— THERE MUST BE ONE OR TWO LEFT IN THESE HILLS. THAT MUCH YOU CAN DO. BUT DON'T BITE OFF MORE THAN YOU CAN CHEW.
MAY I INTRODUCE MYSELF: I AM THE BARON RUDOLF VON SEBOTTENDORF VON DER ROSE. I KNOW PERFECTLY WELL WHO YOU ARE.
YOU'RE A BLEEDIN' EEJIT THEN. NO SURPRISE, WITH A NAME LIKE THAT.
WE'VE BEEN FOLLOWING YOU FOR A YEAR, EVER SINCE YOU MADE A GRAVEYARD OF ONE OF OUR TRAINS. WE, TOO, HAVE SPIES AT PRINCE SAUD'S COURT. YOU HAVE FOUND SOMETHING OF GREAT IMPORTANCE TO US. PLAY YOUR CARDS!
WHAT WOULD YOU KNOW ABOUT CARDS?
YOU WANT TO PLAY, BARON? LET'S PLAY!
PHFFFZZZZZ

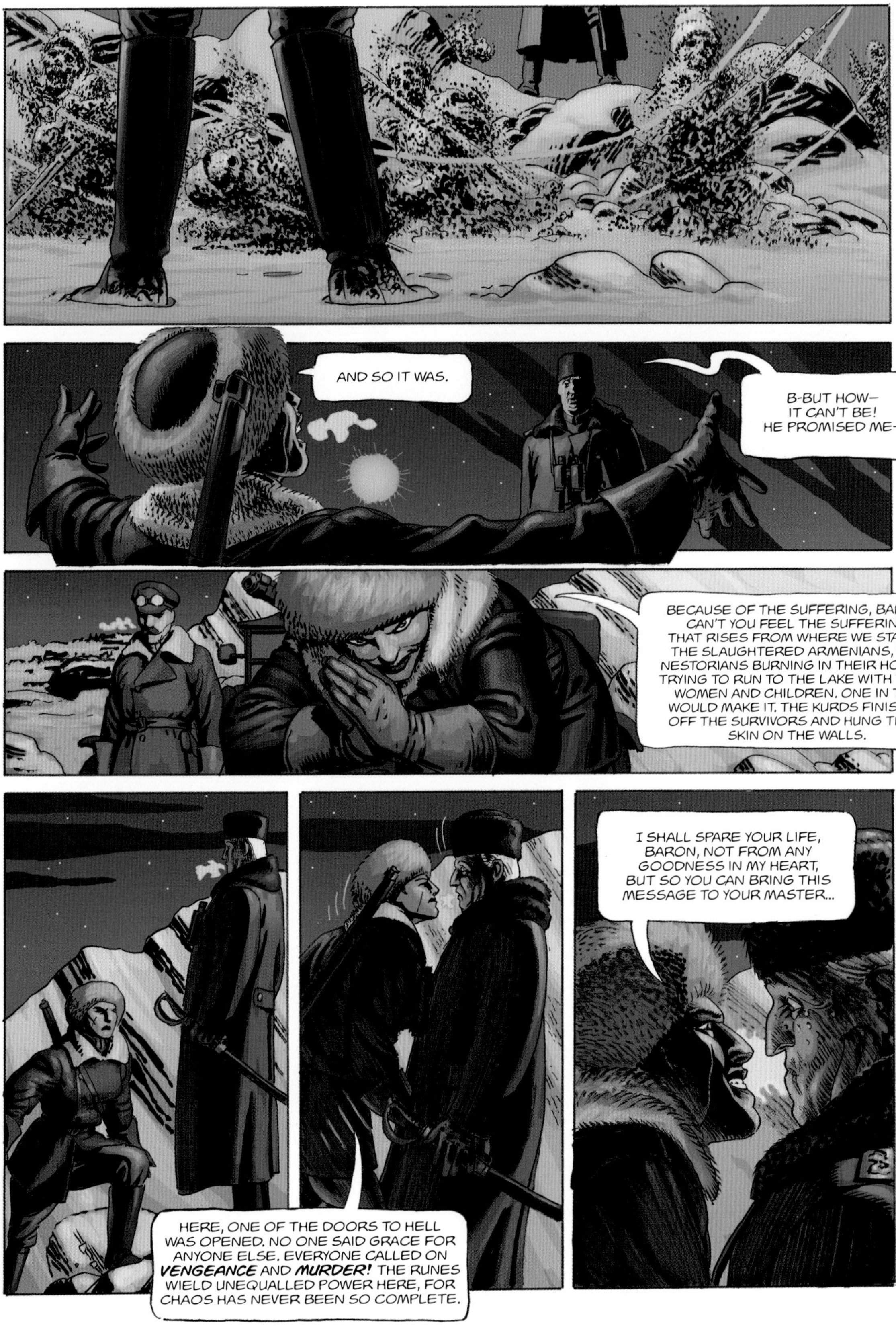
AND SO IT WAS.
B-BUT HOW— IT CAN'T BE! HE PROMISED ME—
BECAUSE OF THE SUFFERING, BARON. CAN'T YOU FEEL THE SUFFERING THAT RISES FROM WHERE WE STAND? THE SLAUGHTERED ARMENIANS, THE NESTORIANS BURNING IN THEIR HOMES, TRYING TO RUN TO THE LAKE WITH THEIR WOMEN AND CHILDREN. ONE IN TEN WOULD MAKE IT. THE KURDS FINISHED OFF THE SURVIVORS AND HUNG THEIR SKIN ON THE WALLS.
HERE, ONE OF THE DOORS TO HELL WAS OPENED. NO ONE SAID GRACE FOR ANYONE ELSE. EVERYONE CALLED ON ***VENGEANCE*** AND ***MURDER!*** THE RUNES WIELD UNEQUALLED POWER HERE, FOR CHAOS HAS NEVER BEEN SO COMPLETE.
I SHALL SPARE YOUR LIFE, BARON, NOT FROM ANY GOODNESS IN MY HEART, BUT SO YOU CAN BRING THIS MESSAGE TO YOUR MASTER...

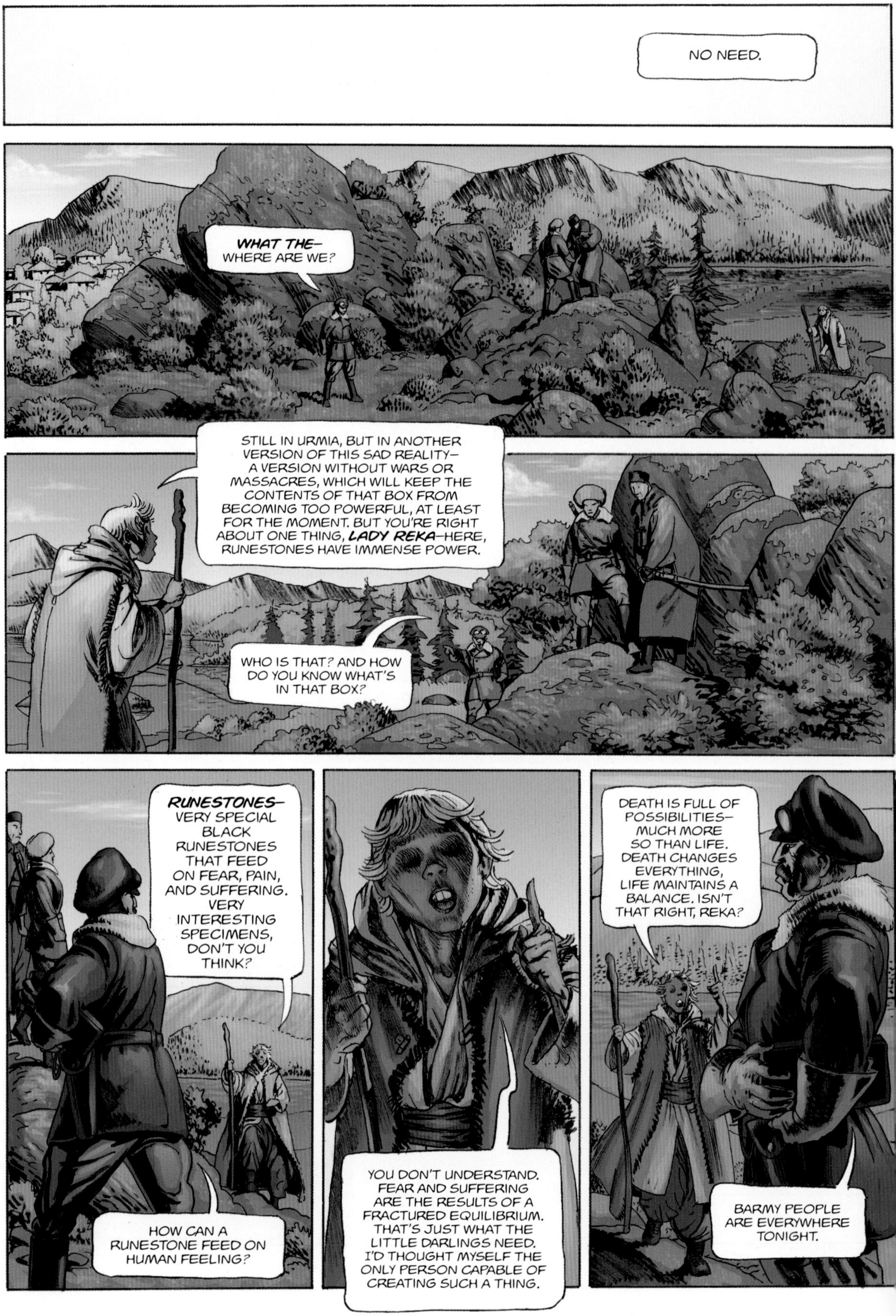
NO NEED.
WHAT THE— WHERE ARE WE?
STILL IN URMIA, BUT IN ANOTHER VERSION OF THIS SAD REALITY— A VERSION WITHOUT WARS OR MASSACRES, WHICH WILL KEEP THE CONTENTS OF THAT BOX FROM BECOMING TOO POWERFUL, AT LEAST FOR THE MOMENT. BUT YOU'RE RIGHT ABOUT ONE THING, LADY REKA—HERE, RUNESTONES HAVE IMMENSE POWER.
WHO IS THAT? AND HOW DO YOU KNOW WHAT'S IN THAT BOX?
RUNESTONES— VERY SPECIAL BLACK RUNESTONES THAT FEED ON FEAR, PAIN, AND SUFFERING. VERY INTERESTING SPECIMENS, DON'T YOU THINK?
HOW CAN A RUNESTONE FEED ON HUMAN FEELING?
YOU DON'T UNDERSTAND. FEAR AND SUFFERING ARE THE RESULTS OF A FRACTURED EQUILIBRIUM. THAT'S JUST WHAT THE LITTLE DARLINGS NEED. I'D THOUGHT MYSELF THE ONLY PERSON CAPABLE OF CREATING SUCH A THING.
DEATH IS FULL OF POSSIBILITIES— MUCH MORE SO THAN LIFE. DEATH CHANGES EVERYTHING, LIFE MAINTAINS A BALANCE. ISN'T THAT RIGHT, REKA?
BARMY PEOPLE ARE EVERYWHERE TONIGHT.

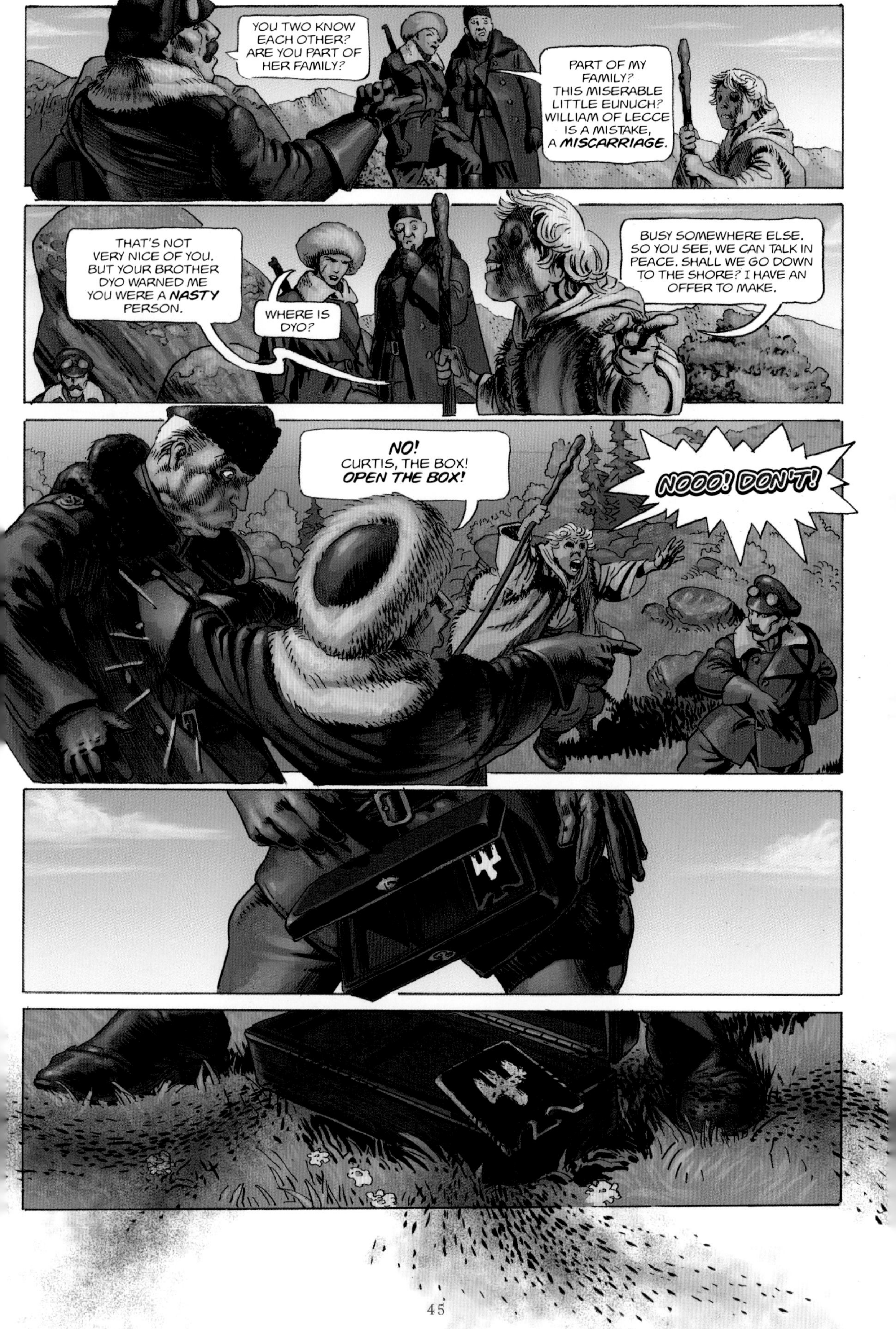
YOU TWO KNOW EACH OTHER? ARE YOU PART OF HER FAMILY?
PART OF MY FAMILY? THIS MISERABLE LITTLE EUNUCH? WILLIAM OF LECCE IS A MISTAKE, A **MISCARRIAGE**.
THAT'S NOT VERY NICE OF YOU. BUT YOUR BROTHER DYO WARNED ME YOU WERE A **NASTY** PERSON.
WHERE IS DYO?
BUSY SOMEWHERE ELSE. SO YOU SEE, WE CAN TALK IN PEACE. SHALL WE GO DOWN TO THE SHORE? I HAVE AN OFFER TO MAKE.
NO! CURTIS, THE BOX! **OPEN THE BOX!**
NOOO! DON'T!

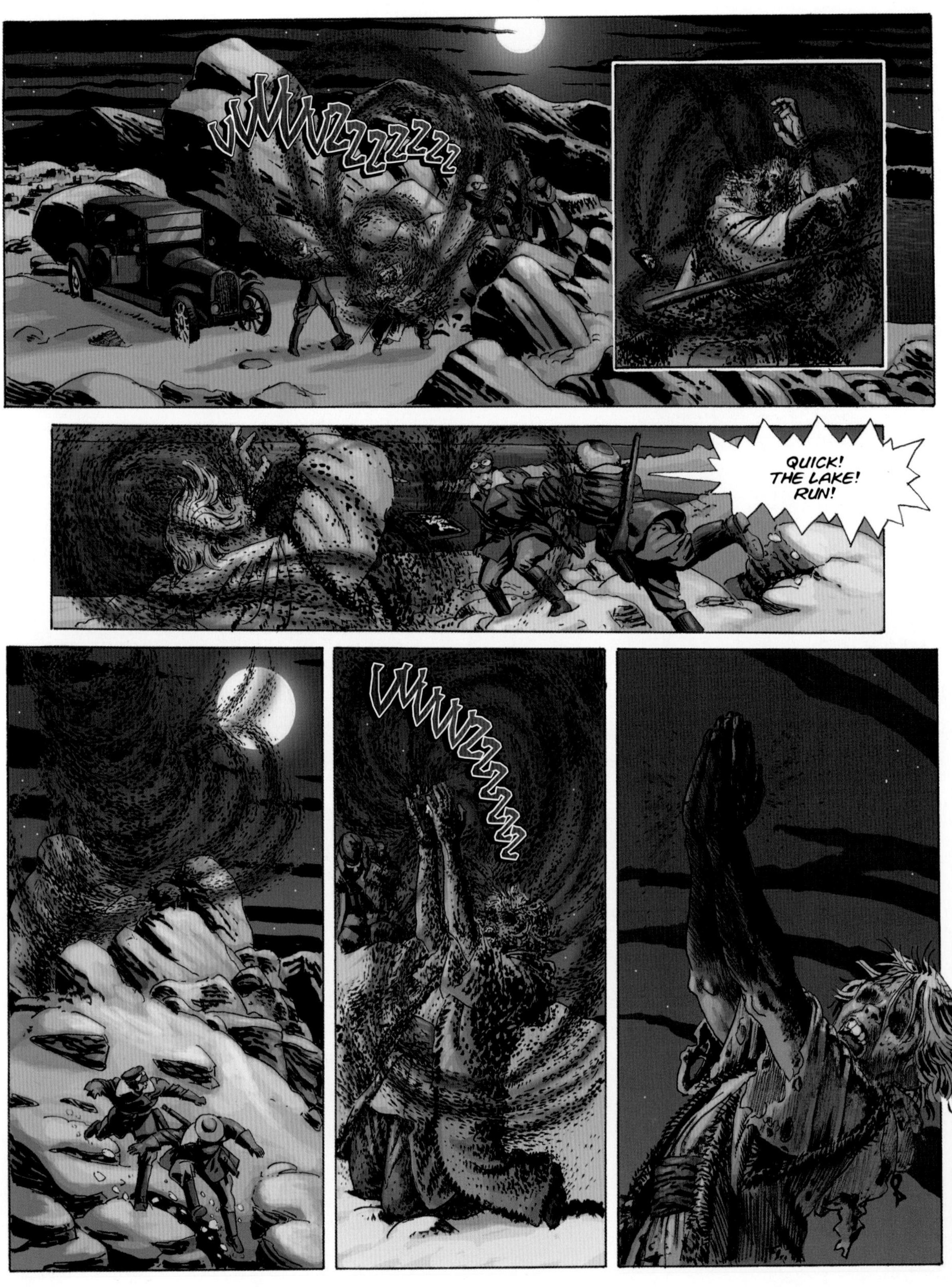
VVVVVZZZZZZZZ
QUICK! THE LAKE! RUN!
VVVVVZZZZZZZZ

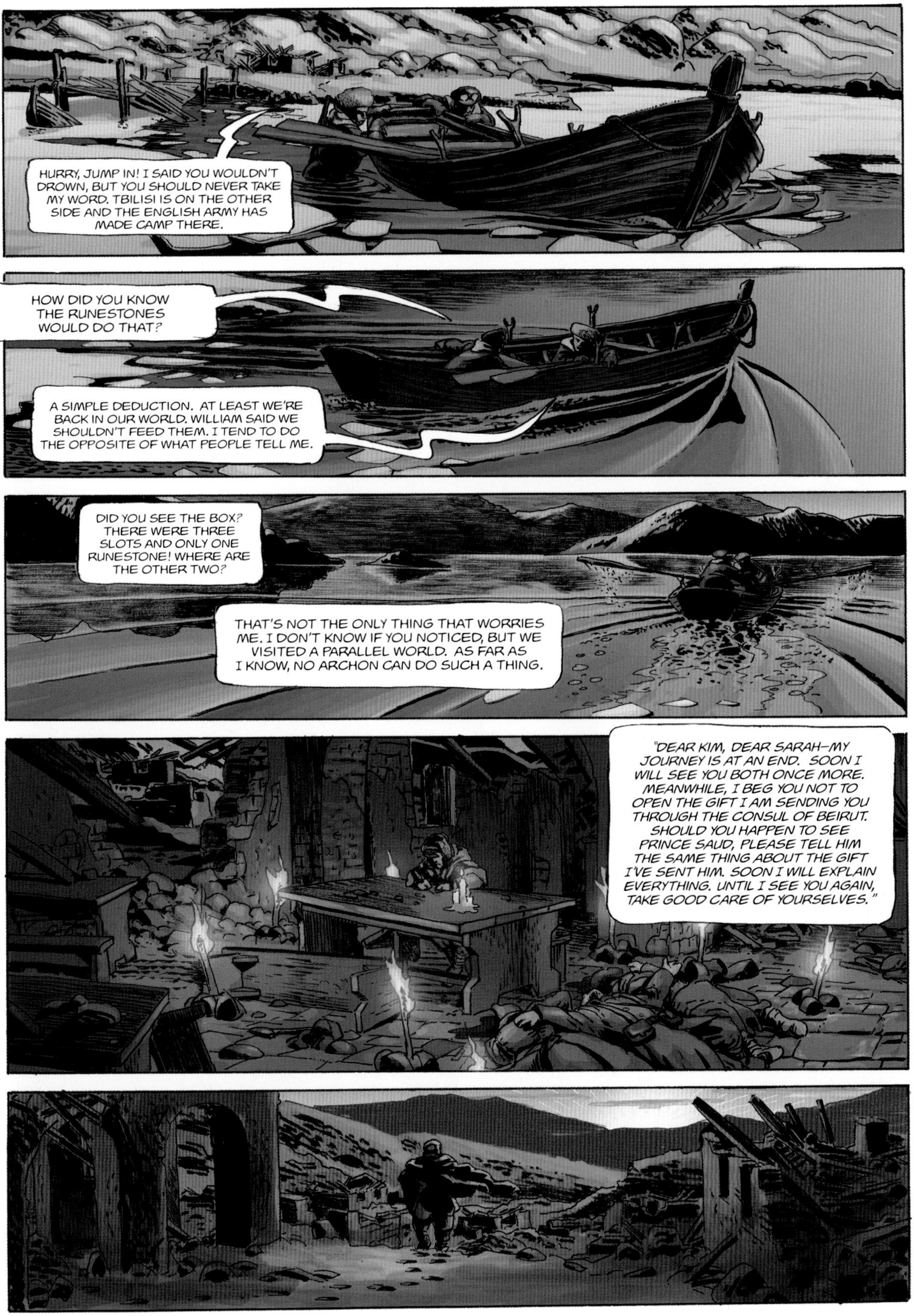
HURRY, JUMP IN! I SAID YOU WOULDN'T DROWN, BUT YOU SHOULD NEVER TAKE MY WORD. TBILISI IS ON THE OTHER SIDE AND THE ENGLISH ARMY HAS MADE CAMP THERE.
HOW DID YOU KNOW THE RUNESTONES WOULD DO THAT?
A SIMPLE DEDUCTION. AT LEAST WE'RE BACK IN OUR WORLD. WILLIAM SAID WE SHOULDN'T FEED THEM. I TEND TO DO THE OPPOSITE OF WHAT PEOPLE TELL ME.
DID YOU SEE THE BOX? THERE WERE THREE SLOTS AND ONLY ONE RUNESTONE! WHERE ARE THE OTHER TWO?
THAT'S NOT THE ONLY THING THAT WORRIES ME. I DON'T KNOW IF YOU NOTICED, BUT WE VISITED A PARALLEL WORLD. AS FAR AS I KNOW, NO ARCHON CAN DO SUCH A THING.
"DEAR KIM, DEAR SARAH—MY JOURNEY IS AT AN END. SOON I WILL SEE YOU BOTH ONCE MORE. MEANWHILE, I BEG YOU NOT TO OPEN THE GIFT I AM SENDING YOU THROUGH THE CONSUL OF BEIRUT. SHOULD YOU HAPPEN TO SEE PRINCE SAUD, PLEASE TELL HIM THE SAME THING ABOUT THE GIFT I'VE SENT HIM. SOON I WILL EXPLAIN EVERYTHING. UNTIL I SEE YOU AGAIN, TAKE GOOD CARE OF YOURSELVES."

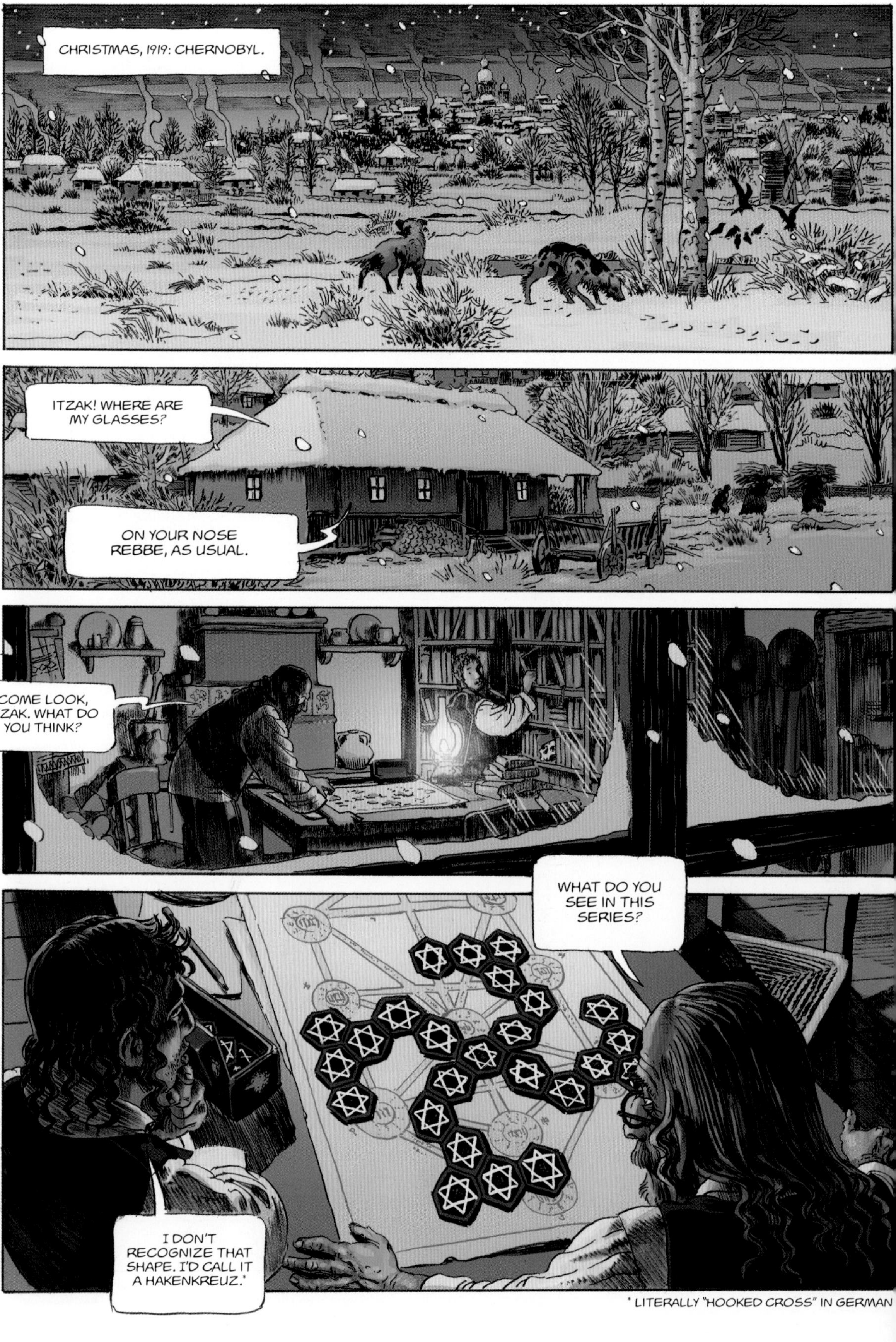
CHRISTMAS, 1919: CHERNOBYL.
ITZAK! WHERE ARE MY GLASSES?
ON YOUR NOSE REBBE, AS USUAL.
COME LOOK, ITZAK. WHAT DO YOU THINK?
WHAT DO YOU SEE IN THIS SERIES?
I DON'T RECOGNIZE THAT SHAPE. I'D CALL IT A HAKENKREUZ.*

* LITERALLY "HOOKED CROSS" IN GERMAN

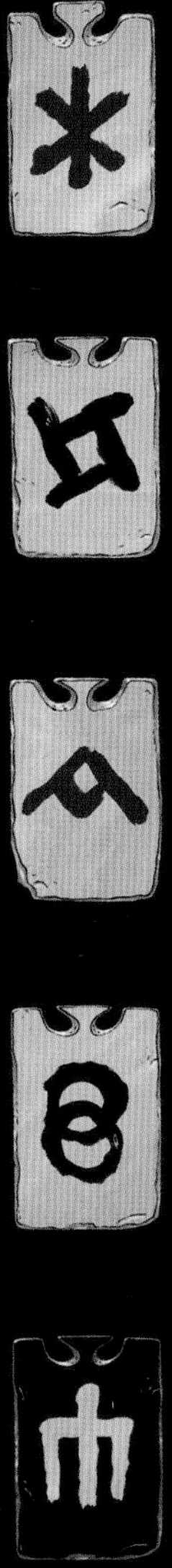

1919 A.D.

Book Nine

The Thule Society

1919 A.D.

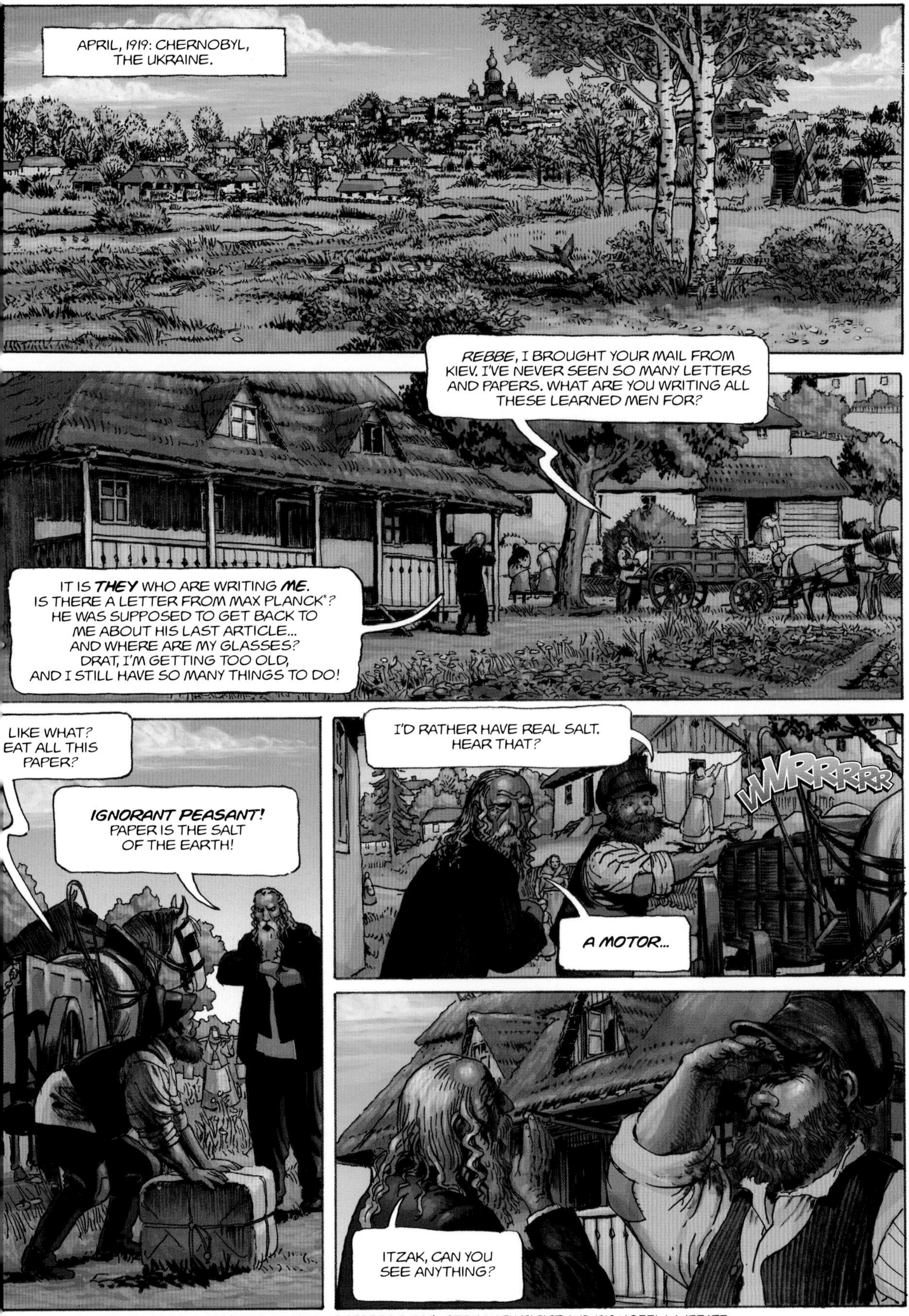
APRIL, 1919: CHERNOBYL, THE UKRAINE.
REBBE, I BROUGHT YOUR MAIL FROM KIEV. I'VE NEVER SEEN SO MANY LETTERS AND PAPERS. WHAT ARE YOU WRITING ALL THESE LEARNED MEN FOR?
IT IS THEY WHO ARE WRITING ME. IS THERE A LETTER FROM MAX PLANCK*? HE WAS SUPPOSED TO GET BACK TO ME ABOUT HIS LAST ARTICLE... AND WHERE ARE MY GLASSES? DRAT, I'M GETTING TOO OLD, AND I STILL HAVE SO MANY THINGS TO DO!
LIKE WHAT? EAT ALL THIS PAPER?
IGNORANT PEASANT! PAPER IS THE SALT OF THE EARTH!
I'D RATHER HAVE REAL SALT. HEAR THAT?
WWRRRRRR
A MOTOR...
ITZAK, CAN YOU SEE ANYTHING?

* MAX KARL ERNST LUDWING PLANCK (APRIL 23, 1858 – OCTOBER 4, 1947): GERMAN PHYSICIST AND 1918 NOBEL LAUREATE.

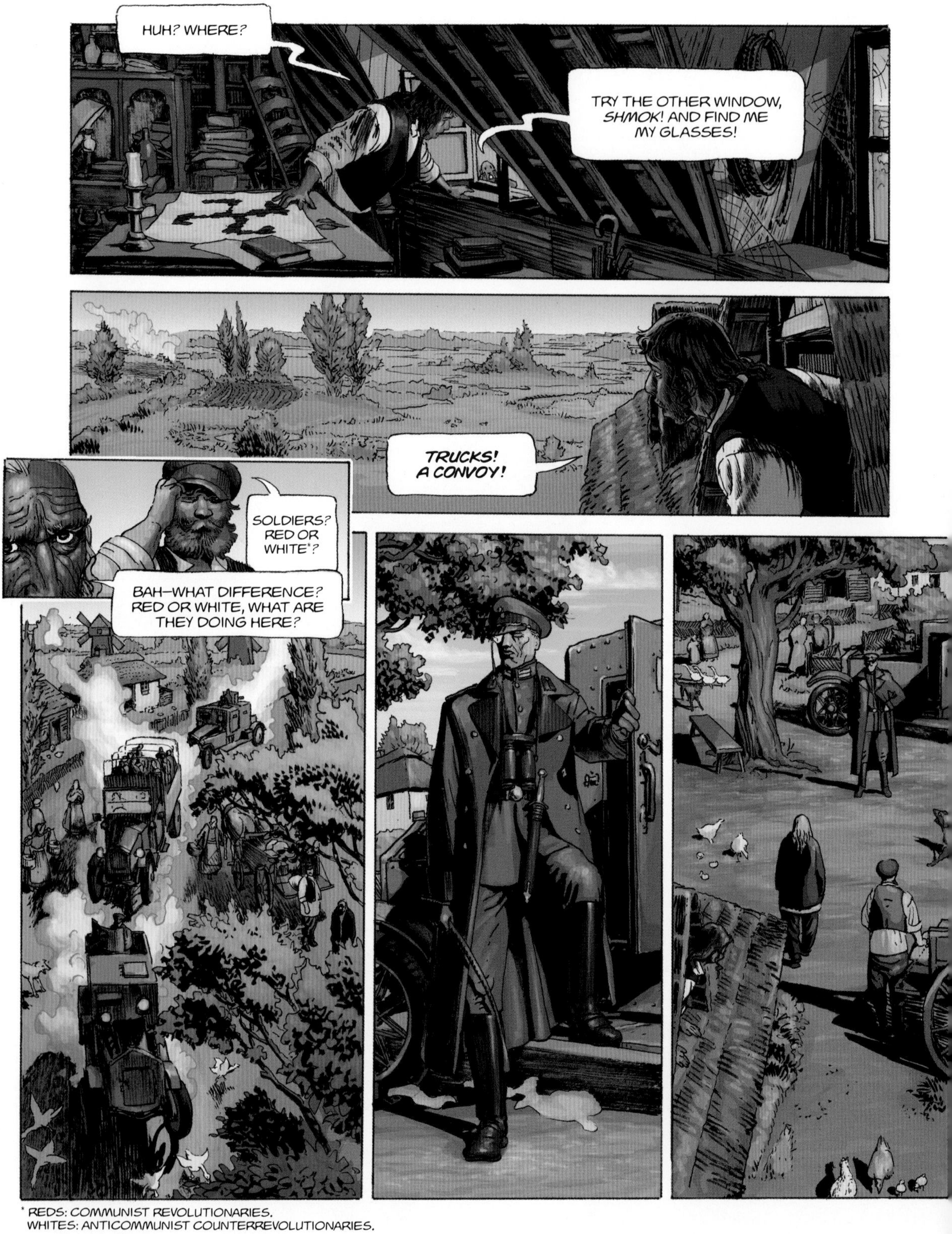
HUH? WHERE?
TRY THE OTHER WINDOW, *SHMOK*! AND FIND ME MY GLASSES!
TRUCKS! A CONVOY!
SOLDIERS? RED OR WHITE*?
BAH—WHAT DIFFERENCE? RED OR WHITE, WHAT ARE THEY DOING HERE?

* REDS: COMMUNIST REVOLUTIONARIES.
WHITES: ANTICOMMUNIST COUNTERREVOLUTIONARIES.

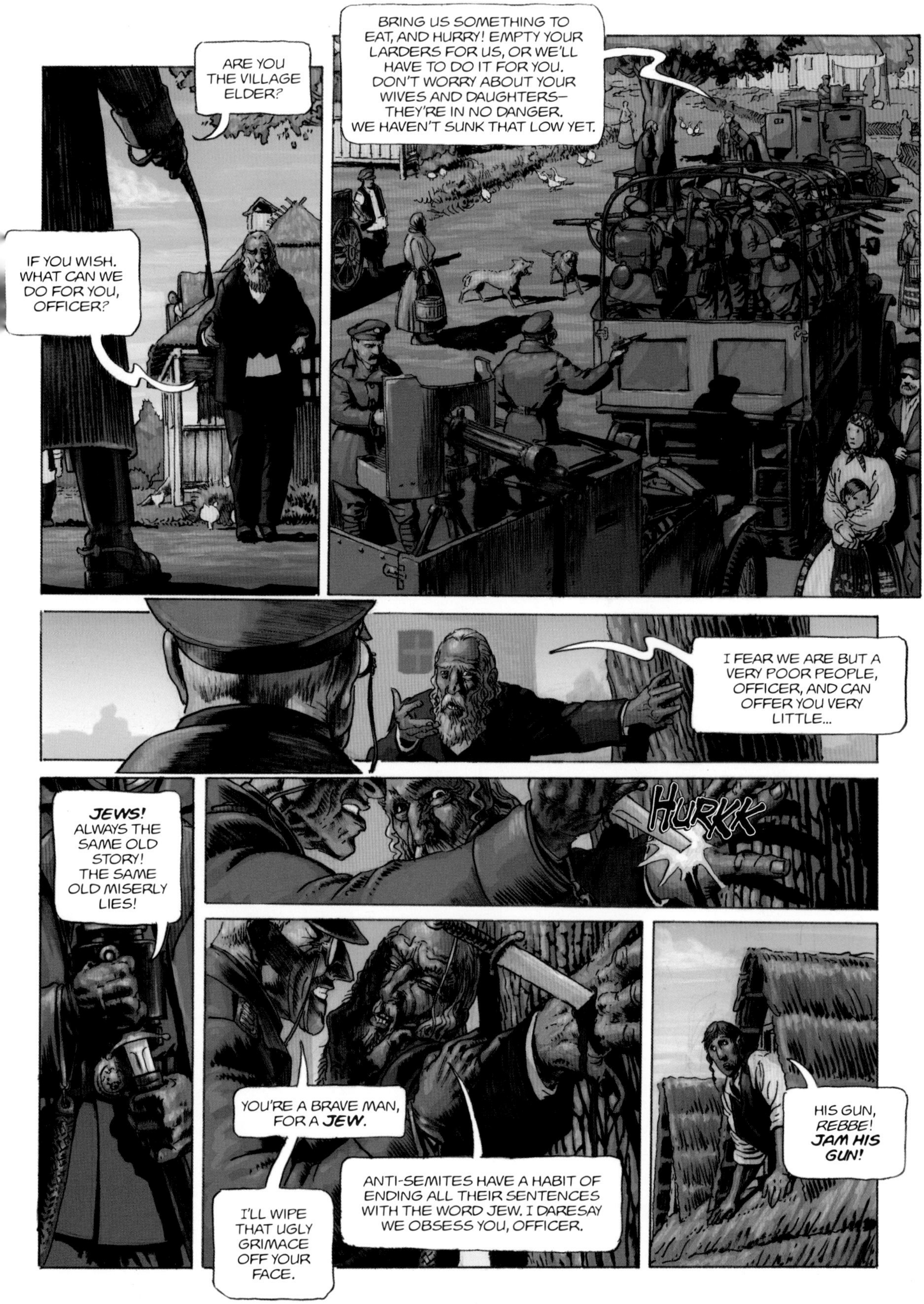
ARE YOU THE VILLAGE ELDER?
IF YOU WISH. WHAT CAN WE DO FOR YOU, OFFICER?
BRING US SOMETHING TO EAT, AND HURRY! EMPTY YOUR LARDERS FOR US, OR WE'LL HAVE TO DO IT FOR YOU. DON'T WORRY ABOUT YOUR WIVES AND DAUGHTERS— THEY'RE IN NO DANGER. WE HAVEN'T SUNK THAT LOW YET.
I FEAR WE ARE BUT A VERY POOR PEOPLE, OFFICER, AND CAN OFFER YOU VERY LITTLE...
JEWS! ALWAYS THE SAME OLD STORY! THE SAME OLD MISERLY LIES!
HURKK
YOU'RE A BRAVE MAN, FOR A JEW.
I'LL WIPE THAT UGLY GRIMACE OFF YOUR FACE.
ANTI-SEMITES HAVE A HABIT OF ENDING ALL THEIR SENTENCES WITH THE WORD JEW. I DARESAY WE OBSESS YOU, OFFICER.
HIS GUN, REBBE! JAM HIS GUN!

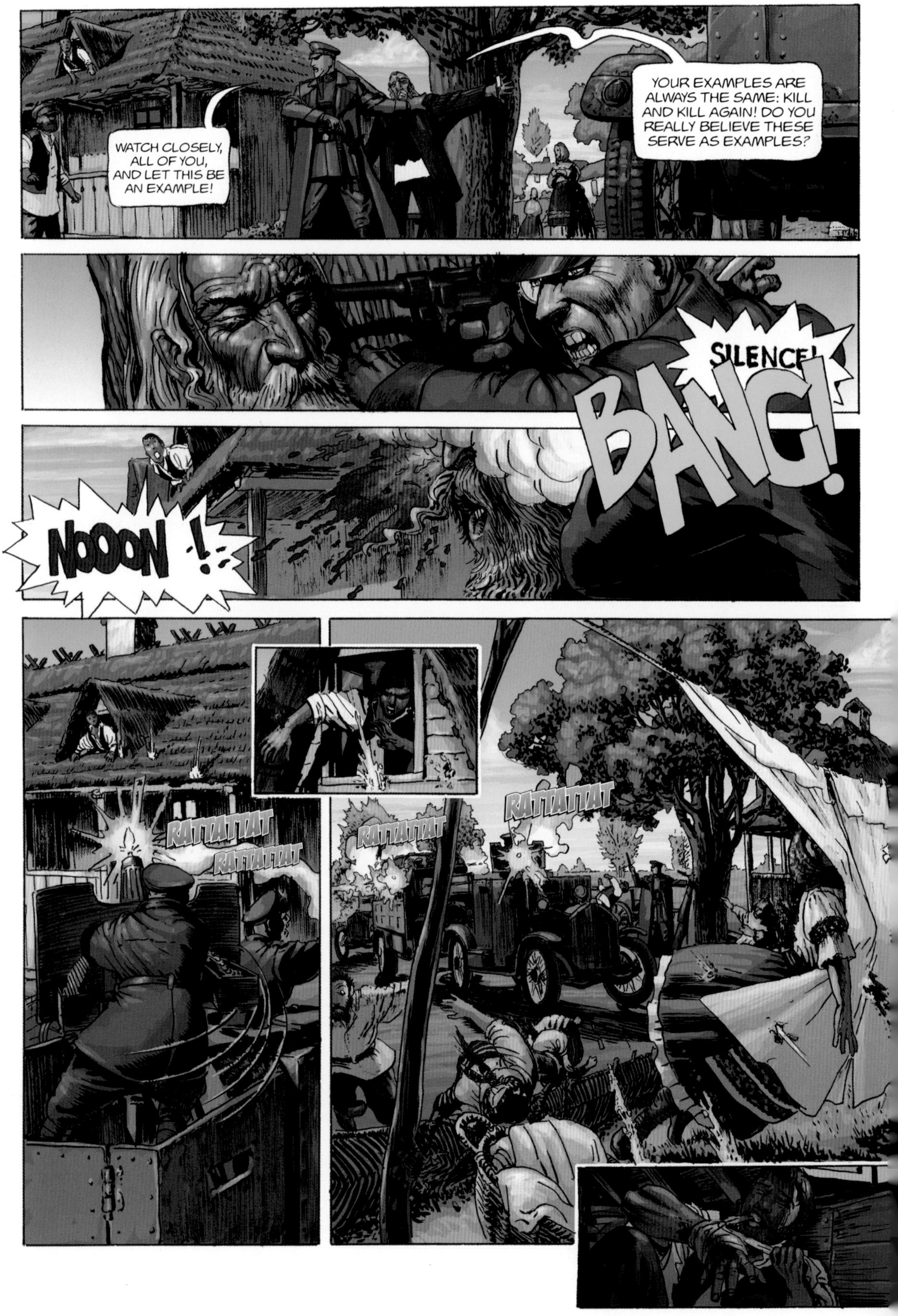
WATCH CLOSELY, ALL OF YOU, AND LET THIS BE AN EXAMPLE!
YOUR EXAMPLES ARE ALWAYS THE SAME: KILL AND KILL AGAIN! DO YOU REALLY BELIEVE THESE SERVE AS EXAMPLES?
SILENCE!
BANG!
NOOON !
RATTATTAT
RATTATTAT
RATTATTAT
RATTATTAT

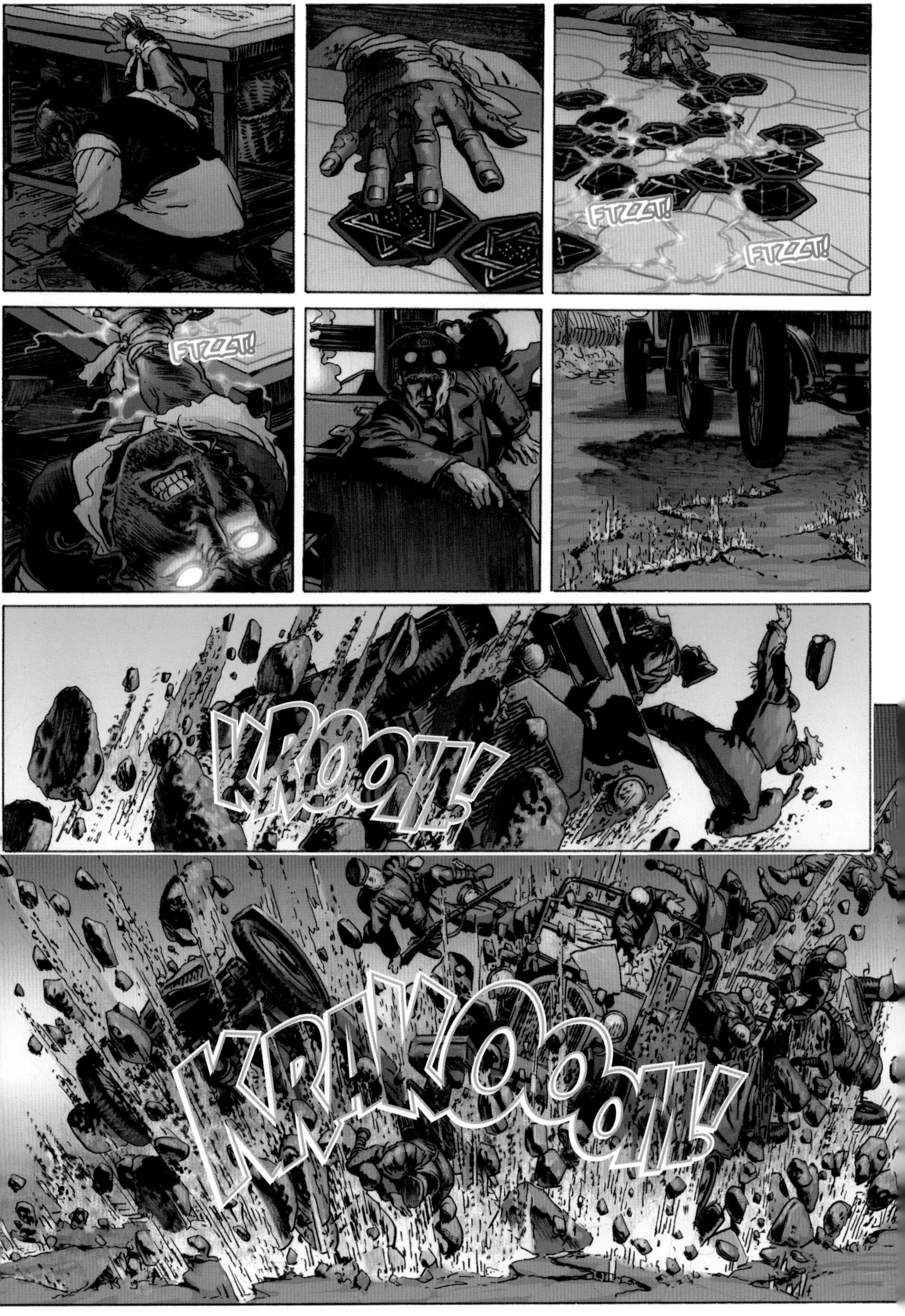
FTZZT!
FTZZT!
FTZZT!
KROOM!
KRAKOOOOM!

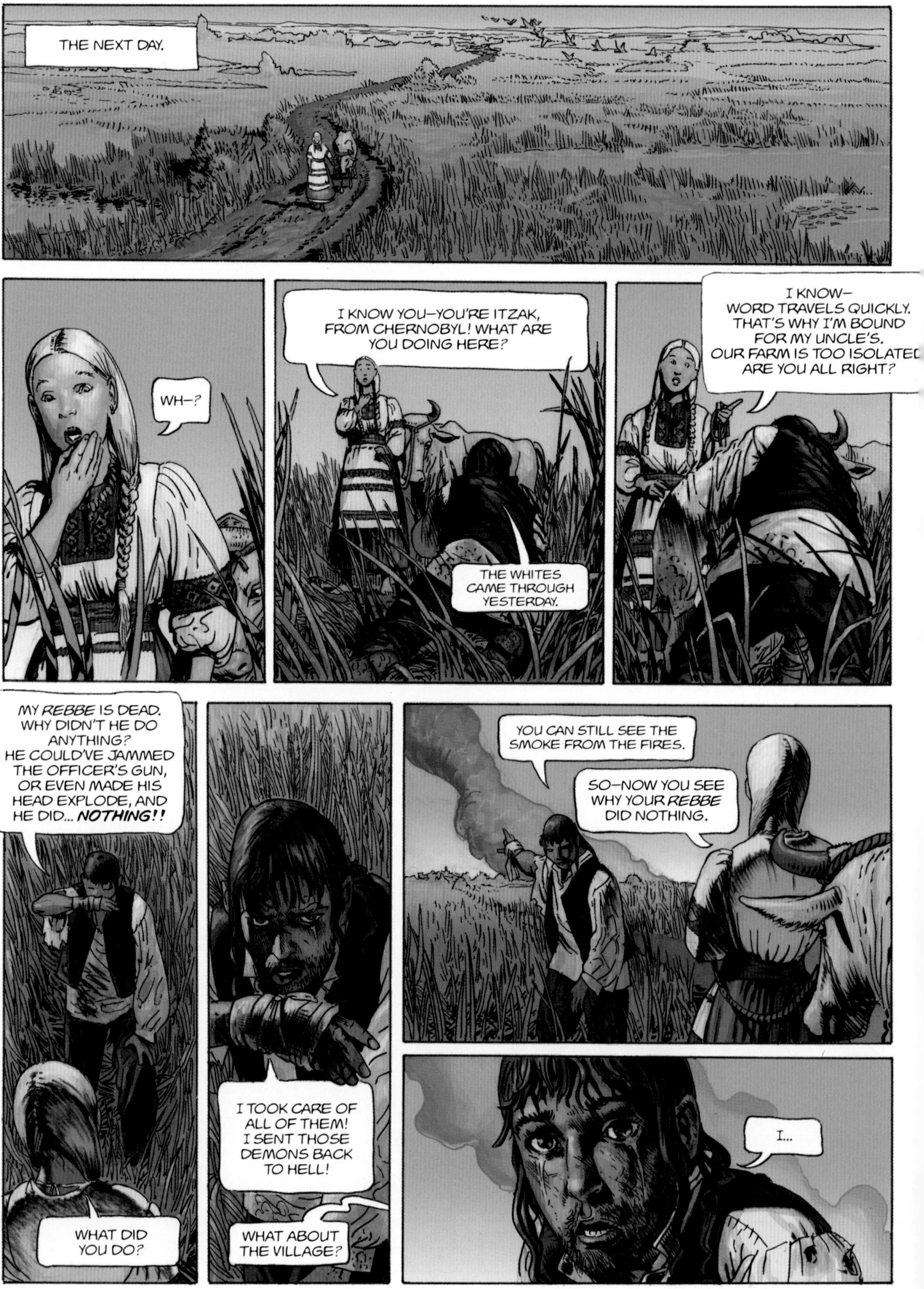
THE NEXT DAY.
WH–?
I KNOW YOU–YOU'RE ITZAK, FROM CHERNOBYL! WHAT ARE YOU DOING HERE?
THE WHITES CAME THROUGH YESTERDAY.
I KNOW– WORD TRAVELS QUICKLY. THAT'S WHY I'M BOUND FOR MY UNCLE'S. OUR FARM IS TOO ISOLATED. ARE YOU ALL RIGHT?
MY *REBBE* IS DEAD. WHY DIDN'T HE DO ANYTHING? HE COULD'VE JAMMED THE OFFICER'S GUN, OR EVEN MADE HIS HEAD EXPLODE, AND HE DID... ***NOTHING!!***
WHAT DID YOU DO?
I TOOK CARE OF ALL OF THEM! I SENT THOSE DEMONS BACK TO HELL!
WHAT ABOUT THE VILLAGE?
YOU CAN STILL SEE THE SMOKE FROM THE FIRES.
SO–NOW YOU SEE WHY YOUR *REBBE* DID NOTHING.
I...

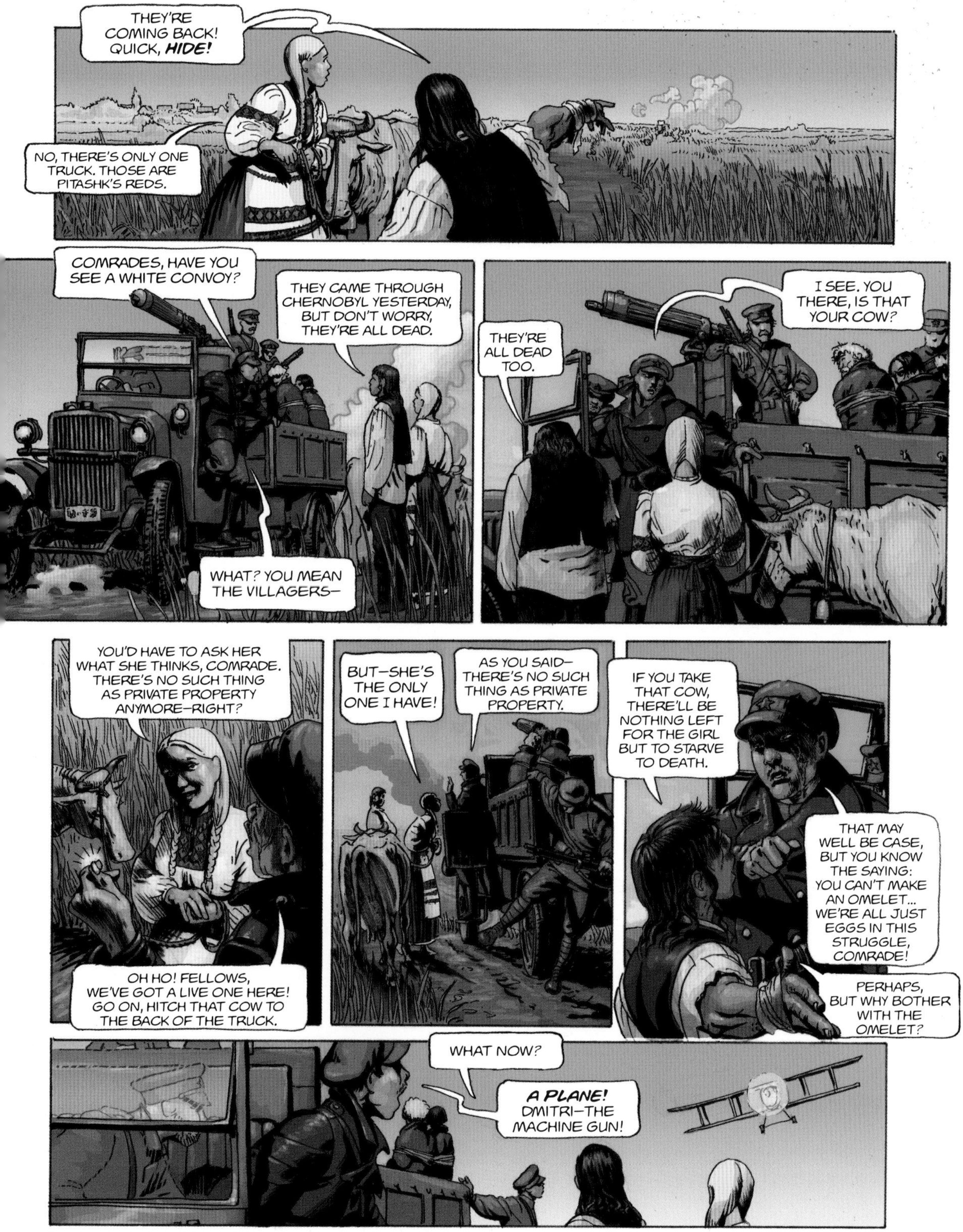
THEY'RE COMING BACK! QUICK, HIDE!
NO, THERE'S ONLY ONE TRUCK. THOSE ARE PITASHK'S REDS.
COMRADES, HAVE YOU SEE A WHITE CONVOY?
THEY CAME THROUGH CHERNOBYL YESTERDAY, BUT DON'T WORRY, THEY'RE ALL DEAD.
WHAT? YOU MEAN THE VILLAGERS—
THEY'RE ALL DEAD TOO.
I SEE. YOU THERE, IS THAT YOUR COW?
YOU'D HAVE TO ASK HER WHAT SHE THINKS, COMRADE. THERE'S NO SUCH THING AS PRIVATE PROPERTY ANYMORE—RIGHT?
OH HO! FELLOWS, WE'VE GOT A LIVE ONE HERE! GO ON, HITCH THAT COW TO THE BACK OF THE TRUCK.
BUT—SHE'S THE ONLY ONE I HAVE!
AS YOU SAID— THERE'S NO SUCH THING AS PRIVATE PROPERTY.
IF YOU TAKE THAT COW, THERE'LL BE NOTHING LEFT FOR THE GIRL BUT TO STARVE TO DEATH.
THAT MAY WELL BE CASE, BUT YOU KNOW THE SAYING: YOU CAN'T MAKE AN OMELET... WE'RE ALL JUST EGGS IN THIS STRUGGLE, COMRADE!
PERHAPS, BUT WHY BOTHER WITH THE OMELET?
WHAT NOW?
A PLANE! DMITRI—THE MACHINE GUN!

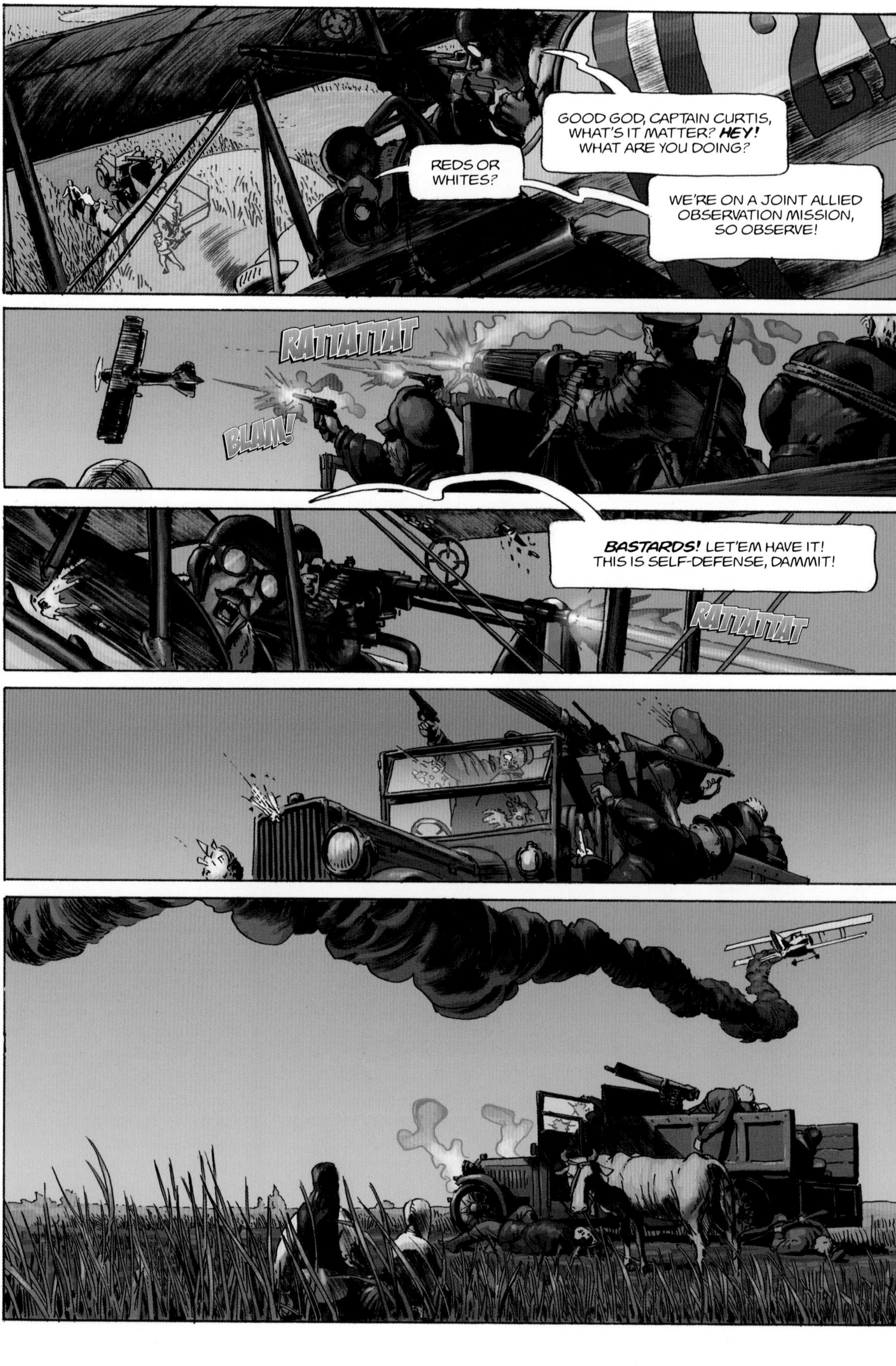
REDS OR WHITES?
GOOD GOD, CAPTAIN CURTIS, WHAT'S IT MATTER? **HEY!** WHAT ARE YOU DOING?
WE'RE ON A JOINT ALLIED OBSERVATION MISSION, SO OBSERVE!
RATTATTAT
BLAM!
BASTARDS! LET'EM HAVE IT! THIS IS SELF-DEFENSE, DAMMIT!
RATTATTAT

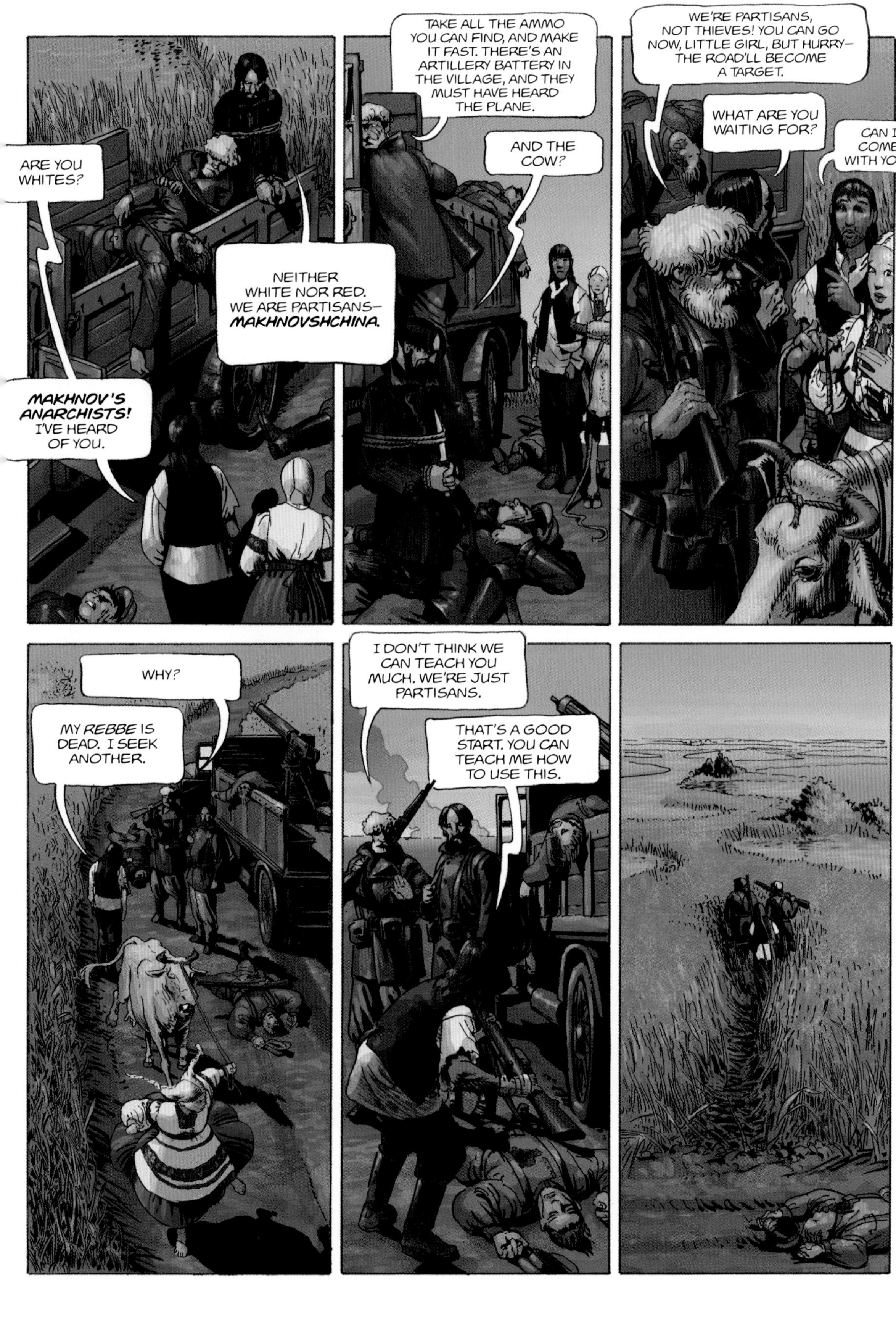
ARE YOU WHITES?
NEITHER WHITE NOR RED. WE ARE PARTISANS— MAKHNOVSHCHINA.
MAKHNOV'S ANARCHISTS! I'VE HEARD OF YOU.
TAKE ALL THE AMMO YOU CAN FIND, AND MAKE IT FAST. THERE'S AN ARTILLERY BATTERY IN THE VILLAGE, AND THEY MUST HAVE HEARD THE PLANE.
AND THE COW?
WE'RE PARTISANS, NOT THIEVES! YOU CAN GO NOW, LITTLE GIRL, BUT HURRY— THE ROAD'LL BECOME A TARGET.
WHAT ARE YOU WAITING FOR?
CAN I COME WITH YOU?
WHY?
MY REBBE IS DEAD. I SEEK ANOTHER.
I DON'T THINK WE CAN TEACH YOU MUCH. WE'RE JUST PARTISANS.
THAT'S A GOOD START. YOU CAN TEACH ME HOW TO USE THIS.

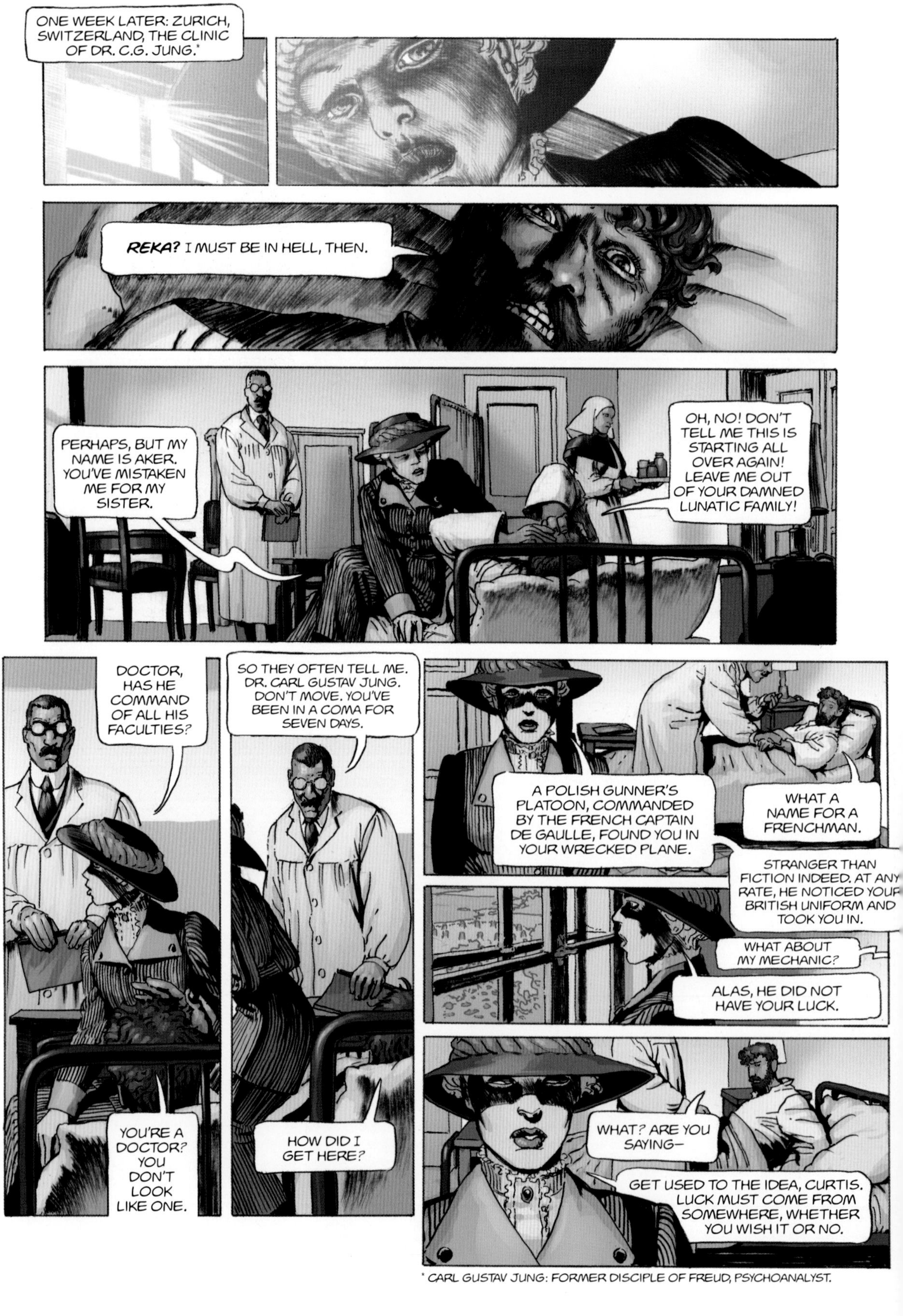
ONE WEEK LATER: ZURICH, SWITZERLAND, THE CLINIC OF DR. C.G. JUNG.*
REKA? I MUST BE IN HELL, THEN.
PERHAPS, BUT MY NAME IS AKER. YOU'VE MISTAKEN ME FOR MY SISTER.
OH, NO! DON'T TELL ME THIS IS STARTING ALL OVER AGAIN! LEAVE ME OUT OF YOUR DAMNED LUNATIC FAMILY!
DOCTOR, HAS HE COMMAND OF ALL HIS FACULTIES?
YOU'RE A DOCTOR? YOU DON'T LOOK LIKE ONE.
SO THEY OFTEN TELL ME. DR. CARL GUSTAV JUNG. DON'T MOVE. YOU'VE BEEN IN A COMA FOR SEVEN DAYS.
HOW DID I GET HERE?
A POLISH GUNNER'S PLATOON, COMMANDED BY THE FRENCH CAPTAIN DE GAULLE, FOUND YOU IN YOUR WRECKED PLANE.
WHAT A NAME FOR A FRENCHMAN.
STRANGER THAN FICTION INDEED. AT ANY RATE, HE NOTICED YOUR BRITISH UNIFORM AND TOOK YOU IN.
WHAT ABOUT MY MECHANIC?
ALAS, HE DID NOT HAVE YOUR LUCK.
WHAT? ARE YOU SAYING–
GET USED TO THE IDEA, CURTIS. LUCK MUST COME FROM SOMEWHERE, WHETHER YOU WISH IT OR NO.

* CARL GUSTAV JUNG: FORMER DISCIPLE OF FREUD, PSYCHOANALYST.

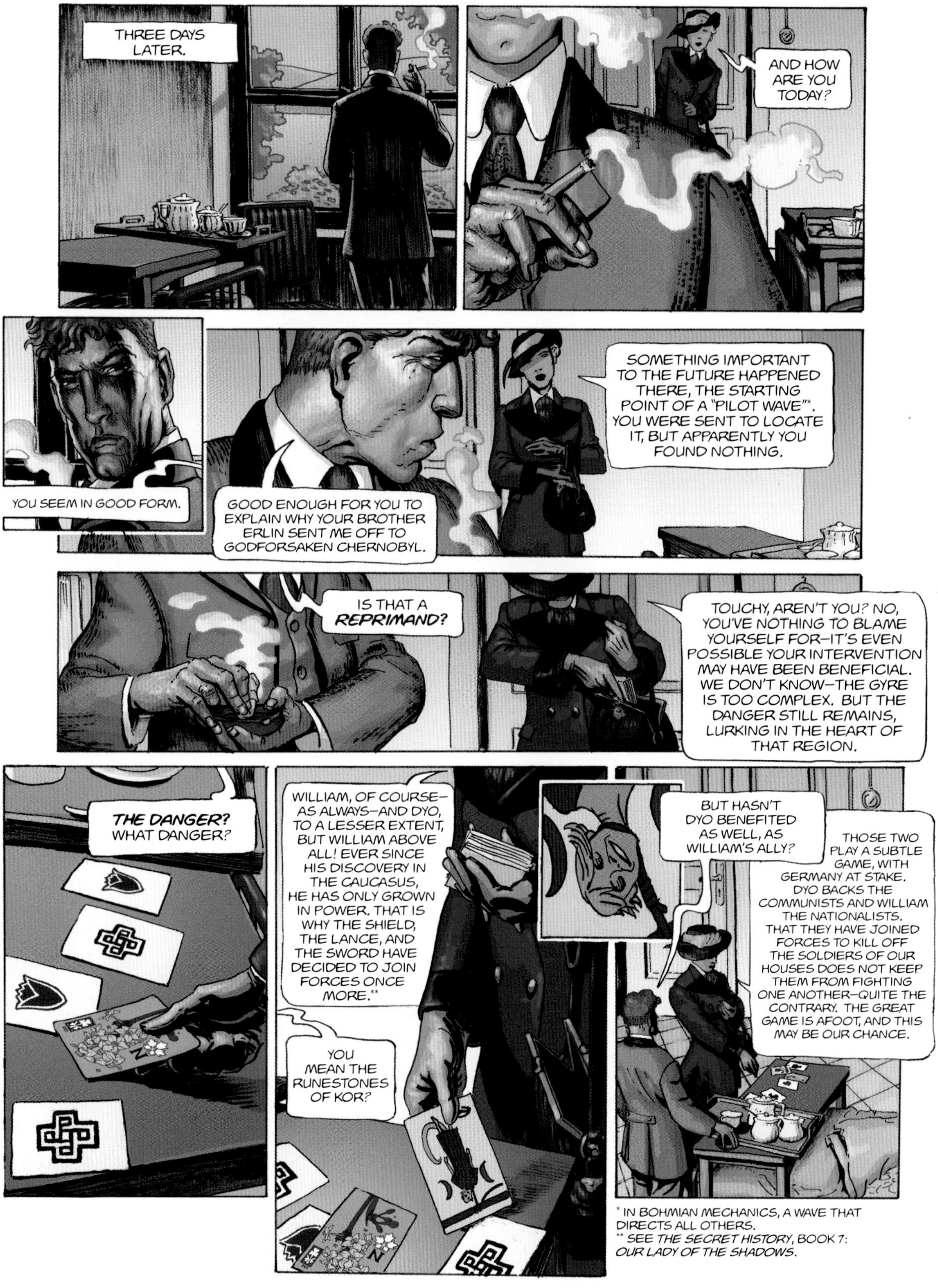
THREE DAYS LATER.
AND HOW ARE YOU TODAY?
YOU SEEM IN GOOD FORM.
GOOD ENOUGH FOR YOU TO EXPLAIN WHY YOUR BROTHER ERLIN SENT ME OFF TO GODFORSAKEN CHERNOBYL.
SOMETHING IMPORTANT TO THE FUTURE HAPPENED THERE, THE STARTING POINT OF A "PILOT WAVE"*. YOU WERE SENT TO LOCATE IT, BUT APPARENTLY YOU FOUND NOTHING.
IS THAT A ***REPRIMAND?***
TOUCHY, AREN'T YOU? NO, YOU'VE NOTHING TO BLAME YOURSELF FOR—IT'S EVEN POSSIBLE YOUR INTERVENTION MAY HAVE BEEN BENEFICIAL. WE DON'T KNOW—THE GYRE IS TOO COMPLEX. BUT THE DANGER STILL REMAINS, LURKING IN THE HEART OF THAT REGION.
THE DANGER? WHAT DANGER?
WILLIAM, OF COURSE—AS ALWAYS—AND DYO, TO A LESSER EXTENT, BUT WILLIAM ABOVE ALL! EVER SINCE HIS DISCOVERY IN THE CAUCASUS, HE HAS ONLY GROWN IN POWER. THAT IS WHY THE SHIELD, THE LANCE, AND THE SWORD HAVE DECIDED TO JOIN FORCES ONCE MORE.**
YOU MEAN THE RUNESTONES OF KOR?
BUT HASN'T DYO BENEFITED AS WELL, AS WILLIAM'S ALLY?
THOSE TWO PLAY A SUBTLE GAME, WITH GERMANY AT STAKE. DYO BACKS THE COMMUNISTS AND WILLIAM THE NATIONALISTS. THAT THEY HAVE JOINED FORCES TO KILL OFF THE SOLDIERS OF OUR HOUSES DOES NOT KEEP THEM FROM FIGHTING ONE ANOTHER—QUITE THE CONTRARY. THE GREAT GAME IS AFOOT, AND THIS MAY BE OUR CHANCE.

* IN BOHMIAN MECHANICS, A WAVE THAT DIRECTS ALL OTHERS.
** SEE *THE SECRET HISTORY*, BOOK 7: *OUR LADY OF THE SHADOWS.*

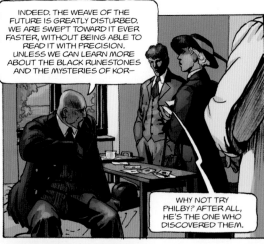

INDEED. THE WEAVE OF THE FUTURE IS GREATLY DISTURBED. WE ARE SWEPT TOWARD IT EVER FASTER, WITHOUT BEING ABLE TO READ IT WITH PRECISION. UNLESS WE CAN LEARN MORE ABOUT THE BLACK RUNESTONES AND THE MYSTERIES OF KOR—

I SEE YOU'VE BEGUN THE BRIEFING.

ERLIN? YOUR SISTER DOESN'T SEEM TO HAVE GOOD NEWS.

WHY NOT TRY PHILBY? AFTER ALL, HE'S THE ONE WHO DISCOVERED THEM.

WE CAN'T FIND HIM! AFTER HIS ENCOUNTER WITH YOU AND REKA, HE LEFT FOR RIYADH AND SAUD'S COURT. HE'S STILL HIDDEN THERE, BUT NONE OF OUR SPIES HAVE BEEN ABLE TO SAY WHERE. THE ARABIAN PENINSULA IS ONE OF THE MOST STABLE PLACES ON THE PLANET: NO RAIN, NO FLORA. YOU KNOW AS WELL AS I THAT THE MORE STABLE A PLACE, THE MORE DIFFICULT IT IS TO USE OUR RUNESTONES.

AND YET YOU'VE SUCCEEDED IN THE PAST.

IN THE PAST, YES—BUT WE ARE WEAKER NOW AND GROW EVER MORE SO. WITH EACH PASSING DAY THE RUNESTONES LOSE THEIR POWER OVER TIME'S GYRE.

SO MAKE A NEW SET OF RUNES!

THE GREAT PATTERNMAKERS ARE LONG SINCE GONE: CELLINI, DA VINCI, MICHELANGELO—

THERE'S NO ONE LEFT WHO CAN MAKE A SET? IMPOSSIBLE! THAT'S NEVER HAPPENED BEFORE!

I DIDN'T SAY THAT. RIGHT NOW, DOCTOR JUNG IS WORKING ON SKETCHES BY A YOUNG PRODIGY: PABLO DIEGO JOSÉ FRANCISCO DE PAULA JUAN NEPOMUCENO CRISPIN CRISPINIANO DE LA SENTISSIMA TRINIDAD RUIZ BLASCO PICASSO Y LOPEZ. IT'S COMING ALONG.

IS THAT ONE MAN OR A WHOLE TEAM?

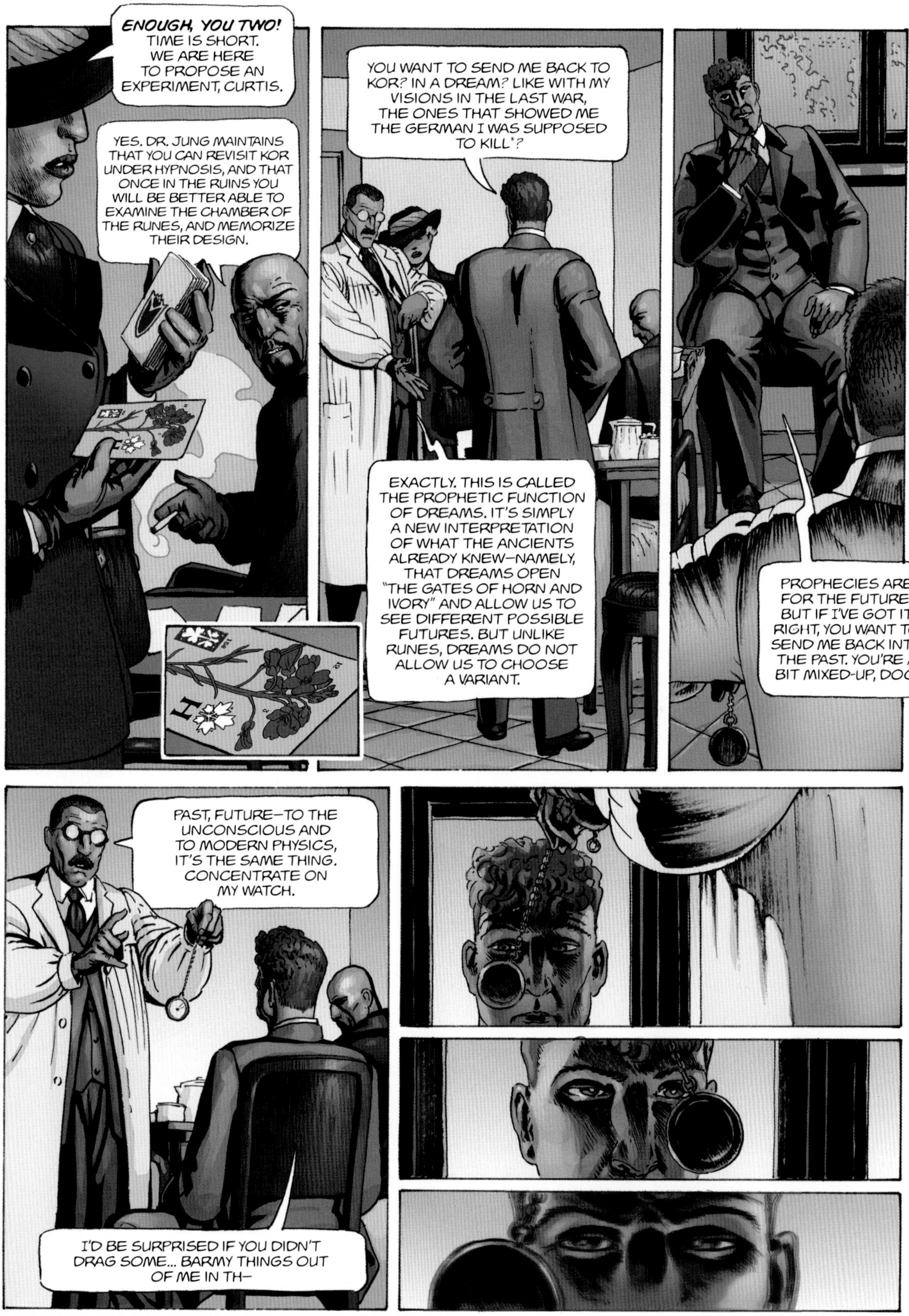
ENOUGH, YOU TWO! TIME IS SHORT. WE ARE HERE TO PROPOSE AN EXPERIMENT, CURTIS.
YES. DR. JUNG MAINTAINS THAT YOU CAN REVISIT KOR UNDER HYPNOSIS, AND THAT ONCE IN THE RUINS YOU WILL BE BETTER ABLE TO EXAMINE THE CHAMBER OF THE RUNES, AND MEMORIZE THEIR DESIGN.
YOU WANT TO SEND ME BACK TO KOR? IN A DREAM? LIKE WITH MY VISIONS IN THE LAST WAR, THE ONES THAT SHOWED ME THE GERMAN I WAS SUPPOSED TO KILL*?
EXACTLY. THIS IS CALLED THE PROPHETIC FUNCTION OF DREAMS. IT'S SIMPLY A NEW INTERPRETATION OF WHAT THE ANCIENTS ALREADY KNEW—NAMELY, THAT DREAMS OPEN "THE GATES OF HORN AND IVORY" AND ALLOW US TO SEE DIFFERENT POSSIBLE FUTURES. BUT UNLIKE RUNES, DREAMS DO NOT ALLOW US TO CHOOSE A VARIANT.
PROPHECIES ARE FOR THE FUTURE. BUT IF I'VE GOT IT RIGHT, YOU WANT TO SEND ME BACK INTO THE PAST. YOU'RE A BIT MIXED-UP, DOC.
PAST, FUTURE—TO THE UNCONSCIOUS AND TO MODERN PHYSICS, IT'S THE SAME THING. CONCENTRATE ON MY WATCH.
I'D BE SURPRISED IF YOU DIDN'T DRAG SOME... BARMY THINGS OUT OF ME IN TH—

* SEE *THE SECRET HISTORY, BOOK 7: OUR LADY OF THE SHADOWS.*

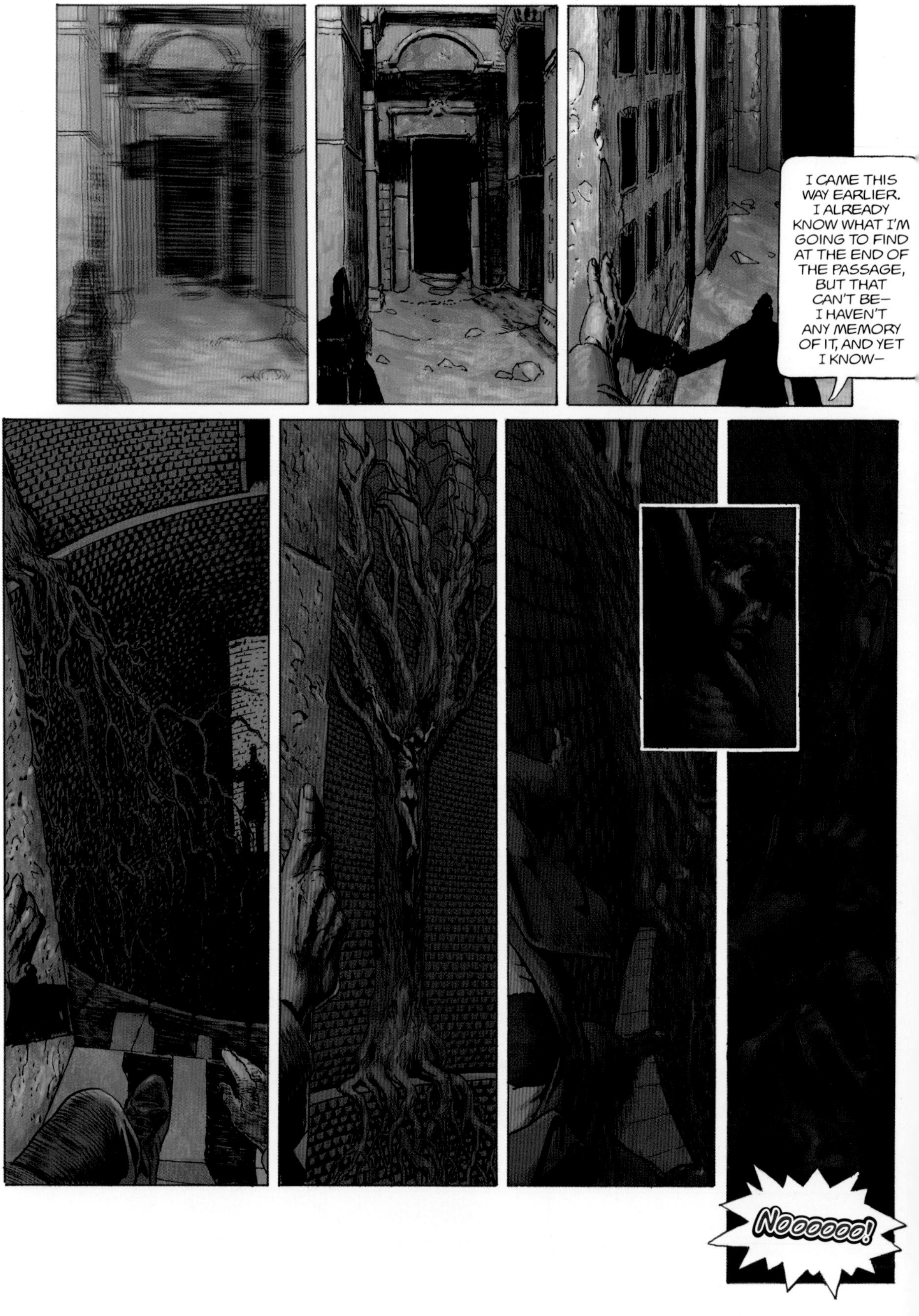
I CAME THIS WAY EARLIER. I ALREADY KNOW WHAT I'M GOING TO FIND AT THE END OF THE PASSAGE, BUT THAT CAN'T BE— I HAVEN'T ANY MEMORY OF IT, AND YET I KNOW—
Noooooo!

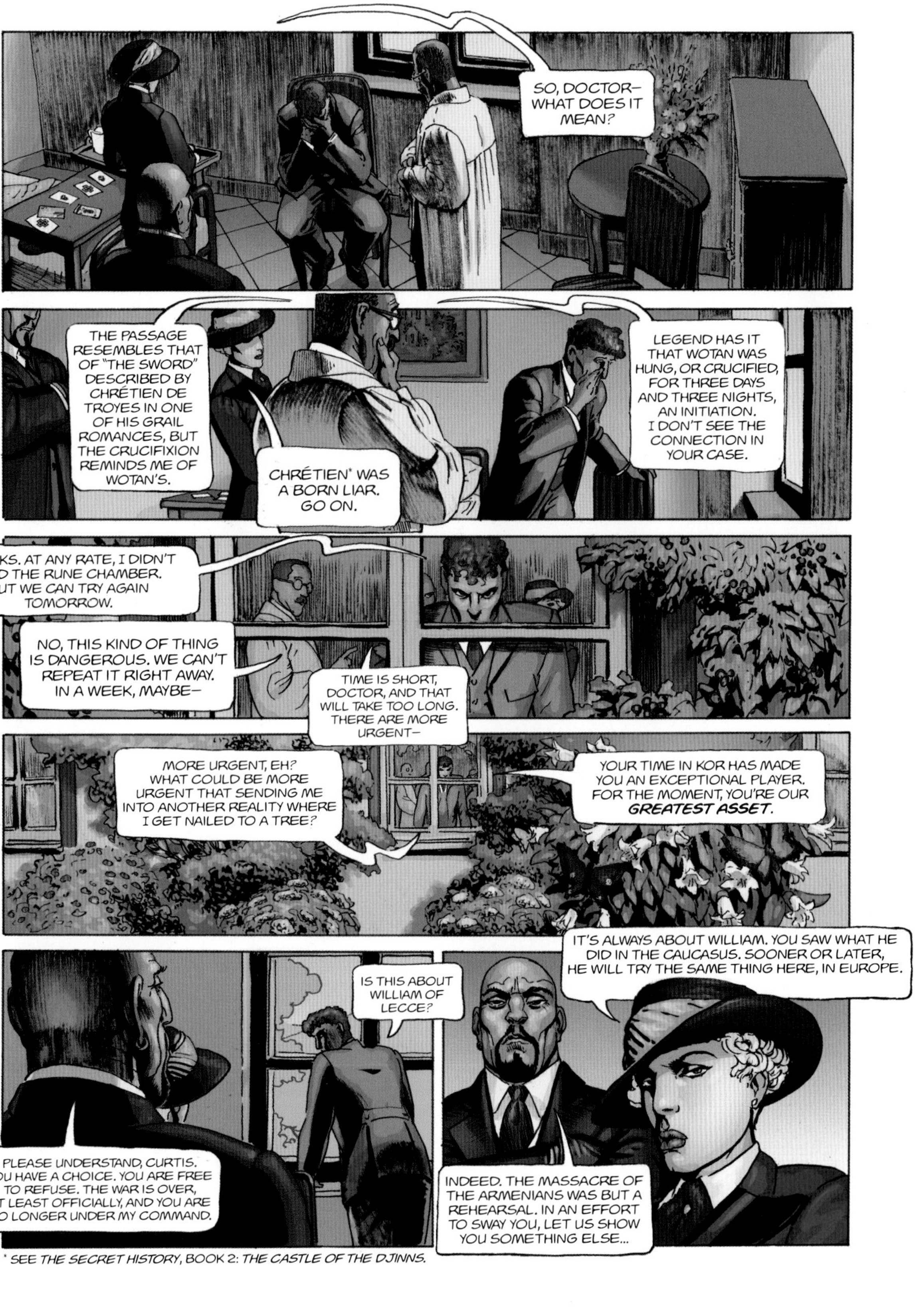
SO, DOCTOR— WHAT DOES IT MEAN?
THE PASSAGE RESEMBLES THAT OF "THE SWORD" DESCRIBED BY CHRÉTIEN DE TROYES IN ONE OF HIS GRAIL ROMANCES, BUT THE CRUCIFIXION REMINDS ME OF WOTAN'S.
CHRÉTIEN* WAS A BORN LIAR. GO ON.
LEGEND HAS IT THAT WOTAN WAS HUNG, OR CRUCIFIED, FOR THREE DAYS AND THREE NIGHTS, AN INITIATION. I DON'T SEE THE CONNECTION IN YOUR CASE.
THANKS. AT ANY RATE, I DIDN'T FIND THE RUNE CHAMBER. BUT WE CAN TRY AGAIN TOMORROW.
NO, THIS KIND OF THING IS DANGEROUS. WE CAN'T REPEAT IT RIGHT AWAY. IN A WEEK, MAYBE—
TIME IS SHORT, DOCTOR, AND THAT WILL TAKE TOO LONG. THERE ARE MORE URGENT—
MORE URGENT, EH? WHAT COULD BE MORE URGENT THAT SENDING ME INTO ANOTHER REALITY WHERE I GET NAILED TO A TREE?
YOUR TIME IN KOR HAS MADE YOU AN EXCEPTIONAL PLAYER. FOR THE MOMENT, YOU'RE OUR GREATEST ASSET.
IS THIS ABOUT WILLIAM OF LECCE?
IT'S ALWAYS ABOUT WILLIAM. YOU SAW WHAT HE DID IN THE CAUCASUS. SOONER OR LATER, HE WILL TRY THE SAME THING HERE, IN EUROPE.
PLEASE UNDERSTAND, CURTIS. YOU HAVE A CHOICE. YOU ARE FREE TO REFUSE. THE WAR IS OVER, AT LEAST OFFICIALLY, AND YOU ARE NO LONGER UNDER MY COMMAND.
INDEED. THE MASSACRE OF THE ARMENIANS WAS BUT A REHEARSAL. IN AN EFFORT TO SWAY YOU, LET US SHOW YOU SOMETHING ELSE...

* SEE *THE SECRET HISTORY*, BOOK 2: *THE CASTLE OF THE DJINNS.*

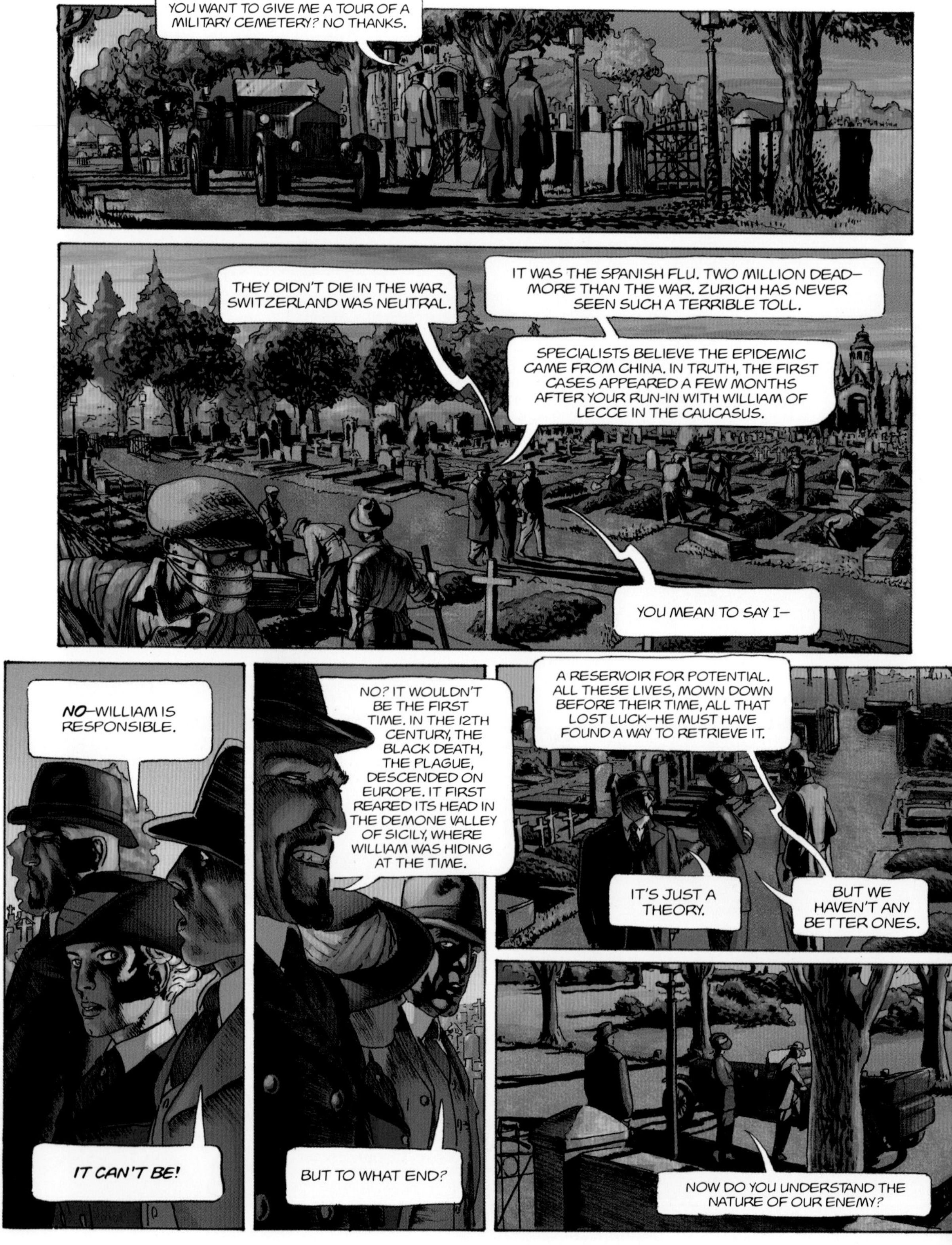
YOU WANT TO GIVE ME A TOUR OF A MILITARY CEMETERY? NO THANKS.
THEY DIDN'T DIE IN THE WAR. SWITZERLAND WAS NEUTRAL.
IT WAS THE SPANISH FLU. TWO MILLION DEAD— MORE THAN THE WAR. ZURICH HAS NEVER SEEN SUCH A TERRIBLE TOLL.
SPECIALISTS BELIEVE THE EPIDEMIC CAME FROM CHINA. IN TRUTH, THE FIRST CASES APPEARED A FEW MONTHS AFTER YOUR RUN-IN WITH WILLIAM OF LECCE IN THE CAUCASUS.
YOU MEAN TO SAY I—
NO—WILLIAM IS RESPONSIBLE.
IT CAN'T BE!
NO? IT WOULDN'T BE THE FIRST TIME. IN THE 12TH CENTURY, THE BLACK DEATH, THE PLAGUE, DESCENDED ON EUROPE. IT FIRST REARED ITS HEAD IN THE DEMONE VALLEY OF SICILY, WHERE WILLIAM WAS HIDING AT THE TIME.
BUT TO WHAT END?
A RESERVOIR FOR POTENTIAL. ALL THESE LIVES, MOWN DOWN BEFORE THEIR TIME, ALL THAT LOST LUCK—HE MUST HAVE FOUND A WAY TO RETRIEVE IT.
IT'S JUST A THEORY.
BUT WE HAVEN'T ANY BETTER ONES.
NOW DO YOU UNDERSTAND THE NATURE OF OUR ENEMY?

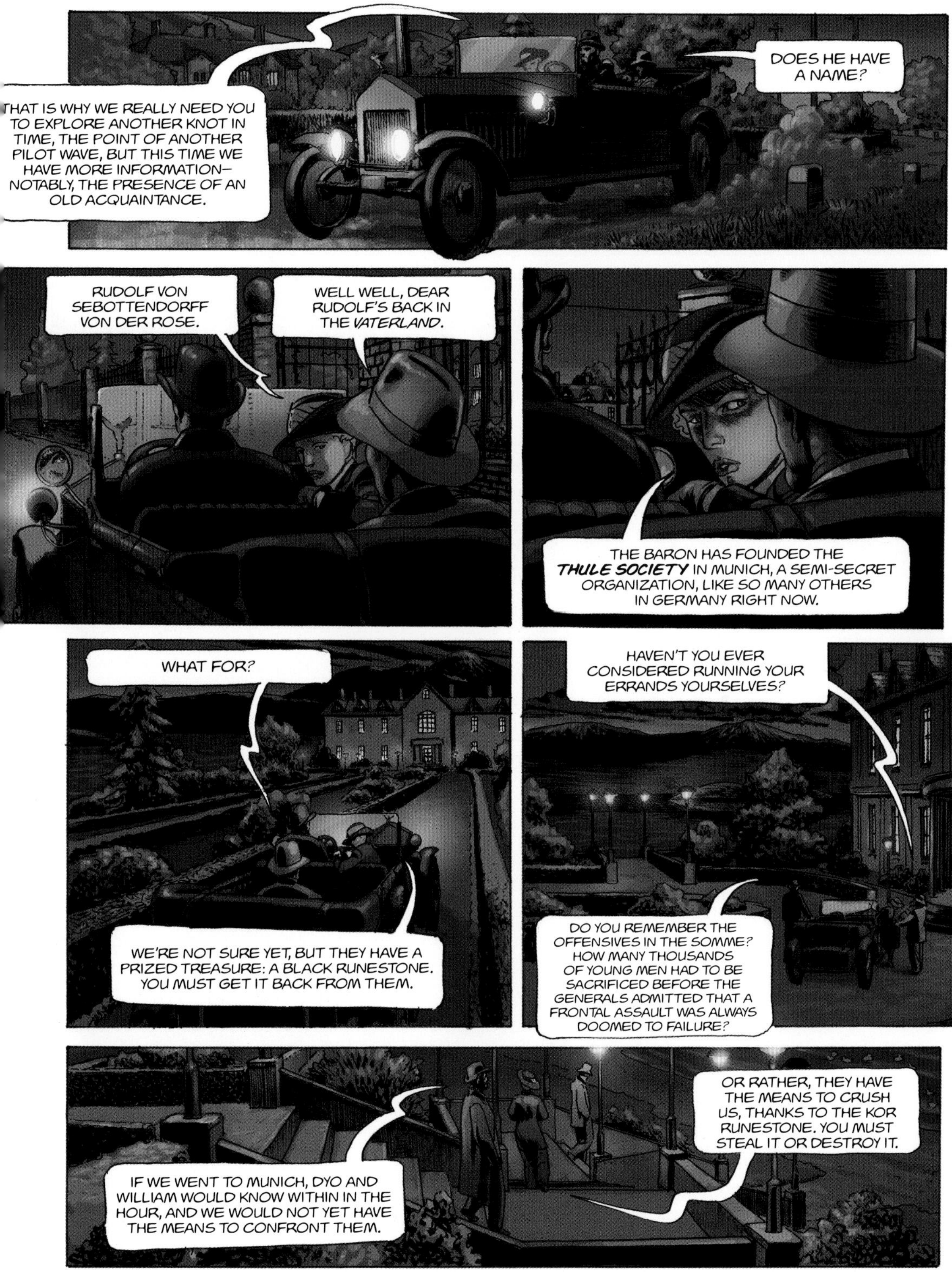
THAT IS WHY WE REALLY NEED YOU TO EXPLORE ANOTHER KNOT IN TIME, THE POINT OF ANOTHER PILOT WAVE, BUT THIS TIME WE HAVE MORE INFORMATION— NOTABLY, THE PRESENCE OF AN OLD ACQUAINTANCE.
DOES HE HAVE A NAME?
RUDOLF VON SEBOTTENDORFF VON DER ROSE.
WELL WELL, DEAR RUDOLF'S BACK IN THE VATERLAND.
THE BARON HAS FOUNDED THE THULE SOCIETY IN MUNICH, A SEMI-SECRET ORGANIZATION, LIKE SO MANY OTHERS IN GERMANY RIGHT NOW.
WHAT FOR?
WE'RE NOT SURE YET, BUT THEY HAVE A PRIZED TREASURE: A BLACK RUNESTONE. YOU MUST GET IT BACK FROM THEM.
HAVEN'T YOU EVER CONSIDERED RUNNING YOUR ERRANDS YOURSELVES?
DO YOU REMEMBER THE OFFENSIVES IN THE SOMME? HOW MANY THOUSANDS OF YOUNG MEN HAD TO BE SACRIFICED BEFORE THE GENERALS ADMITTED THAT A FRONTAL ASSAULT WAS ALWAYS DOOMED TO FAILURE?
IF WE WENT TO MUNICH, DYO AND WILLIAM WOULD KNOW WITHIN IN THE HOUR, AND WE WOULD NOT YET HAVE THE MEANS TO CONFRONT THEM.
OR RATHER, THEY HAVE THE MEANS TO CRUSH US, THANKS TO THE KOR RUNESTONE. YOU MUST STEAL IT OR DESTROY IT.

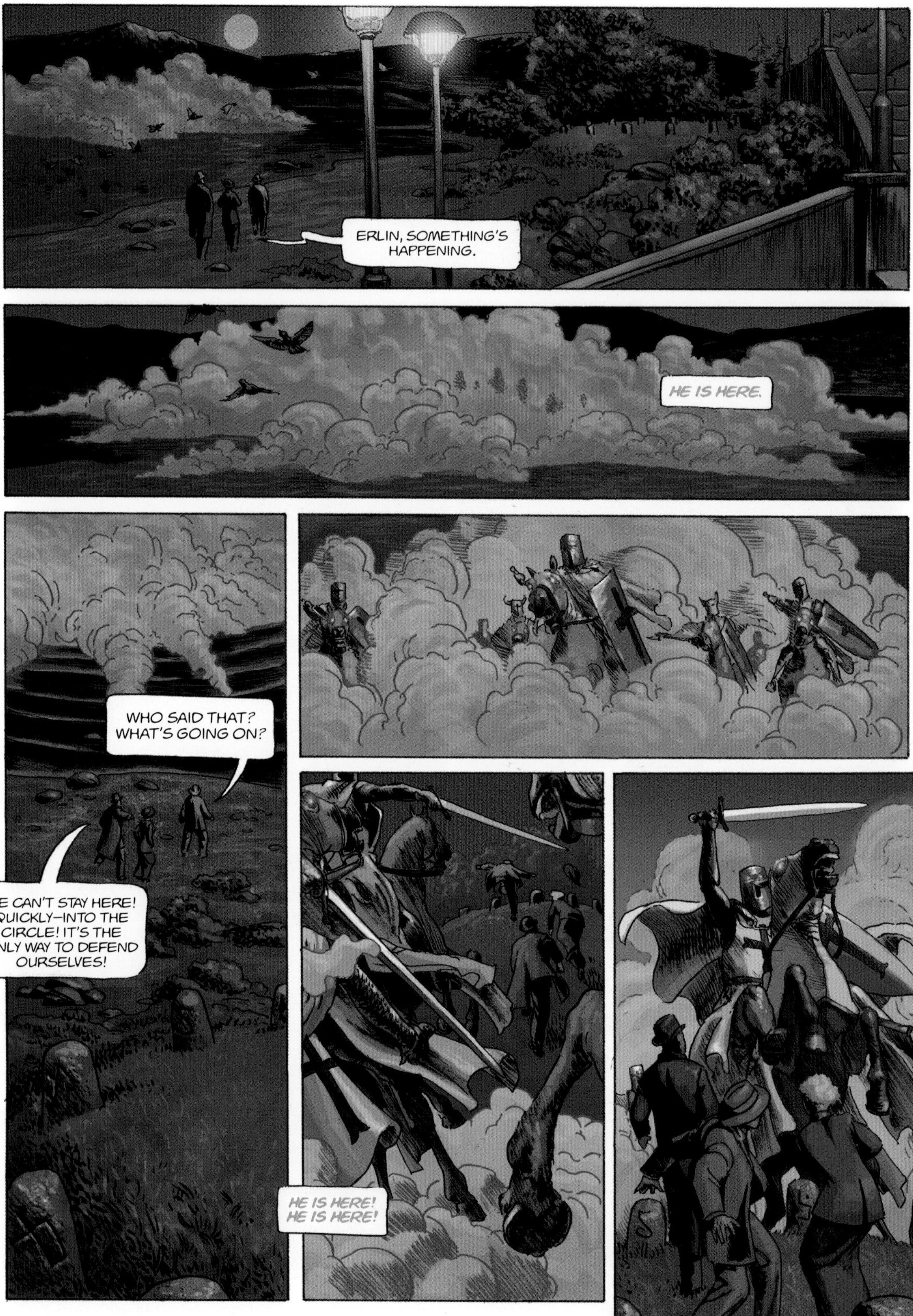

ERLIN, SOMETHING'S HAPPENING.
HE IS HERE.
WHO SAID THAT? WHAT'S GOING ON?
WE CAN'T STAY HERE! QUICKLY—INTO THE CIRCLE! IT'S THE ONLY WAY TO DEFEND OURSELVES!
HE IS HERE! HE IS HERE!

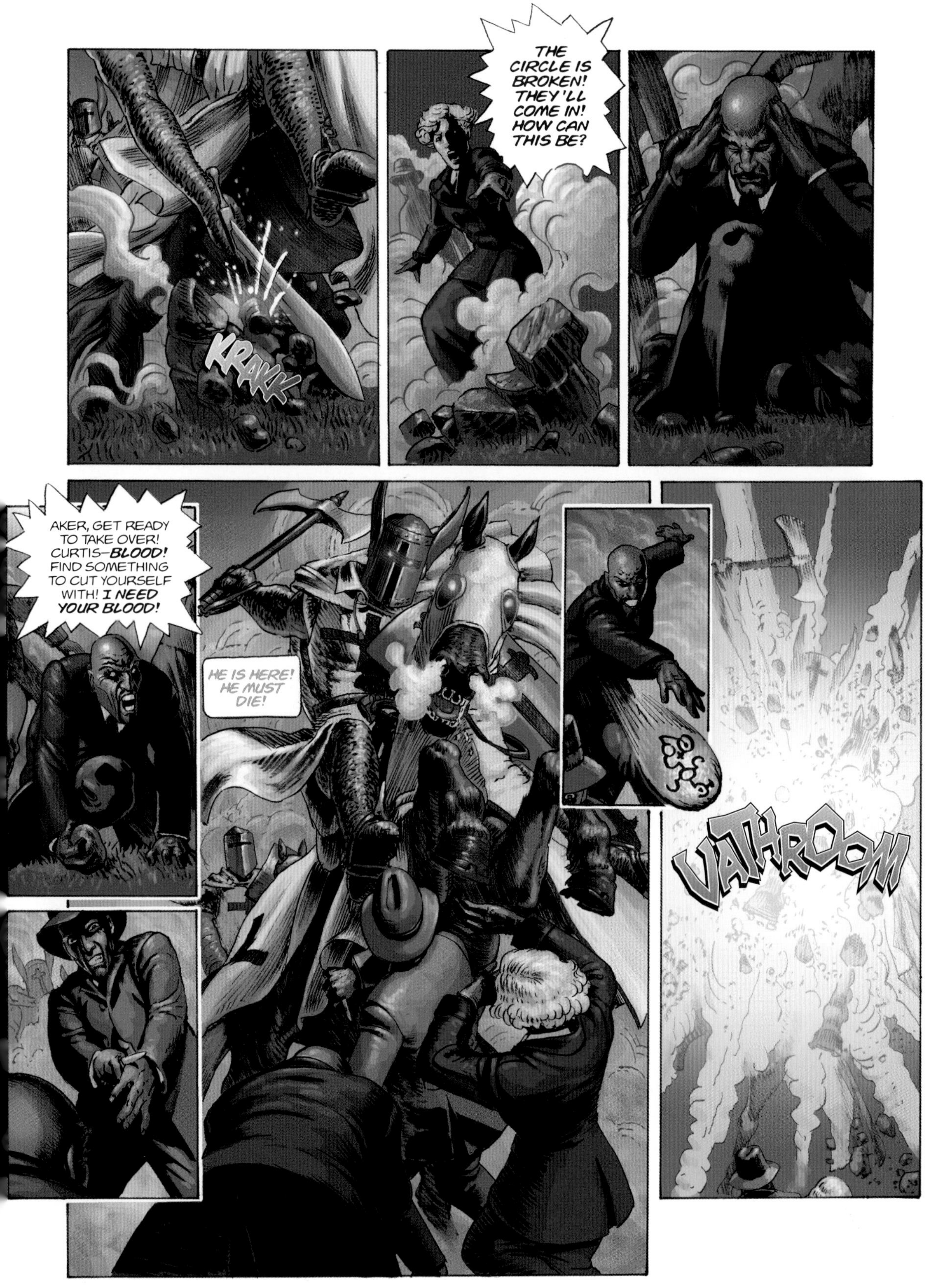
KRAKK
THE CIRCLE IS BROKEN! THEY'LL COME IN! HOW CAN THIS BE?
AKER, GET READY TO TAKE OVER! CURTIS—**BLOOD!** FIND SOMETHING TO CUT YOURSELF WITH! **I NEED YOUR BLOOD!**
HE IS HERE! HE MUST DIE!
VATHROOM

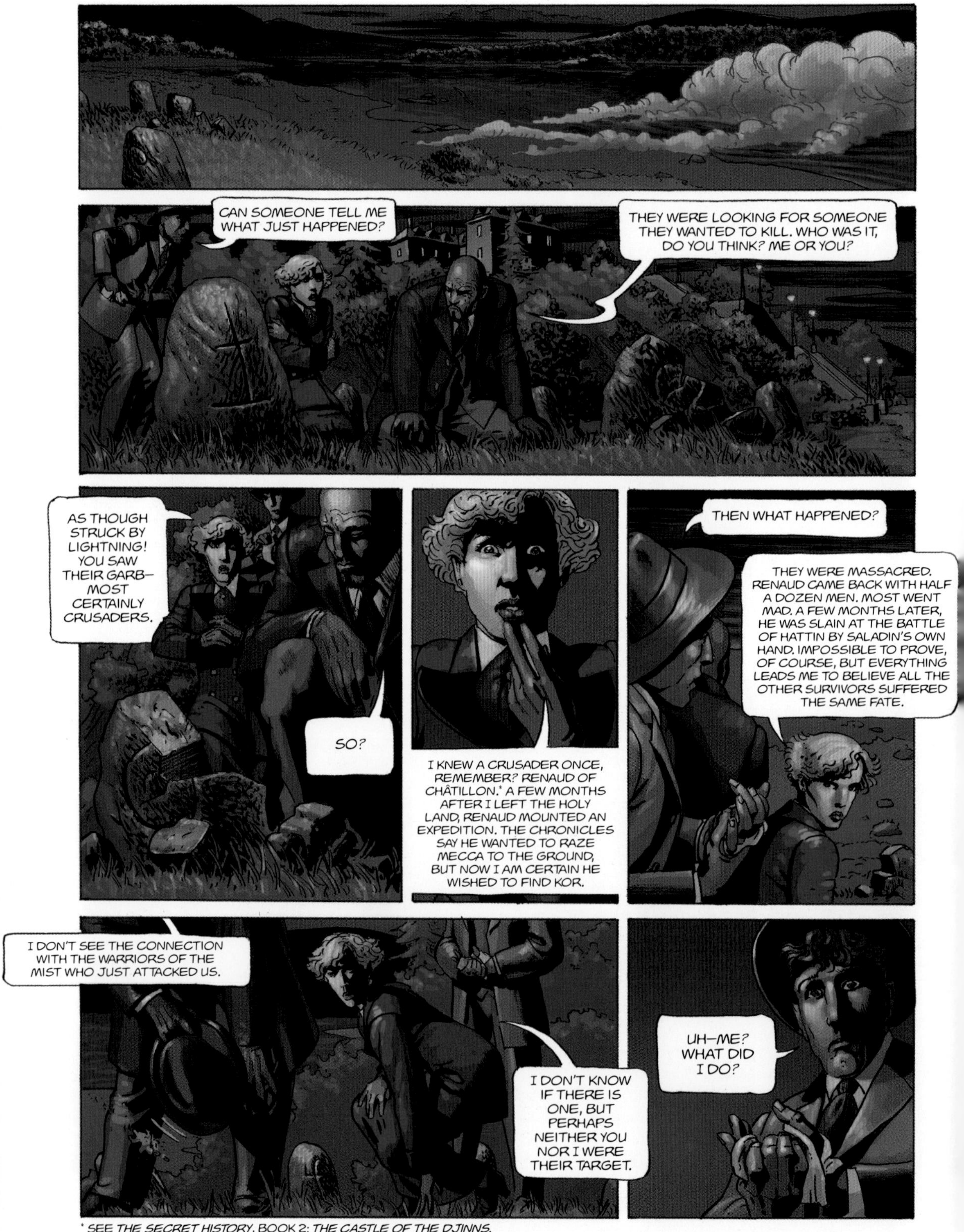
CAN SOMEONE TELL ME WHAT JUST HAPPENED?
THEY WERE LOOKING FOR SOMEONE THEY WANTED TO KILL. WHO WAS IT, DO YOU THINK? ME OR YOU?
AS THOUGH STRUCK BY LIGHTNING! YOU SAW THEIR GARB—MOST CERTAINLY CRUSADERS.
SO?
I KNEW A CRUSADER ONCE, REMEMBER? RENAUD OF CHÂTILLON.* A FEW MONTHS AFTER I LEFT THE HOLY LAND, RENAUD MOUNTED AN EXPEDITION. THE CHRONICLES SAY HE WANTED TO RAZE MECCA TO THE GROUND, BUT NOW I AM CERTAIN HE WISHED TO FIND KOR.
THEN WHAT HAPPENED?
THEY WERE MASSACRED. RENAUD CAME BACK WITH HALF A DOZEN MEN. MOST WENT MAD. A FEW MONTHS LATER, HE WAS SLAIN AT THE BATTLE OF HATTIN BY SALADIN'S OWN HAND. IMPOSSIBLE TO PROVE, OF COURSE, BUT EVERYTHING LEADS ME TO BELIEVE ALL THE OTHER SURVIVORS SUFFERED THE SAME FATE.
I DON'T SEE THE CONNECTION WITH THE WARRIORS OF THE MIST WHO JUST ATTACKED US.
I DON'T KNOW IF THERE IS ONE, BUT PERHAPS NEITHER YOU NOR I WERE THEIR TARGET.
UH—ME? WHAT DID I DO?

* SEE *THE SECRET HISTORY*, BOOK 2: *THE CASTLE OF THE DJINNS.*

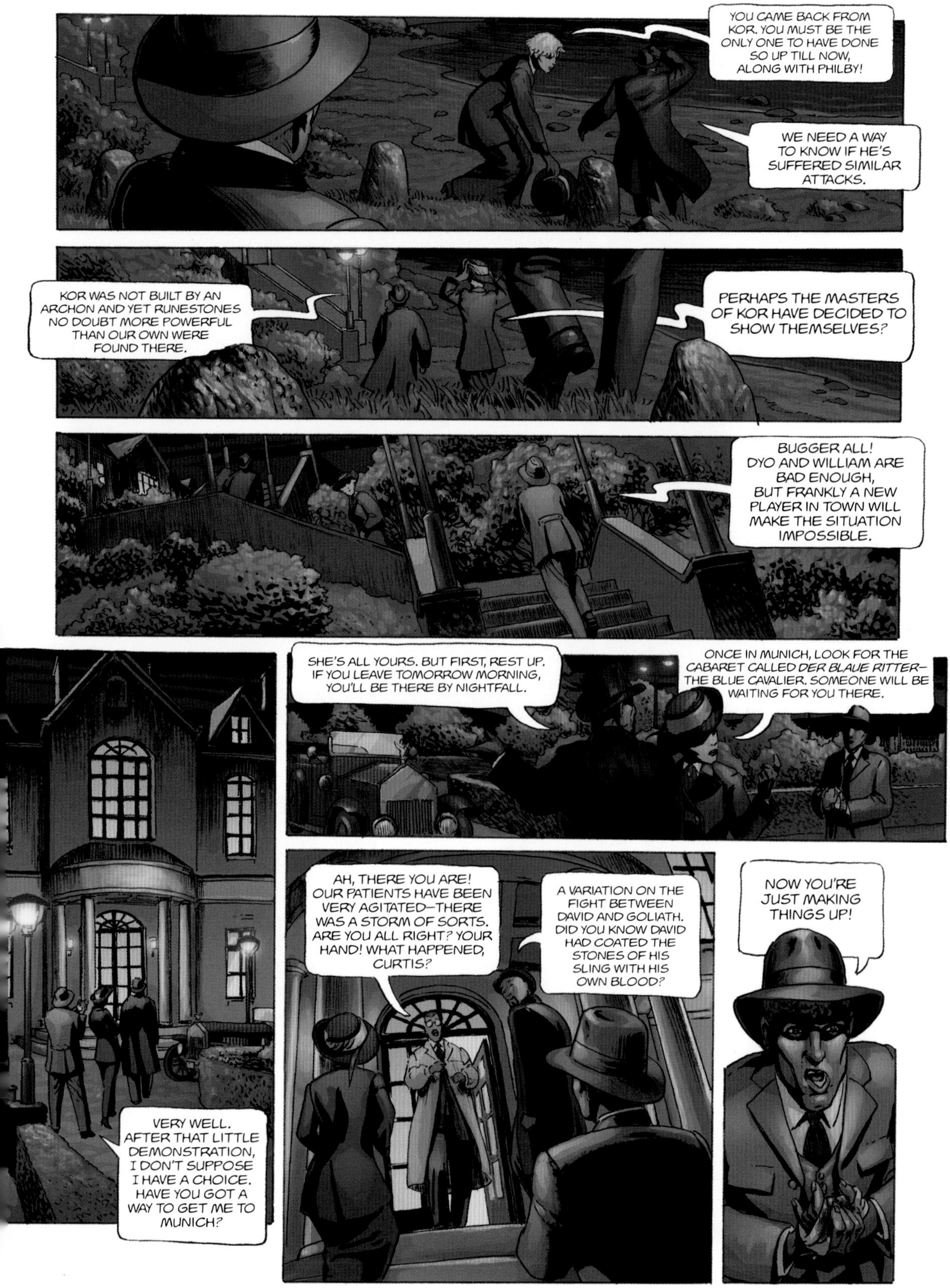
YOU CAME BACK FROM KOR. YOU MUST BE THE ONLY ONE TO HAVE DONE SO UP TILL NOW, ALONG WITH PHILBY!
WE NEED A WAY TO KNOW IF HE'S SUFFERED SIMILAR ATTACKS.
KOR WAS NOT BUILT BY AN ARCHON AND YET RUNESTONES NO DOUBT MORE POWERFUL THAN OUR OWN WERE FOUND THERE.
PERHAPS THE MASTERS OF KOR HAVE DECIDED TO SHOW THEMSELVES?
BUGGER ALL! DYO AND WILLIAM ARE BAD ENOUGH, BUT FRANKLY A NEW PLAYER IN TOWN WILL MAKE THE SITUATION IMPOSSIBLE.
VERY WELL. AFTER THAT LITTLE DEMONSTRATION, I DON'T SUPPOSE I HAVE A CHOICE. HAVE YOU GOT A WAY TO GET ME TO MUNICH?
SHE'S ALL YOURS. BUT FIRST, REST UP. IF YOU LEAVE TOMORROW MORNING, YOU'LL BE THERE BY NIGHTFALL.
ONCE IN MUNICH, LOOK FOR THE CABARET CALLED *DER BLAUE RITTER*— THE BLUE CAVALIER. SOMEONE WILL BE WAITING FOR YOU THERE.
AH, THERE YOU ARE! OUR PATIENTS HAVE BEEN VERY AGITATED—THERE WAS A STORM OF SORTS. ARE YOU ALL RIGHT? YOUR HAND! WHAT HAPPENED, CURTIS?
A VARIATION ON THE FIGHT BETWEEN DAVID AND GOLIATH. DID YOU KNOW DAVID HAD COATED THE STONES OF HIS SLING WITH HIS OWN BLOOD?
NOW YOU'RE JUST MAKING THINGS UP!

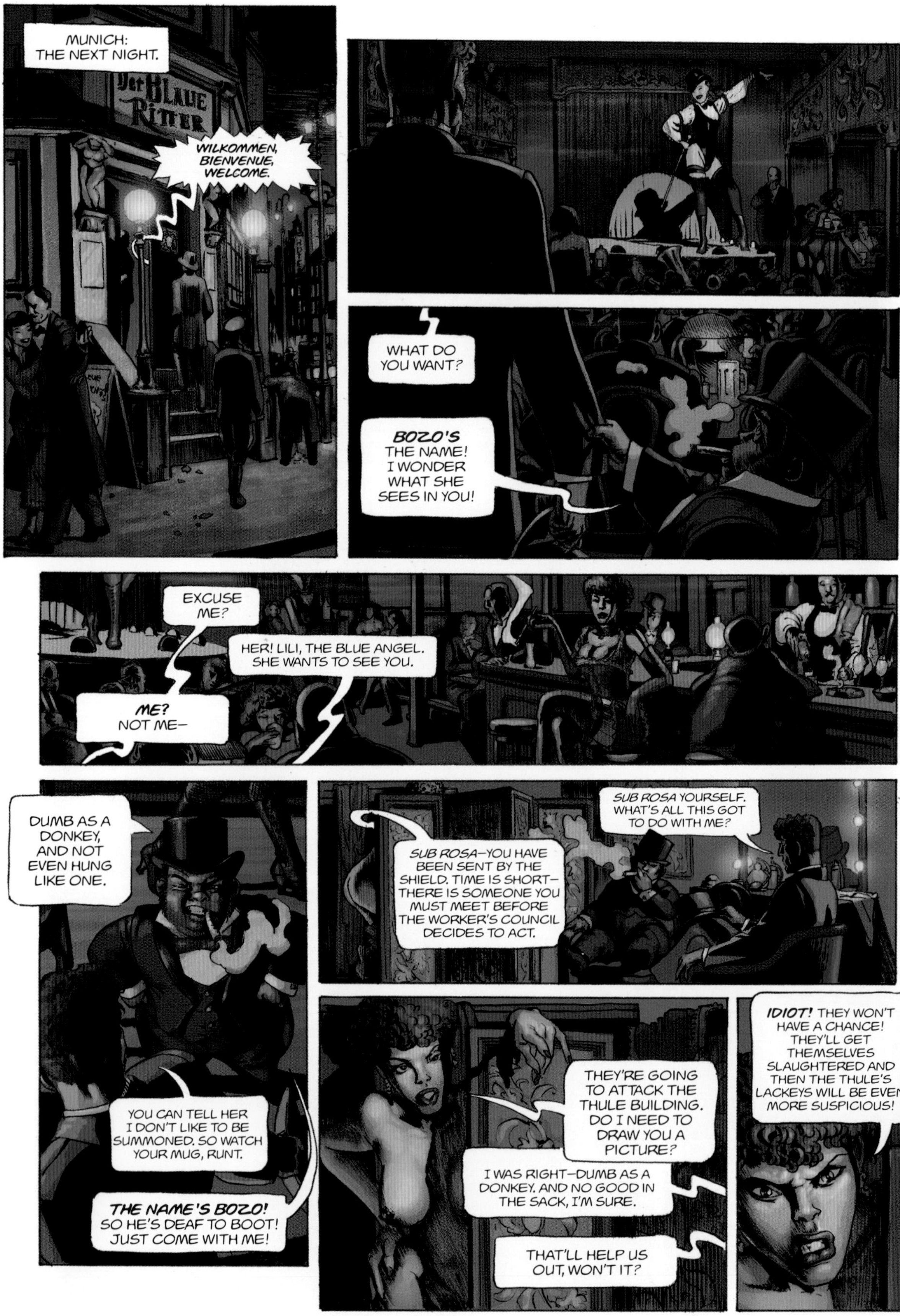
MUNICH: THE NEXT NIGHT.
Der BLAUE RITTER
WILKOMMEN, BIENVENUE, WELCOME.
WHAT DO YOU WANT?
BOZO'S THE NAME! I WONDER WHAT SHE SEES IN YOU!
EXCUSE ME?
HER! LILI, THE BLUE ANGEL. SHE WANTS TO SEE YOU.
ME? NOT ME—
DUMB AS A DONKEY, AND NOT EVEN HUNG LIKE ONE.
YOU CAN TELL HER I DON'T LIKE TO BE SUMMONED. SO WATCH YOUR MUG, RUNT.
THE NAME'S BOZO! SO HE'S DEAF TO BOOT! JUST COME WITH ME!
SUB ROSA—YOU HAVE BEEN SENT BY THE SHIELD. TIME IS SHORT—THERE IS SOMEONE YOU MUST MEET BEFORE THE WORKER'S COUNCIL DECIDES TO ACT.
SUB ROSA YOURSELF. WHAT'S ALL THIS GOT TO DO WITH ME?
THEY'RE GOING TO ATTACK THE THULE BUILDING. DO I NEED TO DRAW YOU A PICTURE?
I WAS RIGHT—DUMB AS A DONKEY. AND NO GOOD IN THE SACK, I'M SURE.
THAT'LL HELP US OUT, WON'T IT?
IDIOT! THEY WON'T HAVE A CHANCE! THEY'LL GET THEMSELVES SLAUGHTERED AND THEN THE THULE'S LACKEYS WILL BE EVEN MORE SUSPICIOUS!

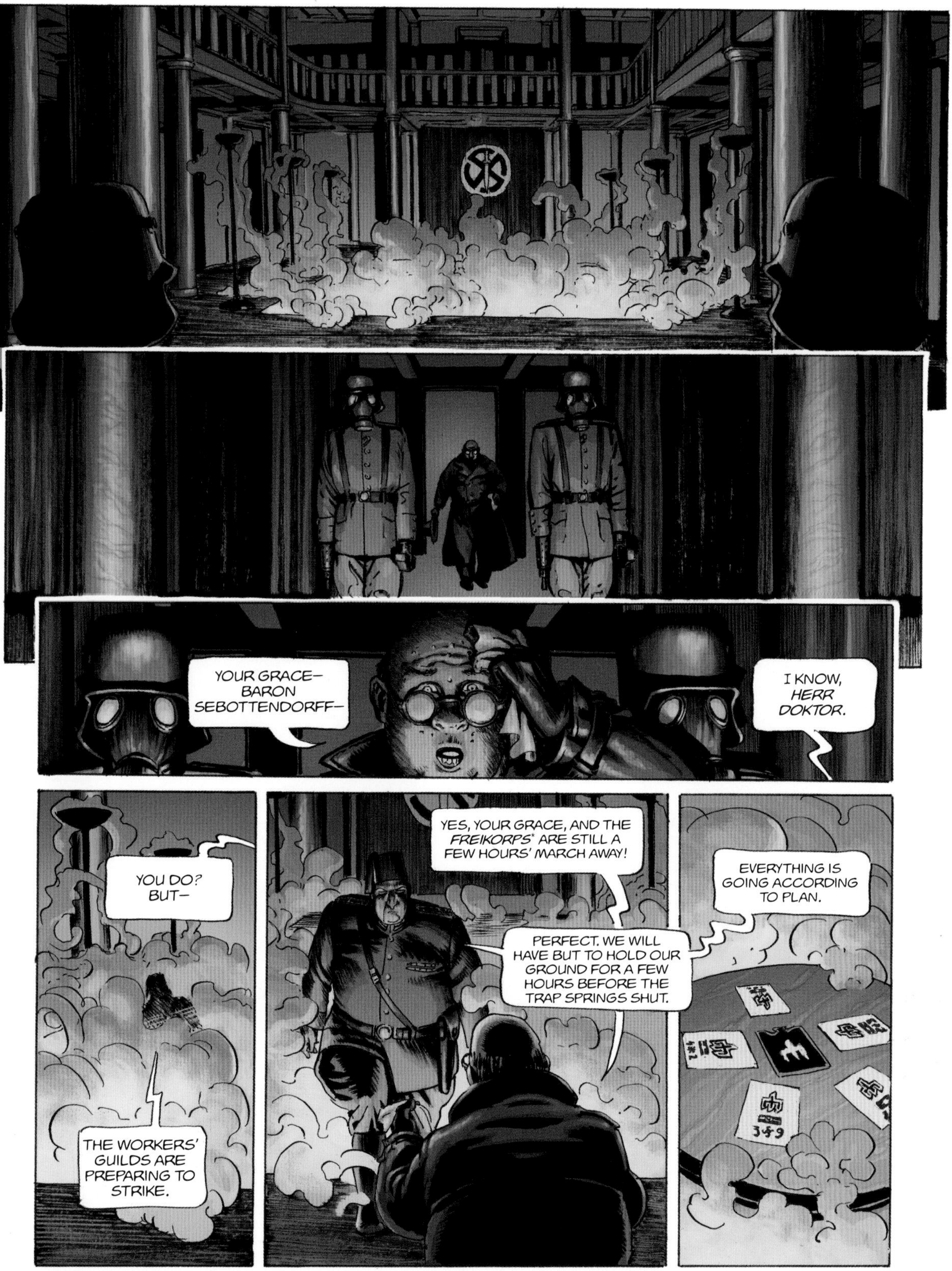
YOUR GRACE—BARON SEBOTTENDORFF—
I KNOW, HERR DOKTOR.
YOU DO? BUT—
THE WORKERS' GUILDS ARE PREPARING TO STRIKE.
YES, YOUR GRACE, AND THE FREIKORPS* ARE STILL A FEW HOURS' MARCH AWAY!
PERFECT. WE WILL HAVE BUT TO HOLD OUR GROUND FOR A FEW HOURS BEFORE THE TRAP SPRINGS SHUT.
EVERYTHING IS GOING ACCORDING TO PLAN.

* "FREE CORPS": PARAMILITARY UNITS.

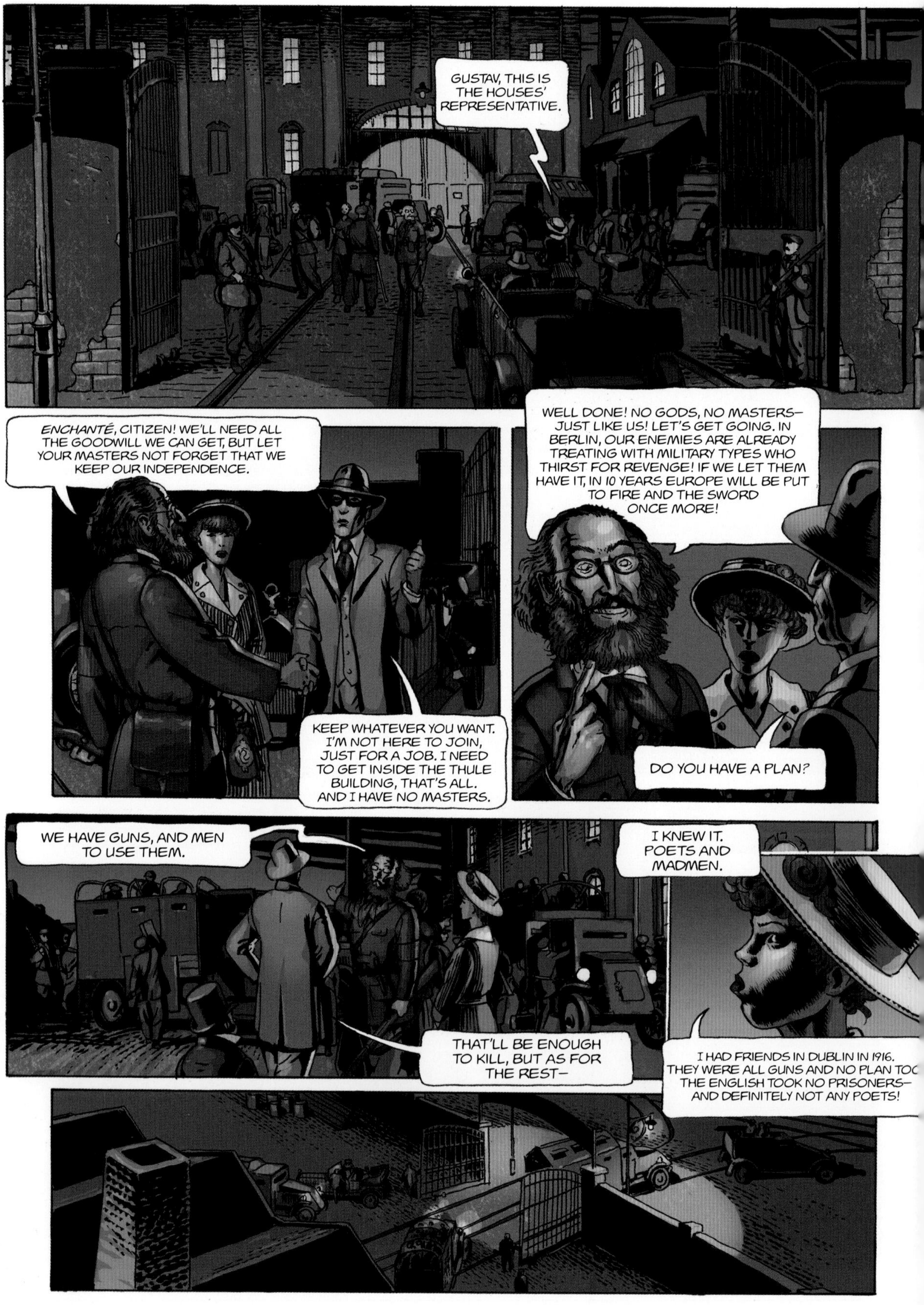
GUSTAV, THIS IS THE HOUSES' REPRESENTATIVE.
ENCHANTÉ, CITIZEN! WE'LL NEED ALL THE GOODWILL WE CAN GET, BUT LET YOUR MASTERS NOT FORGET THAT WE KEEP OUR INDEPENDENCE.
KEEP WHATEVER YOU WANT. I'M NOT HERE TO JOIN, JUST FOR A JOB. I NEED TO GET INSIDE THE THULE BUILDING, THAT'S ALL. AND I HAVE NO MASTERS.
WELL DONE! NO GODS, NO MASTERS— JUST LIKE US! LET'S GET GOING. IN BERLIN, OUR ENEMIES ARE ALREADY TREATING WITH MILITARY TYPES WHO THIRST FOR REVENGE! IF WE LET THEM HAVE IT, IN 10 YEARS EUROPE WILL BE PUT TO FIRE AND THE SWORD ONCE MORE!
DO YOU HAVE A PLAN?
WE HAVE GUNS, AND MEN TO USE THEM.
THAT'LL BE ENOUGH TO KILL, BUT AS FOR THE REST—
I KNEW IT. POETS AND MADMEN.
I HAD FRIENDS IN DUBLIN IN 1916. THEY WERE ALL GUNS AND NO PLAN TOO. THE ENGLISH TOOK NO PRISONERS— AND DEFINITELY NOT ANY POETS!

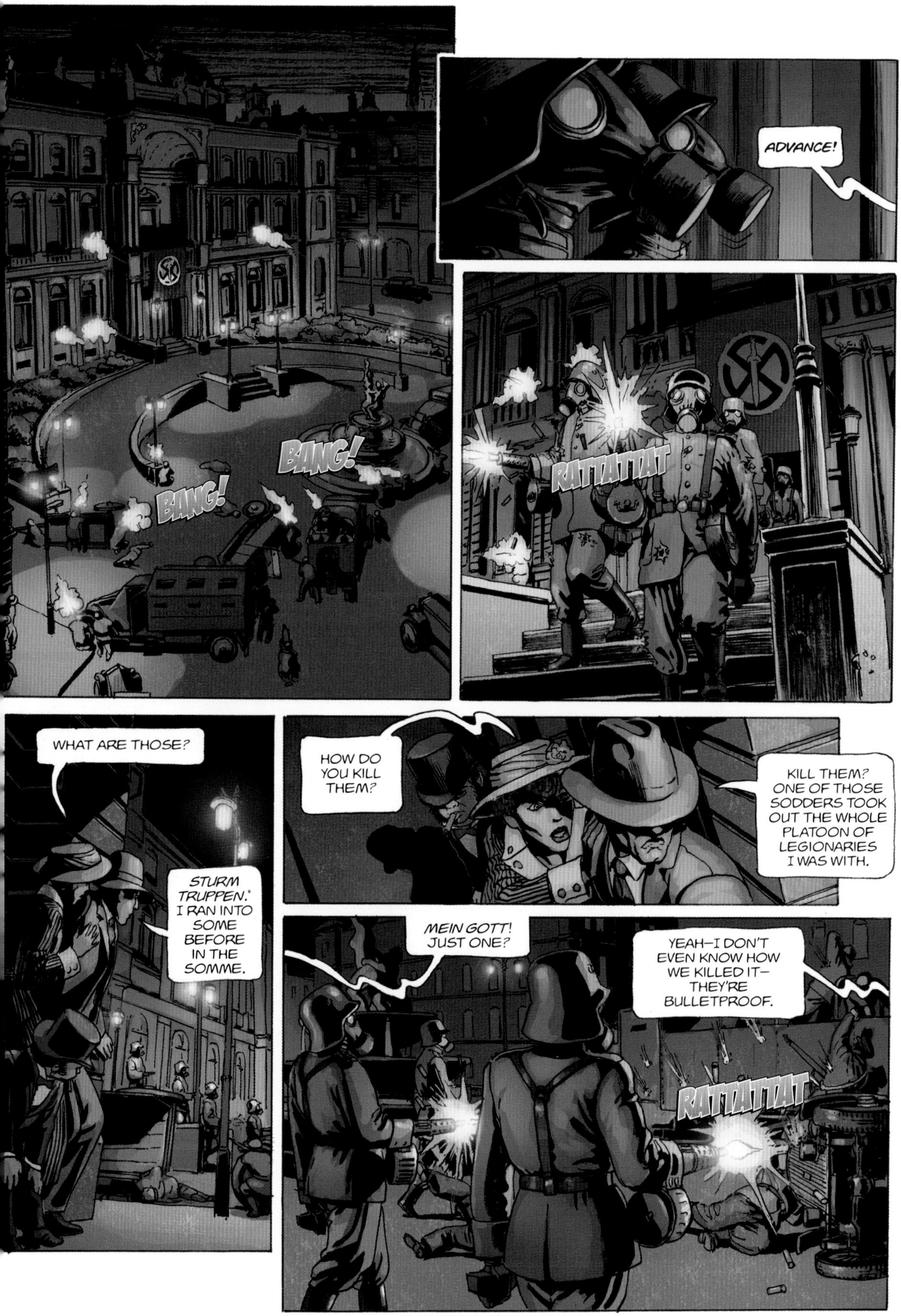
ADVANCE!
BANG!
BANG!
RATTATTAT
WHAT ARE THOSE?
STURM TRUPPEN.* I RAN INTO SOME BEFORE IN THE SOMME.
HOW DO YOU KILL THEM?
KILL THEM? ONE OF THOSE SODDERS TOOK OUT THE WHOLE PLATOON OF LEGIONARIES I WAS WITH.
MEIN GOTT! JUST ONE?
YEAH—I DON'T EVEN KNOW HOW WE KILLED IT— THEY'RE BULLETPROOF.
RATTATTAT

* SEE THE SECRET HISTORY, BOOK 7: OUR LADY OF THE SHADOWS.

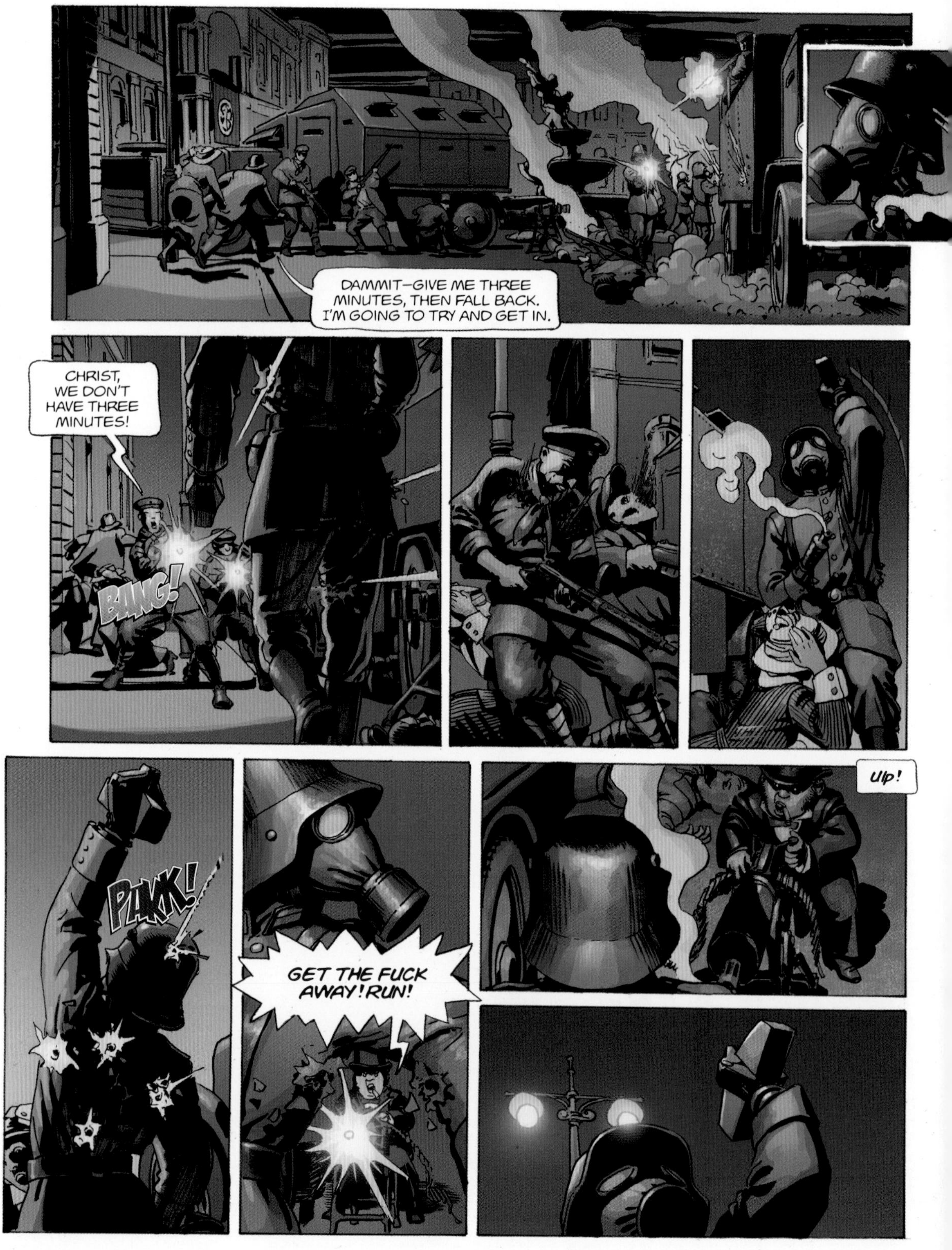
DAMMIT—GIVE ME THREE MINUTES, THEN FALL BACK. I'M GOING TO TRY AND GET IN.
CHRIST, WE DON'T HAVE THREE MINUTES!
BANG!
PAKK!
GET THE FUCK AWAY! RUN!
Ulp!

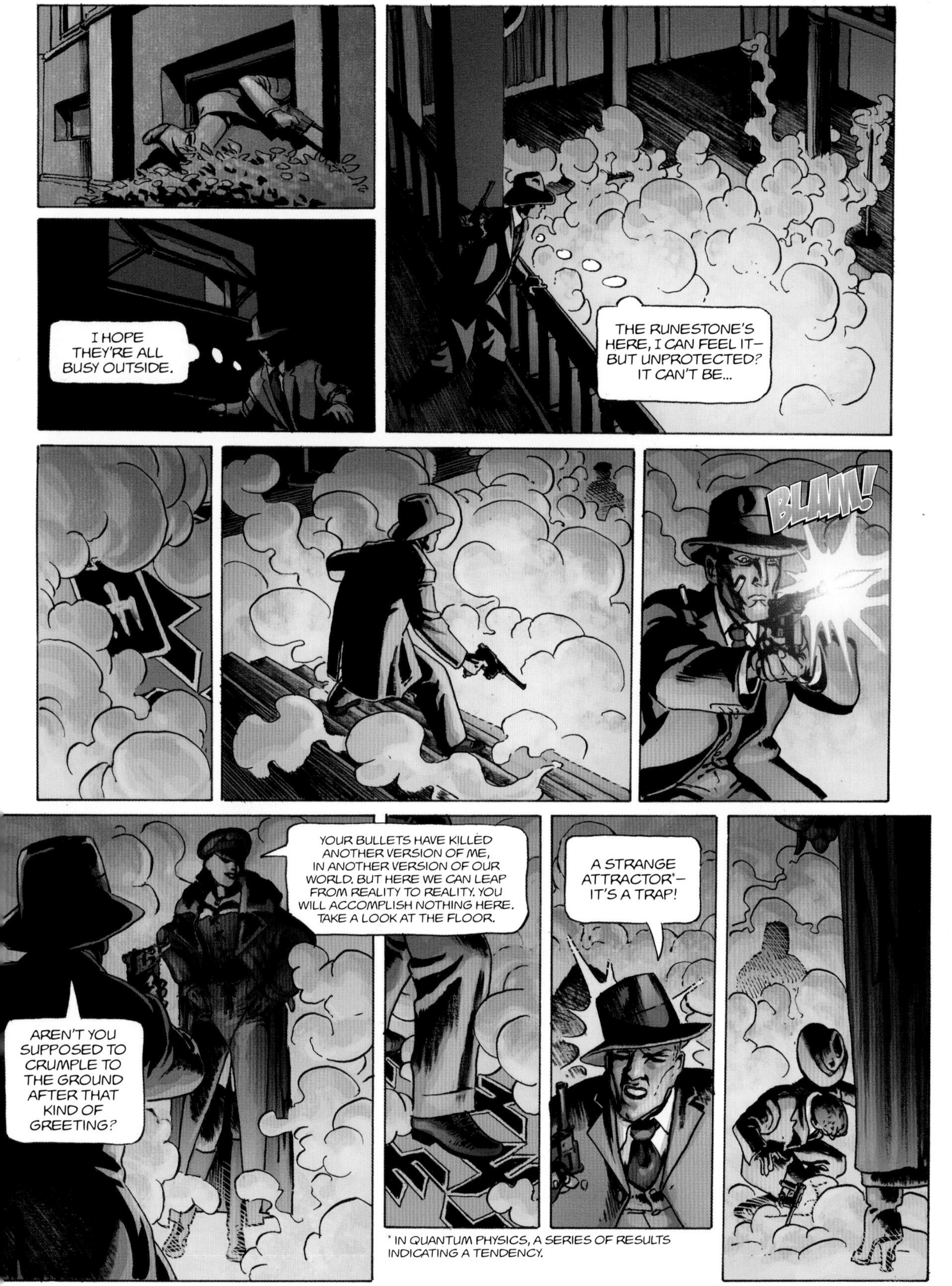
I HOPE THEY'RE ALL BUSY OUTSIDE.
THE RUNESTONE'S HERE, I CAN FEEL IT— BUT UNPROTECTED? IT CAN'T BE...
BLAM!
YOUR BULLETS HAVE KILLED ANOTHER VERSION OF ME, IN ANOTHER VERSION OF OUR WORLD. BUT HERE WE CAN LEAP FROM REALITY TO REALITY. YOU WILL ACCOMPLISH NOTHING HERE. TAKE A LOOK AT THE FLOOR.
AREN'T YOU SUPPOSED TO CRUMPLE TO THE GROUND AFTER THAT KIND OF GREETING?
A STRANGE ATTRACTOR*— IT'S A TRAP!

* IN QUANTUM PHYSICS, A SERIES OF RESULTS INDICATING A TENDENCY.

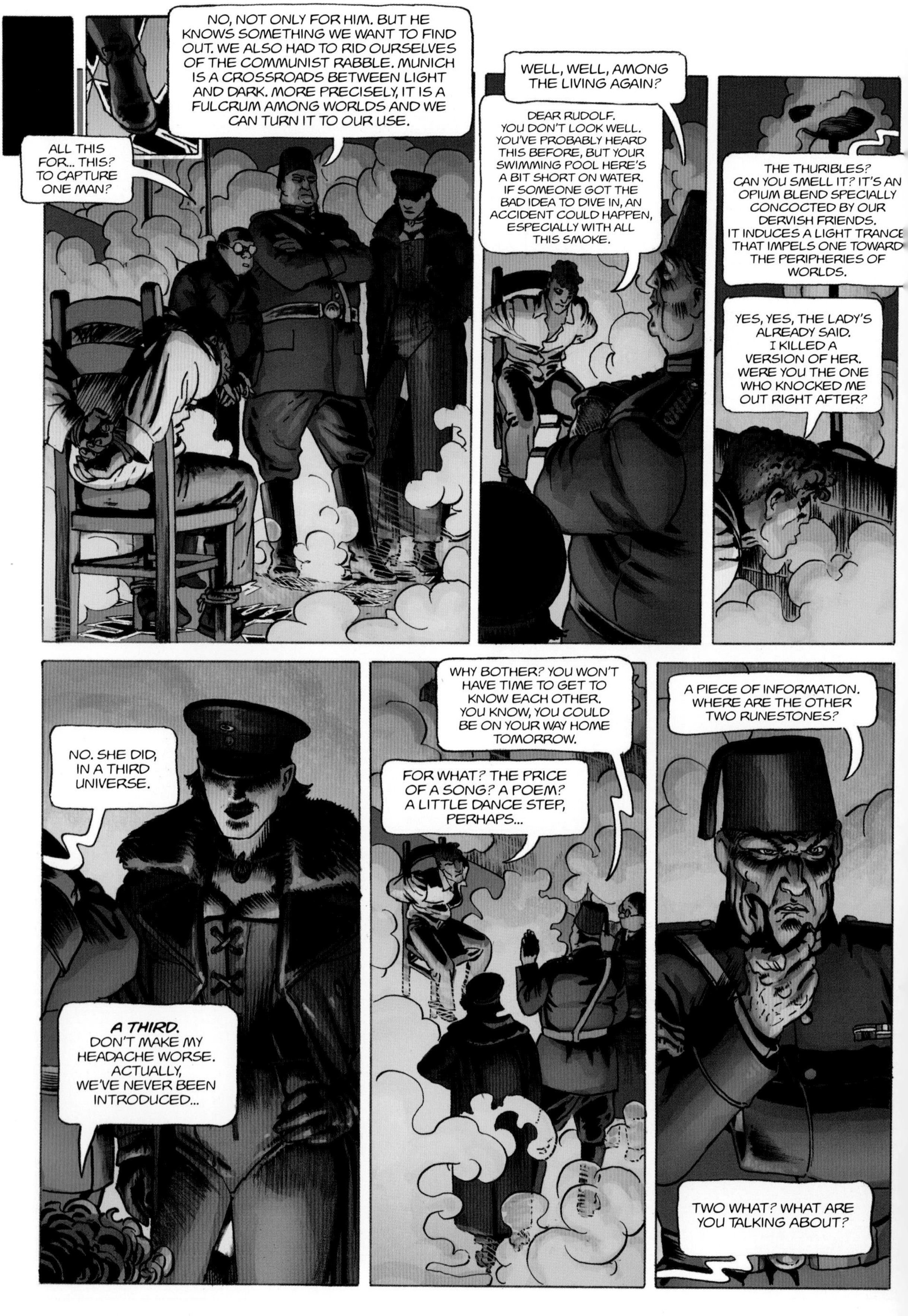
ALL THIS FOR... THIS? TO CAPTURE ONE MAN?
NO, NOT ONLY FOR HIM. BUT HE KNOWS SOMETHING WE WANT TO FIND OUT. WE ALSO HAD TO RID OURSELVES OF THE COMMUNIST RABBLE. MUNICH IS A CROSSROADS BETWEEN LIGHT AND DARK. MORE PRECISELY, IT IS A FULCRUM AMONG WORLDS AND WE CAN TURN IT TO OUR USE.
WELL, WELL, AMONG THE LIVING AGAIN?
DEAR RUDOLF. YOU DON'T LOOK WELL. YOU'VE PROBABLY HEARD THIS BEFORE, BUT YOUR SWIMMING POOL HERE'S A BIT SHORT ON WATER. IF SOMEONE GOT THE BAD IDEA TO DIVE IN, AN ACCIDENT COULD HAPPEN, ESPECIALLY WITH ALL THIS SMOKE.
THE THURIBLES? CAN YOU SMELL IT? IT'S AN OPIUM BLEND SPECIALLY CONCOCTED BY OUR DERVISH FRIENDS. IT INDUCES A LIGHT TRANCE THAT IMPELS ONE TOWARD THE PERIPHERIES OF WORLDS.
YES, YES, THE LADY'S ALREADY SAID. I KILLED A VERSION OF HER. WERE YOU THE ONE WHO KNOCKED ME OUT RIGHT AFTER?
NO. SHE DID, IN A THIRD UNIVERSE.
A THIRD. DON'T MAKE MY HEADACHE WORSE. ACTUALLY, WE'VE NEVER BEEN INTRODUCED...
WHY BOTHER? YOU WON'T HAVE TIME TO GET TO KNOW EACH OTHER. YOU KNOW, YOU COULD BE ON YOUR WAY HOME TOMORROW.
FOR WHAT? THE PRICE OF A SONG? A POEM? A LITTLE DANCE STEP, PERHAPS...
A PIECE OF INFORMATION. WHERE ARE THE OTHER TWO RUNESTONES?
TWO WHAT? WHAT ARE YOU TALKING ABOUT?

THAT CUR PHILBY BROUGHT THREE RUNESTONES BACK FROM KOR.

HOW DO YOU KNOW?

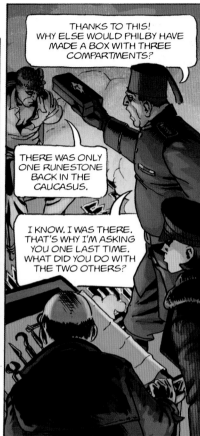

THANKS TO THIS! WHY ELSE WOULD PHILBY HAVE MADE A BOX WITH THREE COMPARTMENTS?

THERE WAS ONLY ONE RUNESTONE BACK IN THE CAUCASUS.

I KNOW. I WAS THERE. THAT'S WHY I'M ASKING YOU ONE LAST TIME. WHAT DID YOU DO WITH THE TWO OTHERS?

YOU'VE MADE A MISTAKE, OLD CHUM. I'VE NEVER SEEN THE OTHERS.

AARRGGHHH!

BLOODY HELL, IF THE SHIELDS HAD THE OTHER TWO BLACK RUNESTONES, DON'T YOU THINK THEY WOULD'VE USED THEM ALREADY?

NOT NECESSARILY. THE RUNESTONES WORK IN VERY STRANGE— AND VERY DANGEROUS— WAYS.

TRY AND THINK A LITTLE. PERHAPS PHILBY PULLED A FAST ONE ON YOU TOO. PERHAPS HE MENTIONED SOMETHING. JUST GIVE US A CLUE.

BUGGER OFF. WHY DON'T YOU ASK HIM YOURSELF—

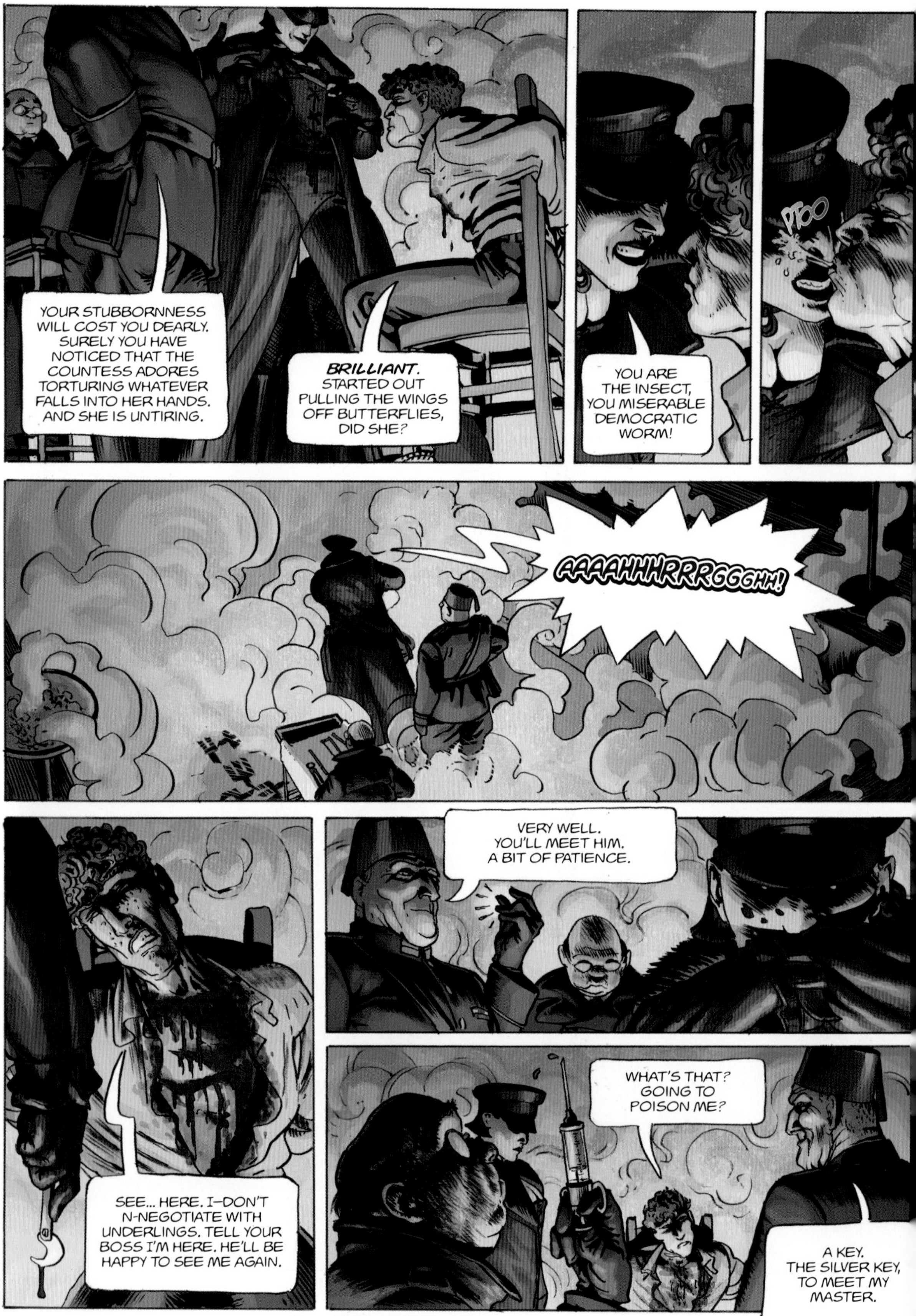
YOUR STUBBORNNESS WILL COST YOU DEARLY. SURELY YOU HAVE NOTICED THAT THE COUNTESS ADORES TORTURING WHATEVER FALLS INTO HER HANDS. AND SHE IS UNTIRING.
BRILLIANT. STARTED OUT PULLING THE WINGS OFF BUTTERFLIES, DID SHE?
YOU ARE THE INSECT, YOU MISERABLE DEMOCRATIC WORM!
PTOO
AAAAHHHRRRGGGHH!
SEE... HERE. I—DON'T N-NEGOTIATE WITH UNDERLINGS. TELL YOUR BOSS I'M HERE. HE'LL BE HAPPY TO SEE ME AGAIN.
VERY WELL. YOU'LL MEET HIM. A BIT OF PATIENCE.
WHAT'S THAT? GOING TO POISON ME?
A KEY. THE SILVER KEY, TO MEET MY MASTER.

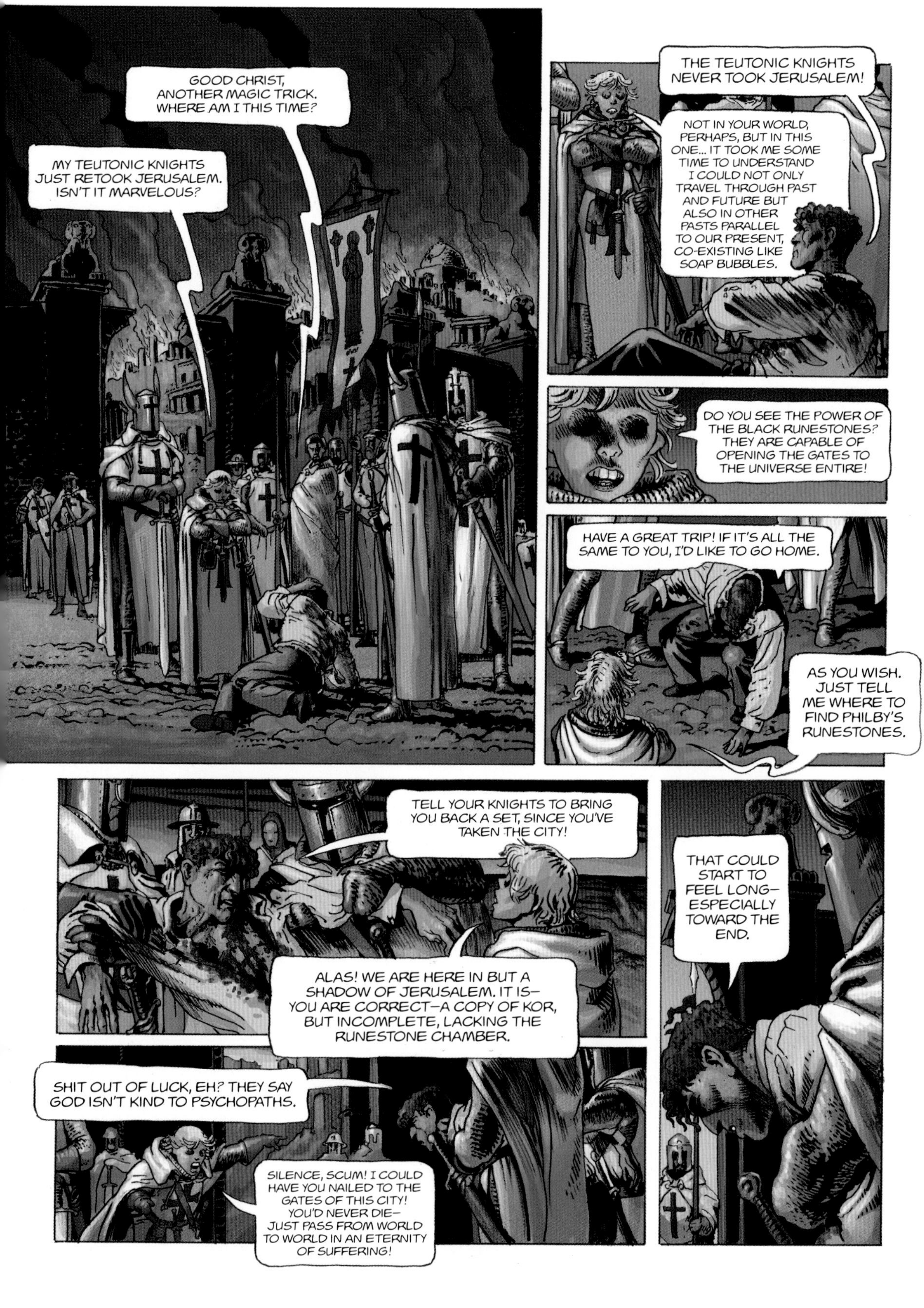
GOOD CHRIST, ANOTHER MAGIC TRICK. WHERE AM I THIS TIME?
MY TEUTONIC KNIGHTS JUST RETOOK JERUSALEM. ISN'T IT MARVELOUS?
THE TEUTONIC KNIGHTS NEVER TOOK JERUSALEM!
NOT IN YOUR WORLD, PERHAPS, BUT IN THIS ONE... IT TOOK ME SOME TIME TO UNDERSTAND I COULD NOT ONLY TRAVEL THROUGH PAST AND FUTURE BUT ALSO IN OTHER PASTS PARALLEL TO OUR PRESENT, CO-EXISTING LIKE SOAP BUBBLES.
DO YOU SEE THE POWER OF THE BLACK RUNESTONES? THEY ARE CAPABLE OF OPENING THE GATES TO THE UNIVERSE ENTIRE!
HAVE A GREAT TRIP! IF IT'S ALL THE SAME TO YOU, I'D LIKE TO GO HOME.
AS YOU WISH. JUST TELL ME WHERE TO FIND PHILBY'S RUNESTONES.
TELL YOUR KNIGHTS TO BRING YOU BACK A SET, SINCE YOU'VE TAKEN THE CITY!
ALAS! WE ARE HERE IN BUT A SHADOW OF JERUSALEM. IT IS—YOU ARE CORRECT—A COPY OF KOR, BUT INCOMPLETE, LACKING THE RUNESTONE CHAMBER.
THAT COULD START TO FEEL LONG—ESPECIALLY TOWARD THE END.
SHIT OUT OF LUCK, EH? THEY SAY GOD ISN'T KIND TO PSYCHOPATHS.
SILENCE, SCUM! I COULD HAVE YOU NAILED TO THE GATES OF THIS CITY! YOU'D NEVER DIE—JUST PASS FROM WORLD TO WORLD IN AN ETERNITY OF SUFFERING!

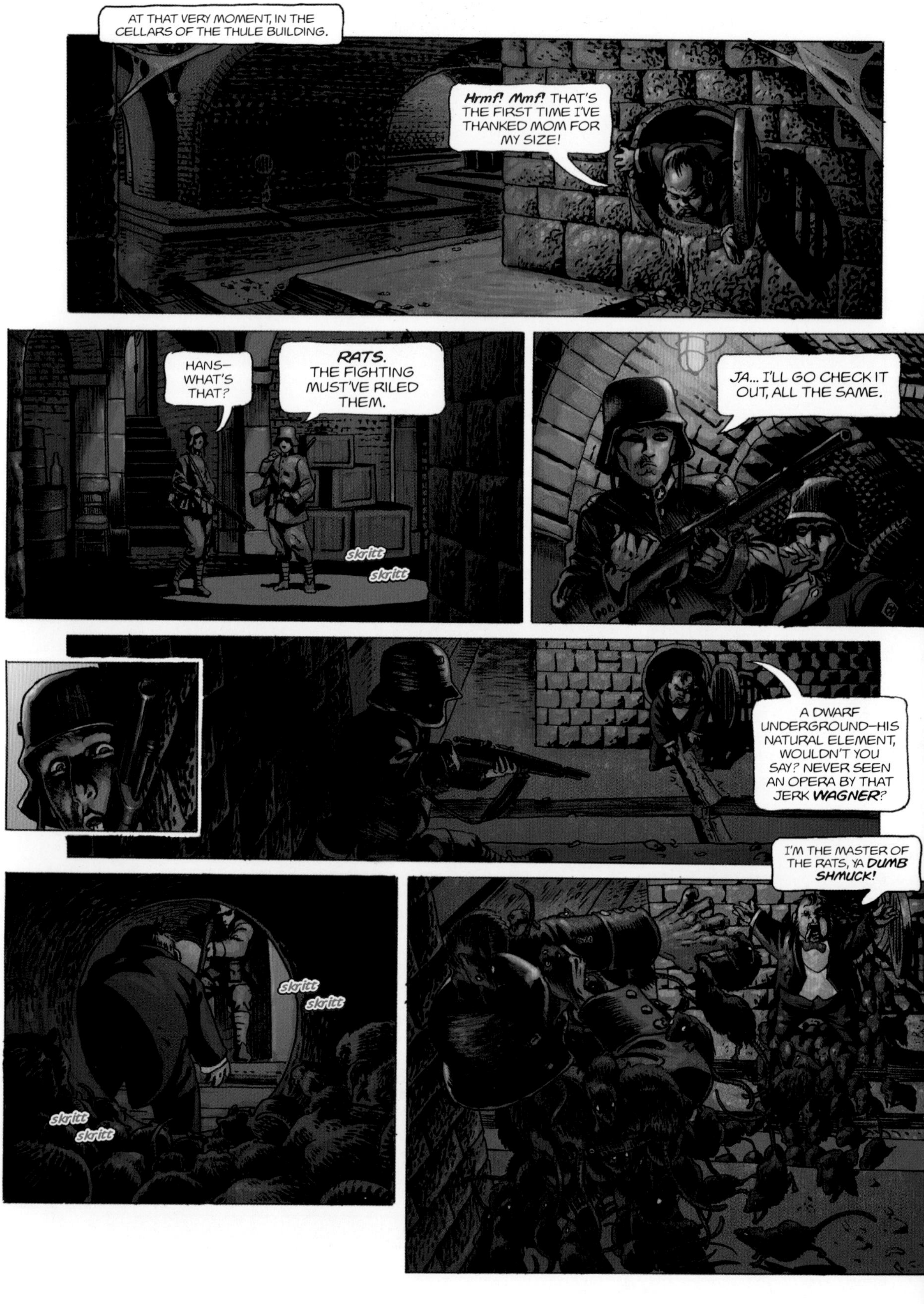

AT THAT VERY MOMENT, IN THE CELLARS OF THE THULE BUILDING.
Hrmf! Mmf! THAT'S THE FIRST TIME I'VE THANKED MOM FOR MY SIZE!
HANS— WHAT'S THAT?
RATS. THE FIGHTING MUST'VE RILED THEM.
skritt
skritt
JA... I'LL GO CHECK IT OUT, ALL THE SAME.
A DWARF UNDERGROUND—HIS NATURAL ELEMENT, WOULDN'T YOU SAY? NEVER SEEN AN OPERA BY THAT JERK WAGNER?
skritt
skritt
skritt
skritt
I'M THE MASTER OF THE RATS, YA DUMB SHMUCK!

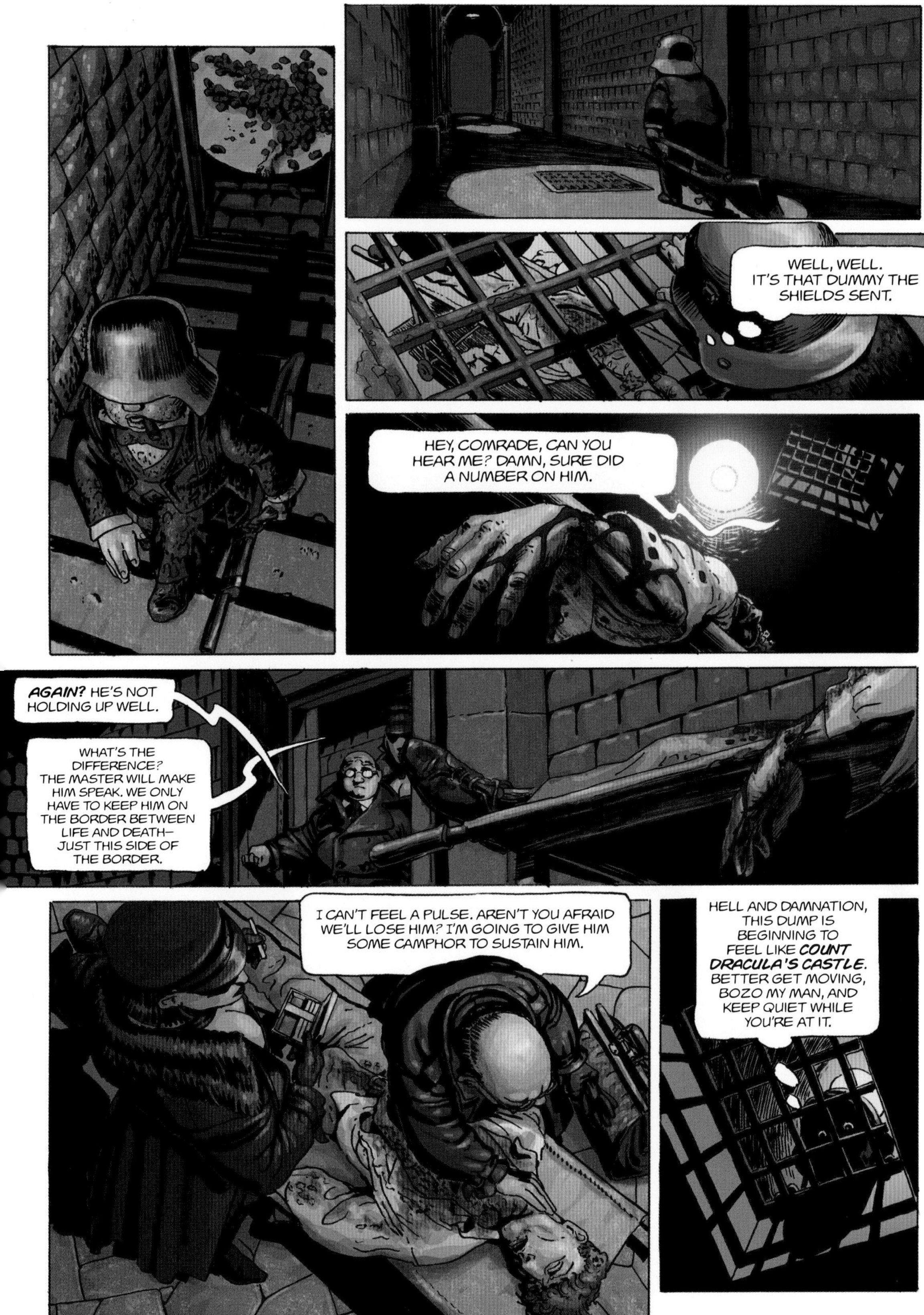
WELL, WELL. IT'S THAT DUMMY THE SHIELDS SENT.
HEY, COMRADE, CAN YOU HEAR ME? DAMN, SURE DID A NUMBER ON HIM.
AGAIN? HE'S NOT HOLDING UP WELL.
WHAT'S THE DIFFERENCE? THE MASTER WILL MAKE HIM SPEAK. WE ONLY HAVE TO KEEP HIM ON THE BORDER BETWEEN LIFE AND DEATH— JUST THIS SIDE OF THE BORDER.
I CAN'T FEEL A PULSE. AREN'T YOU AFRAID WE'LL LOSE HIM? I'M GOING TO GIVE HIM SOME CAMPHOR TO SUSTAIN HIM.
HELL AND DAMNATION, THIS DUMP IS BEGINNING TO FEEL LIKE COUNT DRACULA'S CASTLE. BETTER GET MOVING, BOZO MY MAN, AND KEEP QUIET WHILE YOU'RE AT IT.

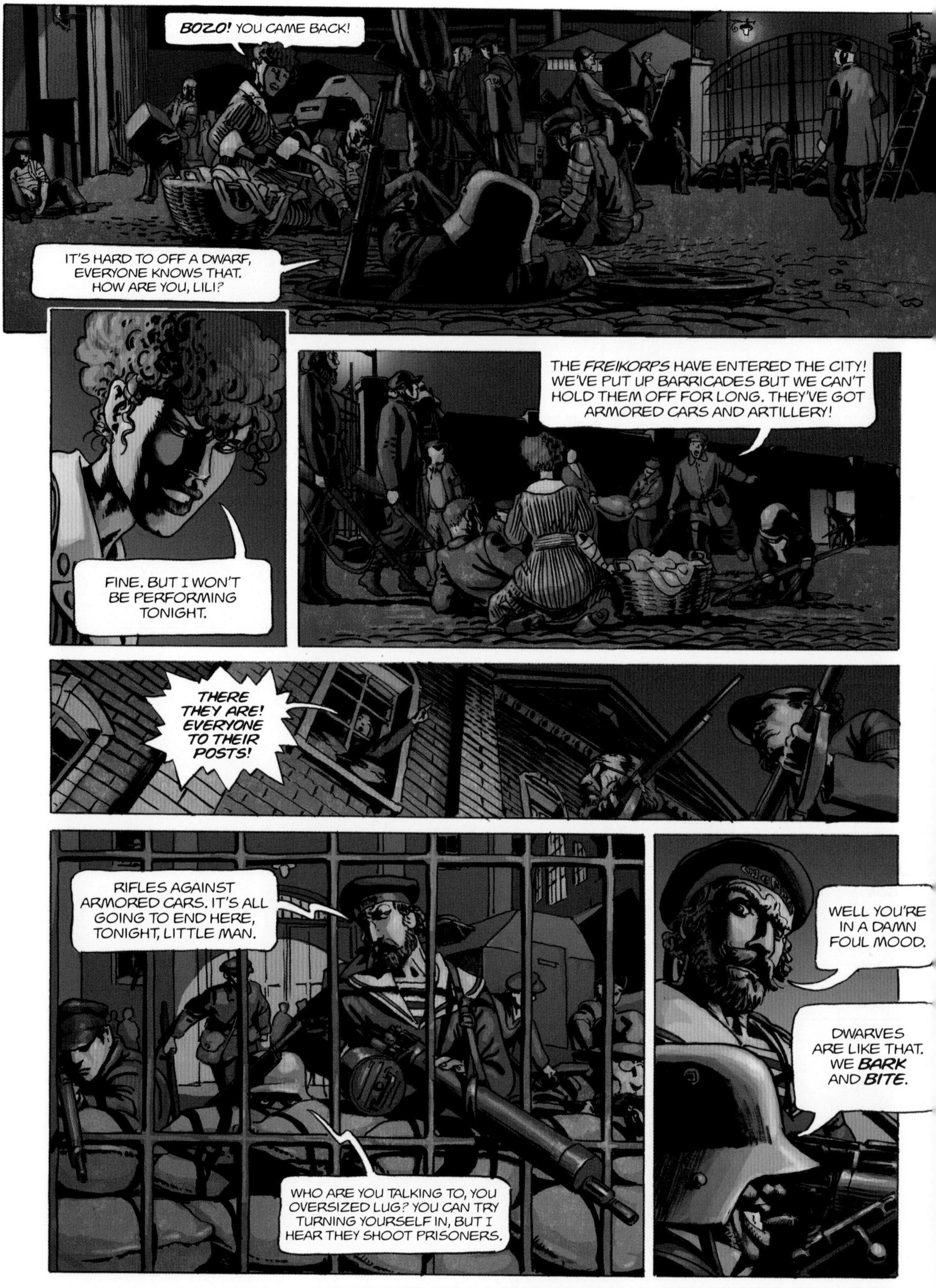
BOZO! YOU CAME BACK!
IT'S HARD TO OFF A DWARF, EVERYONE KNOWS THAT. HOW ARE YOU, LILI?
FINE. BUT I WON'T BE PERFORMING TONIGHT.
THE FREIKORPS HAVE ENTERED THE CITY! WE'VE PUT UP BARRICADES BUT WE CAN'T HOLD THEM OFF FOR LONG. THEY'VE GOT ARMORED CARS AND ARTILLERY!
THERE THEY ARE! EVERYONE TO THEIR POSTS!
RIFLES AGAINST ARMORED CARS. IT'S ALL GOING TO END HERE, TONIGHT, LITTLE MAN.
WHO ARE YOU TALKING TO, YOU OVERSIZED LUG? YOU CAN TRY TURNING YOURSELF IN, BUT I HEAR THEY SHOOT PRISONERS.
WELL YOU'RE IN A DAMN FOUL MOOD.
DWARVES ARE LIKE THAT. WE BARK AND BITE.

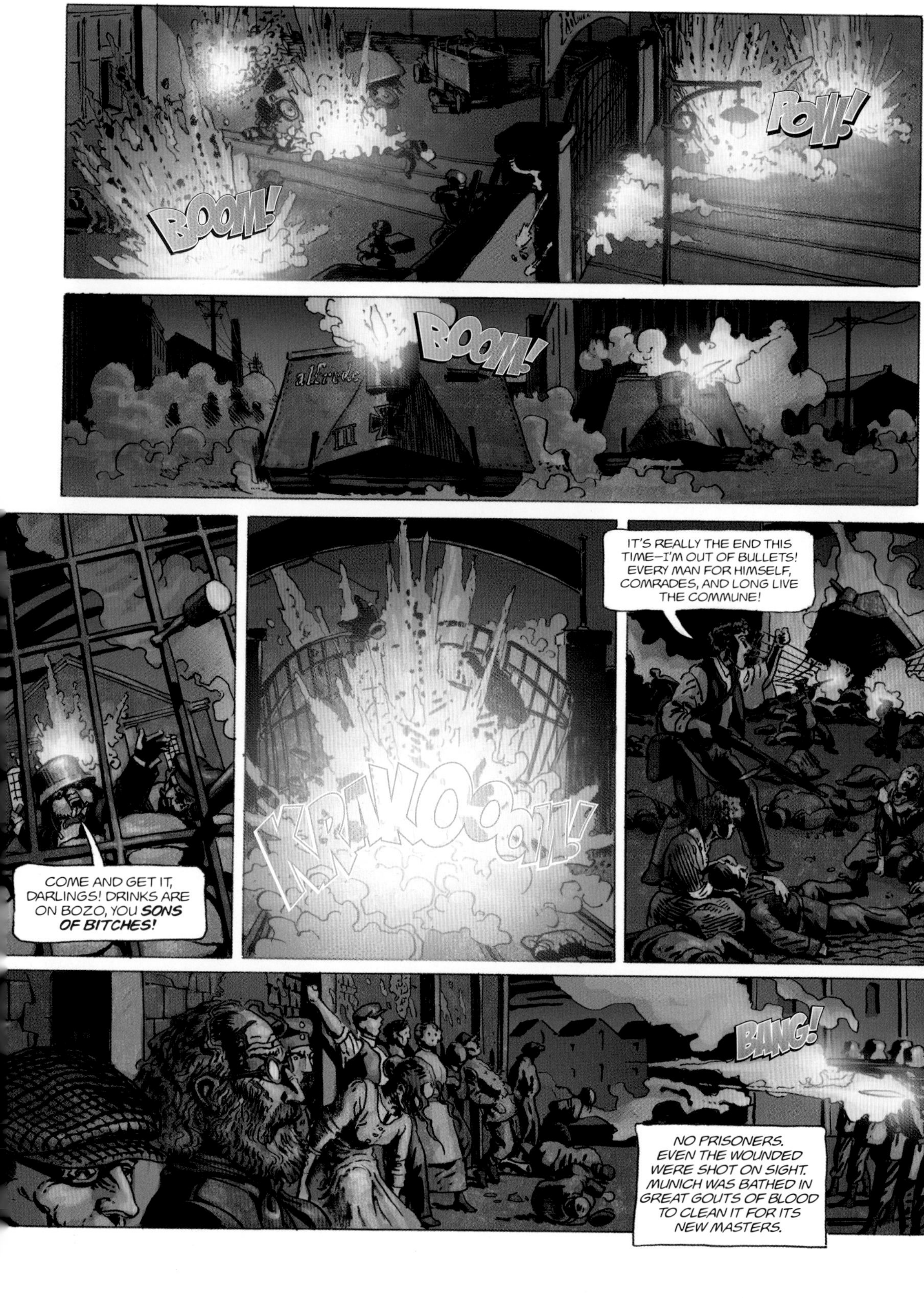
BOOM!
POW!
BOOM!
COME AND GET IT, DARLINGS! DRINKS ARE ON BOZO, YOU **SONS OF BITCHES!**
IT'S REALLY THE END THIS TIME—I'M OUT OF BULLETS! EVERY MAN FOR HIMSELF, COMRADES, AND LONG LIVE THE COMMUNE!
BANG!
NO PRISONERS. EVEN THE WOUNDED WERE SHOT ON SIGHT. MUNICH WAS BATHED IN GREAT GOUTS OF BLOOD TO CLEAN IT FOR ITS NEW MASTERS.

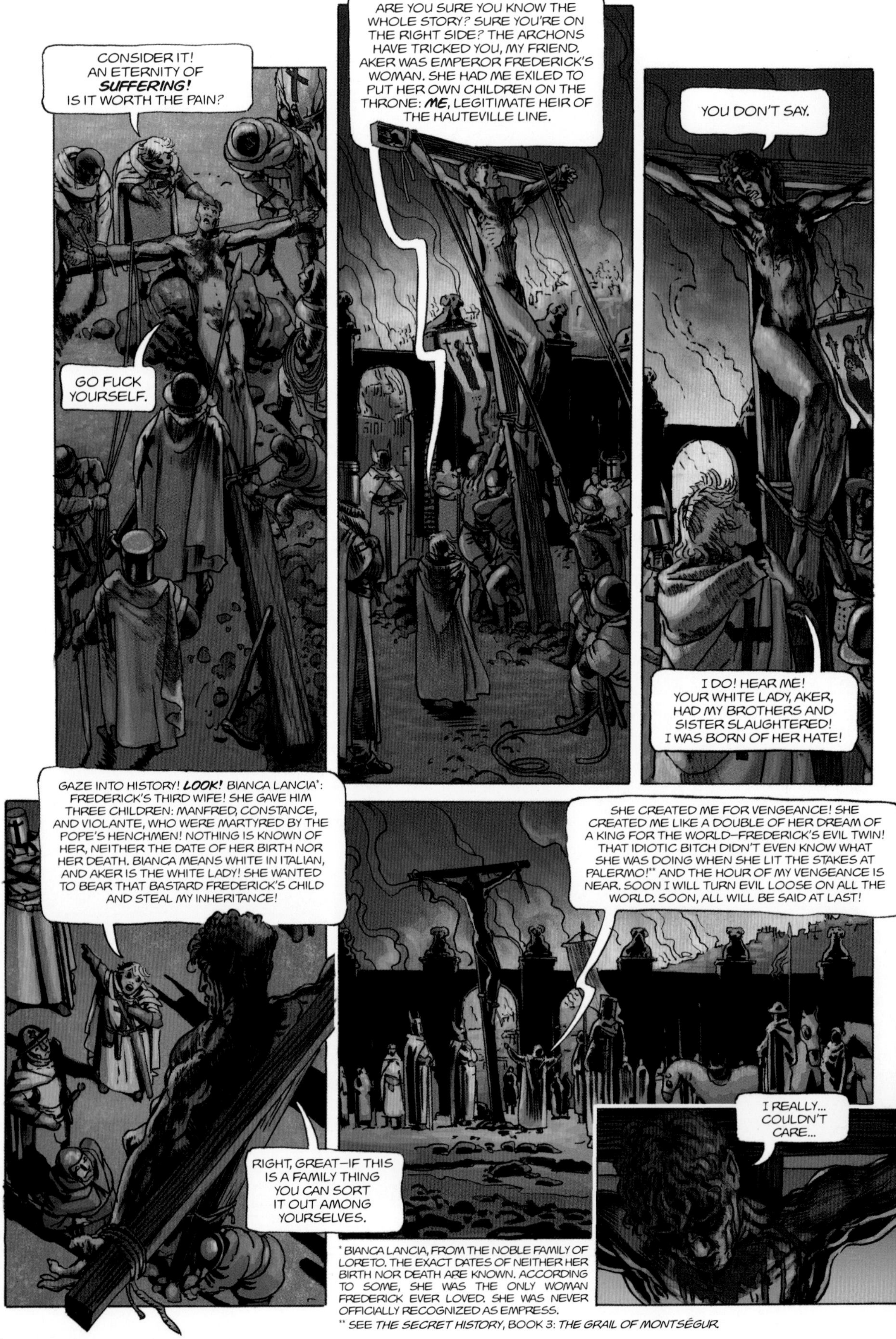

CONSIDER IT! AN ETERNITY OF **SUFFERING!** IS IT WORTH THE PAIN?
GO FUCK YOURSELF.
ARE YOU SURE YOU KNOW THE WHOLE STORY? SURE YOU'RE ON THE RIGHT SIDE? THE ARCHONS HAVE TRICKED YOU, MY FRIEND. AKER WAS EMPEROR FREDERICK'S WOMAN. SHE HAD ME EXILED TO PUT HER OWN CHILDREN ON THE THRONE: **ME**, LEGITIMATE HEIR OF THE HAUTEVILLE LINE.
YOU DON'T SAY.
I DO! HEAR ME! YOUR WHITE LADY, AKER, HAD MY BROTHERS AND SISTER SLAUGHTERED! I WAS BORN OF HER HATE!
GAZE INTO HISTORY! **LOOK!** BIANCA LANCIA*: FREDERICK'S THIRD WIFE! SHE GAVE HIM THREE CHILDREN: MANFRED, CONSTANCE, AND VIOLANTE, WHO WERE MARTYRED BY THE POPE'S HENCHMEN! NOTHING IS KNOWN OF HER, NEITHER THE DATE OF HER BIRTH NOR HER DEATH. BIANCA MEANS WHITE IN ITALIAN, AND AKER IS THE WHITE LADY! SHE WANTED TO BEAR THAT BASTARD FREDERICK'S CHILD AND STEAL MY INHERITANCE!
RIGHT, GREAT—IF THIS IS A FAMILY THING YOU CAN SORT IT OUT AMONG YOURSELVES.
SHE CREATED ME FOR VENGEANCE! SHE CREATED ME LIKE A DOUBLE OF HER DREAM OF A KING FOR THE WORLD—FREDERICK'S EVIL TWIN! THAT IDIOTIC BITCH DIDN'T EVEN KNOW WHAT SHE WAS DOING WHEN SHE LIT THE STAKES AT PALERMO!** AND THE HOUR OF MY VENGEANCE IS NEAR. SOON I WILL TURN EVIL LOOSE ON ALL THE WORLD. SOON, ALL WILL BE SAID AT LAST!
I REALLY... COULDN'T CARE...

* BIANCA LANCIA, FROM THE NOBLE FAMILY OF LORETO. THE EXACT DATES OF NEITHER HER BIRTH NOR DEATH ARE KNOWN. ACCORDING TO SOME, SHE WAS THE ONLY WOMAN FREDERICK EVER LOVED. SHE WAS NEVER OFFICIALLY RECOGNIZED AS EMPRESS.

** SEE *THE SECRET HISTORY*, BOOK 3: *THE GRAIL OF MONTSÉGUR*.

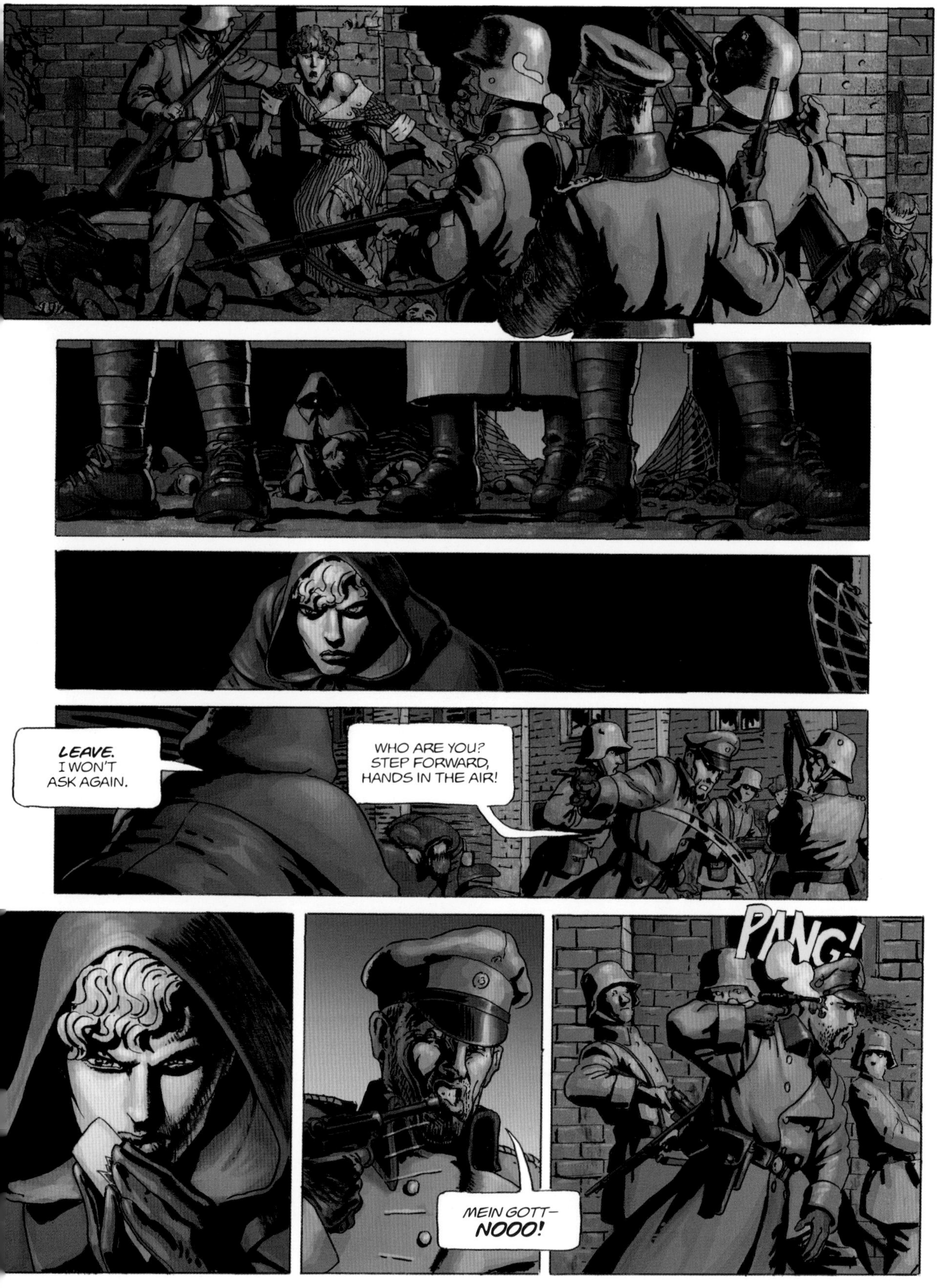
LEAVE. I WON'T ASK AGAIN.
WHO ARE YOU? STEP FORWARD, HANDS IN THE AIR!
MEIN GOTT— NOOO!
PANG!

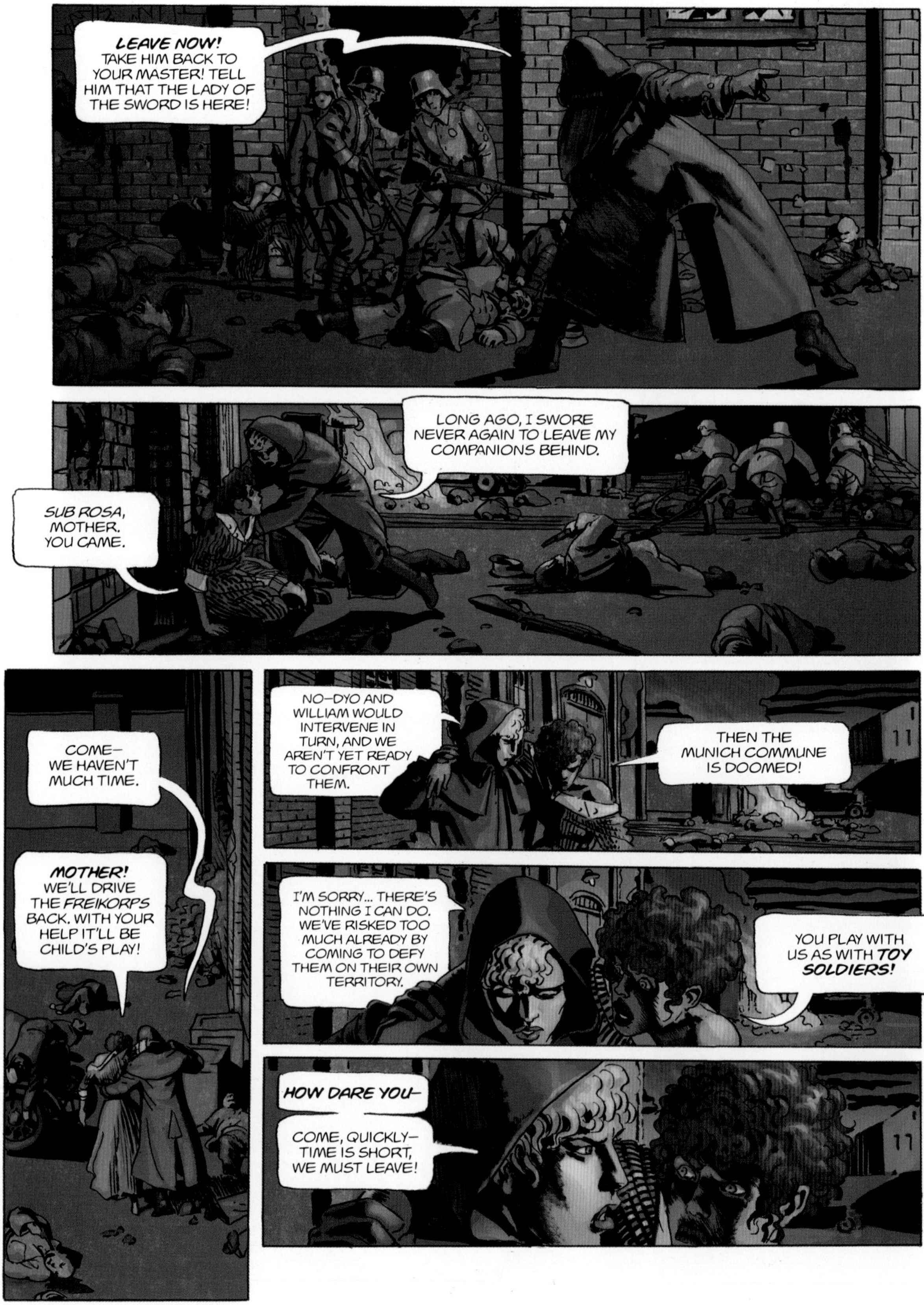
LEAVE NOW! TAKE HIM BACK TO YOUR MASTER! TELL HIM THAT THE LADY OF THE SWORD IS HERE!
LONG AGO, I SWORE NEVER AGAIN TO LEAVE MY COMPANIONS BEHIND.
SUB ROSA, MOTHER. YOU CAME.
COME— WE HAVEN'T MUCH TIME.
MOTHER! WE'LL DRIVE THE FREIKORPS BACK. WITH YOUR HELP IT'LL BE CHILD'S PLAY!
NO-DYO AND WILLIAM WOULD INTERVENE IN TURN, AND WE AREN'T YET READY TO CONFRONT THEM.
THEN THE MUNICH COMMUNE IS DOOMED!
I'M SORRY... THERE'S NOTHING I CAN DO. WE'VE RISKED TOO MUCH ALREADY BY COMING TO DEFY THEM ON THEIR OWN TERRITORY.
YOU PLAY WITH US AS WITH TOY SOLDIERS!
HOW DARE YOU—
COME, QUICKLY— TIME IS SHORT, WE MUST LEAVE!

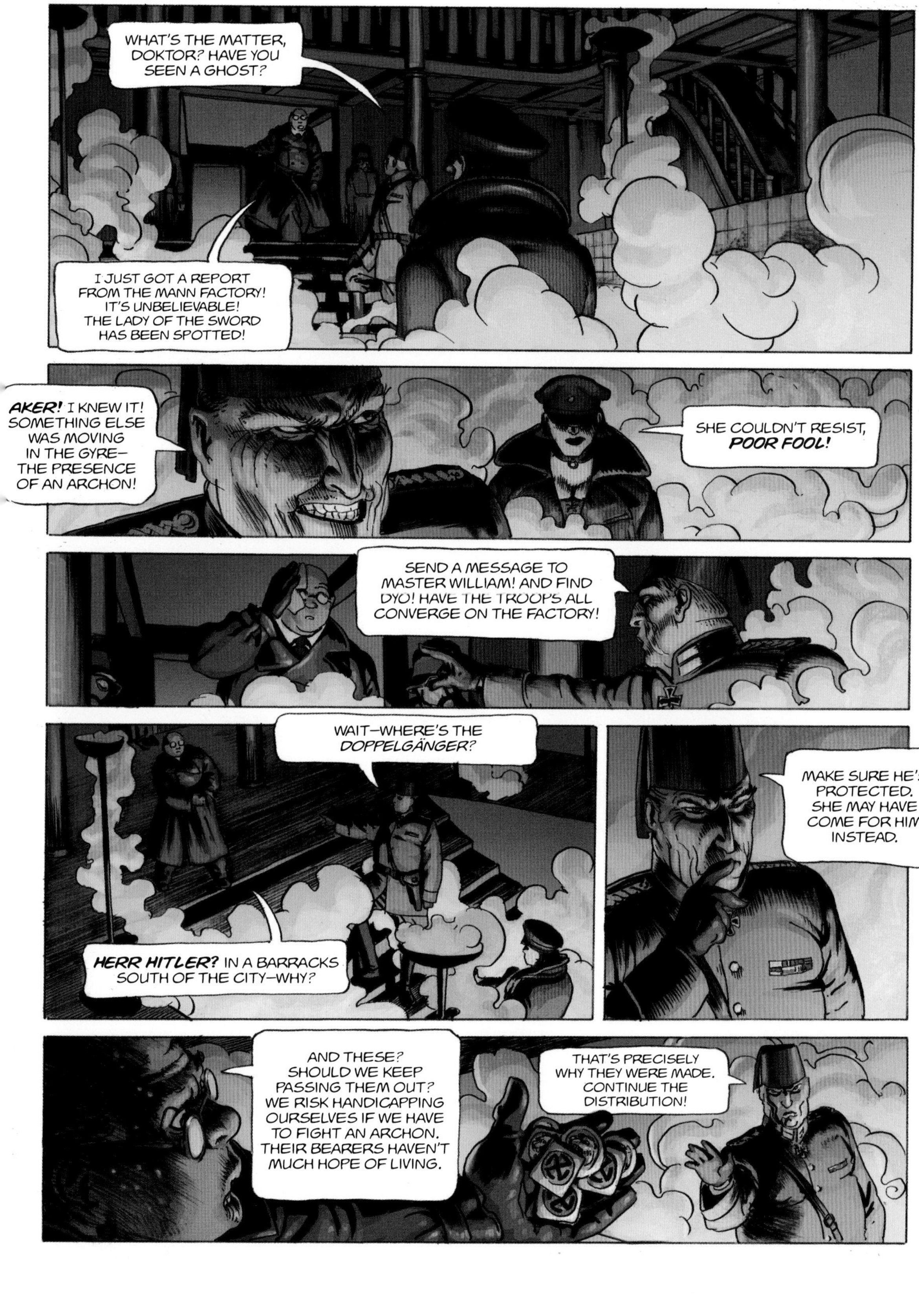
WHAT'S THE MATTER, DOKTOR? HAVE YOU SEEN A GHOST?
I JUST GOT A REPORT FROM THE MANN FACTORY! IT'S UNBELIEVABLE! THE LADY OF THE SWORD HAS BEEN SPOTTED!
AKER! I KNEW IT! SOMETHING ELSE WAS MOVING IN THE GYRE— THE PRESENCE OF AN ARCHON!
SHE COULDN'T RESIST, POOR FOOL!
SEND A MESSAGE TO MASTER WILLIAM! AND FIND DYO! HAVE THE TROOPS ALL CONVERGE ON THE FACTORY!
WAIT—WHERE'S THE DOPPELGÄNGER?
HERR HITLER? IN A BARRACKS SOUTH OF THE CITY—WHY?
MAKE SURE HE'S PROTECTED. SHE MAY HAVE COME FOR HIM INSTEAD.
AND THESE? SHOULD WE KEEP PASSING THEM OUT? WE RISK HANDICAPPING OURSELVES IF WE HAVE TO FIGHT AN ARCHON. THEIR BEARERS HAVEN'T MUCH HOPE OF LIVING.
THAT'S PRECISELY WHY THEY WERE MADE. CONTINUE THE DISTRIBUTION!

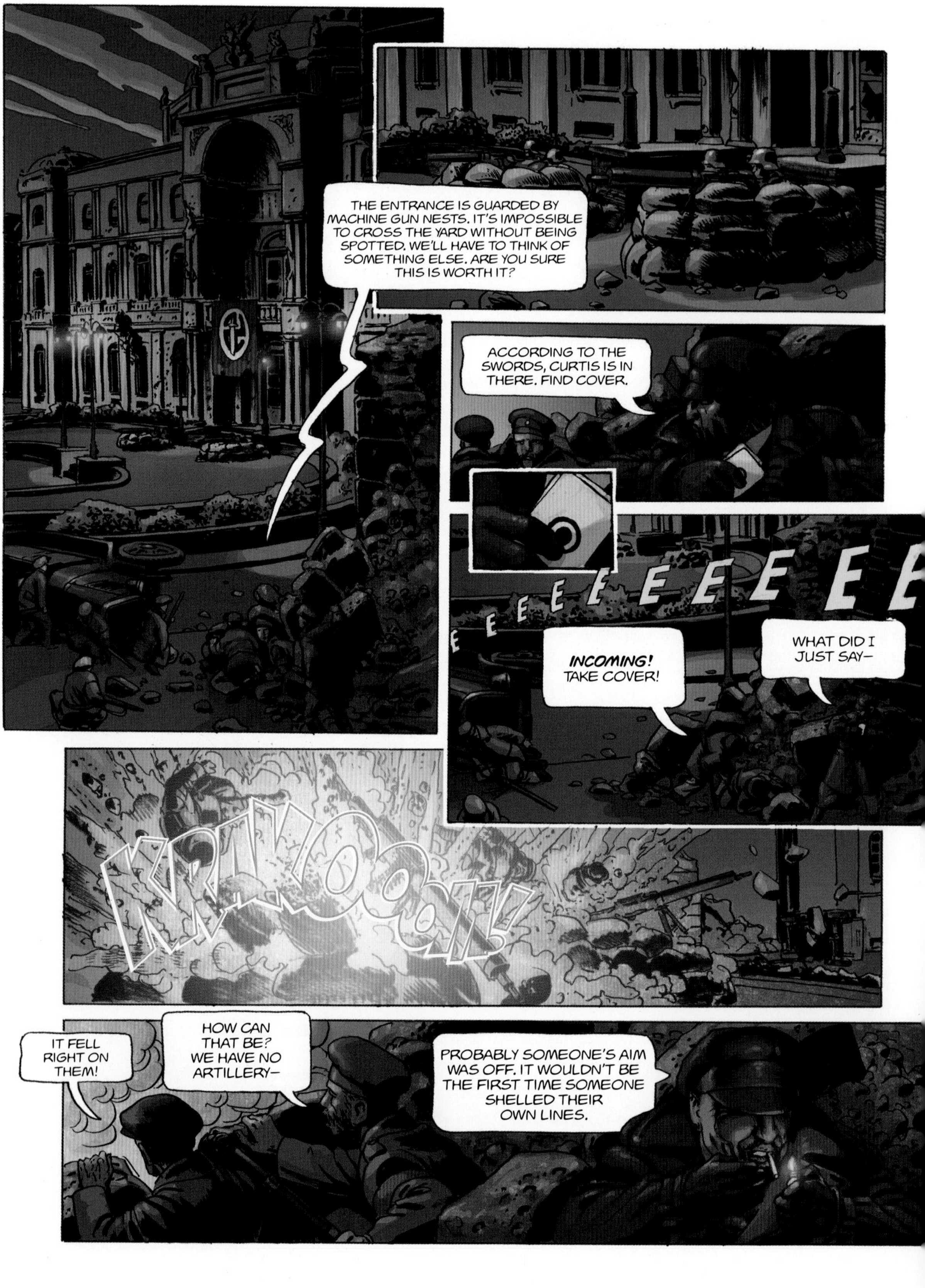
THE ENTRANCE IS GUARDED BY MACHINE GUN NESTS. IT'S IMPOSSIBLE TO CROSS THE YARD WITHOUT BEING SPOTTED. WE'LL HAVE TO THINK OF SOMETHING ELSE. ARE YOU SURE THIS IS WORTH IT?
ACCORDING TO THE SWORDS, CURTIS IS IN THERE. FIND COVER.
EEEEEEEEEEE
INCOMING! TAKE COVER!
WHAT DID I JUST SAY–
KRAKOOOM!
IT FELL RIGHT ON THEM!
HOW CAN THAT BE? WE HAVE NO ARTILLERY–
PROBABLY SOMEONE'S AIM WAS OFF. IT WOULDN'T BE THE FIRST TIME SOMEONE SHELLED THEIR OWN LINES.

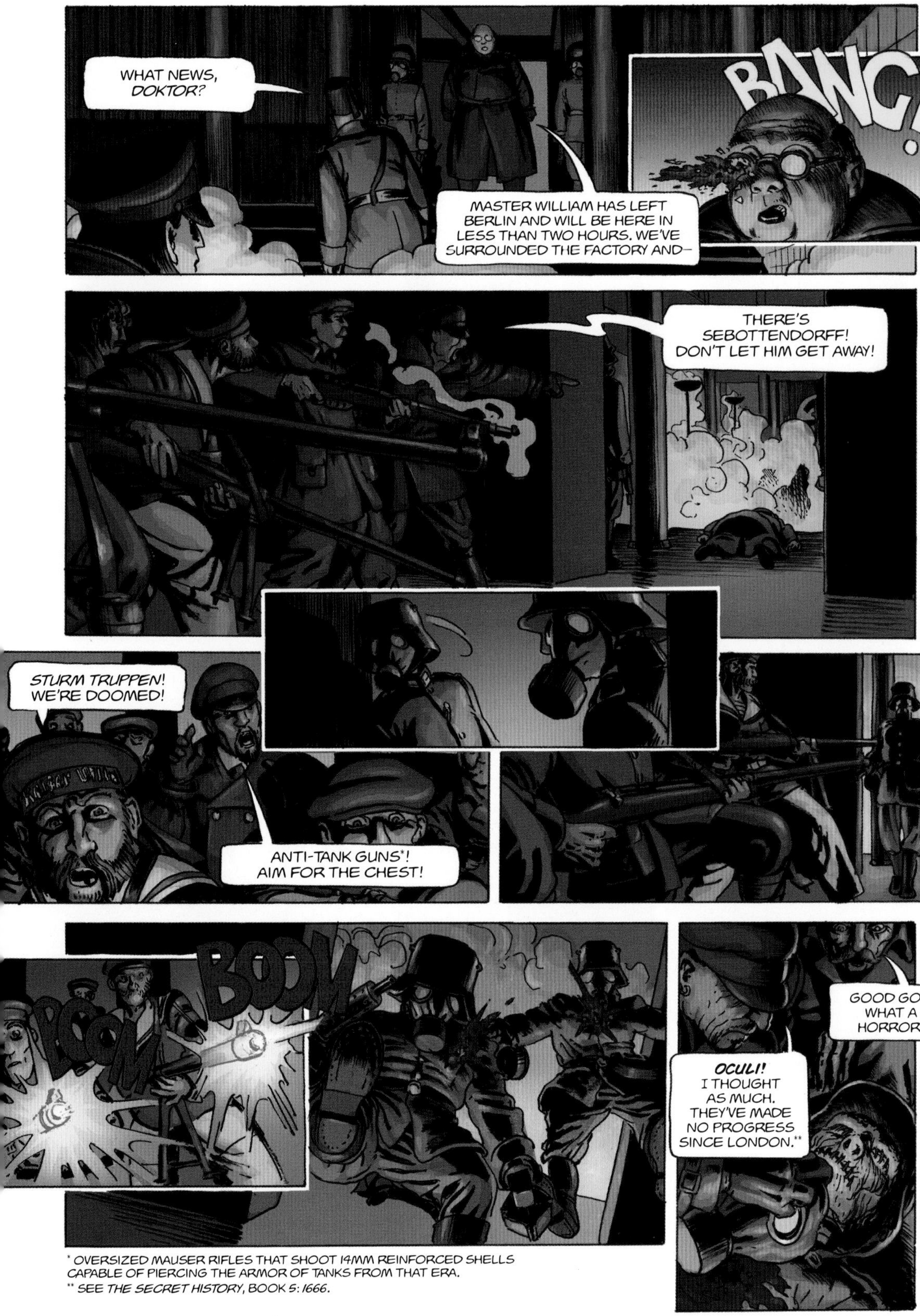
WHAT NEWS, DOKTOR?
MASTER WILLIAM HAS LEFT BERLIN AND WILL BE HERE IN LESS THAN TWO HOURS. WE'VE SURROUNDED THE FACTORY AND—
BANG!
THERE'S SEBOTTENDORFF! DON'T LET HIM GET AWAY!
STURM TRUPPEN! WE'RE DOOMED!
ANTI-TANK GUNS*! AIM FOR THE CHEST!
BOOM
BOOM
GOOD GOD, WHAT A HORROR!
OCULI! I THOUGHT AS MUCH. THEY'VE MADE NO PROGRESS SINCE LONDON.**

* OVERSIZED MAUSER RIFLES THAT SHOOT 14MM REINFORCED SHELLS CAPABLE OF PIERCING THE ARMOR OF TANKS FROM THAT ERA.
** SEE *THE SECRET HISTORY*, BOOK 5: *1666*.

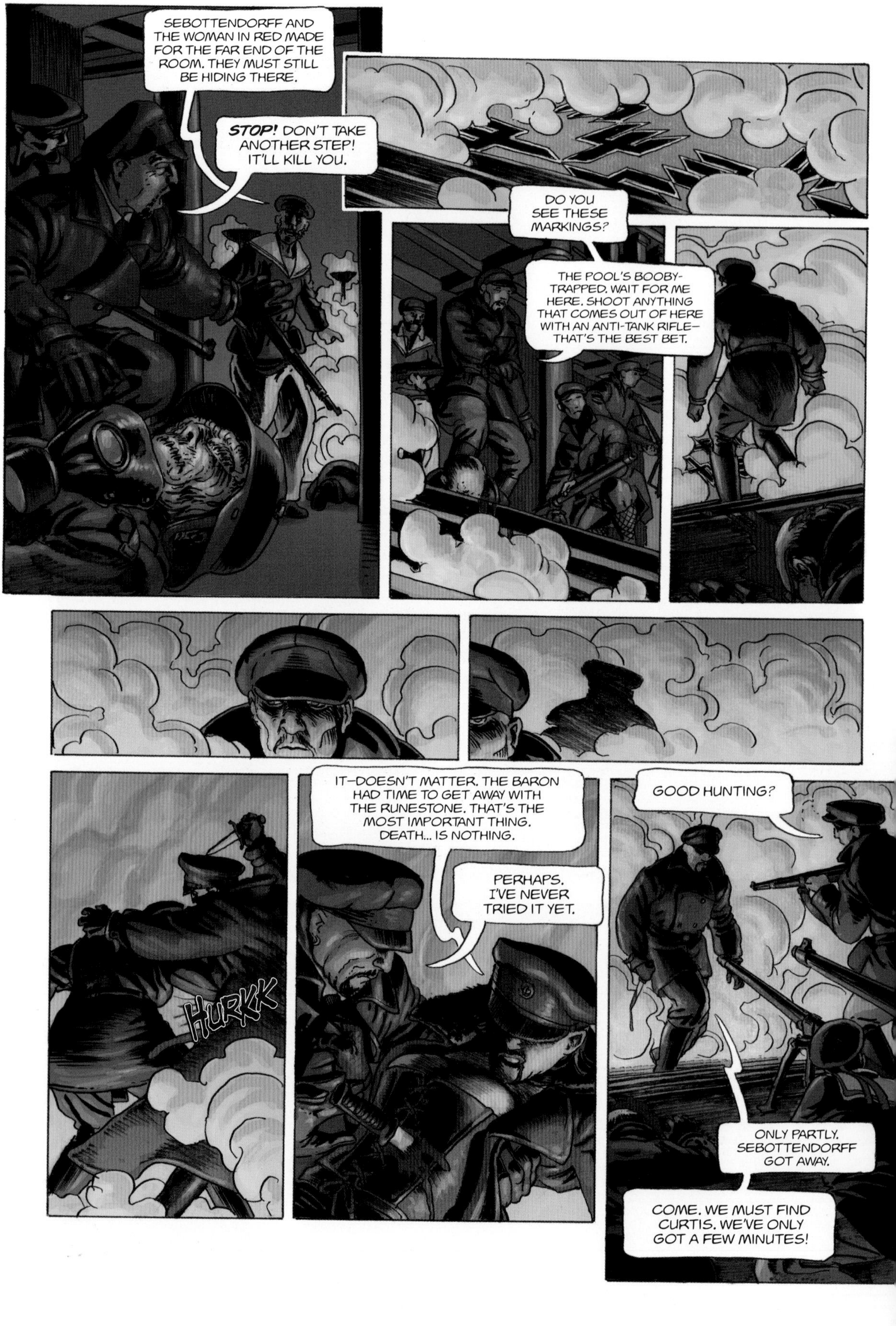
SEBOTTENDORFF AND THE WOMAN IN RED MADE FOR THE FAR END OF THE ROOM. THEY MUST STILL BE HIDING THERE.
STOP! DON'T TAKE ANOTHER STEP! IT'LL KILL YOU.
DO YOU SEE THESE MARKINGS?
THE POOL'S BOOBY-TRAPPED. WAIT FOR ME HERE. SHOOT ANYTHING THAT COMES OUT OF HERE WITH AN ANTI-TANK RIFLE—THAT'S THE BEST BET.
HURKK
IT—DOESN'T MATTER. THE BARON HAD TIME TO GET AWAY WITH THE RUNESTONE. THAT'S THE MOST IMPORTANT THING. DEATH... IS NOTHING.
PERHAPS. I'VE NEVER TRIED IT YET.
GOOD HUNTING?
ONLY PARTLY. SEBOTTENDORFF GOT AWAY.
COME. WE MUST FIND CURTIS. WE'VE ONLY GOT A FEW MINUTES!

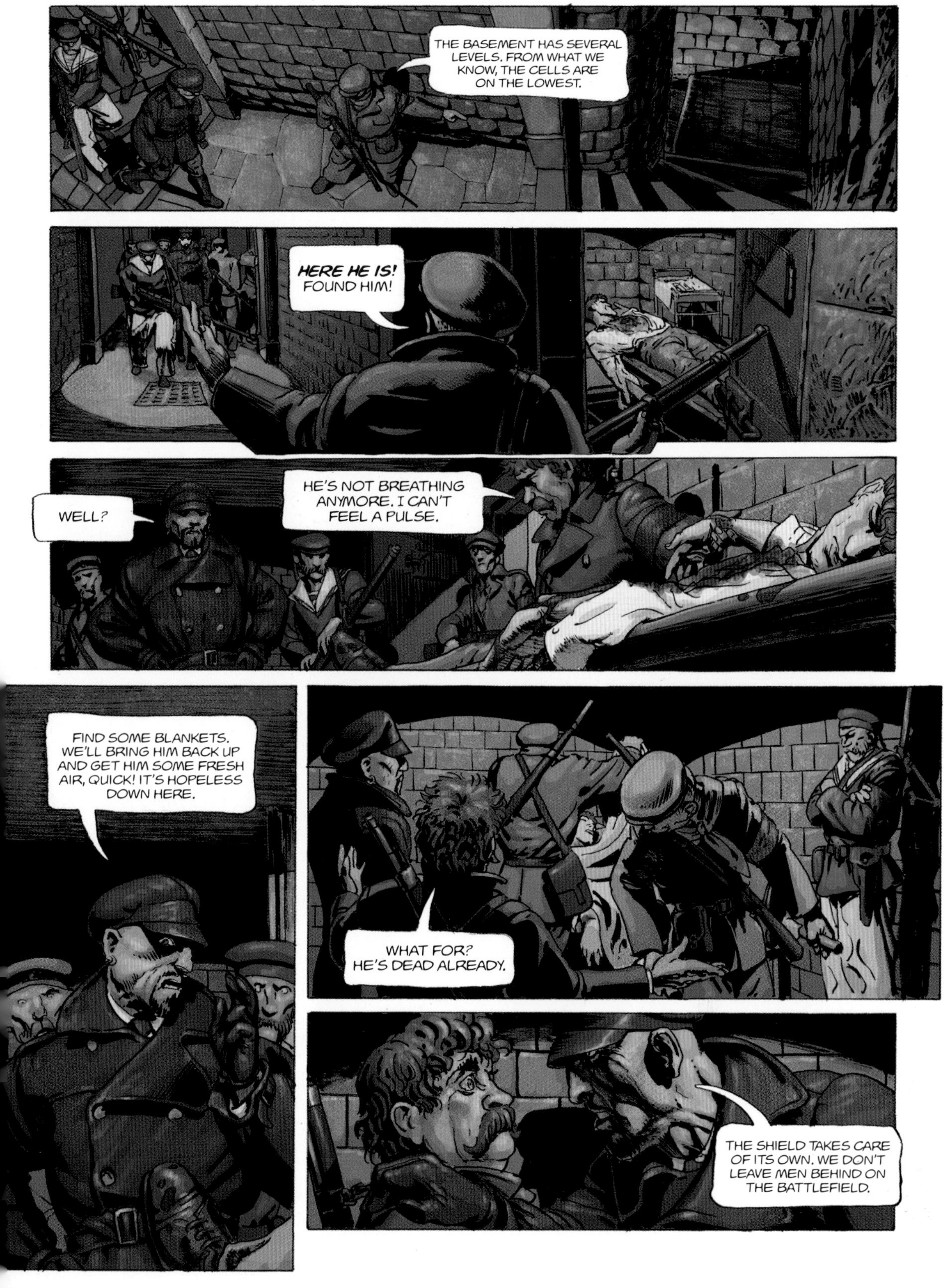
THE BASEMENT HAS SEVERAL LEVELS. FROM WHAT WE KNOW, THE CELLS ARE ON THE LOWEST.
HERE HE IS! FOUND HIM!
WELL?
HE'S NOT BREATHING ANYMORE. I CAN'T FEEL A PULSE.
FIND SOME BLANKETS. WE'LL BRING HIM BACK UP AND GET HIM SOME FRESH AIR, QUICK! IT'S HOPELESS DOWN HERE.
WHAT FOR? HE'S DEAD ALREADY.
THE SHIELD TAKES CARE OF ITS OWN. WE DON'T LEAVE MEN BEHIND ON THE BATTLEFIELD.

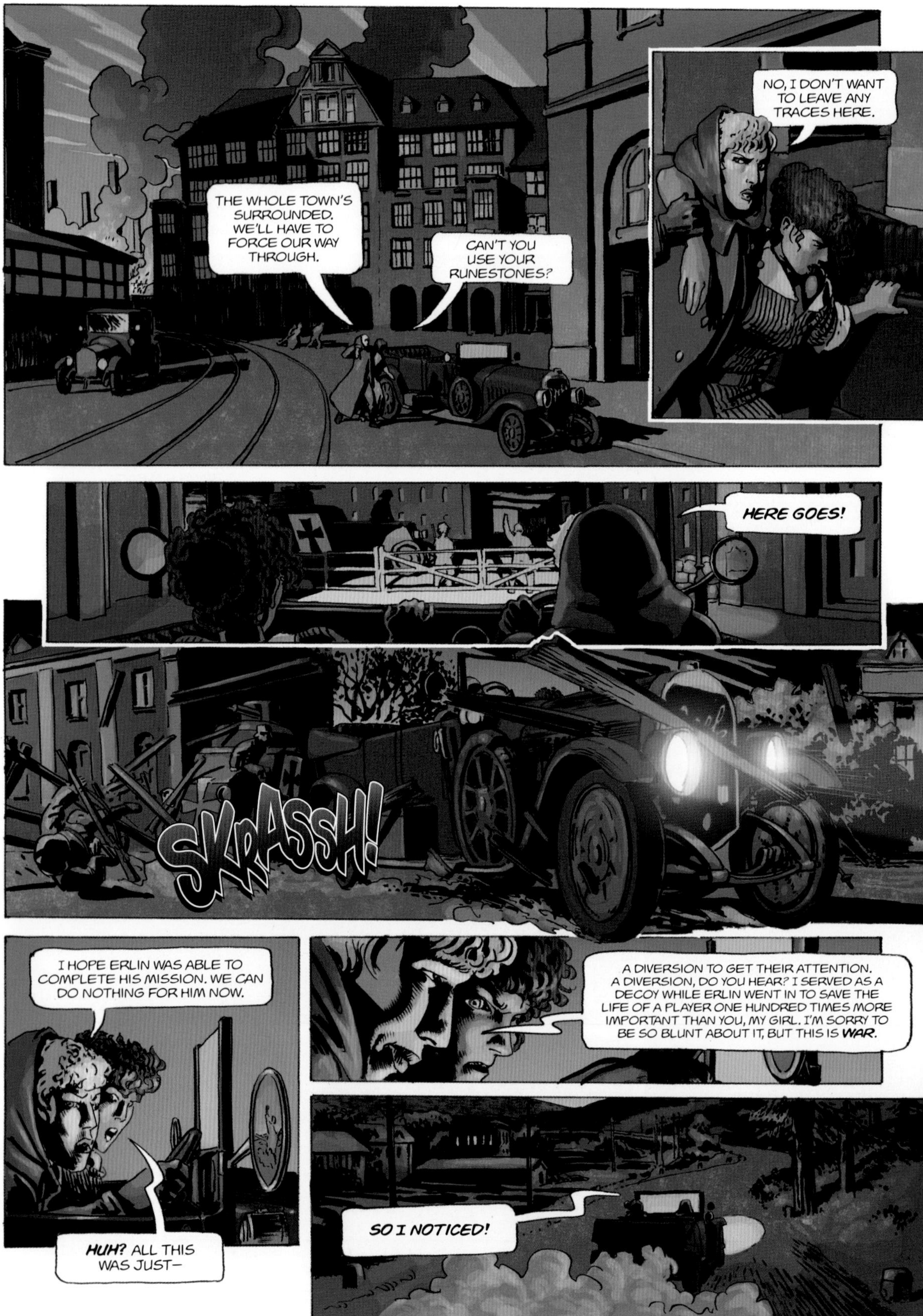
THE WHOLE TOWN'S SURROUNDED. WE'LL HAVE TO FORCE OUR WAY THROUGH.
CAN'T YOU USE YOUR RUNESTONES?
NO, I DON'T WANT TO LEAVE ANY TRACES HERE.
HERE GOES!
SKRASSH!
I HOPE ERLIN WAS ABLE TO COMPLETE HIS MISSION. WE CAN DO NOTHING FOR HIM NOW.
HUH? ALL THIS WAS JUST—
A DIVERSION TO GET THEIR ATTENTION. A DIVERSION, DO YOU HEAR? I SERVED AS A DECOY WHILE ERLIN WENT IN TO SAVE THE LIFE OF A PLAYER ONE HUNDRED TIMES MORE IMPORTANT THAN YOU, MY GIRL. I'M SORRY TO BE SO BLUNT ABOUT IT, BUT THIS IS WAR.
SO I NOTICED!

ZURICH: DOCTOR JUNG'S CLINIC.

DO YOU REMEMBER WHAT DOCTOR JUNG SAID? WOTAN HUNG FOR THREE DAYS AND THREE NIGHTS.

YES. *SO?*

NOTHING HAPPENS BY ACCIDENT. CURTIS HAS BEEN DEAD FOR THREE DAYS.

AT LEAST THEY DIDN'T WONDER WHETHER TO HANG HIM OR TO CRUCIFY HIM. LOOK–KOR IS A RIDDLE, THE CITY OF THE QUEEN OF SHEBA, AND FOR REASONS UNKNOWN TO US CURTIS SEEMS CONNECTED TO THIS MYSTERY. WE MUST TRY ALL WE CAN TO BRING HIM BACK.

HOW DO YOU PROPOSE TO GO ABOUT IT? ONLY A GOD COULD DO SUCH A THING AND WE HAVE ALWAYS REFUSED TO PLAY GOD.

SANDOZ'S LYSERGIC ACID*. IT ALLOWS TRAVEL IN TIME. I'LL GIVE HIM A DOSE.

PICKING UP THE THREAD OF HIS FATE THREATENS THE WEAVE OF THE FUTURE CONSIDERABLY. IT'S A GREAT RISK. YOU ALMOST DIED THE LAST TIME YOU TOOK SOME, IN LUXEMBOURG.

WE HAVE NO CHOICE. CURTIS IS AN ESSENTIAL PART OF THE PUZZLE!

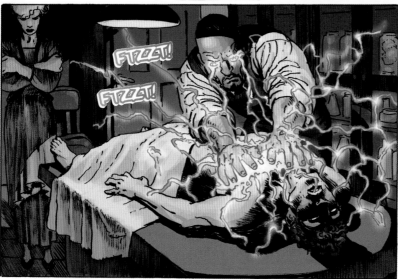

FTZZT!

FTZZT!

* IN SWITZERLAND'S SANDOZ LABORATORIES, THE ACTIVE INGREDIENT IN LSD WAS ISOLATED FOR THE FIRST TIME. SEE *THE SECRET HISTORY, BOOK 7: OUR LADY OF THE SHADOWS.*

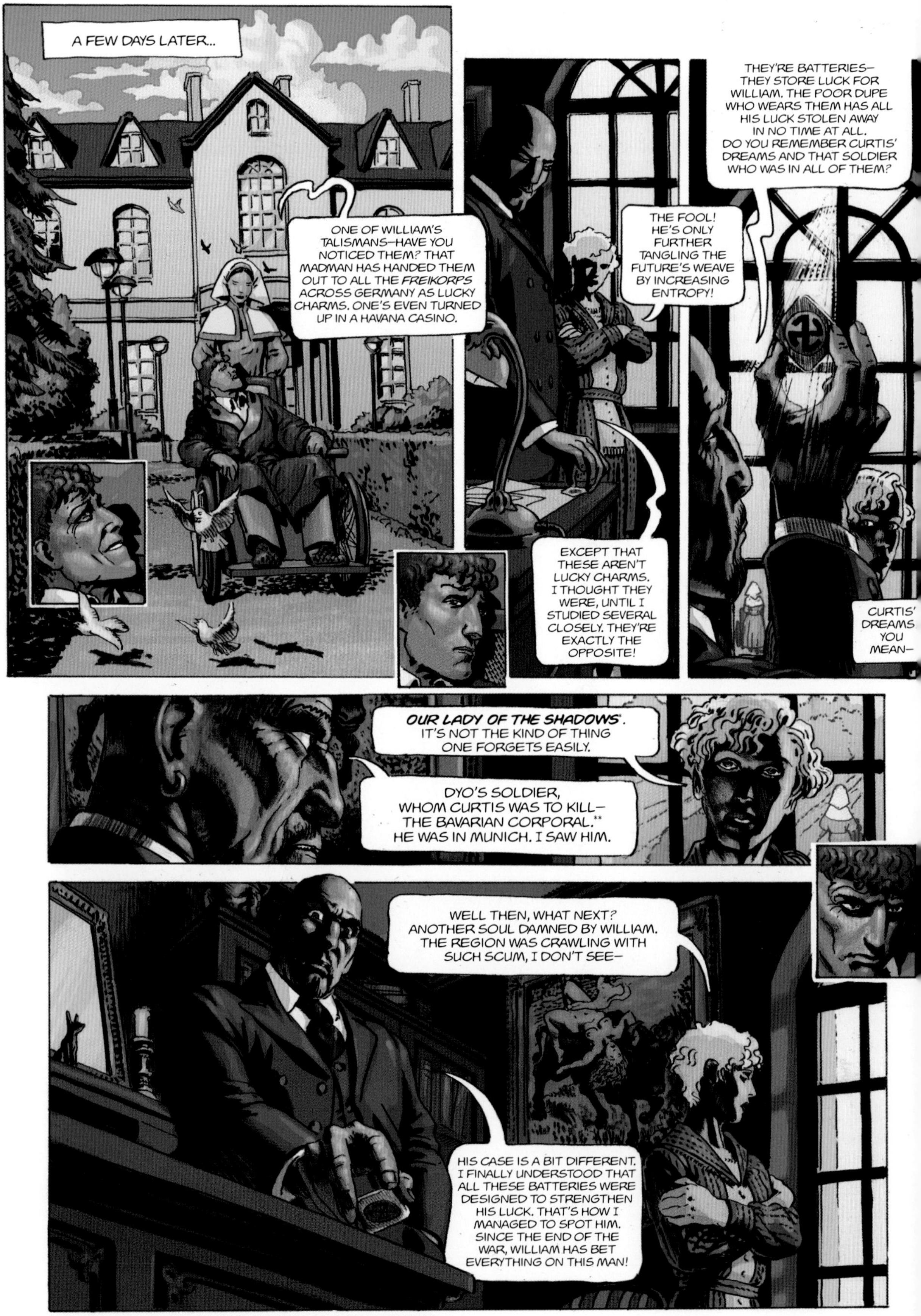
A FEW DAYS LATER...
ONE OF WILLIAM'S TALISMANS—HAVE YOU NOTICED THEM? THAT MADMAN HAS HANDED THEM OUT TO ALL THE FREIKORPS ACROSS GERMANY AS LUCKY CHARMS. ONE'S EVEN TURNED UP IN A HAVANA CASINO.
THE FOOL! HE'S ONLY FURTHER TANGLING THE FUTURE'S WEAVE BY INCREASING ENTROPY!
EXCEPT THAT THESE AREN'T LUCKY CHARMS. I THOUGHT THEY WERE, UNTIL I STUDIED SEVERAL CLOSELY. THEY'RE EXACTLY THE OPPOSITE!
THEY'RE BATTERIES— THEY STORE LUCK FOR WILLIAM. THE POOR DUPE WHO WEARS THEM HAS ALL HIS LUCK STOLEN AWAY IN NO TIME AT ALL. DO YOU REMEMBER CURTIS' DREAMS AND THAT SOLDIER WHO WAS IN ALL OF THEM?
CURTIS' DREAMS YOU MEAN—
OUR LADY OF THE SHADOWS*. IT'S NOT THE KIND OF THING ONE FORGETS EASILY.
DYO'S SOLDIER, WHOM CURTIS WAS TO KILL— THE BAVARIAN CORPORAL.** HE WAS IN MUNICH. I SAW HIM.
WELL THEN, WHAT NEXT? ANOTHER SOUL DAMNED BY WILLIAM. THE REGION WAS CRAWLING WITH SUCH SCUM, I DON'T SEE—
HIS CASE IS A BIT DIFFERENT. I FINALLY UNDERSTOOD THAT ALL THESE BATTERIES WERE DESIGNED TO STRENGTHEN HIS LUCK. THAT'S HOW I MANAGED TO SPOT HIM. SINCE THE END OF THE WAR, WILLIAM HAS BET EVERYTHING ON THIS MAN!

* SEE *THE SECRET HISTORY, BOOK 7: OUR LADY OF THE SHADOWS.*

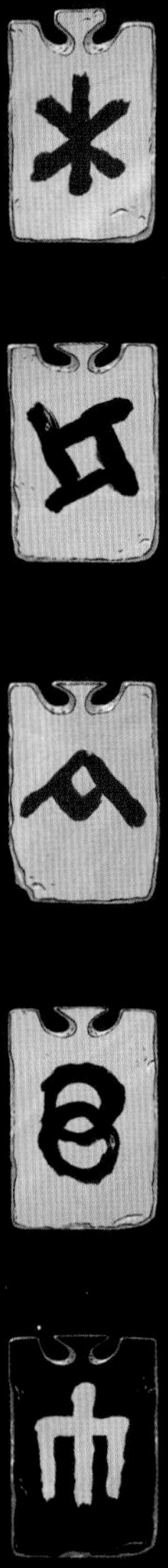

1918 A.D. 1919 A.D.

1926 A.D.

Book Ten

THE BLACK STONE

1926 A.D.

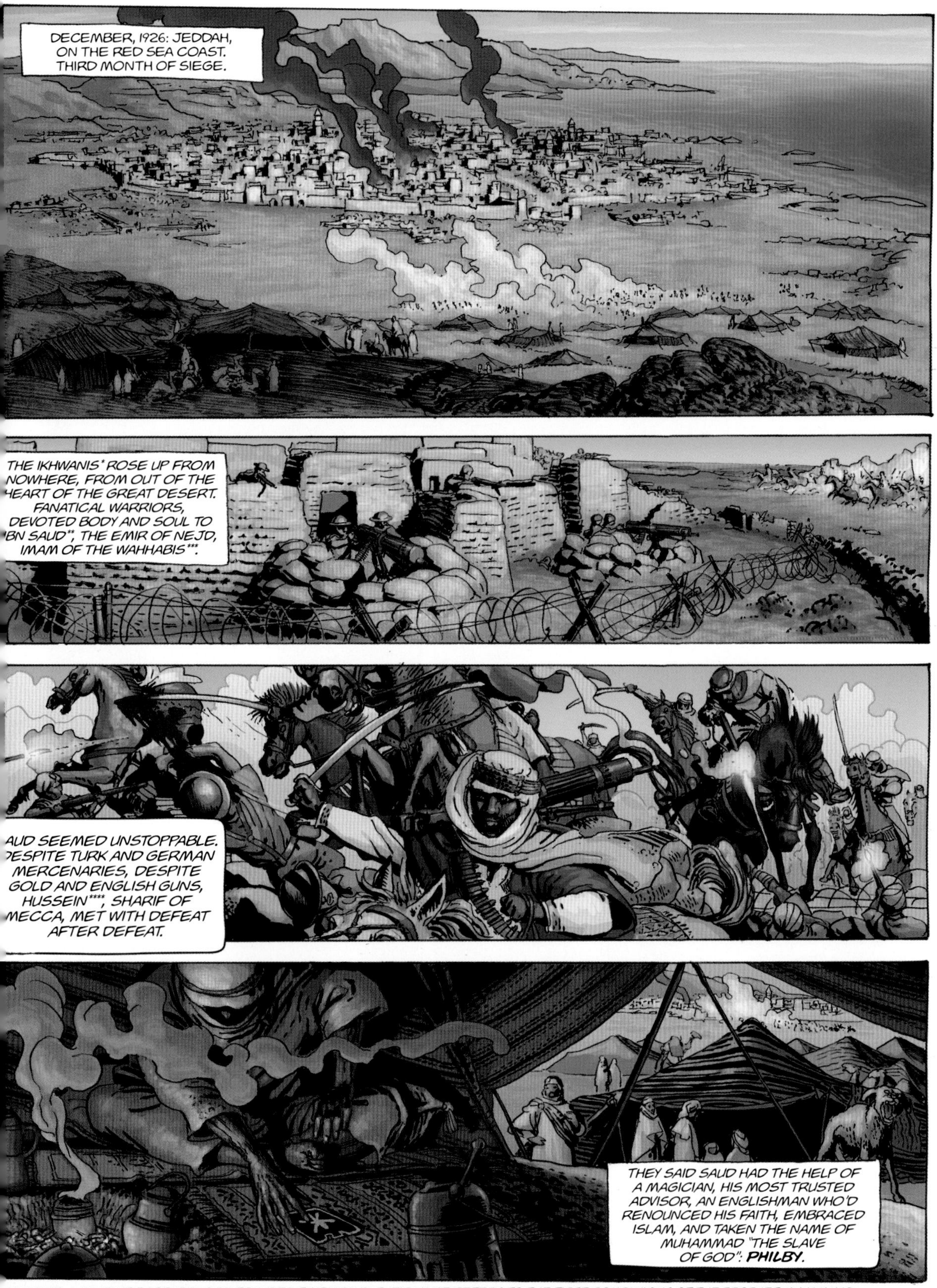
DECEMBER, 1926: JEDDAH, ON THE RED SEA COAST. THIRD MONTH OF SIEGE.
THE IKHWANIS* ROSE UP FROM NOWHERE, FROM OUT OF THE HEART OF THE GREAT DESERT. FANATICAL WARRIORS, DEVOTED BODY AND SOUL TO IBN SAUD**, THE EMIR OF NEJD, IMAM OF THE WAHHABIS***.
AUD SEEMED UNSTOPPABLE. DESPITE TURK AND GERMAN MERCENARIES, DESPITE GOLD AND ENGLISH GUNS, HUSSEIN****, SHARIF OF MECCA, MET WITH DEFEAT AFTER DEFEAT.
THEY SAID SAUD HAD THE HELP OF A MAGICIAN, HIS MOST TRUSTED ADVISOR, AN ENGLISHMAN WHO'D RENOUNCED HIS FAITH, EMBRACED ISLAM, AND TAKEN THE NAME OF MUHAMMAD "THE SLAVE OF GOD": **PHILBY**.

IKHWANIS: A MILITANT BROTHERHOOD FOUNDED BY IBN SAUD. THEIR NAME REFERS TO THE FIRST COMPANIONS OF THE PROPHET MUHAMMAD.

* IBN SAUD: MILITARY AND RELIGIOUS LEADER FROM WHOM THE CURRENT RULER OF SAUDI ARABIA IS DESCENDED.

** WAHHABIS: A VERY CONSERVATIVE REFORMIST SECT OF SUNNI ISLAM FOUNDED BY MUHAMMAD IBN ABD AL-WAHHAB (1703-1792). STILL ACTIVE IN PRESENT-DAY SAUDI ARABIA.

*** HUSSEIN: THE LAST OF THE HASHEMITES, DESCENDANTS OF MUHAMMAD, GUARDIANS OF MECCA AND MEDINA, THE SACRED SITES OF ISLAM.

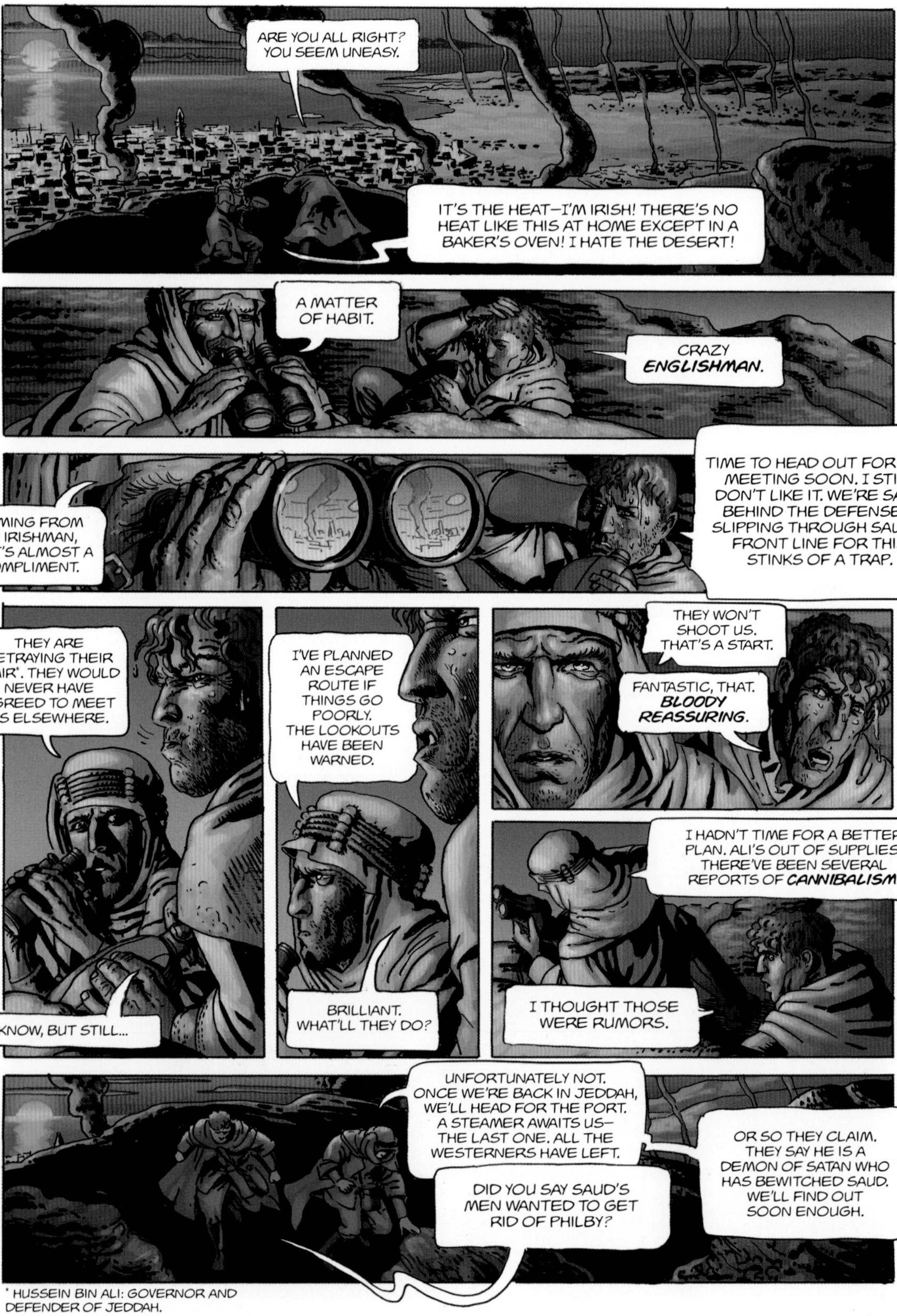
ARE YOU ALL RIGHT? YOU SEEM UNEASY.
IT'S THE HEAT—I'M IRISH! THERE'S NO HEAT LIKE THIS AT HOME EXCEPT IN A BAKER'S OVEN! I HATE THE DESERT!
A MATTER OF HABIT.
CRAZY ENGLISHMAN.
COMING FROM AN IRISHMAN, THAT'S ALMOST A COMPLIMENT.
TIME TO HEAD OUT FOR OUR MEETING SOON. I STILL DON'T LIKE IT. WE'RE SAFE BEHIND THE DEFENSES. SLIPPING THROUGH SAUD'S FRONT LINE FOR THIS STINKS OF A TRAP.
THEY ARE BETRAYING THEIR EMIR*. THEY WOULD NEVER HAVE AGREED TO MEET US ELSEWHERE.
I KNOW, BUT STILL...
I'VE PLANNED AN ESCAPE ROUTE IF THINGS GO POORLY. THE LOOKOUTS HAVE BEEN WARNED.
BRILLIANT. WHAT'LL THEY DO?
THEY WON'T SHOOT US. THAT'S A START.
FANTASTIC, THAT. BLOODY REASSURING.
I HADN'T TIME FOR A BETTER PLAN. ALI'S OUT OF SUPPLIES. THERE'VE BEEN SEVERAL REPORTS OF CANNIBALISM.
I THOUGHT THOSE WERE RUMORS.
UNFORTUNATELY NOT. ONCE WE'RE BACK IN JEDDAH, WE'LL HEAD FOR THE PORT. A STEAMER AWAITS US—THE LAST ONE. ALL THE WESTERNERS HAVE LEFT.
DID YOU SAY SAUD'S MEN WANTED TO GET RID OF PHILBY?
OR SO THEY CLAIM. THEY SAY HE IS A DEMON OF SATAN WHO HAS BEWITCHED SAUD. WE'LL FIND OUT SOON ENOUGH.

* HUSSEIN BIN ALI: GOVERNOR AND DEFENDER OF JEDDAH.

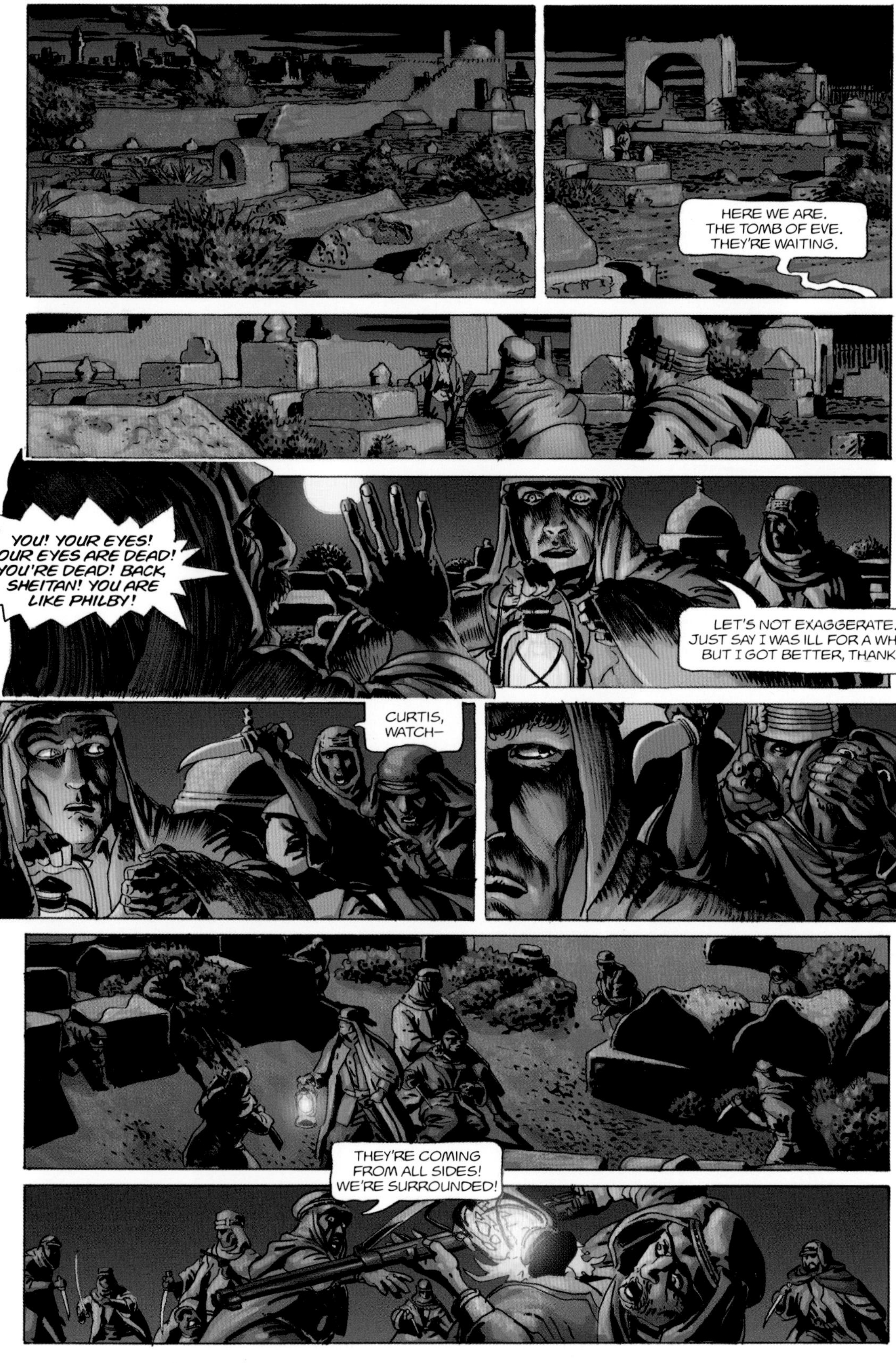
HERE WE ARE. THE TOMB OF EVE. THEY'RE WAITING.
YOU! YOUR EYES! YOUR EYES ARE DEAD! YOU'RE DEAD! BACK, SHEITAN! YOU ARE LIKE PHILBY!
LET'S NOT EXAGGERATE. JUST SAY I WAS ILL FOR A WHILE, BUT I GOT BETTER, THANKS.
CURTIS, WATCH—
THEY'RE COMING FROM ALL SIDES! WE'RE SURROUNDED!

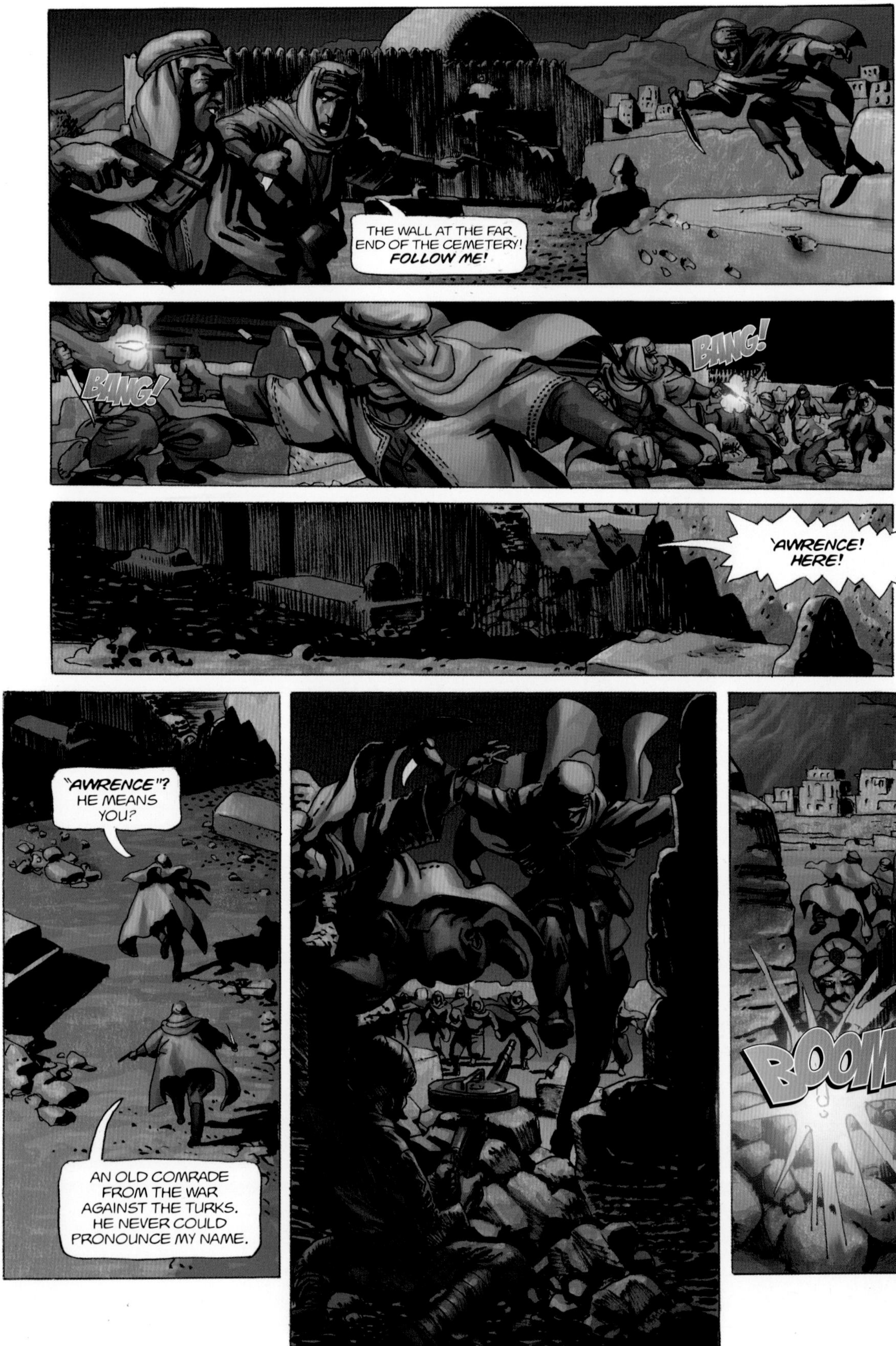
THE WALL AT THE FAR END OF THE CEMETERY! FOLLOW ME!
BANG!
BANG!
'AWRENCE! HERE!
"AWRENCE"? HE MEANS YOU?
AN OLD COMRADE FROM THE WAR AGAINST THE TURKS. HE NEVER COULD PRONOUNCE MY NAME.
BOOM!

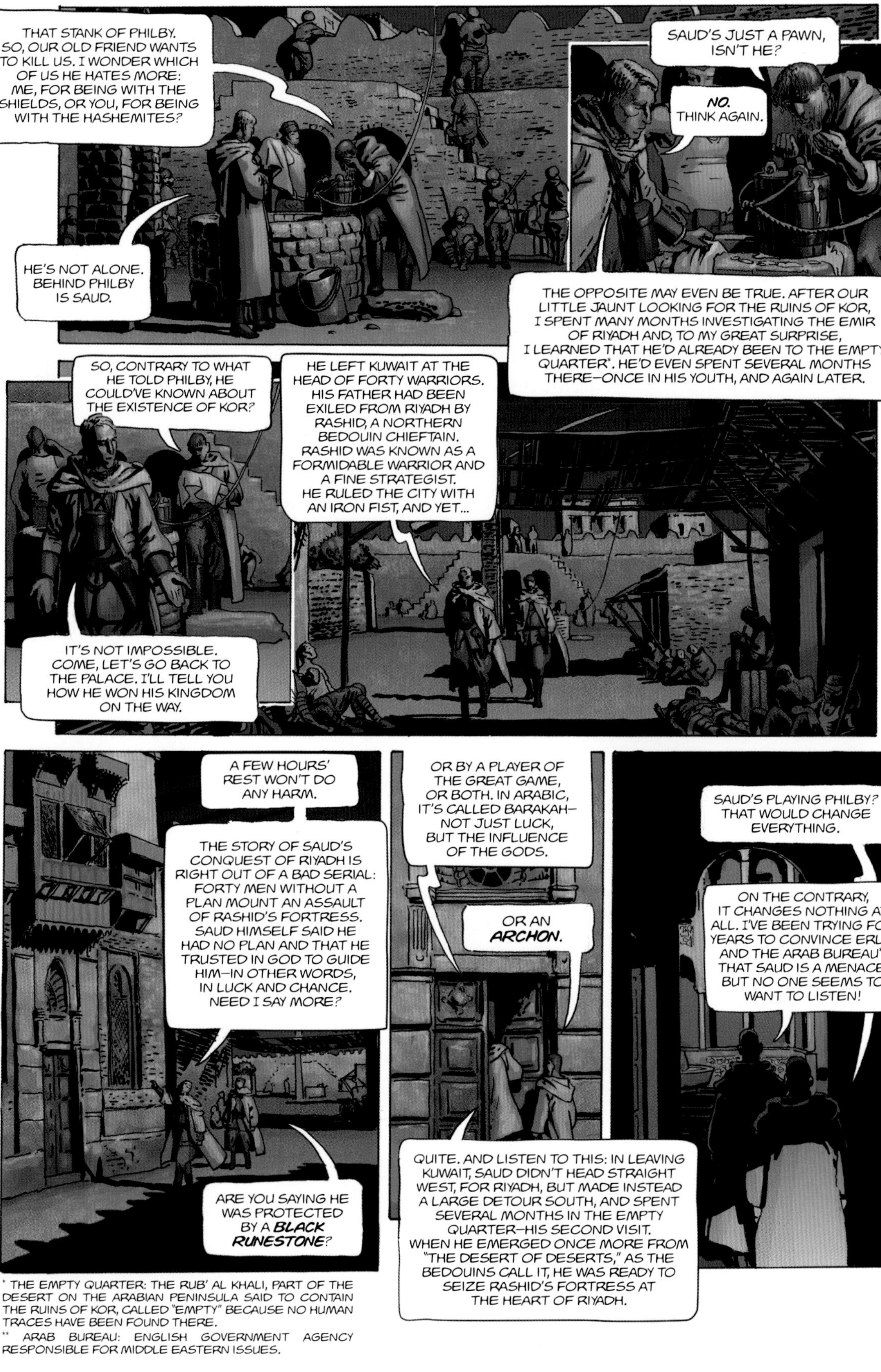
THAT STANK OF PHILBY. SO, OUR OLD FRIEND WANTS TO KILL US. I WONDER WHICH OF US HE HATES MORE: ME, FOR BEING WITH THE SHIELDS, OR YOU, FOR BEING WITH THE HASHEMITES?
HE'S NOT ALONE. BEHIND PHILBY IS SAUD.
SAUD'S JUST A PAWN, ISN'T HE?
NO. THINK AGAIN.
THE OPPOSITE MAY EVEN BE TRUE. AFTER OUR LITTLE JAUNT LOOKING FOR THE RUINS OF KOR, I SPENT MANY MONTHS INVESTIGATING THE EMIR OF RIYADH AND, TO MY GREAT SURPRISE, I LEARNED THAT HE'D ALREADY BEEN TO THE EMPTY QUARTER*. HE'D EVEN SPENT SEVERAL MONTHS THERE—ONCE IN HIS YOUTH, AND AGAIN LATER.
SO, CONTRARY TO WHAT HE TOLD PHILBY, HE COULD'VE KNOWN ABOUT THE EXISTENCE OF KOR?
IT'S NOT IMPOSSIBLE. COME, LET'S GO BACK TO THE PALACE. I'LL TELL YOU HOW HE WON HIS KINGDOM ON THE WAY.
HE LEFT KUWAIT AT THE HEAD OF FORTY WARRIORS. HIS FATHER HAD BEEN EXILED FROM RIYADH BY RASHID, A NORTHERN BEDOUIN CHIEFTAIN. RASHID WAS KNOWN AS A FORMIDABLE WARRIOR AND A FINE STRATEGIST. HE RULED THE CITY WITH AN IRON FIST, AND YET...
A FEW HOURS' REST WON'T DO ANY HARM.
THE STORY OF SAUD'S CONQUEST OF RIYADH IS RIGHT OUT OF A BAD SERIAL: FORTY MEN WITHOUT A PLAN MOUNT AN ASSAULT OF RASHID'S FORTRESS. SAUD HIMSELF SAID HE HAD NO PLAN AND THAT HE TRUSTED IN GOD TO GUIDE HIM—IN OTHER WORDS, IN LUCK AND CHANCE. NEED I SAY MORE?
ARE YOU SAYING HE WAS PROTECTED BY A BLACK RUNESTONE?
OR BY A PLAYER OF THE GREAT GAME, OR BOTH. IN ARABIC, IT'S CALLED BARAKAH—NOT JUST LUCK, BUT THE INFLUENCE OF THE GODS.
OR AN ARCHON.
QUITE. AND LISTEN TO THIS: IN LEAVING KUWAIT, SAUD DIDN'T HEAD STRAIGHT WEST, FOR RIYADH, BUT MADE INSTEAD A LARGE DETOUR SOUTH, AND SPENT SEVERAL MONTHS IN THE EMPTY QUARTER—HIS SECOND VISIT. WHEN HE EMERGED ONCE MORE FROM "THE DESERT OF DESERTS," AS THE BEDOUINS CALL IT, HE WAS READY TO SEIZE RASHID'S FORTRESS AT THE HEART OF RIYADH.
SAUD'S PLAYING PHILBY? THAT WOULD CHANGE EVERYTHING.
ON THE CONTRARY, IT CHANGES NOTHING AT ALL. I'VE BEEN TRYING FOR YEARS TO CONVINCE ERLIN AND THE ARAB BUREAU** THAT SAUD IS A MENACE, BUT NO ONE SEEMS TO WANT TO LISTEN!

* THE EMPTY QUARTER: THE RUB' AL KHALI, PART OF THE DESERT ON THE ARABIAN PENINSULA SAID TO CONTAIN THE RUINS OF KOR, CALLED "EMPTY" BECAUSE NO HUMAN TRACES HAVE BEEN FOUND THERE.

** ARAB BUREAU: ENGLISH GOVERNMENT AGENCY RESPONSIBLE FOR MIDDLE EASTERN ISSUES.

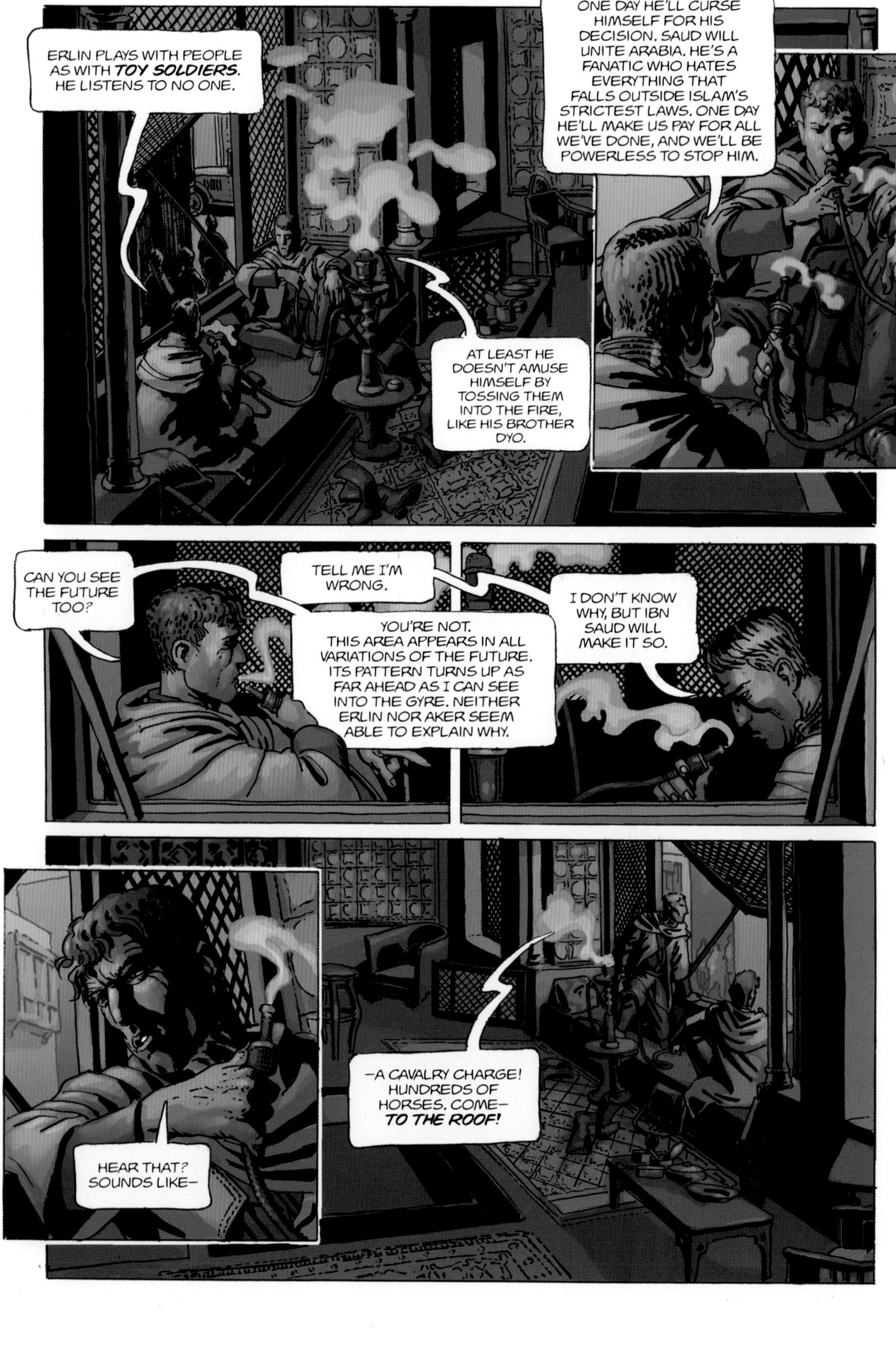
ERLIN PLAYS WITH PEOPLE AS WITH **TOY SOLDIERS**. HE LISTENS TO NO ONE.
AT LEAST HE DOESN'T AMUSE HIMSELF BY TOSSING THEM INTO THE FIRE, LIKE HIS BROTHER DYO.
ONE DAY HE'LL CURSE HIMSELF FOR HIS DECISION. SAUD WILL UNITE ARABIA. HE'S A FANATIC WHO HATES EVERYTHING THAT FALLS OUTSIDE ISLAM'S STRICTEST LAWS. ONE DAY HE'LL MAKE US PAY FOR ALL WE'VE DONE, AND WE'LL BE POWERLESS TO STOP HIM.
CAN YOU SEE THE FUTURE TOO?
TELL ME I'M WRONG.
YOU'RE NOT. THIS AREA APPEARS IN ALL VARIATIONS OF THE FUTURE. ITS PATTERN TURNS UP AS FAR AHEAD AS I CAN SEE INTO THE GYRE. NEITHER ERLIN NOR AKER SEEM ABLE TO EXPLAIN WHY.
I DON'T KNOW WHY, BUT IBN SAUD WILL MAKE IT SO.
HEAR THAT? SOUNDS LIKE–
–A CAVALRY CHARGE! HUNDREDS OF HORSES. COME– **TO THE ROOF!**

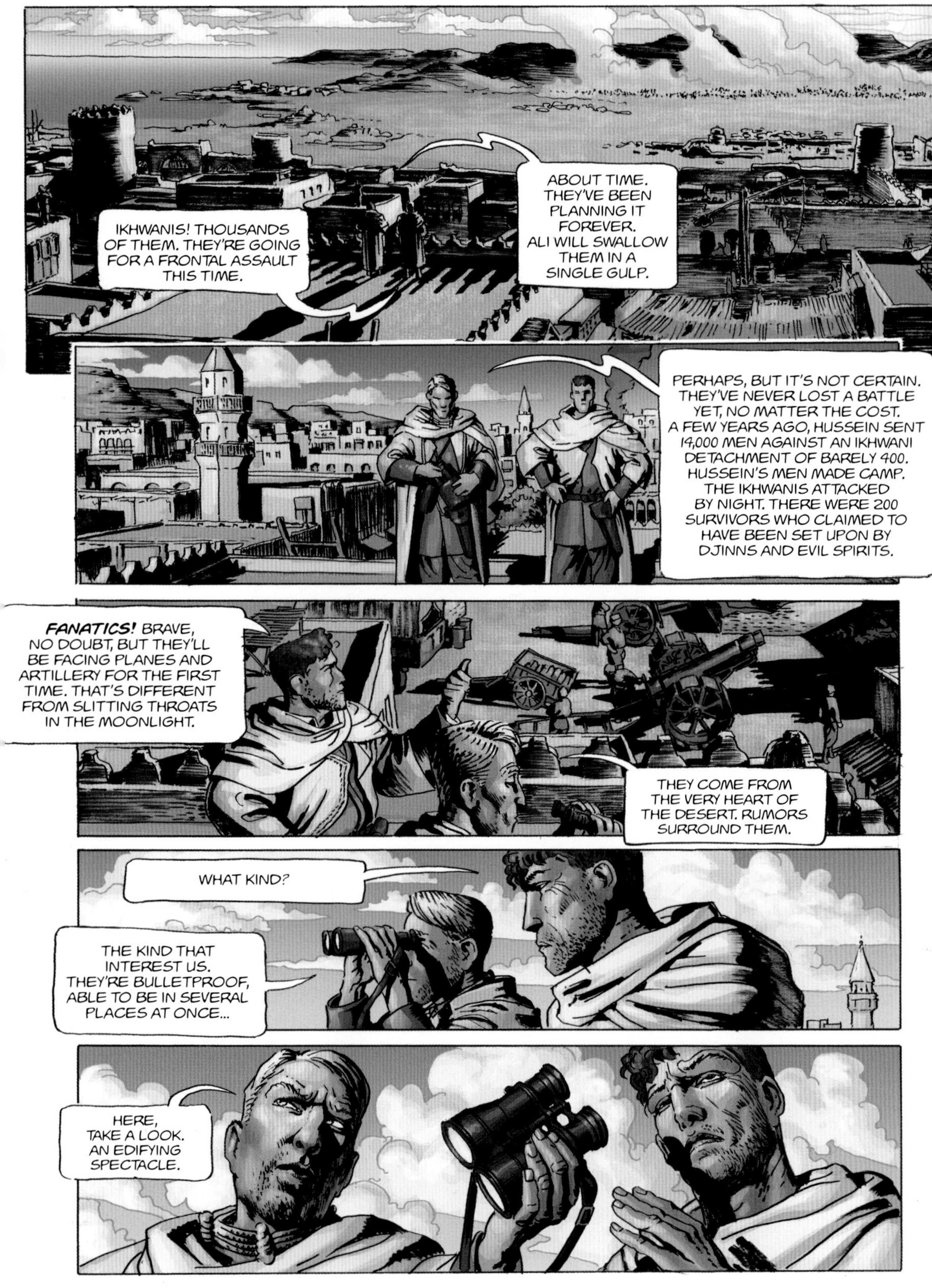
IKHWANIS! THOUSANDS OF THEM. THEY'RE GOING FOR A FRONTAL ASSAULT THIS TIME.
ABOUT TIME. THEY'VE BEEN PLANNING IT FOREVER. ALI WILL SWALLOW THEM IN A SINGLE GULP.
PERHAPS, BUT IT'S NOT CERTAIN. THEY'VE NEVER LOST A BATTLE YET, NO MATTER THE COST. A FEW YEARS AGO, HUSSEIN SENT 14,000 MEN AGAINST AN IKHWANI DETACHMENT OF BARELY 400. HUSSEIN'S MEN MADE CAMP. THE IKHWANIS ATTACKED BY NIGHT. THERE WERE 200 SURVIVORS WHO CLAIMED TO HAVE BEEN SET UPON BY DJINNS AND EVIL SPIRITS.
FANATICS! BRAVE, NO DOUBT, BUT THEY'LL BE FACING PLANES AND ARTILLERY FOR THE FIRST TIME. THAT'S DIFFERENT FROM SLITTING THROATS IN THE MOONLIGHT.
THEY COME FROM THE VERY HEART OF THE DESERT. RUMORS SURROUND THEM.
WHAT KIND?
THE KIND THAT INTEREST US. THEY'RE BULLETPROOF, ABLE TO BE IN SEVERAL PLACES AT ONCE...
HERE, TAKE A LOOK. AN EDIFYING SPECTACLE.

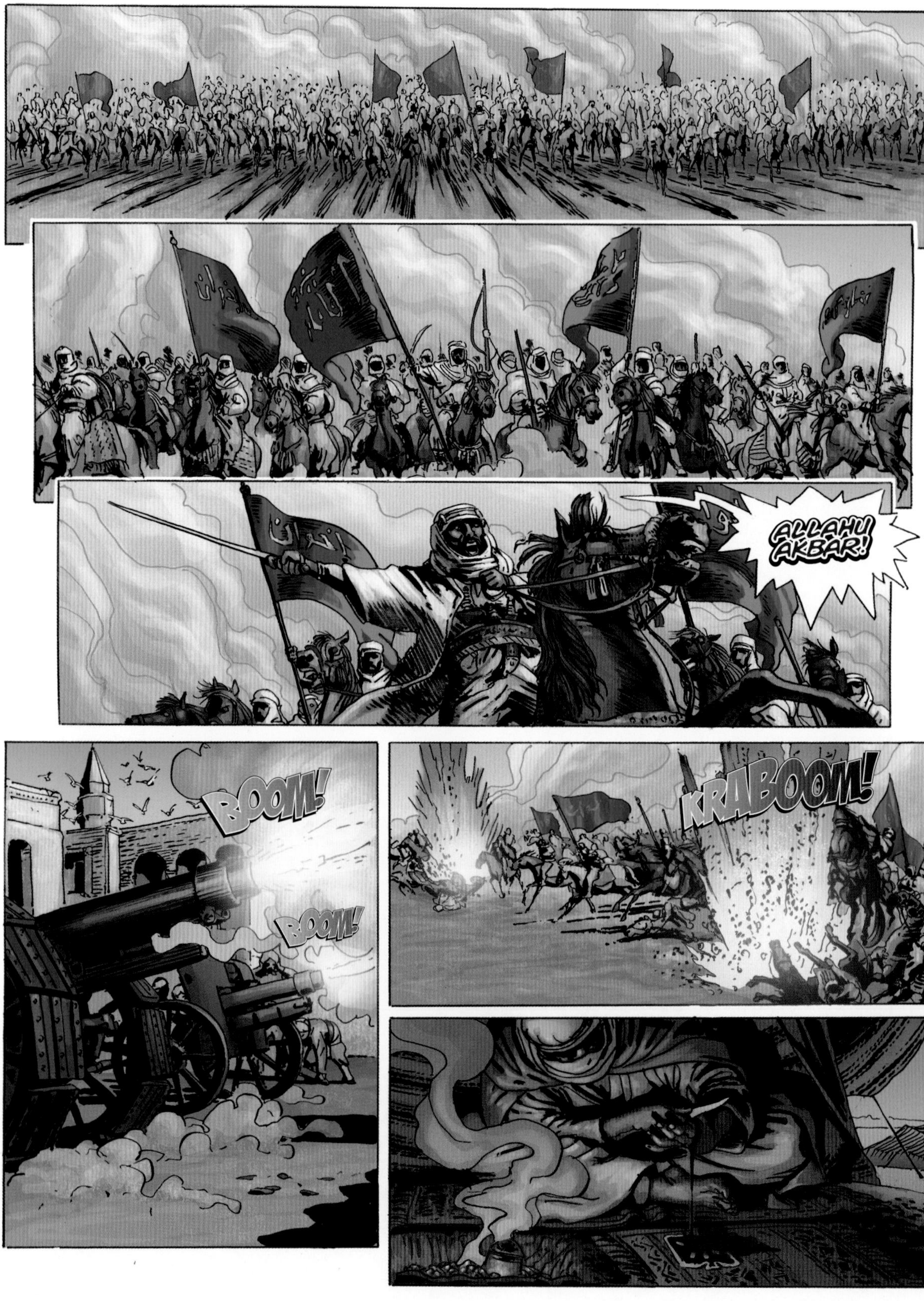
ALLAHU AKBAR!
BOOM!
BOOM!
KRABOOM!

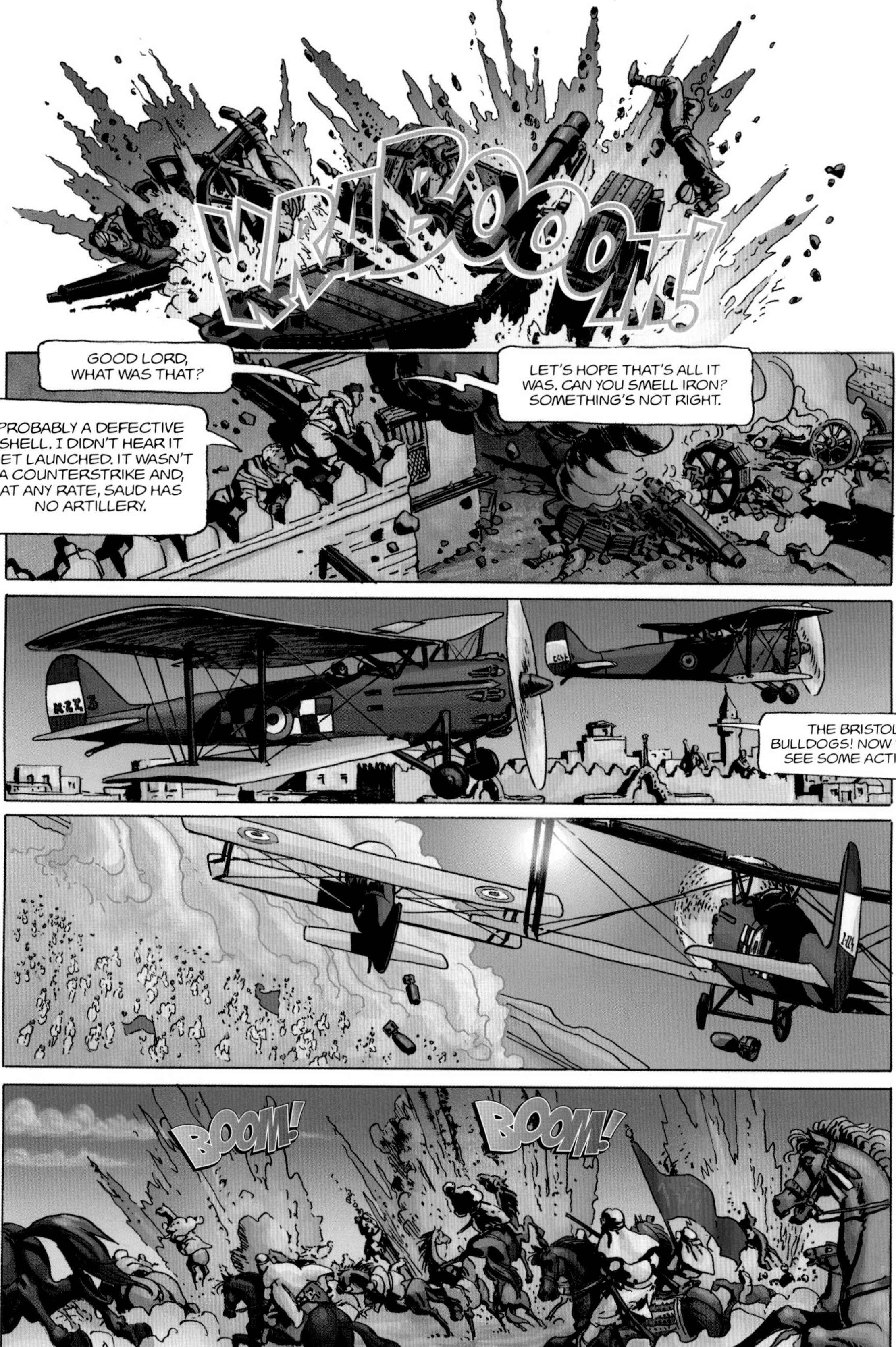
WRABOOOM!
GOOD LORD, WHAT WAS THAT?
LET'S HOPE THAT'S ALL IT WAS. CAN YOU SMELL IRON? SOMETHING'S NOT RIGHT.
PROBABLY A DEFECTIVE SHELL. I DIDN'T HEAR IT GET LAUNCHED. IT WASN'T A COUNTERSTRIKE AND, AT ANY RATE, SAUD HAS NO ARTILLERY.
THE BRISTOL BULLDOGS! NOW WE'LL SEE SOME ACTION!
BOOM!
BOOM!

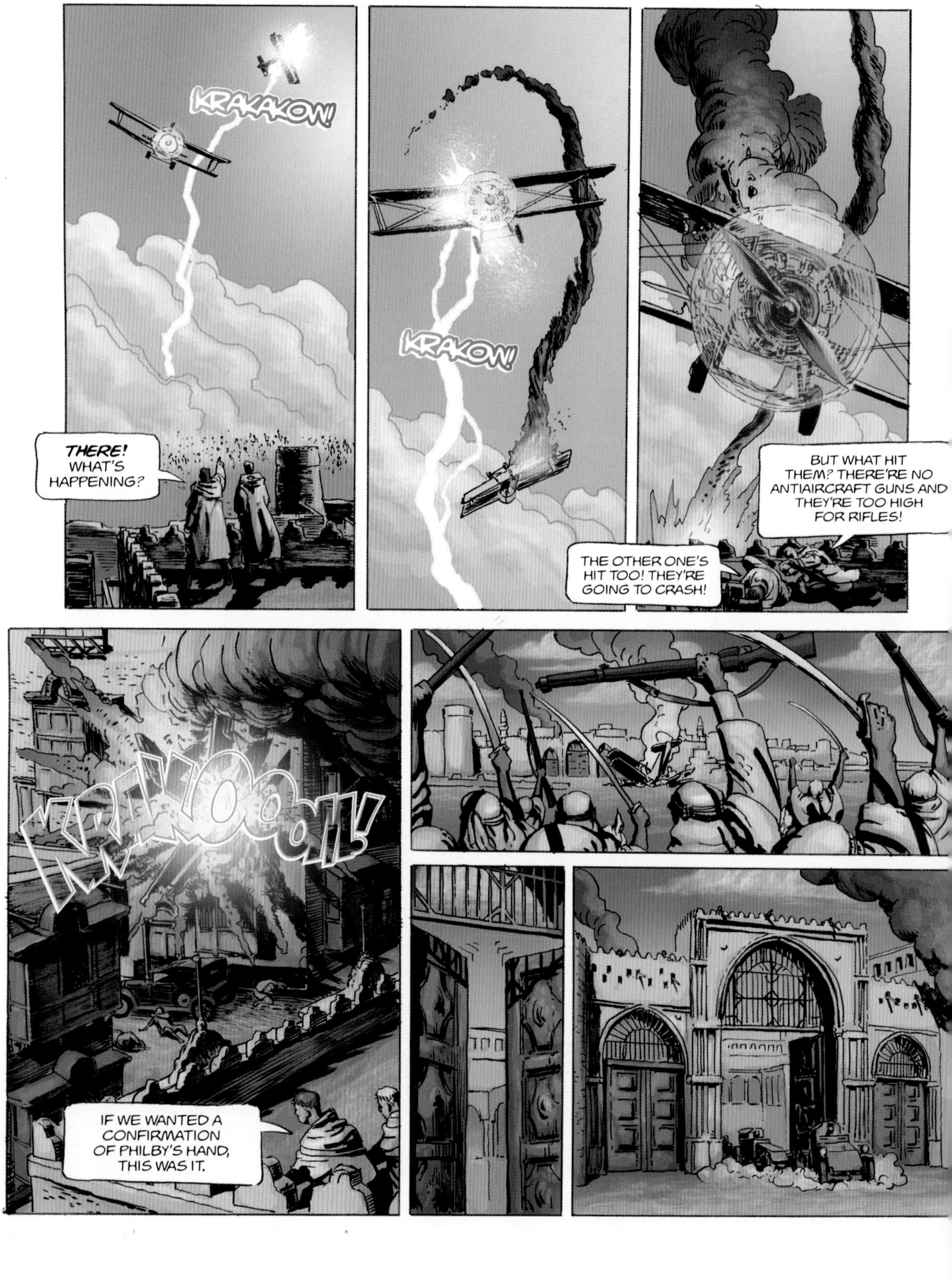
KRAKAKON!
THERE! WHAT'S HAPPENING?
KRAKON!
BUT WHAT HIT THEM? THERE'RE NO ANTIAIRCRAFT GUNS AND THEY'RE TOO HIGH FOR RIFLES!
THE OTHER ONE'S HIT TOO! THEY'RE GOING TO CRASH!
IF WE WANTED A CONFIRMATION OF PHILBY'S HAND, THIS WAS IT.

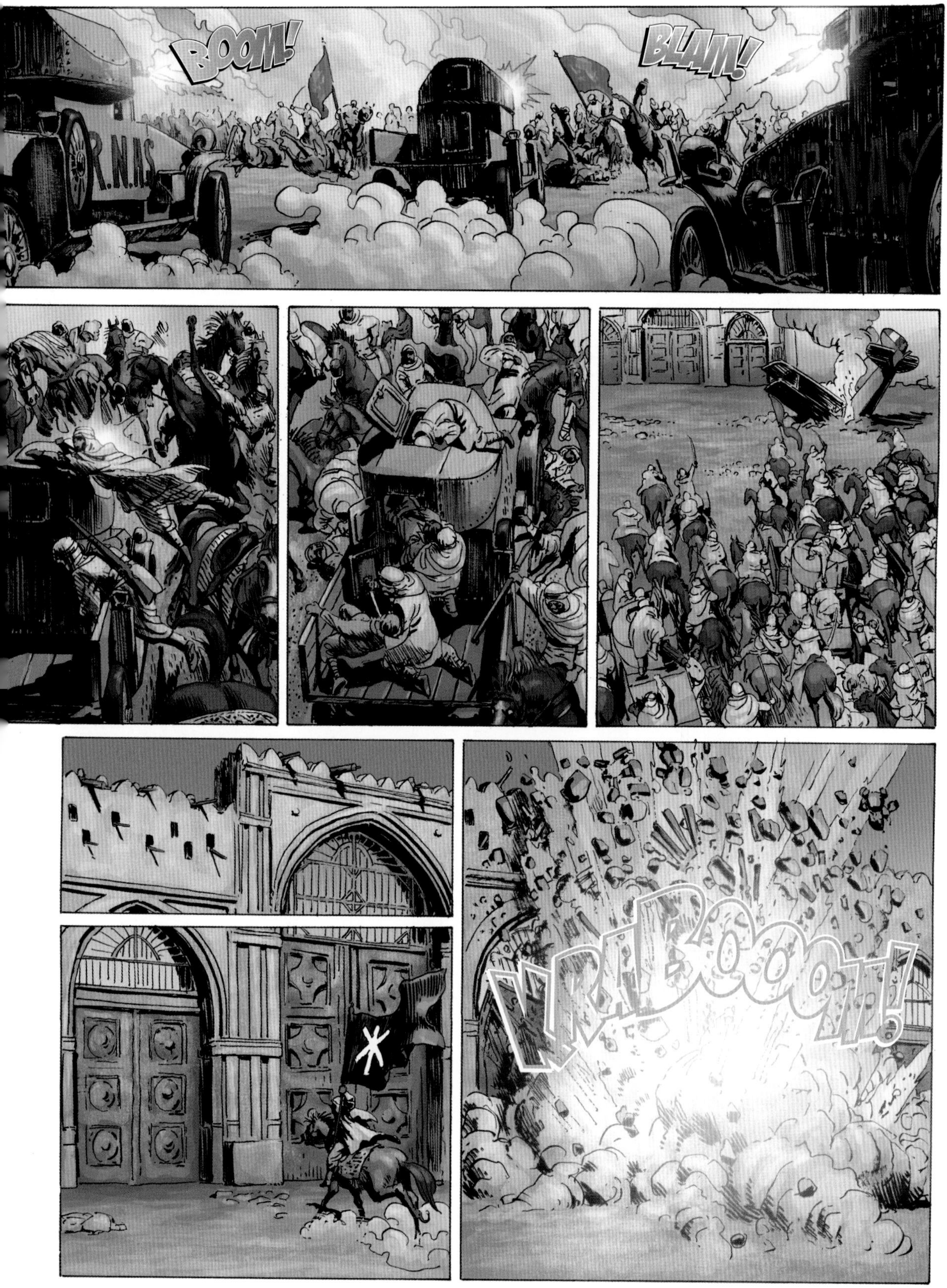
BOOM!
BLAM!
R.N.A.S
KRABOOOM!

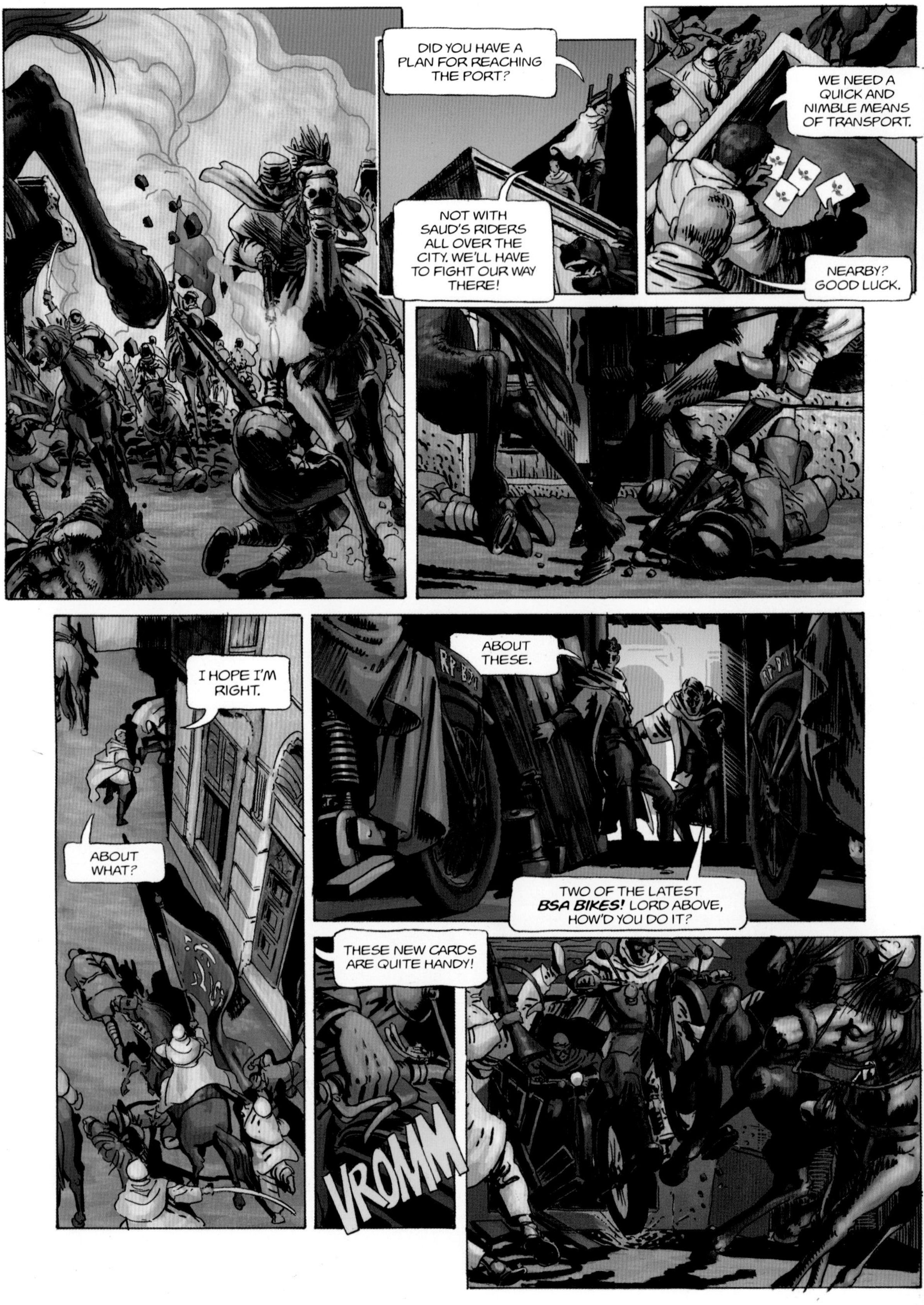
DID YOU HAVE A PLAN FOR REACHING THE PORT?
NOT WITH SAUD'S RIDERS ALL OVER THE CITY. WE'LL HAVE TO FIGHT OUR WAY THERE!
WE NEED A QUICK AND NIMBLE MEANS OF TRANSPORT.
NEARBY? GOOD LUCK.
I HOPE I'M RIGHT.
ABOUT WHAT?
ABOUT THESE.
TWO OF THE LATEST **BSA BIKES!** LORD ABOVE, HOW'D YOU DO IT?
THESE NEW CARDS ARE QUITE HANDY!
VROMM

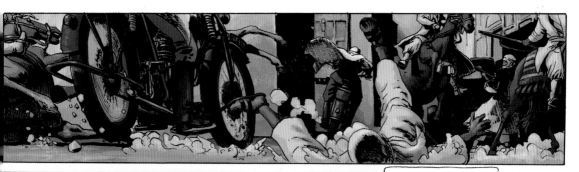

ANY IDEA WHAT THAT IS?

NOT REALLY. BUT IT'S NOT A ROAD REPAIR CREW AND IT'S HEADED RIGHT FOR US.

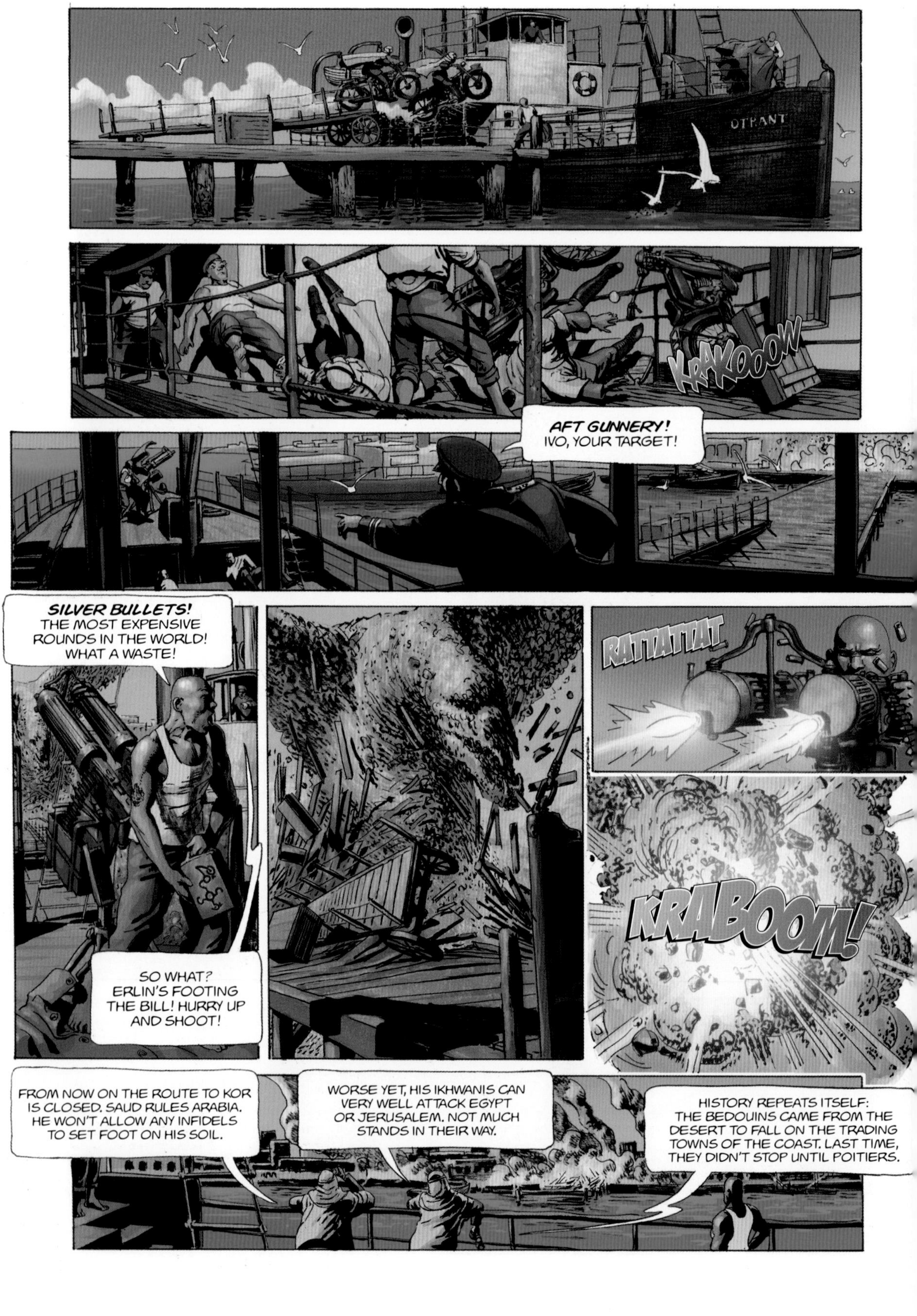
OTRANT
KRAKOOOW
AFT GUNNERY! IVO, YOUR TARGET!
SILVER BULLETS! THE MOST EXPENSIVE ROUNDS IN THE WORLD! WHAT A WASTE!
SO WHAT? ERLIN'S FOOTING THE BILL! HURRY UP AND SHOOT!
RATTATTAT
KRABOOM!
FROM NOW ON THE ROUTE TO KOR IS CLOSED. SAUD RULES ARABIA. HE WON'T ALLOW ANY INFIDELS TO SET FOOT ON HIS SOIL.
WORSE YET, HIS IKHWANIS CAN VERY WELL ATTACK EGYPT OR JERUSALEM. NOT MUCH STANDS IN THEIR WAY.
HISTORY REPEATS ITSELF: THE BEDOUINS CAME FROM THE DESERT TO FALL ON THE TRADING TOWNS OF THE COAST. LAST TIME, THEY DIDN'T STOP UNTIL POITIERS.

THE KAABA* IS NEAR, ALLAH BE PRAISED. I AM THE MASTER OF AL-HEJAZ!

I AM CONVINCED THE **BLACK STONE** WAS BROUGHT HERE FROM KOR. IT AUGMENTS THE RUNESTONES' POWER.

I WOULD ADVISE YOU NOT TO ESPOUSE SUCH THEORIES BEFORE MY IKHWANIS. THEY WILL RUN YOU THROUGH WITH A SWORD FOR YOUR BLASPHEMY.

AND YET, YOUR HIGHNESS, THE BLACK STONE OF MECCA WAS HERE BEFORE THE SERMON OF MUHAMMAD, BLESSED BE HIS NAME. LEGEND HAS IT THAT IT WAS BROUGHT TO MECCA BY BEDOUINS FROM THE GREAT DESERT, FROM THE DIRECTION OF KOR! AL-UZZA: THE POWER WORSHIPPED IN THE FORM OF A BLACK STONE BY PEOPLE OF MUHAMMAD'S TRIBE.

WHICH IS PRECISELY WHY EXPLORATION OF THE GREAT DESERT IS NOW FORBIDDEN TO ALL, INCLUDING THE AMERICAN DIGGERS OF HOLES.

THEY ARE DRILLING, YOUR HIGHNESS! THEY WILL FIND WATER AND, WHAT'S MORE, PETROL!

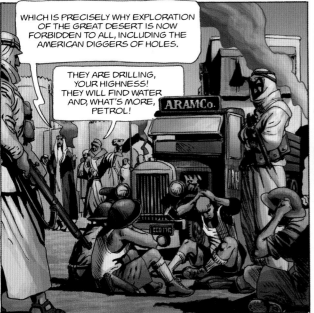

THERE IS NO OIL BENEATH THESE SANDS. WE HAVE NEVER FOUND ANY.

TRUST ME, YOUR HIGHNESS. THEY WILL.

* THE KAABA (LITERALLY, THE CUBE): A SMALL CUBOIDAL BUILDING IN THE CENTER OF THE MOSQUE IN MECCA, WHICH IS THE HOLIEST OF HOLIES OF ISLAM. A SMALL BLACK ROCK IS ENSHRINED THERE.

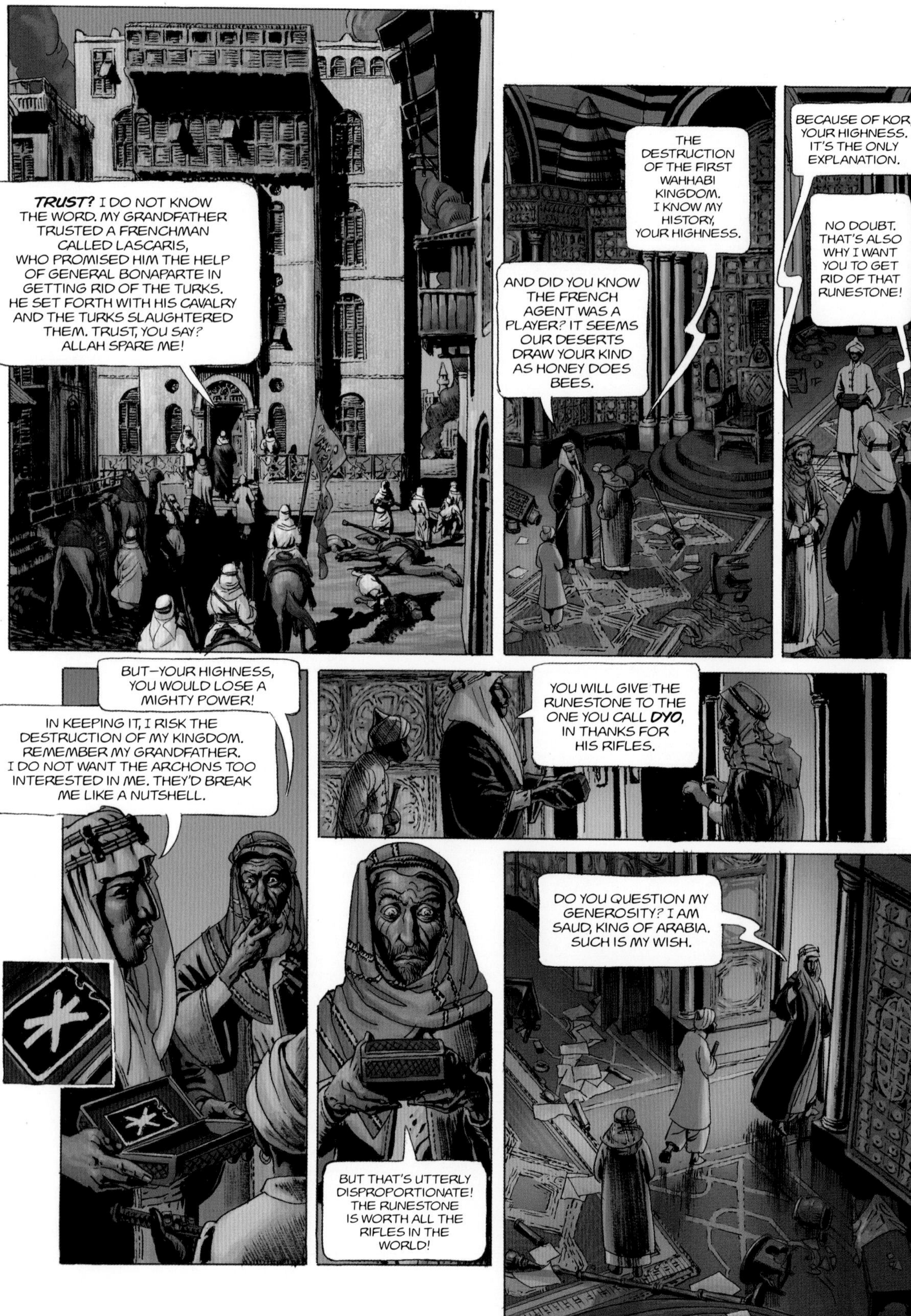
TRUST? I DO NOT KNOW THE WORD. MY GRANDFATHER TRUSTED A FRENCHMAN CALLED LASCARIS, WHO PROMISED HIM THE HELP OF GENERAL BONAPARTE IN GETTING RID OF THE TURKS. HE SET FORTH WITH HIS CAVALRY AND THE TURKS SLAUGHTERED THEM. TRUST, YOU SAY? ALLAH SPARE ME!
THE DESTRUCTION OF THE FIRST WAHHABI KINGDOM. I KNOW MY HISTORY, YOUR HIGHNESS.
AND DID YOU KNOW THE FRENCH AGENT WAS A PLAYER? IT SEEMS OUR DESERTS DRAW YOUR KIND AS HONEY DOES BEES.
BECAUSE OF KOR, YOUR HIGHNESS. IT'S THE ONLY EXPLANATION.
NO DOUBT. THAT'S ALSO WHY I WANT YOU TO GET RID OF THAT RUNESTONE!
BUT—YOUR HIGHNESS, YOU WOULD LOSE A MIGHTY POWER!
IN KEEPING IT, I RISK THE DESTRUCTION OF MY KINGDOM. REMEMBER MY GRANDFATHER. I DO NOT WANT THE ARCHONS TOO INTERESTED IN ME. THEY'D BREAK ME LIKE A NUTSHELL.
YOU WILL GIVE THE RUNESTONE TO THE ONE YOU CALL DYO, IN THANKS FOR HIS RIFLES.
BUT THAT'S UTTERLY DISPROPORTIONATE! THE RUNESTONE IS WORTH ALL THE RIFLES IN THE WORLD!
DO YOU QUESTION MY GENEROSITY? I AM SAUD, KING OF ARABIA. SUCH IS MY WISH.

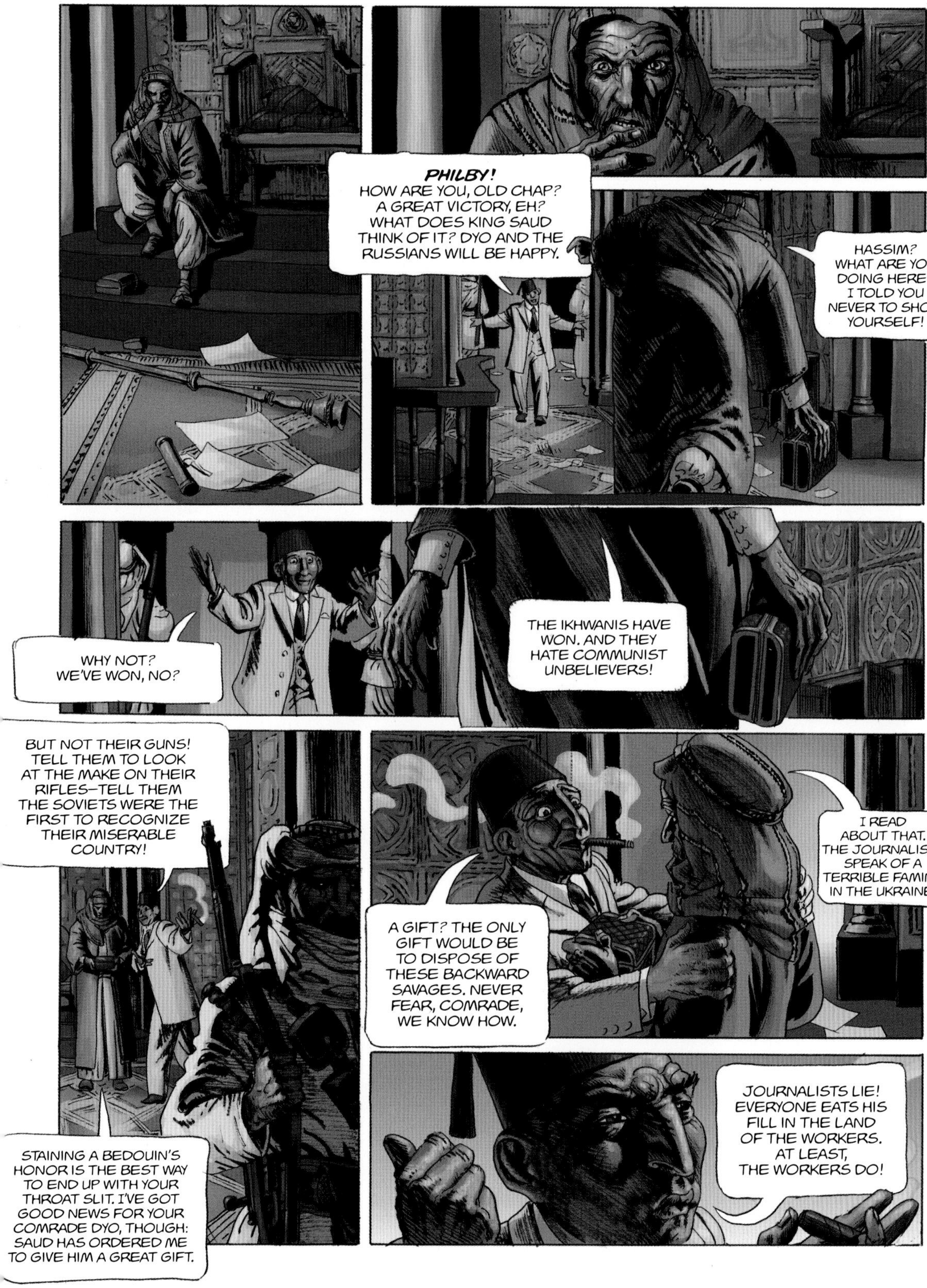
PHILBY!
HOW ARE YOU, OLD CHAP? A GREAT VICTORY, EH? WHAT DOES KING SAUD THINK OF IT? DYO AND THE RUSSIANS WILL BE HAPPY.
HASSIM? WHAT ARE YOU DOING HERE? I TOLD YOU NEVER TO SHOW YOURSELF!
WHY NOT? WE'VE WON, NO?
THE IKHWANIS HAVE WON. AND THEY HATE COMMUNIST UNBELIEVERS!
BUT NOT THEIR GUNS! TELL THEM TO LOOK AT THE MAKE ON THEIR RIFLES—TELL THEM THE SOVIETS WERE THE FIRST TO RECOGNIZE THEIR MISERABLE COUNTRY!
STAINING A BEDOUIN'S HONOR IS THE BEST WAY TO END UP WITH YOUR THROAT SLIT. I'VE GOT GOOD NEWS FOR YOUR COMRADE DYO, THOUGH: SAUD HAS ORDERED ME TO GIVE HIM A GREAT GIFT.
A GIFT? THE ONLY GIFT WOULD BE TO DISPOSE OF THESE BACKWARD SAVAGES. NEVER FEAR, COMRADE, WE KNOW HOW.
I READ ABOUT THAT. THE JOURNALISTS SPEAK OF A TERRIBLE FAMINE IN THE UKRAINE.
JOURNALISTS LIE! EVERYONE EATS HIS FILL IN THE LAND OF THE WORKERS. AT LEAST, THE WORKERS DO!

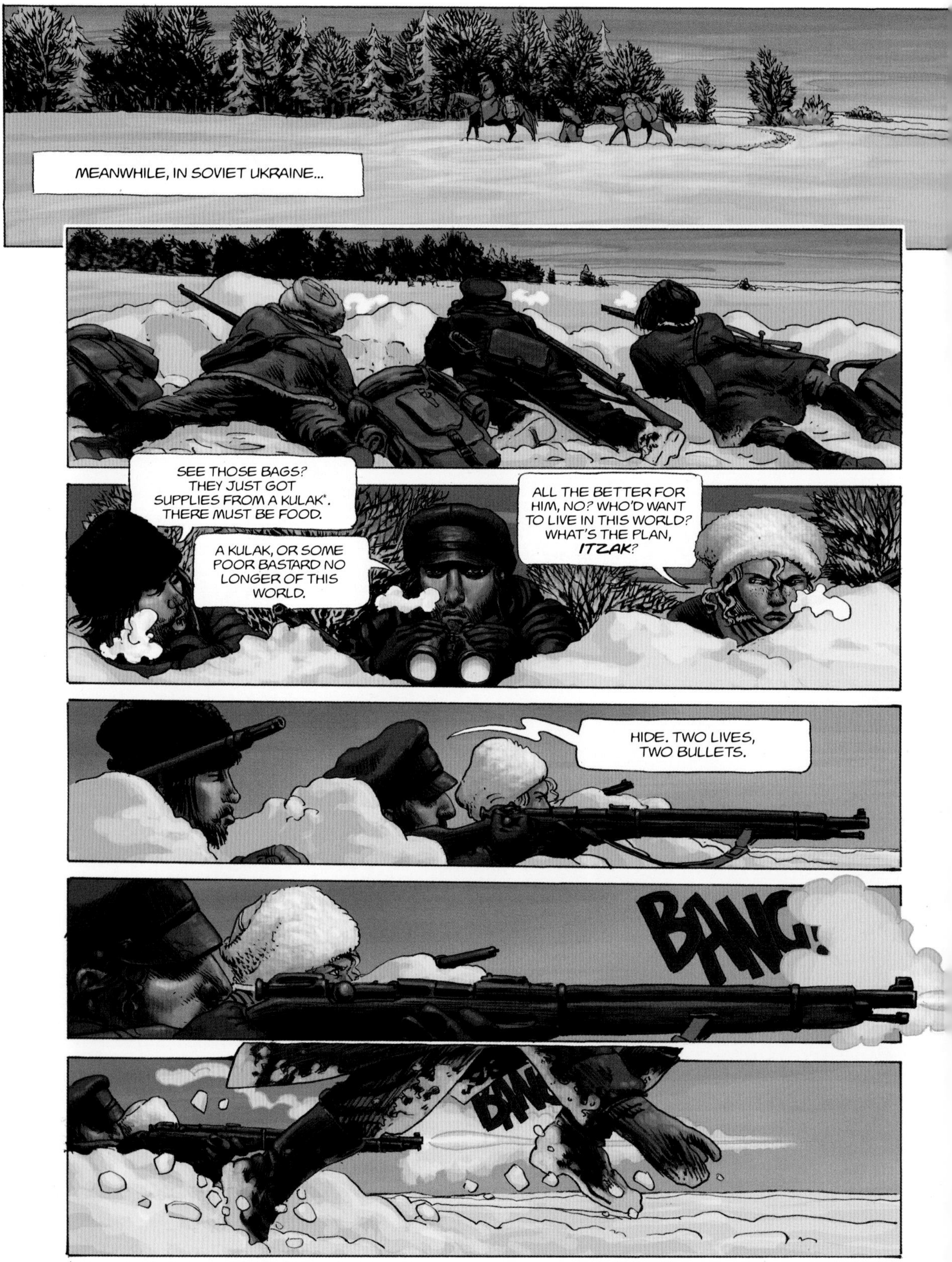
MEANWHILE, IN SOVIET UKRAINE...
SEE THOSE BAGS? THEY JUST GOT SUPPLIES FROM A KULAK*. THERE MUST BE FOOD.
A KULAK, OR SOME POOR BASTARD NO LONGER OF THIS WORLD.
ALL THE BETTER FOR HIM, NO? WHO'D WANT TO LIVE IN THIS WORLD? WHAT'S THE PLAN, ITZAK?
HIDE. TWO LIVES, TWO BULLETS.
BANG!
BANG

* KULAK: PEASANT WHO REFUSED TO GIVE HIS HARVEST TO THE SOVIETS. THEY WERE MASSACRED.

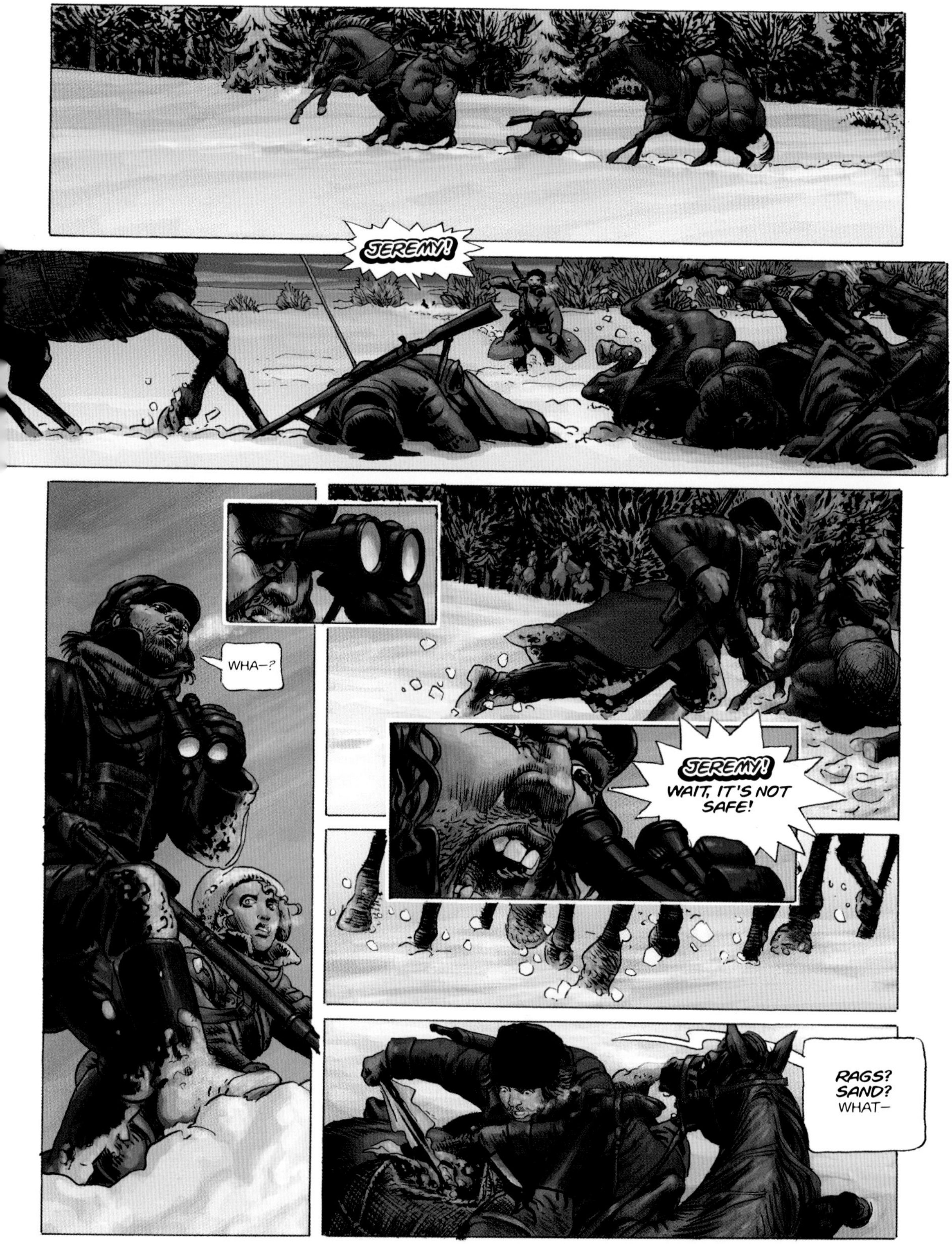
JEREMY!
WHA–?
JEREMY! WAIT, IT'S NOT SAFE!
RAGS? SAND? WHAT–

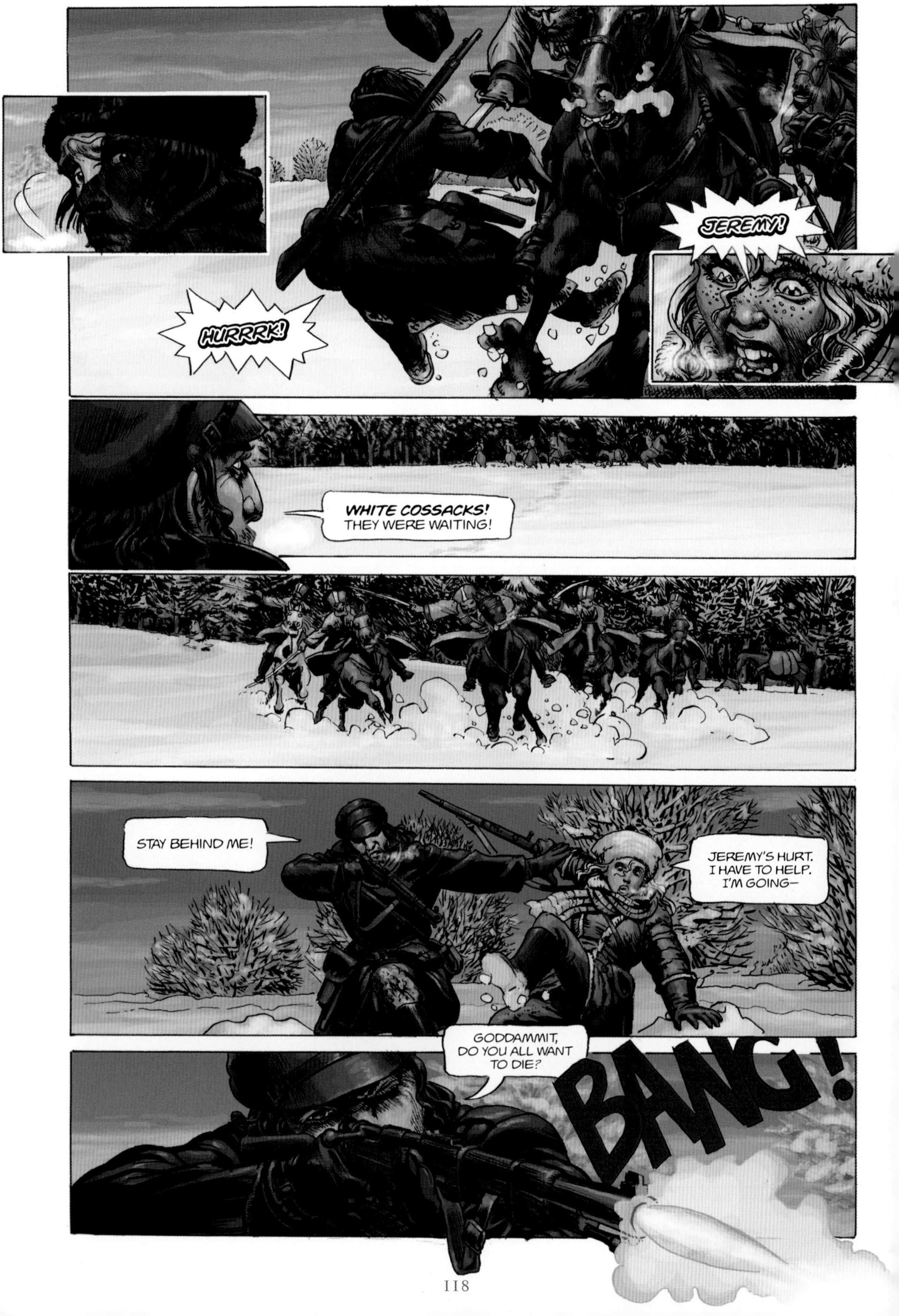
HURRRK!
JEREMY!
WHITE COSSACKS! THEY WERE WAITING!
STAY BEHIND ME!
JEREMY'S HURT. I HAVE TO HELP. I'M GOING–
GODDAMMIT, DO YOU ALL WANT TO DIE?
BANG!

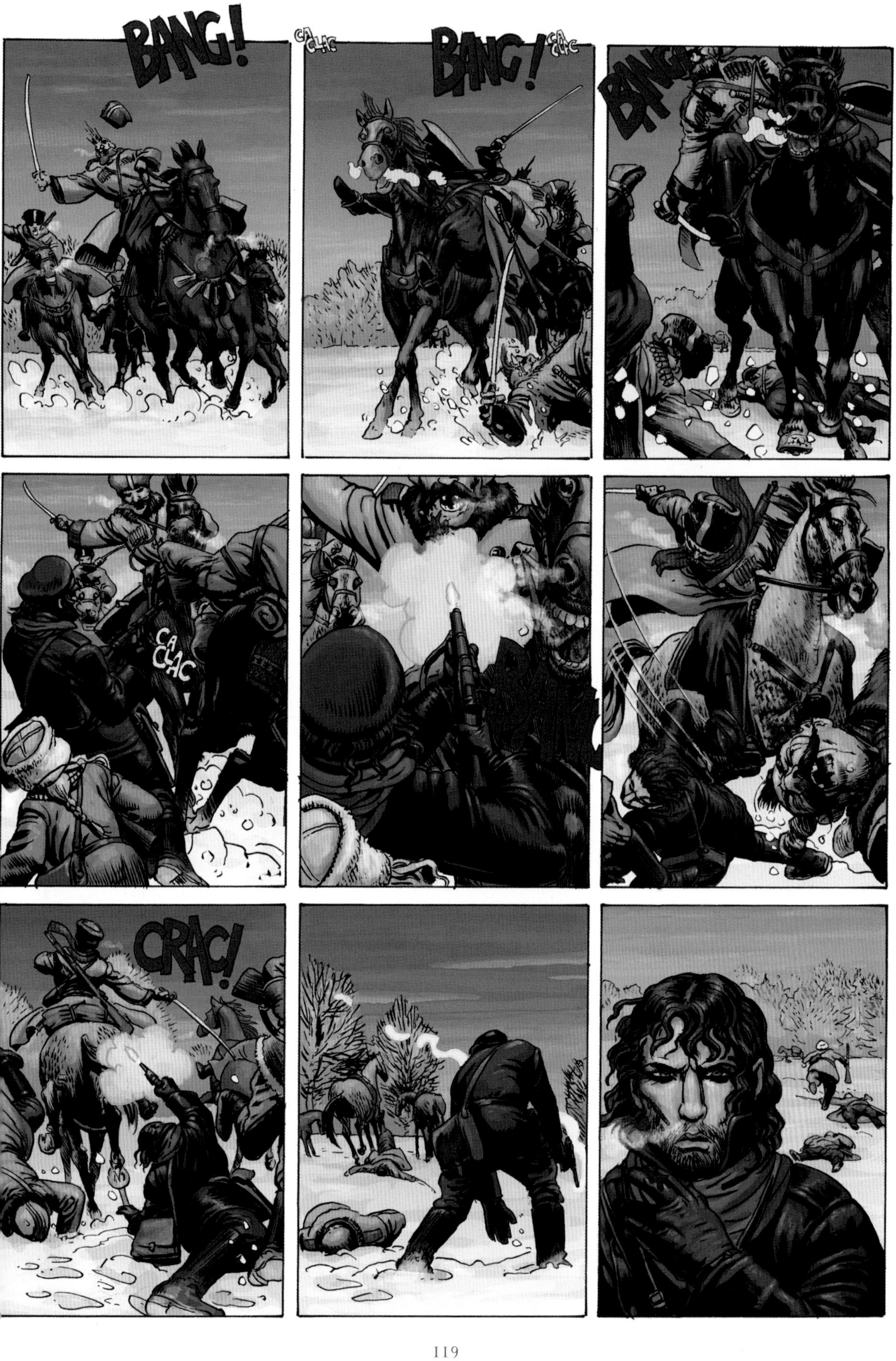
BANG!
CA CLAC
BANG!
CA CLAC
BANG!
CA CLAC
CRAC!

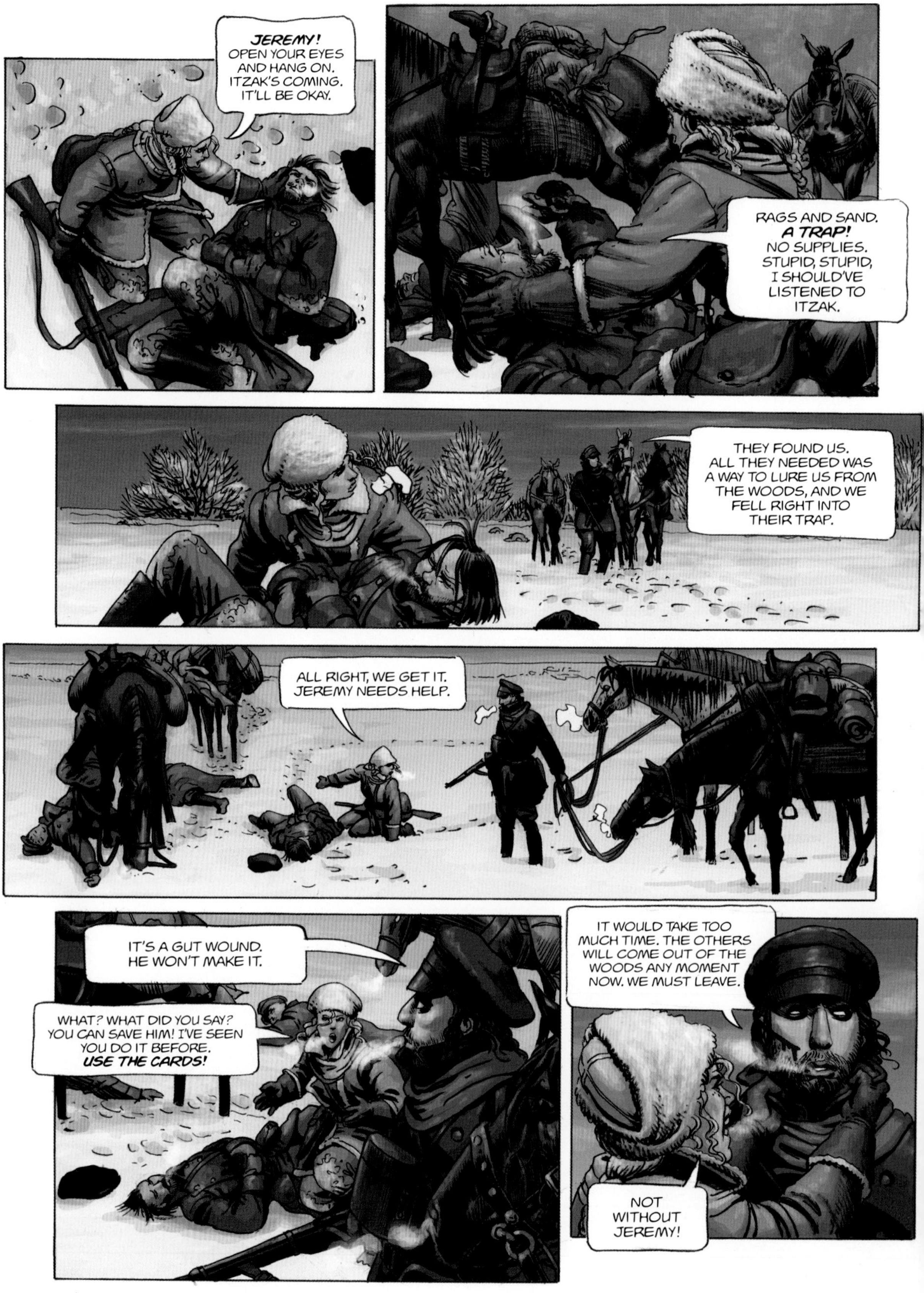
JEREMY! OPEN YOUR EYES AND HANG ON. ITZAK'S COMING. IT'LL BE OKAY.
RAGS AND SAND. A TRAP! NO SUPPLIES. STUPID, STUPID, I SHOULD'VE LISTENED TO ITZAK.
THEY FOUND US. ALL THEY NEEDED WAS A WAY TO LURE US FROM THE WOODS, AND WE FELL RIGHT INTO THEIR TRAP.
ALL RIGHT, WE GET IT. JEREMY NEEDS HELP.
IT'S A GUT WOUND. HE WON'T MAKE IT.
WHAT? WHAT DID YOU SAY? YOU CAN SAVE HIM! I'VE SEEN YOU DO IT BEFORE. USE THE CARDS!
IT WOULD TAKE TOO MUCH TIME. THE OTHERS WILL COME OUT OF THE WOODS ANY MOMENT NOW. WE MUST LEAVE.
NOT WITHOUT JEREMY!

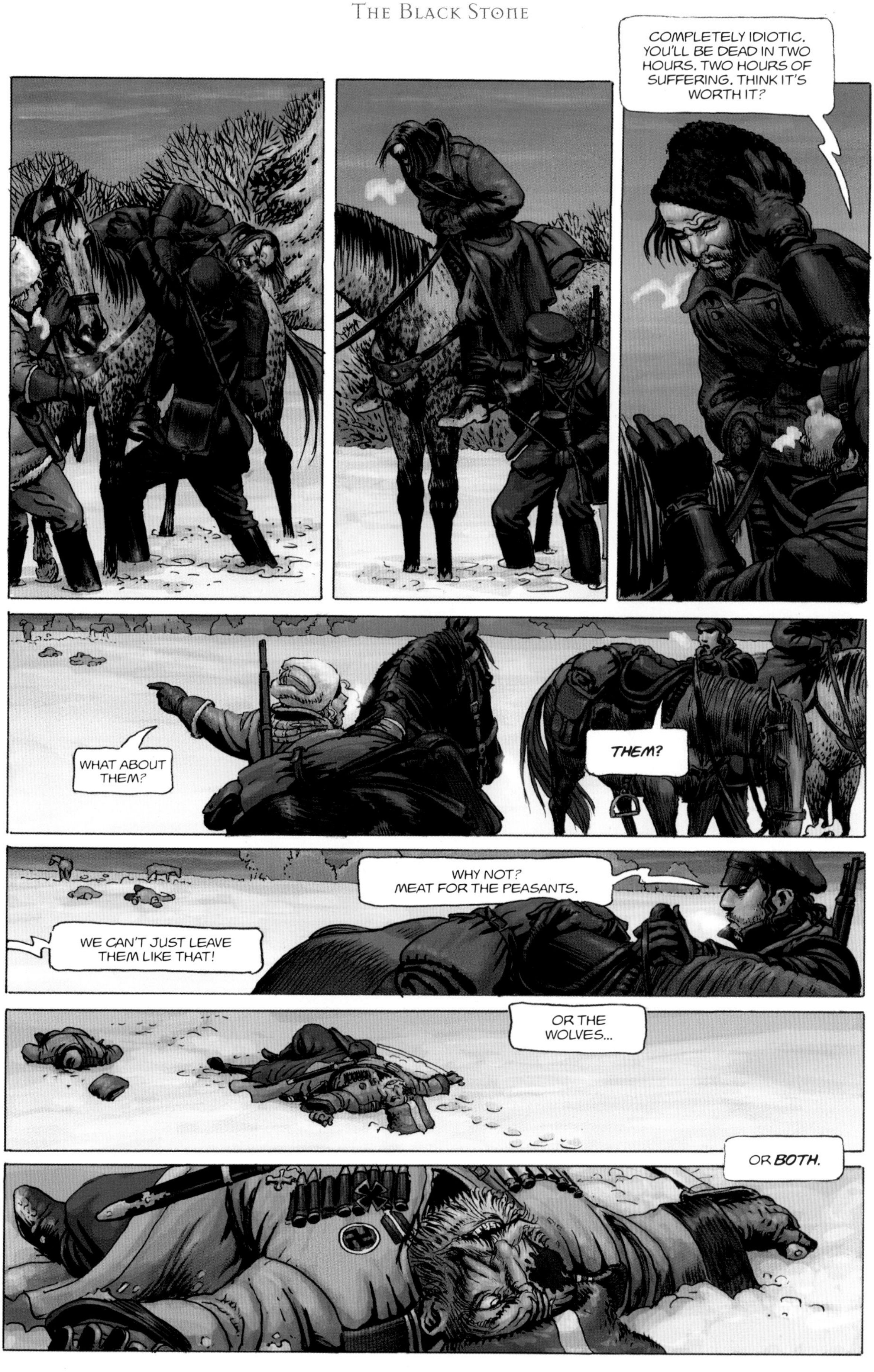
COMPLETELY IDIOTIC. YOU'LL BE DEAD IN TWO HOURS. TWO HOURS OF SUFFERING. THINK IT'S WORTH IT?
WHAT ABOUT THEM?
THEM?
WHY NOT? MEAT FOR THE PEASANTS.
WE CAN'T JUST LEAVE THEM LIKE THAT!
OR THE WOLVES...
OR BOTH.

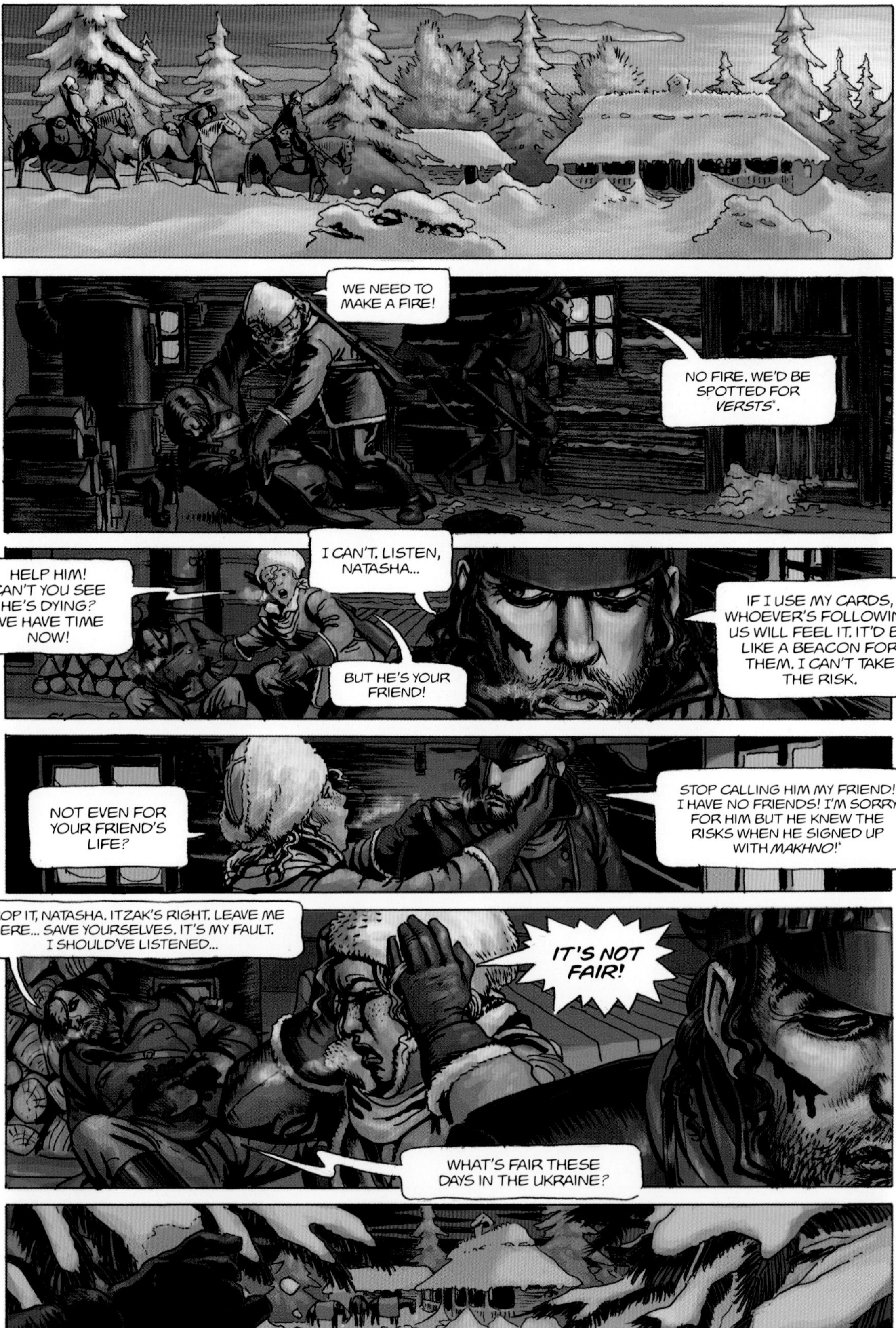
WE NEED TO MAKE A FIRE!
NO FIRE. WE'D BE SPOTTED FOR *VERSTS**.
HELP HIM! CAN'T YOU SEE HE'S DYING? WE HAVE TIME NOW!
I CAN'T. LISTEN, NATASHA...
BUT HE'S YOUR FRIEND!
IF I USE MY CARDS, WHOEVER'S FOLLOWING US WILL FEEL IT. IT'D BE LIKE A BEACON FOR THEM. I CAN'T TAKE THE RISK.
NOT EVEN FOR YOUR FRIEND'S LIFE?
STOP CALLING HIM MY FRIEND! I HAVE NO FRIENDS! I'M SORRY FOR HIM BUT HE KNEW THE RISKS WHEN HE SIGNED UP WITH *MAKHNO*!**
DROP IT, NATASHA. ITZAK'S RIGHT. LEAVE ME HERE... SAVE YOURSELVES. IT'S MY FAULT. I SHOULD'VE LISTENED...
IT'S NOT FAIR!
WHAT'S FAIR THESE DAYS IN THE UKRAINE?

* VERST: A RUSSIAN UNIT OF DISTANCE EQUAL TO 2/3 OF A MILE.

** MAKNO: NESTOR IVANOVICH MAKHNO, UKRANIAN ANARCHIST, ORGANIZED AN ARMY OF PARTISANS WHO FOUGHT AGAINST THE BOLSHEVIKS AND THE WHITE COUNTER-REVOLUTIONARIES.

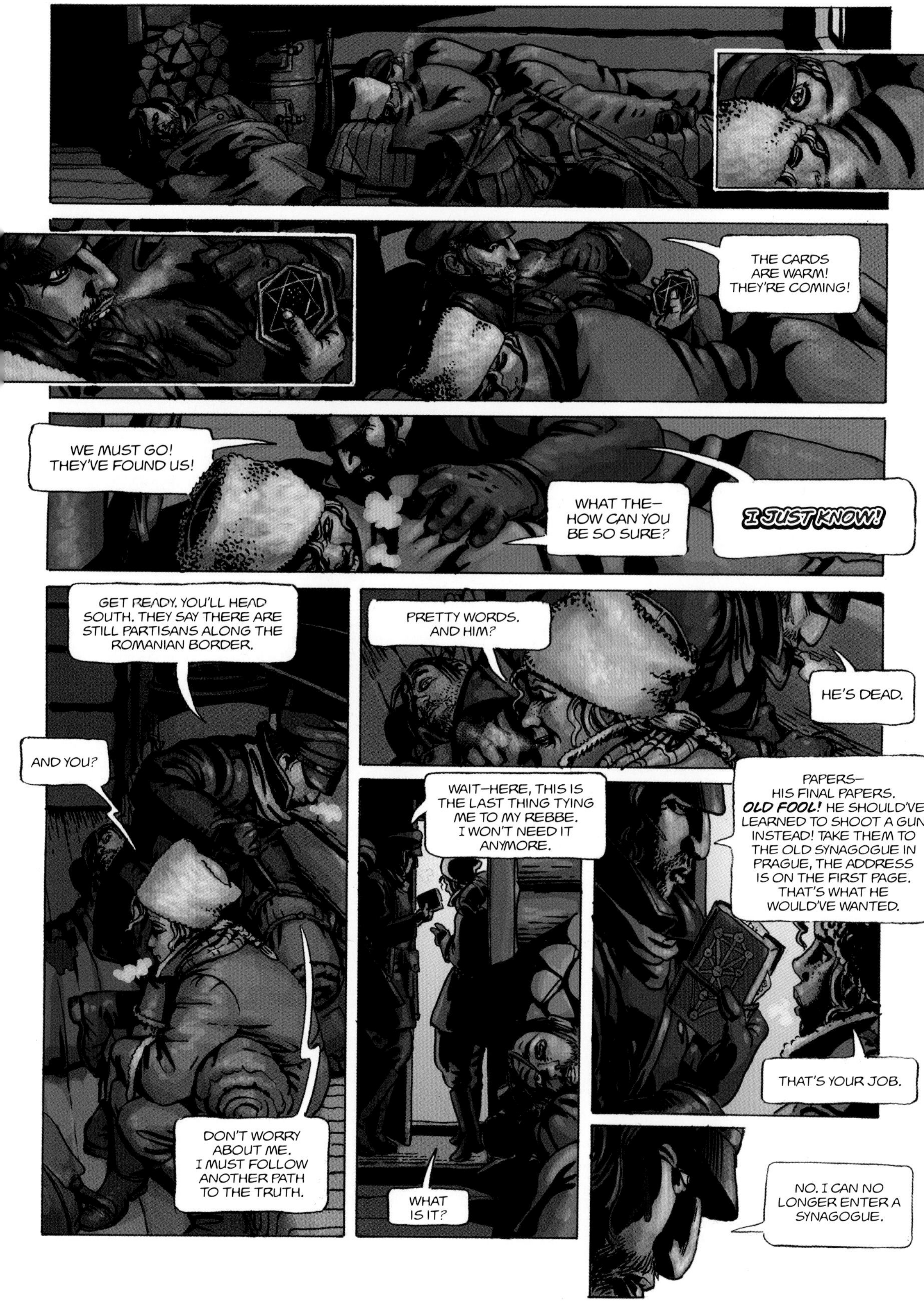
THE CARDS ARE WARM! THEY'RE COMING!
WE MUST GO! THEY'VE FOUND US!
WHAT THE— HOW CAN YOU BE SO SURE?
I JUST KNOW!
GET READY. YOU'LL HEAD SOUTH. THEY SAY THERE ARE STILL PARTISANS ALONG THE ROMANIAN BORDER.
AND YOU?
DON'T WORRY ABOUT ME. I MUST FOLLOW ANOTHER PATH TO THE TRUTH.
PRETTY WORDS. AND HIM?
HE'S DEAD.
WAIT—HERE, THIS IS THE LAST THING TYING ME TO MY REBBE. I WON'T NEED IT ANYMORE.
WHAT IS IT?
PAPERS— HIS FINAL PAPERS. OLD FOOL! HE SHOULD'VE LEARNED TO SHOOT A GUN INSTEAD! TAKE THEM TO THE OLD SYNAGOGUE IN PRAGUE, THE ADDRESS IS ON THE FIRST PAGE. THAT'S WHAT HE WOULD'VE WANTED.
THAT'S YOUR JOB.
NO. I CAN NO LONGER ENTER A SYNAGOGUE.

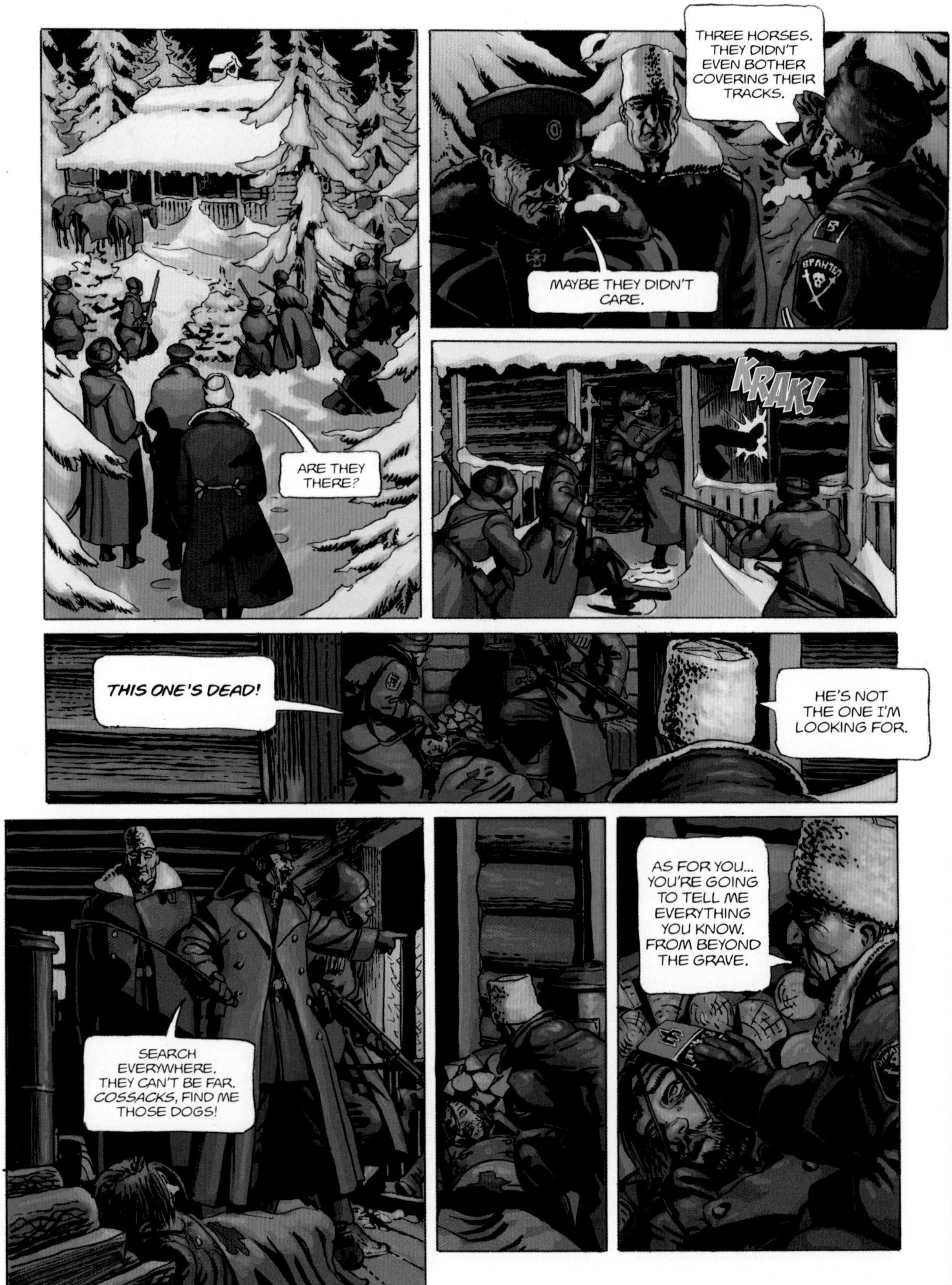
ARE THEY THERE?
THREE HORSES. THEY DIDN'T EVEN BOTHER COVERING THEIR TRACKS.
MAYBE THEY DIDN'T CARE.
KRAK!
THIS ONE'S DEAD!
HE'S NOT THE ONE I'M LOOKING FOR.
SEARCH EVERYWHERE. THEY CAN'T BE FAR. COSSACKS, FIND ME THOSE DOGS!
AS FOR YOU... YOU'RE GOING TO TELL ME EVERYTHING YOU KNOW. FROM BEYOND THE GRAVE.

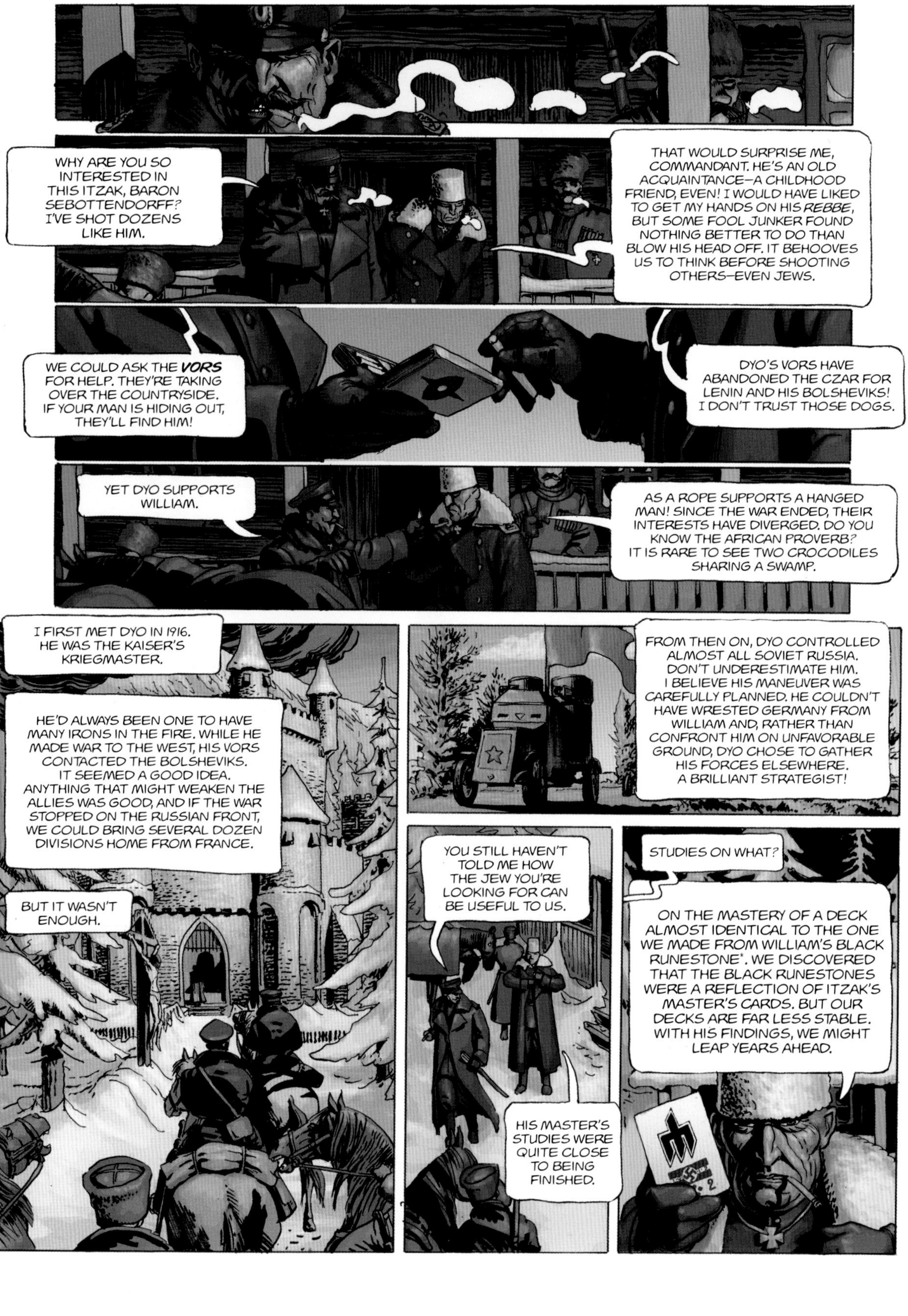
WHY ARE YOU SO INTERESTED IN THIS ITZAK, BARON SEBOTTENDORFF? I'VE SHOT DOZENS LIKE HIM.
THAT WOULD SURPRISE ME, COMMANDANT. HE'S AN OLD ACQUAINTANCE—A CHILDHOOD FRIEND, EVEN! I WOULD HAVE LIKED TO GET MY HANDS ON HIS *REBBE*, BUT SOME FOOL JUNKER FOUND NOTHING BETTER TO DO THAN BLOW HIS HEAD OFF. IT BEHOOVES US TO THINK BEFORE SHOOTING OTHERS—EVEN JEWS.
WE COULD ASK THE ***VORS*** FOR HELP. THEY'RE TAKING OVER THE COUNTRYSIDE. IF YOUR MAN IS HIDING OUT, THEY'LL FIND HIM!
DYO'S VORS HAVE ABANDONED THE CZAR FOR LENIN AND HIS BOLSHEVIKS! I DON'T TRUST THOSE DOGS.
YET DYO SUPPORTS WILLIAM.
AS A ROPE SUPPORTS A HANGED MAN! SINCE THE WAR ENDED, THEIR INTERESTS HAVE DIVERGED. DO YOU KNOW THE AFRICAN PROVERB? IT IS RARE TO SEE TWO CROCODILES SHARING A SWAMP.
I FIRST MET DYO IN 1916. HE WAS THE KAISER'S KRIEGMASTER.
HE'D ALWAYS BEEN ONE TO HAVE MANY IRONS IN THE FIRE. WHILE HE MADE WAR TO THE WEST, HIS VORS CONTACTED THE BOLSHEVIKS. IT SEEMED A GOOD IDEA. ANYTHING THAT MIGHT WEAKEN THE ALLIES WAS GOOD, AND IF THE WAR STOPPED ON THE RUSSIAN FRONT, WE COULD BRING SEVERAL DOZEN DIVISIONS HOME FROM FRANCE.
BUT IT WASN'T ENOUGH.
FROM THEN ON, DYO CONTROLLED ALMOST ALL SOVIET RUSSIA. DON'T UNDERESTIMATE HIM. I BELIEVE HIS MANEUVER WAS CAREFULLY PLANNED. HE COULDN'T HAVE WRESTED GERMANY FROM WILLIAM AND, RATHER THAN CONFRONT HIM ON UNFAVORABLE GROUND, DYO CHOSE TO GATHER HIS FORCES ELSEWHERE. A BRILLIANT STRATEGIST!
YOU STILL HAVEN'T TOLD ME HOW THE JEW YOU'RE LOOKING FOR CAN BE USEFUL TO US.
HIS MASTER'S STUDIES WERE QUITE CLOSE TO BEING FINISHED.
STUDIES ON WHAT?
ON THE MASTERY OF A DECK ALMOST IDENTICAL TO THE ONE WE MADE FROM WILLIAM'S BLACK RUNESTONE*. WE DISCOVERED THAT THE BLACK RUNESTONES WERE A REFLECTION OF ITZAK'S MASTER'S CARDS. BUT OUR DECKS ARE FAR LESS STABLE. WITH HIS FINDINGS, WE MIGHT LEAP YEARS AHEAD.

THE COUNTER-REVOLUTIONARY ARMIES HAD BEEN DEFEATED EVERYWHERE. IN THE URALS, SAILORS FROM KRONSTADT* HELPED, FIGHTING TOOTH AND NAIL AGAINST THE CZECH LEGION AND ADMIRAL KOLCHAK OF SIBERIA.

THE THREAT WAS PAST, BUT THE BOLSHEVIKS REALIZED THAT TO REMAIN IN POWER, THEY WOULD NEED TO RID THEMSELVES OF THEIR UNPREDICTABLE ALLIES.

AS BEFORE, IN THE UKRAINE, THE TIME HAD COME TO SETTLE ACCOUNTS. FOR THE FIRST TIME IN A LONG TIME, DYO ALONE HEADED AN EMPIRE.

WHAT WOULD HE DO WITH IT?

* KRONSTADT: AN ISLAND FORTRESS FACING ST. PETERSBURG. A SPEARHEAD OF THE RUSSIAN REVOLUTIONS BEFORE BEING TAKEN OVER BY THE BOLSHEVIKS.

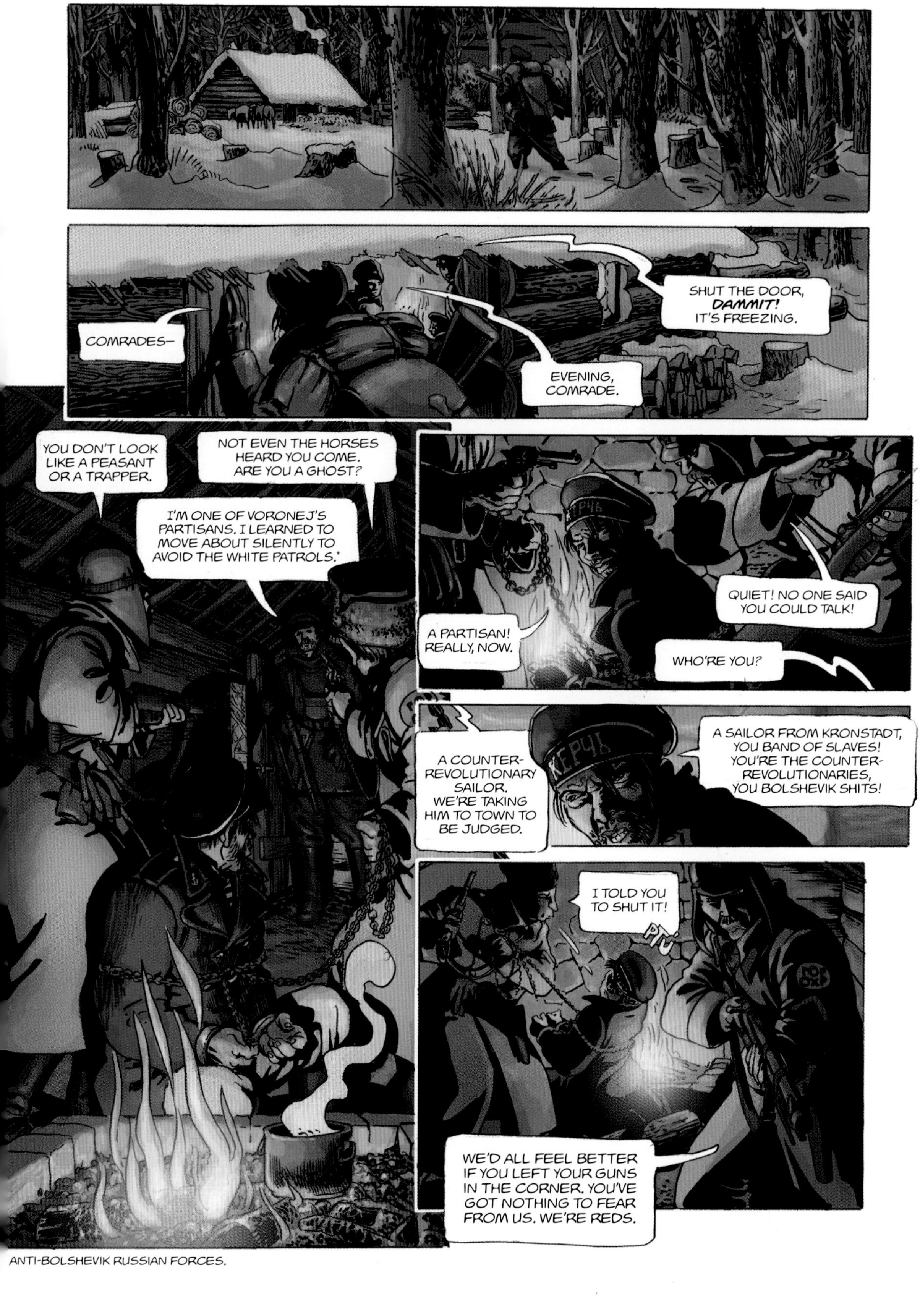
COMRADES—
SHUT THE DOOR, DAMMIT! IT'S FREEZING.
EVENING, COMRADE.
YOU DON'T LOOK LIKE A PEASANT OR A TRAPPER.
NOT EVEN THE HORSES HEARD YOU COME. ARE YOU A GHOST?
I'M ONE OF VORONEJ'S PARTISANS. I LEARNED TO MOVE ABOUT SILENTLY TO AVOID THE WHITE PATROLS.*
A PARTISAN! REALLY, NOW.
QUIET! NO ONE SAID YOU COULD TALK!
WHO'RE YOU?
A COUNTER-REVOLUTIONARY SAILOR. WE'RE TAKING HIM TO TOWN TO BE JUDGED.
A SAILOR FROM KRONSTADT, YOU BAND OF SLAVES! YOU'RE THE COUNTER-REVOLUTIONARIES, YOU BOLSHEVIK SHITS!
I TOLD YOU TO SHUT IT!
WE'D ALL FEEL BETTER IF YOU LEFT YOUR GUNS IN THE CORNER. YOU'VE GOT NOTHING TO FEAR FROM US. WE'RE REDS.

*ANTI-BOLSHEVIK RUSSIAN FORCES.

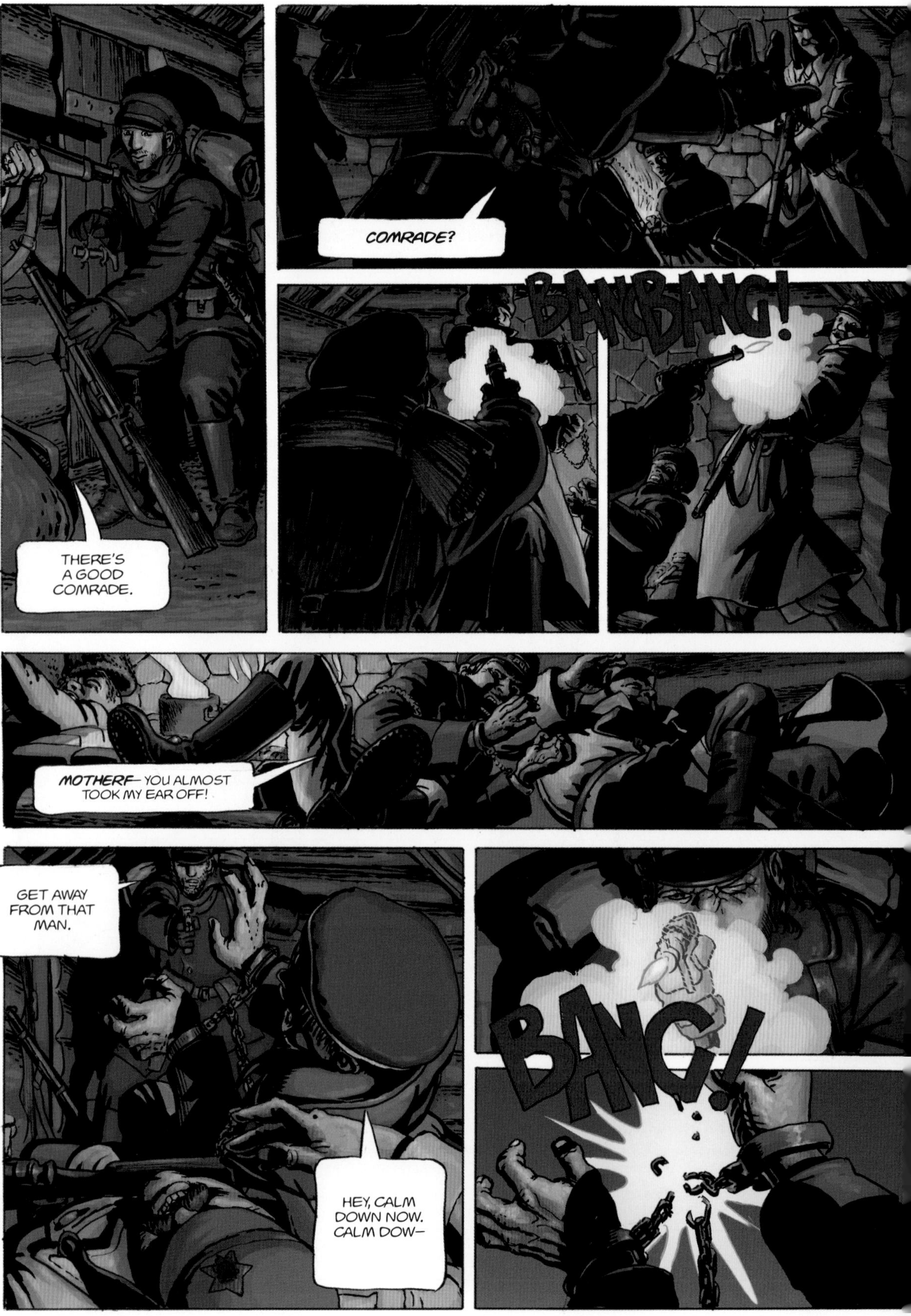
COMRADE?
THERE'S A GOOD COMRADE.
BANBANG!
MOTHERF— YOU ALMOST TOOK MY EAR OFF!
GET AWAY FROM THAT MAN.
HEY, CALM DOWN NOW. CALM DOW—
BANG!

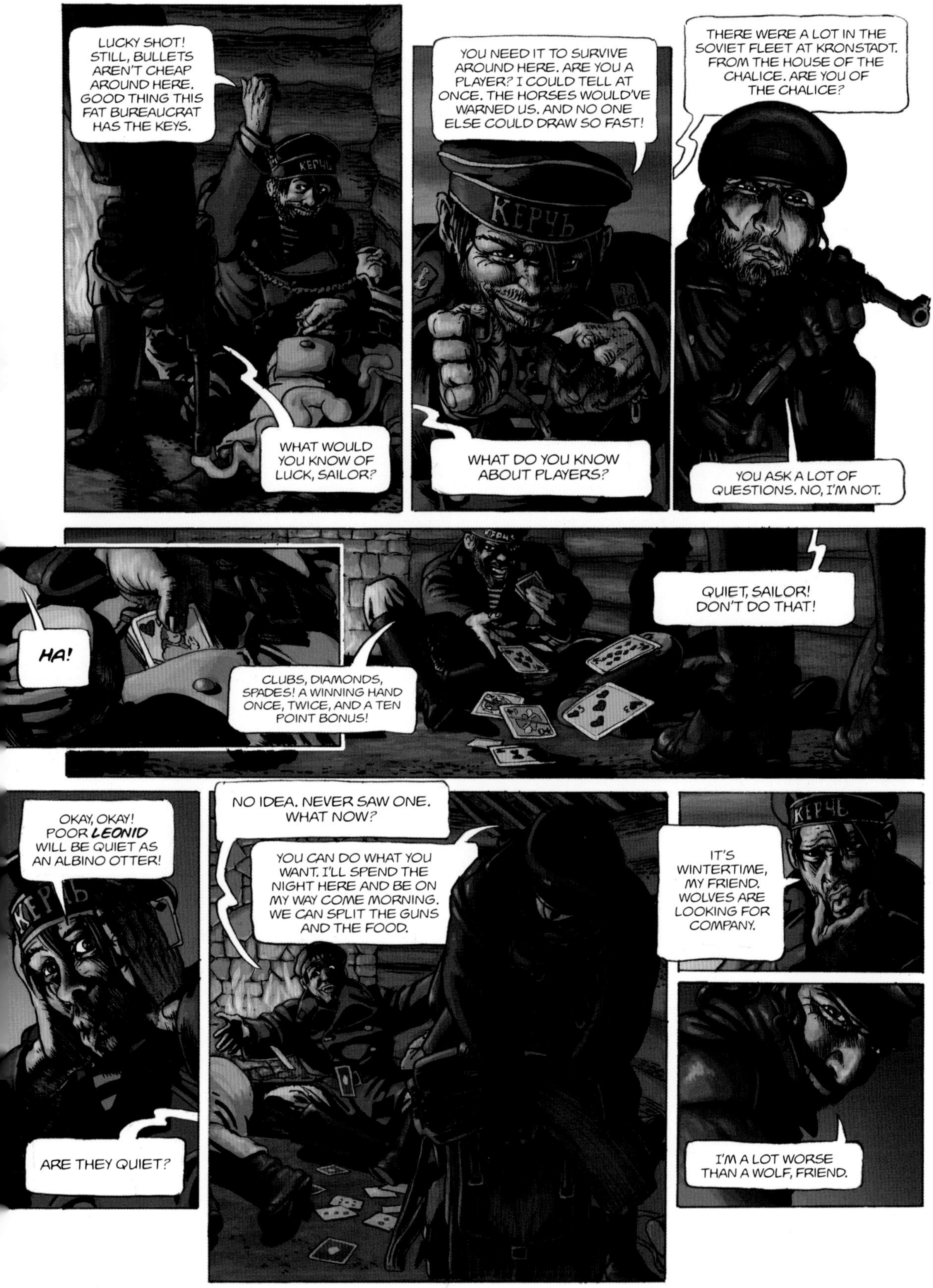
LUCKY SHOT! STILL, BULLETS AREN'T CHEAP AROUND HERE. GOOD THING THIS FAT BUREAUCRAT HAS THE KEYS.
WHAT WOULD YOU KNOW OF LUCK, SAILOR?
КЕРЧЬ
YOU NEED IT TO SURVIVE AROUND HERE. ARE YOU A PLAYER? I COULD TELL AT ONCE. THE HORSES WOULD'VE WARNED US. AND NO ONE ELSE COULD DRAW SO FAST!
WHAT DO YOU KNOW ABOUT PLAYERS?
THERE WERE A LOT IN THE SOVIET FLEET AT KRONSTADT. FROM THE HOUSE OF THE CHALICE. ARE YOU OF THE CHALICE?
YOU ASK A LOT OF QUESTIONS. NO, I'M NOT.
HA!
CLUBS, DIAMONDS, SPADES! A WINNING HAND ONCE, TWICE, AND A TEN POINT BONUS!
QUIET, SAILOR! DON'T DO THAT!
OKAY, OKAY! POOR LEONID WILL BE QUIET AS AN ALBINO OTTER!
ARE THEY QUIET?
NO IDEA. NEVER SAW ONE. WHAT NOW?
YOU CAN DO WHAT YOU WANT. I'LL SPEND THE NIGHT HERE AND BE ON MY WAY COME MORNING. WE CAN SPLIT THE GUNS AND THE FOOD.
IT'S WINTERTIME, MY FRIEND. WOLVES ARE LOOKING FOR COMPANY.
I'M A LOT WORSE THAN A WOLF, FRIEND.

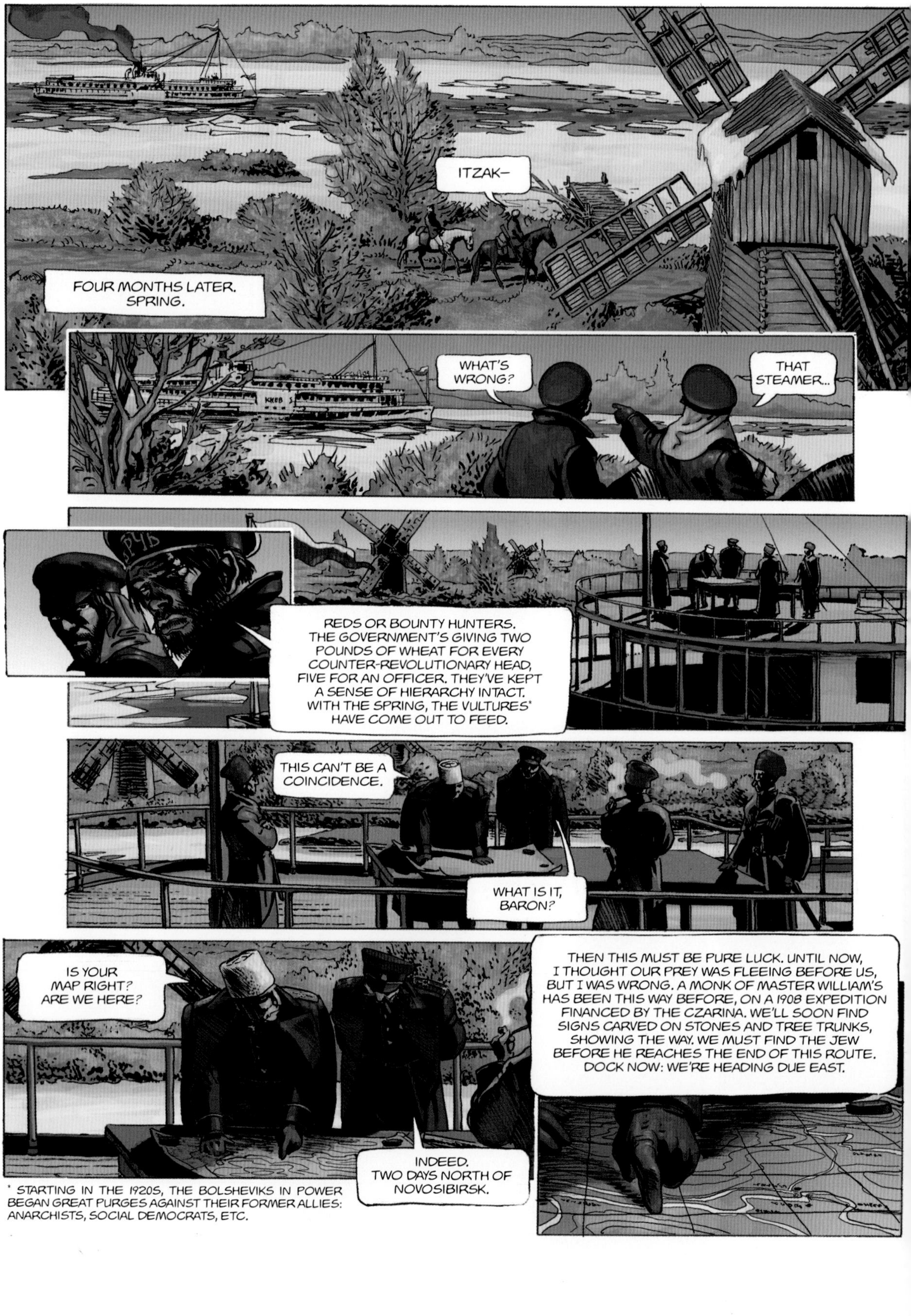
FOUR MONTHS LATER. SPRING.
ITZAK—
WHAT'S WRONG?
THAT STEAMER...
REDS OR BOUNTY HUNTERS. THE GOVERNMENT'S GIVING TWO POUNDS OF WHEAT FOR EVERY COUNTER-REVOLUTIONARY HEAD, FIVE FOR AN OFFICER. THEY'VE KEPT A SENSE OF HIERARCHY INTACT. WITH THE SPRING, THE VULTURES* HAVE COME OUT TO FEED.
THIS CAN'T BE A COINCIDENCE.
WHAT IS IT, BARON?
IS YOUR MAP RIGHT? ARE WE HERE?
INDEED. TWO DAYS NORTH OF NOVOSIBIRSK.
THEN THIS MUST BE PURE LUCK. UNTIL NOW, I THOUGHT OUR PREY WAS FLEEING BEFORE US, BUT I WAS WRONG. A MONK OF MASTER WILLIAM'S HAS BEEN THIS WAY BEFORE, ON A 1908 EXPEDITION FINANCED BY THE CZARINA. WE'LL SOON FIND SIGNS CARVED ON STONES AND TREE TRUNKS, SHOWING THE WAY. WE MUST FIND THE JEW BEFORE HE REACHES THE END OF THIS ROUTE. DOCK NOW: WE'RE HEADING DUE EAST.

* STARTING IN THE 1920S, THE BOLSHEVIKS IN POWER BEGAN GREAT PURGES AGAINST THEIR FORMER ALLIES: ANARCHISTS, SOCIAL DEMOCRATS, ETC.

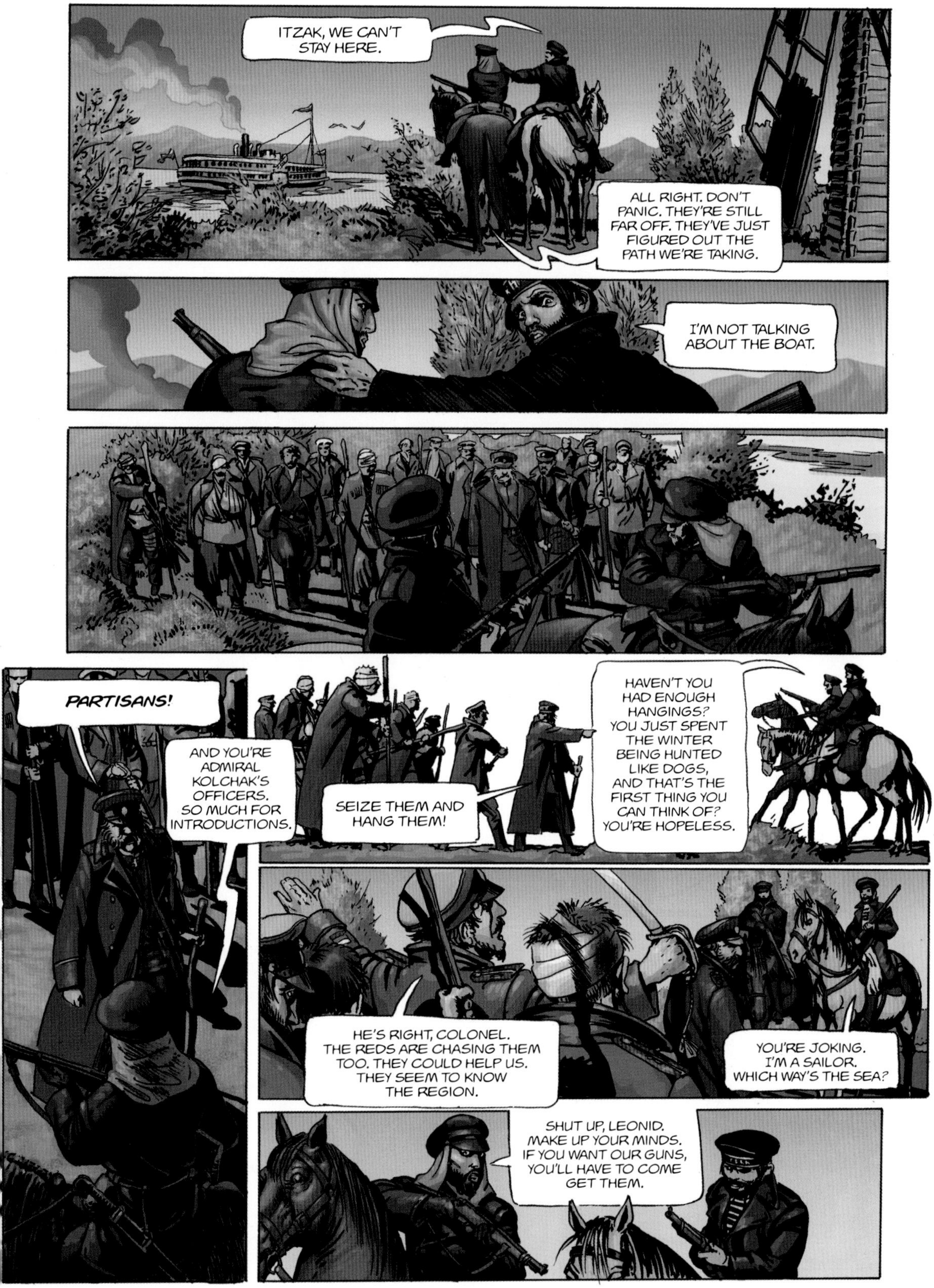
ITZAK, WE CAN'T STAY HERE.
ALL RIGHT. DON'T PANIC. THEY'RE STILL FAR OFF. THEY'VE JUST FIGURED OUT THE PATH WE'RE TAKING.
I'M NOT TALKING ABOUT THE BOAT.
PARTISANS!
AND YOU'RE ADMIRAL KOLCHAK'S OFFICERS. SO MUCH FOR INTRODUCTIONS.
SEIZE THEM AND HANG THEM!
HAVEN'T YOU HAD ENOUGH HANGINGS? YOU JUST SPENT THE WINTER BEING HUNTED LIKE DOGS, AND THAT'S THE FIRST THING YOU CAN THINK OF? YOU'RE HOPELESS.
HE'S RIGHT, COLONEL. THE REDS ARE CHASING THEM TOO. THEY COULD HELP US. THEY SEEM TO KNOW THE REGION.
YOU'RE JOKING. I'M A SAILOR. WHICH WAY'S THE SEA?
SHUT UP, LEONID. MAKE UP YOUR MINDS. IF YOU WANT OUR GUNS, YOU'LL HAVE TO COME GET THEM.

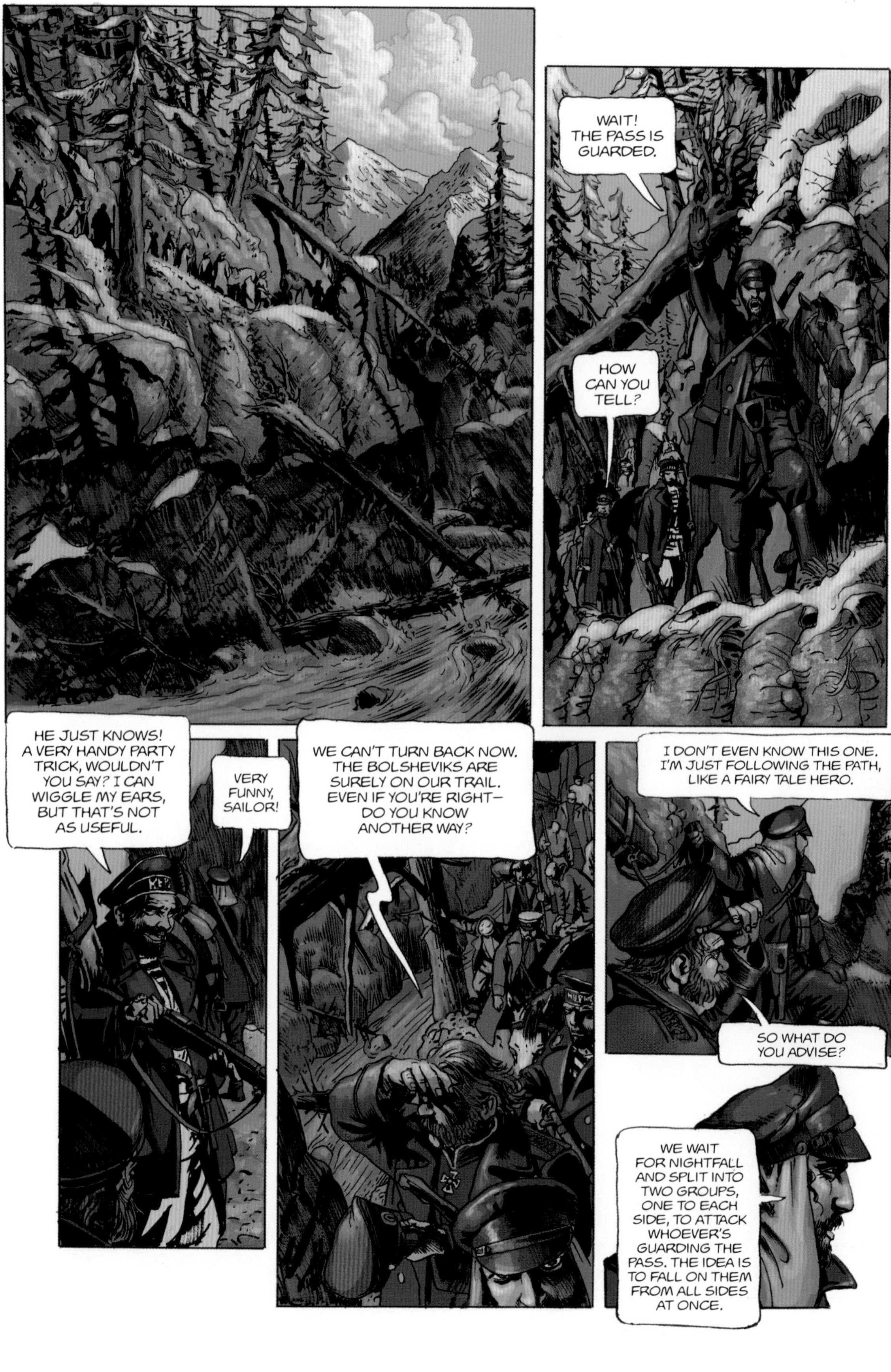
WAIT! THE PASS IS GUARDED.
HOW CAN YOU TELL?
HE JUST KNOWS! A VERY HANDY PARTY TRICK, WOULDN'T YOU SAY? I CAN WIGGLE MY EARS, BUT THAT'S NOT AS USEFUL.
VERY FUNNY, SAILOR!
WE CAN'T TURN BACK NOW. THE BOLSHEVIKS ARE SURELY ON OUR TRAIL. EVEN IF YOU'RE RIGHT– DO YOU KNOW ANOTHER WAY?
I DON'T EVEN KNOW THIS ONE. I'M JUST FOLLOWING THE PATH, LIKE A FAIRY TALE HERO.
SO WHAT DO YOU ADVISE?
WE WAIT FOR NIGHTFALL AND SPLIT INTO TWO GROUPS, ONE TO EACH SIDE, TO ATTACK WHOEVER'S GUARDING THE PASS. THE IDEA IS TO FALL ON THEM FROM ALL SIDES AT ONCE.

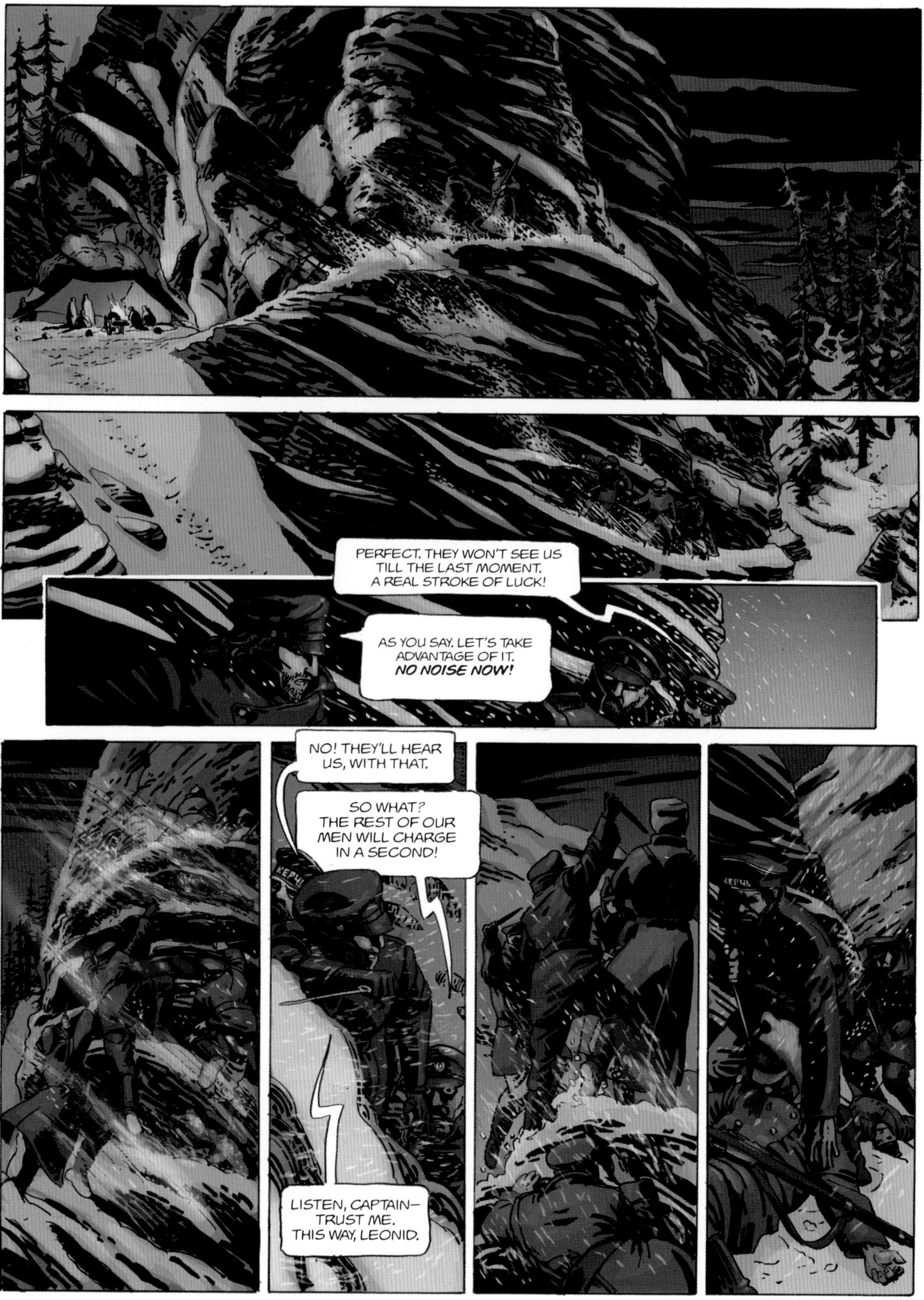
PERFECT. THEY WON'T SEE US TILL THE LAST MOMENT. A REAL STROKE OF LUCK!
AS YOU SAY. LET'S TAKE ADVANTAGE OF IT. ***NO NOISE NOW!***
NO! THEY'LL HEAR US, WITH THAT.
SO WHAT? THE REST OF OUR MEN WILL CHARGE IN A SECOND!
LISTEN, CAPTAIN— TRUST ME. THIS WAY, LEONID.

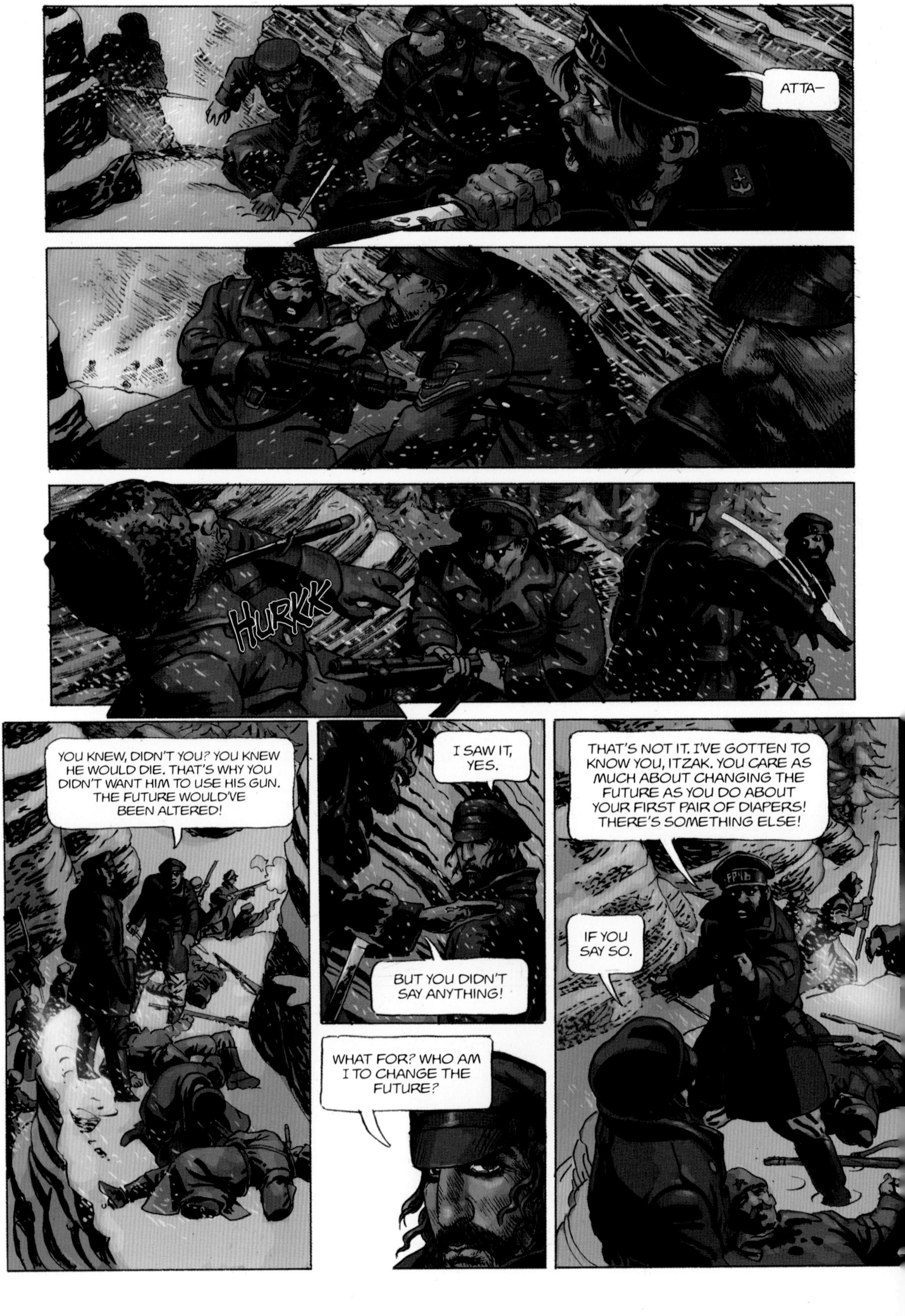
ATTA–
HURKK
YOU KNEW, DIDN'T YOU? YOU KNEW HE WOULD DIE. THAT'S WHY YOU DIDN'T WANT HIM TO USE HIS GUN. THE FUTURE WOULD'VE BEEN ALTERED!
I SAW IT, YES.
BUT YOU DIDN'T SAY ANYTHING!
WHAT FOR? WHO AM I TO CHANGE THE FUTURE?
THAT'S NOT IT. I'VE GOTTEN TO KNOW YOU, ITZAK. YOU CARE AS MUCH ABOUT CHANGING THE FUTURE AS YOU DO ABOUT YOUR FIRST PAIR OF DIAPERS! THERE'S SOMETHING ELSE!
IF YOU SAY SO.

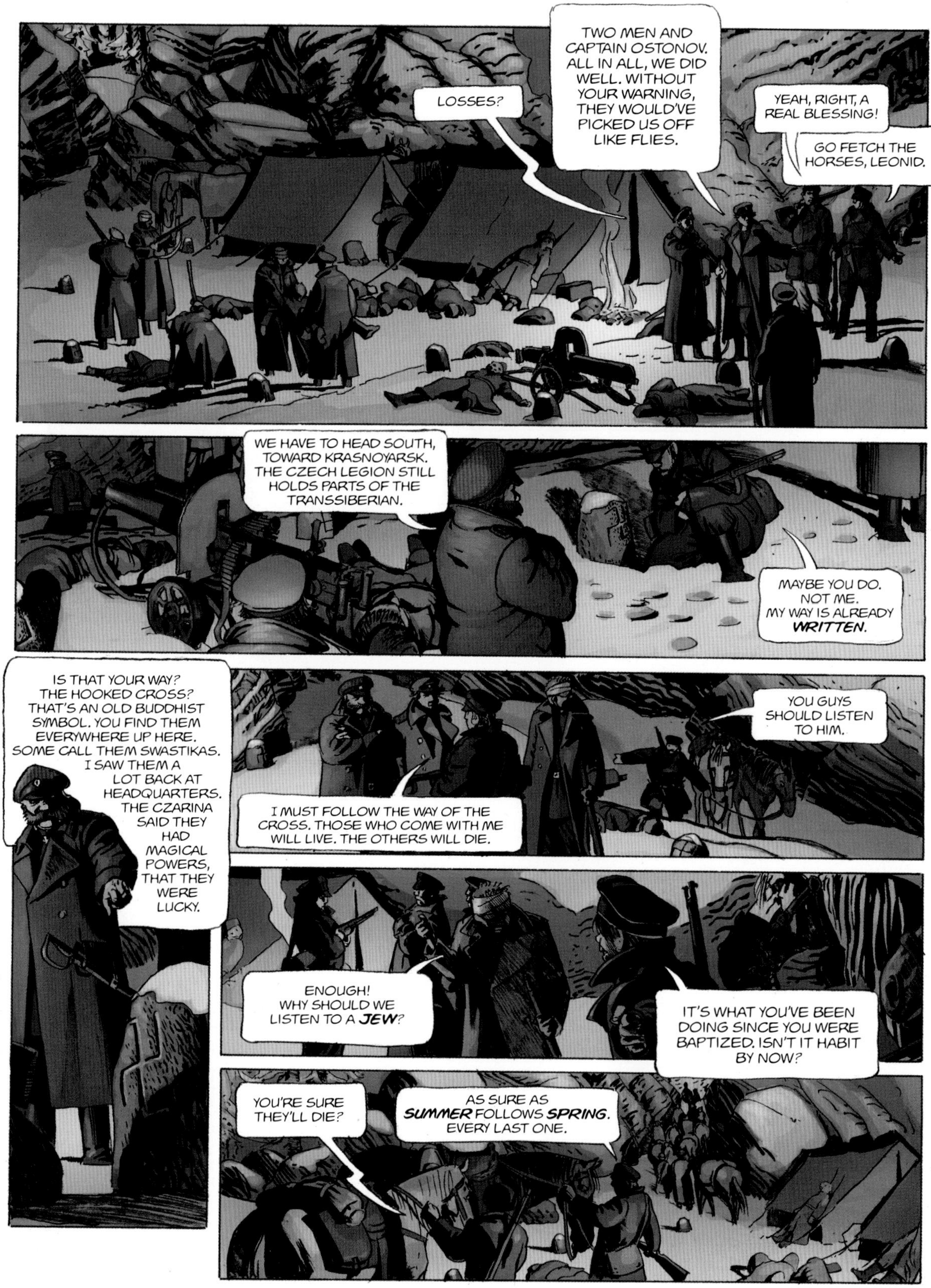
LOSSES?
TWO MEN AND CAPTAIN OSTONOV. ALL IN ALL, WE DID WELL. WITHOUT YOUR WARNING, THEY WOULD'VE PICKED US OFF LIKE FLIES.
YEAH, RIGHT, A REAL BLESSING!
GO FETCH THE HORSES, LEONID.
WE HAVE TO HEAD SOUTH, TOWARD KRASNOYARSK. THE CZECH LEGION STILL HOLDS PARTS OF THE TRANSSIBERIAN.
MAYBE YOU DO. NOT ME. MY WAY IS ALREADY WRITTEN.
IS THAT YOUR WAY? THE HOOKED CROSS? THAT'S AN OLD BUDDHIST SYMBOL. YOU FIND THEM EVERYWHERE UP HERE. SOME CALL THEM SWASTIKAS. I SAW THEM A LOT BACK AT HEADQUARTERS. THE CZARINA SAID THEY HAD MAGICAL POWERS, THAT THEY WERE LUCKY.
I MUST FOLLOW THE WAY OF THE CROSS. THOSE WHO COME WITH ME WILL LIVE. THE OTHERS WILL DIE.
YOU GUYS SHOULD LISTEN TO HIM.
ENOUGH! WHY SHOULD WE LISTEN TO A JEW?
IT'S WHAT YOU'VE BEEN DOING SINCE YOU WERE BAPTIZED. ISN'T IT HABIT BY NOW?
YOU'RE SURE THEY'LL DIE?
AS SURE AS SUMMER FOLLOWS SPRING. EVERY LAST ONE.

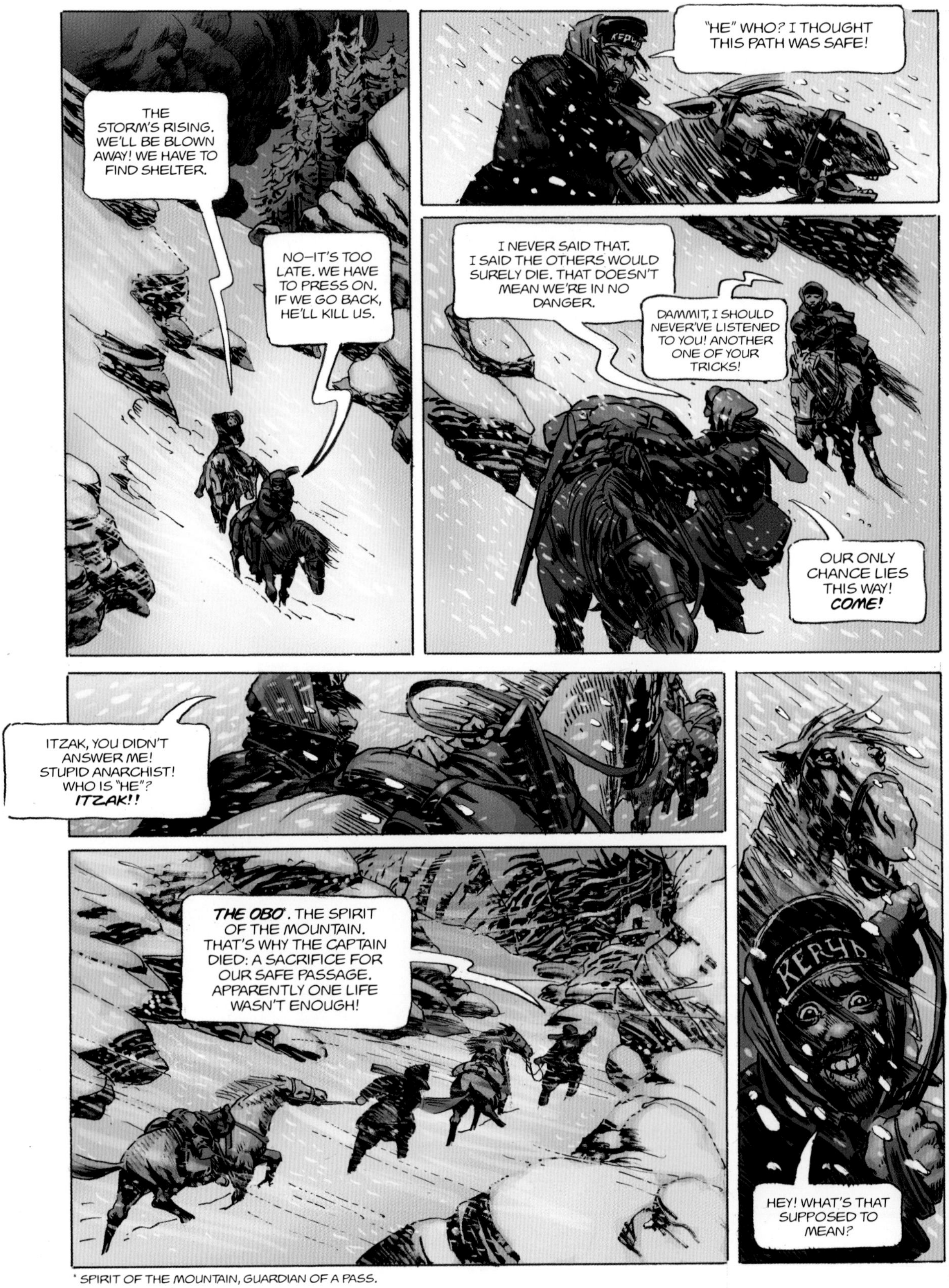
THE STORM'S RISING. WE'LL BE BLOWN AWAY! WE HAVE TO FIND SHELTER.
NO–IT'S TOO LATE. WE HAVE TO PRESS ON. IF WE GO BACK, HE'LL KILL US.
"HE" WHO? I THOUGHT THIS PATH WAS SAFE!
KERYB
I NEVER SAID THAT. I SAID THE OTHERS WOULD SURELY DIE. THAT DOESN'T MEAN WE'RE IN NO DANGER.
DAMMIT, I SHOULD NEVER'VE LISTENED TO YOU! ANOTHER ONE OF YOUR TRICKS!
OUR ONLY CHANCE LIES THIS WAY! **COME!**
ITZAK, YOU DIDN'T ANSWER ME! STUPID ANARCHIST! WHO IS "HE"? **ITZAK!!**
THE OBO*. THE SPIRIT OF THE MOUNTAIN. THAT'S WHY THE CAPTAIN DIED: A SACRIFICE FOR OUR SAFE PASSAGE. APPARENTLY ONE LIFE WASN'T ENOUGH!
KERYB
HEY! WHAT'S THAT SUPPOSED TO MEAN?

* SPIRIT OF THE MOUNTAIN, GUARDIAN OF A PASS.

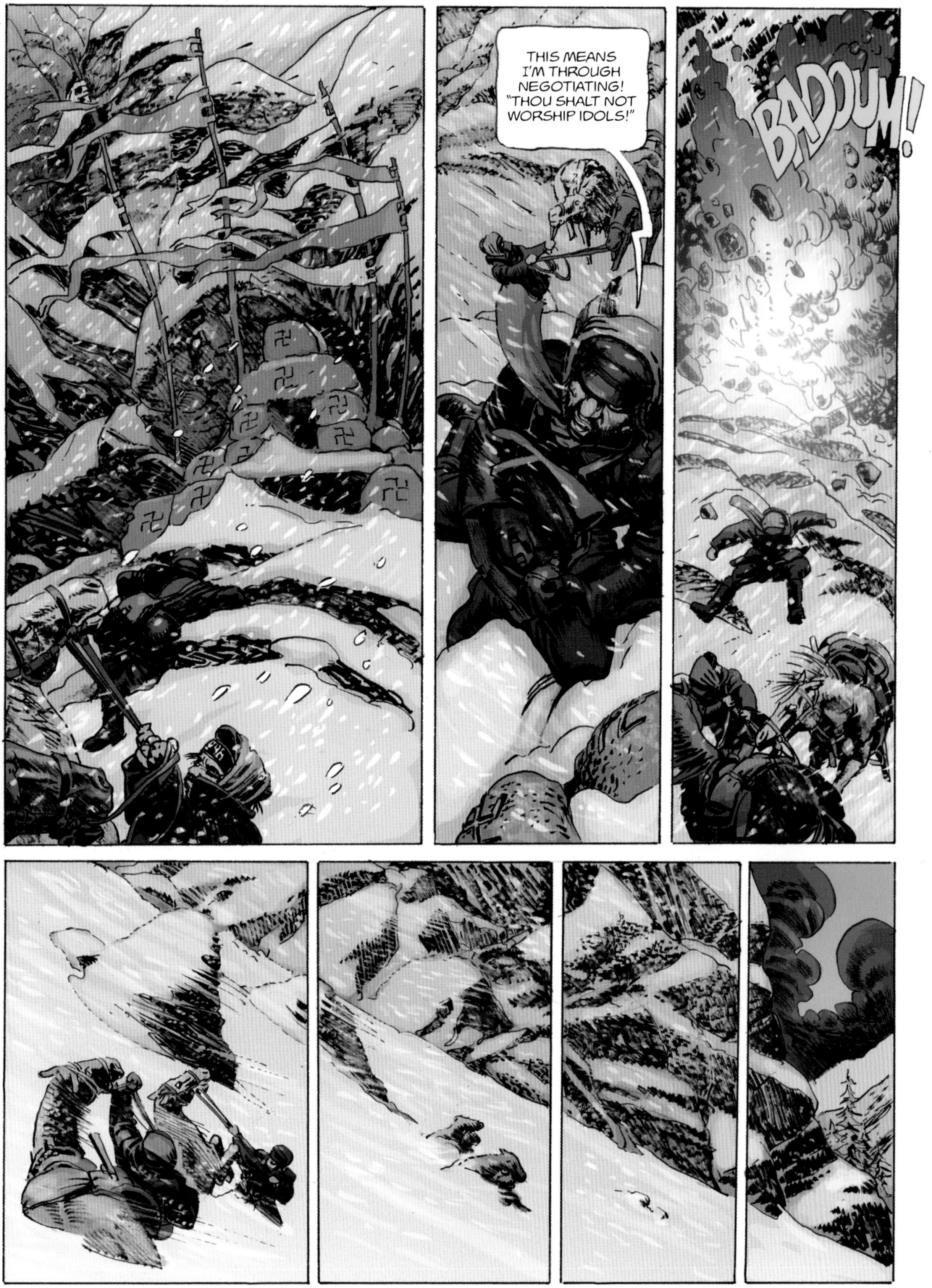
THIS MEANS I'M THROUGH NEGOTIATING! "THOU SHALT NOT WORSHIP IDOLS!"
BADOUM!

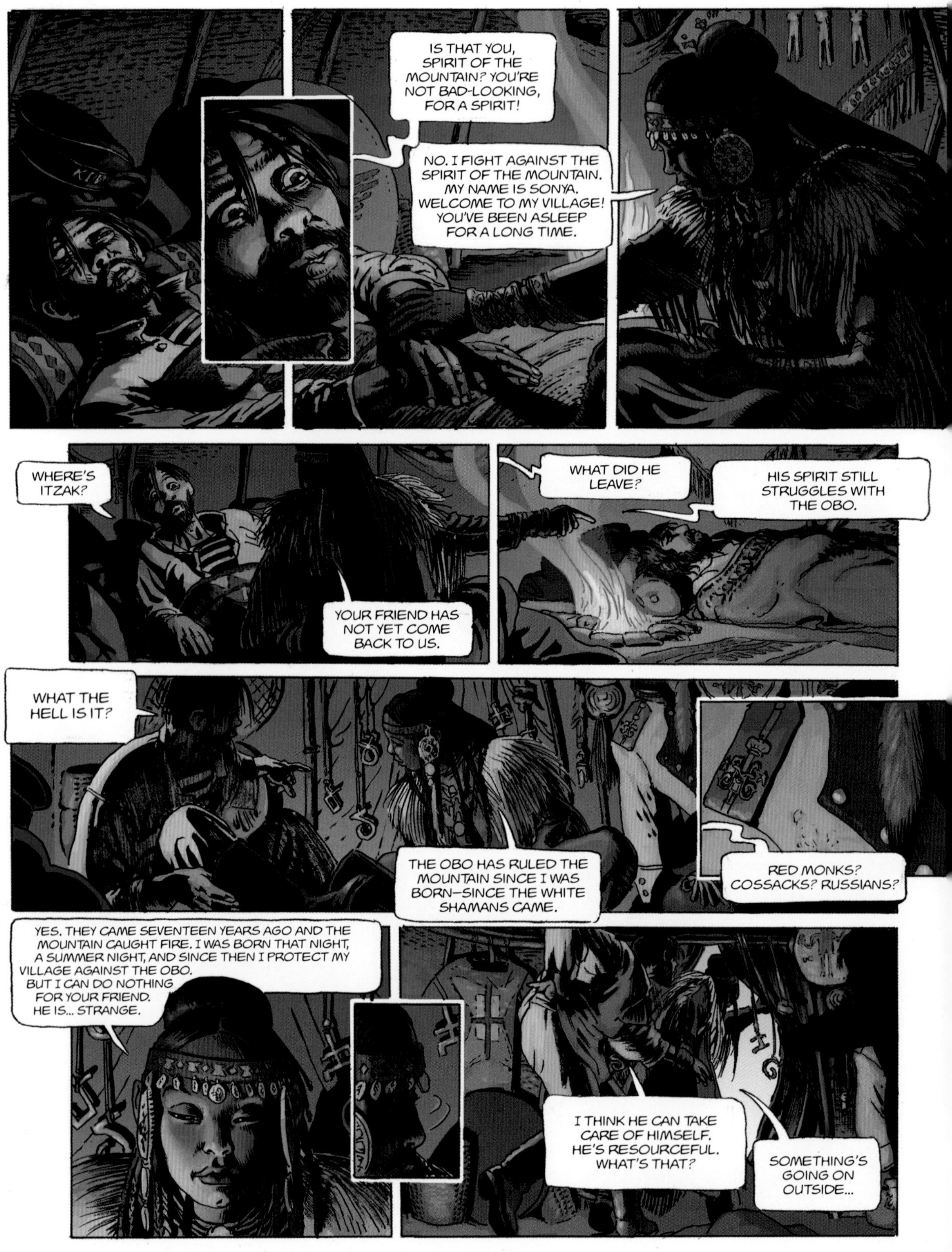
IS THAT YOU, SPIRIT OF THE MOUNTAIN? YOU'RE NOT BAD-LOOKING, FOR A SPIRIT!
NO. I FIGHT AGAINST THE SPIRIT OF THE MOUNTAIN. MY NAME IS SONYA. WELCOME TO MY VILLAGE! YOU'VE BEEN ASLEEP FOR A LONG TIME.
WHERE'S ITZAK?
YOUR FRIEND HAS NOT YET COME BACK TO US.
WHAT DID HE LEAVE?
HIS SPIRIT STILL STRUGGLES WITH THE OBO.
WHAT THE HELL IS IT?
THE OBO HAS RULED THE MOUNTAIN SINCE I WAS BORN—SINCE THE WHITE SHAMANS CAME.
RED MONKS? COSSACKS? RUSSIANS?
YES. THEY CAME SEVENTEEN YEARS AGO AND THE MOUNTAIN CAUGHT FIRE. I WAS BORN THAT NIGHT, A SUMMER NIGHT, AND SINCE THEN I PROTECT MY VILLAGE AGAINST THE OBO. BUT I CAN DO NOTHING FOR YOUR FRIEND. HE IS... STRANGE.
I THINK HE CAN TAKE CARE OF HIMSELF. HE'S RESOURCEFUL. WHAT'S THAT?
SOMETHING'S GOING ON OUTSIDE...

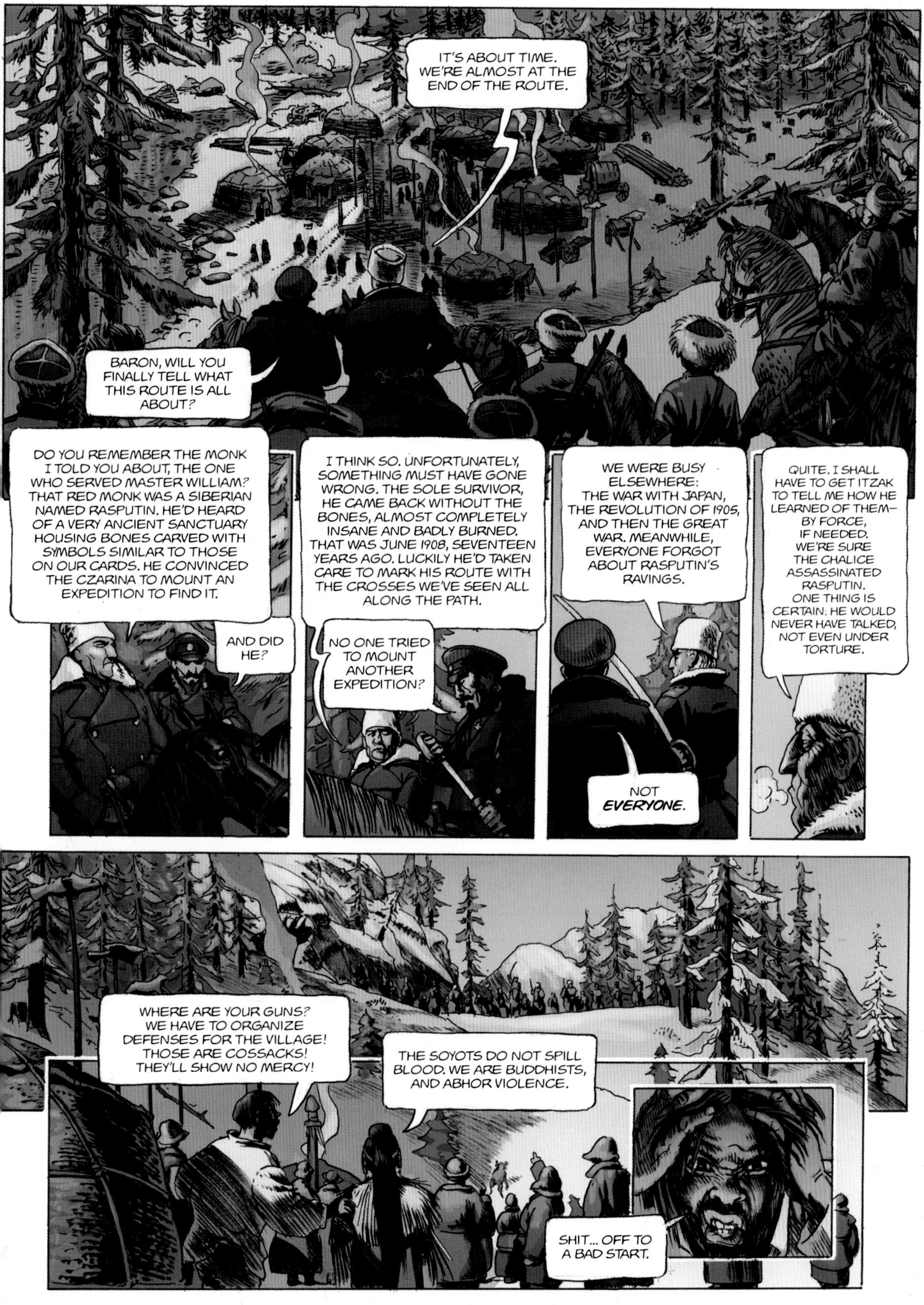
IT'S ABOUT TIME. WE'RE ALMOST AT THE END OF THE ROUTE.
BARON, WILL YOU FINALLY TELL WHAT THIS ROUTE IS ALL ABOUT?
DO YOU REMEMBER THE MONK I TOLD YOU ABOUT, THE ONE WHO SERVED MASTER WILLIAM? THAT RED MONK WAS A SIBERIAN NAMED RASPUTIN. HE'D HEARD OF A VERY ANCIENT SANCTUARY HOUSING BONES CARVED WITH SYMBOLS SIMILAR TO THOSE ON OUR CARDS. HE CONVINCED THE CZARINA TO MOUNT AN EXPEDITION TO FIND IT.
AND DID HE?
I THINK SO. UNFORTUNATELY, SOMETHING MUST HAVE GONE WRONG. THE SOLE SURVIVOR, HE CAME BACK WITHOUT THE BONES, ALMOST COMPLETELY INSANE AND BADLY BURNED. THAT WAS JUNE 1908, SEVENTEEN YEARS AGO. LUCKILY HE'D TAKEN CARE TO MARK HIS ROUTE WITH THE CROSSES WE'VE SEEN ALL ALONG THE PATH.
NO ONE TRIED TO MOUNT ANOTHER EXPEDITION?
WE WERE BUSY ELSEWHERE: THE WAR WITH JAPAN, THE REVOLUTION OF 1905, AND THEN THE GREAT WAR. MEANWHILE, EVERYONE FORGOT ABOUT RASPUTIN'S RAVINGS.
NOT *EVERYONE*.
QUITE. I SHALL HAVE TO GET ITZAK TO TELL ME HOW HE LEARNED OF THEM— BY FORCE, IF NEEDED. WE'RE SURE THE CHALICE ASSASSINATED RASPUTIN. ONE THING IS CERTAIN: HE WOULD NEVER HAVE TALKED, NOT EVEN UNDER TORTURE.
WHERE ARE YOUR GUNS? WE HAVE TO ORGANIZE DEFENSES FOR THE VILLAGE! THOSE ARE COSSACKS! THEY'LL SHOW NO MERCY!
THE SOYOTS DO NOT SPILL BLOOD. WE ARE BUDDHISTS, AND ABHOR VIOLENCE.
SHIT... OFF TO A BAD START.

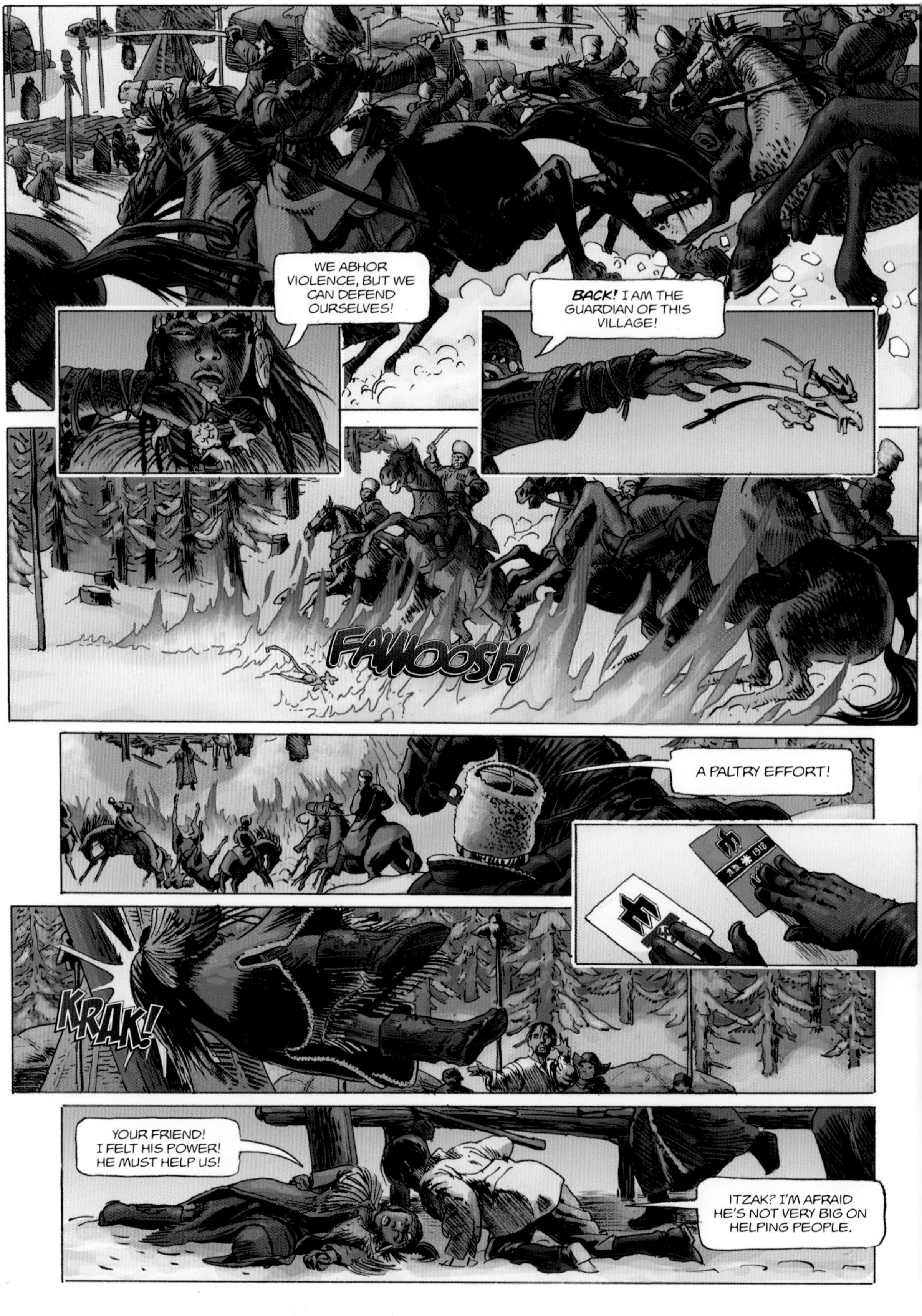
WE ABHOR VIOLENCE, BUT WE CAN DEFEND OURSELVES!
BACK! I AM THE GUARDIAN OF THIS VILLAGE!
FAWOOSH
A PALTRY EFFORT!
1918
KRAK!
YOUR FRIEND! I FELT HIS POWER! HE MUST HELP US!
ITZAK? I'M AFRAID HE'S NOT VERY BIG ON HELPING PEOPLE.

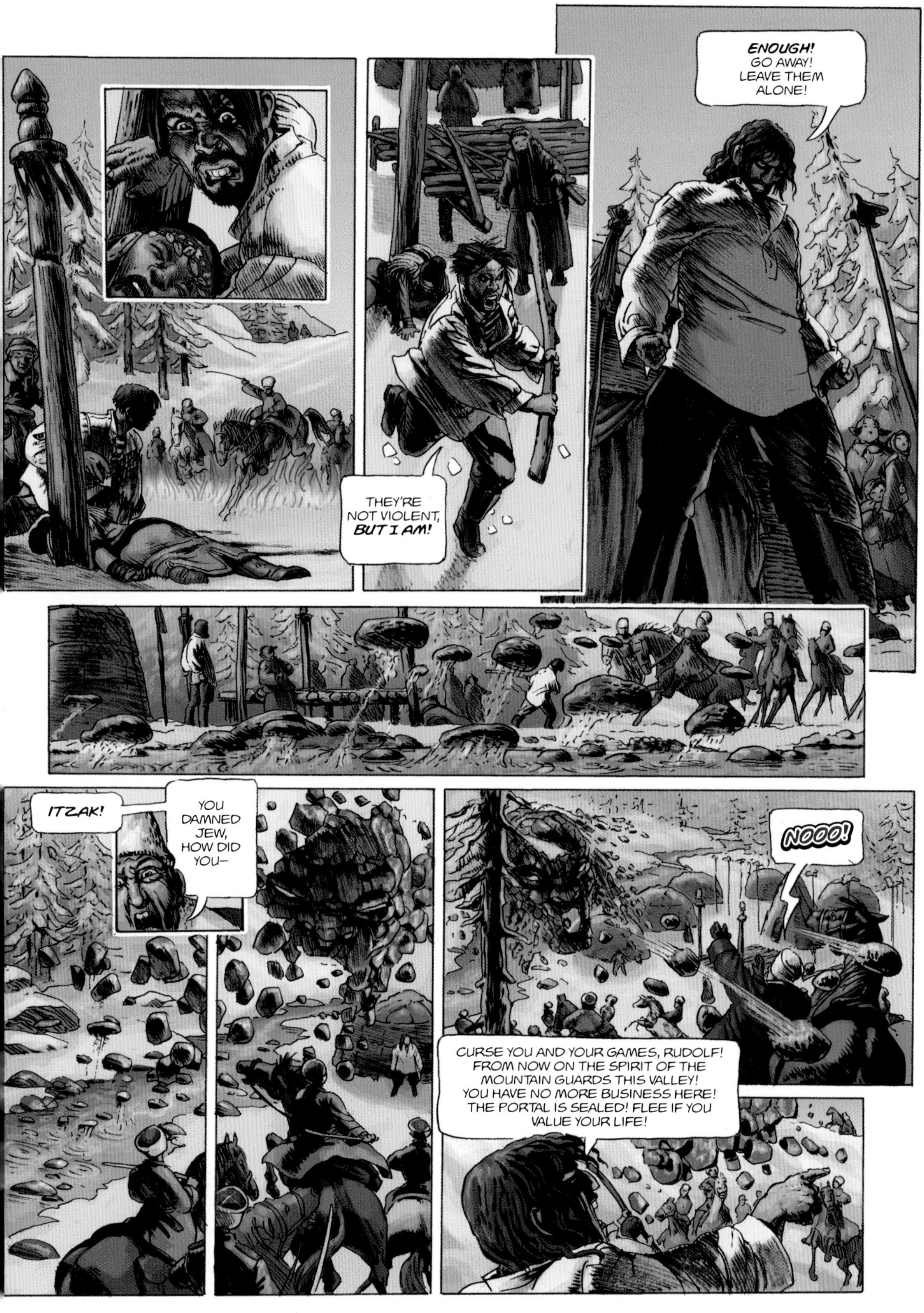
THEY'RE NOT VIOLENT, BUT I AM!
ENOUGH! GO AWAY! LEAVE THEM ALONE!
ITZAK!
YOU DAMNED JEW, HOW DID YOU–
NOOO!
CURSE YOU AND YOUR GAMES, RUDOLF! FROM NOW ON THE SPIRIT OF THE MOUNTAIN GUARDS THIS VALLEY! YOU HAVE NO MORE BUSINESS HERE! THE PORTAL IS SEALED! FLEE IF YOU VALUE YOUR LIFE!

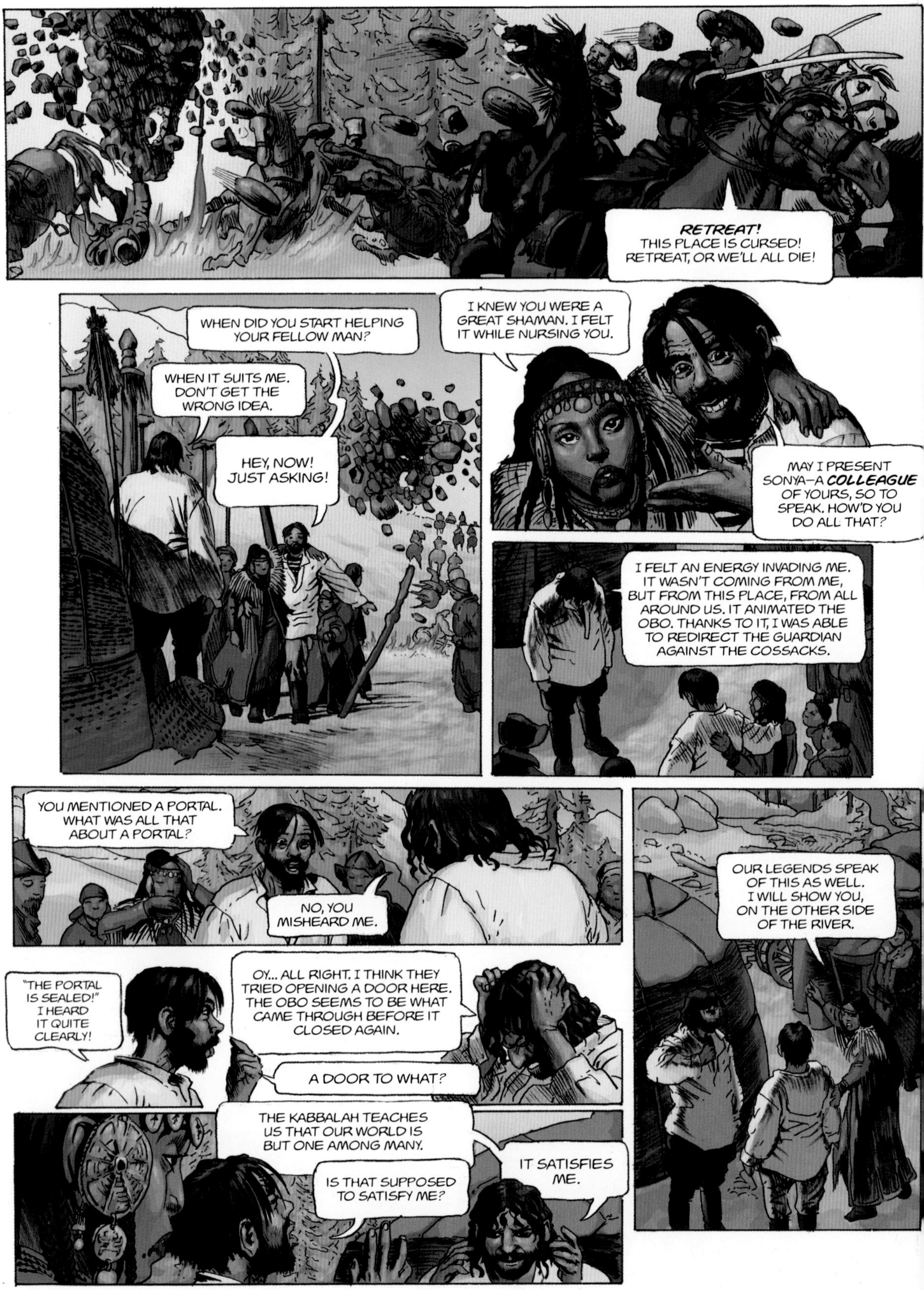
RETREAT! THIS PLACE IS CURSED! RETREAT, OR WE'LL ALL DIE!
WHEN DID YOU START HELPING YOUR FELLOW MAN?
WHEN IT SUITS ME. DON'T GET THE WRONG IDEA.
HEY, NOW! JUST ASKING!
I KNEW YOU WERE A GREAT SHAMAN. I FELT IT WHILE NURSING YOU.
MAY I PRESENT SONYA—A COLLEAGUE OF YOURS, SO TO SPEAK. HOW'D YOU DO ALL THAT?
I FELT AN ENERGY INVADING ME. IT WASN'T COMING FROM ME, BUT FROM THIS PLACE, FROM ALL AROUND US. IT ANIMATED THE OBO. THANKS TO IT, I WAS ABLE TO REDIRECT THE GUARDIAN AGAINST THE COSSACKS.
YOU MENTIONED A PORTAL. WHAT WAS ALL THAT ABOUT A PORTAL?
NO, YOU MISHEARD ME.
"THE PORTAL IS SEALED!" I HEARD IT QUITE CLEARLY!
OY... ALL RIGHT. I THINK THEY TRIED OPENING A DOOR HERE. THE OBO SEEMS TO BE WHAT CAME THROUGH BEFORE IT CLOSED AGAIN.
A DOOR TO WHAT?
THE KABBALAH TEACHES US THAT OUR WORLD IS BUT ONE AMONG MANY.
IS THAT SUPPOSED TO SATISFY ME?
IT SATISFIES ME.
OUR LEGENDS SPEAK OF THIS AS WELL. I WILL SHOW YOU, ON THE OTHER SIDE OF THE RIVER.

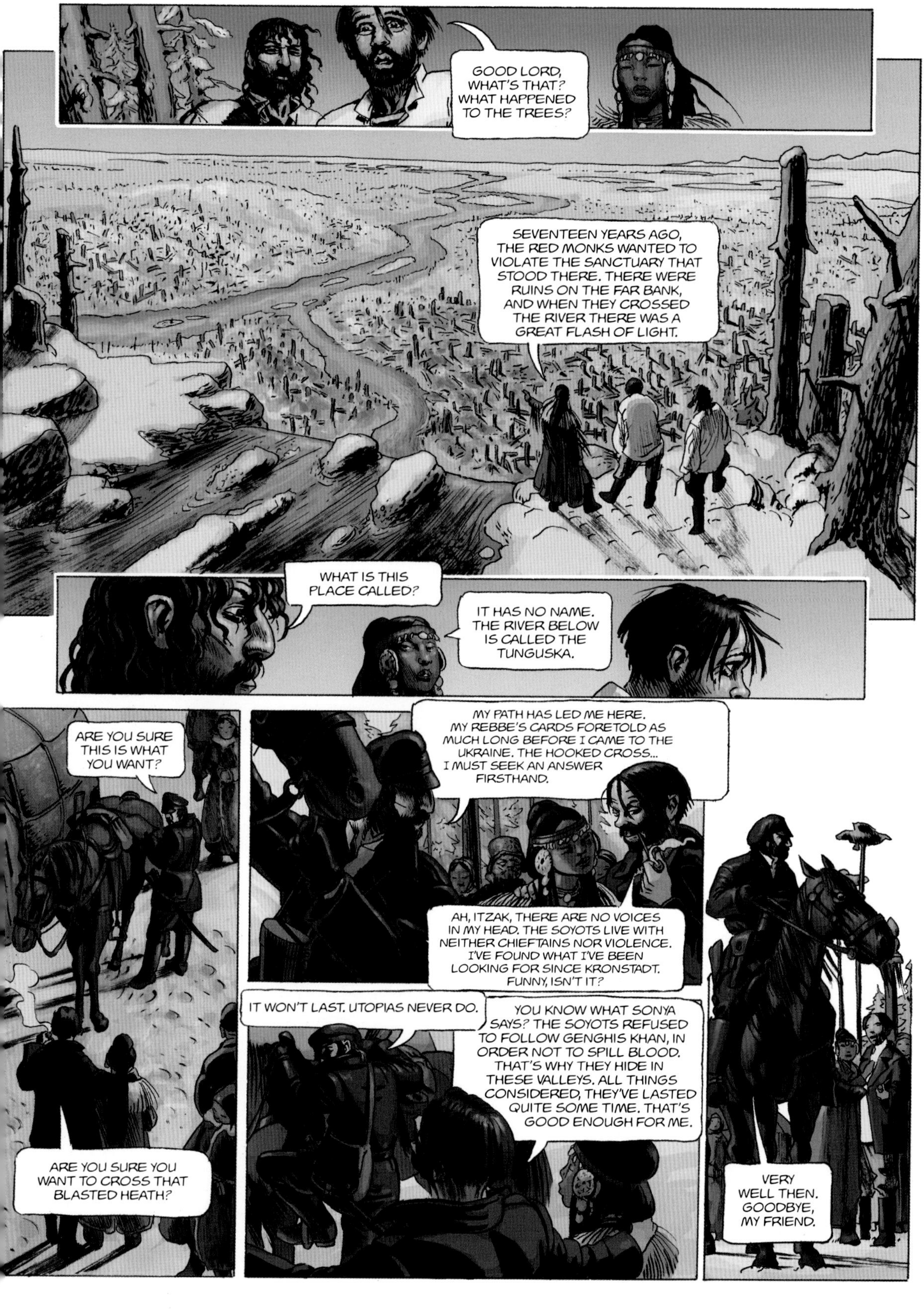
GOOD LORD, WHAT'S THAT? WHAT HAPPENED TO THE TREES?
SEVENTEEN YEARS AGO, THE RED MONKS WANTED TO VIOLATE THE SANCTUARY THAT STOOD THERE. THERE WERE RUINS ON THE FAR BANK, AND WHEN THEY CROSSED THE RIVER THERE WAS A GREAT FLASH OF LIGHT.
WHAT IS THIS PLACE CALLED?
IT HAS NO NAME. THE RIVER BELOW IS CALLED THE TUNGUSKA.
ARE YOU SURE THIS IS WHAT YOU WANT?
MY PATH HAS LED ME HERE. MY REBBE'S CARDS FORETOLD AS MUCH LONG BEFORE I CAME TO THE UKRAINE. THE HOOKED CROSS... I MUST SEEK AN ANSWER FIRSTHAND.
AH, ITZAK, THERE ARE NO VOICES IN MY HEAD. THE SOYOTS LIVE WITH NEITHER CHIEFTAINS NOR VIOLENCE. I'VE FOUND WHAT I'VE BEEN LOOKING FOR SINCE KRONSTADT. FUNNY, ISN'T IT?
ARE YOU SURE YOU WANT TO CROSS THAT BLASTED HEATH?
IT WON'T LAST. UTOPIAS NEVER DO.
YOU KNOW WHAT SONYA SAYS? THE SOYOTS REFUSED TO FOLLOW GENGHIS KHAN, IN ORDER NOT TO SPILL BLOOD. THAT'S WHY THEY HIDE IN THESE VALLEYS. ALL THINGS CONSIDERED, THEY'VE LASTED QUITE SOME TIME. THAT'S GOOD ENOUGH FOR ME.
VERY WELL THEN. GOODBYE, MY FRIEND.

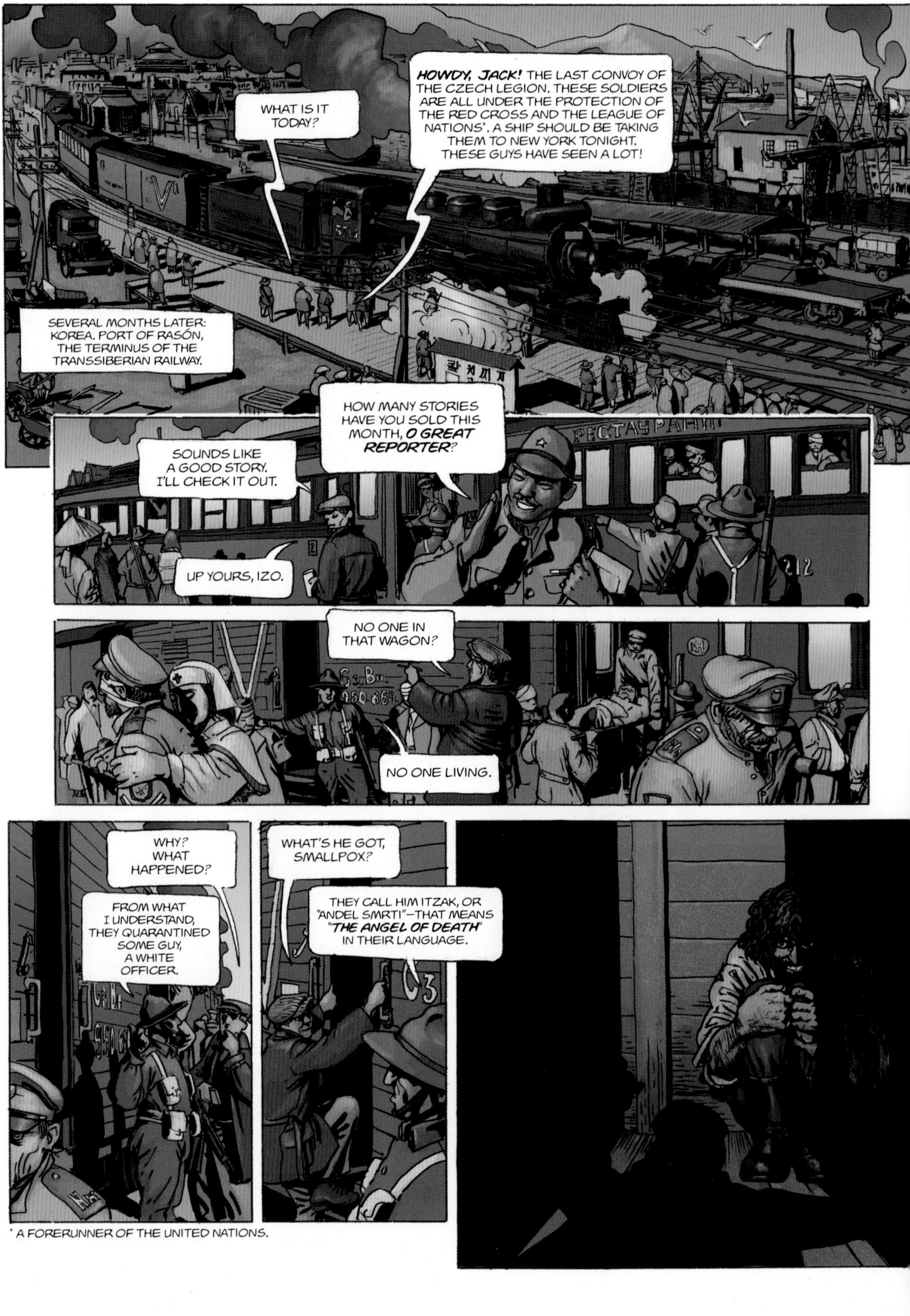
SEVERAL MONTHS LATER: KOREA. PORT OF RASÓN, THE TERMINUS OF THE TRANSSIBERIAN RAILWAY.
WHAT IS IT TODAY?
HOWDY, JACK! THE LAST CONVOY OF THE CZECH LEGION. THESE SOLDIERS ARE ALL UNDER THE PROTECTION OF THE RED CROSS AND THE LEAGUE OF NATIONS*. A SHIP SHOULD BE TAKING THEM TO NEW YORK TONIGHT. THESE GUYS HAVE SEEN A LOT!
SOUNDS LIKE A GOOD STORY. I'LL CHECK IT OUT.
HOW MANY STORIES HAVE YOU SOLD THIS MONTH, O GREAT REPORTER?
UP YOURS, IZO.
NO ONE IN THAT WAGON?
NO ONE LIVING.
WHY? WHAT HAPPENED?
FROM WHAT I UNDERSTAND, THEY QUARANTINED SOME GUY, A WHITE OFFICER.
WHAT'S HE GOT, SMALLPOX?
THEY CALL HIM ITZAK, OR "ANDEL SMRTI"—THAT MEANS "THE ANGEL OF DEATH" IN THEIR LANGUAGE.

* A FORERUNNER OF THE UNITED NATIONS.

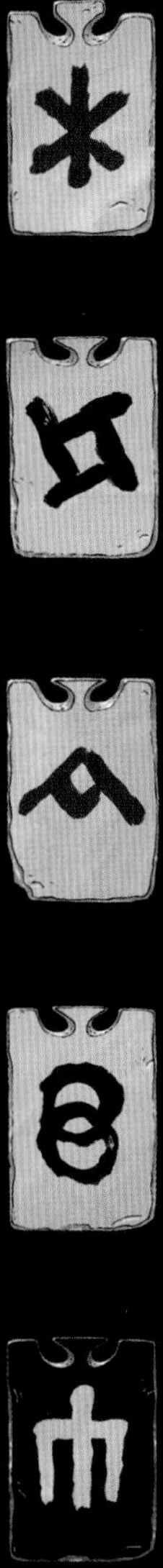

1940 A.D.

BOOK ELEVEN
NADJA

1940 A.D.

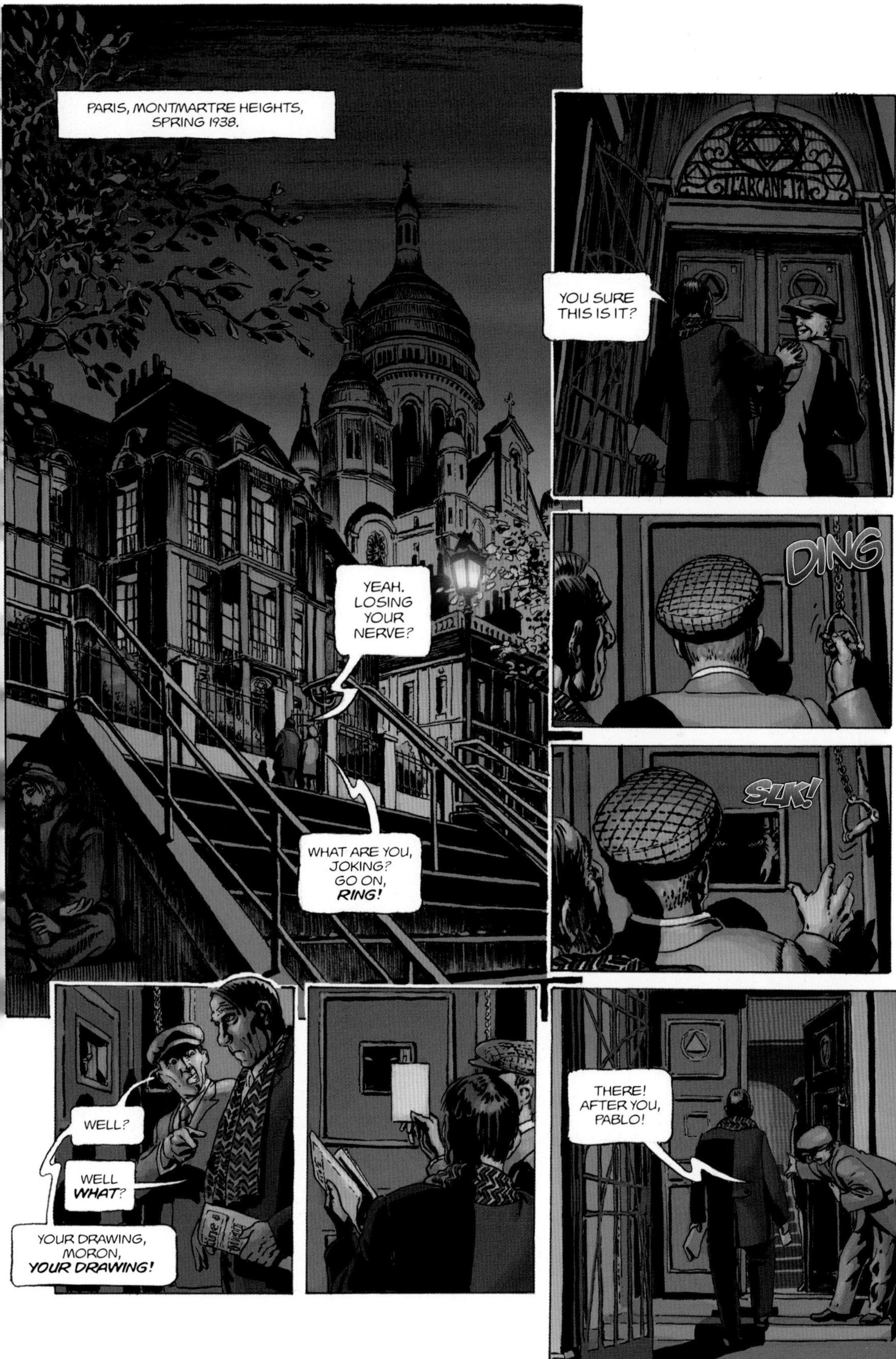
PARIS, MONTMARTRE HEIGHTS, SPRING 1938.
YOU SURE THIS IS IT?
YEAH. LOSING YOUR NERVE?
WHAT ARE YOU, JOKING? GO ON, **RING!**
DING
SLIK!
WELL?
WELL **WHAT**?
YOUR DRAWING, MORON, **YOUR DRAWING!**
THERE! AFTER YOU, PABLO!

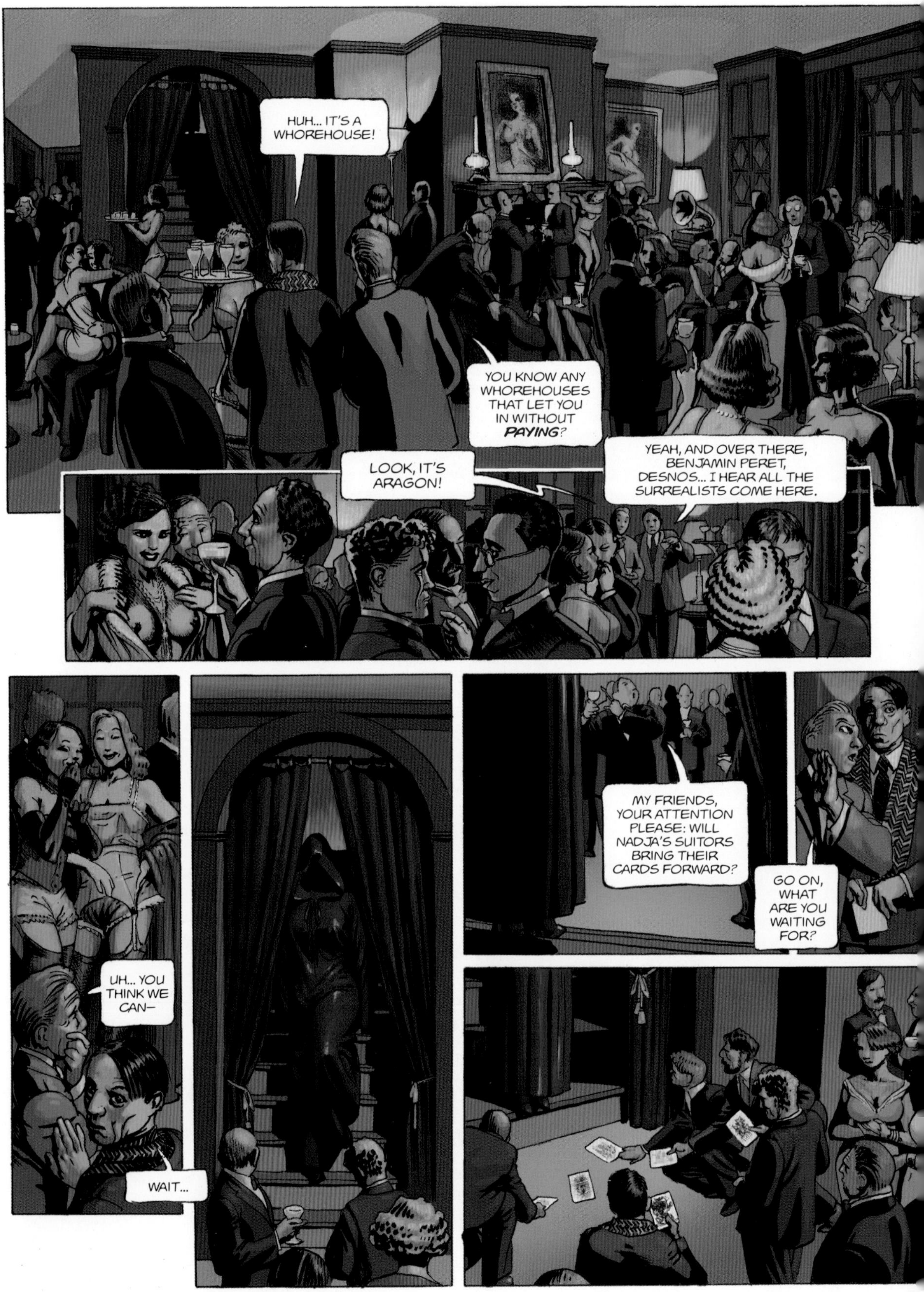
HUH... IT'S A WHOREHOUSE!
YOU KNOW ANY WHOREHOUSES THAT LET YOU IN WITHOUT PAYING?
LOOK, IT'S ARAGON!
YEAH, AND OVER THERE, BENJAMIN PERET, DESNOS... I HEAR ALL THE SURREALISTS COME HERE.
UH... YOU THINK WE CAN–
WAIT...
MY FRIENDS, YOUR ATTENTION PLEASE: WILL NADJA'S SUITORS BRING THEIR CARDS FORWARD?
GO ON, WHAT ARE YOU WAITING FOR?

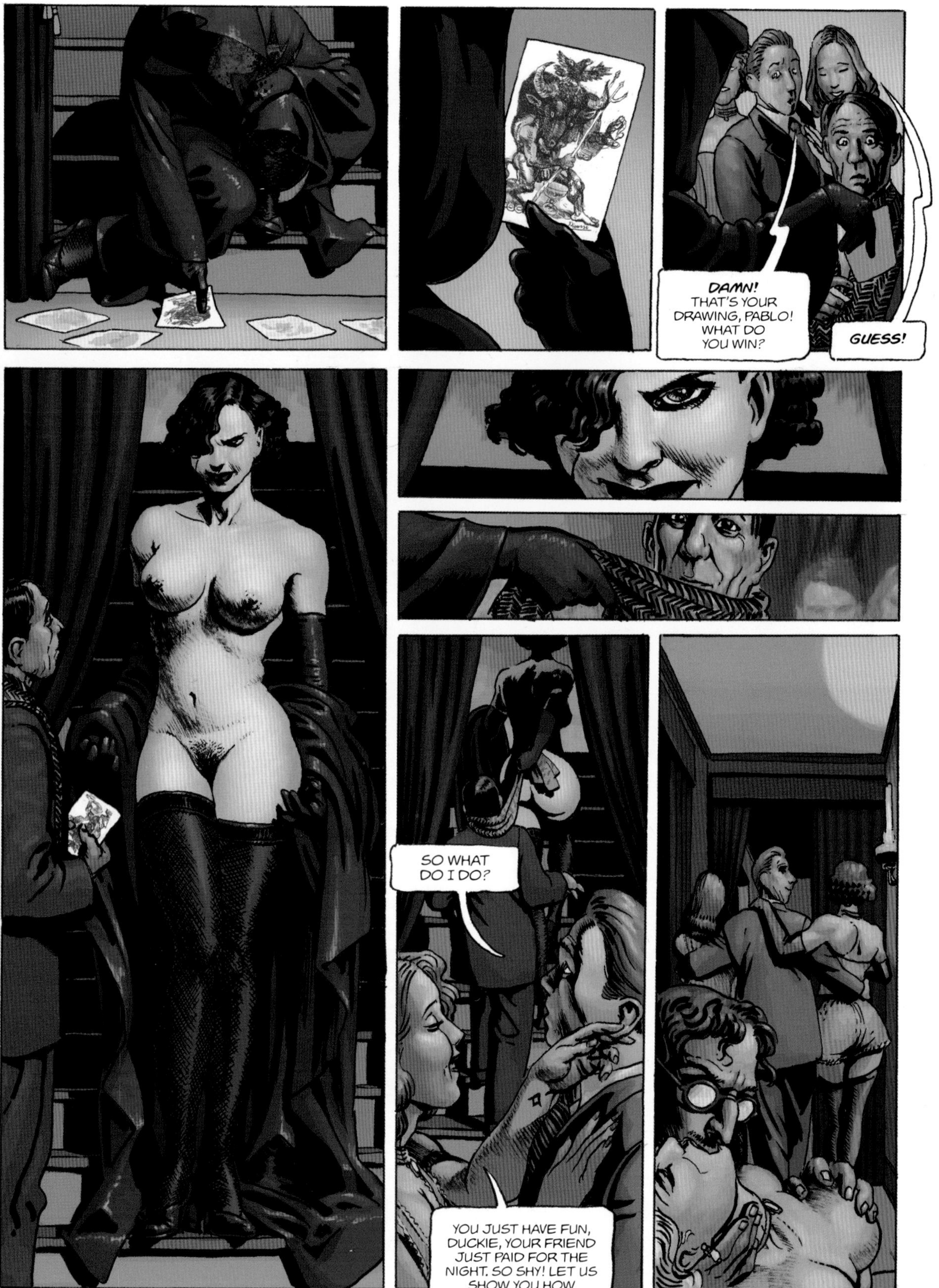
DAMN! THAT'S YOUR DRAWING, PABLO! WHAT DO YOU WIN?
GUESS!
SO WHAT DO I DO?
YOU JUST HAVE FUN, DUCKIE, YOUR FRIEND JUST PAID FOR THE NIGHT. SO SHY! LET US SHOW YOU HOW IT'S DONE.

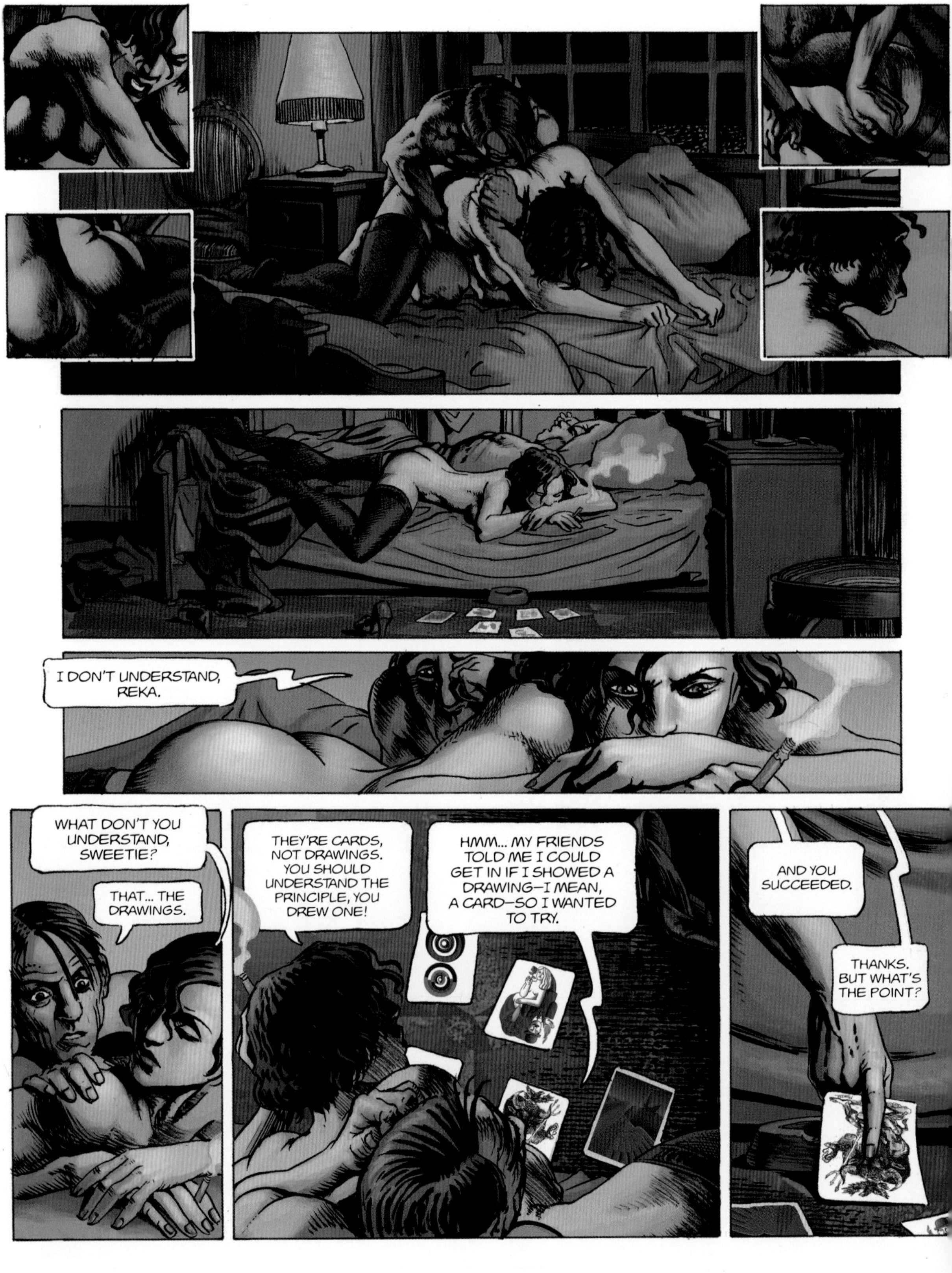
I DON'T UNDERSTAND, REKA.
WHAT DON'T YOU UNDERSTAND, SWEETIE?
THAT... THE DRAWINGS.
THEY'RE CARDS, NOT DRAWINGS. YOU SHOULD UNDERSTAND THE PRINCIPLE, YOU DREW ONE!
HMM... MY FRIENDS TOLD ME I COULD GET IN IF I SHOWED A DRAWING—I MEAN, A CARD—SO I WANTED TO TRY.
AND YOU SUCCEEDED.
THANKS. BUT WHAT'S THE POINT?

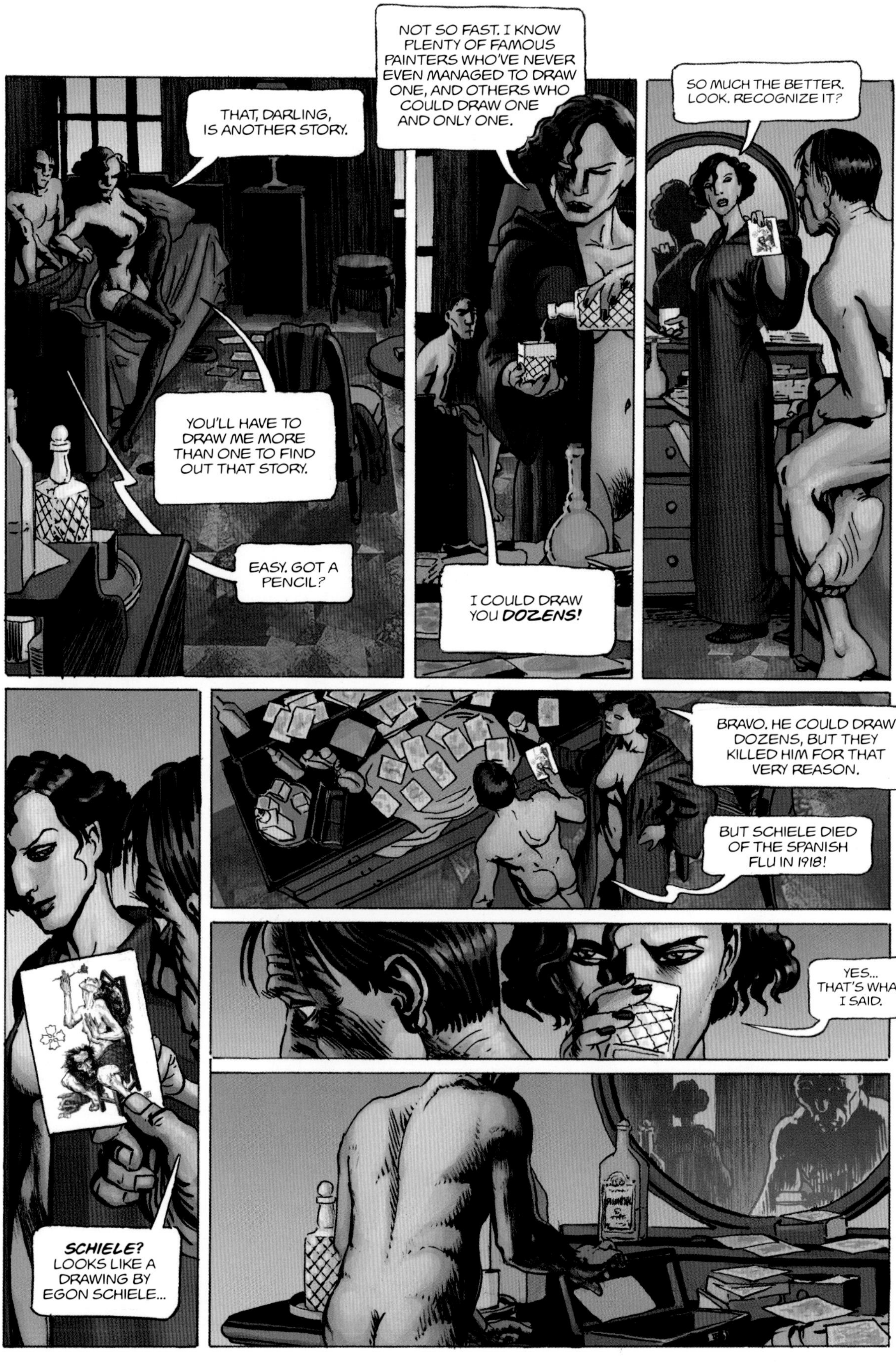
THAT, DARLING, IS ANOTHER STORY.
YOU'LL HAVE TO DRAW ME MORE THAN ONE TO FIND OUT THAT STORY.
EASY. GOT A PENCIL?
NOT SO FAST. I KNOW PLENTY OF FAMOUS PAINTERS WHO'VE NEVER EVEN MANAGED TO DRAW ONE, AND OTHERS WHO COULD DRAW ONE AND ONLY ONE.
I COULD DRAW YOU **DOZENS!**
SO MUCH THE BETTER. LOOK. RECOGNIZE IT?
SCHIELE? LOOKS LIKE A DRAWING BY EGON SCHIELE...
BRAVO. HE COULD DRAW DOZENS, BUT THEY KILLED HIM FOR THAT VERY REASON.
BUT SCHIELE DIED OF THE SPANISH FLU IN 1918!
YES... THAT'S WHAT I SAID.

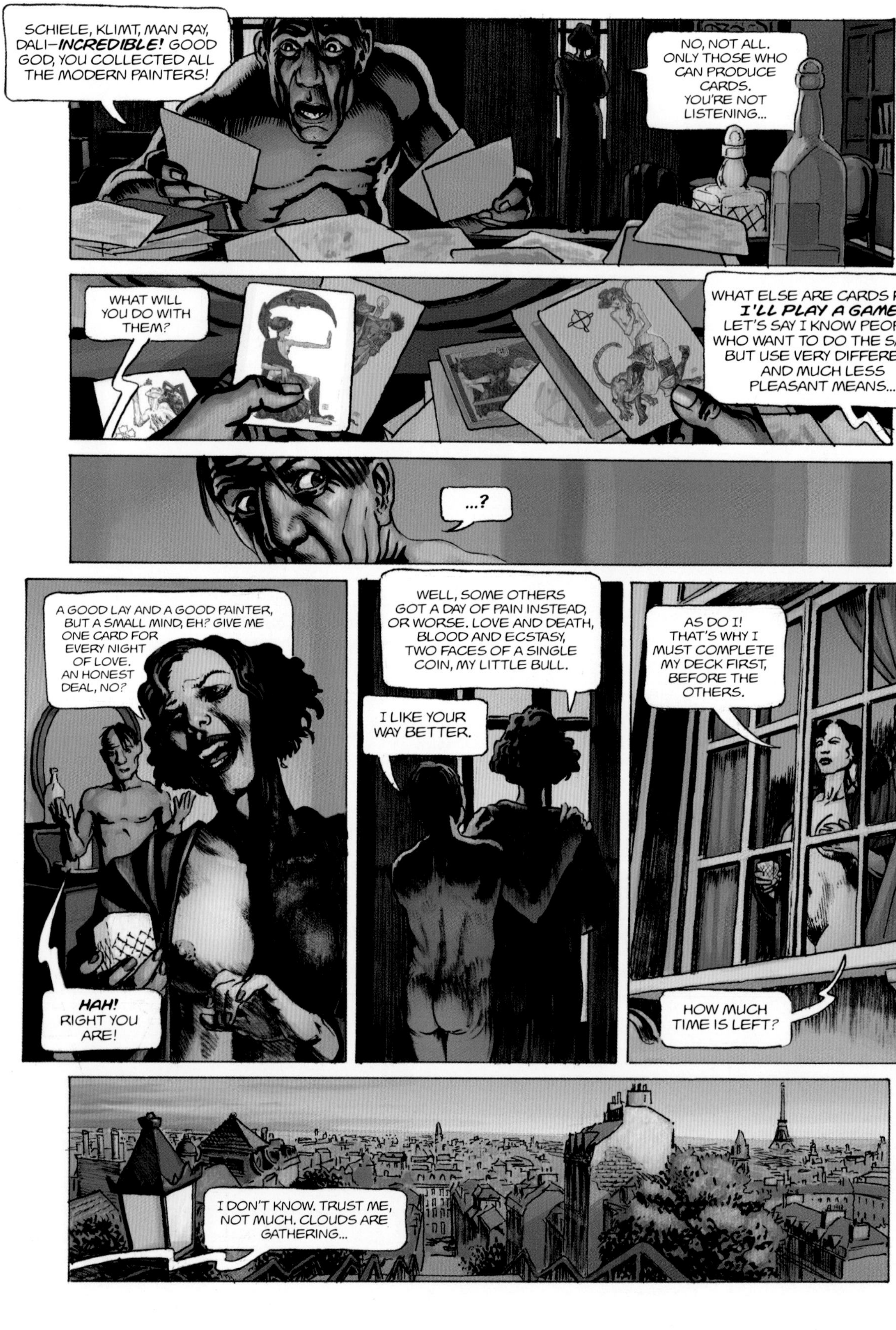
SCHIELE, KLIMT, MAN RAY, DALI—INCREDIBLE! GOOD GOD, YOU COLLECTED ALL THE MODERN PAINTERS!
NO, NOT ALL. ONLY THOSE WHO CAN PRODUCE CARDS. YOU'RE NOT LISTENING...
WHAT WILL YOU DO WITH THEM?
WHAT ELSE ARE CARDS FOR? I'LL PLAY A GAME! LET'S SAY I KNOW PEOPLE WHO WANT TO DO THE SAME, BUT USE VERY DIFFERENT AND MUCH LESS PLEASANT MEANS...
...?
A GOOD LAY AND A GOOD PAINTER, BUT A SMALL MIND, EH? GIVE ME ONE CARD FOR EVERY NIGHT OF LOVE. AN HONEST DEAL, NO?
HAH! RIGHT YOU ARE!
WELL, SOME OTHERS GOT A DAY OF PAIN INSTEAD, OR WORSE. LOVE AND DEATH, BLOOD AND ECSTASY, TWO FACES OF A SINGLE COIN, MY LITTLE BULL.
I LIKE YOUR WAY BETTER.
AS DO I! THAT'S WHY I MUST COMPLETE MY DECK FIRST, BEFORE THE OTHERS.
HOW MUCH TIME IS LEFT?
I DON'T KNOW. TRUST ME, NOT MUCH. CLOUDS ARE GATHERING...

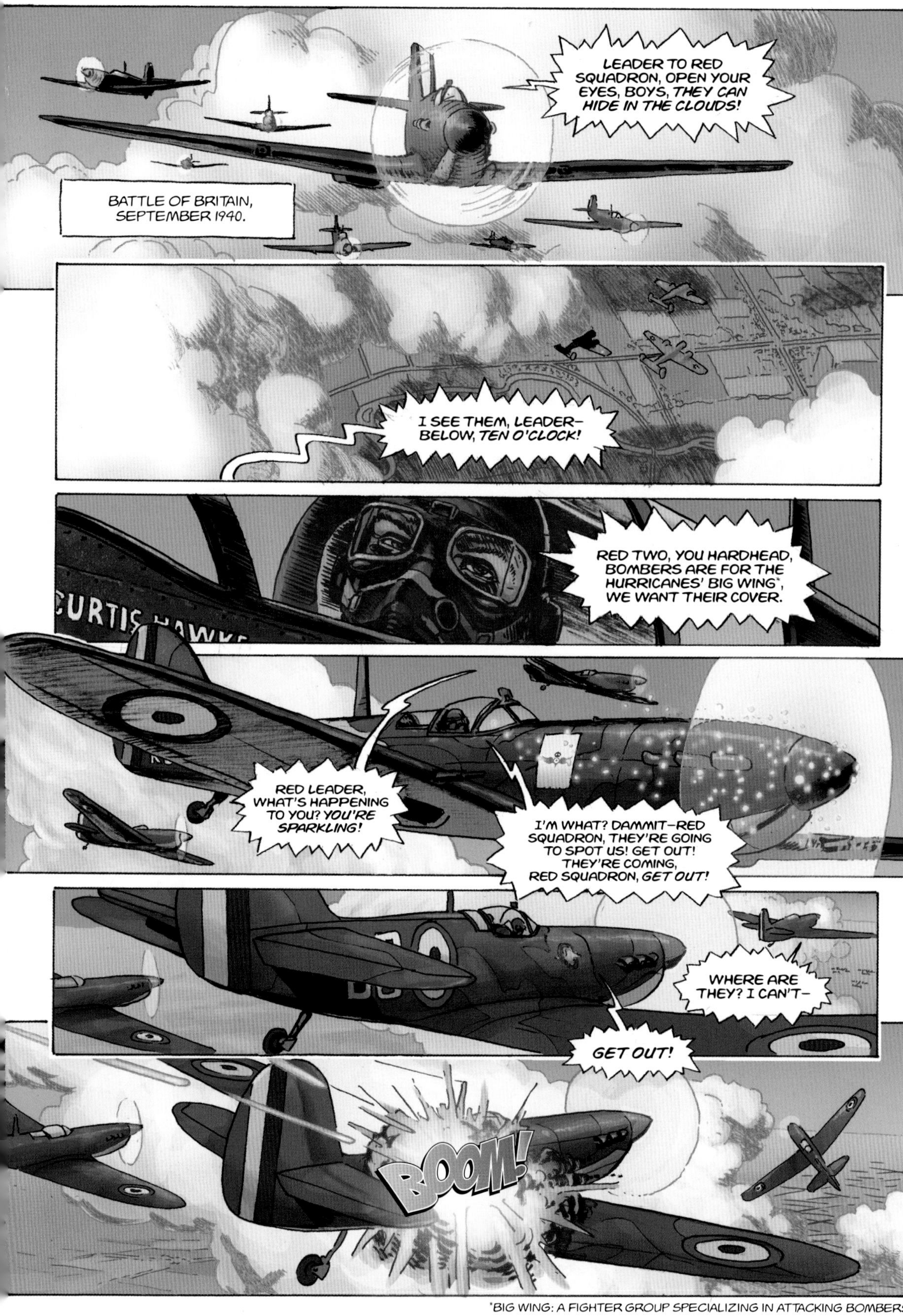
LEADER TO RED SQUADRON, OPEN YOUR EYES, BOYS, THEY CAN HIDE IN THE CLOUDS!
BATTLE OF BRITAIN, SEPTEMBER 1940.
I SEE THEM, LEADER— BELOW, TEN O'CLOCK!
RED TWO, YOU HARDHEAD, BOMBERS ARE FOR THE HURRICANES' BIG WING*, WE WANT THEIR COVER.
CURTIS HAWK
RED LEADER, WHAT'S HAPPENING TO YOU? YOU'RE SPARKLING!
I'M WHAT? DAMMIT—RED SQUADRON, THEY'RE GOING TO SPOT US! GET OUT! THEY'RE COMING, RED SQUADRON, GET OUT!
WHERE ARE THEY? I CAN'T—
GET OUT!
BOOM!

*BIG WING: A FIGHTER GROUP SPECIALIZING IN ATTACKING BOMBERS.

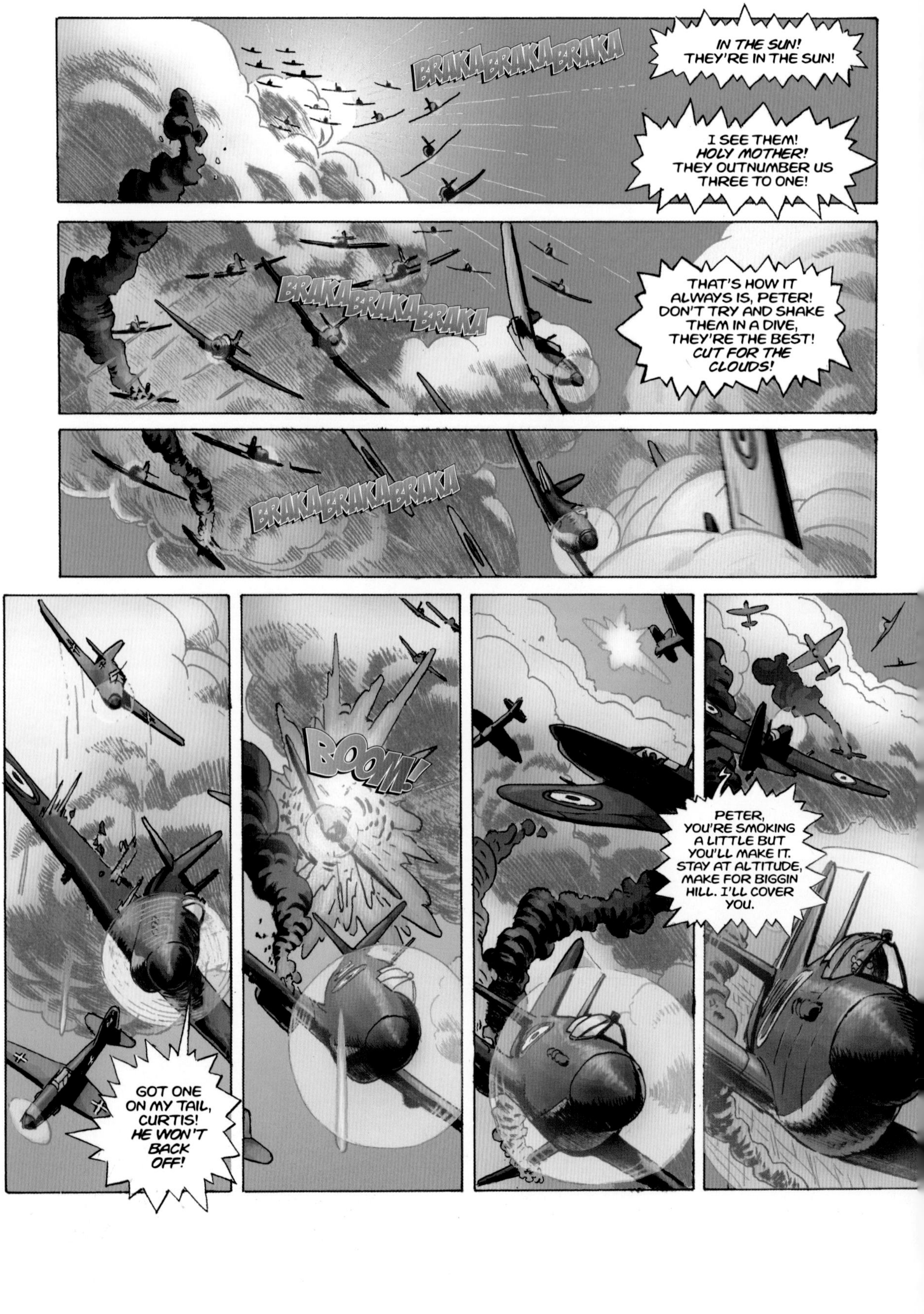
BRAKABRAKABRAKA
IN THE SUN! THEY'RE IN THE SUN!
I SEE THEM! HOLY MOTHER! THEY OUTNUMBER US THREE TO ONE!
BRAKABRAKABRAKA
THAT'S HOW IT ALWAYS IS, PETER! DON'T TRY AND SHAKE THEM IN A DIVE, THEY'RE THE BEST! CUT FOR THE CLOUDS!
BRAKABRAKABRAKA
GOT ONE ON MY TAIL, CURTIS! HE WON'T BACK OFF!
BOOM!
PETER, YOU'RE SMOKING A LITTLE BUT YOU'LL MAKE IT. STAY AT ALTITUDE, MAKE FOR BIGGIN HILL. I'LL COVER YOU.

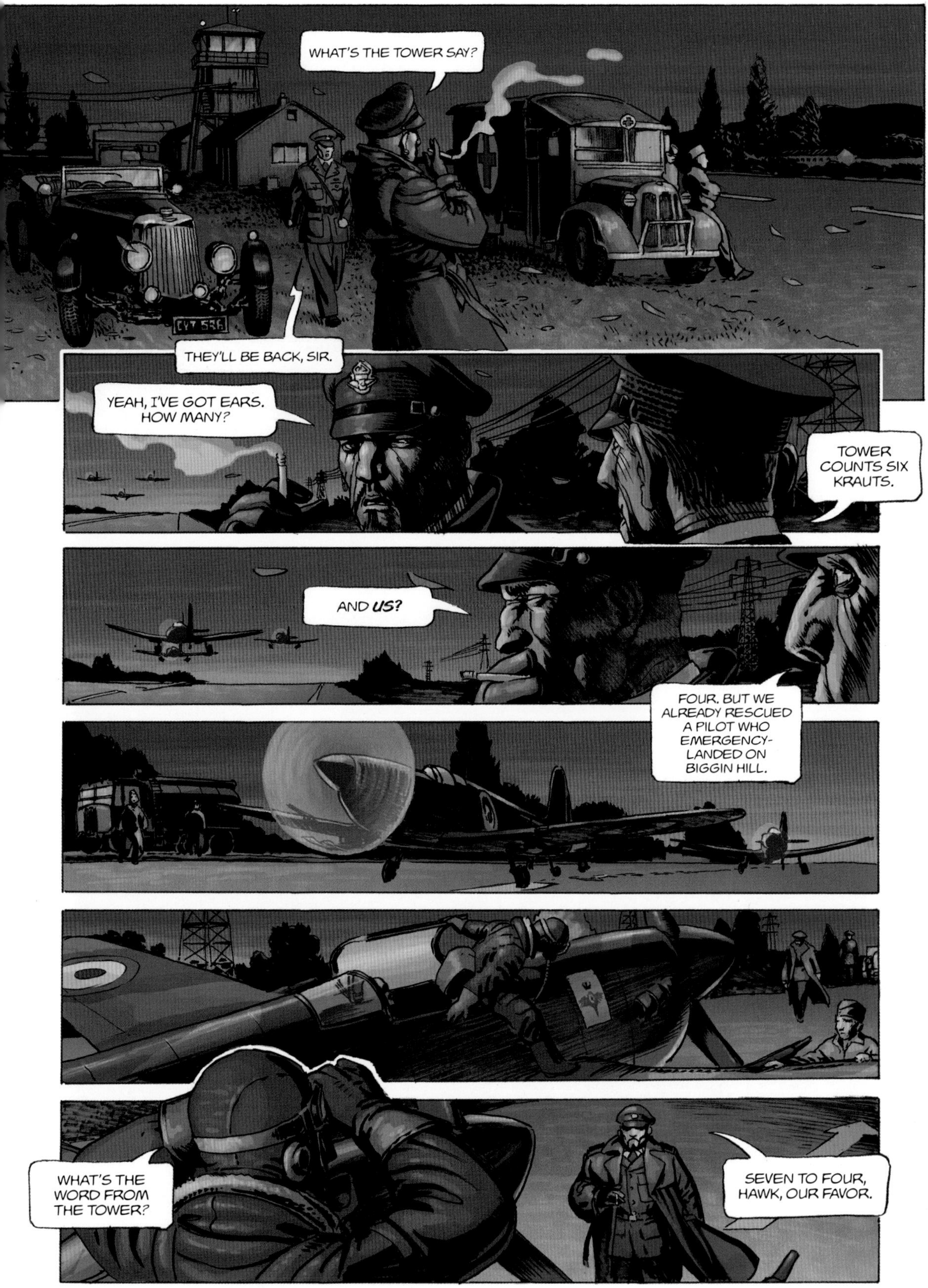
WHAT'S THE TOWER SAY?
THEY'LL BE BACK, SIR.
YEAH, I'VE GOT EARS. HOW MANY?
TOWER COUNTS SIX KRAUTS.
AND US?
FOUR. BUT WE ALREADY RESCUED A PILOT WHO EMERGENCY-LANDED ON BIGGIN HILL.
WHAT'S THE WORD FROM THE TOWER?
SEVEN TO FOUR, HAWK, OUR FAVOR.

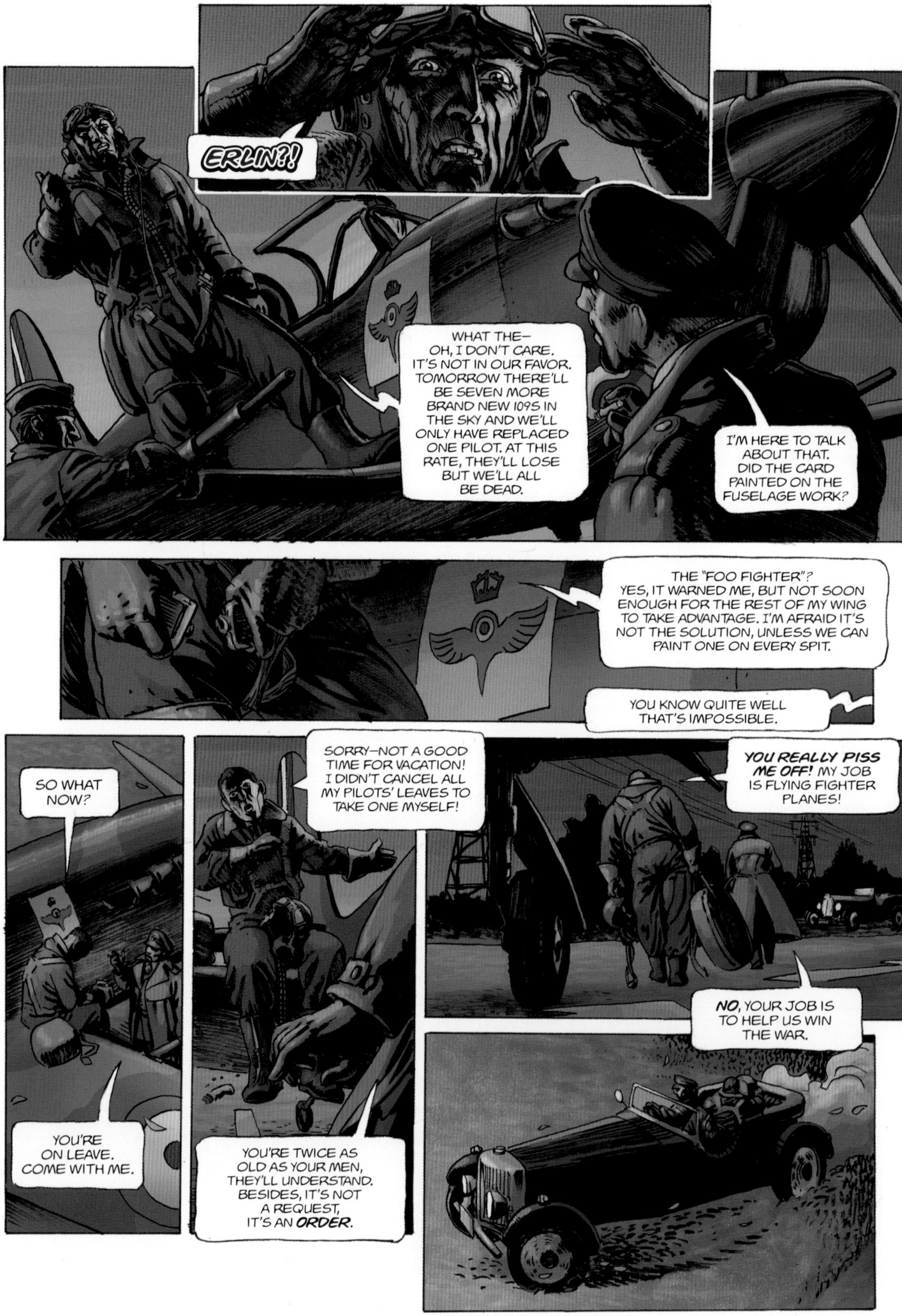
ERLIN?!
WHAT THE— OH, I DON'T CARE. IT'S NOT IN OUR FAVOR. TOMORROW THERE'LL BE SEVEN MORE BRAND NEW 109S IN THE SKY AND WE'LL ONLY HAVE REPLACED ONE PILOT. AT THIS RATE, THEY'LL LOSE BUT WE'LL ALL BE DEAD.
I'M HERE TO TALK ABOUT THAT. DID THE CARD PAINTED ON THE FUSELAGE WORK?
THE "FOO FIGHTER"? YES, IT WARNED ME, BUT NOT SOON ENOUGH FOR THE REST OF MY WING TO TAKE ADVANTAGE. I'M AFRAID IT'S NOT THE SOLUTION, UNLESS WE CAN PAINT ONE ON EVERY SPIT.
YOU KNOW QUITE WELL THAT'S IMPOSSIBLE.
SO WHAT NOW?
YOU'RE ON LEAVE. COME WITH ME.
SORRY—NOT A GOOD TIME FOR VACATION! I DIDN'T CANCEL ALL MY PILOTS' LEAVES TO TAKE ONE MYSELF!
YOU'RE TWICE AS OLD AS YOUR MEN, THEY'LL UNDERSTAND. BESIDES, IT'S NOT A REQUEST, IT'S AN ORDER.
YOU REALLY PISS ME OFF! MY JOB IS FLYING FIGHTER PLANES!
NO, YOUR JOB IS TO HELP US WIN THE WAR.

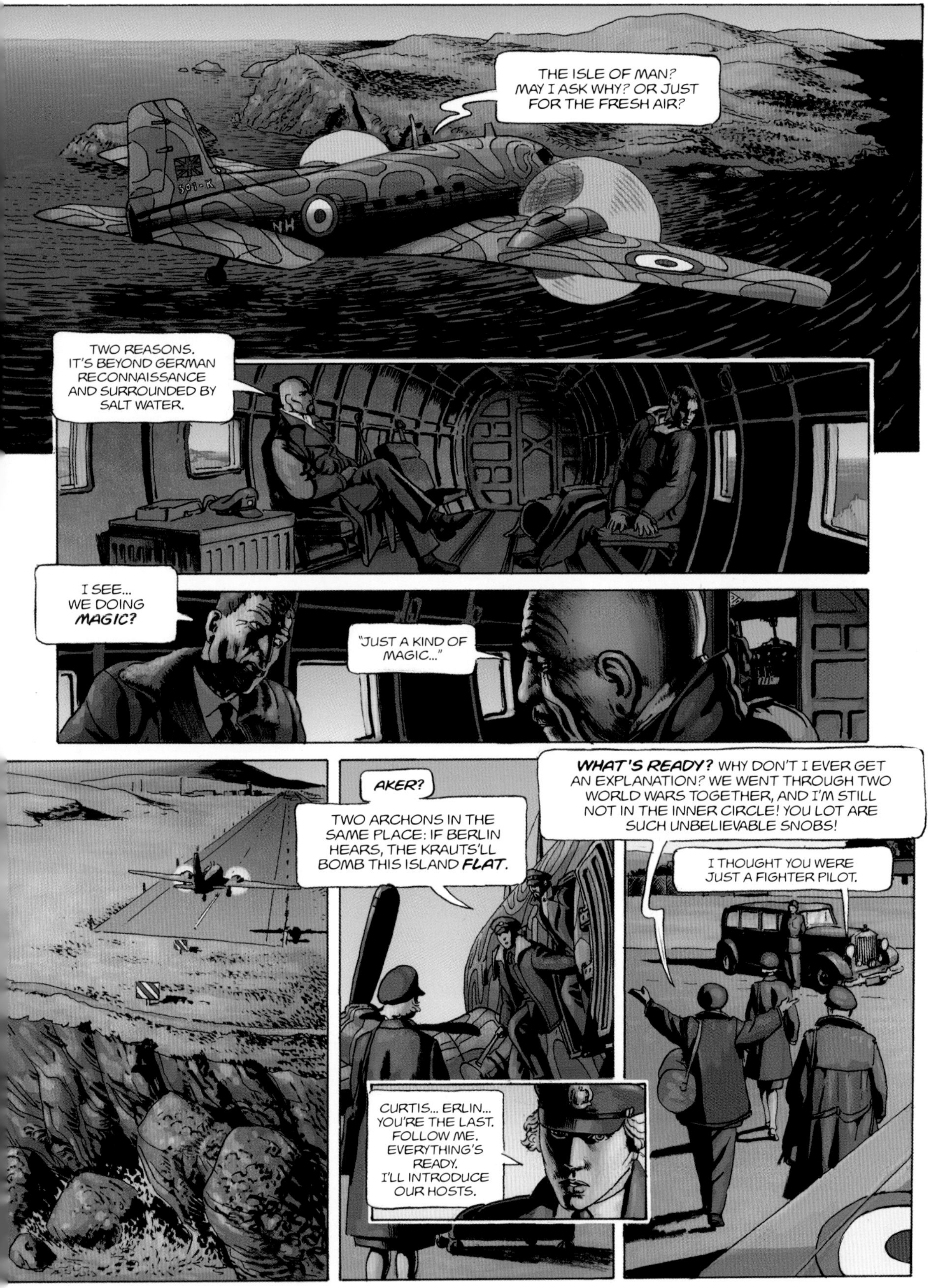
THE ISLE OF MAN? MAY I ASK WHY? OR JUST FOR THE FRESH AIR?
NH
TWO REASONS. IT'S BEYOND GERMAN RECONNAISSANCE AND SURROUNDED BY SALT WATER.
I SEE... WE DOING MAGIC?
"JUST A KIND OF MAGIC..."
AKER?
TWO ARCHONS IN THE SAME PLACE: IF BERLIN HEARS, THE KRAUTS'LL BOMB THIS ISLAND FLAT.
CURTIS... ERLIN... YOU'RE THE LAST. FOLLOW ME. EVERYTHING'S READY. I'LL INTRODUCE OUR HOSTS.
WHAT'S READY? WHY DON'T I EVER GET AN EXPLANATION? WE WENT THROUGH TWO WORLD WARS TOGETHER, AND I'M STILL NOT IN THE INNER CIRCLE! YOU LOT ARE SUCH UNBELIEVABLE SNOBS!
I THOUGHT YOU WERE JUST A FIGHTER PILOT.

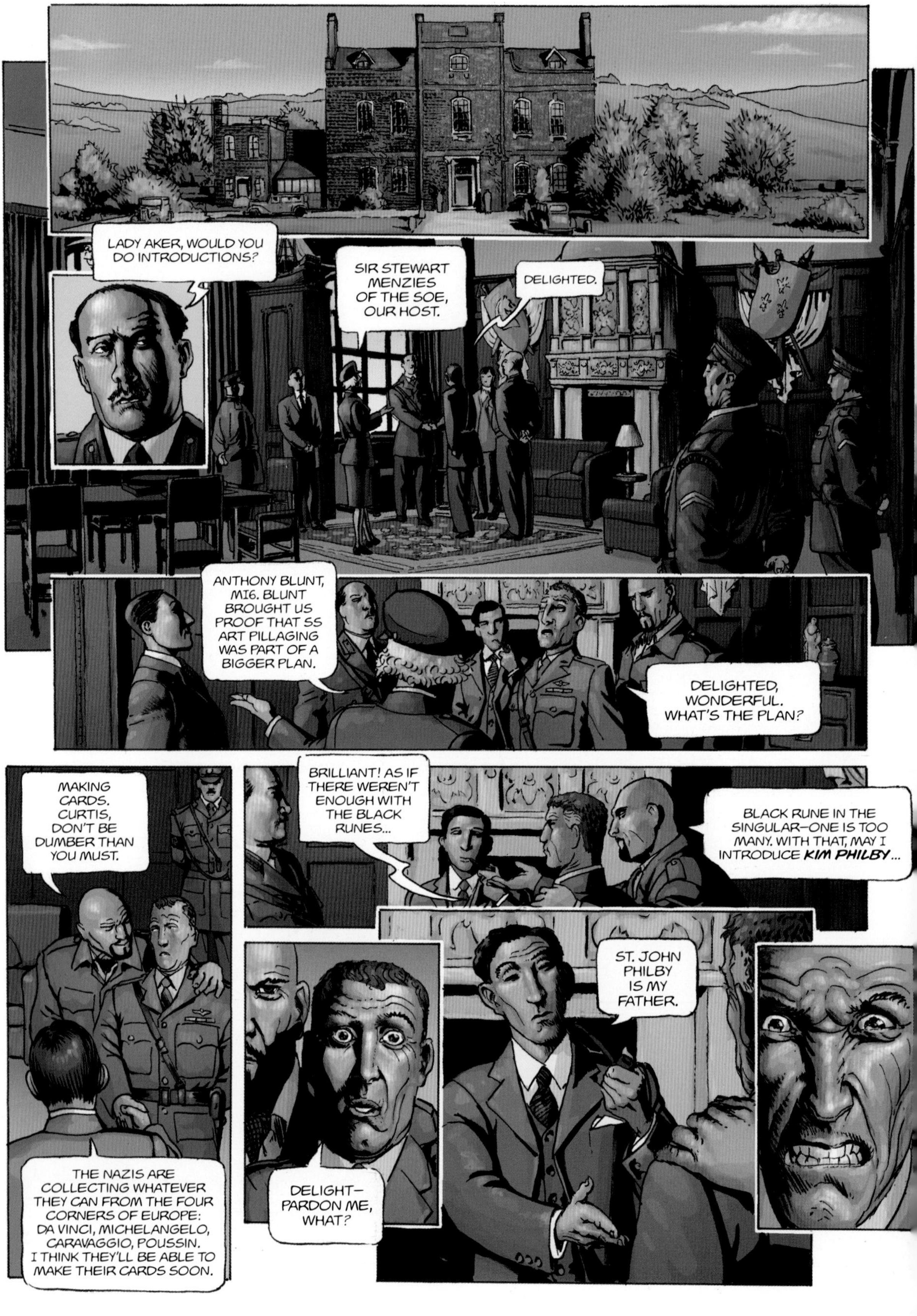
LADY AKER, WOULD YOU DO INTRODUCTIONS?
SIR STEWART MENZIES OF THE SOE, OUR HOST.
DELIGHTED.
ANTHONY BLUNT, MI6. BLUNT BROUGHT US PROOF THAT SS ART PILLAGING WAS PART OF A BIGGER PLAN.
DELIGHTED, WONDERFUL. WHAT'S THE PLAN?
MAKING CARDS. CURTIS, DON'T BE DUMBER THAN YOU MUST.
THE NAZIS ARE COLLECTING WHATEVER THEY CAN FROM THE FOUR CORNERS OF EUROPE: DA VINCI, MICHELANGELO, CARAVAGGIO, POUSSIN. I THINK THEY'LL BE ABLE TO MAKE THEIR CARDS SOON.
BRILLIANT! AS IF THERE WEREN'T ENOUGH WITH THE BLACK RUNES...
BLACK RUNE IN THE SINGULAR—ONE IS TOO MANY. WITH THAT, MAY I INTRODUCE **KIM PHILBY**...
DELIGHT— PARDON ME, WHAT?
ST. JOHN PHILBY IS MY FATHER.

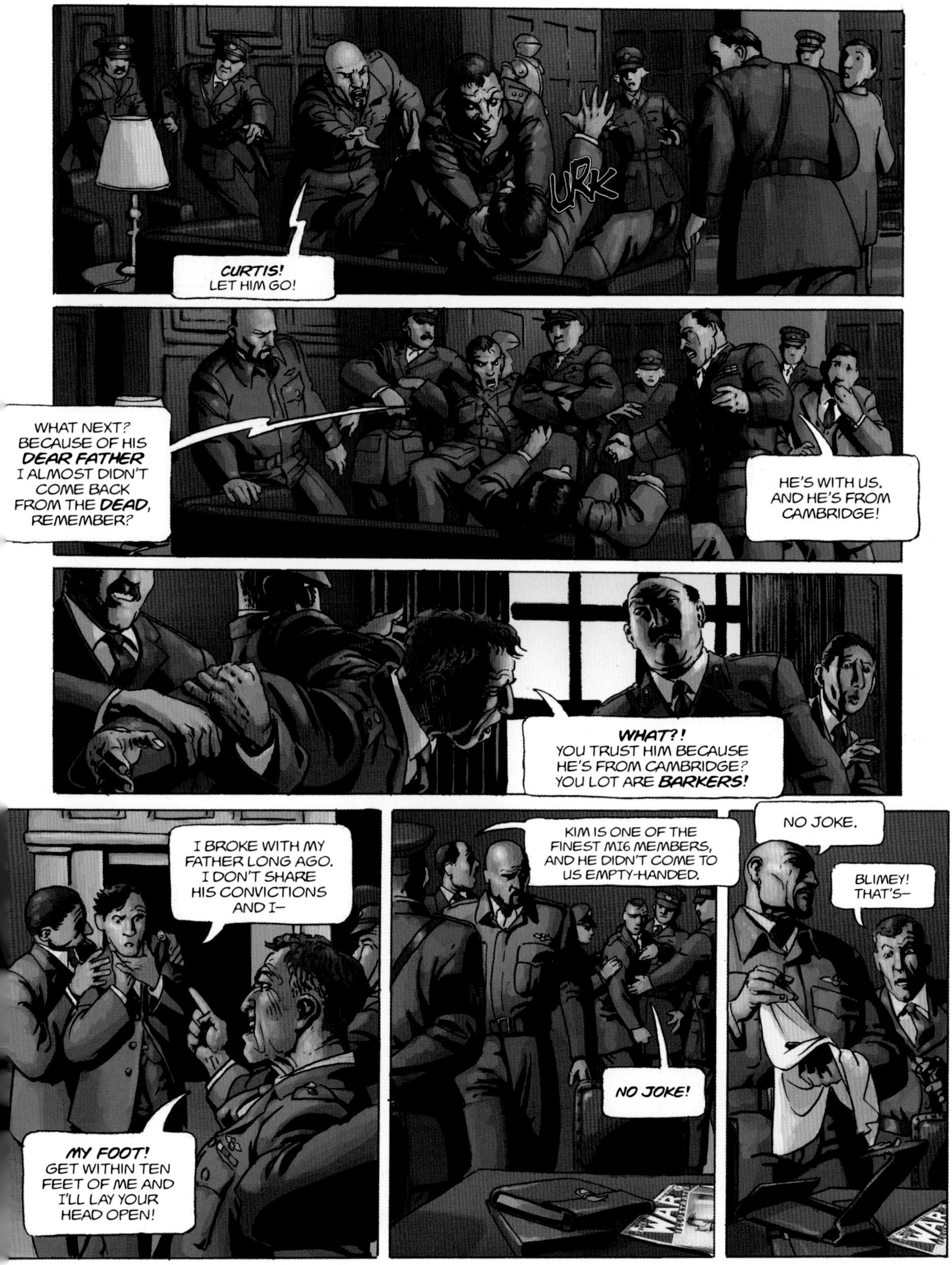
URK
CURTIS! LET HIM GO!
WHAT NEXT? BECAUSE OF HIS DEAR FATHER I ALMOST DIDN'T COME BACK FROM THE DEAD, REMEMBER?
HE'S WITH US. AND HE'S FROM CAMBRIDGE!
WHAT?! YOU TRUST HIM BECAUSE HE'S FROM CAMBRIDGE? YOU LOT ARE BARKERS!
I BROKE WITH MY FATHER LONG AGO. I DON'T SHARE HIS CONVICTIONS AND I–
MY FOOT! GET WITHIN TEN FEET OF ME AND I'LL LAY YOUR HEAD OPEN!
KIM IS ONE OF THE FINEST MI6 MEMBERS, AND HE DIDN'T COME TO US EMPTY-HANDED.
NO JOKE!
NO JOKE.
BLIMEY! THAT'S–

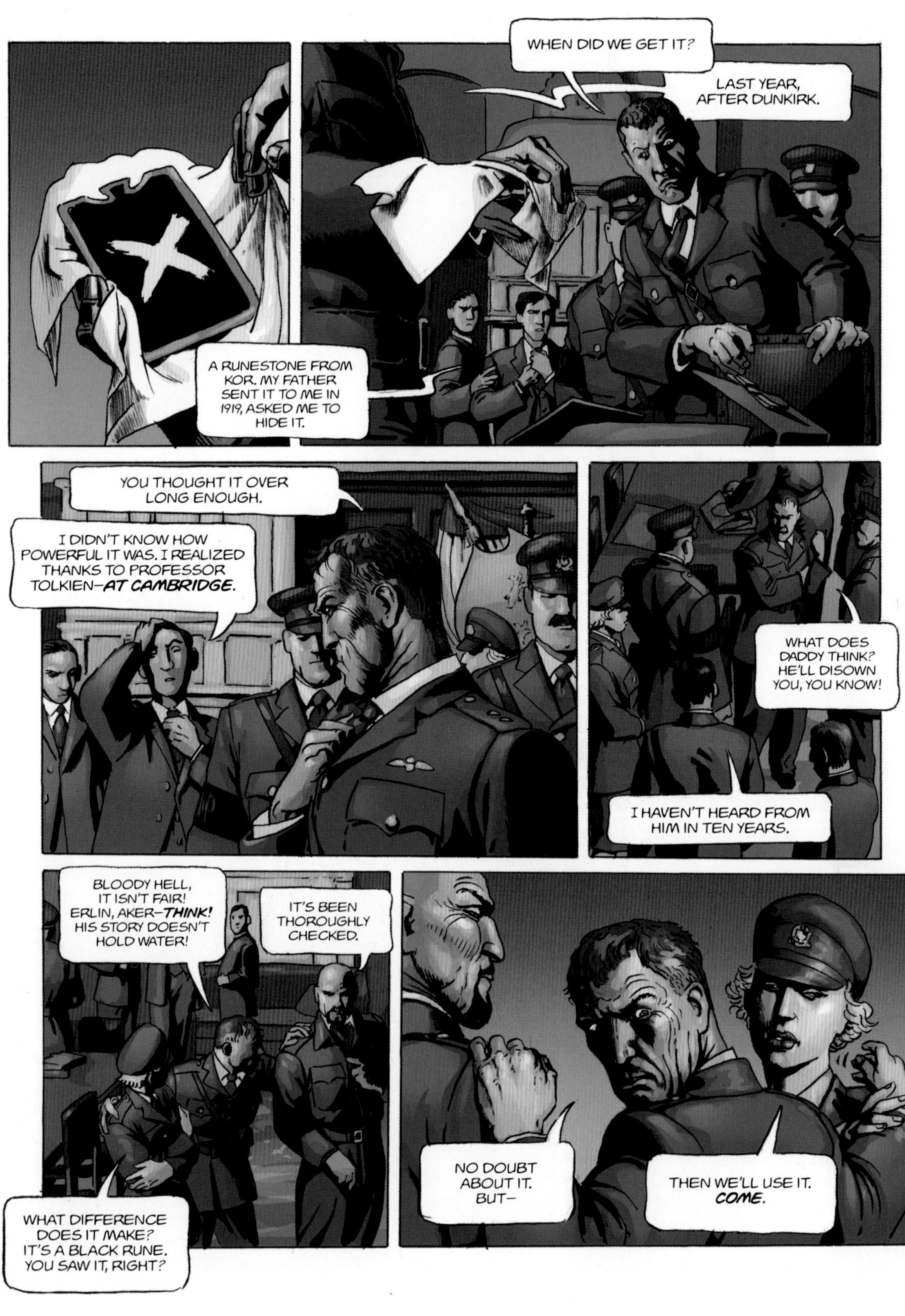
WHEN DID WE GET IT?
LAST YEAR, AFTER DUNKIRK.
A RUNESTONE FROM KOR. MY FATHER SENT IT TO ME IN 1919, ASKED ME TO HIDE IT.
YOU THOUGHT IT OVER LONG ENOUGH.
I DIDN'T KNOW HOW POWERFUL IT WAS. I REALIZED THANKS TO PROFESSOR TOLKIEN—AT CAMBRIDGE.
WHAT DOES DADDY THINK? HE'LL DISOWN YOU, YOU KNOW!
I HAVEN'T HEARD FROM HIM IN TEN YEARS.
BLOODY HELL, IT ISN'T FAIR! ERLIN, AKER—THINK! HIS STORY DOESN'T HOLD WATER!
IT'S BEEN THOROUGHLY CHECKED.
WHAT DIFFERENCE DOES IT MAKE? IT'S A BLACK RUNE. YOU SAW IT, RIGHT?
NO DOUBT ABOUT IT. BUT—
THEN WE'LL USE IT. COME.

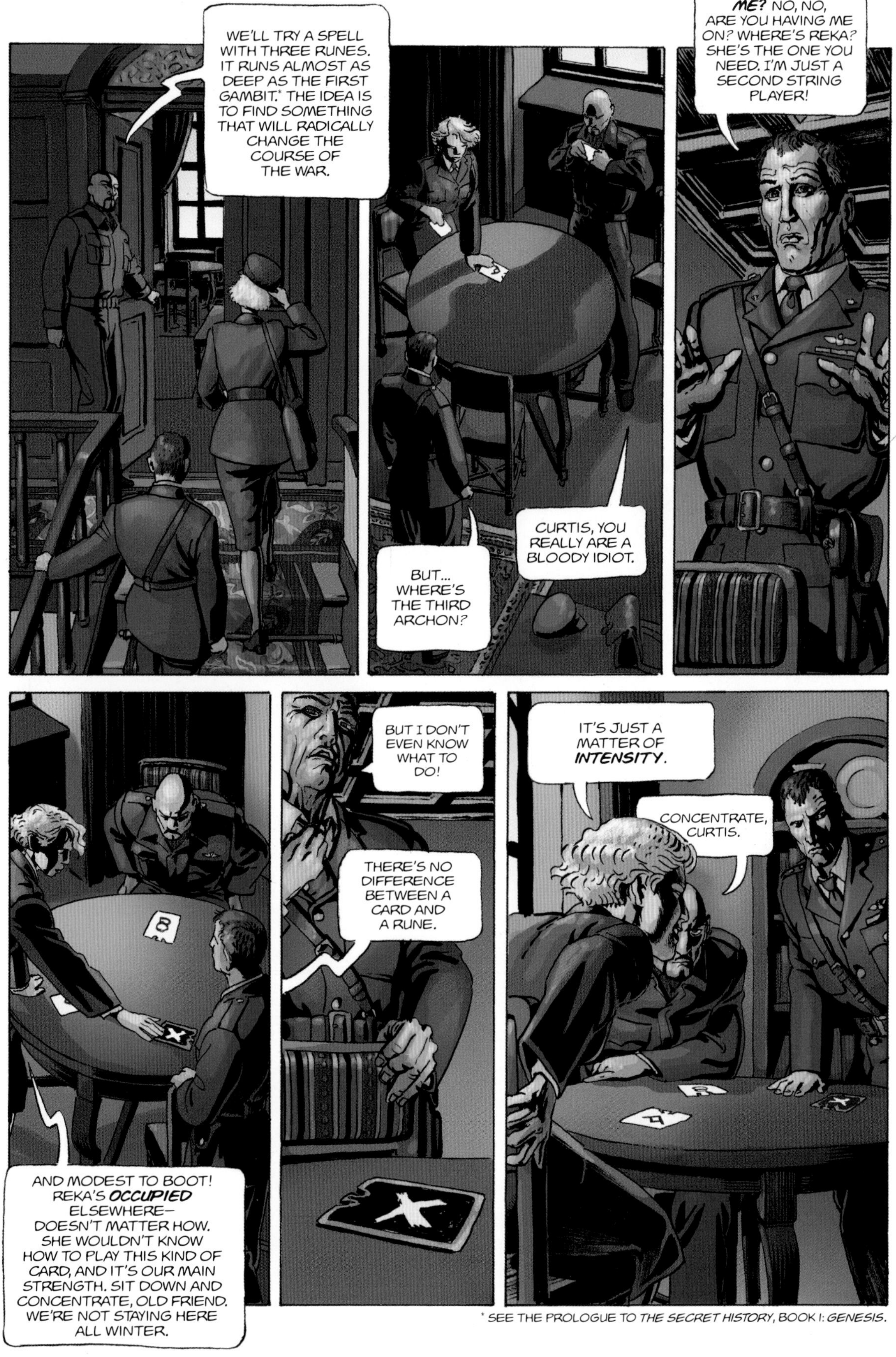
WE'LL TRY A SPELL WITH THREE RUNES. IT RUNS ALMOST AS DEEP AS THE FIRST GAMBIT.* THE IDEA IS TO FIND SOMETHING THAT WILL RADICALLY CHANGE THE COURSE OF THE WAR.
BUT... WHERE'S THE THIRD ARCHON?
CURTIS, YOU REALLY ARE A BLOODY IDIOT.
ME? NO, NO, ARE YOU HAVING ME ON? WHERE'S REKA? SHE'S THE ONE YOU NEED. I'M JUST A SECOND STRING PLAYER!
AND MODEST TO BOOT! REKA'S *OCCUPIED* ELSEWHERE— DOESN'T MATTER HOW. SHE WOULDN'T KNOW HOW TO PLAY THIS KIND OF CARD, AND IT'S OUR MAIN STRENGTH. SIT DOWN AND CONCENTRATE, OLD FRIEND. WE'RE NOT STAYING HERE ALL WINTER.
BUT I DON'T EVEN KNOW WHAT TO DO!
THERE'S NO DIFFERENCE BETWEEN A CARD AND A RUNE.
IT'S JUST A MATTER OF *INTENSITY*.
CONCENTRATE, CURTIS.

* SEE THE PROLOGUE TO *THE SECRET HISTORY*, BOOK I: *GENESIS*.

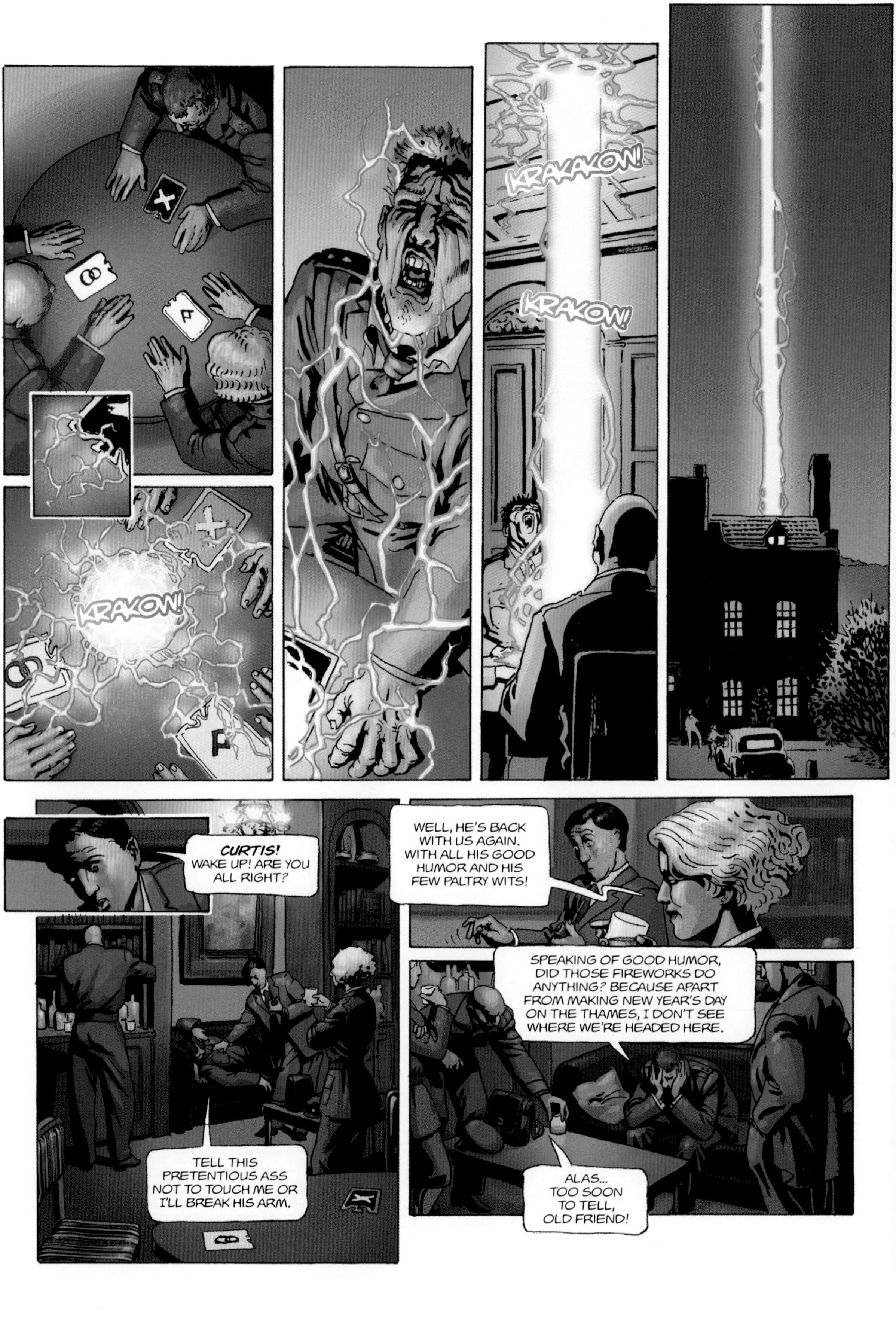
KRAKON!
KRAKAKON!
KRAKON!
CURTIS! WAKE UP! ARE YOU ALL RIGHT?
TELL THIS PRETENTIOUS ASS NOT TO TOUCH ME OR I'LL BREAK HIS ARM.
WELL, HE'S BACK WITH US AGAIN. WITH ALL HIS GOOD HUMOR AND HIS FEW PALTRY WITS!
SPEAKING OF GOOD HUMOR, DID THOSE FIREWORKS DO ANYTHING? BECAUSE APART FROM MAKING NEW YEAR'S DAY ON THE THAMES, I DON'T SEE WHERE WE'RE HEADED HERE.
ALAS... TOO SOON TO TELL, OLD FRIEND!

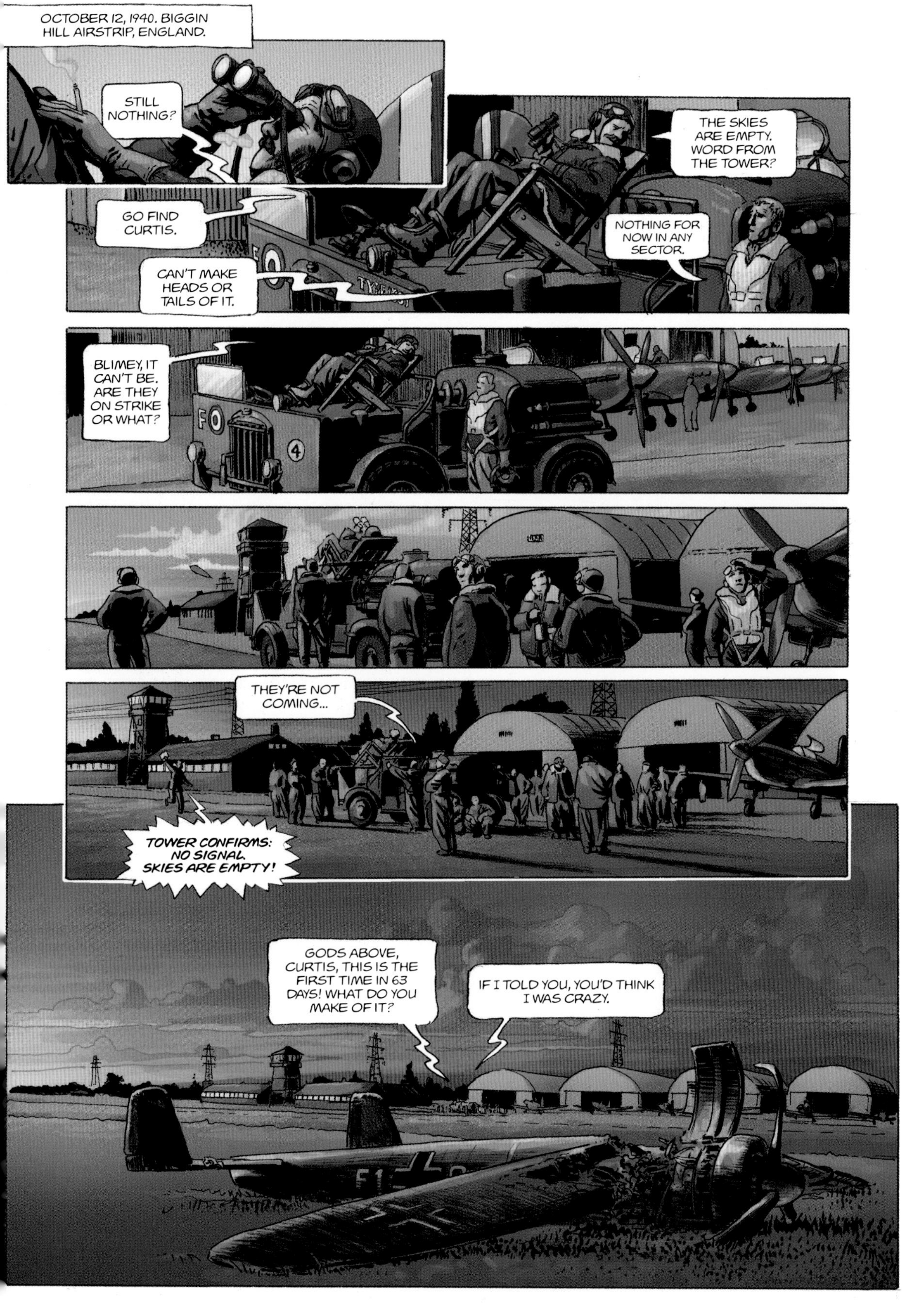

OCTOBER 12, 1940. BIGGIN HILL AIRSTRIP, ENGLAND.
STILL NOTHING?
THE SKIES ARE EMPTY. WORD FROM THE TOWER?
GO FIND CURTIS.
NOTHING FOR NOW IN ANY SECTOR.
CAN'T MAKE HEADS OR TAILS OF IT.
BLIMEY, IT CAN'T BE. ARE THEY ON STRIKE OR WHAT?
THEY'RE NOT COMING...
TOWER CONFIRMS: NO SIGNAL. SKIES ARE EMPTY!
GODS ABOVE, CURTIS, THIS IS THE FIRST TIME IN 63 DAYS! WHAT DO YOU MAKE OF IT?
IF I TOLD YOU, YOU'D THINK I WAS CRAZY.

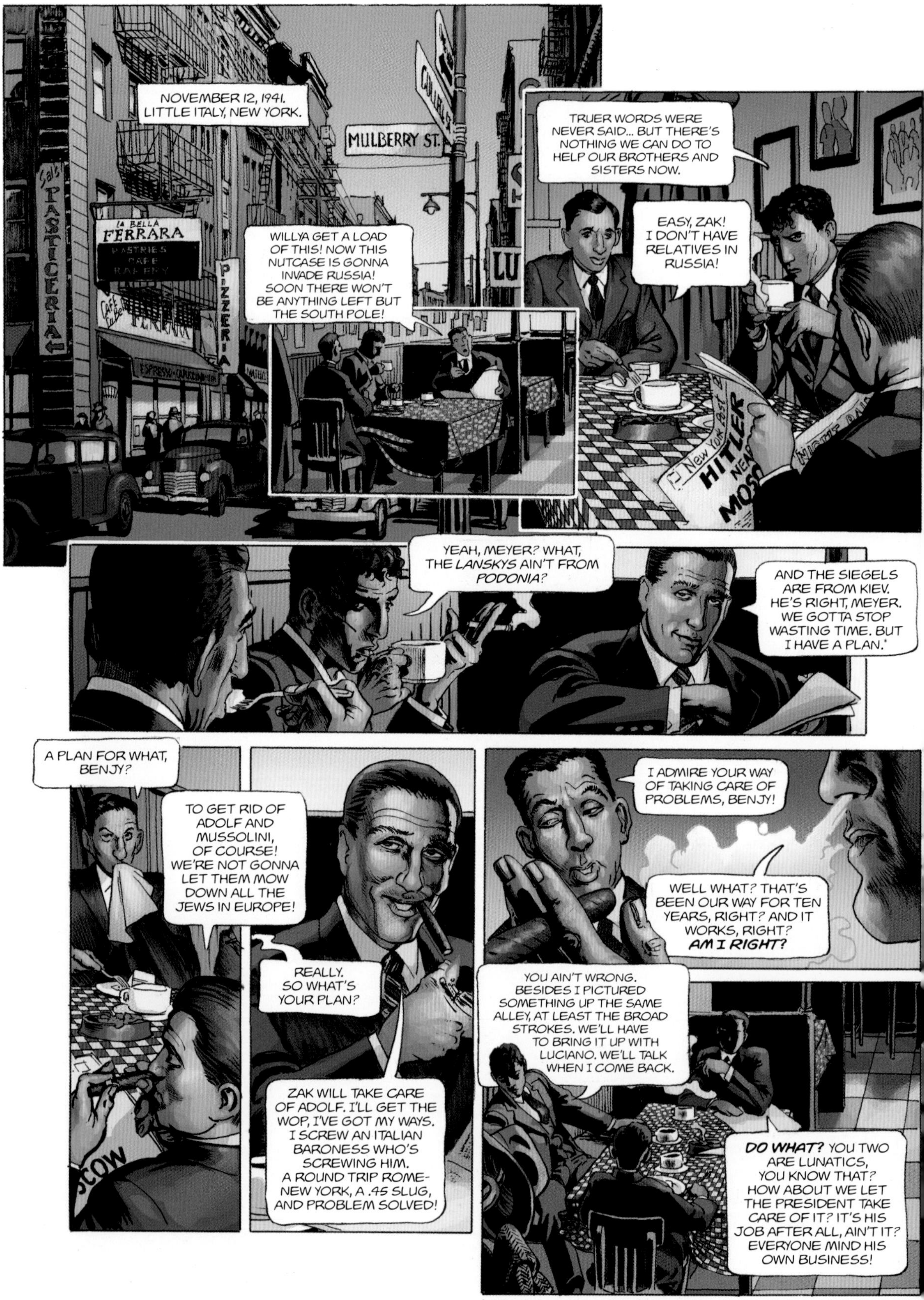
NOVEMBER 12, 1941. LITTLE ITALY, NEW YORK.
MULBERRY ST.
LA BELLA FERRARA PASTRIES CAFE BAKERY
PASTICERIA
PIZZERIA
WILLYA GET A LOAD OF THIS! NOW THIS NUTCASE IS GONNA INVADE RUSSIA! SOON THERE WON'T BE ANYTHING LEFT BUT THE SOUTH POLE!
TRUER WORDS WERE NEVER SAID... BUT THERE'S NOTHING WE CAN DO TO HELP OUR BROTHERS AND SISTERS NOW.
EASY, ZAK! I DON'T HAVE RELATIVES IN RUSSIA!
New York Post
HITLER
YEAH, MEYER? WHAT, THE *LANSKYS* AIN'T FROM *PODONIA*?
AND THE SIEGELS ARE FROM KIEV. HE'S RIGHT, MEYER. WE GOTTA STOP WASTING TIME. BUT I HAVE A PLAN.*
A PLAN FOR WHAT, BENJY?
TO GET RID OF ADOLF AND MUSSOLINI, OF COURSE! WE'RE NOT GONNA LET THEM MOW DOWN ALL THE JEWS IN EUROPE!
REALLY. SO WHAT'S YOUR PLAN?
ZAK WILL TAKE CARE OF ADOLF. I'LL GET THE WOP, I'VE GOT MY WAYS. I SCREW AN ITALIAN BARONESS WHO'S SCREWING HIM. A ROUND TRIP ROME-NEW YORK, A .45 SLUG, AND PROBLEM SOLVED!
I ADMIRE YOUR WAY OF TAKING CARE OF PROBLEMS, BENJY!
WELL WHAT? THAT'S BEEN OUR WAY FOR TEN YEARS, RIGHT? AND IT WORKS, RIGHT? **AM I RIGHT?**
YOU AIN'T WRONG. BESIDES I PICTURED SOMETHING UP THE SAME ALLEY, AT LEAST THE BROAD STROKES. WE'LL HAVE TO BRING IT UP WITH LUCIANO. WE'LL TALK WHEN I COME BACK.
DO WHAT? YOU TWO ARE LUNATICS, YOU KNOW THAT? HOW ABOUT WE LET THE PRESIDENT TAKE CARE OF IT? IT'S HIS JOB AFTER ALL, AIN'T IT? EVERYONE MIND HIS OWN BUSINESS!

* TRUE! MULTIPLE WITNESSES WOULD CONFIRM THE SIEGEL PLAN AFTER THE WAR.

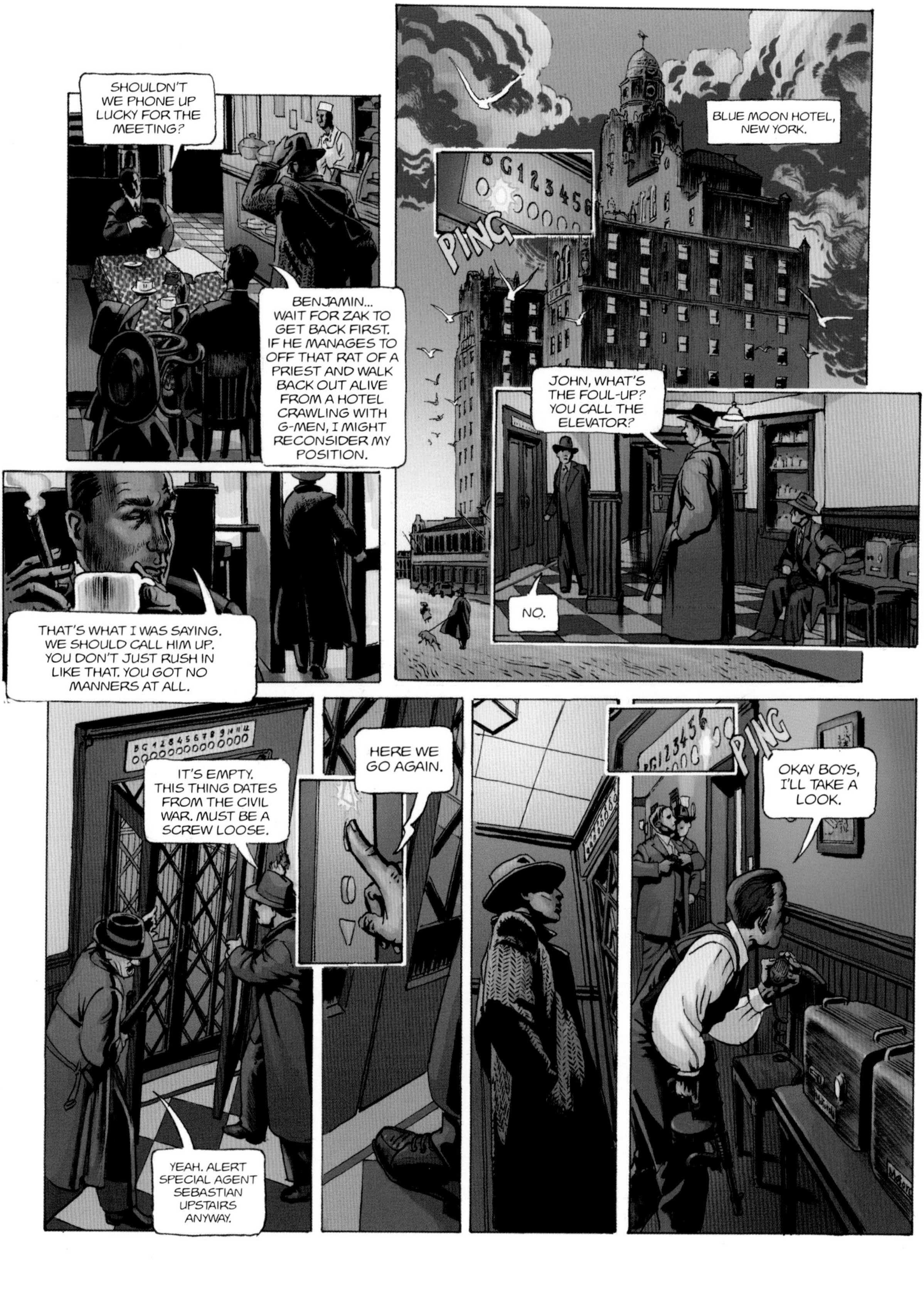
SHOULDN'T WE PHONE UP LUCKY FOR THE MEETING?
BENJAMIN... WAIT FOR ZAK TO GET BACK FIRST. IF HE MANAGES TO OFF THAT RAT OF A PRIEST AND WALK BACK OUT ALIVE FROM A HOTEL CRAWLING WITH G-MEN, I MIGHT RECONSIDER MY POSITION.
THAT'S WHAT I WAS SAYING. WE SHOULD CALL HIM UP. YOU DON'T JUST RUSH IN LIKE THAT. YOU GOT NO MANNERS AT ALL.
BLUE MOON HOTEL, NEW YORK.
PING
JOHN, WHAT'S THE FOUL-UP? YOU CALL THE ELEVATOR?
NO.
IT'S EMPTY. THIS THING DATES FROM THE CIVIL WAR. MUST BE A SCREW LOOSE.
YEAH. ALERT SPECIAL AGENT SEBASTIAN UPSTAIRS ANYWAY.
HERE WE GO AGAIN.
PING
OKAY BOYS, I'LL TAKE A LOOK.

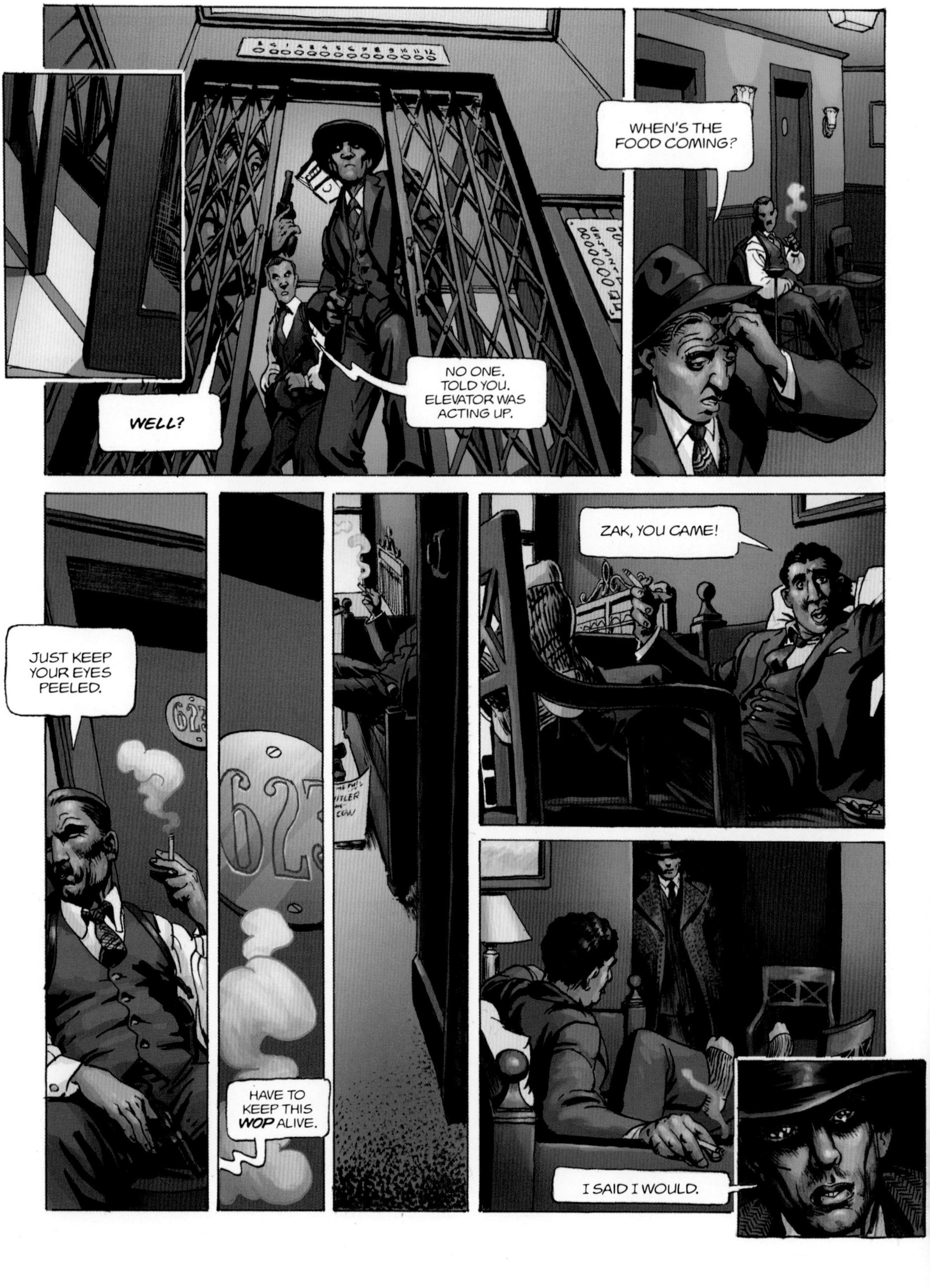
WELL?
NO ONE. TOLD YOU. ELEVATOR WAS ACTING UP.
WHEN'S THE FOOD COMING?
JUST KEEP YOUR EYES PEELED.
HAVE TO KEEP THIS WOP ALIVE.
ZAK, YOU CAME!
I SAID I WOULD.

YEAH! WE'LL GO SEE MEYER AND I'LL EXPLAIN IT ALL. LET ME GET MY LOAFERS ON.

TRUST ME. HALLWAY'S CRAWLING WITH FEDS.

C'MERE. BY THE WINDOW.

UH, I'M AFRAID OF HEIGHTS.

DID YOU TALK TO MEYER FOR ME?

TIME'S A-WASTING. HE UNDERSTANDS FINE. YOU HAD NO CHOICE. IT'S OKAY, NO FOUL. BLANK SLATE.

GODDAMMIT, SOMEONE TELL ME WHAT JUST HAPPENED!*

HE MUST'VE *JUMPED!*

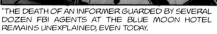

JUMPED? THE ONLY WITNESS AGAINST LANSKY, AND YOU'RE TELLING ME HE THREW HIMSELF OUT THE WINDOW?

YOU SAW HIM. HE'S DRESSED LIKE HE WAS ABOUT TO GO OUT FOR A WALK!

THAT WAS ONE HELL OF A *WALK.*

*THE DEATH OF AN INFORMER GUARDED BY SEVERAL DOZEN FBI AGENTS AT THE BLUE MOON HOTEL REMAINS UNEXPLAINED, EVEN TODAY.

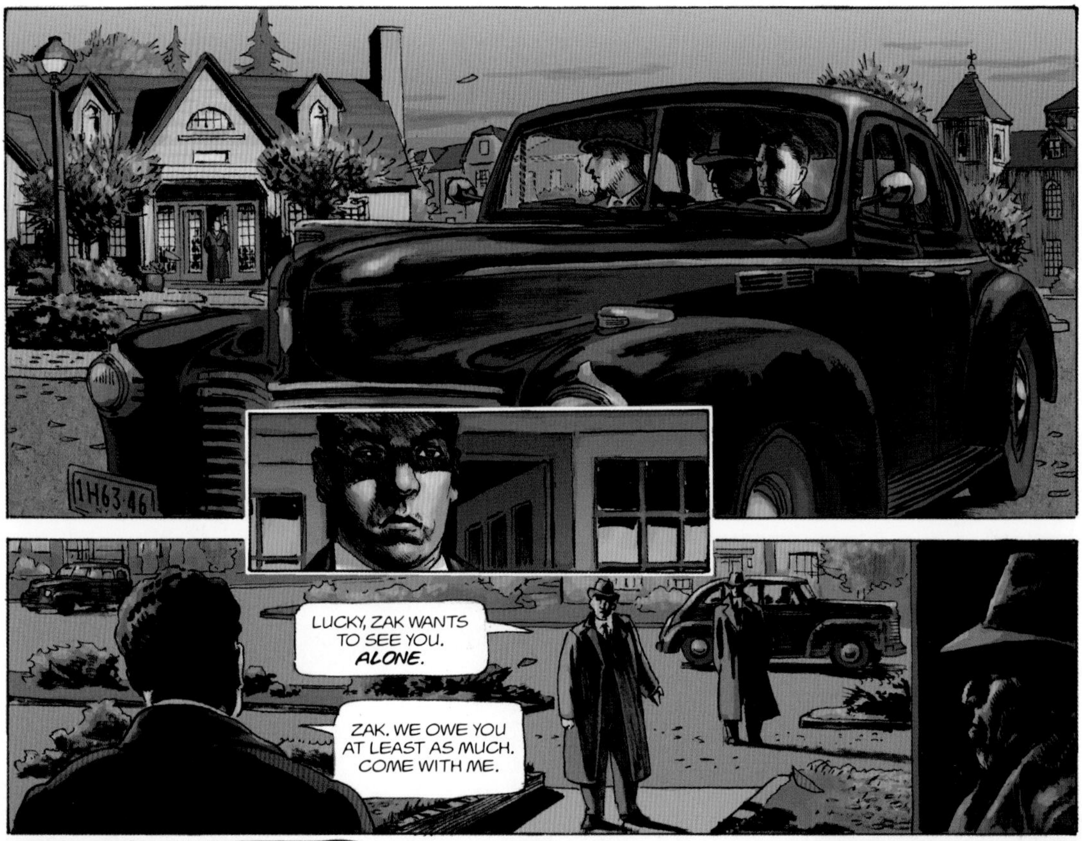
1H63-46
LUCKY, ZAK WANTS TO SEE YOU. ***ALONE.***
ZAK. WE OWE YOU AT LEAST AS MUCH. COME WITH ME.

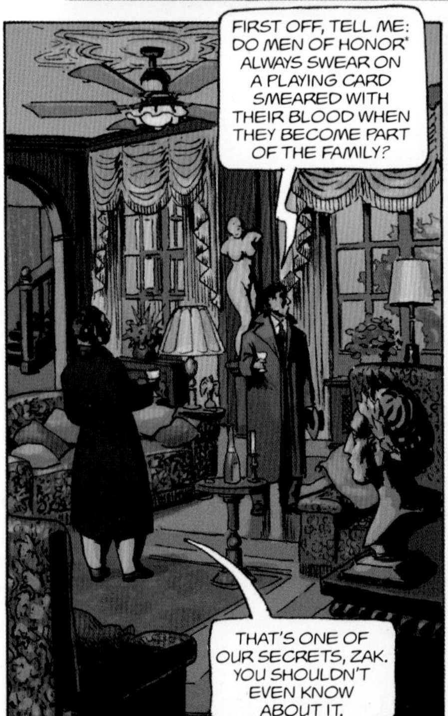
FIRST OFF, TELL ME: DO MEN OF HONOR* ALWAYS SWEAR ON A PLAYING CARD SMEARED WITH THEIR BLOOD WHEN THEY BECOME PART OF THE FAMILY?
THAT'S ONE OF OUR SECRETS, ZAK. YOU SHOULDN'T EVEN KNOW ABOUT IT.

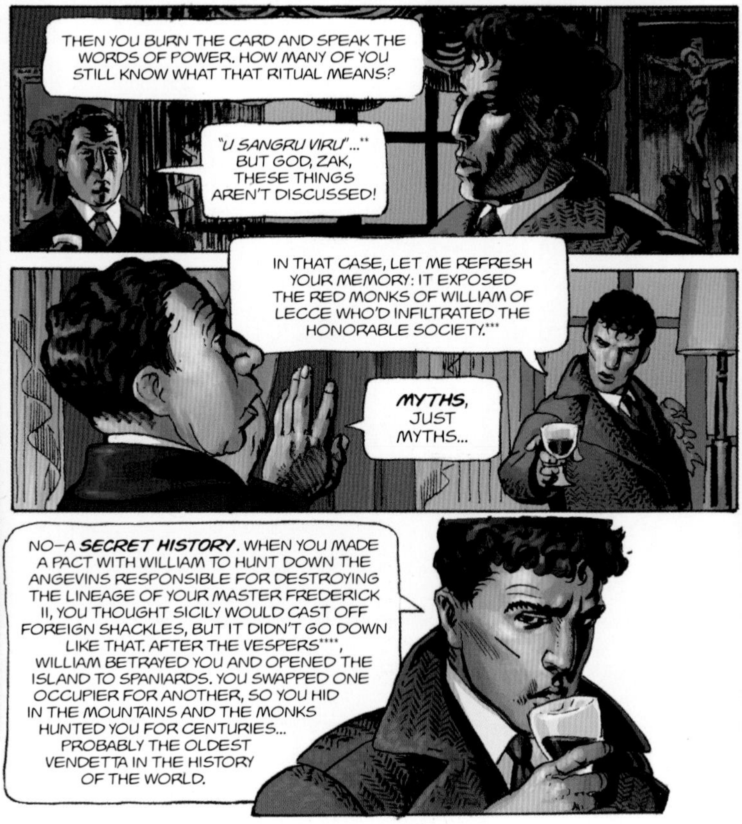
THEN YOU BURN THE CARD AND SPEAK THE WORDS OF POWER. HOW MANY OF YOU STILL KNOW WHAT THAT RITUAL MEANS?
"U SANGRU VIRU"...** BUT GOD, ZAK, THESE THINGS AREN'T DISCUSSED!
IN THAT CASE, LET ME REFRESH YOUR MEMORY: IT EXPOSED THE RED MONKS OF WILLIAM OF LECCE WHO'D INFILTRATED THE HONORABLE SOCIETY.***
MYTHS, JUST MYTHS...
NO—A ***SECRET HISTORY***. WHEN YOU MADE A PACT WITH WILLIAM TO HUNT DOWN THE ANGEVINS RESPONSIBLE FOR DESTROYING THE LINEAGE OF YOUR MASTER FREDERICK II, YOU THOUGHT SICILY WOULD CAST OFF FOREIGN SHACKLES, BUT IT DIDN'T GO DOWN LIKE THAT. AFTER THE VESPERS****, WILLIAM BETRAYED YOU AND OPENED THE ISLAND TO SPANIARDS. YOU SWAPPED ONE OCCUPIER FOR ANOTHER, SO YOU HID IN THE MOUNTAINS AND THE MONKS HUNTED YOU FOR CENTURIES... PROBABLY THE OLDEST VENDETTA IN THE HISTORY OF THE WORLD.

* MAFIOSOS.
** "THE TRUTH OF BLOOD," OR BLOOD DOESN'T LIE.
*** THE MAFIA.
**** SICILIAN VESPERS. SEE *THE SECRET HISTORY, BOOK 3: THE GRAIL OF MONTSÉGUR,* AND BOOK 4: *THE KEYS OF SAINT PETER.* ACCORDING TO SOME AUTHORS, THE SICILIAN VESPERS WERE THE BIRTH OF THE MAFIA.

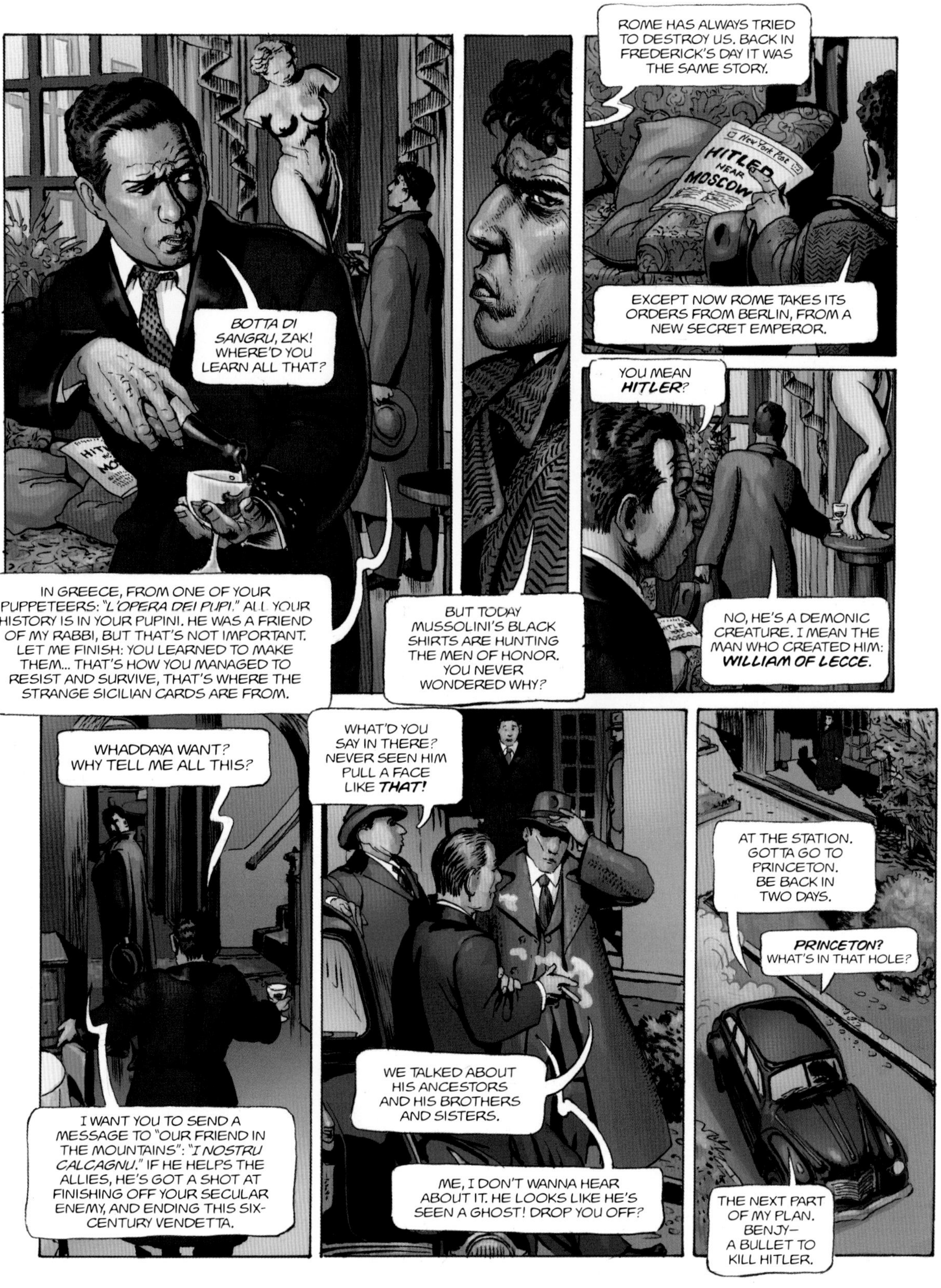
BOTTA DI SANGRU, ZAK! WHERE'D YOU LEARN ALL THAT?
IN GREECE, FROM ONE OF YOUR PUPPETEERS: "L'OPERA DEI PUPI." ALL YOUR HISTORY IS IN YOUR PUPINI. HE WAS A FRIEND OF MY RABBI, BUT THAT'S NOT IMPORTANT. LET ME FINISH: YOU LEARNED TO MAKE THEM... THAT'S HOW YOU MANAGED TO RESIST AND SURVIVE, THAT'S WHERE THE STRANGE SICILIAN CARDS ARE FROM.
BUT TODAY MUSSOLINI'S BLACK SHIRTS ARE HUNTING THE MEN OF HONOR. YOU NEVER WONDERED WHY?
ROME HAS ALWAYS TRIED TO DESTROY US. BACK IN FREDERICK'S DAY IT WAS THE SAME STORY.
New York Post
HITLER NEAR MOSCOW
EXCEPT NOW ROME TAKES ITS ORDERS FROM BERLIN, FROM A NEW SECRET EMPEROR.
YOU MEAN HITLER?
NO, HE'S A DEMONIC CREATURE. I MEAN THE MAN WHO CREATED HIM: WILLIAM OF LECCE.
WHADDAYA WANT? WHY TELL ME ALL THIS?
I WANT YOU TO SEND A MESSAGE TO "OUR FRIEND IN THE MOUNTAINS": "I NOSTRU CALCAGNU." IF HE HELPS THE ALLIES, HE'S GOT A SHOT AT FINISHING OFF YOUR SECULAR ENEMY, AND ENDING THIS SIX-CENTURY VENDETTA.
WHAT'D YOU SAY IN THERE? NEVER SEEN HIM PULL A FACE LIKE THAT!
WE TALKED ABOUT HIS ANCESTORS AND HIS BROTHERS AND SISTERS.
ME, I DON'T WANNA HEAR ABOUT IT. HE LOOKS LIKE HE'S SEEN A GHOST! DROP YOU OFF?
AT THE STATION. GOTTA GO TO PRINCETON. BE BACK IN TWO DAYS.
PRINCETON? WHAT'S IN THAT HOLE?
THE NEXT PART OF MY PLAN. BENJY— A BULLET TO KILL HITLER.

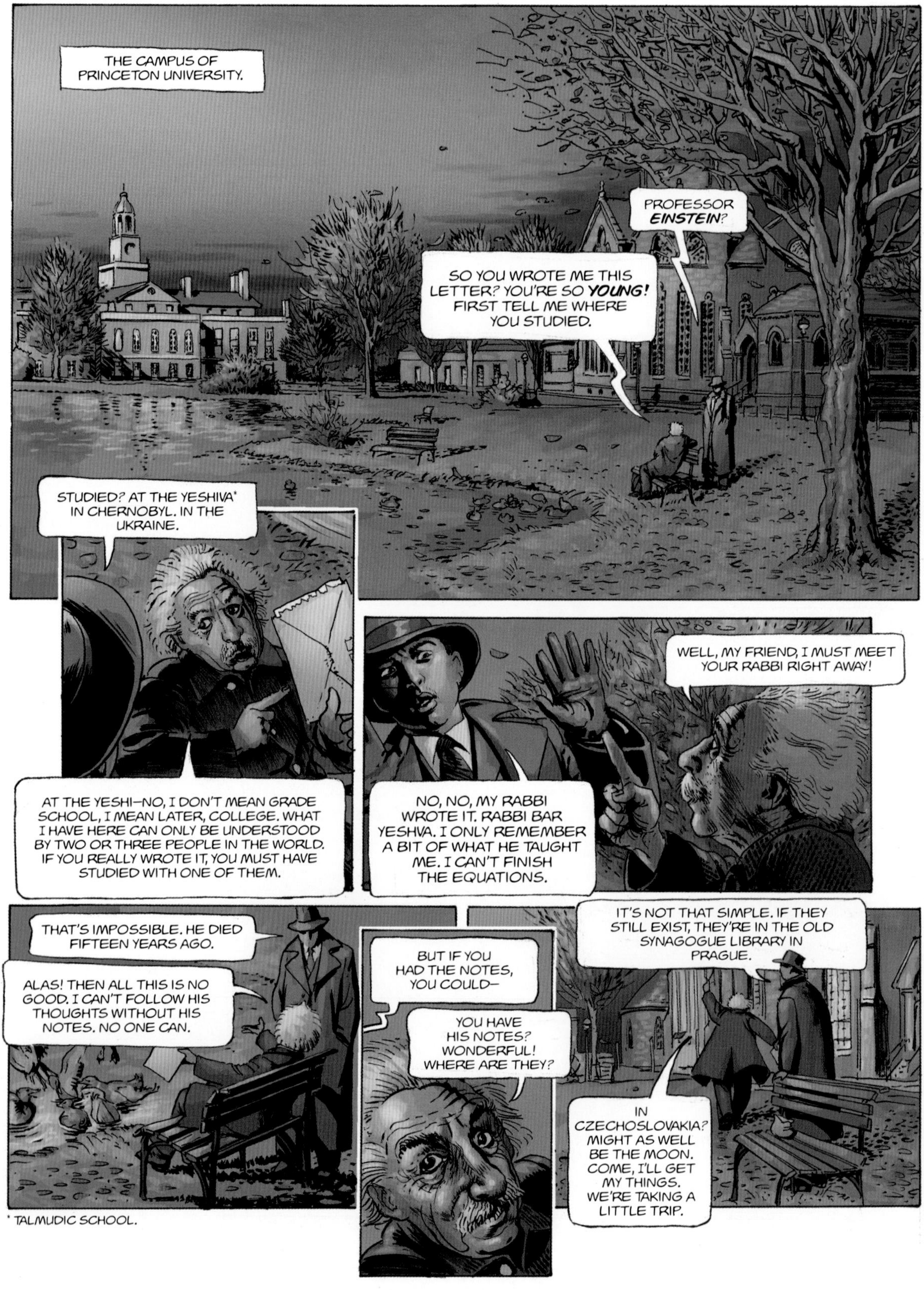
THE CAMPUS OF PRINCETON UNIVERSITY.
PROFESSOR EINSTEIN?
SO YOU WROTE ME THIS LETTER? YOU'RE SO YOUNG! FIRST TELL ME WHERE YOU STUDIED.
STUDIED? AT THE YESHIVA* IN CHERNOBYL. IN THE UKRAINE.
AT THE YESHI—NO, I DON'T MEAN GRADE SCHOOL, I MEAN LATER, COLLEGE. WHAT I HAVE HERE CAN ONLY BE UNDERSTOOD BY TWO OR THREE PEOPLE IN THE WORLD. IF YOU REALLY WROTE IT, YOU MUST HAVE STUDIED WITH ONE OF THEM.
NO, NO, MY RABBI WROTE IT. RABBI BAR YESHVA. I ONLY REMEMBER A BIT OF WHAT HE TAUGHT ME. I CAN'T FINISH THE EQUATIONS.
WELL, MY FRIEND, I MUST MEET YOUR RABBI RIGHT AWAY!
THAT'S IMPOSSIBLE. HE DIED FIFTEEN YEARS AGO.
ALAS! THEN ALL THIS IS NO GOOD. I CAN'T FOLLOW HIS THOUGHTS WITHOUT HIS NOTES. NO ONE CAN.
BUT IF YOU HAD THE NOTES, YOU COULD—
YOU HAVE HIS NOTES? WONDERFUL! WHERE ARE THEY?
IT'S NOT THAT SIMPLE. IF THEY STILL EXIST, THEY'RE IN THE OLD SYNAGOGUE LIBRARY IN PRAGUE.
IN CZECHOSLOVAKIA? MIGHT AS WELL BE THE MOON. COME, I'LL GET MY THINGS. WE'RE TAKING A LITTLE TRIP.
* TALMUDIC SCHOOL.

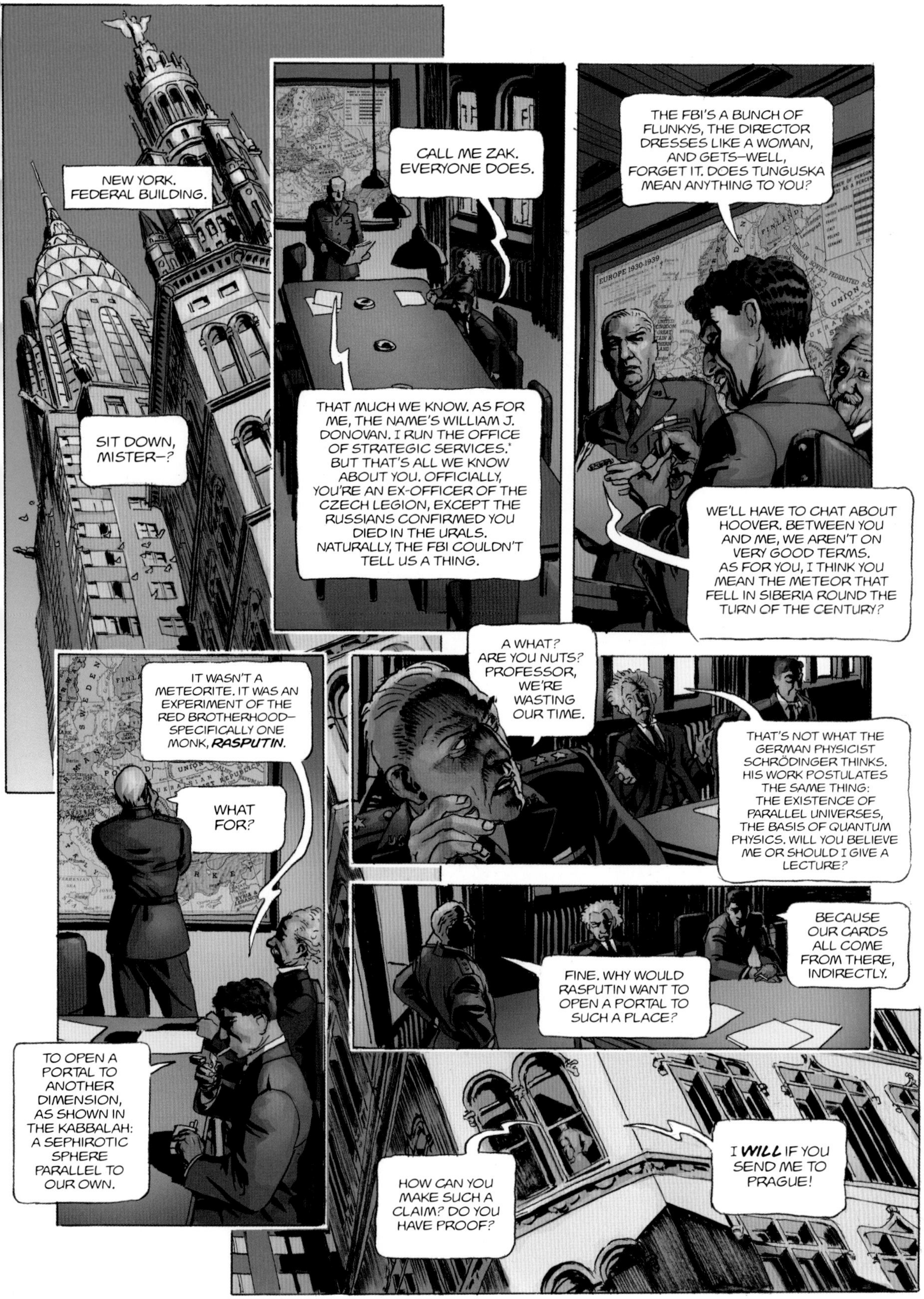
NEW YORK. FEDERAL BUILDING.
SIT DOWN, MISTER–?
CALL ME ZAK. EVERYONE DOES.
THAT MUCH WE KNOW. AS FOR ME, THE NAME'S WILLIAM J. DONOVAN. I RUN THE OFFICE OF STRATEGIC SERVICES.* BUT THAT'S ALL WE KNOW ABOUT YOU. OFFICIALLY, YOU'RE AN EX-OFFICER OF THE CZECH LEGION, EXCEPT THE RUSSIANS CONFIRMED YOU DIED IN THE URALS. NATURALLY, THE FBI COULDN'T TELL US A THING.
THE FBI'S A BUNCH OF FLUNKYS, THE DIRECTOR DRESSES LIKE A WOMAN, AND GETS–WELL, FORGET IT. DOES TUNGUSKA MEAN ANYTHING TO YOU?
WE'LL HAVE TO CHAT ABOUT HOOVER. BETWEEN YOU AND ME, WE AREN'T ON VERY GOOD TERMS. AS FOR YOU, I THINK YOU MEAN THE METEOR THAT FELL IN SIBERIA ROUND THE TURN OF THE CENTURY?
IT WASN'T A METEORITE. IT WAS AN EXPERIMENT OF THE RED BROTHERHOOD–SPECIFICALLY ONE MONK, ***RASPUTIN***.
WHAT FOR?
TO OPEN A PORTAL TO ANOTHER DIMENSION, AS SHOWN IN THE KABBALAH: A SEPHIROTIC SPHERE PARALLEL TO OUR OWN.
A WHAT? ARE YOU NUTS? PROFESSOR, WE'RE WASTING OUR TIME.
THAT'S NOT WHAT THE GERMAN PHYSICIST SCHRÖDINGER THINKS. HIS WORK POSTULATES THE SAME THING: THE EXISTENCE OF PARALLEL UNIVERSES, THE BASIS OF QUANTUM PHYSICS. WILL YOU BELIEVE ME OR SHOULD I GIVE A LECTURE?
FINE. WHY WOULD RASPUTIN WANT TO OPEN A PORTAL TO SUCH A PLACE?
BECAUSE OUR CARDS ALL COME FROM THERE, INDIRECTLY.
HOW CAN YOU MAKE SUCH A CLAIM? DO YOU HAVE PROOF?
I ***WILL*** IF YOU SEND ME TO PRAGUE!

*OSS: AMERICAN SECRET SERVICE, FORERUNNER OF THE CIA.

BIGGAN HILL AIRSTRIP, ENGLAND.

AKER, ALL THIS SEEMS QUITE NEBULOUS. AT ANY RATE, YOU SURELY NEEDN'T BE INVOLVED IN THIS MISSION.

NO? WE KNOW THAT REINHARD HEYDRICH* WAS SENT TO PRAGUE WITH THE TITLE OF *REICHSPROTEKTOR* OF BOHEMIA-MORAVIA. THINK THAT'S JUST COINCIDENCE?

THERE'VE BEEN LEAKS. THE SS IS AFTER THE SAME THING WE ARE. THE YANKS ARE SENDING ZAK, WHO'S VERY GOOD, BUT HE'LL NEED HELP. IT'S A RACE AGAINST TIME, AND THIS TIME WE CAN'T AFFORD TO LOSE.

OF COURSE, AKER, BUT I—

WE'VE BEEN GETTING STRANGE INFORMATION FOR A FEW MONTHS NOW.

YOU MEAN THOSE STORIES OF MASS KILLINGS? WE'VE SEEN SO MANY WARS: CAN YOU NAME ONE WITHOUT ITS OWN HOST OF ATROCITIES? I HAVE TROUBLE TELLING BETWEEN THE PROPAGANDA OF WILLIAM AND DYO!

FINE, BUT THIS TIME IT'S DIFFERENT. HEYDRICH SEEMS TO HAVE SOME ORGANIZATION IN PLACE BEHIND THE FRONT. JEWS AND GYPSIES ARE SYSTEMATICALLY TAKEN INTO THE WOODS AND KILLED EN MASSE. WHAT DOES THE SS WANT? THERE'S NO SENSE TO IT; MOST AREN'T EVEN COMMUNIST! *NO SENSE AT ALL!*

NO, BUT I THINK HIS DEATH WILL KEEP THE MADNESS AT BAY FOR A BIT. PLUS REMEMBER WHAT HAPPENED AT THE ISLE OF MAN, WITH CURTIS. YOU FELT IT TOO, RIGHT?

IT'S NOT JUST THAT. THERE'S SOMETHING ELSE MUCH *DARKER* AT WORK.

OF COURSE. JOACHIM OF FIORE SPOKE OF THE *ANTICHRIST*, THE RESPONSE TO THE KING YOU TRIED TO GIVE THE WORLD**. HERE WE ARE...

YOU HOPING HEYDRICH WILL EXPLAIN?

THE DEATH OF AN ARCHON. MIGHT AS WELL CALL A SPADE A SPADE.

* REINHARD HEYDRICH: SS OFFICER WHO, WITH ADOLF EICHMANN, WAS ONE OF THE ARCHITECTS OF THE SHOAH.

** SEE *THE SECRET HISTORY* BOOK 3: *THE GRAIL OF MONTSÉGUR.*

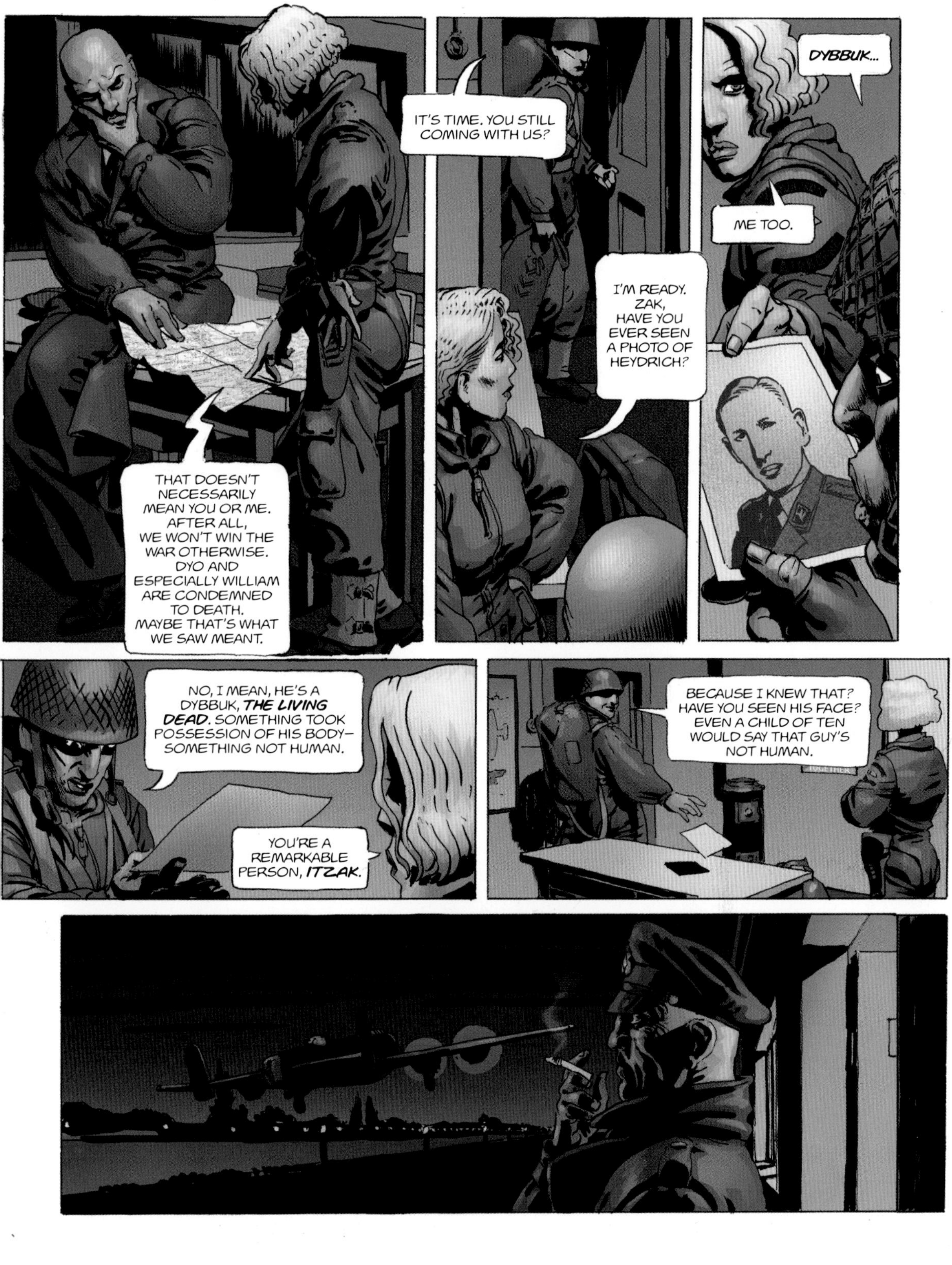
THAT DOESN'T NECESSARILY MEAN YOU OR ME. AFTER ALL, WE WON'T WIN THE WAR OTHERWISE. DYO AND ESPECIALLY WILLIAM ARE CONDEMNED TO DEATH. MAYBE THAT'S WHAT WE SAW MEANT.
IT'S TIME. YOU STILL COMING WITH US?
I'M READY. ZAK, HAVE YOU EVER SEEN A PHOTO OF HEYDRICH?
DYBBUK...
ME TOO.
NO, I MEAN, HE'S A DYBBUK, THE LIVING DEAD. SOMETHING TOOK POSSESSION OF HIS BODY— SOMETHING NOT HUMAN.
YOU'RE A REMARKABLE PERSON, ITZAK.
BECAUSE I KNEW THAT? HAVE YOU SEEN HIS FACE? EVEN A CHILD OF TEN WOULD SAY THAT GUY'S NOT HUMAN.

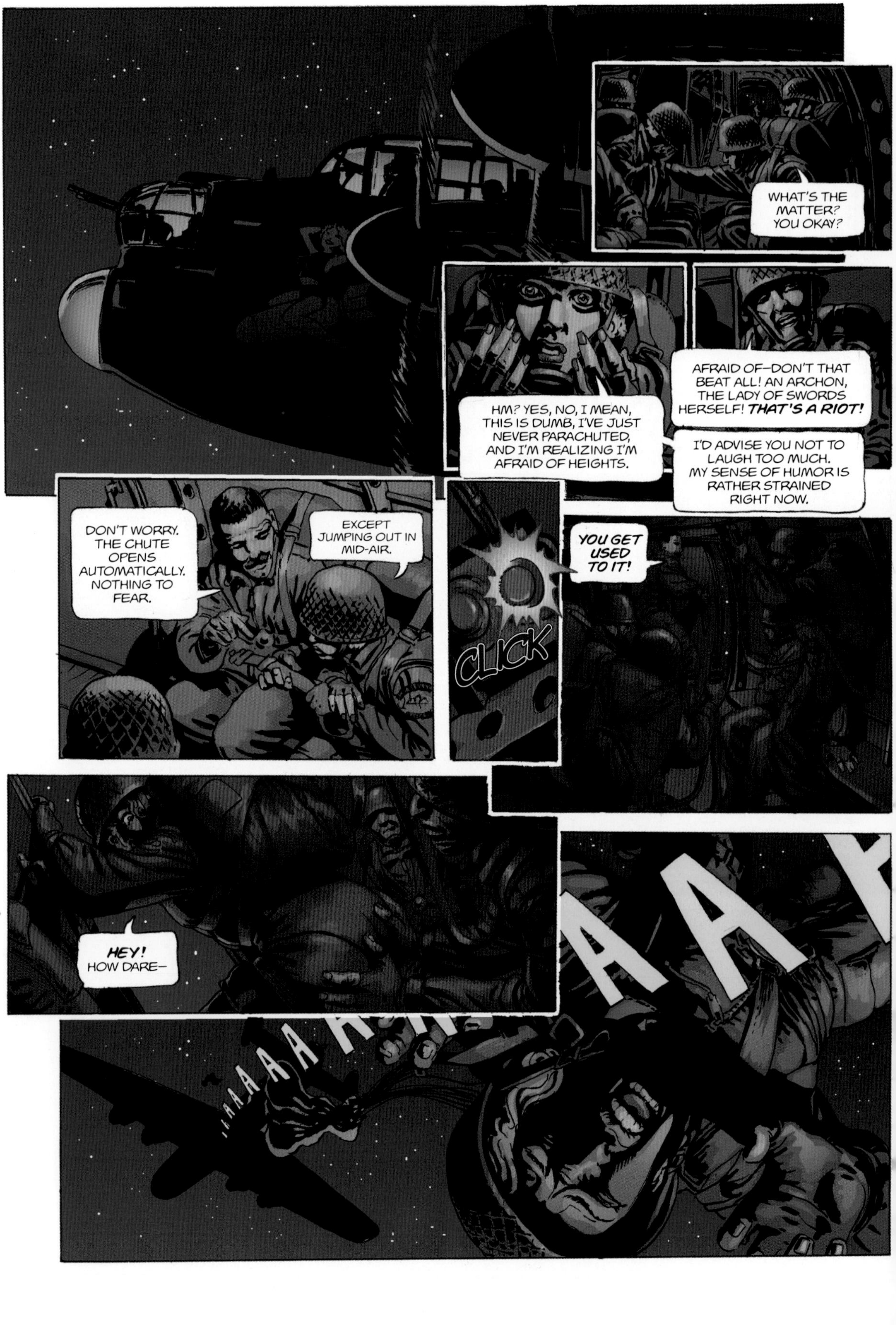
WHAT'S THE MATTER? YOU OKAY?
HM? YES, NO, I MEAN, THIS IS DUMB, I'VE JUST NEVER PARACHUTED, AND I'M REALIZING I'M AFRAID OF HEIGHTS.
AFRAID OF—DON'T THAT BEAT ALL! AN ARCHON, THE LADY OF SWORDS HERSELF! THAT'S A RIOT!
I'D ADVISE YOU NOT TO LAUGH TOO MUCH. MY SENSE OF HUMOR IS RATHER STRAINED RIGHT NOW.
DON'T WORRY. THE CHUTE OPENS AUTOMATICALLY. NOTHING TO FEAR.
EXCEPT JUMPING OUT IN MID-AIR.
CLICK
YOU GET USED TO IT!
HEY! HOW DARE—

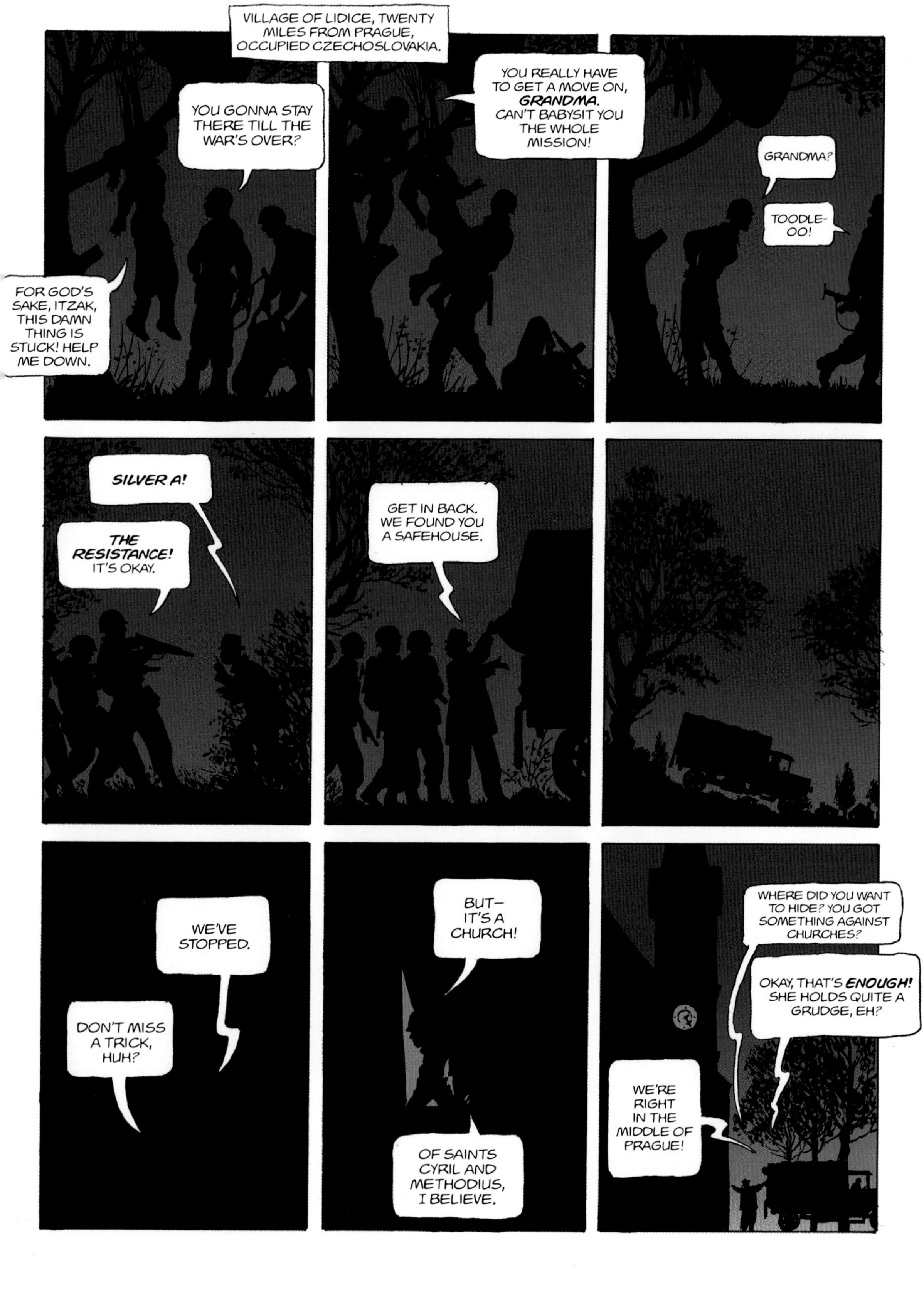
VILLAGE OF LIDICE, TWENTY MILES FROM PRAGUE, OCCUPIED CZECHOSLOVAKIA.
FOR GOD'S SAKE, ITZAK, THIS DAMN THING IS STUCK! HELP ME DOWN.
YOU GONNA STAY THERE TILL THE WAR'S OVER?
YOU REALLY HAVE TO GET A MOVE ON, GRANDMA. CAN'T BABYSIT YOU THE WHOLE MISSION!
GRANDMA?
TOODLE-OO!
SILVER A!
THE RESISTANCE! IT'S OKAY.
GET IN BACK. WE FOUND YOU A SAFEHOUSE.
WE'VE STOPPED.
DON'T MISS A TRICK, HUH?
BUT— IT'S A CHURCH!
OF SAINTS CYRIL AND METHODIUS, I BELIEVE.
WHERE DID YOU WANT TO HIDE? YOU GOT SOMETHING AGAINST CHURCHES?
OKAY, THAT'S ENOUGH! SHE HOLDS QUITE A GRUDGE, EH?
WE'RE RIGHT IN THE MIDDLE OF PRAGUE!

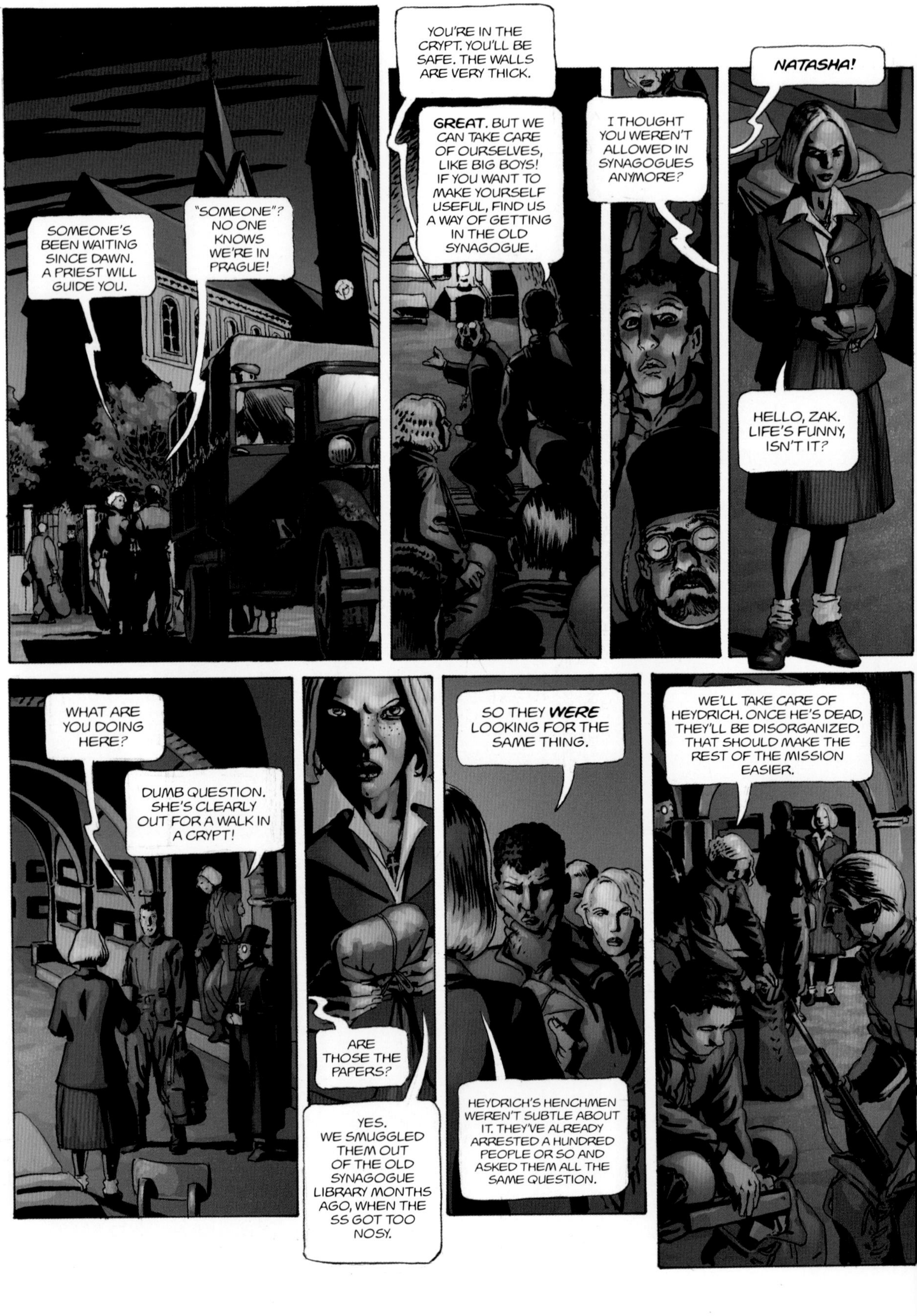
SOMEONE'S BEEN WAITING SINCE DAWN. A PRIEST WILL GUIDE YOU.
"SOMEONE"? NO ONE KNOWS WE'RE IN PRAGUE!
YOU'RE IN THE CRYPT. YOU'LL BE SAFE. THE WALLS ARE VERY THICK.
GREAT. BUT WE CAN TAKE CARE OF OURSELVES, LIKE BIG BOYS! IF YOU WANT TO MAKE YOURSELF USEFUL, FIND US A WAY OF GETTING IN THE OLD SYNAGOGUE.
I THOUGHT YOU WEREN'T ALLOWED IN SYNAGOGUES ANYMORE?
NATASHA!
HELLO, ZAK. LIFE'S FUNNY, ISN'T IT?
WHAT ARE YOU DOING HERE?
DUMB QUESTION. SHE'S CLEARLY OUT FOR A WALK IN A CRYPT!
ARE THOSE THE PAPERS?
YES. WE SMUGGLED THEM OUT OF THE OLD SYNAGOGUE LIBRARY MONTHS AGO, WHEN THE SS GOT TOO NOSY.
SO THEY WERE LOOKING FOR THE SAME THING.
HEYDRICH'S HENCHMEN WEREN'T SUBTLE ABOUT IT. THEY'VE ALREADY ARRESTED A HUNDRED PEOPLE OR SO AND ASKED THEM ALL THE SAME QUESTION.
WE'LL TAKE CARE OF HEYDRICH. ONCE HE'S DEAD, THEY'LL BE DISORGANIZED. THAT SHOULD MAKE THE REST OF THE MISSION EASIER.

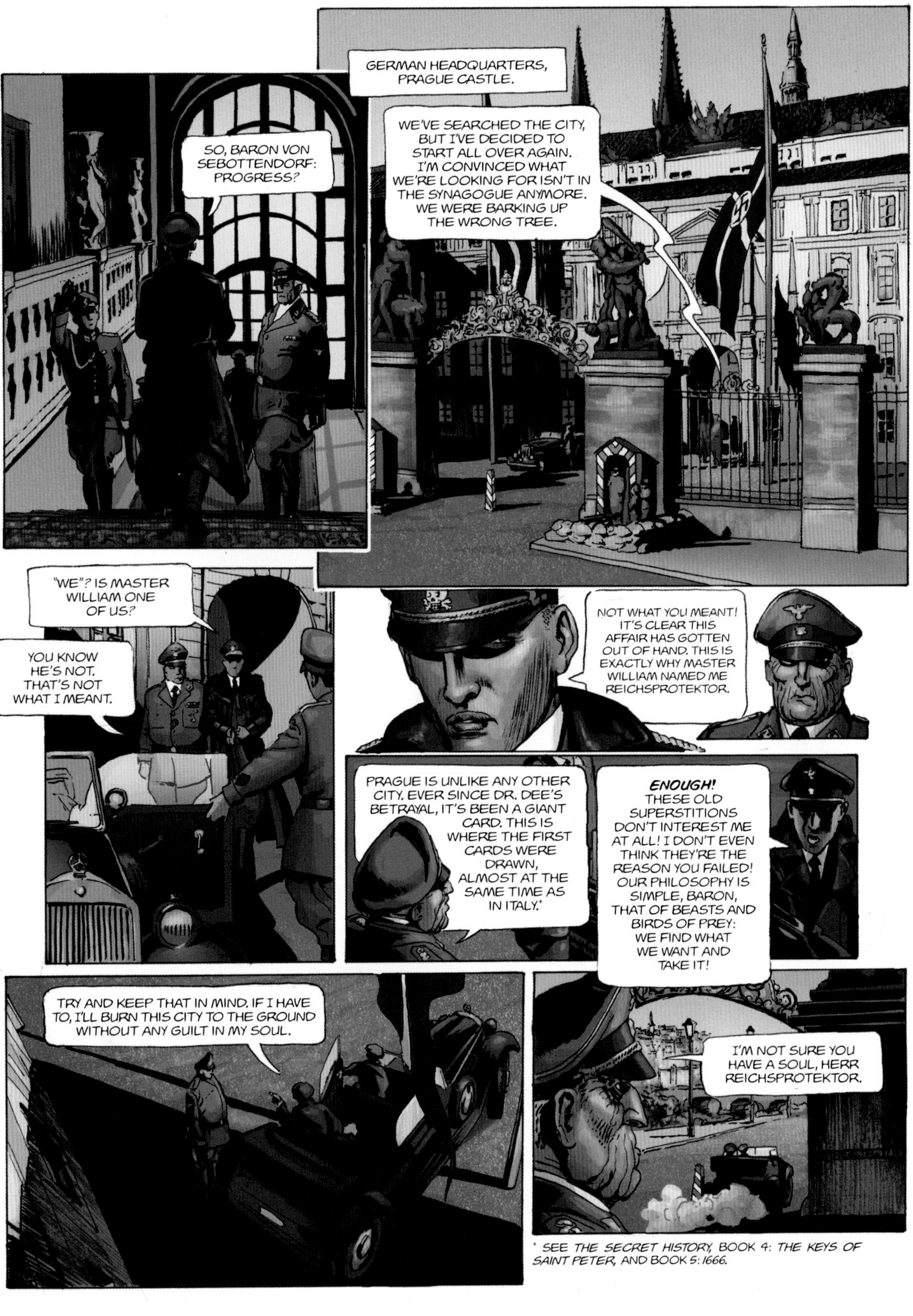
GERMAN HEADQUARTERS, PRAGUE CASTLE.
SO, BARON VON SEBOTTENDORF: PROGRESS?
WE'VE SEARCHED THE CITY, BUT I'VE DECIDED TO START ALL OVER AGAIN. I'M CONVINCED WHAT WE'RE LOOKING FOR ISN'T IN THE SYNAGOGUE ANYMORE. WE WERE BARKING UP THE WRONG TREE.
"WE"? IS MASTER WILLIAM ONE OF US?
YOU KNOW HE'S NOT. THAT'S NOT WHAT I MEANT.
NOT WHAT YOU MEANT! IT'S CLEAR THIS AFFAIR HAS GOTTEN OUT OF HAND. THIS IS EXACTLY WHY MASTER WILLIAM NAMED ME REICHSPROTEKTOR.
PRAGUE IS UNLIKE ANY OTHER CITY. EVER SINCE DR. DEE'S BETRAYAL, IT'S BEEN A GIANT CARD. THIS IS WHERE THE FIRST CARDS WERE DRAWN, ALMOST AT THE SAME TIME AS IN ITALY.*
ENOUGH! THESE OLD SUPERSTITIONS DON'T INTEREST ME AT ALL! I DON'T EVEN THINK THEY'RE THE REASON YOU FAILED! OUR PHILOSOPHY IS SIMPLE, BARON, THAT OF BEASTS AND BIRDS OF PREY: WE FIND WHAT WE WANT AND TAKE IT!
TRY AND KEEP THAT IN MIND. IF I HAVE TO, I'LL BURN THIS CITY TO THE GROUND WITHOUT ANY GUILT IN MY SOUL.
I'M NOT SURE YOU HAVE A SOUL, HERR REICHSPROTEKTOR.

* SEE *THE SECRET HISTORY, BOOK 4: THE KEYS OF SAINT PETER*, AND BOOK 5: *1666*.

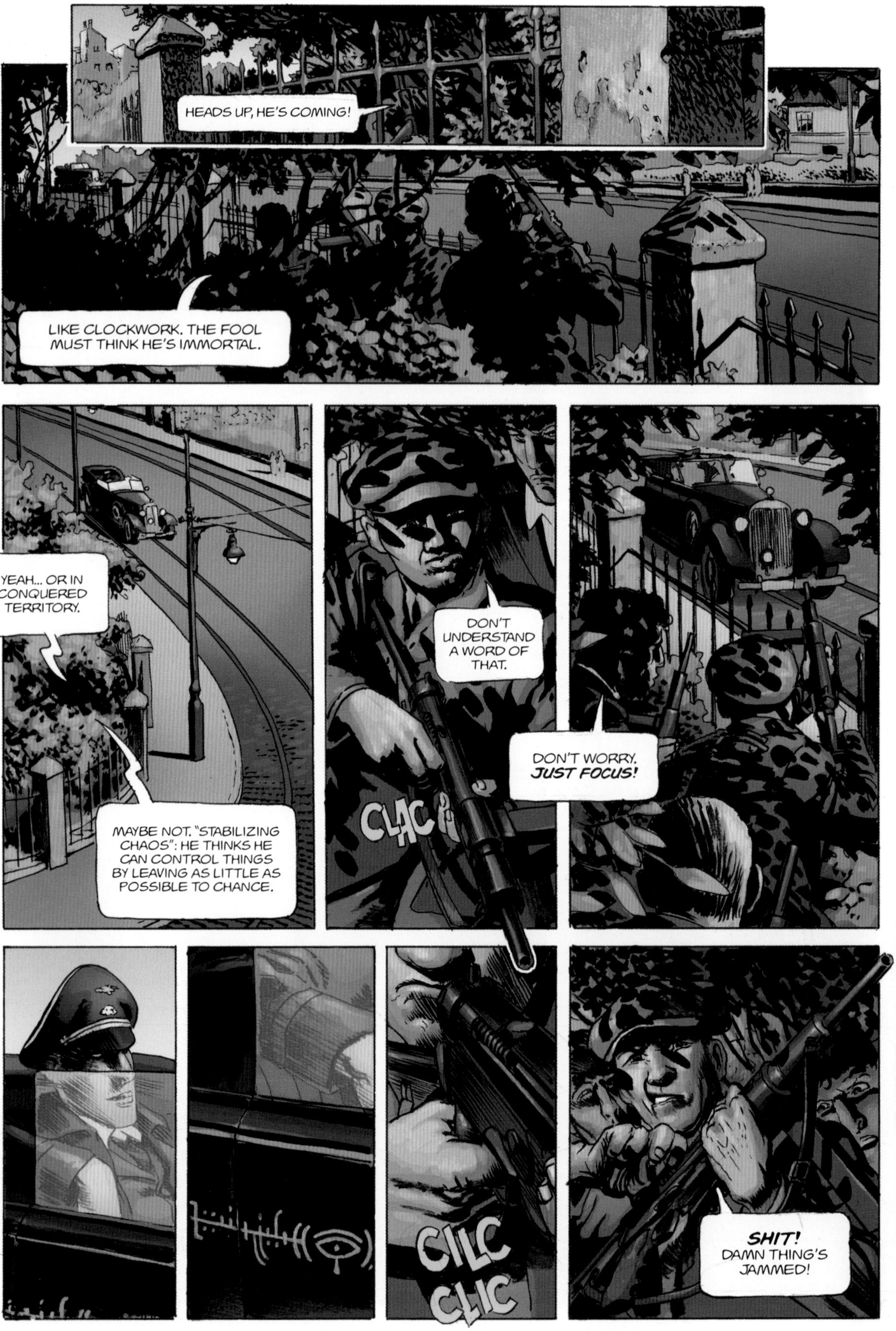
HEADS UP, HE'S COMING!
LIKE CLOCKWORK. THE FOOL MUST THINK HE'S IMMORTAL.
YEAH... OR IN CONQUERED TERRITORY.
MAYBE NOT. "STABILIZING CHAOS": HE THINKS HE CAN CONTROL THINGS BY LEAVING AS LITTLE AS POSSIBLE TO CHANCE.
DON'T UNDERSTAND A WORD OF THAT.
CLAC
DON'T WORRY. JUST FOCUS!
CLIC
CLIC
SHIT! DAMN THING'S JAMMED!

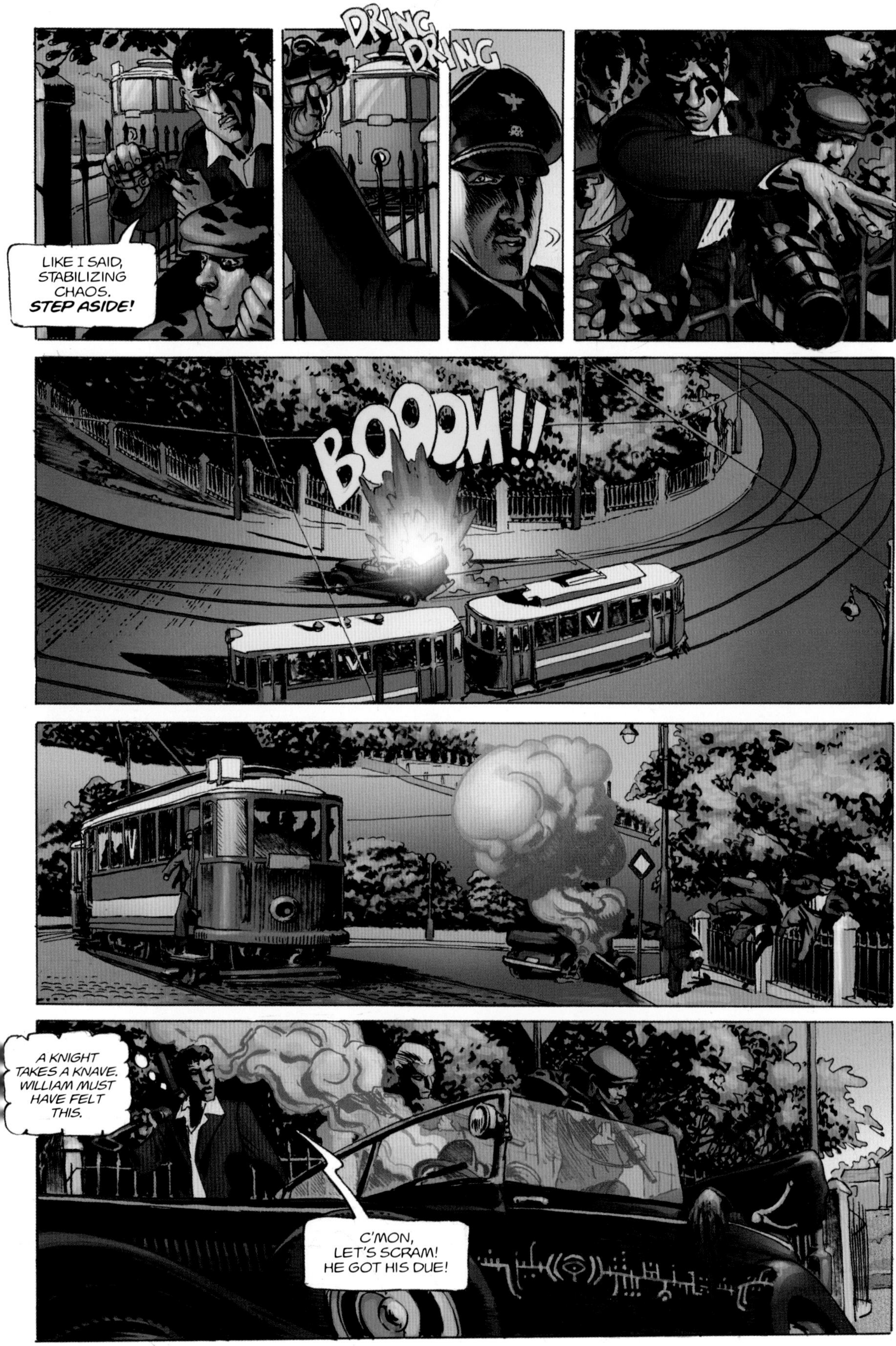
DRING DRING
LIKE I SAID, STABILIZING CHAOS. STEP ASIDE!
BOOOOM!!
A KNIGHT TAKES A KNAVE. WILLIAM MUST HAVE FELT THIS.
C'MON, LET'S SCRAM! HE GOT HIS DUE!

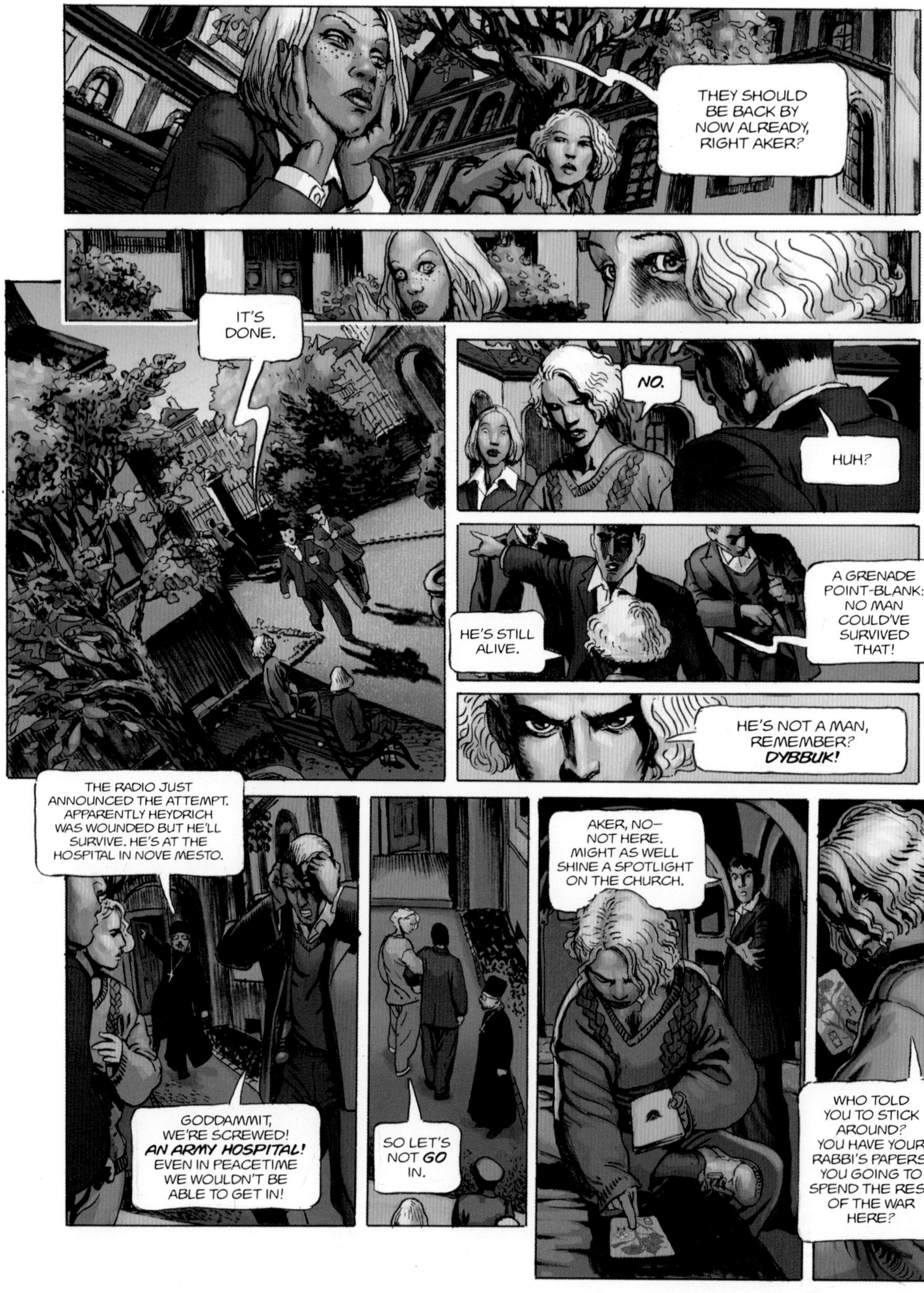
THEY SHOULD BE BACK BY NOW ALREADY, RIGHT AKER?
IT'S DONE.
NO.
HUH?
HE'S STILL ALIVE.
A GRENADE POINT-BLANK: NO MAN COULD'VE SURVIVED THAT!
HE'S NOT A MAN, REMEMBER? DYBBUK!
THE RADIO JUST ANNOUNCED THE ATTEMPT. APPARENTLY HEYDRICH WAS WOUNDED BUT HE'LL SURVIVE. HE'S AT THE HOSPITAL IN NOVE MESTO.
GODDAMMIT, WE'RE SCREWED! AN ARMY HOSPITAL! EVEN IN PEACETIME WE WOULDN'T BE ABLE TO GET IN!
SO LET'S NOT GO IN.
AKER, NO— NOT HERE. MIGHT AS WELL SHINE A SPOTLIGHT ON THE CHURCH.
WHO TOLD YOU TO STICK AROUND? YOU HAVE YOUR RABBI'S PAPERS. YOU GOING TO SPEND THE REST OF THE WAR HERE?

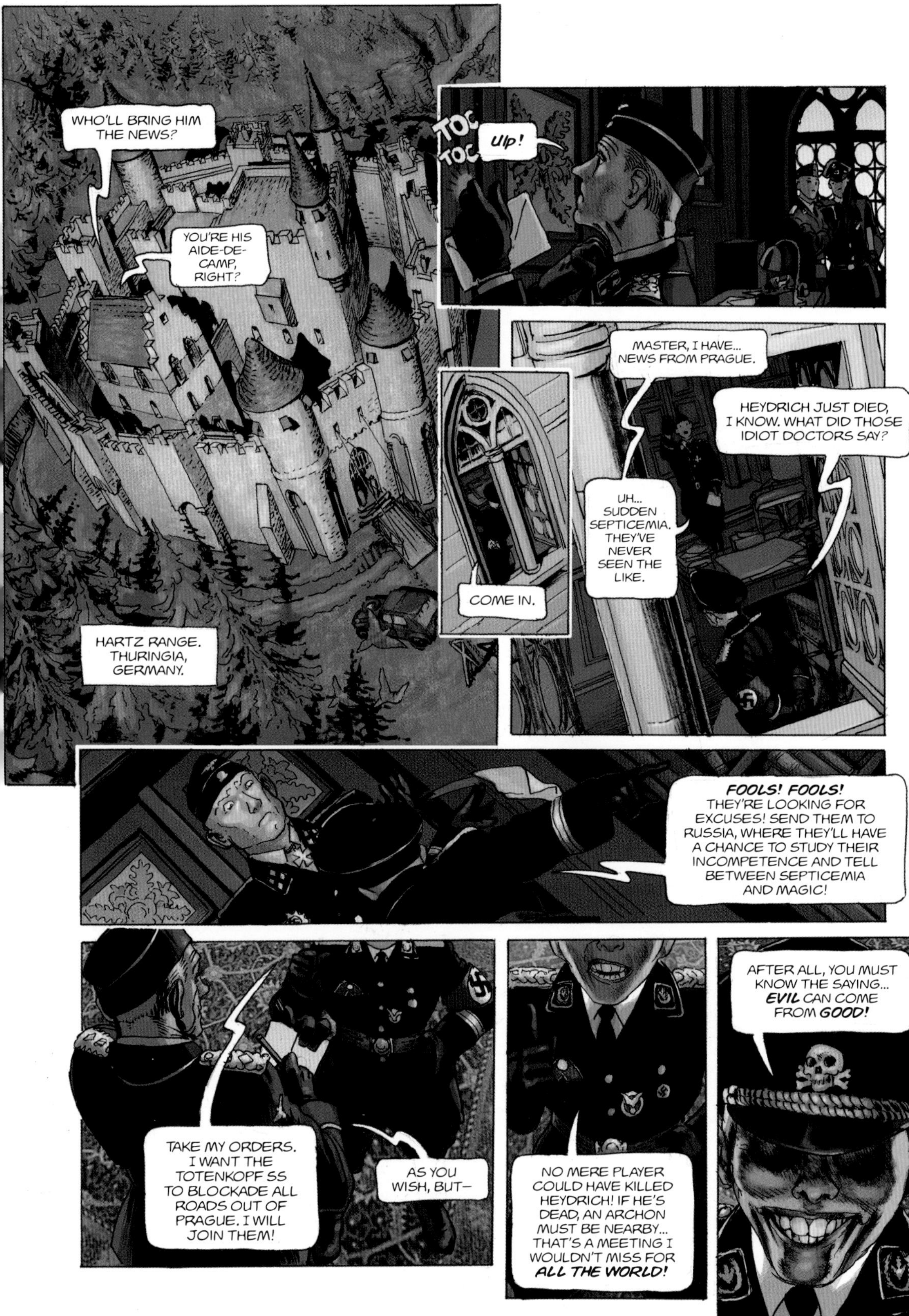

WHO'LL BRING HIM THE NEWS?
YOU'RE HIS AIDE-DE-CAMP, RIGHT?
HARTZ RANGE. THURINGIA, GERMANY.
TOC TOC
Up!
COME IN.
MASTER, I HAVE... NEWS FROM PRAGUE.
HEYDRICH JUST DIED, I KNOW. WHAT DID THOSE IDIOT DOCTORS SAY?
UH... SUDDEN SEPTICEMIA. THEY'VE NEVER SEEN THE LIKE.
FOOLS! FOOLS! THEY'RE LOOKING FOR EXCUSES! SEND THEM TO RUSSIA, WHERE THEY'LL HAVE A CHANCE TO STUDY THEIR INCOMPETENCE AND TELL BETWEEN SEPTICEMIA AND MAGIC!
TAKE MY ORDERS. I WANT THE TOTENKOPF SS TO BLOCKADE ALL ROADS OUT OF PRAGUE. I WILL JOIN THEM!
AS YOU WISH, BUT—
NO MERE PLAYER COULD HAVE KILLED HEYDRICH! IF HE'S DEAD, AN ARCHON MUST BE NEARBY... THAT'S A MEETING I WOULDN'T MISS FOR ALL THE WORLD!
AFTER ALL, YOU MUST KNOW THE SAYING... EVIL CAN COME FROM GOOD!

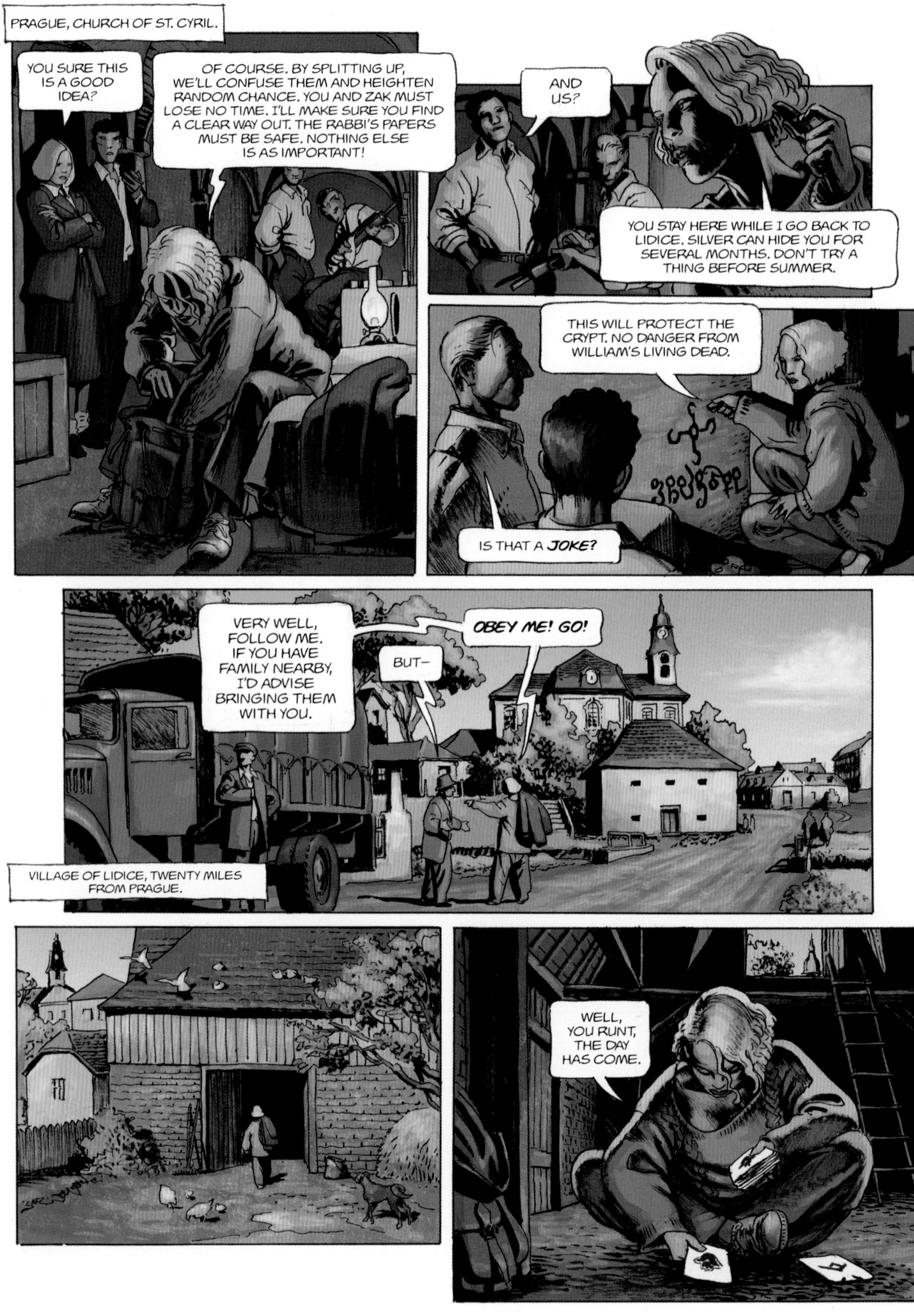
PRAGUE, CHURCH OF ST. CYRIL.
YOU SURE THIS IS A GOOD IDEA?
OF COURSE. BY SPLITTING UP, WE'LL CONFUSE THEM AND HEIGHTEN RANDOM CHANCE. YOU AND ZAK MUST LOSE NO TIME. I'LL MAKE SURE YOU FIND A CLEAR WAY OUT. THE RABBI'S PAPERS MUST BE SAFE. NOTHING ELSE IS AS IMPORTANT!
AND US?
YOU STAY HERE WHILE I GO BACK TO LIDICE. SILVER CAN HIDE YOU FOR SEVERAL MONTHS. DON'T TRY A THING BEFORE SUMMER.
THIS WILL PROTECT THE CRYPT. NO DANGER FROM WILLIAM'S LIVING DEAD.
IS THAT A JOKE?
VERY WELL, FOLLOW ME. IF YOU HAVE FAMILY NEARBY, I'D ADVISE BRINGING THEM WITH YOU.
BUT–
OBEY ME! GO!
VILLAGE OF LIDICE, TWENTY MILES FROM PRAGUE.
WELL, YOU RUNT, THE DAY HAS COME.

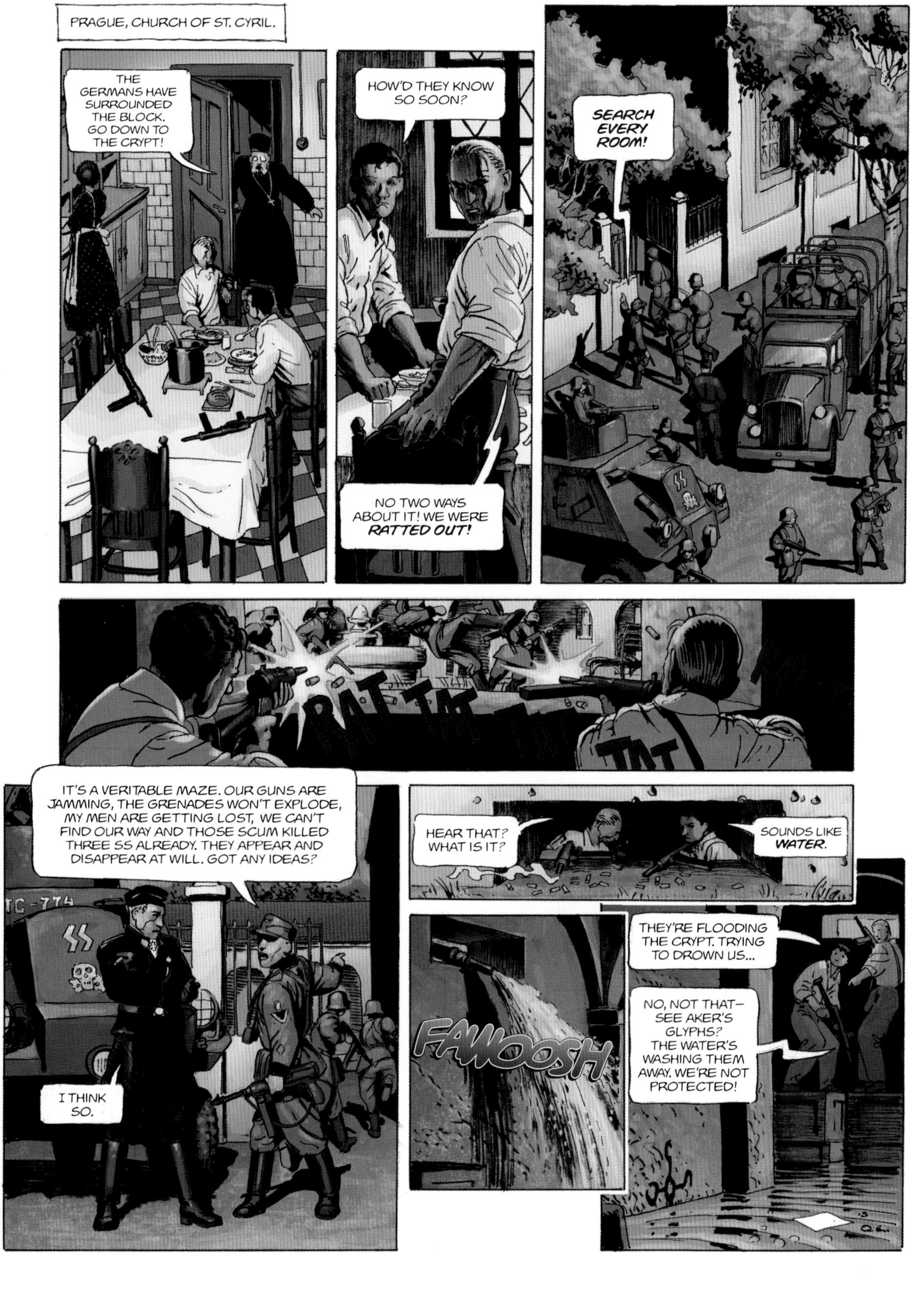
PRAGUE, CHURCH OF ST. CYRIL.
THE GERMANS HAVE SURROUNDED THE BLOCK. GO DOWN TO THE CRYPT!
HOW'D THEY KNOW SO SOON?
NO TWO WAYS ABOUT IT! WE WERE RATTED OUT!
SEARCH EVERY ROOM!
RAT TAT TAT
TAT
IT'S A VERITABLE MAZE. OUR GUNS ARE JAMMING, THE GRENADES WON'T EXPLODE, MY MEN ARE GETTING LOST, WE CAN'T FIND OUR WAY AND THOSE SCUM KILLED THREE SS ALREADY. THEY APPEAR AND DISAPPEAR AT WILL. GOT ANY IDEAS?
I THINK SO.
HEAR THAT? WHAT IS IT?
SOUNDS LIKE WATER.
FAWOOSH
THEY'RE FLOODING THE CRYPT. TRYING TO DROWN US...
NO, NOT THAT—SEE AKER'S GLYPHS? THE WATER'S WASHING THEM AWAY. WE'RE NOT PROTECTED!

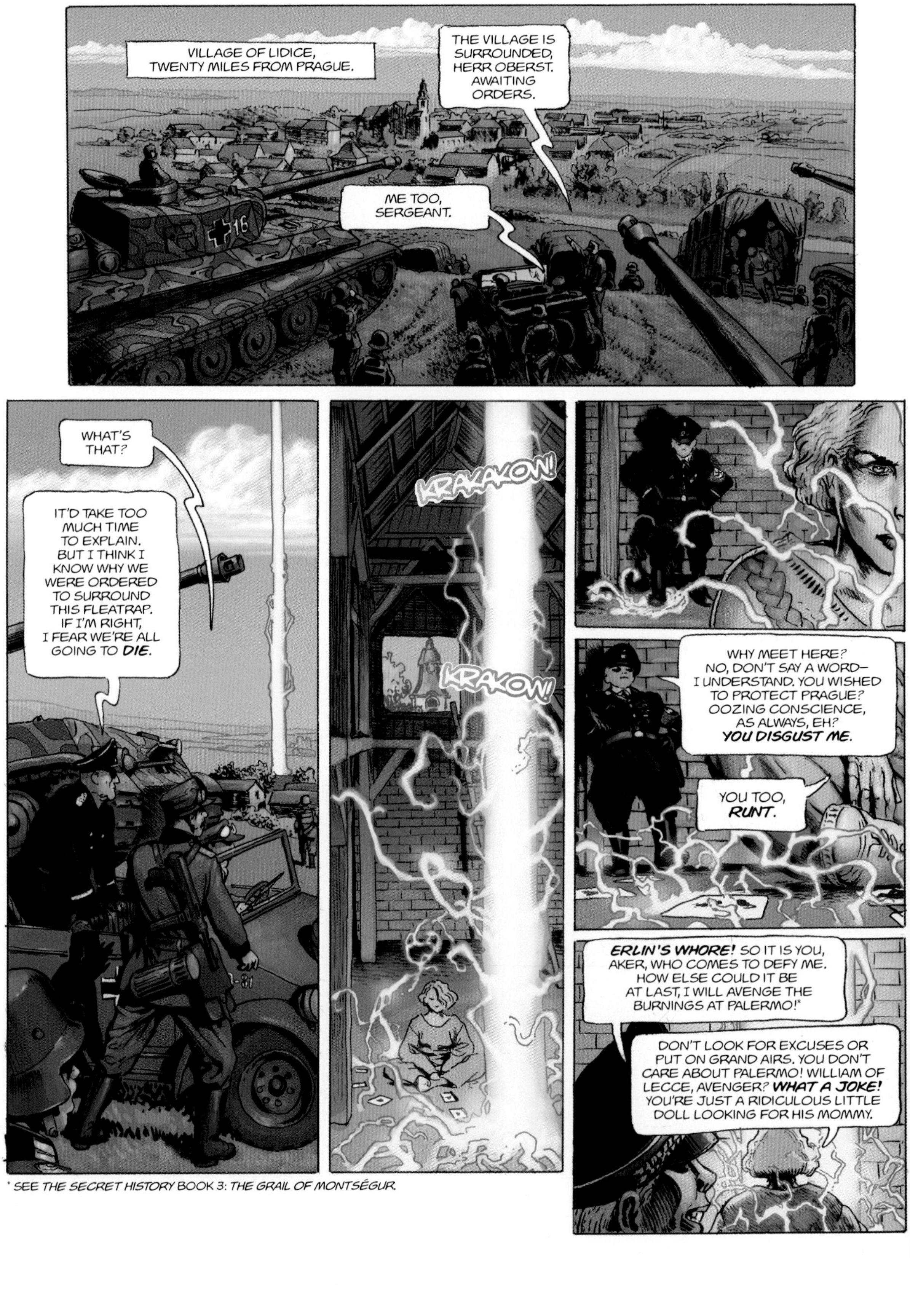
VILLAGE OF LIDICE, TWENTY MILES FROM PRAGUE.
THE VILLAGE IS SURROUNDED, HERR OBERST. AWAITING ORDERS.
ME TOO, SERGEANT.
WHAT'S THAT?
IT'D TAKE TOO MUCH TIME TO EXPLAIN. BUT I THINK I KNOW WHY WE WERE ORDERED TO SURROUND THIS FLEATRAP. IF I'M RIGHT, I FEAR WE'RE ALL GOING TO DIE.
KRAKAKOW!
KRAKOW!
WHY MEET HERE? NO, DON'T SAY A WORD– I UNDERSTAND. YOU WISHED TO PROTECT PRAGUE? OOZING CONSCIENCE, AS ALWAYS, EH? YOU DISGUST ME.
YOU TOO, RUNT.
ERLIN'S WHORE! SO IT IS YOU, AKER, WHO COMES TO DEFY ME. HOW ELSE COULD IT BE AT LAST, I WILL AVENGE THE BURNINGS AT PALERMO!*
DON'T LOOK FOR EXCUSES OR PUT ON GRAND AIRS. YOU DON'T CARE ABOUT PALERMO! WILLIAM OF LECCE, AVENGER? WHAT A JOKE! YOU'RE JUST A RIDICULOUS LITTLE DOLL LOOKING FOR HIS MOMMY.

* SEE *THE SECRET HISTORY BOOK 3: THE GRAIL OF MONTSÉGUR.*

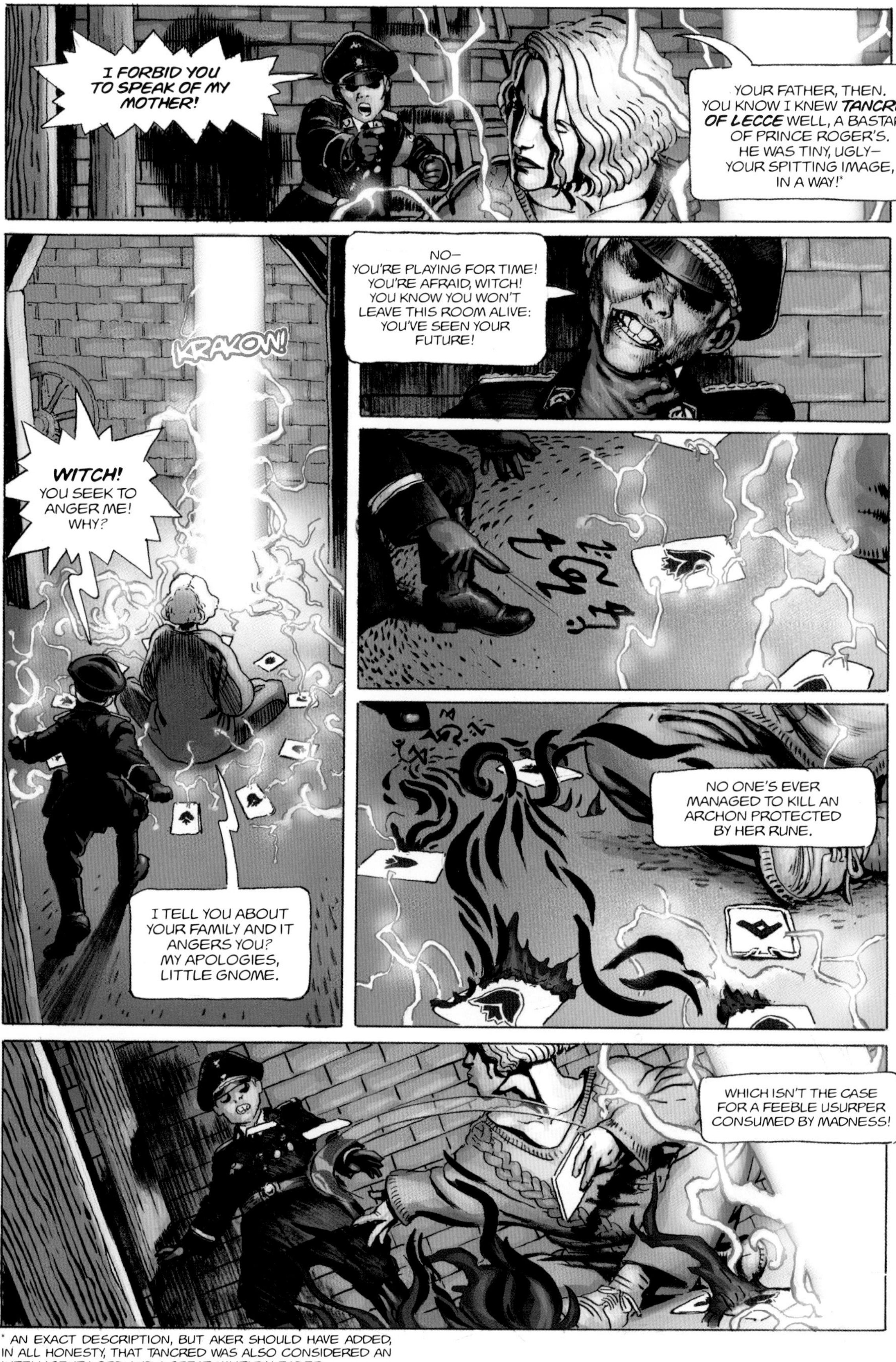
I FORBID YOU TO SPEAK OF MY MOTHER!
YOUR FATHER, THEN. YOU KNOW I KNEW TANCRED OF LECCE WELL, A BASTARD OF PRINCE ROGER'S. HE WAS TINY, UGLY— YOUR SPITTING IMAGE, IN A WAY!*
NO— YOU'RE PLAYING FOR TIME! YOU'RE AFRAID, WITCH! YOU KNOW YOU WON'T LEAVE THIS ROOM ALIVE: YOU'VE SEEN YOUR FUTURE!
KRAKOW!
WITCH! YOU SEEK TO ANGER ME! WHY?
I TELL YOU ABOUT YOUR FAMILY AND IT ANGERS YOU? MY APOLOGIES, LITTLE GNOME.
NO ONE'S EVER MANAGED TO KILL AN ARCHON PROTECTED BY HER RUNE.
WHICH ISN'T THE CASE FOR A FEEBLE USURPER CONSUMED BY MADNESS!

* AN EXACT DESCRIPTION, BUT AKER SHOULD HAVE ADDED, IN ALL HONESTY, THAT TANCRED WAS ALSO CONSIDERED AN INTELLIGENT LORD AND A GREAT MILITARY LEADER.

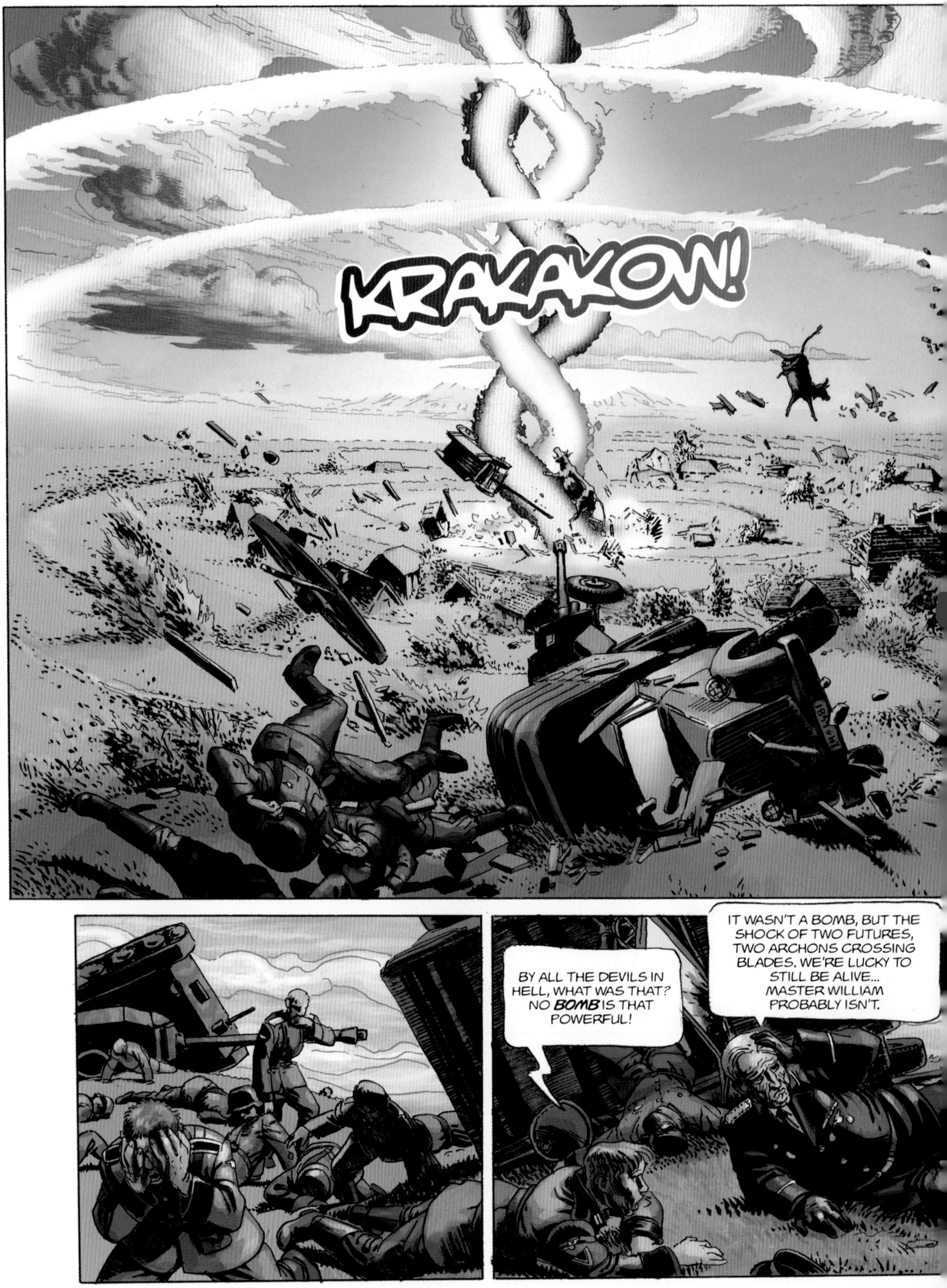
KRAKAKOW!
BY ALL THE DEVILS IN HELL, WHAT WAS THAT? NO BOMB IS THAT POWERFUL!
IT WASN'T A BOMB, BUT THE SHOCK OF TWO FUTURES, TWO ARCHONS CROSSING BLADES. WE'RE LUCKY TO STILL BE ALIVE... MASTER WILLIAM PROBABLY ISN'T.

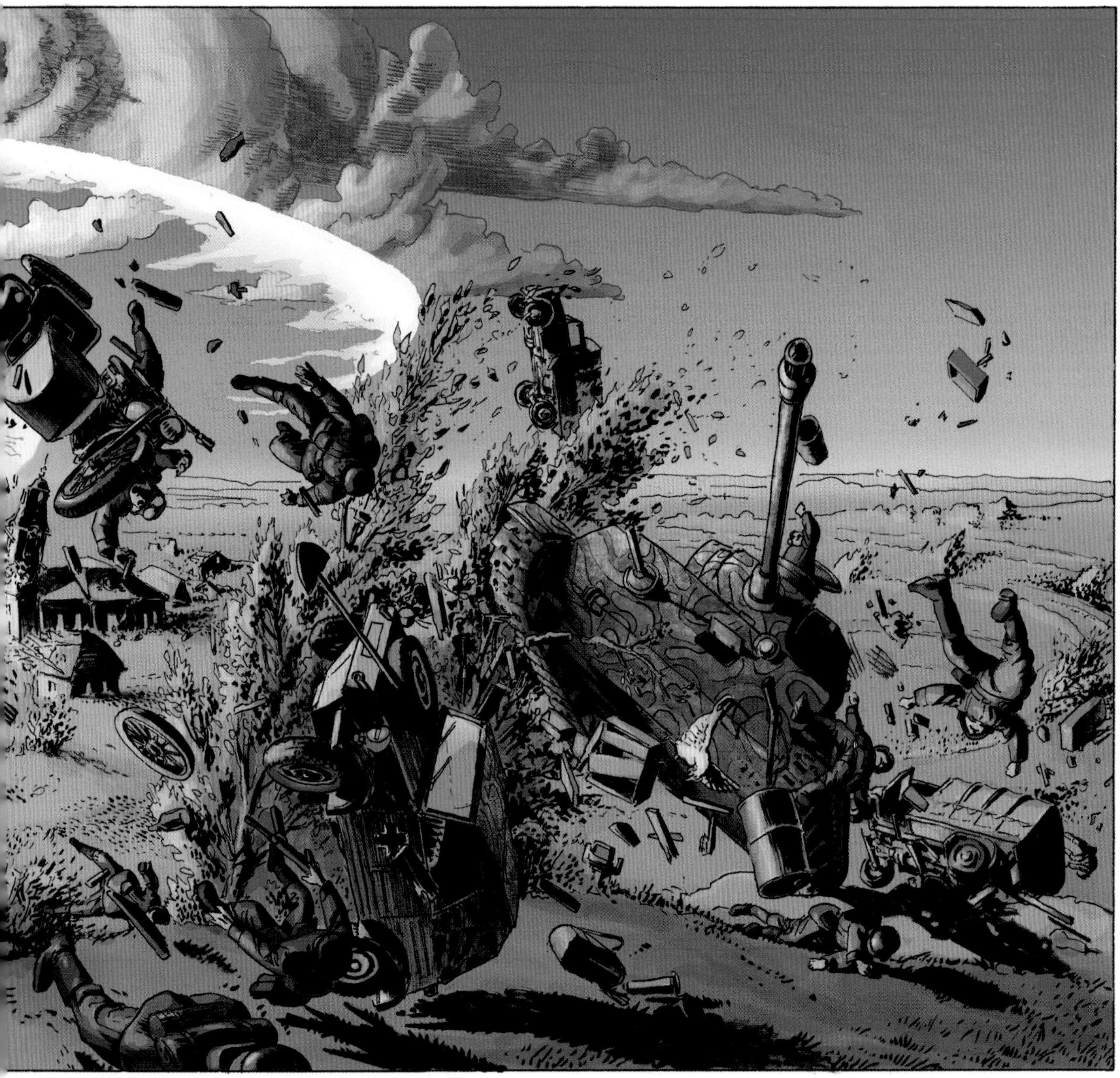

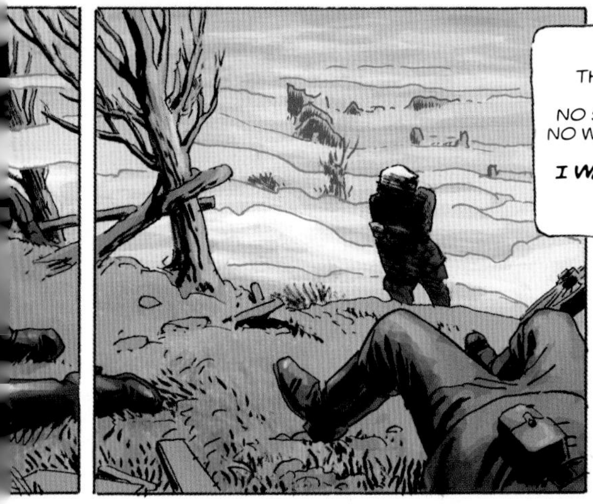

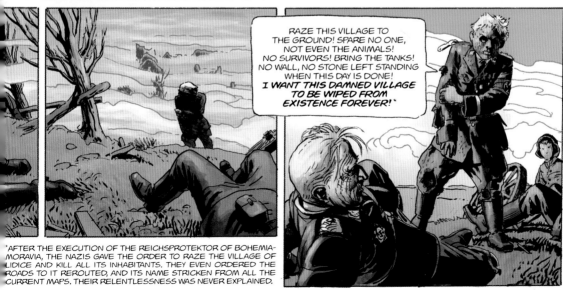

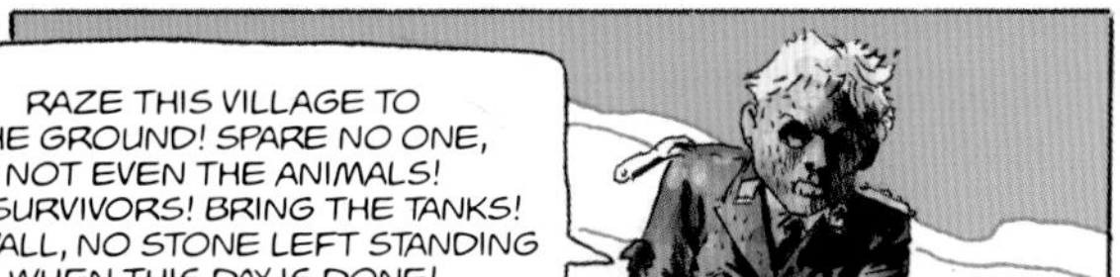
RAZE THIS VILLAGE TO THE GROUND! SPARE NO ONE, NOT EVEN THE ANIMALS! NO SURVIVORS! BRING THE TANKS! NO WALL, NO STONE LEFT STANDING WHEN THIS DAY IS DONE! ***I WANT THIS DAMNED VILLAGE TO BE WIPED FROM EXISTENCE FOREVER!****

*AFTER THE EXECUTION OF THE REICHSPROTEKTOR OF BOHEMIA-MORAVIA, THE NAZIS GAVE THE ORDER TO RAZE THE VILLAGE OF LIDICE AND KILL ALL ITS INHABITANTS. THEY EVEN ORDERED THE ROADS TO IT REROUTED, AND ITS NAME STRICKEN FROM ALL THE CURRENT MAPS. THEIR RELENTLESSNESS WAS NEVER EXPLAINED.

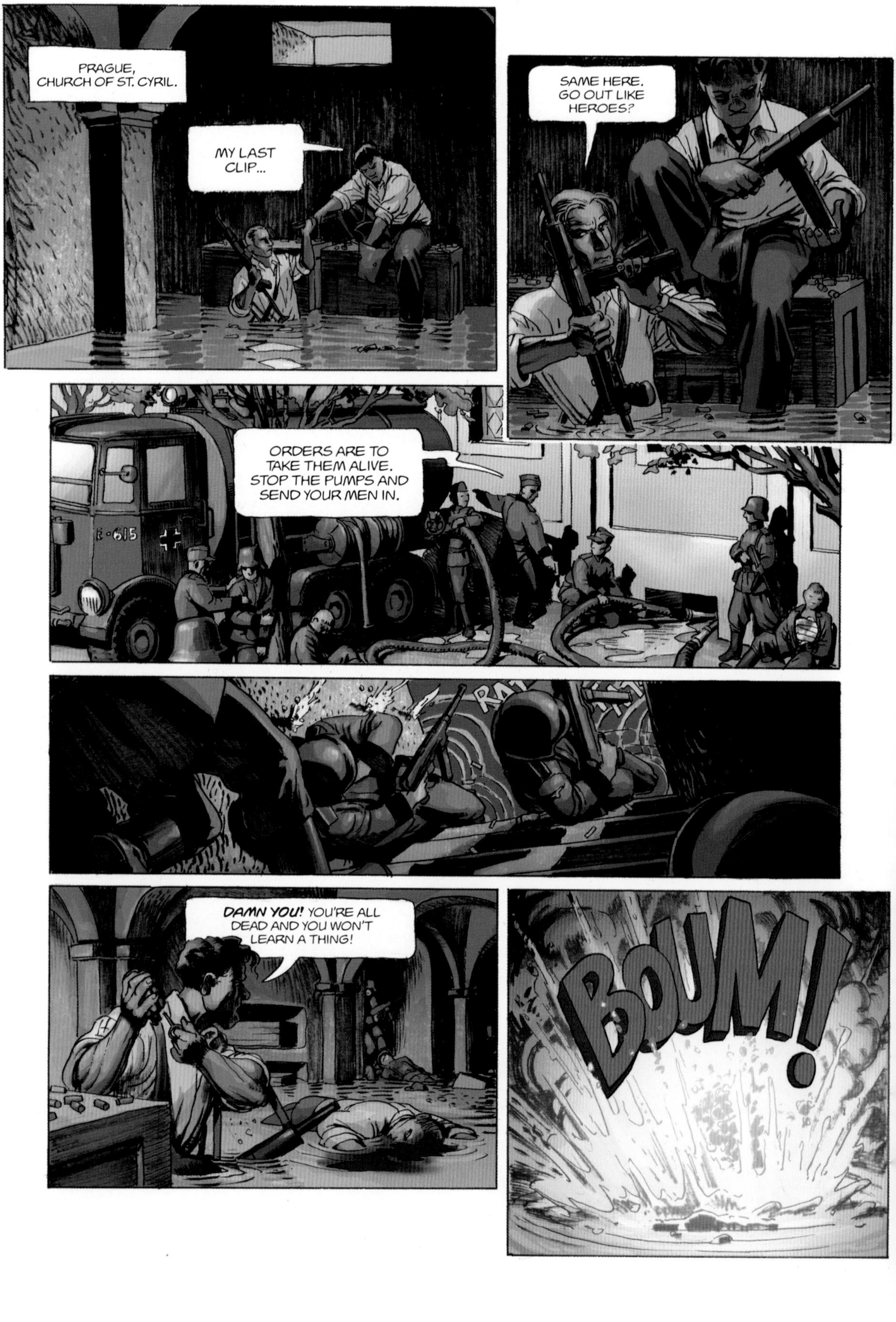
PRAGUE, CHURCH OF ST. CYRIL.
MY LAST CLIP...
SAME HERE. GO OUT LIKE HEROES?
E-615
ORDERS ARE TO TAKE THEM ALIVE. STOP THE PUMPS AND SEND YOUR MEN IN.
DAMN YOU! YOU'RE ALL DEAD AND YOU WON'T LEARN A THING!
BOUM!

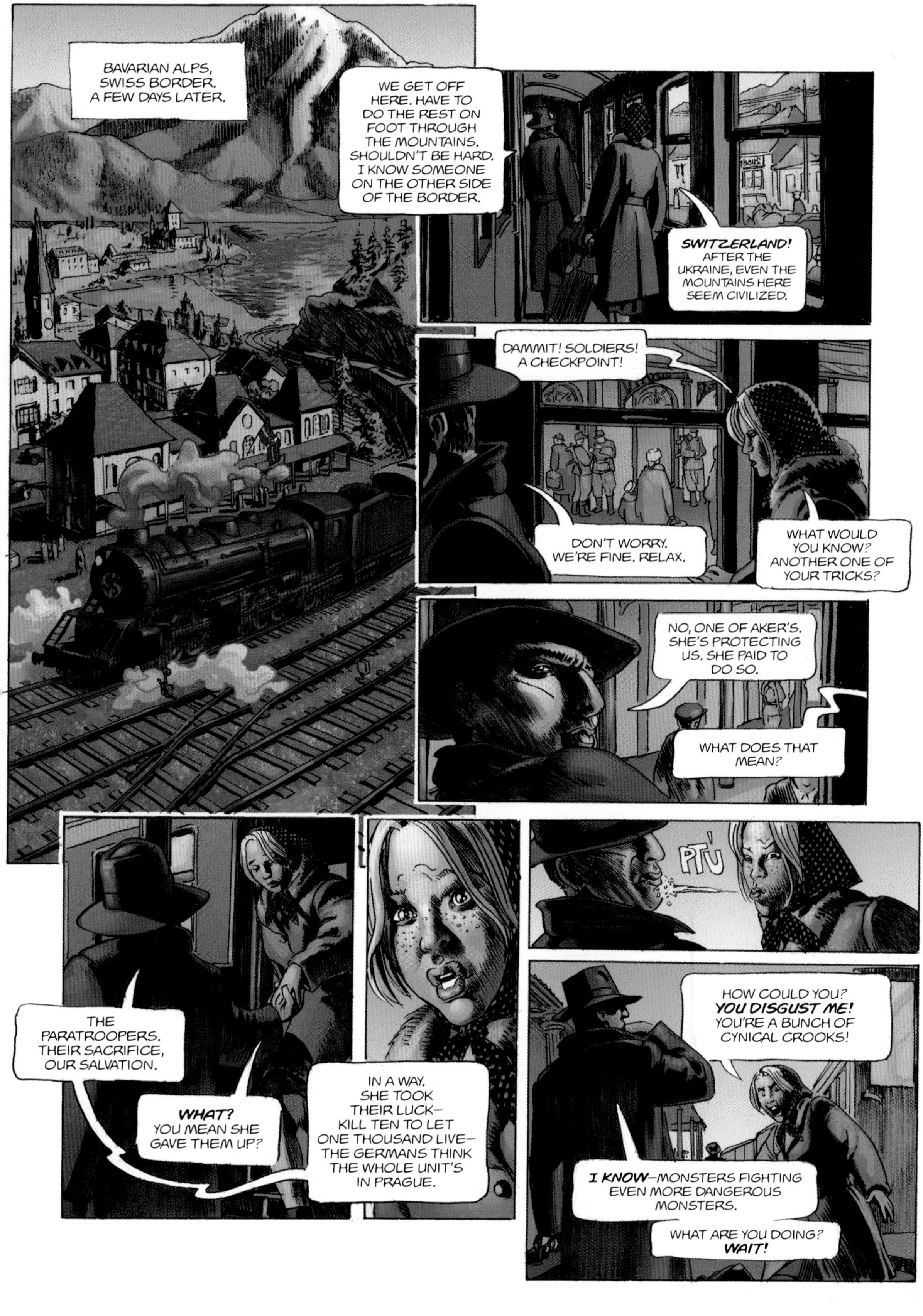
BAVARIAN ALPS, SWISS BORDER. A FEW DAYS LATER.
WE GET OFF HERE. HAVE TO DO THE REST ON FOOT THROUGH THE MOUNTAINS. SHOULDN'T BE HARD. I KNOW SOMEONE ON THE OTHER SIDE OF THE BORDER.
SWITZERLAND! AFTER THE UKRAINE, EVEN THE MOUNTAINS HERE SEEM CIVILIZED.
DAMMIT! SOLDIERS! A CHECKPOINT!
DON'T WORRY. WE'RE FINE. RELAX.
WHAT WOULD YOU KNOW? ANOTHER ONE OF YOUR TRICKS?
NO, ONE OF AKER'S. SHE'S PROTECTING US. SHE PAID TO DO SO.
WHAT DOES THAT MEAN?
THE PARATROOPERS. THEIR SACRIFICE, OUR SALVATION.
WHAT? YOU MEAN SHE GAVE THEM UP?
IN A WAY. SHE TOOK THEIR LUCK— KILL TEN TO LET ONE THOUSAND LIVE— THE GERMANS THINK THE WHOLE UNIT'S IN PRAGUE.
PTU
HOW COULD YOU? YOU DISGUST ME! YOU'RE A BUNCH OF CYNICAL CROOKS!
I KNOW—MONSTERS FIGHTING EVEN MORE DANGEROUS MONSTERS.
WHAT ARE YOU DOING? WAIT!

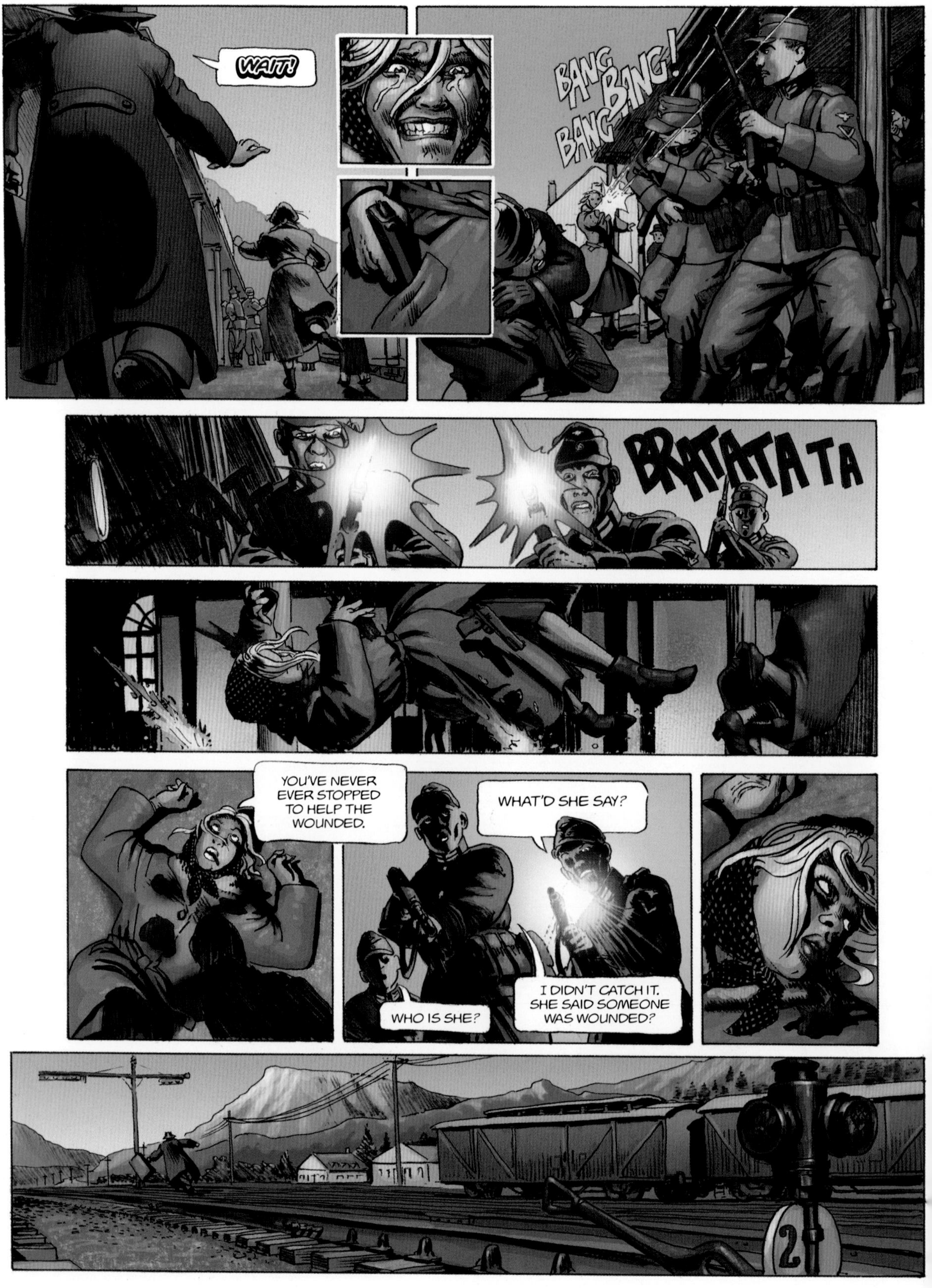
WAIT!
BANG BANG BANG!
BRATATATA TA
YOU'VE NEVER EVER STOPPED TO HELP THE WOUNDED.
WHAT'D SHE SAY?
WHO IS SHE?
I DIDN'T CATCH IT. SHE SAID SOMEONE WAS WOUNDED?
2

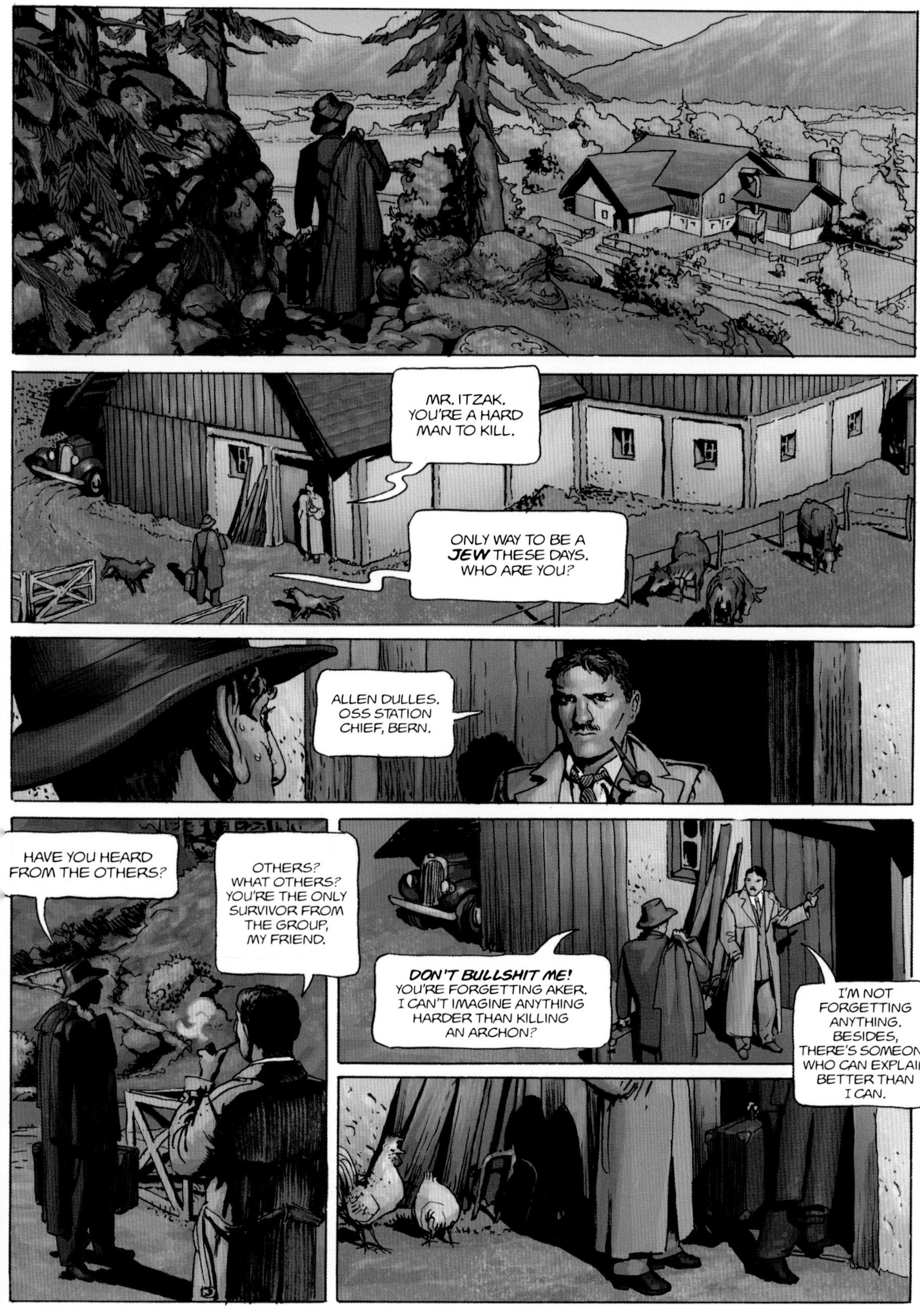
MR. ITZAK. YOU'RE A HARD MAN TO KILL.
ONLY WAY TO BE A JEW THESE DAYS. WHO ARE YOU?
ALLEN DULLES. OSS STATION CHIEF, BERN.
HAVE YOU HEARD FROM THE OTHERS?
OTHERS? WHAT OTHERS? YOU'RE THE ONLY SURVIVOR FROM THE GROUP, MY FRIEND.
DON'T BULLSHIT ME! YOU'RE FORGETTING AKER. I CAN'T IMAGINE ANYTHING HARDER THAN KILLING AN ARCHON?
I'M NOT FORGETTING ANYTHING. BESIDES, THERE'S SOMEONE WHO CAN EXPLAIN BETTER THAN I CAN.

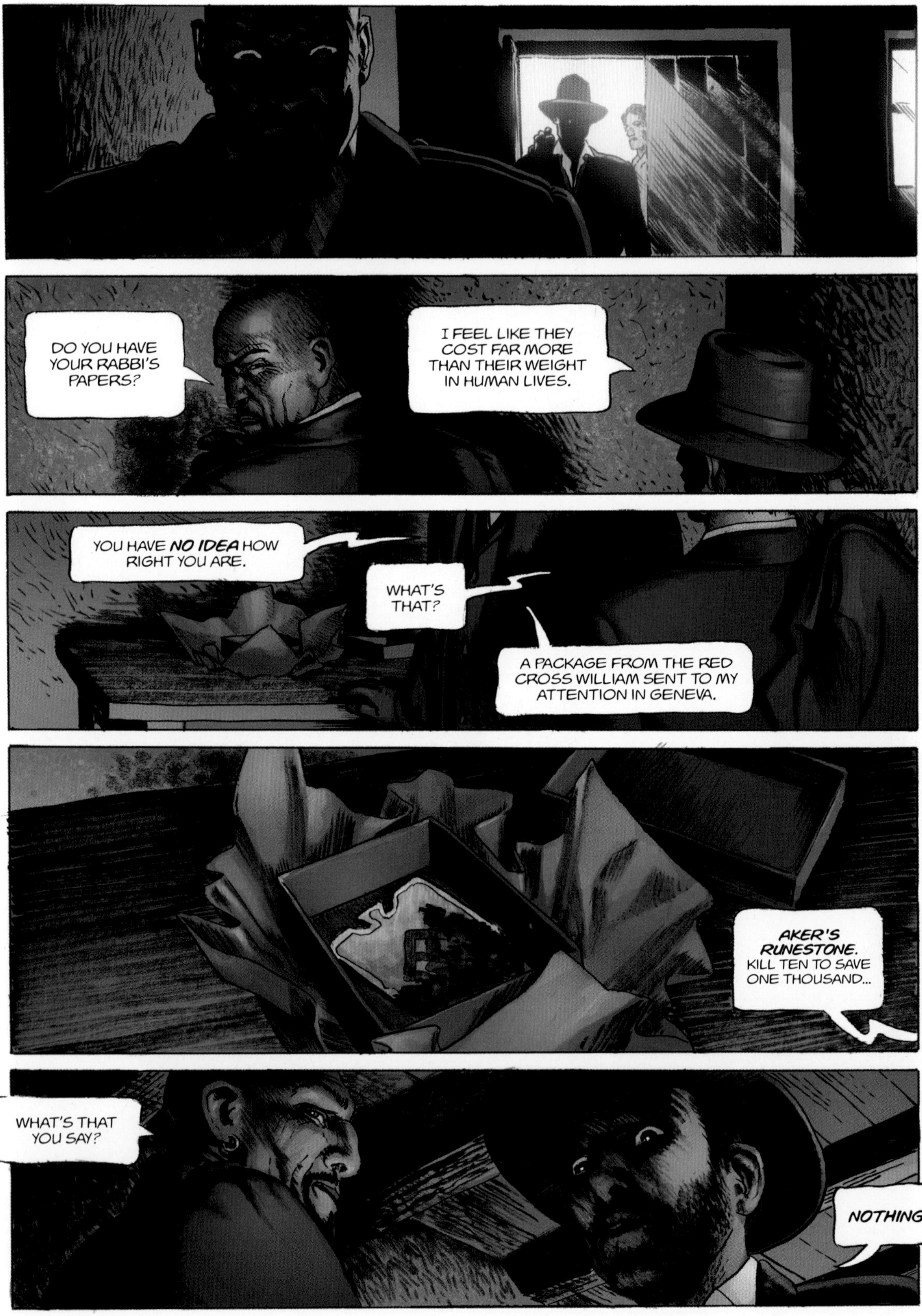
DO YOU HAVE YOUR RABBI'S PAPERS?
I FEEL LIKE THEY COST FAR MORE THAN THEIR WEIGHT IN HUMAN LIVES.
YOU HAVE **NO IDEA** HOW RIGHT YOU ARE.
WHAT'S THAT?
A PACKAGE FROM THE RED CROSS WILLIAM SENT TO MY ATTENTION IN GENEVA.
AKER'S RUNESTONE. KILL TEN TO SAVE ONE THOUSAND...
WHAT'S THAT YOU SAY?
NOTHING.

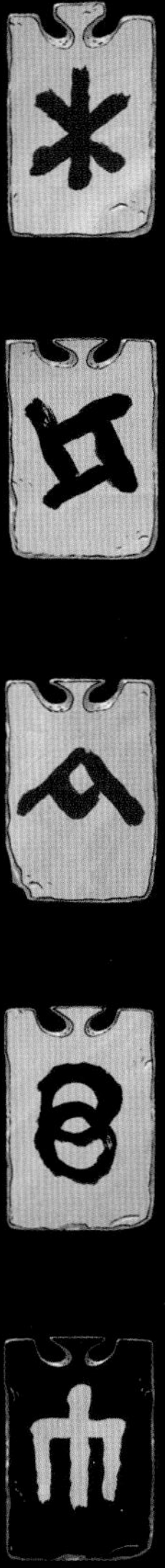

1918 A.D. 1919 A.D. 1926 A.D. 1940 A.D.

1942 A.D.

BOOK TWELVE
LUCKY POINT

1942 A.D.

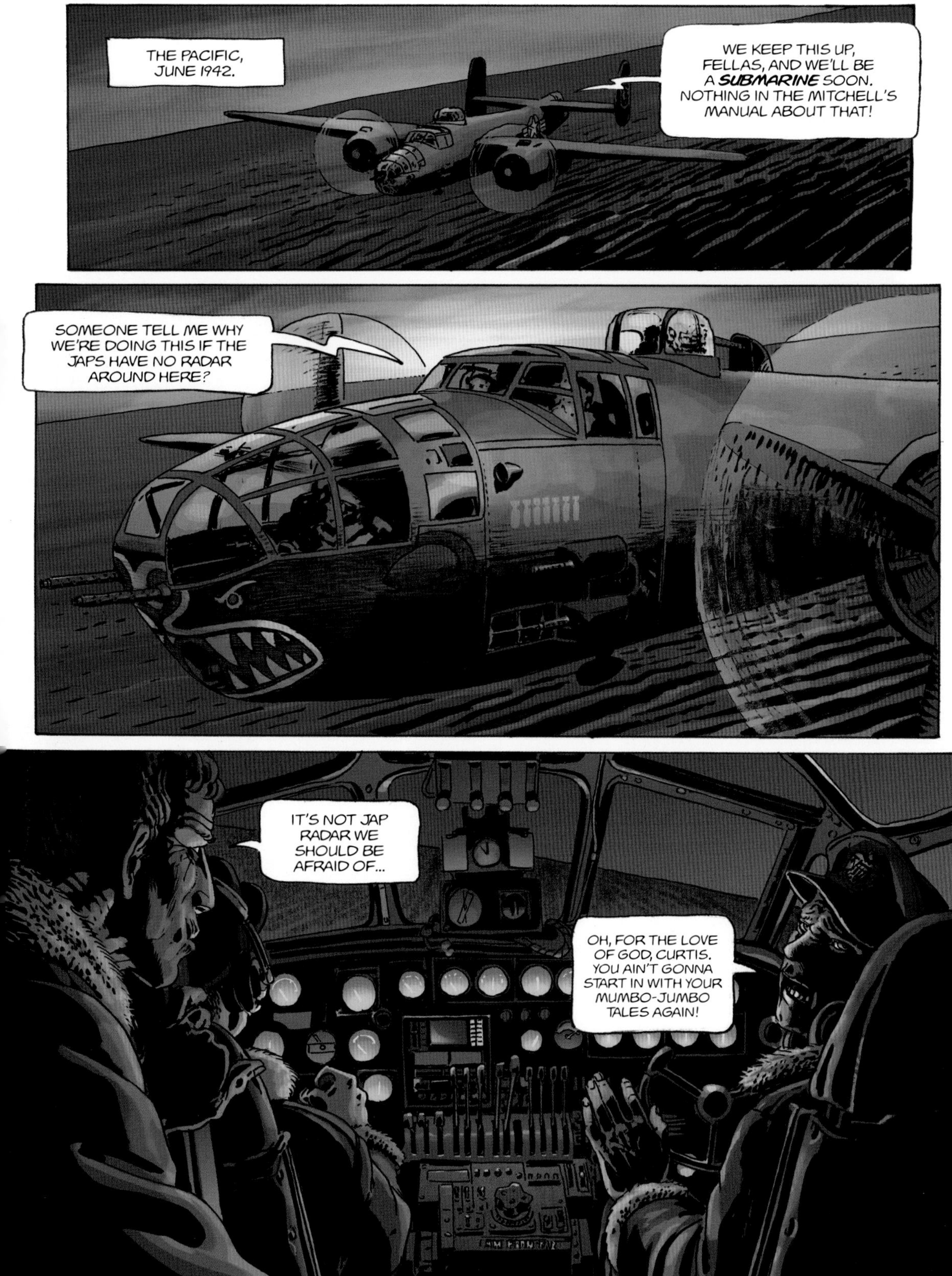
THE PACIFIC, JUNE 1942.
WE KEEP THIS UP, FELLAS, AND WE'LL BE A SUBMARINE SOON. NOTHING IN THE MITCHELL'S MANUAL ABOUT THAT!
SOMEONE TELL ME WHY WE'RE DOING THIS IF THE JAPS HAVE NO RADAR AROUND HERE?
IT'S NOT JAP RADAR WE SHOULD BE AFRAID OF...
OH, FOR THE LOVE OF GOD, CURTIS. YOU AIN'T GONNA START IN WITH YOUR MUMBO-JUMBO TALES AGAIN!

SHARK ISLAND, FRENCH FRIGATE SHOALS. 560 MILES NORTHWEST OF HONOLULU.

I NOTE WITH REGRET, *HERR* OBERST, THAT YOUR SUPERIORS *STILL* DO NOT TRUST YOU.

WHY DO YOU SAY THAT, IKO SAN?

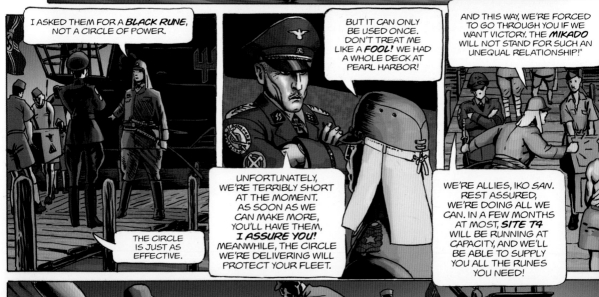

I ASKED THEM FOR A *BLACK RUNE*, NOT A CIRCLE OF POWER.

BUT IT CAN ONLY BE USED ONCE. DON'T TREAT ME LIKE A *FOOL!* WE HAD A WHOLE DECK AT PEARL HARBOR!

AND THIS WAY, WE'RE FORCED TO GO THROUGH YOU IF WE WANT VICTORY. THE *MIKADO* WILL NOT STAND FOR SUCH AN UNEQUAL RELATIONSHIP!*

THE CIRCLE IS JUST AS EFFECTIVE.

UNFORTUNATELY, WE'RE TERRIBLY SHORT AT THE MOMENT. AS SOON AS WE CAN MAKE MORE, YOU'LL HAVE THEM, *I ASSURE YOU!* MEANWHILE, THE CIRCLE WE'RE DELIVERING WILL PROTECT YOUR FLEET.

WE'RE ALLIES, IKO *SAN.* REST ASSURED, WE'RE DOING ALL WE CAN. IN A FEW MONTHS AT MOST, *SITE T4* WILL BE RUNNING AT CAPACITY, AND WE'LL BE ABLE TO SUPPLY YOU ALL THE RUNES YOU NEED!

*DURING WWII, THE MIKADO WAS THE JAPANESE HIGH STRATEGIC COMMAN

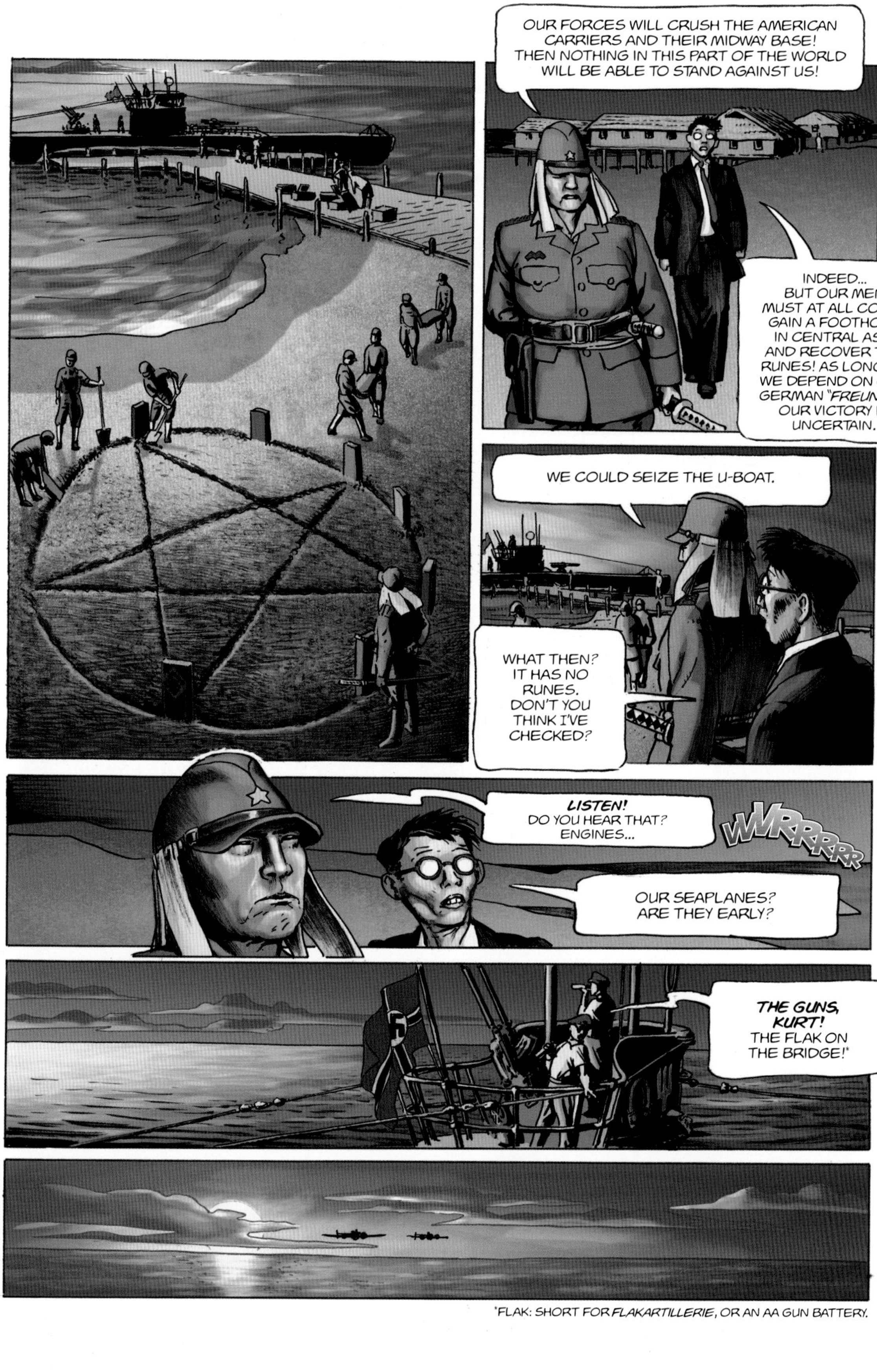
OUR FORCES WILL CRUSH THE AMERICAN CARRIERS AND THEIR MIDWAY BASE! THEN NOTHING IN THIS PART OF THE WORLD WILL BE ABLE TO STAND AGAINST US!
INDEED... BUT OUR MEN MUST AT ALL COSTS GAIN A FOOTHOLD IN CENTRAL ASIA AND RECOVER THE RUNES! AS LONG AS WE DEPEND ON OUR GERMAN "FREUNDS," OUR VICTORY IS UNCERTAIN.
WE COULD SEIZE THE U-BOAT.
WHAT THEN? IT HAS NO RUNES. DON'T YOU THINK I'VE CHECKED?
LISTEN! DO YOU HEAR THAT? ENGINES...
WWRRRRRR
OUR SEAPLANES? ARE THEY EARLY?
THE GUNS, KURT! THE FLAK ON THE BRIDGE!*

*FLAK: SHORT FOR *FLAKARTILLERIE*, OR AN AA GUN BATTERY.

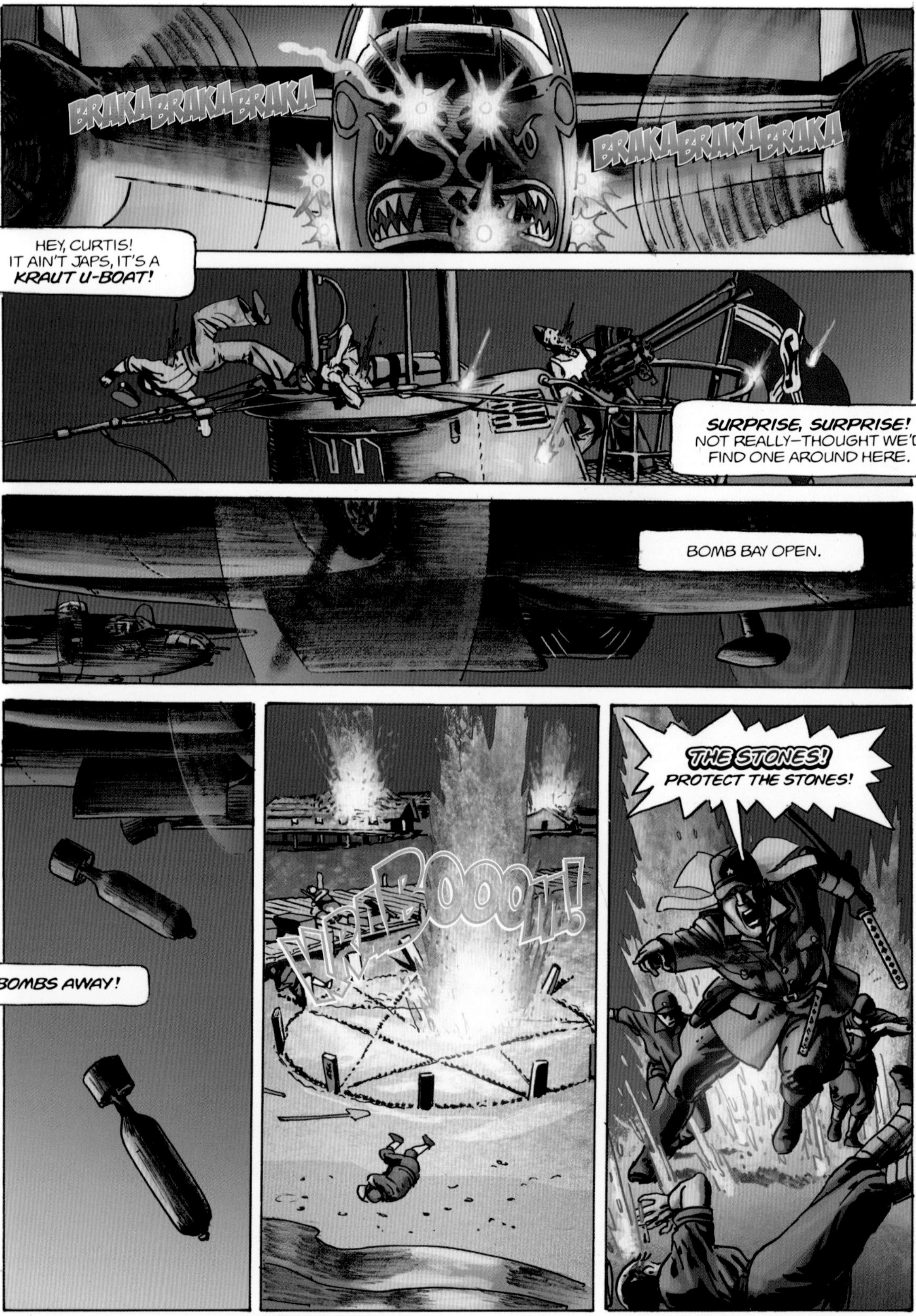
BRAKABRAKABRAKA
BRAKABRAKABRAKA
HEY, CURTIS! IT AIN'T JAPS, IT'S A KRAUT U-BOAT!
SURPRISE, SURPRISE! NOT REALLY—THOUGHT WE'D FIND ONE AROUND HERE.
BOMB BAY OPEN.
BOMBS AWAY!
VRABOOOM!
THE STONES! PROTECT THE STONES!

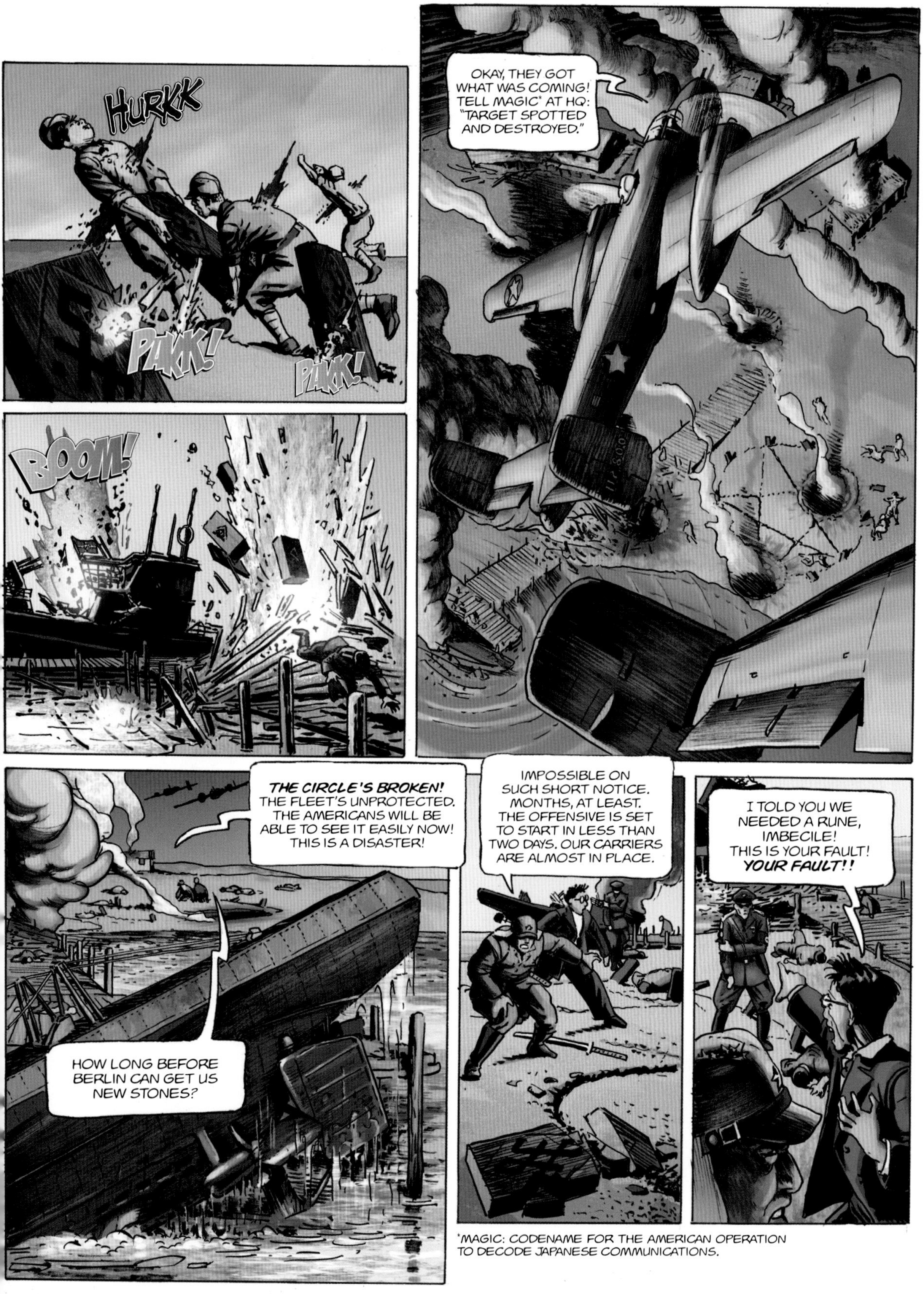
HURKK
PAKK!
PAKK!
OKAY, THEY GOT WHAT WAS COMING! TELL MAGIC* AT HQ: "TARGET SPOTTED AND DESTROYED."
BOOM!
THE CIRCLE'S BROKEN! THE FLEET'S UNPROTECTED. THE AMERICANS WILL BE ABLE TO SEE IT EASILY NOW! THIS IS A DISASTER!
HOW LONG BEFORE BERLIN CAN GET US NEW STONES?
IMPOSSIBLE ON SUCH SHORT NOTICE. MONTHS, AT LEAST. THE OFFENSIVE IS SET TO START IN LESS THAN TWO DAYS. OUR CARRIERS ARE ALMOST IN PLACE.
I TOLD YOU WE NEEDED A RUNE, IMBECILE! THIS IS YOUR FAULT! YOUR FAULT!!

*MAGIC: CODENAME FOR THE AMERICAN OPERATION TO DECODE JAPANESE COMMUNICATIONS.

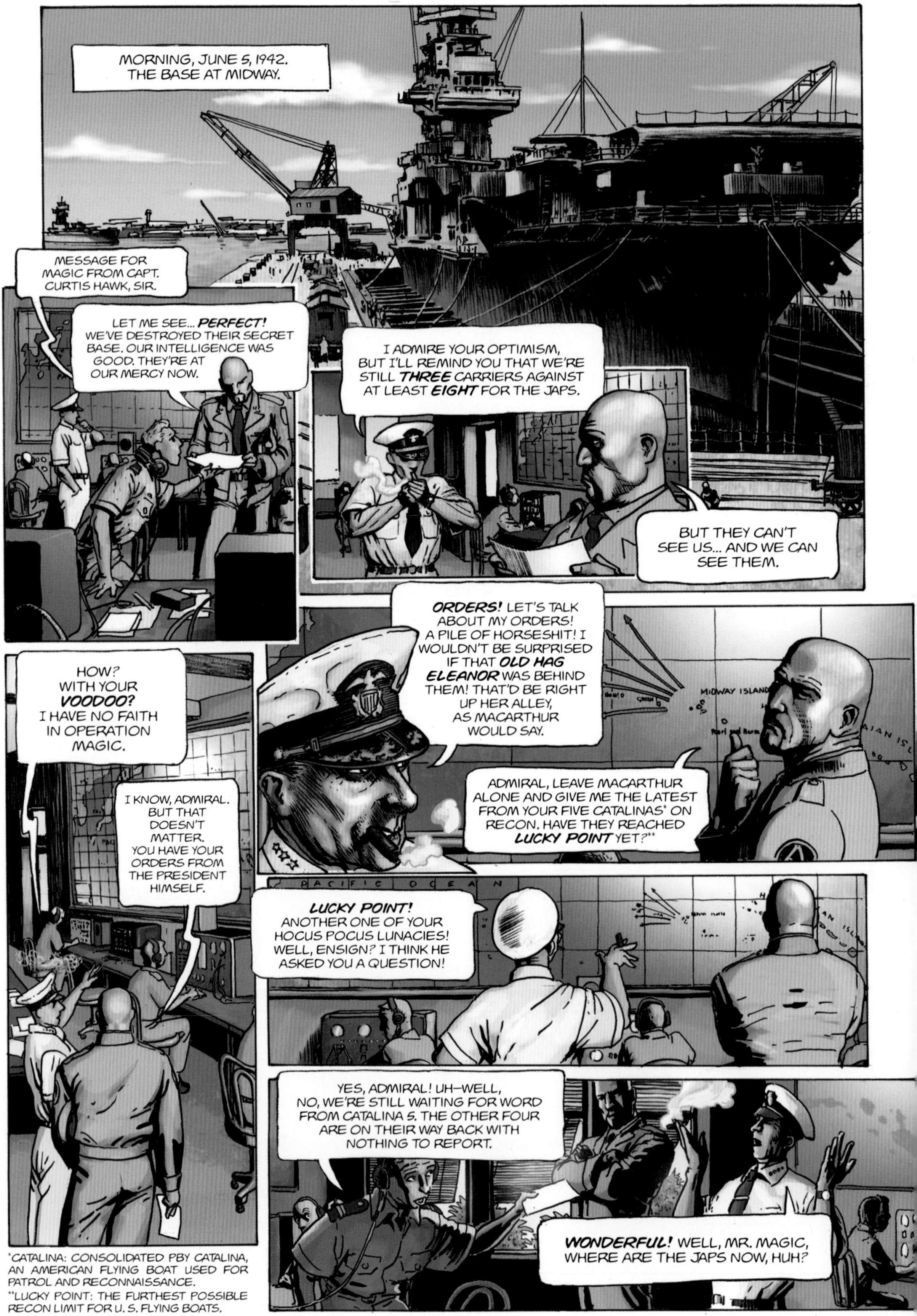
MORNING, JUNE 5, 1942. THE BASE AT MIDWAY.
MESSAGE FOR MAGIC FROM CAPT. CURTIS HAWK, SIR.
LET ME SEE... PERFECT! WE'VE DESTROYED THEIR SECRET BASE. OUR INTELLIGENCE WAS GOOD. THEY'RE AT OUR MERCY NOW.
I ADMIRE YOUR OPTIMISM, BUT I'LL REMIND YOU THAT WE'RE STILL THREE CARRIERS AGAINST AT LEAST EIGHT FOR THE JAPS.
BUT THEY CAN'T SEE US... AND WE CAN SEE THEM.
HOW? WITH YOUR VOODOO? I HAVE NO FAITH IN OPERATION MAGIC.
I KNOW, ADMIRAL. BUT THAT DOESN'T MATTER. YOU HAVE YOUR ORDERS FROM THE PRESIDENT HIMSELF.
ORDERS! LET'S TALK ABOUT MY ORDERS! A PILE OF HORSESHIT! I WOULDN'T BE SURPRISED IF THAT OLD HAG ELEANOR WAS BEHIND THEM! THAT'D BE RIGHT UP HER ALLEY, AS MACARTHUR WOULD SAY.
MIDWAY ISLAND
ADMIRAL, LEAVE MACARTHUR ALONE AND GIVE ME THE LATEST FROM YOUR FIVE CATALINAS* ON RECON. HAVE THEY REACHED LUCKY POINT YET?**
PACIFIC OCEAN
LUCKY POINT! ANOTHER ONE OF YOUR HOCUS POCUS LUNACIES! WELL, ENSIGN? I THINK HE ASKED YOU A QUESTION!
YES, ADMIRAL! UH—WELL, NO, WE'RE STILL WAITING FOR WORD FROM CATALINA 5. THE OTHER FOUR ARE ON THEIR WAY BACK WITH NOTHING TO REPORT.
WONDERFUL! WELL, MR. MAGIC, WHERE ARE THE JAPS NOW, HUH?

*CATALINA: CONSOLIDATED PBY CATALINA, AN AMERICAN FLYING BOAT USED FOR PATROL AND RECONNAISSANCE.
**LUCKY POINT: THE FURTHEST POSSIBLE RECON LIMIT FOR U. S. FLYING BOATS.

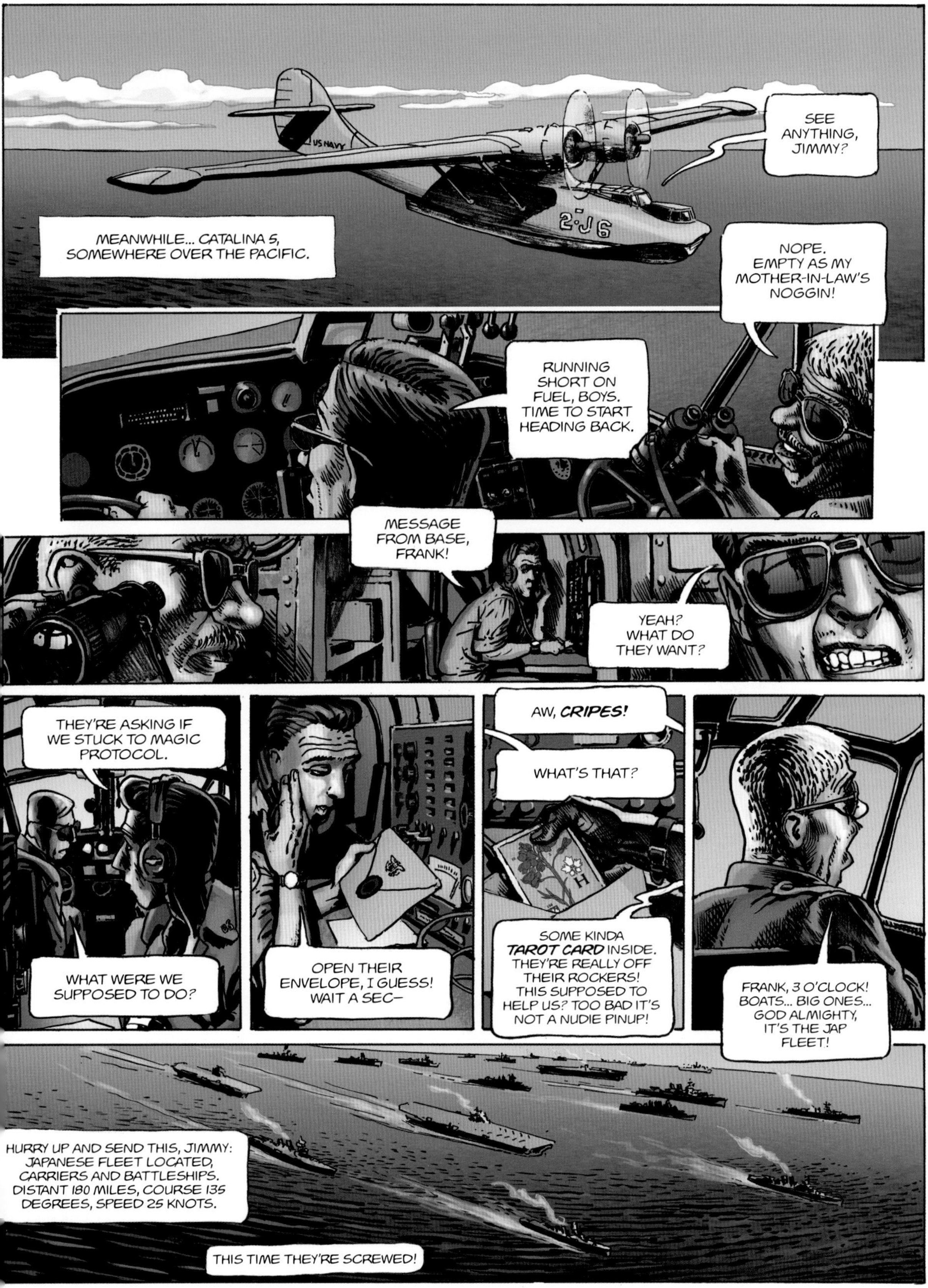
MEANWHILE... CATALINA 5, SOMEWHERE OVER THE PACIFIC.
US NAVY
2-J6
SEE ANYTHING, JIMMY?
NOPE. EMPTY AS MY MOTHER-IN-LAW'S NOGGIN!
RUNNING SHORT ON FUEL, BOYS. TIME TO START HEADING BACK.
MESSAGE FROM BASE, FRANK!
YEAH? WHAT DO THEY WANT?
THEY'RE ASKING IF WE STUCK TO MAGIC PROTOCOL.
WHAT WERE WE SUPPOSED TO DO?
OPEN THEIR ENVELOPE, I GUESS! WAIT A SEC—
AW, **CRIPES!**
WHAT'S THAT?
SOME KINDA **TAROT CARD** INSIDE. THEY'RE REALLY OFF THEIR ROCKERS! THIS SUPPOSED TO HELP US? TOO BAD IT'S NOT A NUDIE PINUP!
FRANK, 3 O'CLOCK! BOATS... BIG ONES... GOD ALMIGHTY, IT'S THE JAP FLEET!
HURRY UP AND SEND THIS, JIMMY: JAPANESE FLEET LOCATED, CARRIERS AND BATTLESHIPS. DISTANT 180 MILES, COURSE 135 DEGREES, SPEED 25 KNOTS.
THIS TIME THEY'RE SCREWED!

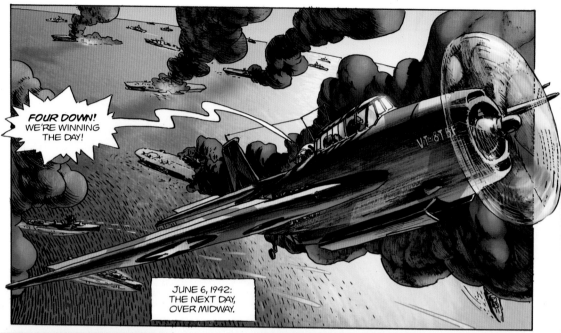

FOUR DOWN! WE'RE WINNING THE DAY!

JUNE 6, 1942: THE NEXT DAY, OVER MIDWAY.

NOW THEY'LL PAY FOR *PEARL HARBOR!*

ERLIN?

ADMIRAL.

THERE'S NO PROOF YOUR ST. ANTHONY MEDALS WERE BEHIND OUR VICTORY.

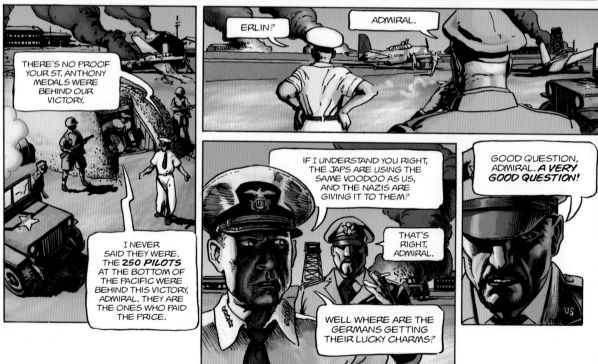

I NEVER SAID THEY WERE. THE *250 PILOTS* AT THE BOTTOM OF THE PACIFIC WERE BEHIND THIS VICTORY, ADMIRAL. THEY ARE THE ONES WHO PAID THE PRICE.

IF I UNDERSTAND YOU RIGHT, THE JAPS ARE USING THE SAME VOODOO AS US, AND THE NAZIS ARE GIVING IT TO THEM?

THAT'S RIGHT, ADMIRAL.

WELL WHERE ARE THE GERMANS GETTING THEIR LUCKY CHARMS?

GOOD QUESTION, ADMIRAL. *A VERY GOOD QUESTION!*

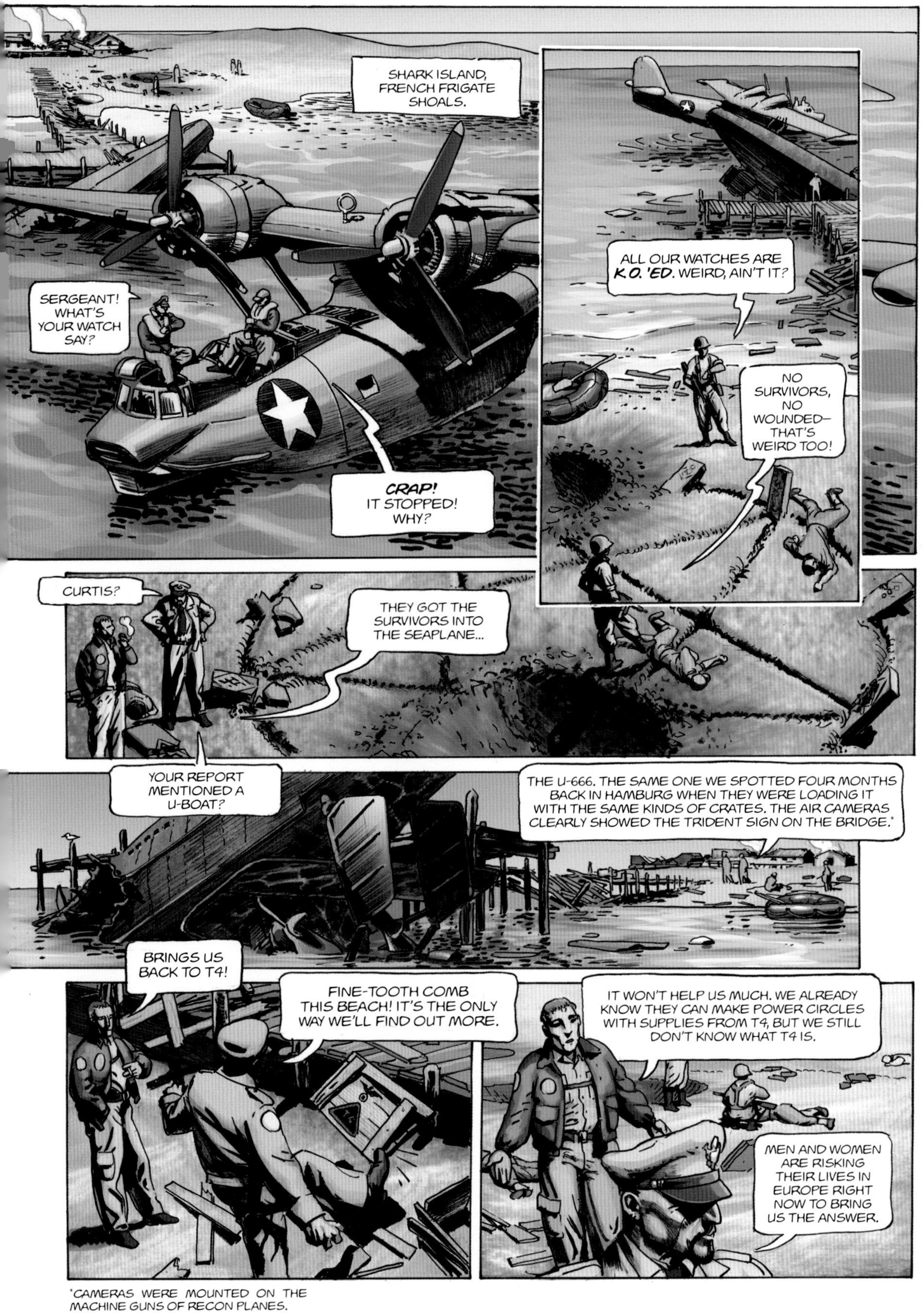
SHARK ISLAND, FRENCH FRIGATE SHOALS.
SERGEANT! WHAT'S YOUR WATCH SAY?
CRAP! IT STOPPED! WHY?
ALL OUR WATCHES ARE K.O.'ED. WEIRD, AIN'T IT?
NO SURVIVORS, NO WOUNDED— THAT'S WEIRD TOO!
CURTIS?
THEY GOT THE SURVIVORS INTO THE SEAPLANE...
YOUR REPORT MENTIONED A U-BOAT?
THE U-666. THE SAME ONE WE SPOTTED FOUR MONTHS BACK IN HAMBURG WHEN THEY WERE LOADING IT WITH THE SAME KINDS OF CRATES. THE AIR CAMERAS CLEARLY SHOWED THE TRIDENT SIGN ON THE BRIDGE.*
BRINGS US BACK TO T4!
FINE-TOOTH COMB THIS BEACH! IT'S THE ONLY WAY WE'LL FIND OUT MORE.
IT WON'T HELP US MUCH. WE ALREADY KNOW THEY CAN MAKE POWER CIRCLES WITH SUPPLIES FROM T4, BUT WE STILL DON'T KNOW WHAT T4 IS.
MEN AND WOMEN ARE RISKING THEIR LIVES IN EUROPE RIGHT NOW TO BRING US THE ANSWER.

*CAMERAS WERE MOUNTED ON THE MACHINE GUNS OF RECON PLANES.

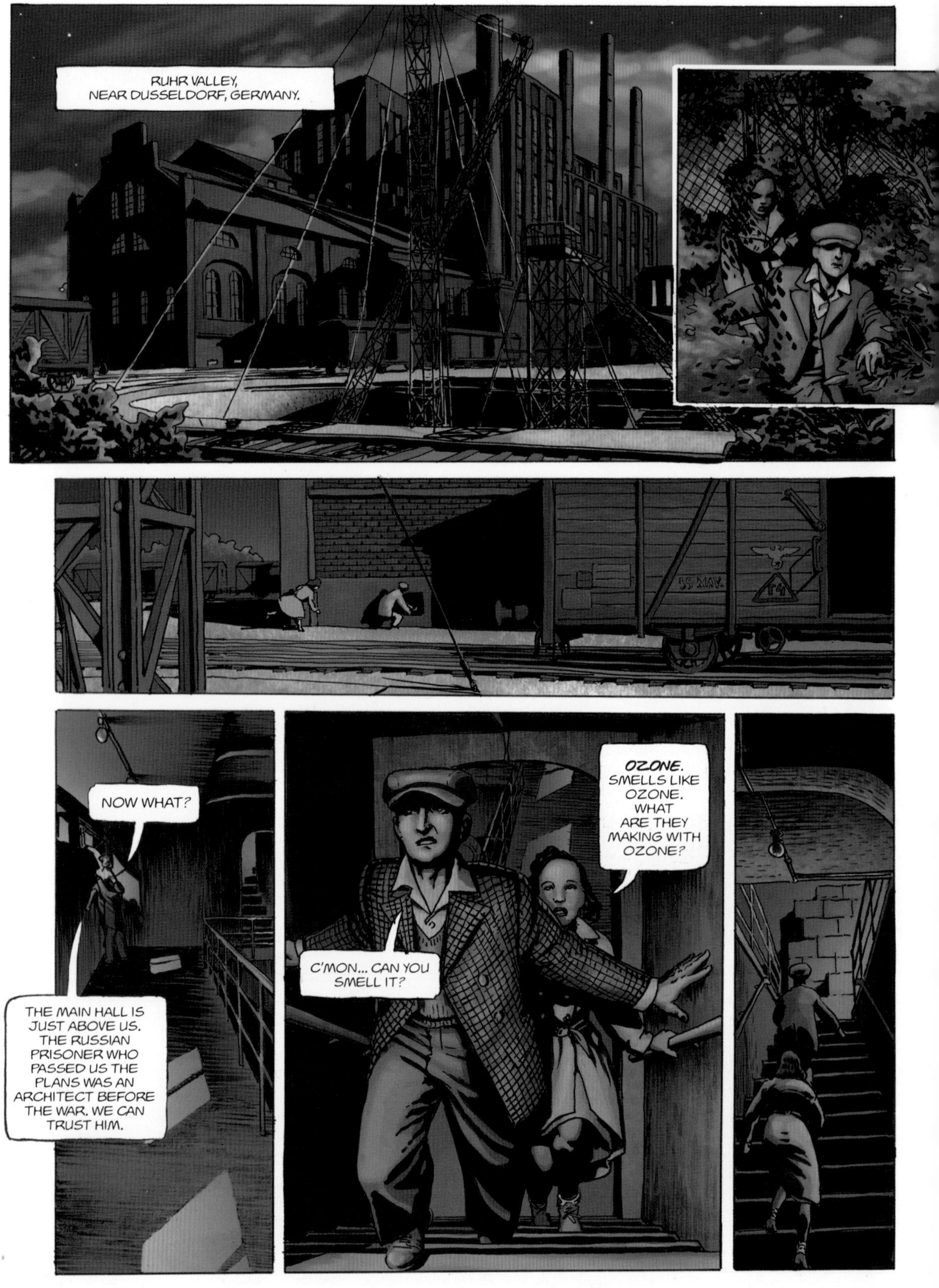
RUHR VALLEY,
NEAR DUSSELDORF, GERMANY.
NOW WHAT?
THE MAIN HALL IS JUST ABOVE US. THE RUSSIAN PRISONER WHO PASSED US THE PLANS WAS AN ARCHITECT BEFORE THE WAR. WE CAN TRUST HIM.
C'MON... CAN YOU SMELL IT?
OZONE. SMELLS LIKE OZONE. WHAT ARE THEY MAKING WITH OZONE?

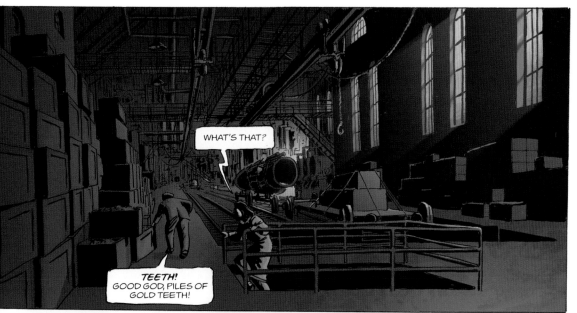

WHAT'S THAT?

TEETH!
GOOD GOD, PILES OF
GOLD TEETH!

AND HAIR—
WOMEN'S HAIR!
WHERE ARE WE,
FLORIAN? I DON'T
WANT TO BE HERE.

C'MON! WE JUST
NEED TO TAKE
PHOTOS OF THE
ROOM AND WE CAN
GO, I PROMISE.

FLORIAN,
I—I CAN'T KEEP
MY TEETH FROM
CHATTERING.
WE HAVE TO GO,
NOW!

NOT BEFORE WE
GET SOME PROOF!
C'MON, **TRY!**

IT'S COMPLETELY
QUIET. DID YOU NOTICE?
THERE'S ALWAYS NOISE IN
FACTORIES...

BUT NOT IN
CEMETERIES.

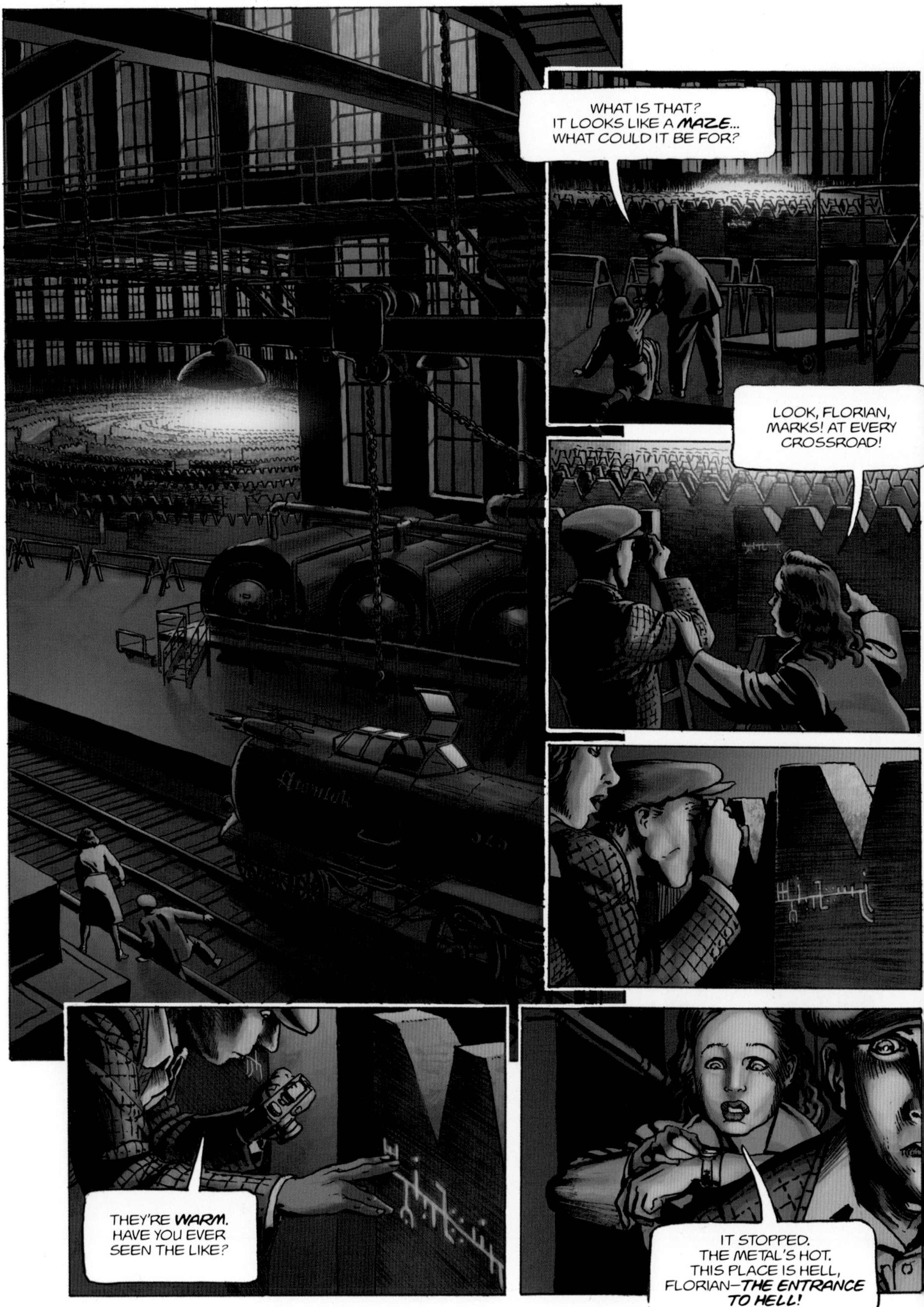
WHAT IS THAT? IT LOOKS LIKE A ***MAZE***... WHAT COULD IT BE FOR?
LOOK, FLORIAN, MARKS! AT EVERY CROSSROAD!
THEY'RE ***WARM***. HAVE YOU EVER SEEN THE LIKE?
IT STOPPED. THE METAL'S HOT. THIS PLACE IS HELL, FLORIAN—***THE ENTRANCE TO HELL!***

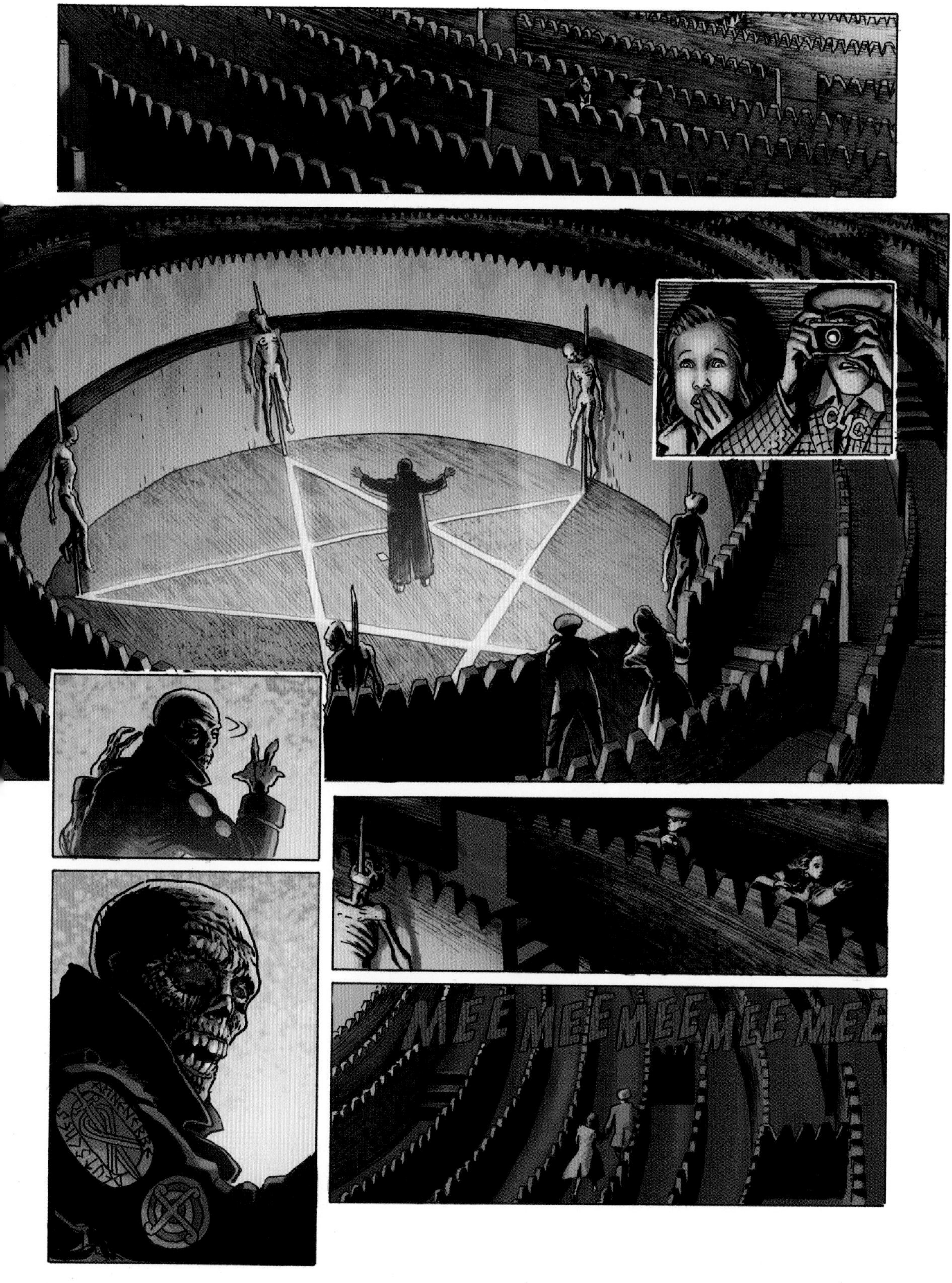
CLIC
MEE MEE MEE MEE MEE

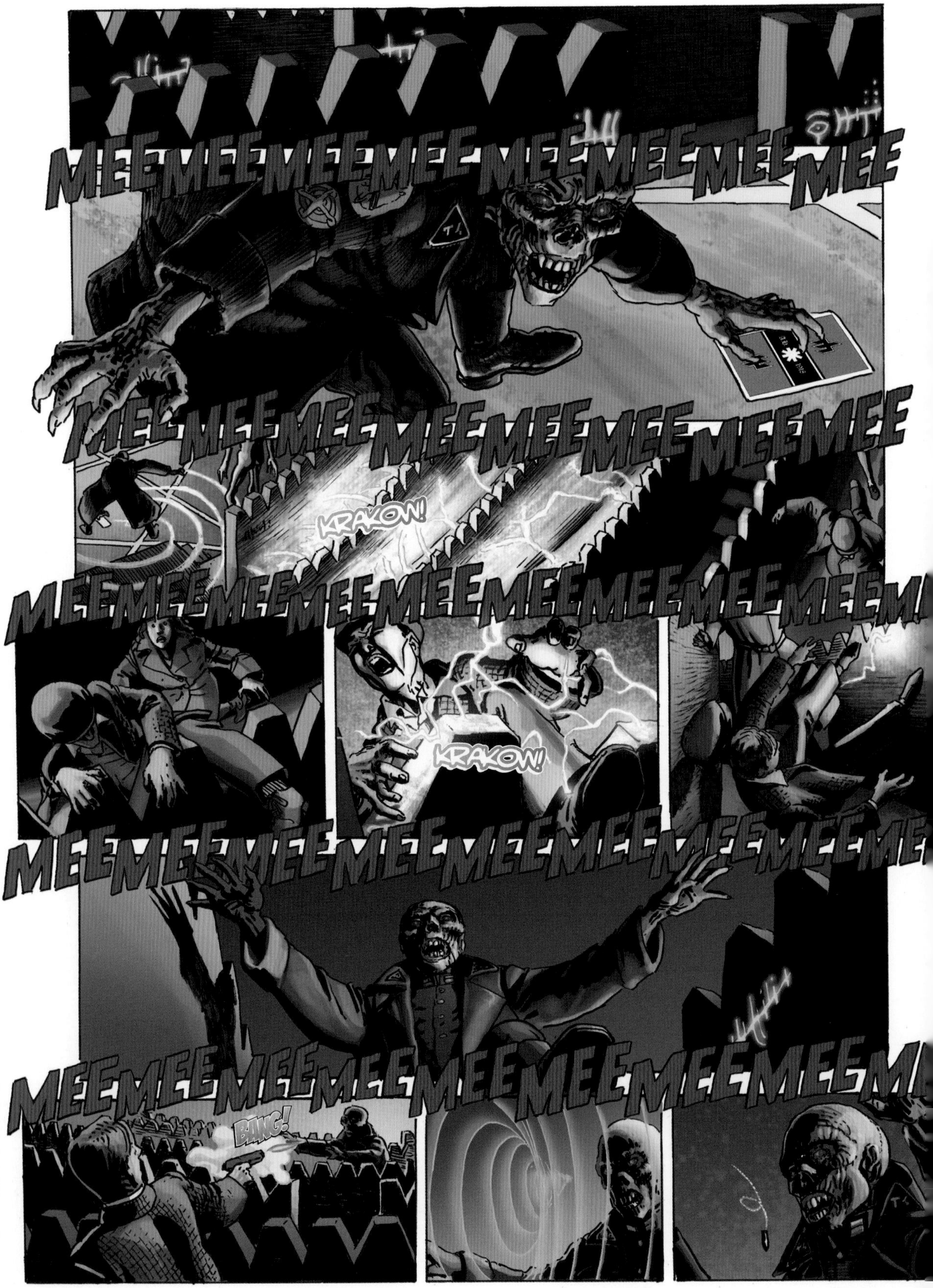
MEEMEEMEEMEEMEE MEEMEEMEE MEE
MEEMEEMEEMEEMEEMEEMEEMEE
KRAKOW!
MEEMEEMEEMEEMEEMEEMEEMEEMEE
KRAKOW!
MEEMEEMEEMEEMEEMEEMEEMEEMEE
MEEMEEMEEMEEMEEMEEMEEMEEMEE
BANG!

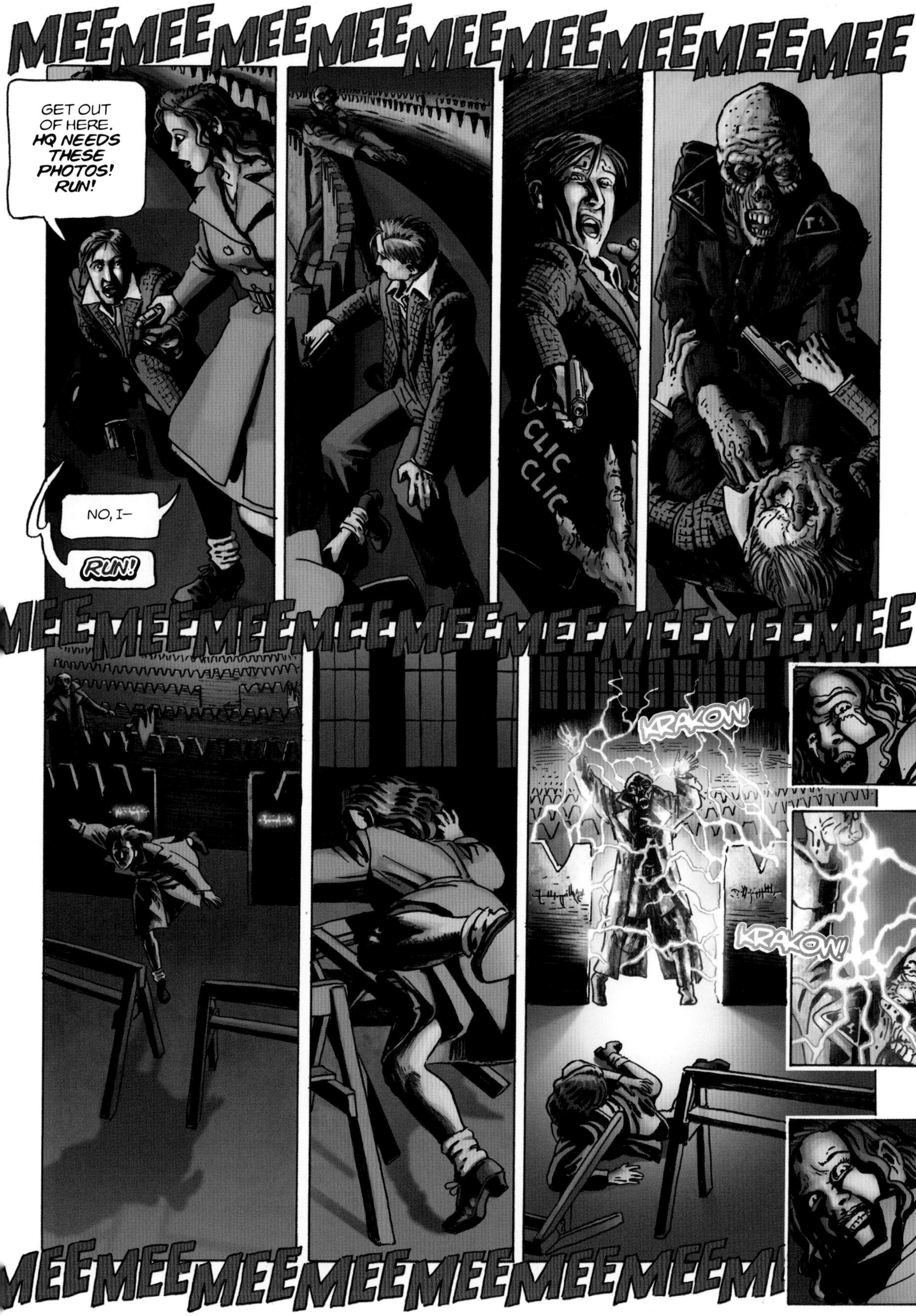
MEEMEEMEEMEEMEEMEEMEEMEEMEE
GET OUT OF HERE. HQ NEEDS THESE PHOTOS! RUN!
NO, I–
RUN!
CLIC CLIC
MEEMEEMEEMEEMEEMEEMEEMEEMEEMEE
KRAKOW!
KRAKOW!
MEEMEEMEEMEEMEEMEEMEEMEEMEEMI

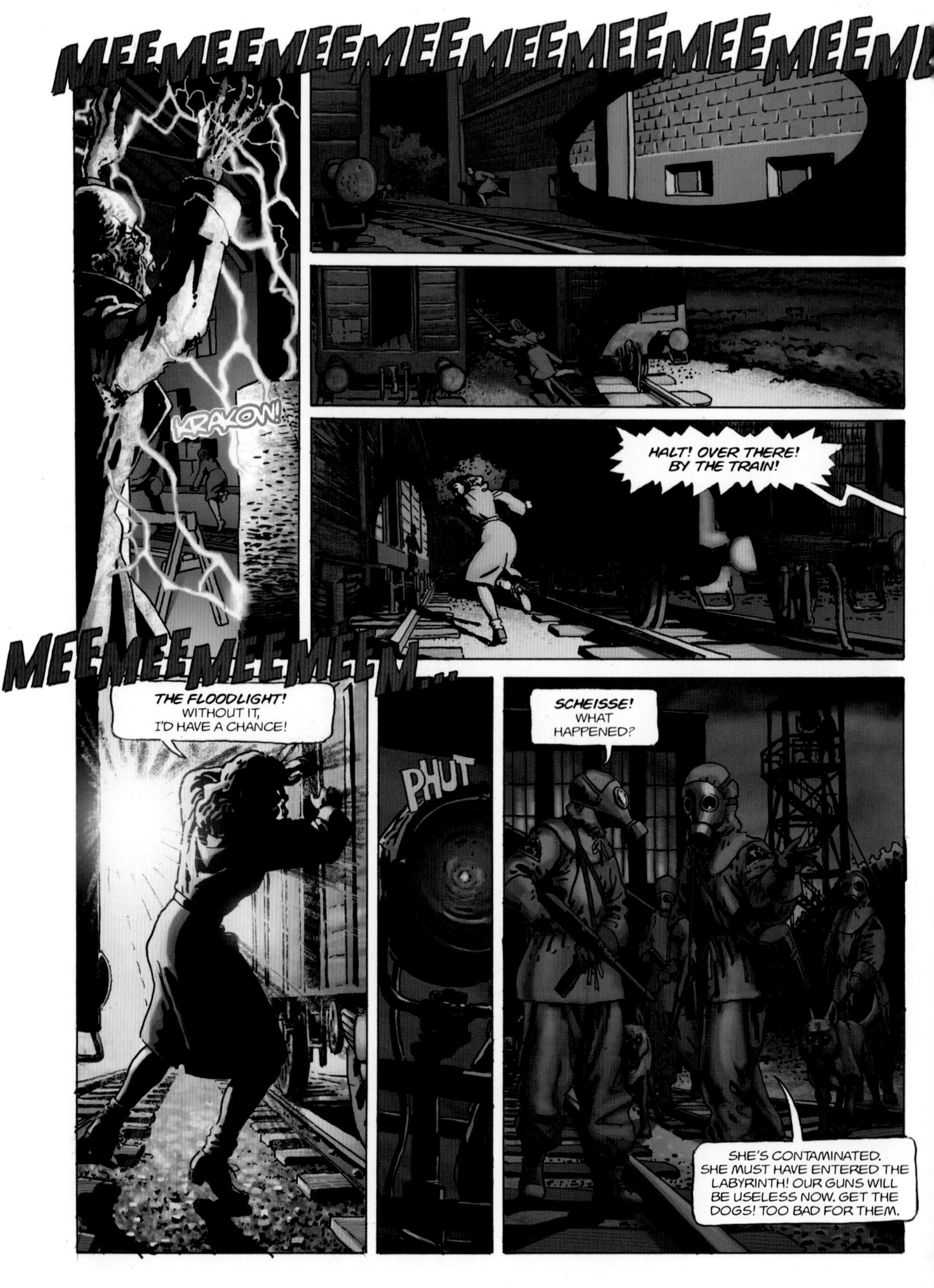
MEEMEEMEEMEEMEEMEEMEEMEEM
KRAKOW!
HALT! OVER THERE! BY THE TRAIN!
MEEMEEMEEMEEM...
THE FLOODLIGHT! WITHOUT IT, I'D HAVE A CHANCE!
PHUT
SCHEISSE! WHAT HAPPENED?
SHE'S CONTAMINATED. SHE MUST HAVE ENTERED THE LABYRINTH! OUR GUNS WILL BE USELESS NOW. GET THE DOGS! TOO BAD FOR THEM.

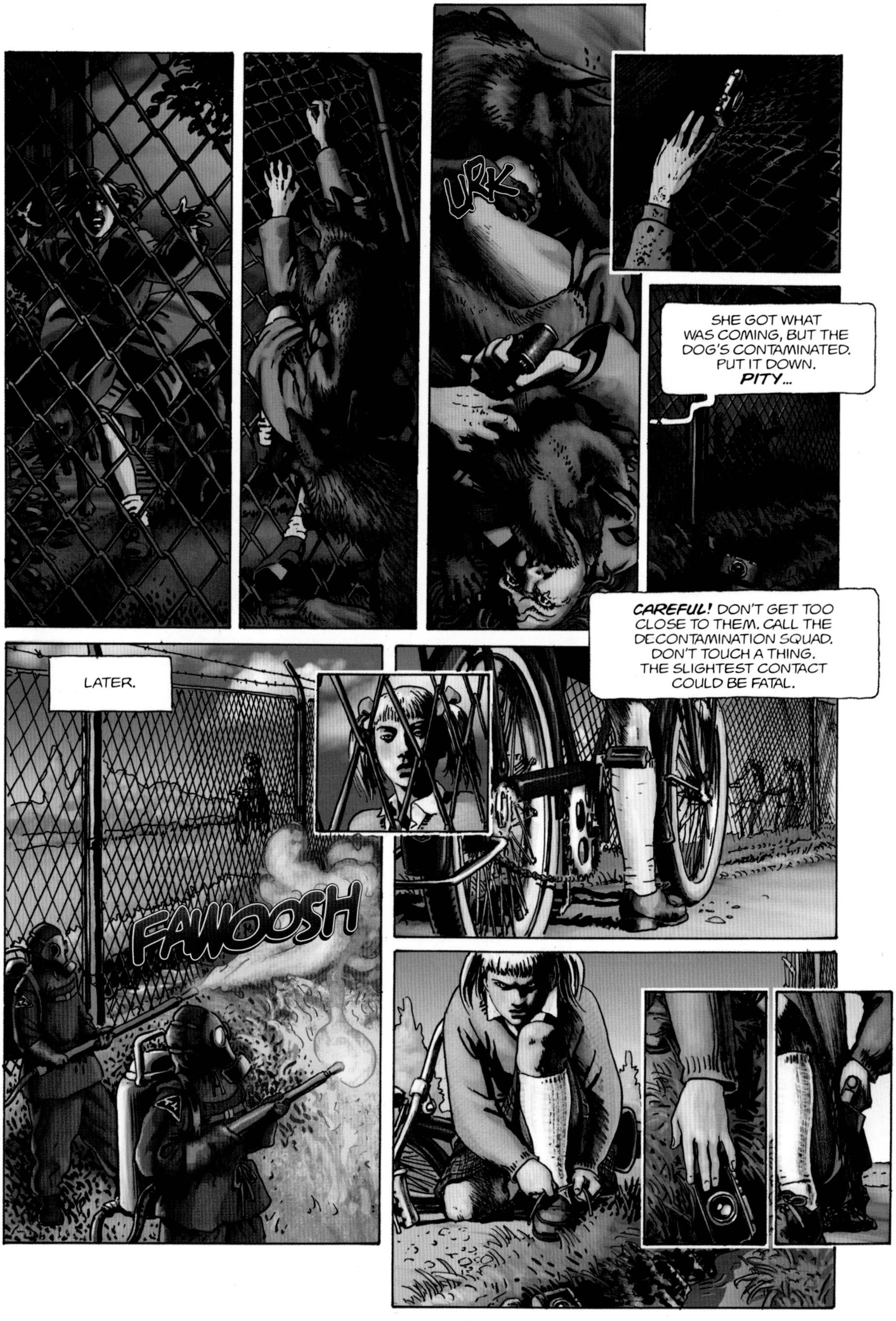
URK
SHE GOT WHAT WAS COMING, BUT THE DOG'S CONTAMINATED. PUT IT DOWN. PITY...
CAREFUL! DON'T GET TOO CLOSE TO THEM. CALL THE DECONTAMINATION SQUAD. DON'T TOUCH A THING. THE SLIGHTEST CONTACT COULD BE FATAL.
LATER.
FAWOOSH

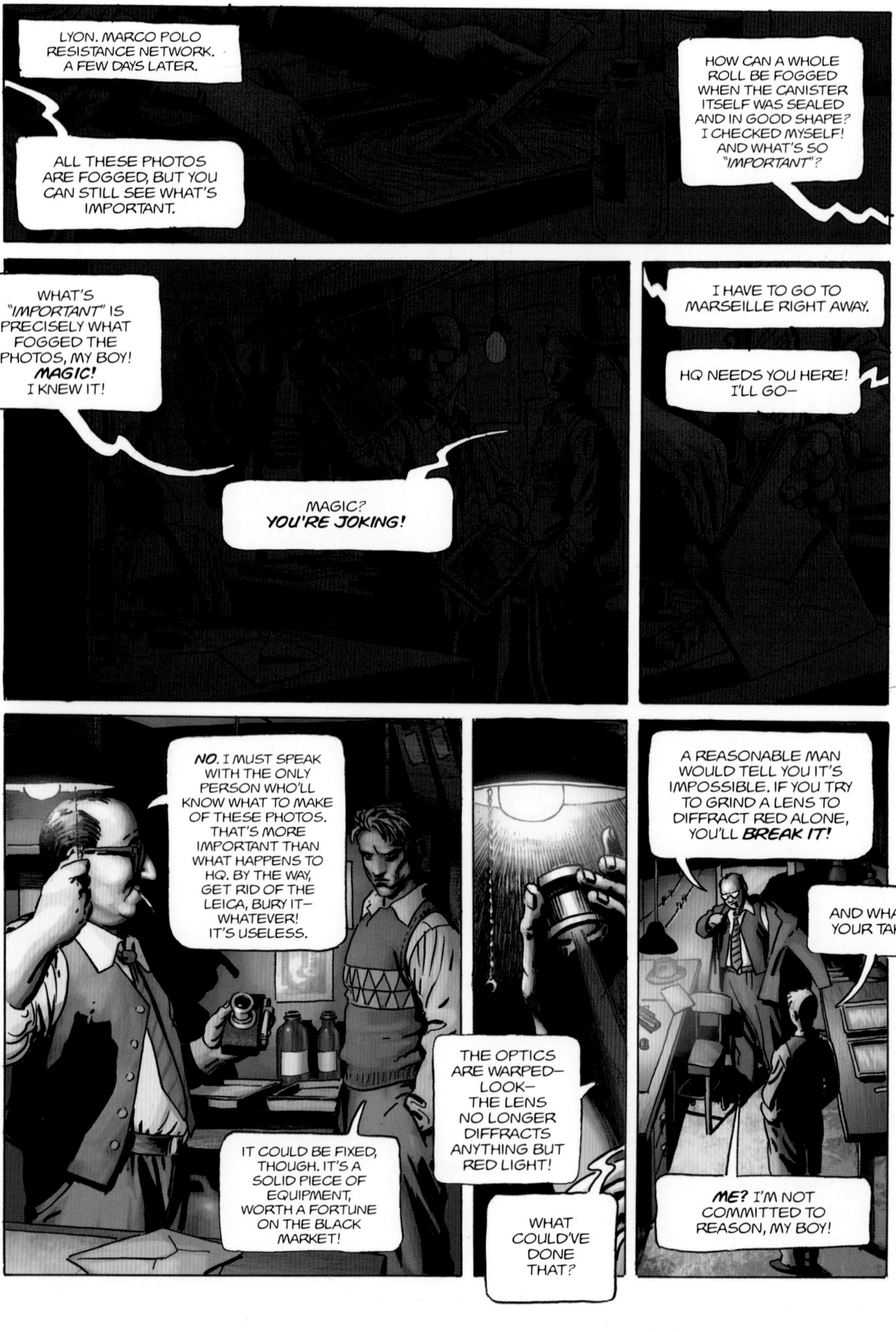
LYON. MARCO POLO RESISTANCE NETWORK. A FEW DAYS LATER.
ALL THESE PHOTOS ARE FOGGED, BUT YOU CAN STILL SEE WHAT'S IMPORTANT.
HOW CAN A WHOLE ROLL BE FOGGED WHEN THE CANISTER ITSELF WAS SEALED AND IN GOOD SHAPE? I CHECKED MYSELF! AND WHAT'S SO "IMPORTANT"?
WHAT'S "IMPORTANT" IS PRECISELY WHAT FOGGED THE PHOTOS, MY BOY! MAGIC! I KNEW IT!
MAGIC? YOU'RE JOKING!
I HAVE TO GO TO MARSEILLE RIGHT AWAY.
HQ NEEDS YOU HERE! I'LL GO—
NO. I MUST SPEAK WITH THE ONLY PERSON WHO'LL KNOW WHAT TO MAKE OF THESE PHOTOS. THAT'S MORE IMPORTANT THAN WHAT HAPPENS TO HQ. BY THE WAY, GET RID OF THE LEICA, BURY IT—WHATEVER! IT'S USELESS.
IT COULD BE FIXED, THOUGH. IT'S A SOLID PIECE OF EQUIPMENT, WORTH A FORTUNE ON THE BLACK MARKET!
THE OPTICS ARE WARPED—LOOK—THE LENS NO LONGER DIFFRACTS ANYTHING BUT RED LIGHT!
WHAT COULD'VE DONE THAT?
A REASONABLE MAN WOULD TELL YOU IT'S IMPOSSIBLE. IF YOU TRY TO GRIND A LENS TO DIFFRACT RED ALONE, YOU'LL BREAK IT!
AND WHAT'S YOUR TAKE?
ME? I'M NOT COMMITTED TO REASON, MY BOY!

SOMEONE FOR YOU, MATER. I PATTED HIM DOWN, HE'S-A CLEAN.
TRY NOT TO TALK LIKE THAT, GRANNY. ONE OF THESE DAYS IT'LL GET YOU IN TROUBLE.
PANIER DISTRICT, MARSEILLE.
WHATSA MATTER, MATER? I'M-A CORSICAN AND PROUD OF IT.
KLAUS BARBIE'S SECRET POLICE KNOW OUR NETWORK IS PROTECTED BY THE UNION CORSE. THEY'RE FAR FROM STUPID.
AND I SAY I'M-A **CORSICAN** SO FUCK YOU AND YOUR BARBIE.
WIZARD*... I'VE HEARD A LOT ABOUT YOU THESE PAST MONTHS. YOUR MARCO POLO NETWORK HAS CANARIS** IN A COLD SWEAT!
I HOPE SO! THAT'S THE IDEA. HAVE YOU HAD TIME TO LOOK AT MY PHOTOS? WHAT DO YOU THINK?
AT LAST WE KNOW WHAT'S GOING ON IN FACTORY T4!
WE DO? HOW LUCKY YOU ARE! ALL I HAVE ARE GUESSES.

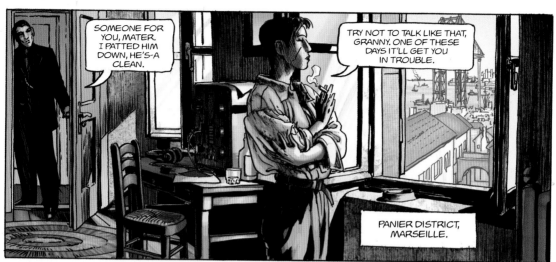

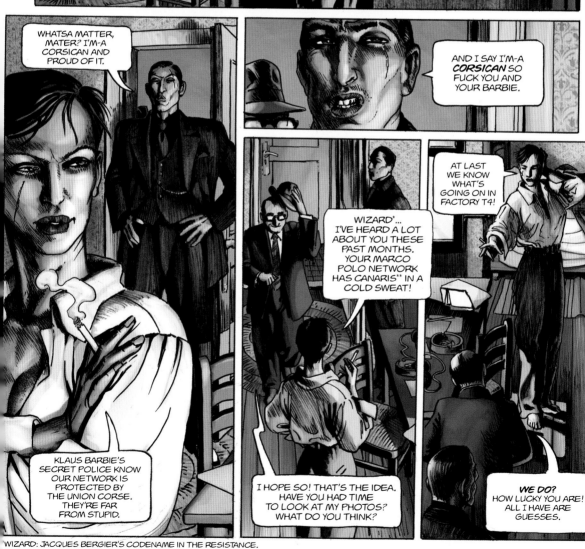

*WIZARD: JACQUES BERGIER'S CODENAME IN THE RESISTANCE.
**ADMIRAL CANARIS: CHIEF OF GERMAN INTELLIGENCE.

THAT'S BECAUSE YOU DON'T HAVE ALL FACTS AT HAND, MY DEAR! YOU DID INDEED SAY THE FACTORY RECEIVES MULTIPLE CONVOYS FROM THE GERMAN CAMPS?

THAT'S RIGHT. AT LEAST TWO A DAY.

HOW MANY PEOPLE ARE THEY KILLING AT THAT RATE? *INCREDIBLE!*

KILLING?

THEY'RE MAKING RUNES, BERGIER! FACTORY T4 MAKES DECKS, USING A PROCESS I'D THOUGHT FORGOTTEN. WILLIAM OF LECCE INVENTED IT IN SICILY ALMOST SEVEN CENTURIES AGO! HE WAS ALSO CALLED KLINGSOR.

KLINGSOR? LIKE IN WAGNER'S OPERA*?

BASED ON WOLFRAM VON ESCHENBACH'S EPIC POEM, YES.

WHAT WAS THE NATURE OF THIS PROCESS?

PAIN... FEAR... THE ACCUMULATION OF THE FEAR AND PAIN OF THOSE TORTURED, TO MAKE *BLACK DECKS!*

GODS ABOVE, ARE SUCH THINGS POSSIBLE?

LONG AGO IN PALERMO, A YOUNG MAN NAMED WILLIAM OF LECCE FIRST EXPERIMENTED WITH THEM, UNFORTUNATELY...**

*WAGNER'S OPERA *PARSIFAL*, ITSELF INSPIRED BY WOLFRAM VON ESCHENBACH'S *PARZIVAL*, A VARIANT OF *PERCEVAL* BY CHRÉTIEN DE TROYES.
**SEE *THE SECRET HISTORY*, BOOK 3: *THE GRAIL OF MONTSÉGUR*.

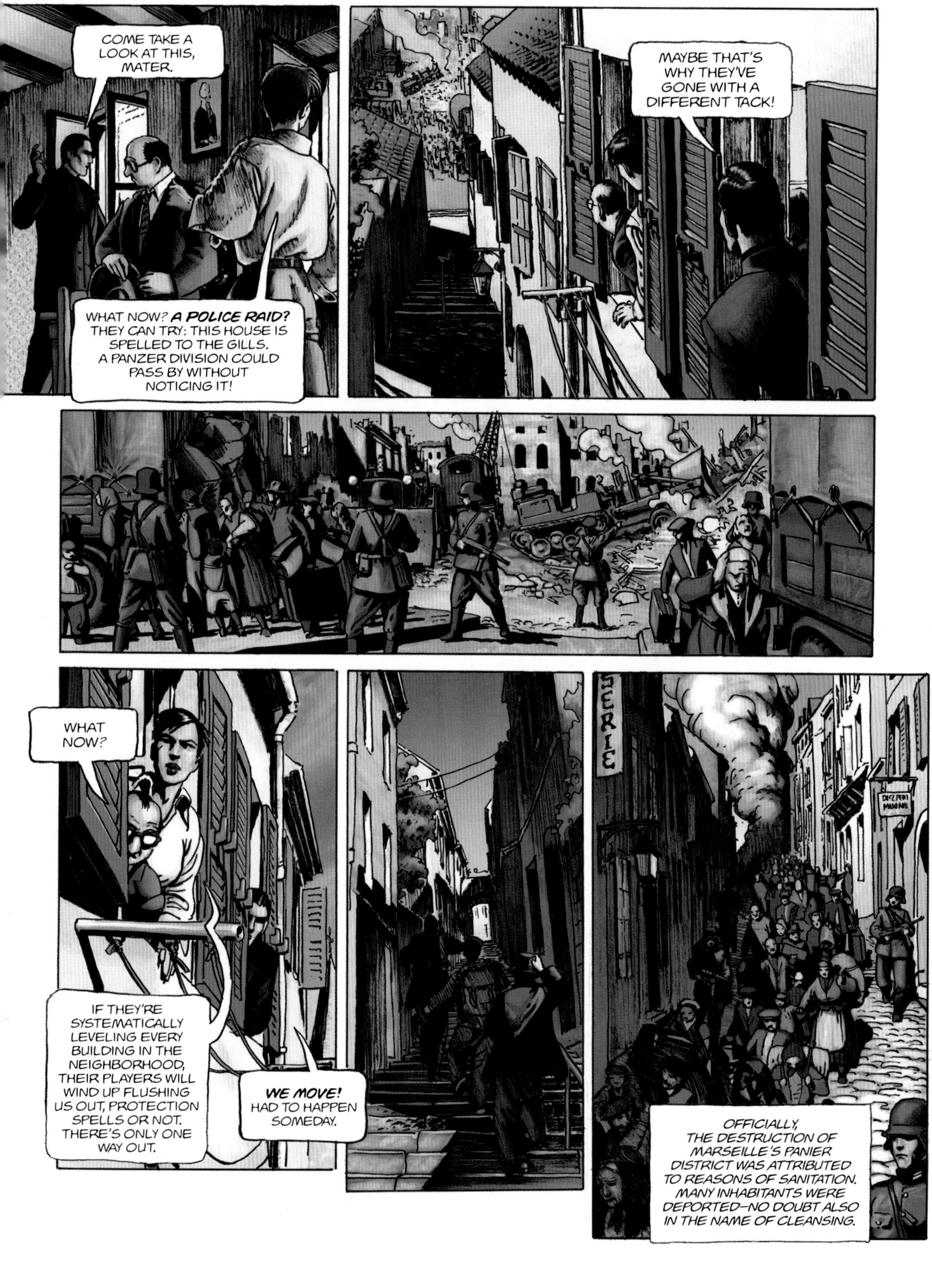
COME TAKE A LOOK AT THIS, MATER.
WHAT NOW? **A POLICE RAID?** THEY CAN TRY: THIS HOUSE IS SPELLED TO THE GILLS. A PANZER DIVISION COULD PASS BY WITHOUT NOTICING IT!
MAYBE THAT'S WHY THEY'VE GONE WITH A DIFFERENT TACK!
WHAT NOW?
IF THEY'RE SYSTEMATICALLY LEVELING EVERY BUILDING IN THE NEIGHBORHOOD, THEIR PLAYERS WILL WIND UP FLUSHING US OUT, PROTECTION SPELLS OR NOT. THERE'S ONLY ONE WAY OUT.
WE MOVE! HAD TO HAPPEN SOMEDAY.
OFFICIALLY, THE DESTRUCTION OF MARSEILLE'S PANIER DISTRICT WAS ATTRIBUTED TO REASONS OF SANITATION. MANY INHABITANTS WERE DEPORTED—NO DOUBT ALSO IN THE NAME OF CLEANSING.

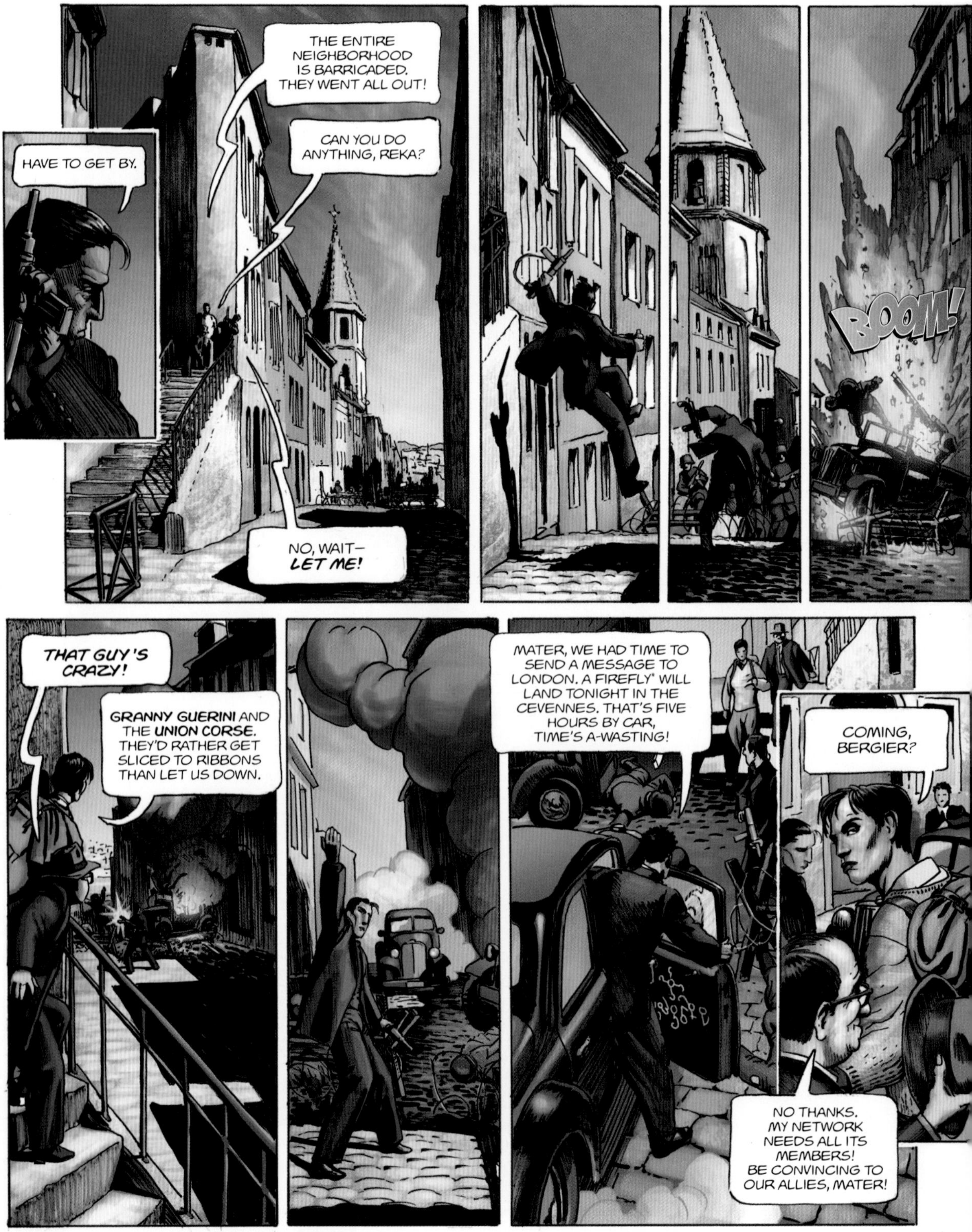
HAVE TO GET BY.
THE ENTIRE NEIGHBORHOOD IS BARRICADED. THEY WENT ALL OUT!
CAN YOU DO ANYTHING, REKA?
NO, WAIT— LET ME!
BOOM!
THAT GUY'S CRAZY!
GRANNY GUERINI AND THE UNION CORSE. THEY'D RATHER GET SLICED TO RIBBONS THAN LET US DOWN.
MATER, WE HAD TIME TO SEND A MESSAGE TO LONDON. A FIREFLY* WILL LAND TONIGHT IN THE CEVENNES. THAT'S FIVE HOURS BY CAR, TIME'S A-WASTING!
COMING, BERGIER?
NO THANKS. MY NETWORK NEEDS ALL ITS MEMBERS! BE CONVINCING TO OUR ALLIES, MATER!

*FIREFLY: A LYSANDER SHORT-FIELD AIRCRAFT USED TO DROP OR PICK UP AGENTS OF THE FRENCH RESISTANCE.

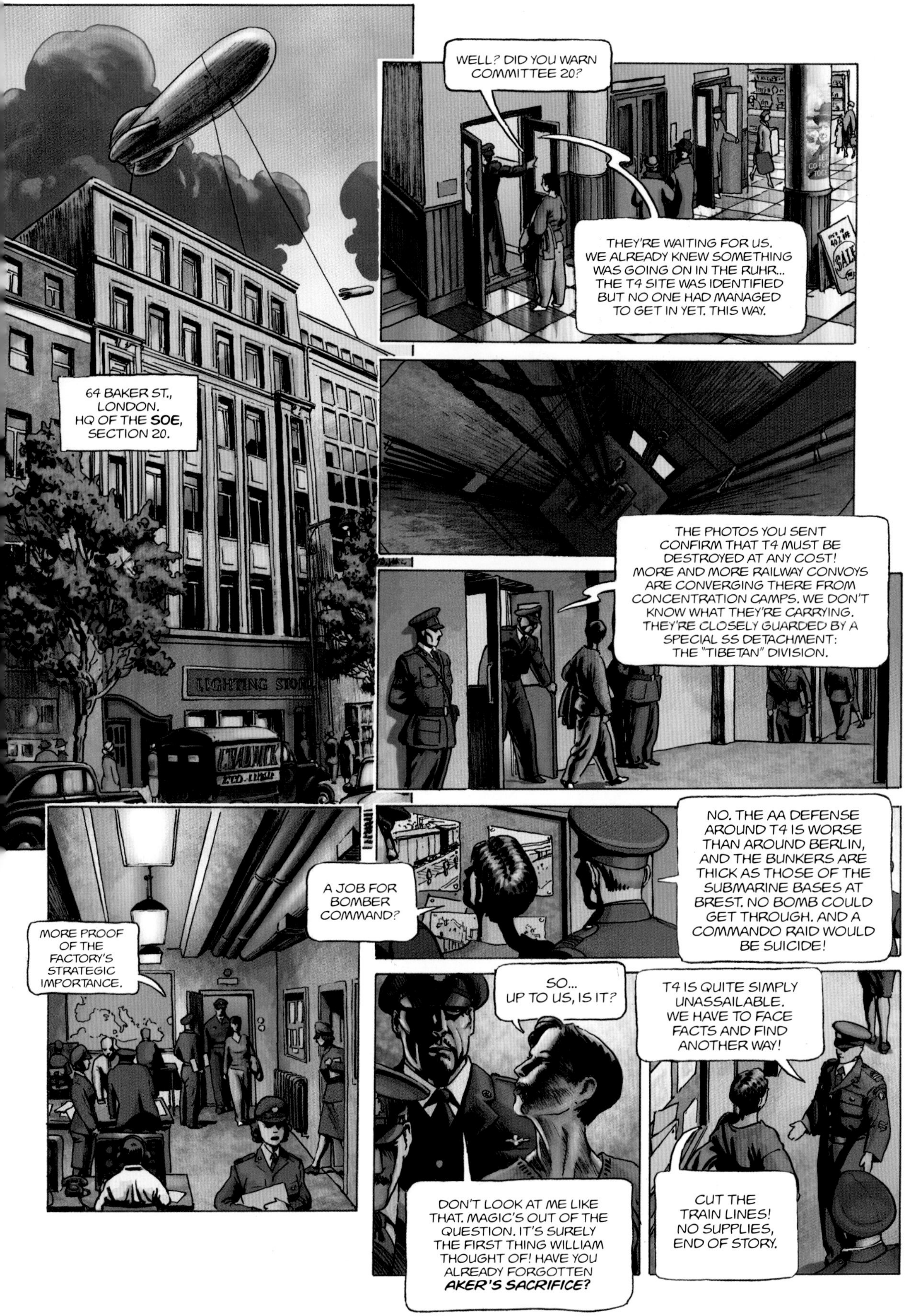
64 BAKER ST., LONDON. HQ OF THE **SOE**, SECTION 20.
LIGHTING STORE
WELL? DID YOU WARN COMMITTEE 20?
THEY'RE WAITING FOR US. WE ALREADY KNEW SOMETHING WAS GOING ON IN THE RUHR... THE T4 SITE WAS IDENTIFIED BUT NO ONE HAD MANAGED TO GET IN YET. THIS WAY.
THE PHOTOS YOU SENT CONFIRM THAT T4 MUST BE DESTROYED AT ANY COST! MORE AND MORE RAILWAY CONVOYS ARE CONVERGING THERE FROM CONCENTRATION CAMPS. WE DON'T KNOW WHAT THEY'RE CARRYING. THEY'RE CLOSELY GUARDED BY A SPECIAL SS DETACHMENT: THE "TIBETAN" DIVISION.
MORE PROOF OF THE FACTORY'S STRATEGIC IMPORTANCE.
A JOB FOR BOMBER COMMAND?
NO. THE AA DEFENSE AROUND T4 IS WORSE THAN AROUND BERLIN, AND THE BUNKERS ARE THICK AS THOSE OF THE SUBMARINE BASES AT BREST. NO BOMB COULD GET THROUGH. AND A COMMANDO RAID WOULD BE SUICIDE!
SO... UP TO US, IS IT?
DON'T LOOK AT ME LIKE THAT. MAGIC'S OUT OF THE QUESTION. IT'S SURELY THE FIRST THING WILLIAM THOUGHT OF! HAVE YOU ALREADY FORGOTTEN ***AKER'S SACRIFICE***?
T4 IS QUITE SIMPLY UNASSAILABLE. WE HAVE TO FACE FACTS AND FIND ANOTHER WAY!
CUT THE TRAIN LINES! NO SUPPLIES, END OF STORY.

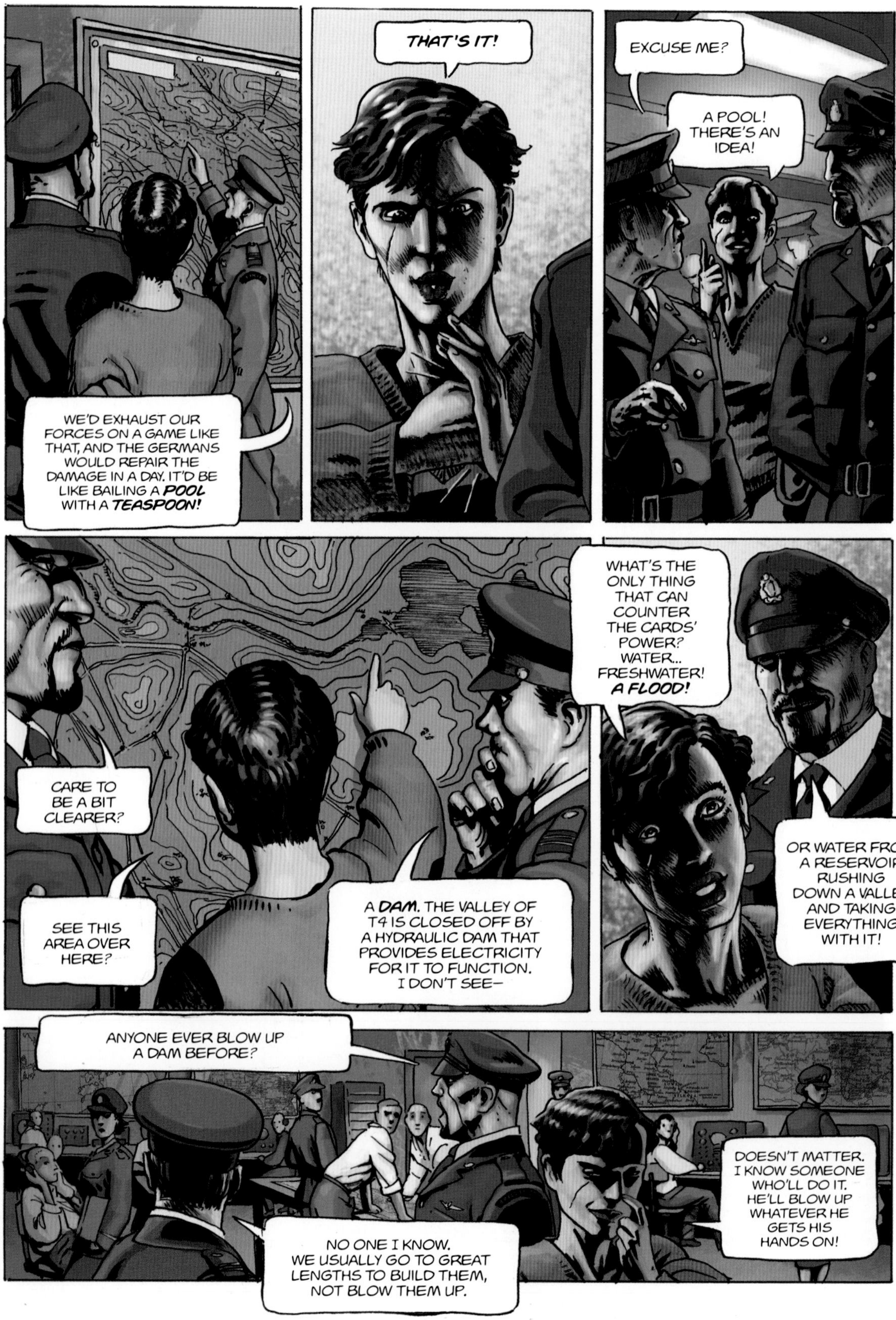
WE'D EXHAUST OUR FORCES ON A GAME LIKE THAT, AND THE GERMANS WOULD REPAIR THE DAMAGE IN A DAY. IT'D BE LIKE BAILING A **POOL** WITH A **TEASPOON!**
THAT'S IT!
EXCUSE ME?
A POOL! THERE'S AN IDEA!
CARE TO BE A BIT CLEARER?
SEE THIS AREA OVER HERE?
A **DAM**. THE VALLEY OF T4 IS CLOSED OFF BY A HYDRAULIC DAM THAT PROVIDES ELECTRICITY FOR IT TO FUNCTION. I DON'T SEE–
WHAT'S THE ONLY THING THAT CAN COUNTER THE CARDS' POWER? WATER... FRESHWATER! **A FLOOD!**
OR WATER FROM A RESERVOIR RUSHING DOWN A VALLEY AND TAKING EVERYTHING WITH IT!
ANYONE EVER BLOW UP A DAM BEFORE?
NO ONE I KNOW. WE USUALLY GO TO GREAT LENGTHS TO BUILD THEM, NOT BLOW THEM UP.
DOESN'T MATTER. I KNOW SOMEONE WHO'LL DO IT. HE'LL BLOW UP WHATEVER HE GETS HIS HANDS ON!

CAPTAIN, SOMEONE'S ASKING FOR YOU AT THE MESS!

BIGGIN HILL AERODROME, ENGLAND.

BIG BALD FELLOW? TELL HIM I'M DEAD...

NO, NOT BALD, REALLY... AND NOT A FELLOW AT THAT! SHE'S CHEERING UP THE WHOLE WING!

HER? OH CHRIST, PLEASE, NO...

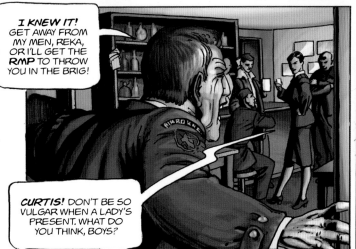

I KNEW IT! GET AWAY FROM MY MEN, REKA, OR I'LL GET THE **RMP** TO THROW YOU IN THE BRIG!

CURTIS! DON'T BE SO VULGAR WHEN A LADY'S PRESENT. WHAT DO YOU THINK, BOYS?

GET OUT OF HERE, YOU LOT! THAT'S AN ORDER! **GO!**

WHAT'S THIS? CAN'T STAY AWAY FROM FLYBOYS AT WAR?* WHAT DO YOUR PAPERS SAY THIS TIME? YOU PART OF THE **SOE** NOW?

THAT'S RIGHT, CAPTAIN. THAT'S WHY I LET HER IN.

I DIDN'T ASK YOU, SERGEANT! GET OUT AND SHUT THE DOOR!

LEAVE THE DOOR OPEN, SERGEANT, WE'RE GOING. CAPTAIN HAWK IS COMING WITH ME: HQ'S ORDERS.

*SEE THE SECRET HISTORY, BOOK 7: OUR LADY OF THE SHADOWS.

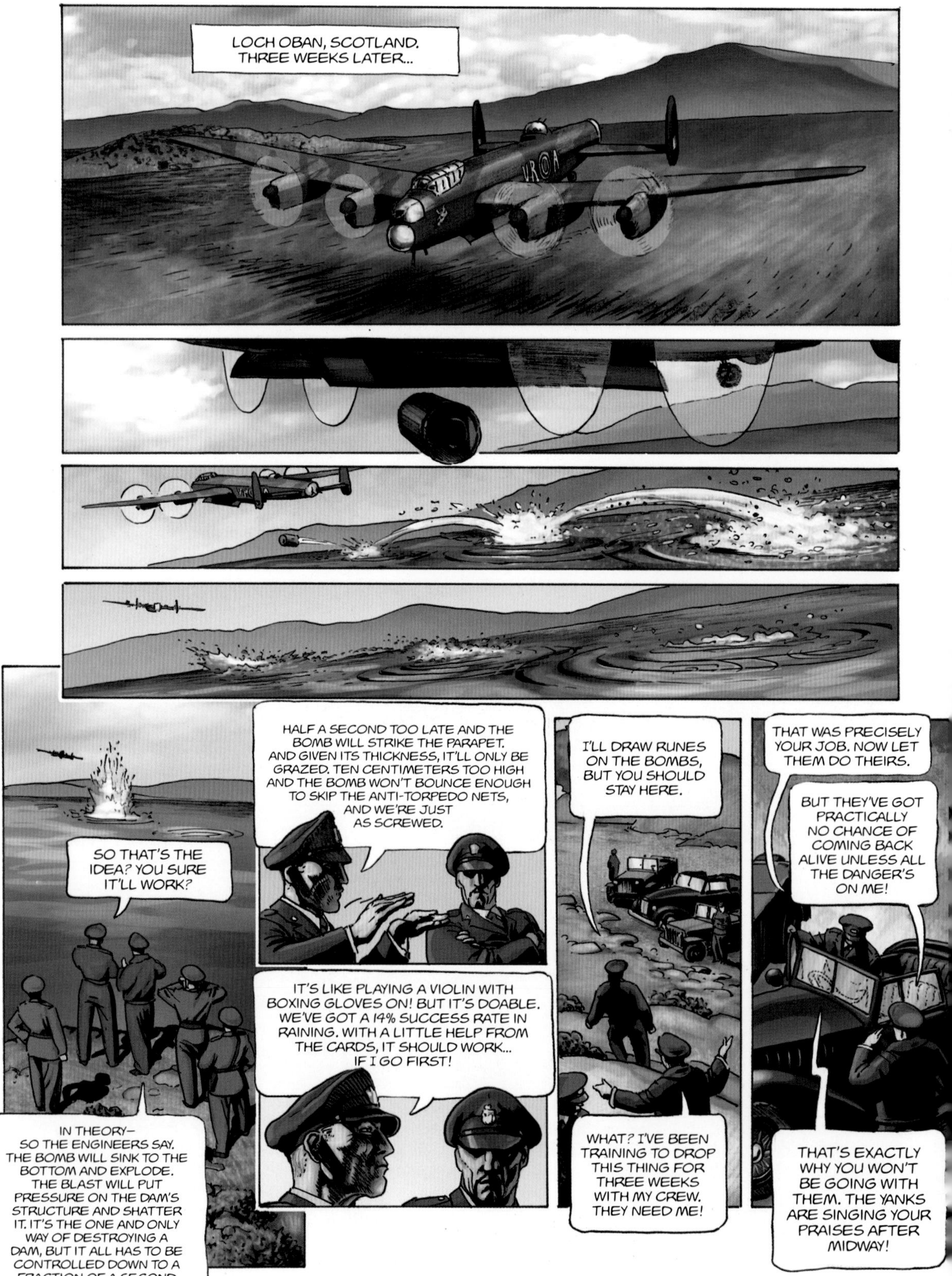
LOCH OBAN, SCOTLAND.
THREE WEEKS LATER...
VR A
SO THAT'S THE IDEA? YOU SURE IT'LL WORK?
IN THEORY– SO THE ENGINEERS SAY. THE BOMB WILL SINK TO THE BOTTOM AND EXPLODE. THE BLAST WILL PUT PRESSURE ON THE DAM'S STRUCTURE AND SHATTER IT. IT'S THE ONE AND ONLY WAY OF DESTROYING A DAM, BUT IT ALL HAS TO BE CONTROLLED DOWN TO A FRACTION OF A SECOND AND A CENTIMETER!
HALF A SECOND TOO LATE AND THE BOMB WILL STRIKE THE PARAPET. AND GIVEN ITS THICKNESS, IT'LL ONLY BE GRAZED. TEN CENTIMETERS TOO HIGH AND THE BOMB WON'T BOUNCE ENOUGH TO SKIP THE ANTI-TORPEDO NETS, AND WE'RE JUST AS SCREWED.
IT'S LIKE PLAYING A VIOLIN WITH BOXING GLOVES ON! BUT IT'S DOABLE. WE'VE GOT A 14% SUCCESS RATE IN RAINING. WITH A LITTLE HELP FROM THE CARDS, IT SHOULD WORK... IF I GO FIRST!
I'LL DRAW RUNES ON THE BOMBS, BUT YOU SHOULD STAY HERE.
WHAT? I'VE BEEN TRAINING TO DROP THIS THING FOR THREE WEEKS WITH MY CREW. THEY NEED ME!
THAT WAS PRECISELY YOUR JOB. NOW LET THEM DO THEIRS.
BUT THEY'VE GOT PRACTICALLY NO CHANCE OF COMING BACK ALIVE UNLESS ALL THE DANGER'S ON ME!
THAT'S EXACTLY WHY YOU WON'T BE GOING WITH THEM. THE YANKS ARE SINGING YOUR PRAISES AFTER MIDWAY!

OPERATION PUNISHMENT, DAY J, HOUR H.

THEY KNOW WHAT THEY HAVE TO DO, AND YOU'VE TRAINED THEM WELL. THIS IS NO TIME FOR SENTIMENT.

ERLIN, YOU JUST DON'T LIKE PEOPLE!

I DON'T LIKE PEOPLE? I'VE BEEN TRYING TO SAVE THEIR ASSES FOR 10,000 YEARS, OLD FRIEND, SO DON'T TELL ME I DON'T LIKE THEM. I MUST BE THE ONE WHO LIKES THEM THE MOST IN ALL MY FAMILY. *AKER* WANTED TO IMPROVE THEM AT ANY COST, *REKA* DOESN'T CARE SO LONG AS SHE HAS A GOOD TIME, AND AS FOR DEAR *DYO*...

WELL, YES, HE DOESN'T LIKE PEOPLE. HE EVEN TOLD ME ONE DAY THAT PEOPLE MADE TOO MUCH NOISE AND THE WORLD WOULD BE BETTER WITHOUT THEM! NOW THERE'S A TRUE MISANTHROPE! AND HE'S SPENT HIS LIFE TRYING TO MAKE GOOD ON HIS WORDS!

DON'T MISS YOUR TARGET, CURTIS! AND GET A MOVE ON, OR YOU'LL MISS YOUR PLANE FOR THE STATES!

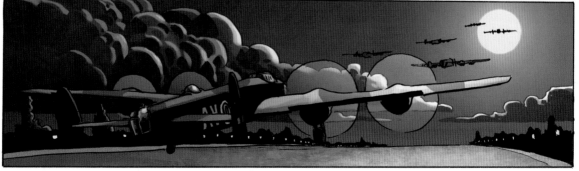

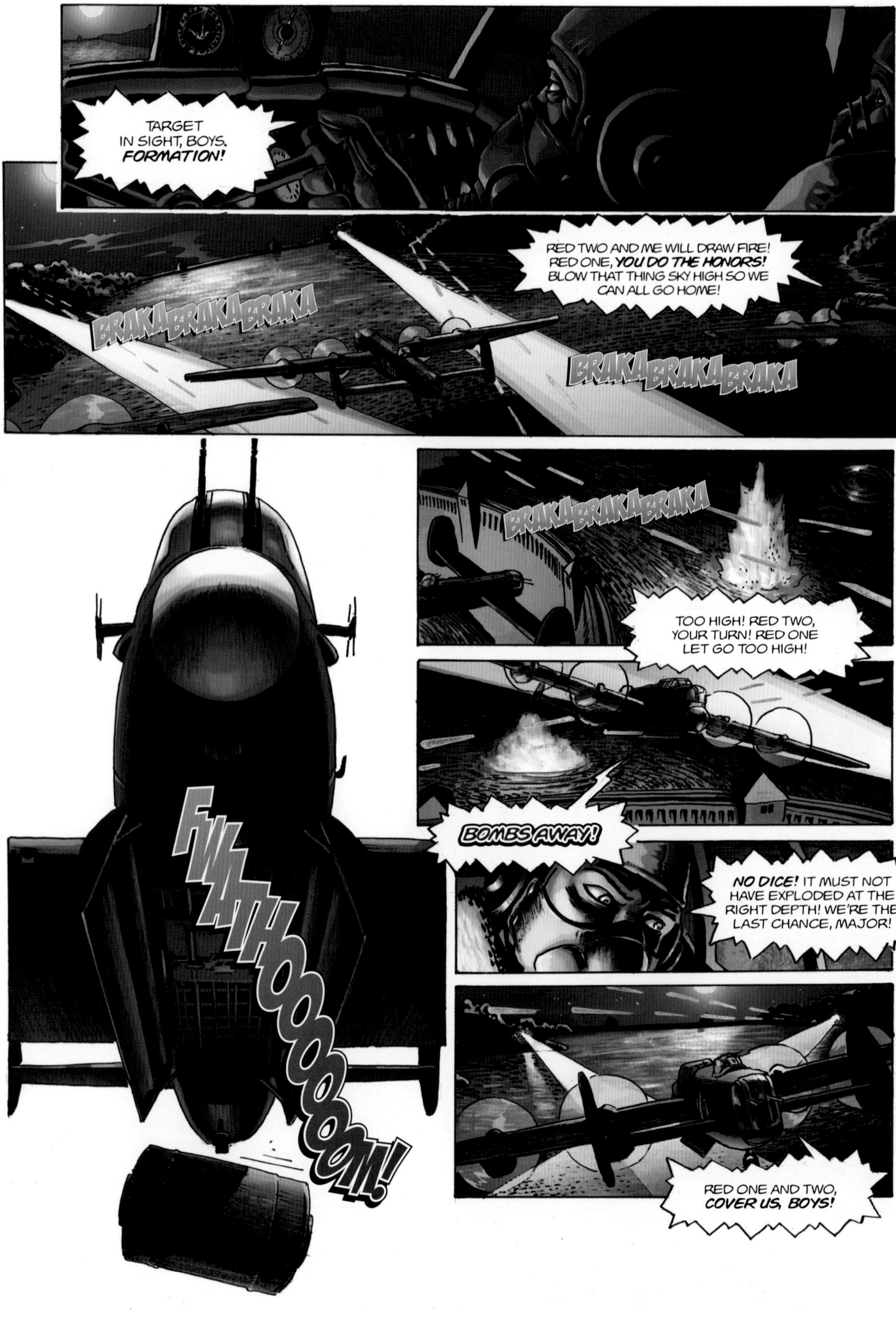
TARGET IN SIGHT, BOYS. *FORMATION!*
RED TWO AND ME WILL DRAW FIRE! RED ONE, *YOU DO THE HONORS!* BLOW THAT THING SKY HIGH SO WE CAN ALL GO HOME!
BRAKABRAKABRAKA
BRAKABRAKABRAKA
FWATHOOOOOOM!
BRAKABRAKABRAKA
TOO HIGH! RED TWO, YOUR TURN! RED ONE LET GO TOO HIGH!
BOMBS AWAY!
NO DICE! IT MUST NOT HAVE EXPLODED AT THE RIGHT DEPTH! WE'RE THE LAST CHANCE, MAJOR!
RED ONE AND TWO, *COVER US, BOYS!*

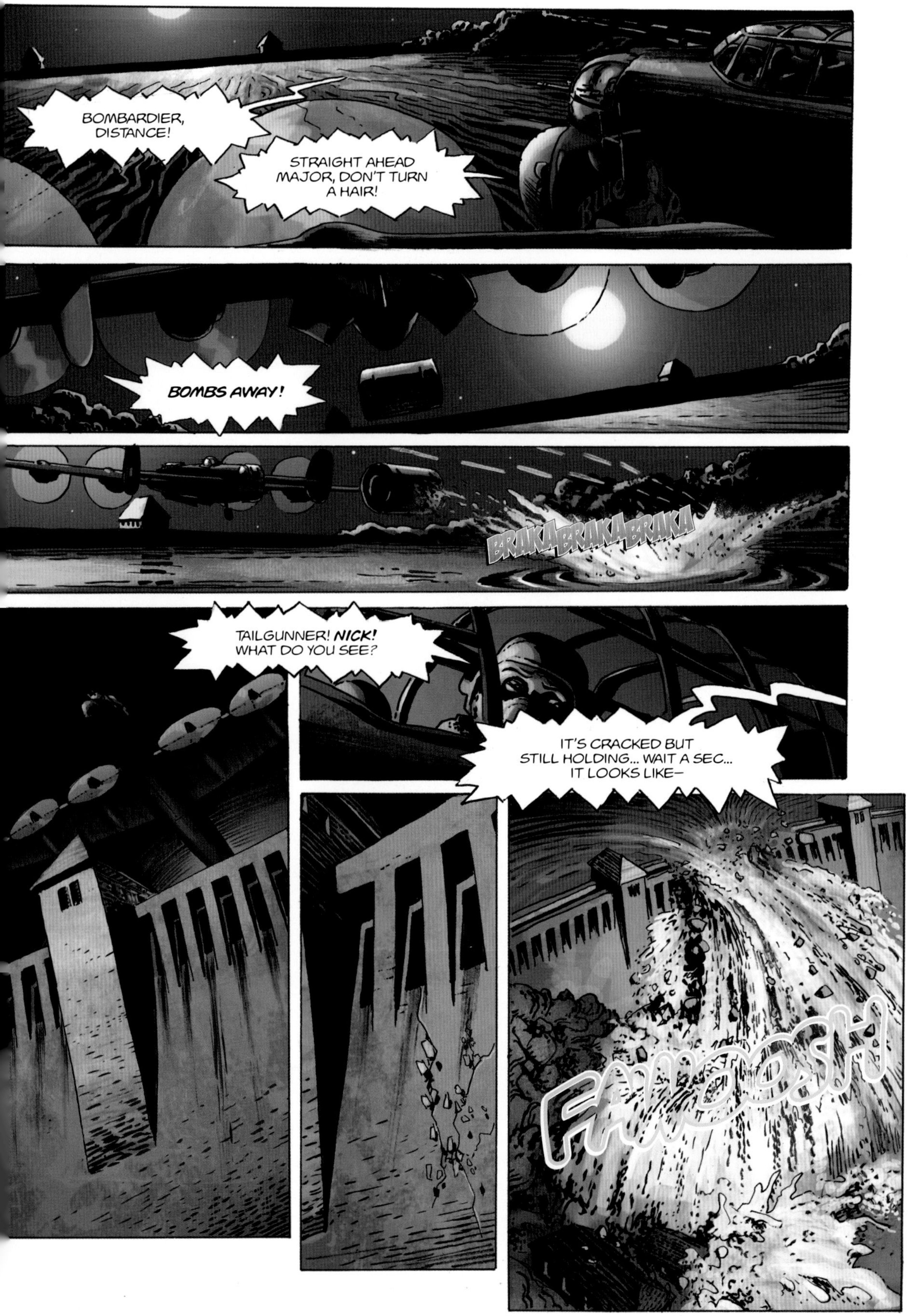
BOMBARDIER, DISTANCE!
STRAIGHT AHEAD MAJOR, DON'T TURN A HAIR!
BOMBS AWAY!
BRAKABRAKABRAKA
TAILGUNNER! NICK! WHAT DO YOU SEE?
IT'S CRACKED BUT STILL HOLDING... WAIT A SEC... IT LOOKS LIKE–
FAWOOSH

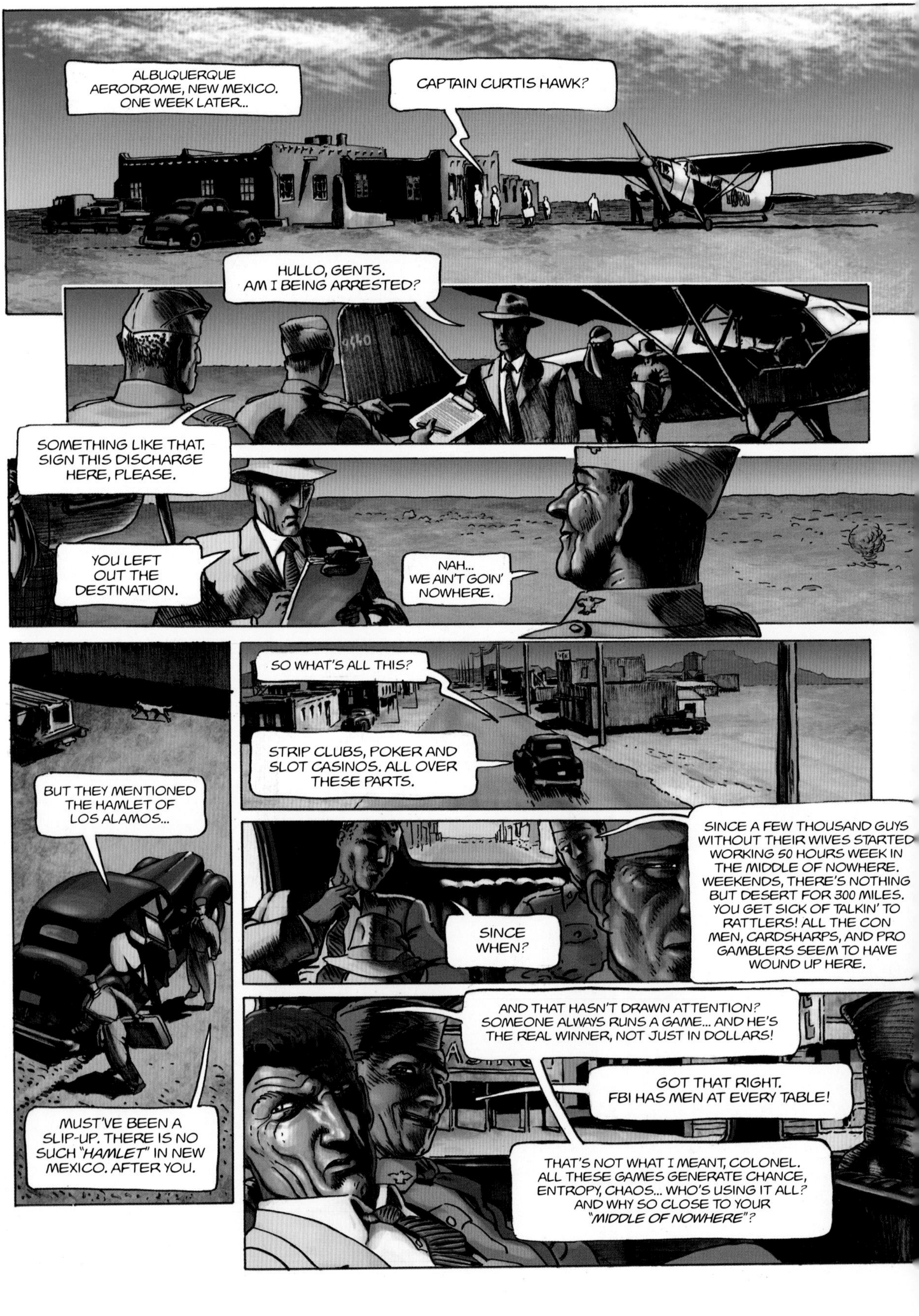
ALBUQUERQUE AERODROME, NEW MEXICO. ONE WEEK LATER...
CAPTAIN CURTIS HAWK?
HULLO, GENTS. AM I BEING ARRESTED?
SOMETHING LIKE THAT. SIGN THIS DISCHARGE HERE, PLEASE.
YOU LEFT OUT THE DESTINATION.
NAH... WE AIN'T GOIN' NOWHERE.
BUT THEY MENTIONED THE HAMLET OF LOS ALAMOS...
MUST'VE BEEN A SLIP-UP. THERE IS NO SUCH "HAMLET" IN NEW MEXICO. AFTER YOU.
SO WHAT'S ALL THIS?
STRIP CLUBS, POKER AND SLOT CASINOS. ALL OVER THESE PARTS.
SINCE WHEN?
SINCE A FEW THOUSAND GUYS WITHOUT THEIR WIVES STARTED WORKING 50 HOURS WEEK IN THE MIDDLE OF NOWHERE. WEEKENDS, THERE'S NOTHING BUT DESERT FOR 300 MILES. YOU GET SICK OF TALKIN' TO RATTLERS! ALL THE CON MEN, CARDSHARPS, AND PRO GAMBLERS SEEM TO HAVE WOUND UP HERE.
AND THAT HASN'T DRAWN ATTENTION? SOMEONE ALWAYS RUNS A GAME... AND HE'S THE REAL WINNER, NOT JUST IN DOLLARS!
GOT THAT RIGHT. FBI HAS MEN AT EVERY TABLE!
THAT'S NOT WHAT I MEANT, COLONEL. ALL THESE GAMES GENERATE CHANCE, ENTROPY, CHAOS... WHO'S USING IT ALL? AND WHY SO CLOSE TO YOUR "MIDDLE OF NOWHERE"?

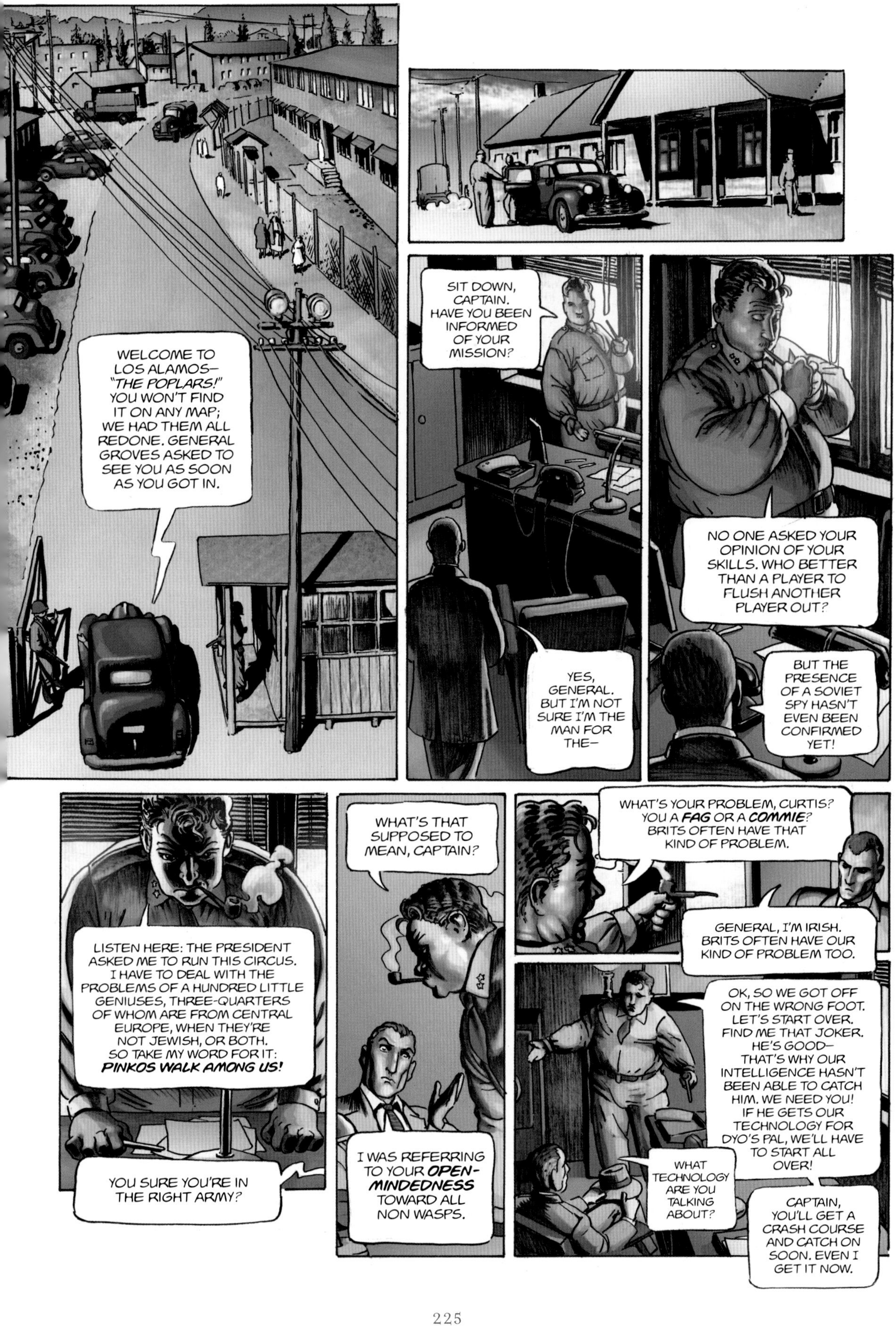
WELCOME TO LOS ALAMOS— "THE POPLARS!" YOU WON'T FIND IT ON ANY MAP; WE HAD THEM ALL REDONE. GENERAL GROVES ASKED TO SEE YOU AS SOON AS YOU GOT IN.
SIT DOWN, CAPTAIN. HAVE YOU BEEN INFORMED OF YOUR MISSION?
YES, GENERAL. BUT I'M NOT SURE I'M THE MAN FOR THE—
NO ONE ASKED YOUR OPINION OF YOUR SKILLS. WHO BETTER THAN A PLAYER TO FLUSH ANOTHER PLAYER OUT?
BUT THE PRESENCE OF A SOVIET SPY HASN'T EVEN BEEN CONFIRMED YET!
LISTEN HERE: THE PRESIDENT ASKED ME TO RUN THIS CIRCUS. I HAVE TO DEAL WITH THE PROBLEMS OF A HUNDRED LITTLE GENIUSES, THREE-QUARTERS OF WHOM ARE FROM CENTRAL EUROPE, WHEN THEY'RE NOT JEWISH, OR BOTH. SO TAKE MY WORD FOR IT: **PINKOS WALK AMONG US!**
YOU SURE YOU'RE IN THE RIGHT ARMY?
WHAT'S THAT SUPPOSED TO MEAN, CAPTAIN?
I WAS REFERRING TO YOUR **OPEN-MINDEDNESS** TOWARD ALL NON WASPS.
WHAT'S YOUR PROBLEM, CURTIS? YOU A **FAG** OR A **COMMIE**? BRITS OFTEN HAVE THAT KIND OF PROBLEM.
GENERAL, I'M IRISH. BRITS OFTEN HAVE OUR KIND OF PROBLEM TOO.
OK, SO WE GOT OFF ON THE WRONG FOOT. LET'S START OVER. FIND ME THAT JOKER. HE'S GOOD— THAT'S WHY OUR INTELLIGENCE HASN'T BEEN ABLE TO CATCH HIM. WE NEED YOU! IF HE GETS OUR TECHNOLOGY FOR DYO'S PAL, WE'LL HAVE TO START ALL OVER!
WHAT TECHNOLOGY ARE YOU TALKING ABOUT?
CAPTAIN, YOU'LL GET A CRASH COURSE AND CATCH ON SOON. EVEN I GET IT NOW.

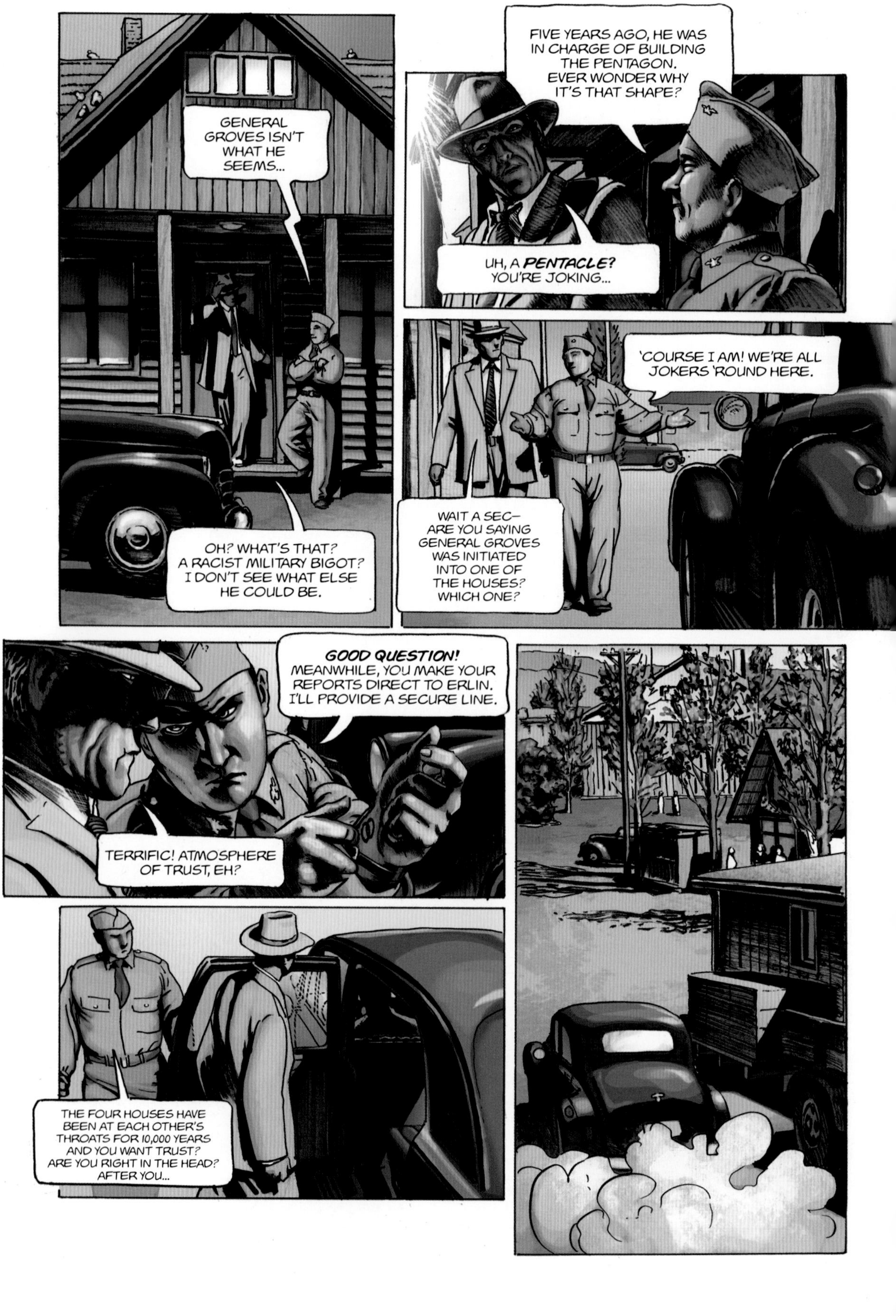
GENERAL GROVES ISN'T WHAT HE SEEMS...
OH? WHAT'S THAT? A RACIST MILITARY BIGOT? I DON'T SEE WHAT ELSE HE COULD BE.
FIVE YEARS AGO, HE WAS IN CHARGE OF BUILDING THE PENTAGON. EVER WONDER WHY IT'S THAT SHAPE?
UH, A PENTACLE? YOU'RE JOKING...
'COURSE I AM! WE'RE ALL JOKERS 'ROUND HERE.
WAIT A SEC— ARE YOU SAYING GENERAL GROVES WAS INITIATED INTO ONE OF THE HOUSES? WHICH ONE?
GOOD QUESTION! MEANWHILE, YOU MAKE YOUR REPORTS DIRECT TO ERLIN. I'LL PROVIDE A SECURE LINE.
TERRIFIC! ATMOSPHERE OF TRUST, EH?
THE FOUR HOUSES HAVE BEEN AT EACH OTHER'S THROATS FOR 10,000 YEARS AND YOU WANT TRUST? ARE YOU RIGHT IN THE HEAD? AFTER YOU...

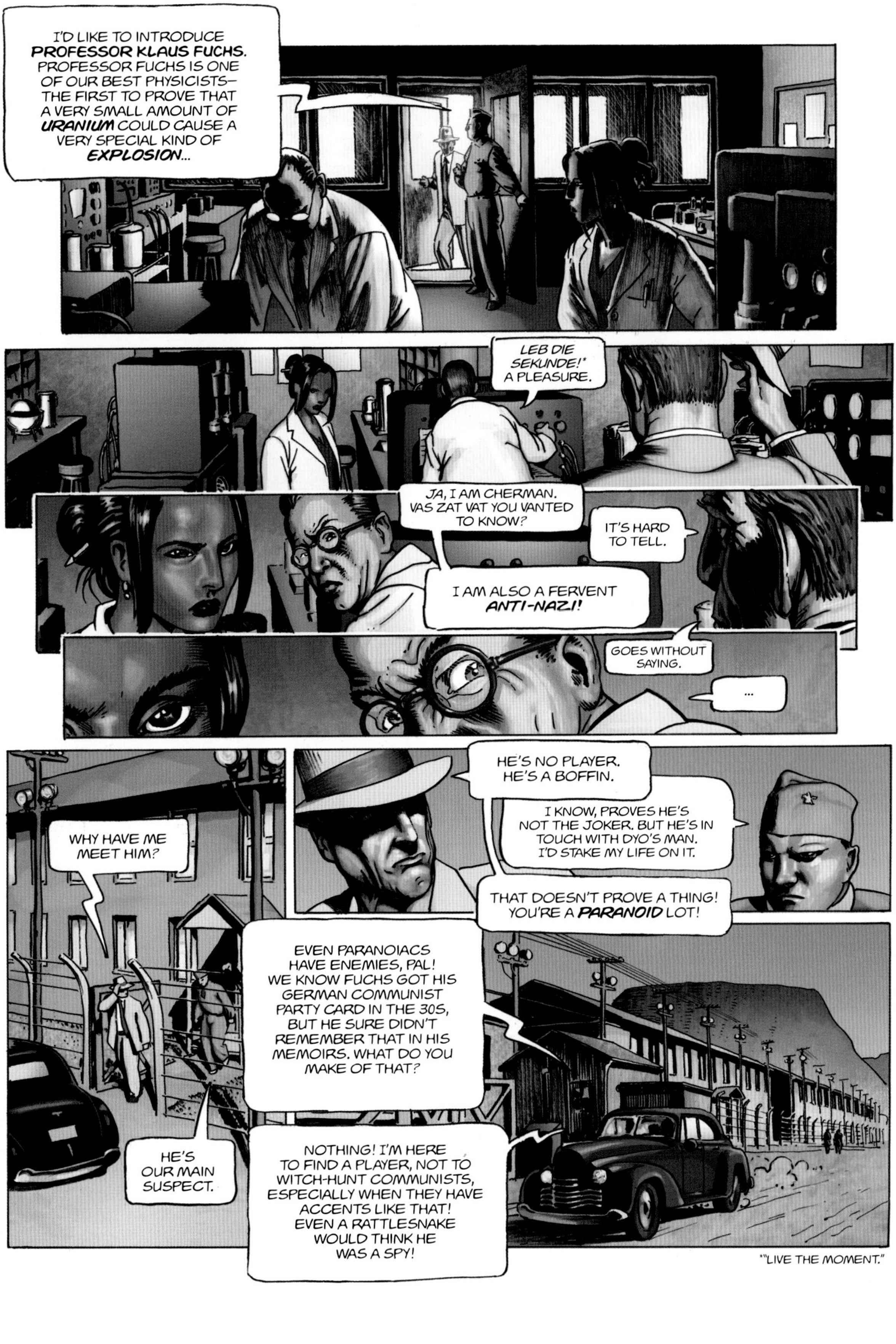
I'D LIKE TO INTRODUCE **PROFESSOR KLAUS FUCHS.** PROFESSOR FUCHS IS ONE OF OUR BEST PHYSICISTS— THE FIRST TO PROVE THAT A VERY SMALL AMOUNT OF ***URANIUM*** COULD CAUSE A VERY SPECIAL KIND OF ***EXPLOSION***...
*LEB DIE SEKUNDE!** A PLEASURE.
JA, I AM CHERMAN. VAS ZAT VAT YOU VANTED TO KNOW?
IT'S HARD TO TELL.
I AM ALSO A FERVENT ***ANTI-NAZI!***
GOES WITHOUT SAYING.
...
WHY HAVE ME MEET HIM?
HE'S NO PLAYER. HE'S A BOFFIN.
I KNOW, PROVES HE'S NOT THE JOKER. BUT HE'S IN TOUCH WITH DYO'S MAN. I'D STAKE MY LIFE ON IT.
THAT DOESN'T PROVE A THING! YOU'RE A ***PARANOID*** LOT!
EVEN PARANOIACS HAVE ENEMIES, PAL! WE KNOW FUCHS GOT HIS GERMAN COMMUNIST PARTY CARD IN THE 30S, BUT HE SURE DIDN'T REMEMBER THAT IN HIS MEMOIRS. WHAT DO YOU MAKE OF THAT?
HE'S OUR MAIN SUSPECT.
NOTHING! I'M HERE TO FIND A PLAYER, NOT TO WITCH-HUNT COMMUNISTS, ESPECIALLY WHEN THEY HAVE ACCENTS LIKE THAT! EVEN A RATTLESNAKE WOULD THINK HE WAS A SPY!

*"LIVE THE MOMENT."

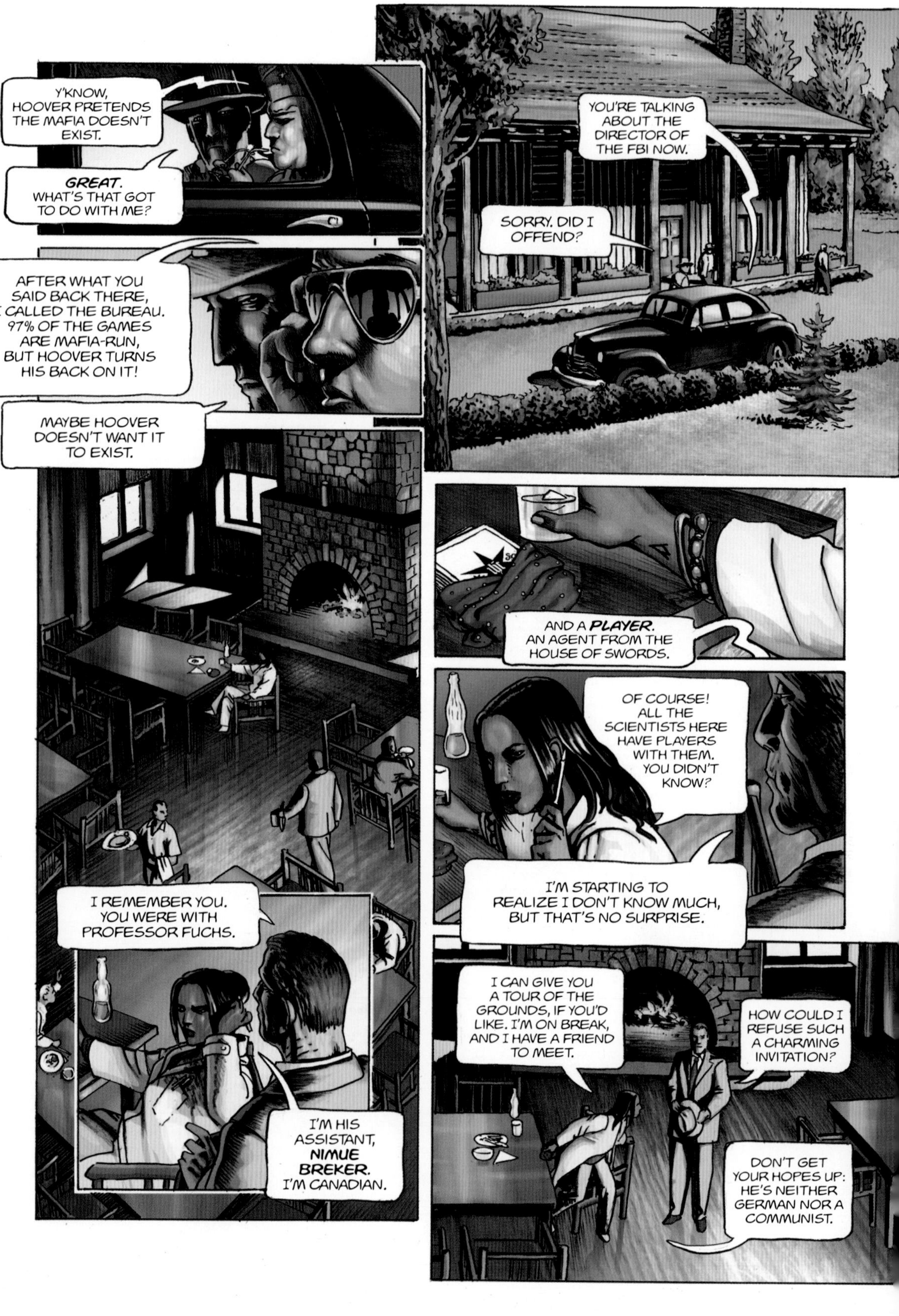
Y'KNOW, HOOVER PRETENDS THE MAFIA DOESN'T EXIST.
GREAT. WHAT'S THAT GOT TO DO WITH ME?
AFTER WHAT YOU SAID BACK THERE, I CALLED THE BUREAU. 97% OF THE GAMES ARE MAFIA-RUN, BUT HOOVER TURNS HIS BACK ON IT!
MAYBE HOOVER DOESN'T WANT IT TO EXIST.
YOU'RE TALKING ABOUT THE DIRECTOR OF THE FBI NOW.
SORRY. DID I OFFEND?
I REMEMBER YOU. YOU WERE WITH PROFESSOR FUCHS.
I'M HIS ASSISTANT, NIMUE BREKER. I'M CANADIAN.
AND A PLAYER. AN AGENT FROM THE HOUSE OF SWORDS.
OF COURSE! ALL THE SCIENTISTS HERE HAVE PLAYERS WITH THEM. YOU DIDN'T KNOW?
I'M STARTING TO REALIZE I DON'T KNOW MUCH, BUT THAT'S NO SURPRISE.
I CAN GIVE YOU A TOUR OF THE GROUNDS, IF YOU'D LIKE. I'M ON BREAK, AND I HAVE A FRIEND TO MEET.
HOW COULD I REFUSE SUCH A CHARMING INVITATION?
DON'T GET YOUR HOPES UP: HE'S NEITHER GERMAN NOR A COMMUNIST.

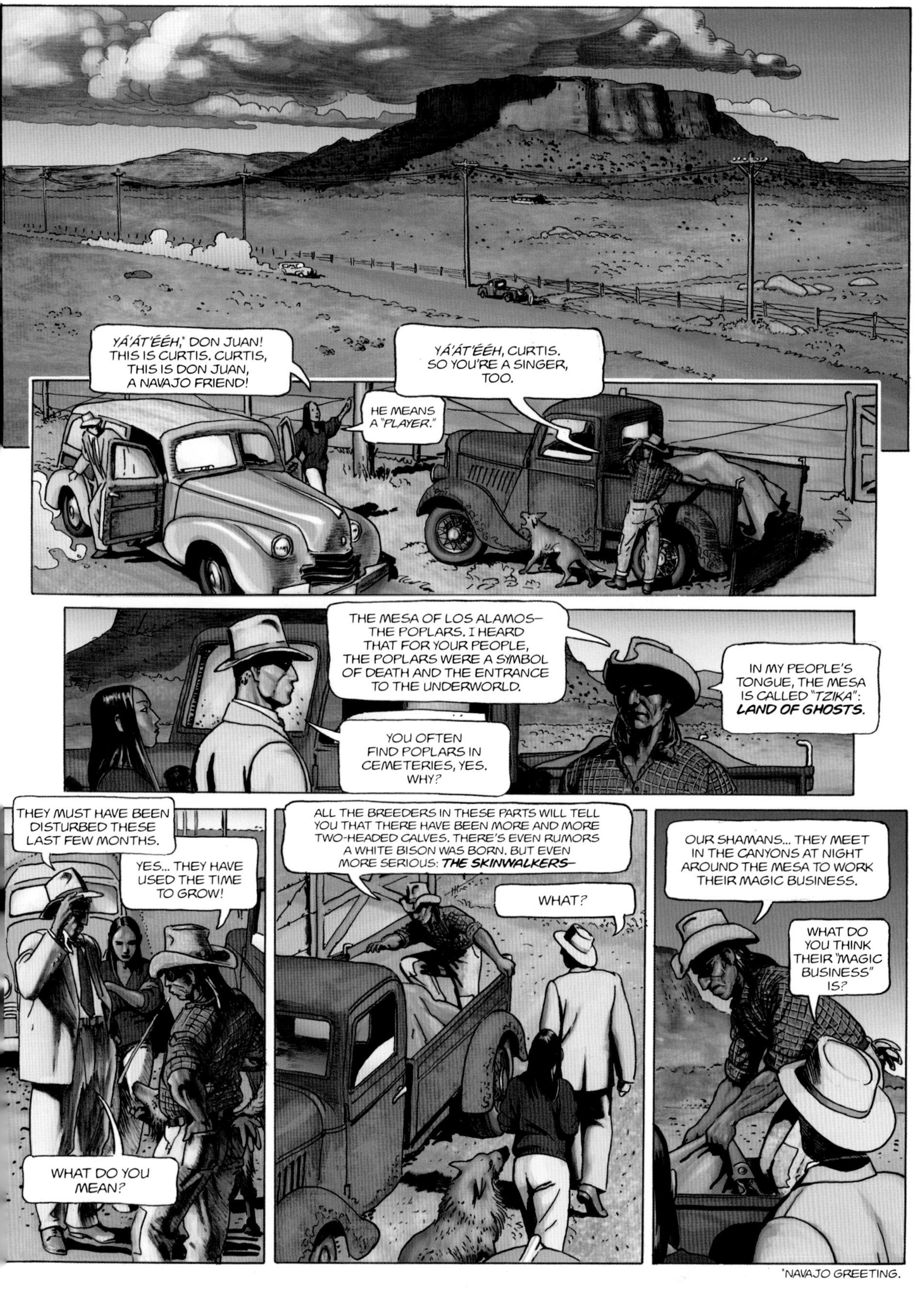
YÁ'ÁT'ÉÉH,* DON JUAN! THIS IS CURTIS. CURTIS, THIS IS DON JUAN, A NAVAJO FRIEND!
YÁ'ÁT'ÉÉH, CURTIS. SO YOU'RE A SINGER, TOO.
HE MEANS A "PLAYER."
THE MESA OF LOS ALAMOS— THE POPLARS. I HEARD THAT FOR YOUR PEOPLE, THE POPLARS WERE A SYMBOL OF DEATH AND THE ENTRANCE TO THE UNDERWORLD.
IN MY PEOPLE'S TONGUE, THE MESA IS CALLED "TZIKA": LAND OF GHOSTS.
YOU OFTEN FIND POPLARS IN CEMETERIES, YES. WHY?
THEY MUST HAVE BEEN DISTURBED THESE LAST FEW MONTHS.
YES... THEY HAVE USED THE TIME TO GROW!
WHAT DO YOU MEAN?
ALL THE BREEDERS IN THESE PARTS WILL TELL YOU THAT THERE HAVE BEEN MORE AND MORE TWO-HEADED CALVES. THERE'S EVEN RUMORS A WHITE BISON WAS BORN. BUT EVEN MORE SERIOUS: THE SKINWALKERS—
WHAT?
OUR SHAMANS... THEY MEET IN THE CANYONS AT NIGHT AROUND THE MESA TO WORK THEIR MAGIC BUSINESS.
WHAT DO YOU THINK THEIR "MAGIC BUSINESS" IS?

*NAVAJO GREETING.

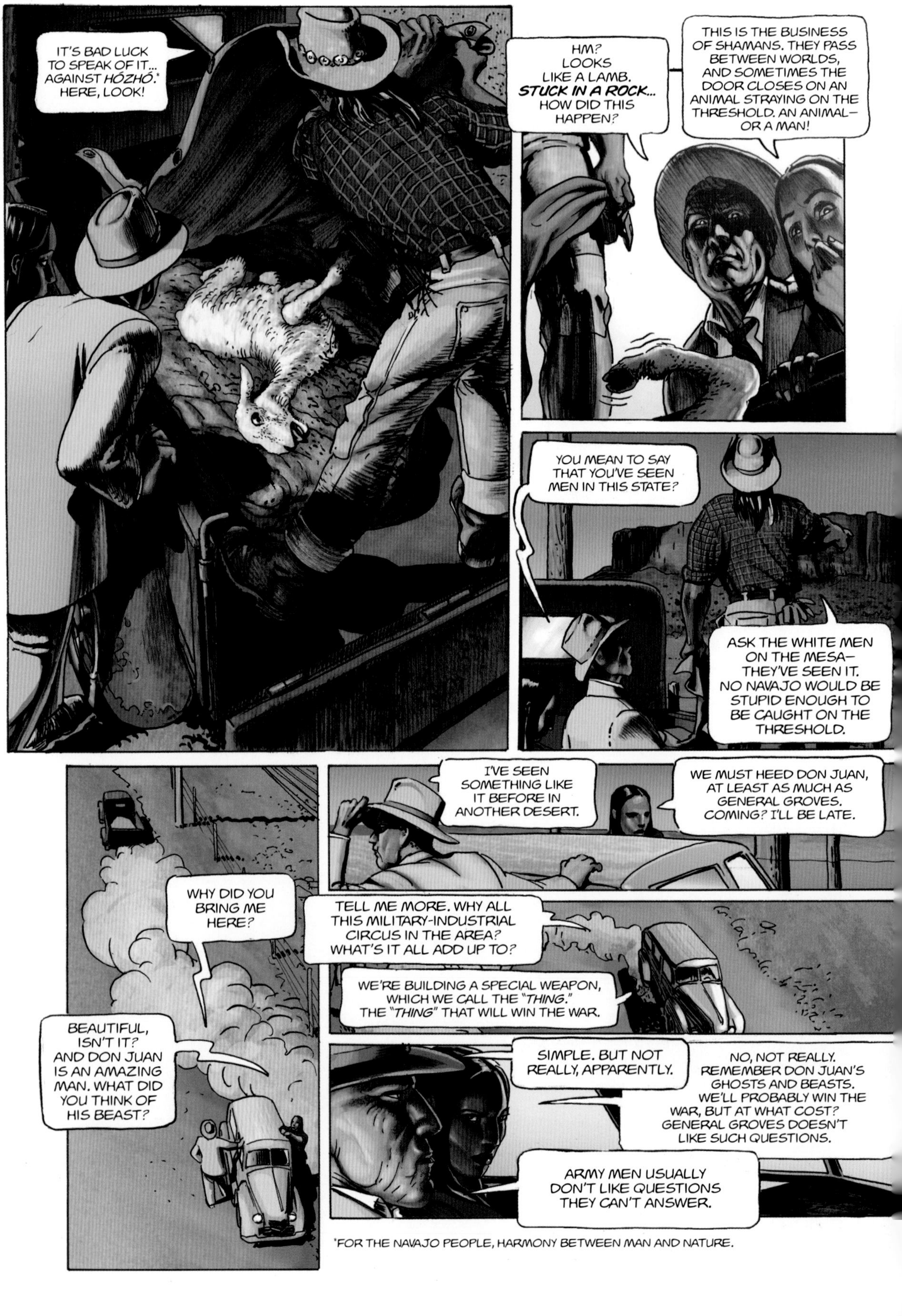
IT'S BAD LUCK TO SPEAK OF IT... AGAINST HÓZHÓ.* HERE, LOOK!
HM? LOOKS LIKE A LAMB. STUCK IN A ROCK... HOW DID THIS HAPPEN?
THIS IS THE BUSINESS OF SHAMANS. THEY PASS BETWEEN WORLDS, AND SOMETIMES THE DOOR CLOSES ON AN ANIMAL STRAYING ON THE THRESHOLD. AN ANIMAL— OR A MAN!
YOU MEAN TO SAY THAT YOU'VE SEEN MEN IN THIS STATE?
ASK THE WHITE MEN ON THE MESA— THEY'VE SEEN IT. NO NAVAJO WOULD BE STUPID ENOUGH TO BE CAUGHT ON THE THRESHOLD.
I'VE SEEN SOMETHING LIKE IT BEFORE IN ANOTHER DESERT.
WE MUST HEED DON JUAN, AT LEAST AS MUCH AS GENERAL GROVES. COMING? I'LL BE LATE.
WHY DID YOU BRING ME HERE?
BEAUTIFUL, ISN'T IT? AND DON JUAN IS AN AMAZING MAN. WHAT DID YOU THINK OF HIS BEAST?
TELL ME MORE. WHY ALL THIS MILITARY-INDUSTRIAL CIRCUS IN THE AREA? WHAT'S IT ALL ADD UP TO?
WE'RE BUILDING A SPECIAL WEAPON, WHICH WE CALL THE "THING." THE "THING" THAT WILL WIN THE WAR.
SIMPLE. BUT NOT REALLY, APPARENTLY.
NO, NOT REALLY. REMEMBER DON JUAN'S GHOSTS AND BEASTS. WE'LL PROBABLY WIN THE WAR, BUT AT WHAT COST? GENERAL GROVES DOESN'T LIKE SUCH QUESTIONS.
ARMY MEN USUALLY DON'T LIKE QUESTIONS THEY CAN'T ANSWER.

*FOR THE NAVAJO PEOPLE, HARMONY BETWEEN MAN AND NATURE.

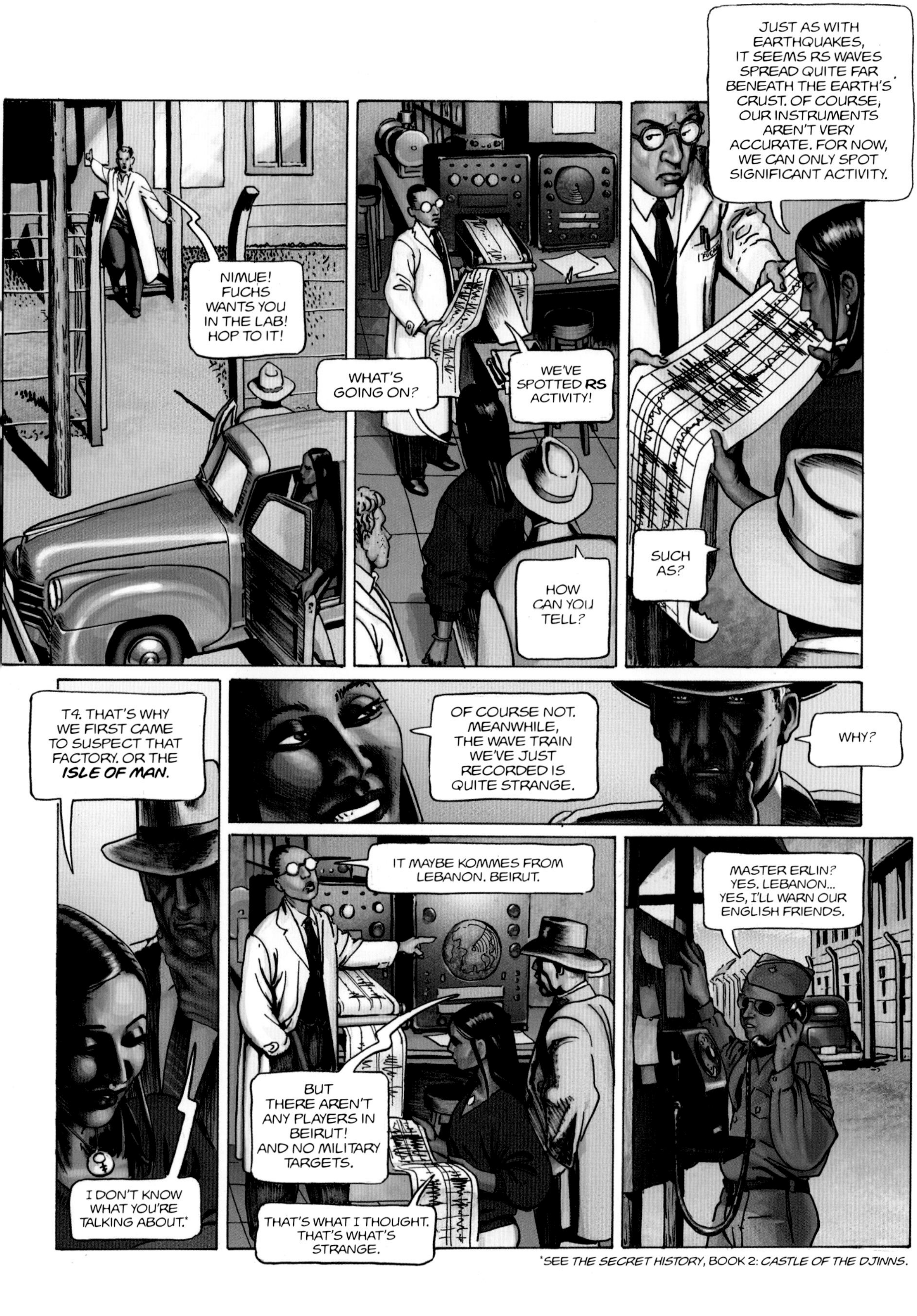
NIMUE! FUCHS WANTS YOU IN THE LAB! HOP TO IT!
WHAT'S GOING ON?
WE'VE SPOTTED RS ACTIVITY!
HOW CAN YOU TELL?
JUST AS WITH EARTHQUAKES, IT SEEMS RS WAVES SPREAD QUITE FAR BENEATH THE EARTH'S CRUST. OF COURSE, OUR INSTRUMENTS AREN'T VERY ACCURATE. FOR NOW, WE CAN ONLY SPOT SIGNIFICANT ACTIVITY.
SUCH AS?
T4. THAT'S WHY WE FIRST CAME TO SUSPECT THAT FACTORY. OR THE ISLE OF MAN.
I DON'T KNOW WHAT YOU'RE TALKING ABOUT.*
OF COURSE NOT. MEANWHILE, THE WAVE TRAIN WE'VE JUST RECORDED IS QUITE STRANGE.
WHY?
IT MAYBE KOMMES FROM LEBANON. BEIRUT.
BUT THERE AREN'T ANY PLAYERS IN BEIRUT! AND NO MILITARY TARGETS.
THAT'S WHAT I THOUGHT. THAT'S WHAT'S STRANGE.
MASTER ERLIN? YES. LEBANON... YES, I'LL WARN OUR ENGLISH FRIENDS.

*SEE *THE SECRET HISTORY*, BOOK 2: *CASTLE OF THE DJINNS*.

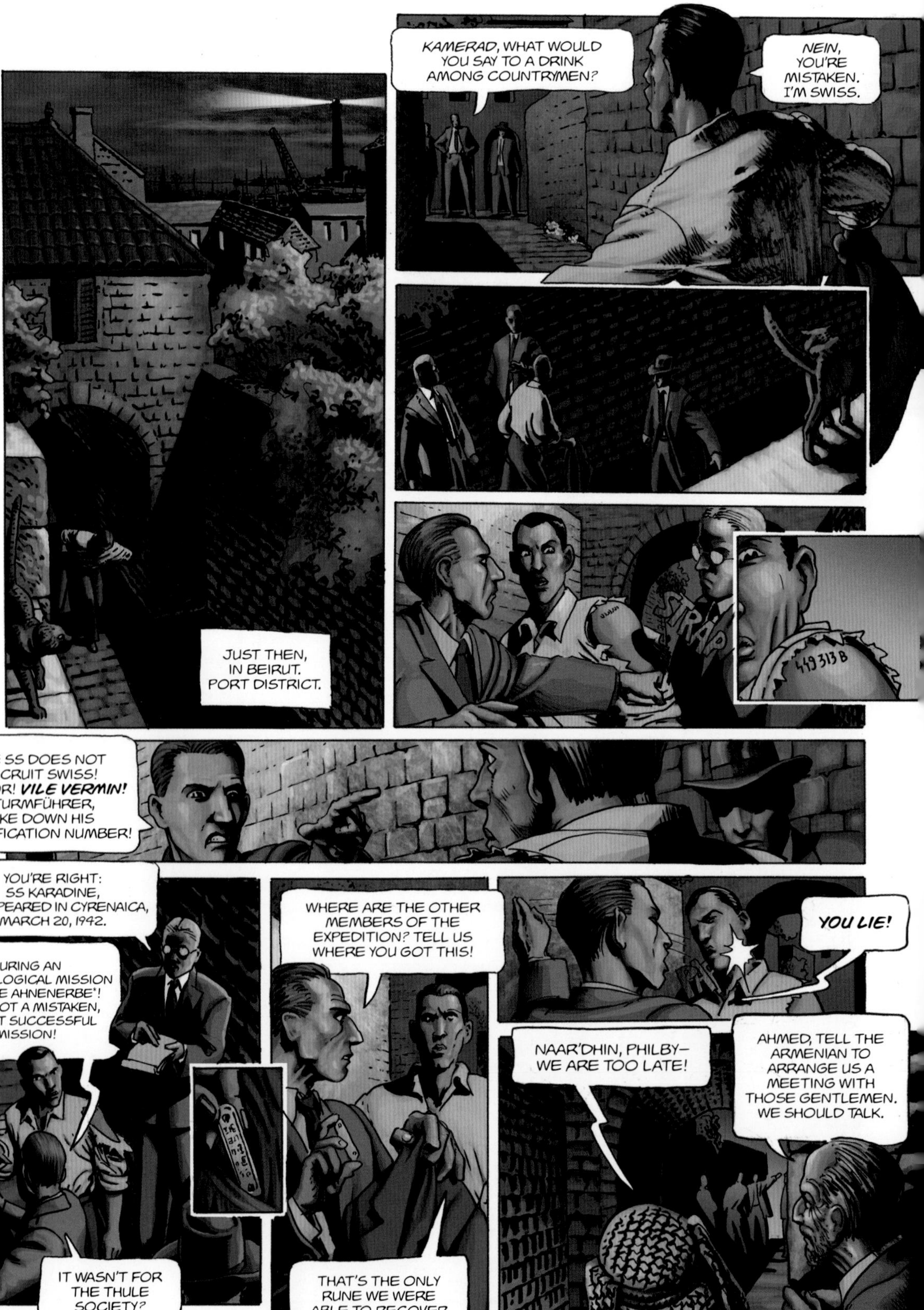
JUST THEN, IN BEIRUT. PORT DISTRICT.
KAMERAD, WHAT WOULD YOU SAY TO A DRINK AMONG COUNTRYMEN?
NEIN, YOU'RE MISTAKEN. I'M SWISS.
STRAP
449 313 B
THE SS DOES NOT RECRUIT SWISS! TRAITOR! VILE VERMIN! STURMFÜHRER, TAKE DOWN HIS IDENTIFICATION NUMBER!
YOU'RE RIGHT: SS KARADINE, DISAPPEARED IN CYRENAICA, MARCH 20, 1942.
DURING AN ARCHEOLOGICAL MISSION FOR THE AHNENERBE*! IF I'M NOT A MISTAKEN, A MOST SUCCESSFUL MISSION!
IT WASN'T FOR THE THULE SOCIETY?
WHERE ARE THE OTHER MEMBERS OF THE EXPEDITION? TELL US WHERE YOU GOT THIS!
THAT'S THE ONLY RUNE WE WERE ABLE TO RECOVER FROM THE DIG SITE BEFORE THE ENGLISH BOMBING!
YOU LIE!
NAAR'DHIN, PHILBY— WE ARE TOO LATE!
AHMED, TELL THE ARMENIAN TO ARRANGE US A MEETING WITH THOSE GENTLEMEN. WE SHOULD TALK.

*"GERMAN ANCESTRAL HERITAGE": THE SS DEPARTMENT OF ESOTERIC STUDIES. EVEN TO THIS DAY, NO ONE REALLY KNOWS WHAT ITS FUNCTION AND THE TRUE NATURE OF ITS STUDIES WERE

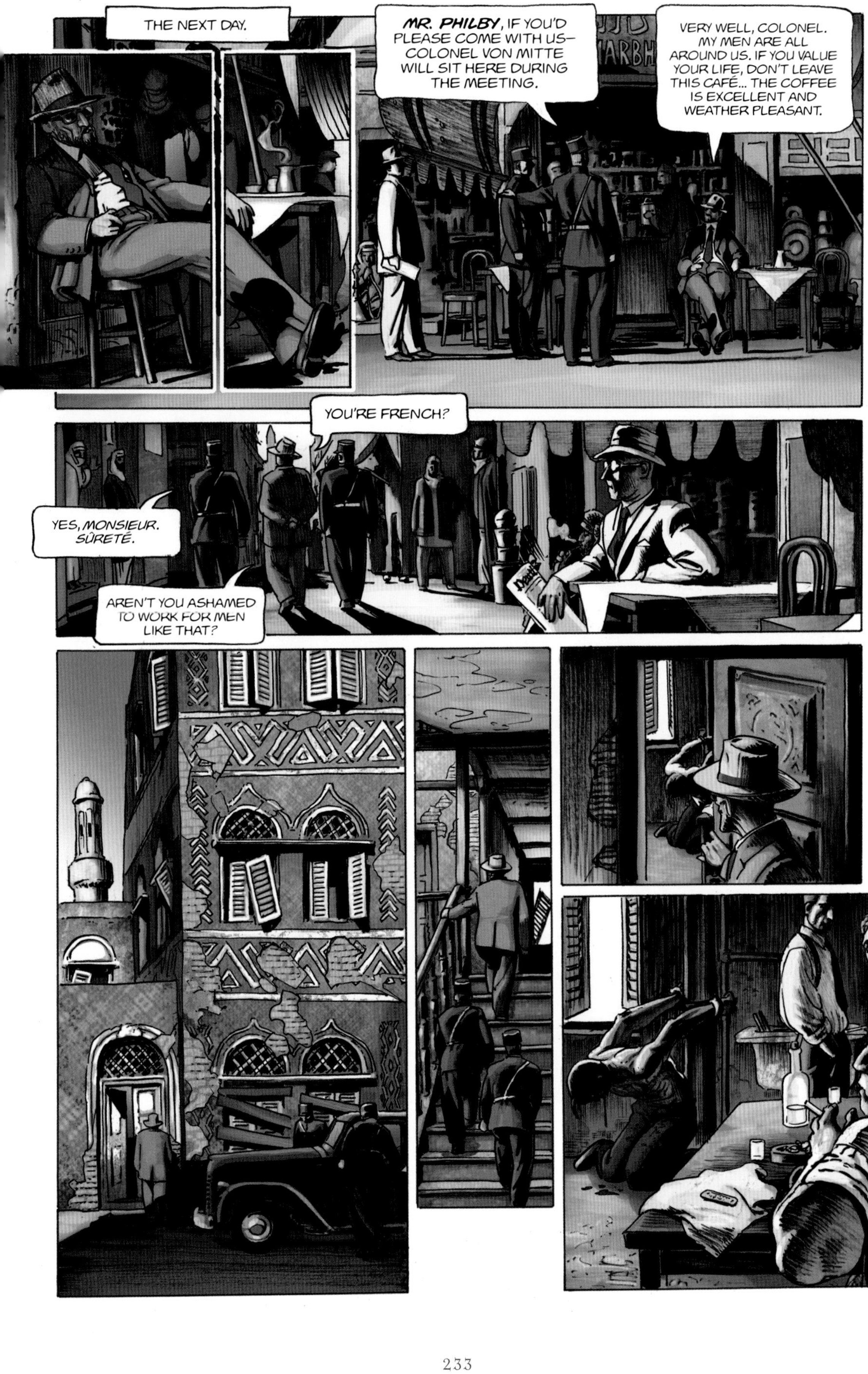
THE NEXT DAY.
MR. PHILBY, IF YOU'D PLEASE COME WITH US— COLONEL VON MITTE WILL SIT HERE DURING THE MEETING.
VERY WELL, COLONEL. MY MEN ARE ALL AROUND US. IF YOU VALUE YOUR LIFE, DON'T LEAVE THIS CAFÉ... THE COFFEE IS EXCELLENT AND WEATHER PLEASANT.
YOU'RE FRENCH?
YES, MONSIEUR. SÛRETÉ.
AREN'T YOU ASHAMED TO WORK FOR MEN LIKE THAT?

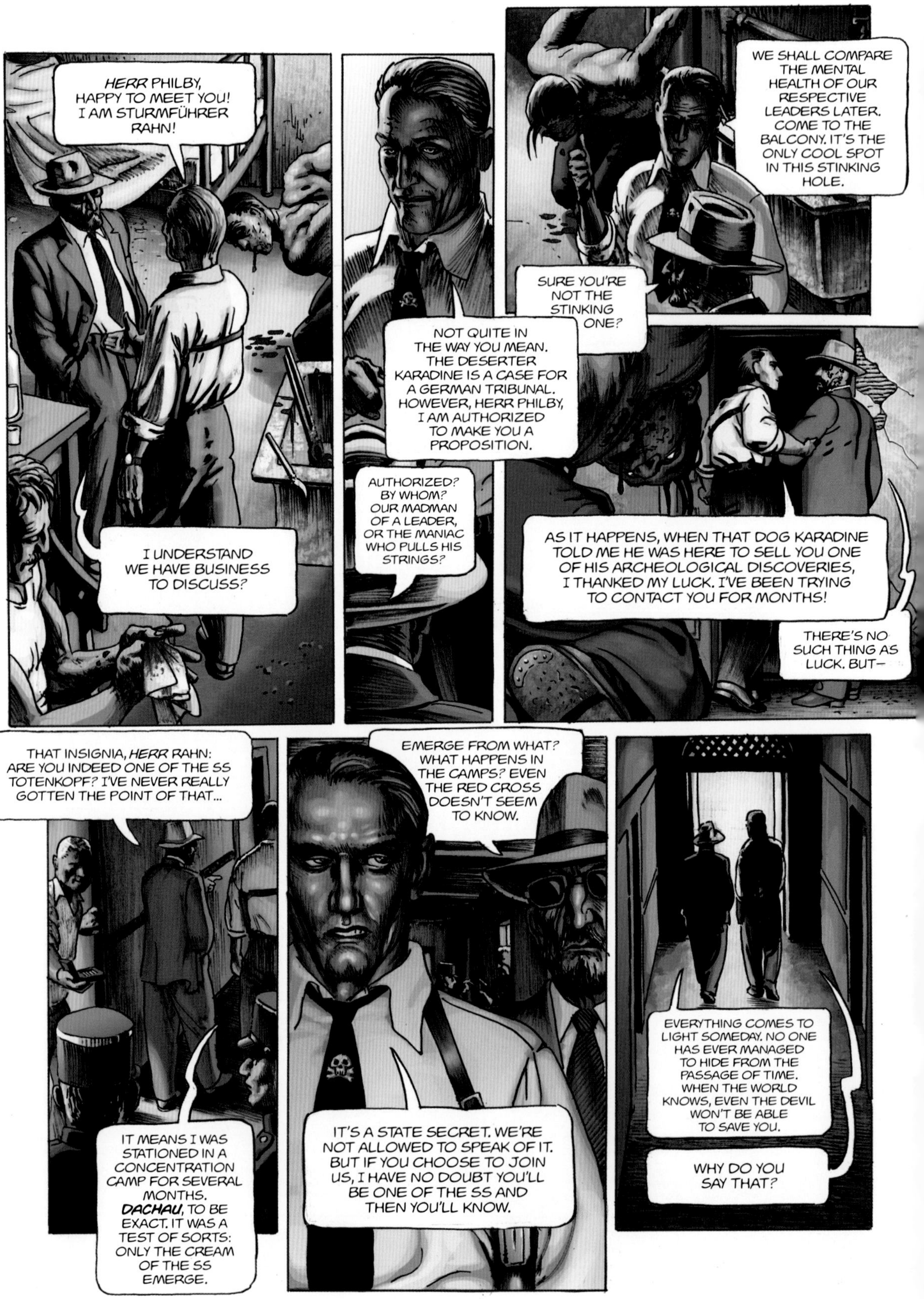
HERR PHILBY, HAPPY TO MEET YOU! I AM STURMFÜHRER RAHN!
I UNDERSTAND WE HAVE BUSINESS TO DISCUSS?
NOT QUITE IN THE WAY YOU MEAN. THE DESERTER KARADINE IS A CASE FOR A GERMAN TRIBUNAL. HOWEVER, HERR PHILBY, I AM AUTHORIZED TO MAKE YOU A PROPOSITION.
AUTHORIZED? BY WHOM? OUR MADMAN OF A LEADER, OR THE MANIAC WHO PULLS HIS STRINGS?
WE SHALL COMPARE THE MENTAL HEALTH OF OUR RESPECTIVE LEADERS LATER. COME TO THE BALCONY. IT'S THE ONLY COOL SPOT IN THIS STINKING HOLE.
SURE YOU'RE NOT THE STINKING ONE?
AS IT HAPPENS, WHEN THAT DOG KARADINE TOLD ME HE WAS HERE TO SELL YOU ONE OF HIS ARCHEOLOGICAL DISCOVERIES, I THANKED MY LUCK. I'VE BEEN TRYING TO CONTACT YOU FOR MONTHS!
THERE'S NO SUCH THING AS LUCK. BUT—
THAT INSIGNIA, HERR RAHN: ARE YOU INDEED ONE OF THE SS TOTENKOPF? I'VE NEVER REALLY GOTTEN THE POINT OF THAT...
IT MEANS I WAS STATIONED IN A CONCENTRATION CAMP FOR SEVERAL MONTHS. DACHAU, TO BE EXACT. IT WAS A TEST OF SORTS: ONLY THE CREAM OF THE SS EMERGE.
EMERGE FROM WHAT? WHAT HAPPENS IN THE CAMPS? EVEN THE RED CROSS DOESN'T SEEM TO KNOW.
IT'S A STATE SECRET. WE'RE NOT ALLOWED TO SPEAK OF IT. BUT IF YOU CHOOSE TO JOIN US, I HAVE NO DOUBT YOU'LL BE ONE OF THE SS AND THEN YOU'LL KNOW.
EVERYTHING COMES TO LIGHT SOMEDAY. NO ONE HAS EVER MANAGED TO HIDE FROM THE PASSAGE OF TIME. WHEN THE WORLD KNOWS, EVEN THE DEVIL WON'T BE ABLE TO SAVE YOU.
WHY DO YOU SAY THAT?

YOU'RE **WILLIAM'S SPAWN**. ALL THAT COMES FROM YOU IS EVIL AND CURSED!

SHOULD I TAKE THAT AS A FLAT REFUSAL? YOU'RE MAD. JUST PASS OUR PROPOSITION ON TO SAUD! YOUR KING RULES A FISTFUL OF SAND AND A FEW DATES. WE CAN OFFER HIM ALL THE MIDDLE EAST FROM PALESTINE TO IRAN! *A NEW CALIPHATE!* THE GRAND MUFTI OF JERUSALEM HAS ALREADY PLEDGED HIS SUPPORT!

THE GRAND MUFTI IS A GREEDY IDIOT!

?!!

YOU WON'T WIN THE WAR, NOT AGAINST RUSSIA AND THE US COMBINED. SAUD IS A FINE TACTICIAN. HE'S KNOWN THAT FOR SOME TIME. SO HE WON'T HELP YOU—QUITE THE OPPOSITE.

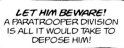

LET HIM BEWARE! A PARATROOPER DIVISION IS ALL IT WOULD TAKE TO DEPOSE HIM!

THINK SO? LIKE IN IRAQ TWO YEARS AGO?* YOU'RE VERY FAR FROM HOME, *HERR* RAHN, AND YOU'D DO BETTER TO GO BACK BEFORE RUBBING A BEDOUIN THE WRONG WAY AND WINDING UP WITH A SLIT THROAT. WE ARE SAVAGES, SO THEY SAY—AT LEAST IN MOST WESTERN COUNTRIES.

A STORM FROM SEA. *STRANGE.* YOU WOULDN'T DARE—

YOU HAVEN'T THE FAINTEST OF HOW POWERFUL THE RUNES OF KOR ARE!

BUT IF OUR INFORMATION IS CORRECT, YOU NO LONGER HAVE THE KOR RUNES IN YOUR POSSESSION.

UNLESS I WENT BACK TO KOR.

THAT'S IMPOSSIBLE! BESIDES, I'M NOT EVEN SURE ANYONE CAN. KOR MOVES IN TIME AND SPACE: THE VALLEY CAN ONLY BE ENTERED DURING VERY SPECIFIC ASTRAL CONJUNCTIONS!

CONGRATULATIONS! AHNENERBE HAS DONE ITS HOMEWORK!

*IN 1942, THE GERMANS FOMENTED A REVOLT IN IRAQ AGAINST THE ENGLISH. IT WAS AN UTTER FAILURE.

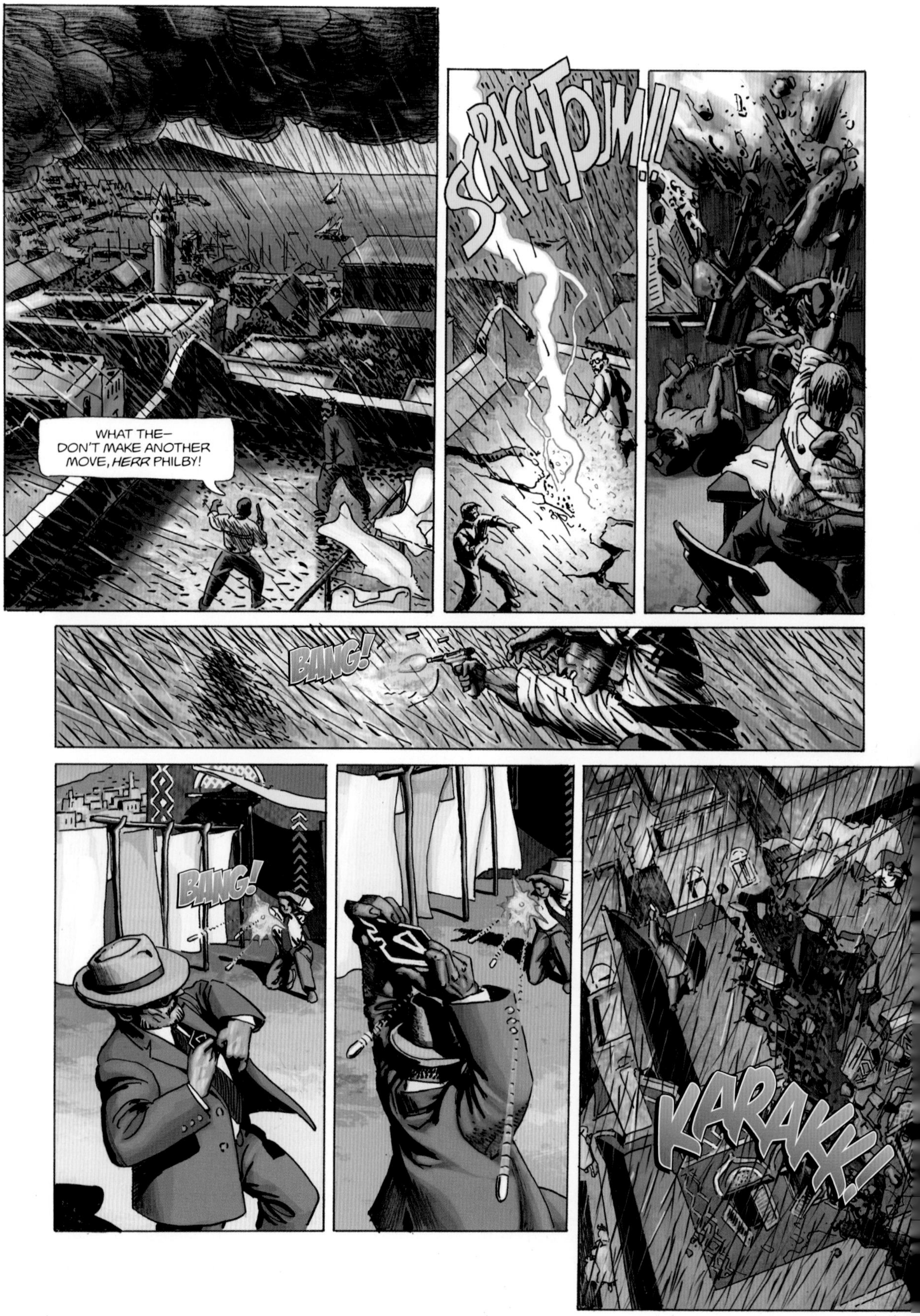
WHAT THE—
DON'T MAKE ANOTHER MOVE, HERR PHILBY!
SCRACATOUM!!
BANG!
BANG!
KARAKK!

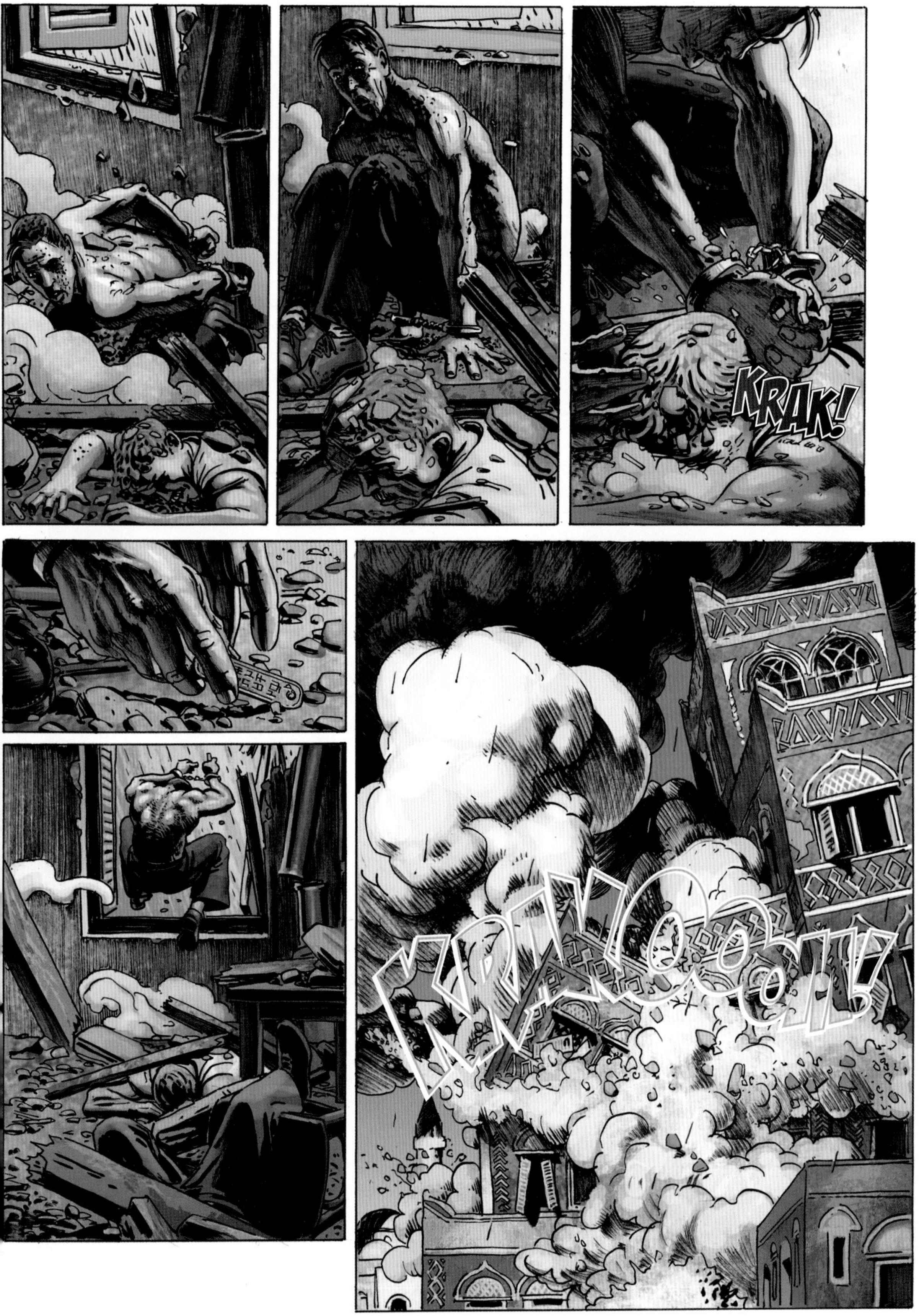
KRAK!
KRAKOOOOM!

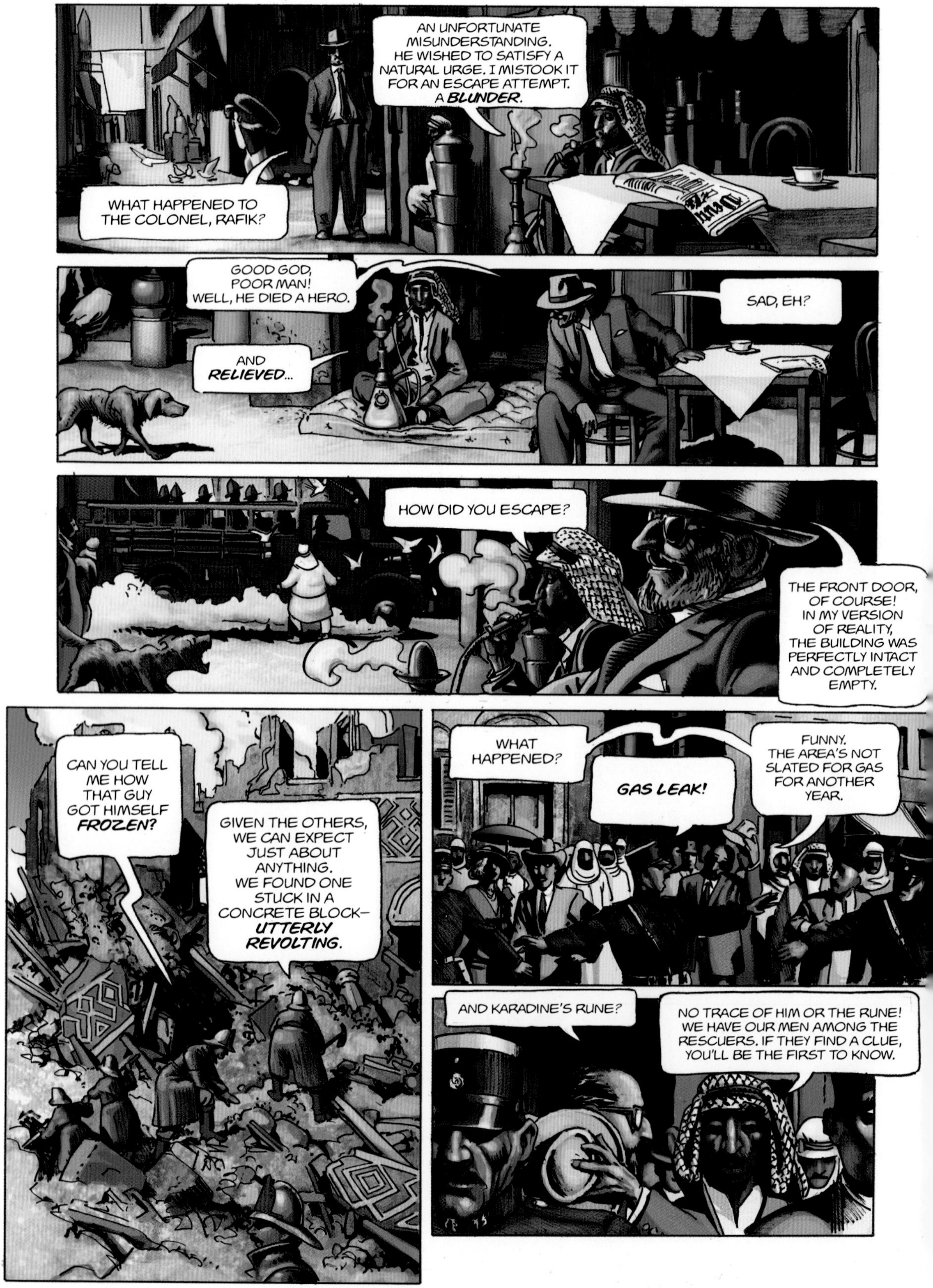
AN UNFORTUNATE MISUNDERSTANDING. HE WISHED TO SATISFY A NATURAL URGE. I MISTOOK IT FOR AN ESCAPE ATTEMPT. A BLUNDER.
WHAT HAPPENED TO THE COLONEL, RAFIK?
GOOD GOD, POOR MAN! WELL, HE DIED A HERO.
AND RELIEVED...
SAD, EH?
HOW DID YOU ESCAPE?
THE FRONT DOOR, OF COURSE! IN MY VERSION OF REALITY, THE BUILDING WAS PERFECTLY INTACT AND COMPLETELY EMPTY.
CAN YOU TELL ME HOW THAT GUY GOT HIMSELF FROZEN?
GIVEN THE OTHERS, WE CAN EXPECT JUST ABOUT ANYTHING. WE FOUND ONE STUCK IN A CONCRETE BLOCK— UTTERLY REVOLTING.
WHAT HAPPENED?
GAS LEAK!
FUNNY. THE AREA'S NOT SLATED FOR GAS FOR ANOTHER YEAR.
AND KARADINE'S RUNE?
NO TRACE OF HIM OR THE RUNE! WE HAVE OUR MEN AMONG THE RESCUERS. IF THEY FIND A CLUE, YOU'LL BE THE FIRST TO KNOW.

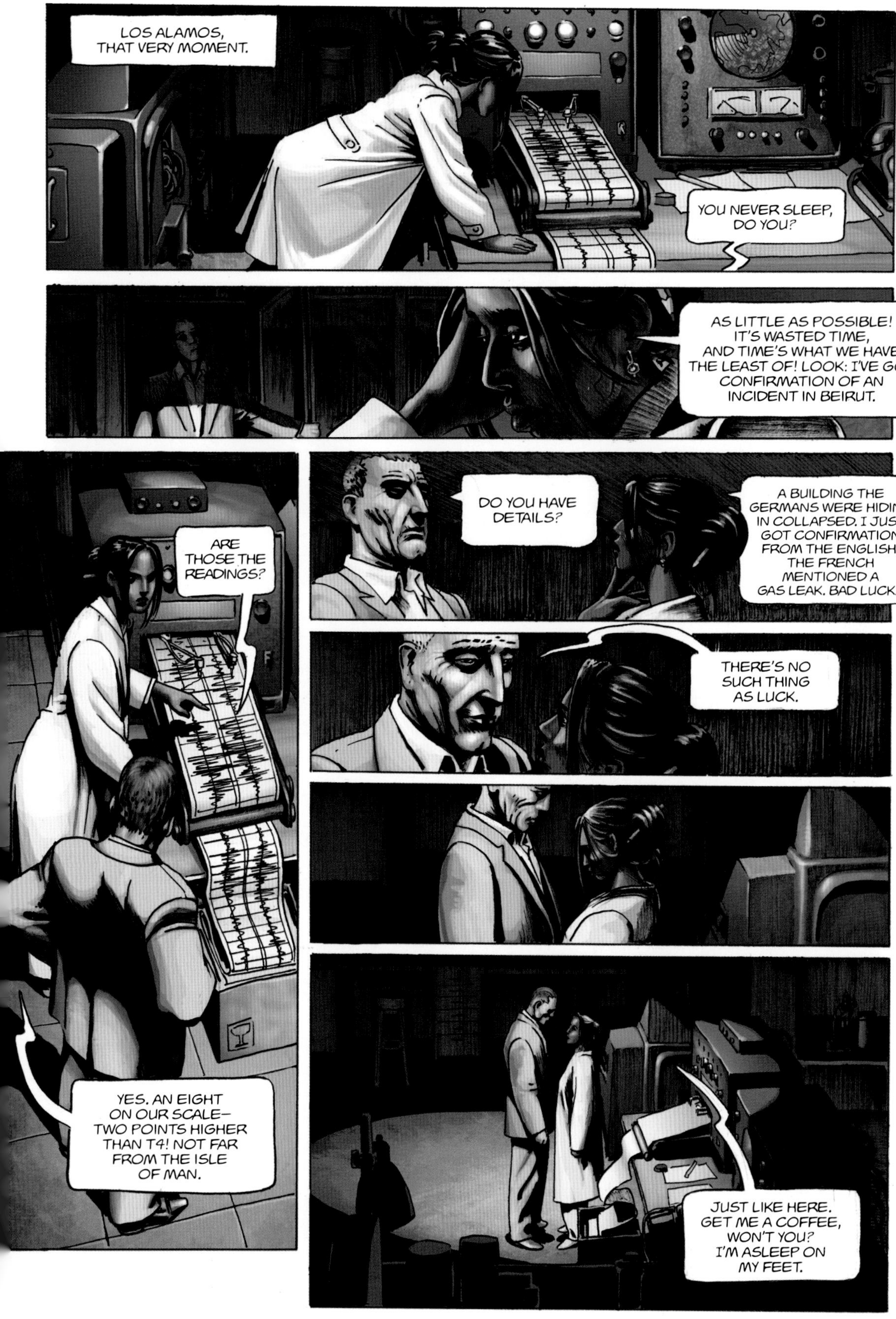
LOS ALAMOS, THAT VERY MOMENT.
YOU NEVER SLEEP, DO YOU?
AS LITTLE AS POSSIBLE! IT'S WASTED TIME, AND TIME'S WHAT WE HAVE THE LEAST OF! LOOK: I'VE GOT CONFIRMATION OF AN INCIDENT IN BEIRUT.
DO YOU HAVE DETAILS?
A BUILDING THE GERMANS WERE HIDING IN COLLAPSED. I JUST GOT CONFIRMATION FROM THE ENGLISH. THE FRENCH MENTIONED A GAS LEAK. BAD LUCK...
ARE THOSE THE READINGS?
YES. AN EIGHT ON OUR SCALE– TWO POINTS HIGHER THAN T4! NOT FAR FROM THE ISLE OF MAN.
THERE'S NO SUCH THING AS LUCK.
JUST LIKE HERE. GET ME A COFFEE, WON'T YOU? I'M ASLEEP ON MY FEET.

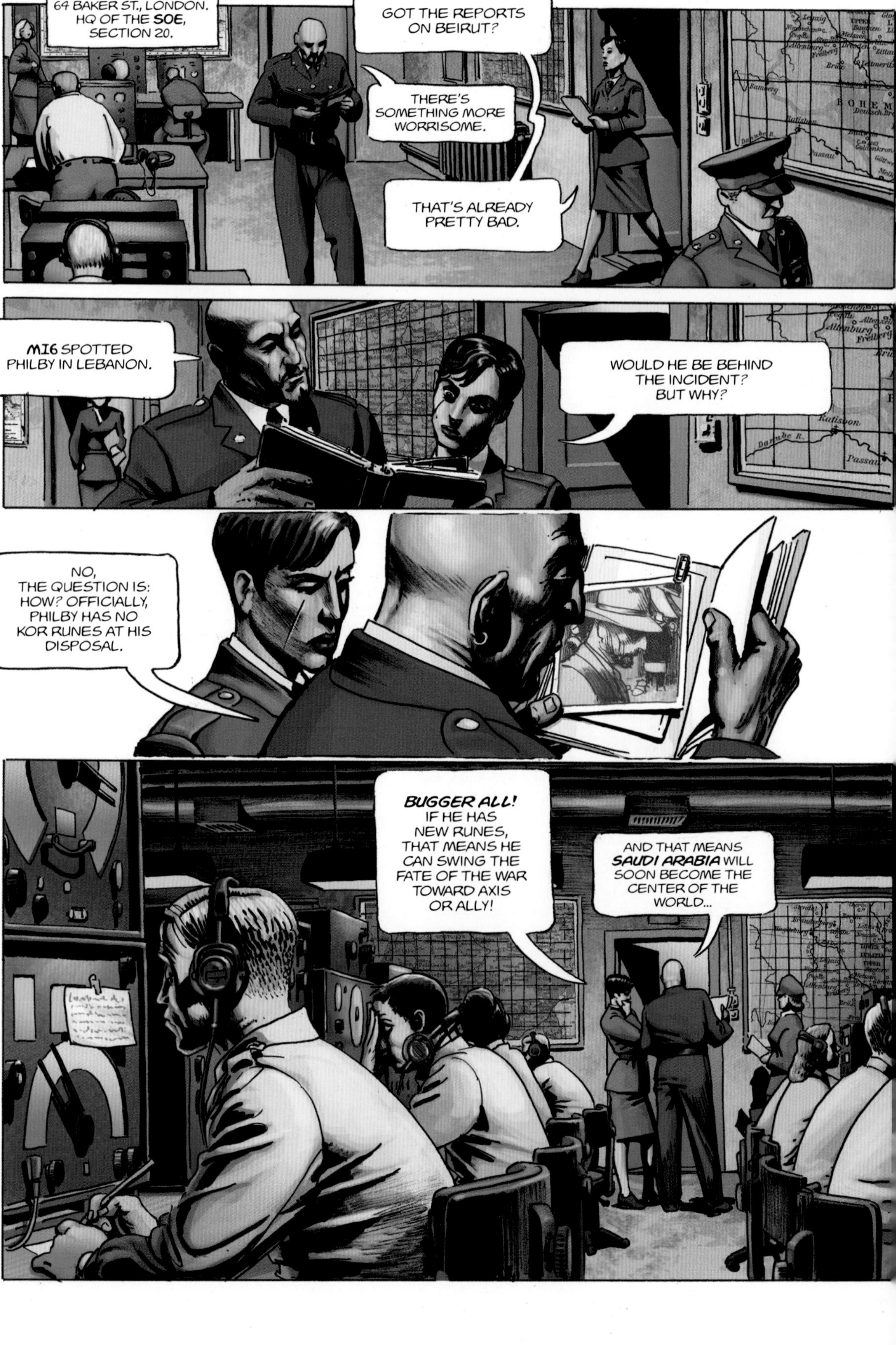
64 BAKER ST., LONDON. HQ OF THE **SOE**, SECTION 20.
GOT THE REPORTS ON BEIRUT?
THERE'S SOMETHING MORE WORRISOME.
THAT'S ALREADY PRETTY BAD.
MI6 SPOTTED PHILBY IN LEBANON.
WOULD HE BE BEHIND THE INCIDENT? BUT WHY?
NO, THE QUESTION IS: HOW? OFFICIALLY, PHILBY HAS NO KOR RUNES AT HIS DISPOSAL.
BUGGER ALL! IF HE HAS NEW RUNES, THAT MEANS HE CAN SWING THE FATE OF THE WAR TOWARD AXIS OR ALLY!
AND THAT MEANS ***SAUDI ARABIA*** WILL SOON BECOME THE CENTER OF THE WORLD...

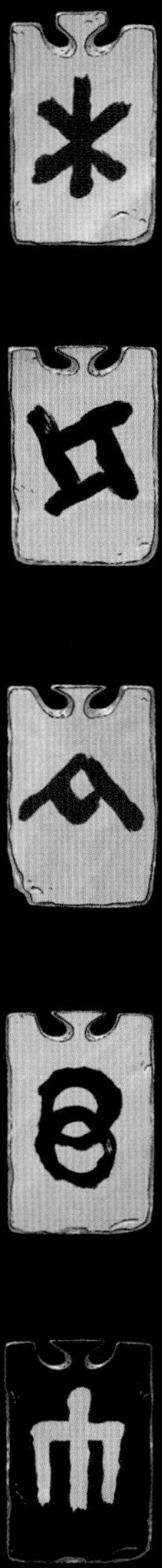

1943 A.D.

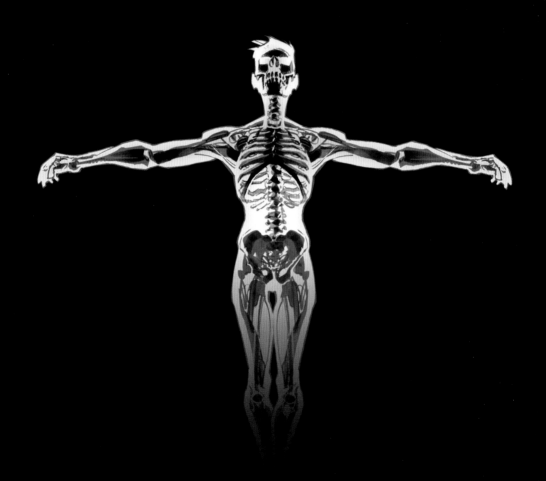

Book Thirteen

Twilight of the Gods | 1943 A.D.

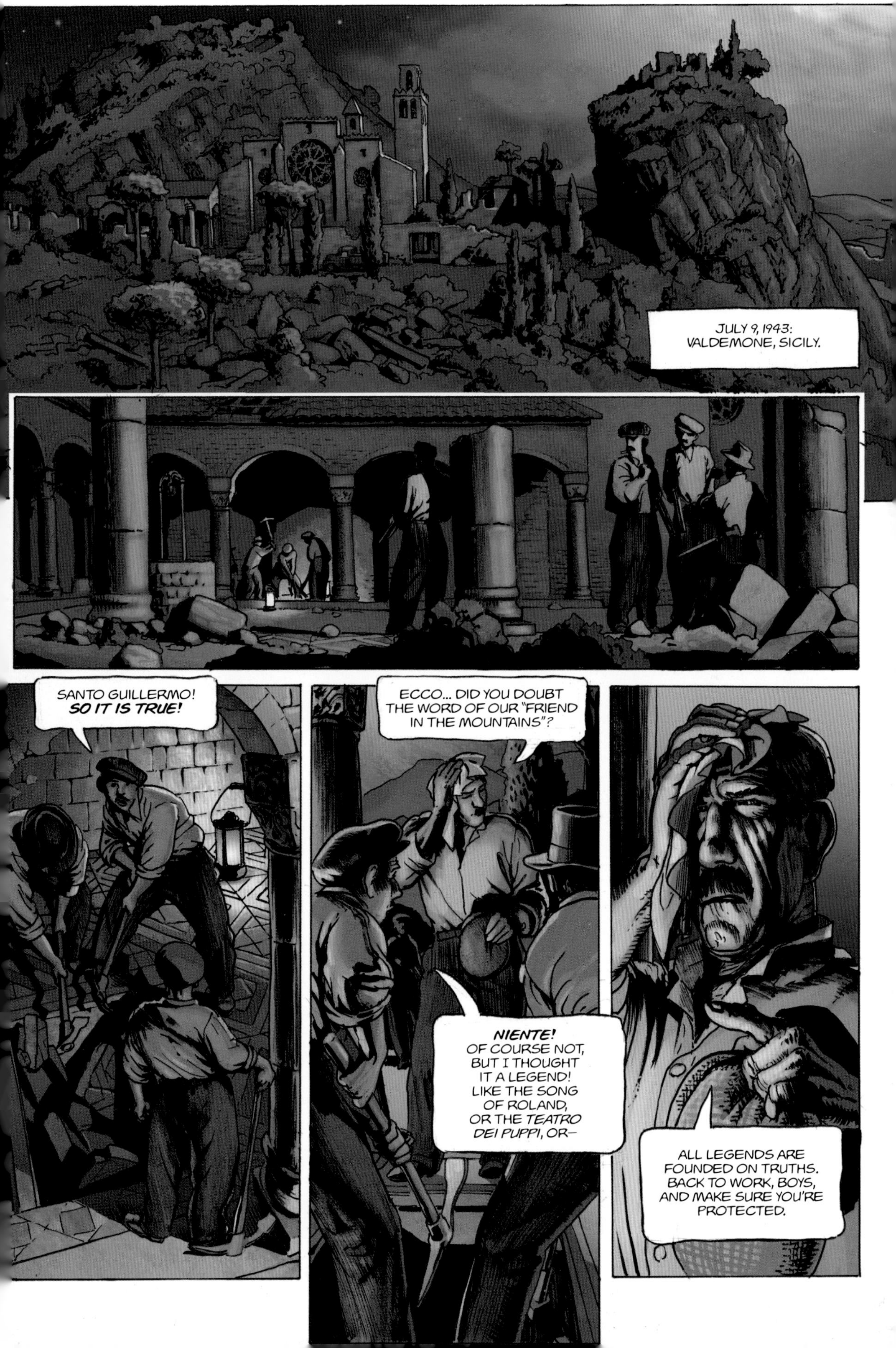
JULY 9, 1943:
VALDEMONE, SICILY.
SANTO GUILLERMO! **SO IT IS TRUE!**
ECCO... DID YOU DOUBT THE WORD OF OUR "FRIEND IN THE MOUNTAINS"?
NIENTE! OF COURSE NOT, BUT I THOUGHT IT A LEGEND! LIKE THE SONG OF ROLAND, OR THE *TEATRO DEI PUPPI*, OR—
ALL LEGENDS ARE FOUNDED ON TRUTHS. BACK TO WORK, BOYS, AND MAKE SURE YOU'RE PROTECTED.

VAI! IT'S TOO HOT TO WEAR THESE!
THIS IS SERIOUS, PIETRO! DO AS YOU'RE TOLD. REMEMBER WHAT THE BIBLE SAYS ABOUT THE ARK OF THE COVENANT? THE SOLDIER WHO TOUCHED IT WAS STRUCK DEAD ON THE SPOT!
VA BENE...
MADRE SANTI, FEEL THAT? MY HANDS ARE FREEZING AND I CAN'T BREATHE, LIKE THE AIR'S GONE ALL STICKY!
DUCE, I HOPE WE WON'T REGRET THIS.
THE OLD MAN'S CONSIGLIERE GAVE US AN ORDER, SO WE OBEY. THAT'S ALL THERE IS TO IT. NOT WORTH THINKING ABOUT.
HEH... EASY FOR YOU TO SAY, ARTICHOKE.
EASY, EASY NOW... GO GET THE TRUCK, TONIO.

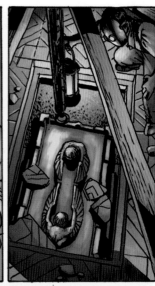

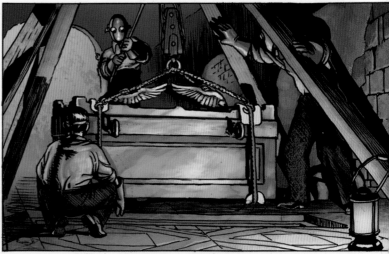

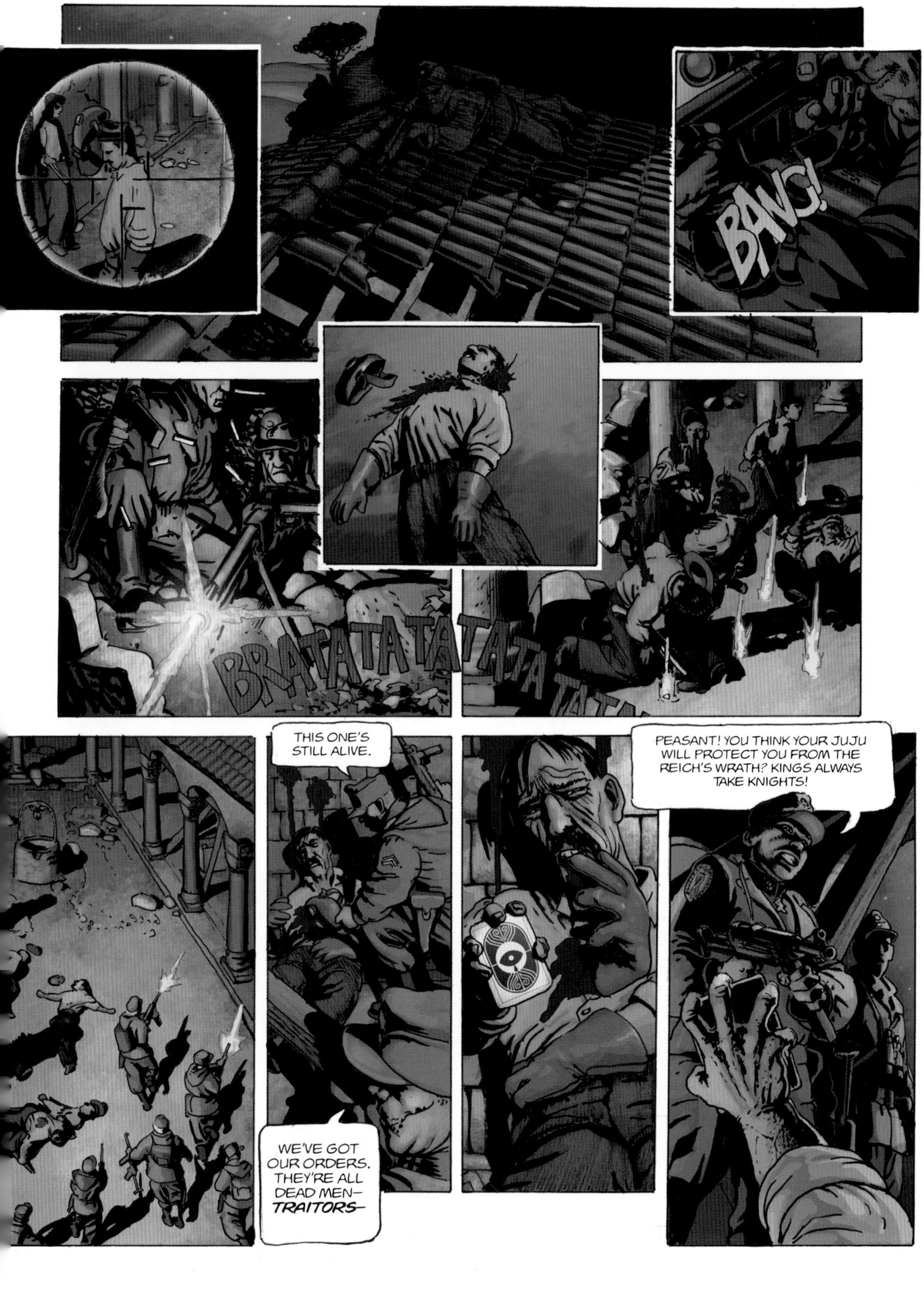
BANG!
BRATATATATATATATA
THIS ONE'S STILL ALIVE.
WE'VE GOT OUR ORDERS. THEY'RE ALL DEAD MEN— *TRAITORS*—
PEASANT! YOU THINK YOUR JUJU WILL PROTECT YOU FROM THE REICH'S WRATH? KINGS ALWAYS TAKE KNIGHTS!

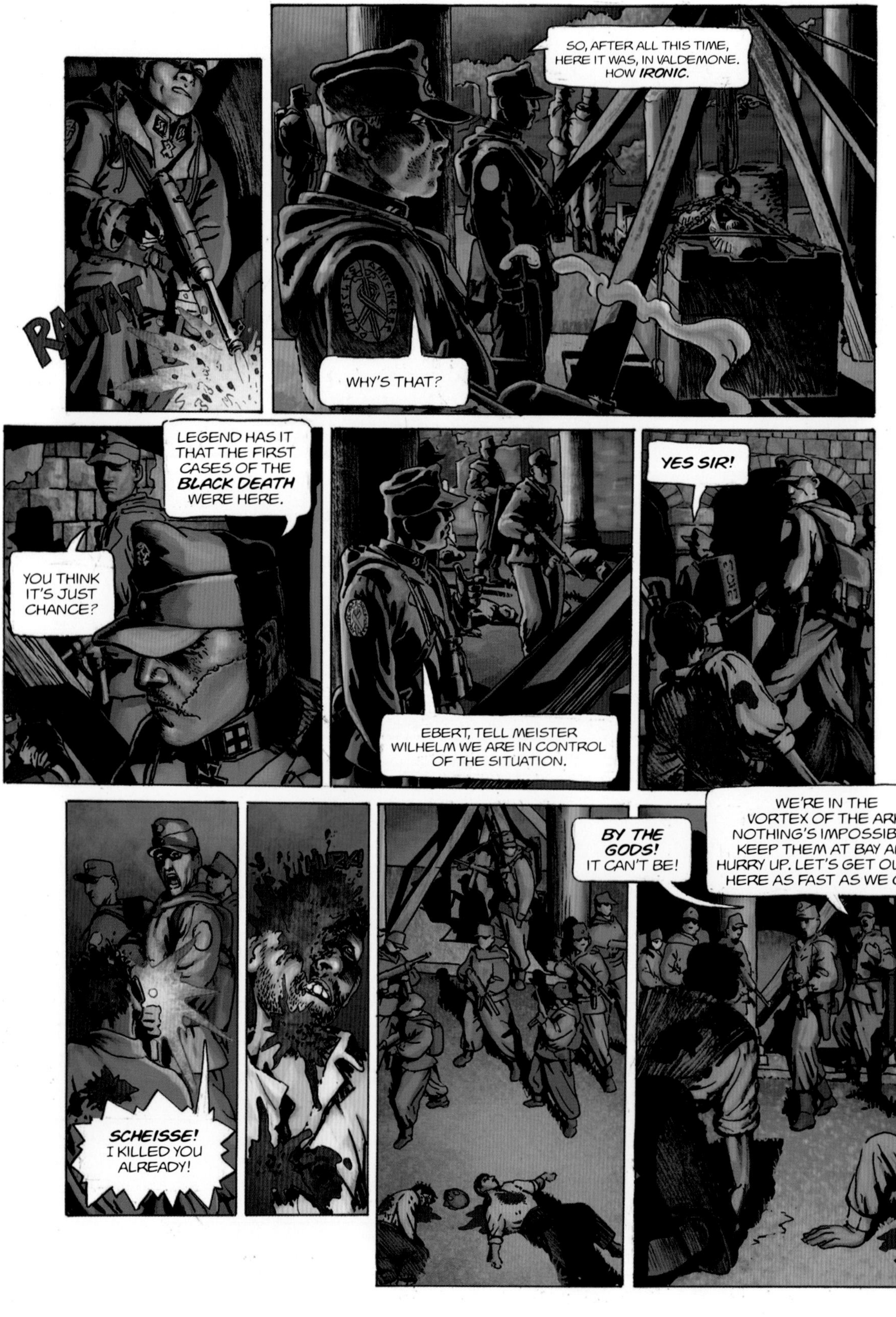
RATTAT
SO, AFTER ALL THIS TIME, HERE IT WAS, IN VALDEMONE. HOW IRONIC.
WHY'S THAT?
LEGEND HAS IT THAT THE FIRST CASES OF THE BLACK DEATH WERE HERE.
YOU THINK IT'S JUST CHANCE?
EBERT, TELL MEISTER WILHELM WE ARE IN CONTROL OF THE SITUATION.
YES SIR!
SCHEISSE! I KILLED YOU ALREADY!
BY THE GODS! IT CAN'T BE!
WE'RE IN THE VORTEX OF THE ARK, NOTHING'S IMPOSSIBLE! KEEP THEM AT BAY AND HURRY UP. LET'S GET OUT OF HERE AS FAST AS WE CAN!

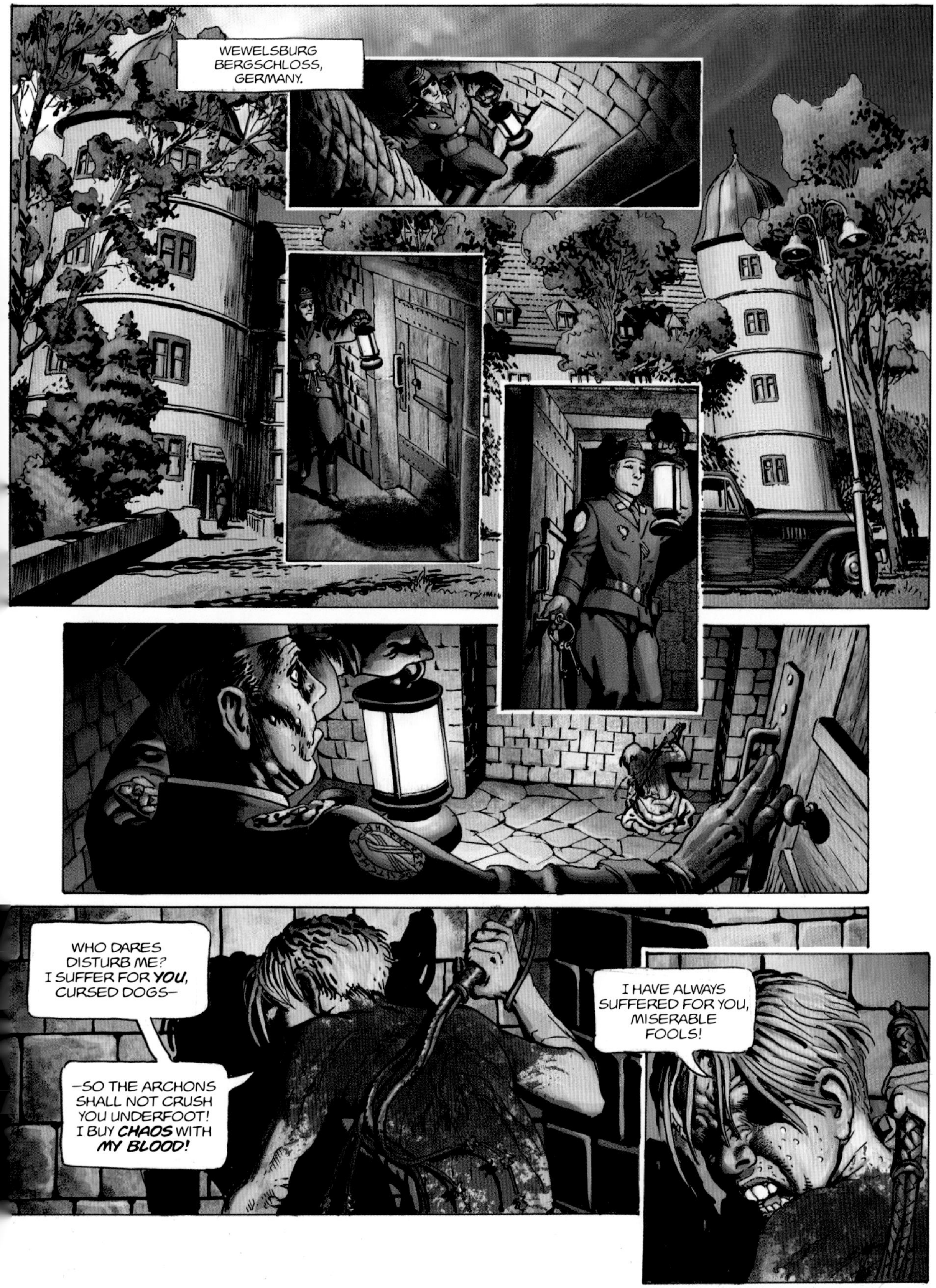
WEWELSBURG BERGSCHLOSS, GERMANY.
WHO DARES DISTURB ME? I SUFFER FOR YOU, CURSED DOGS–
–SO THE ARCHONS SHALL NOT CRUSH YOU UNDERFOOT! I BUY CHAOS WITH MY BLOOD!
I HAVE ALWAYS SUFFERED FOR YOU, MISERABLE FOOLS!

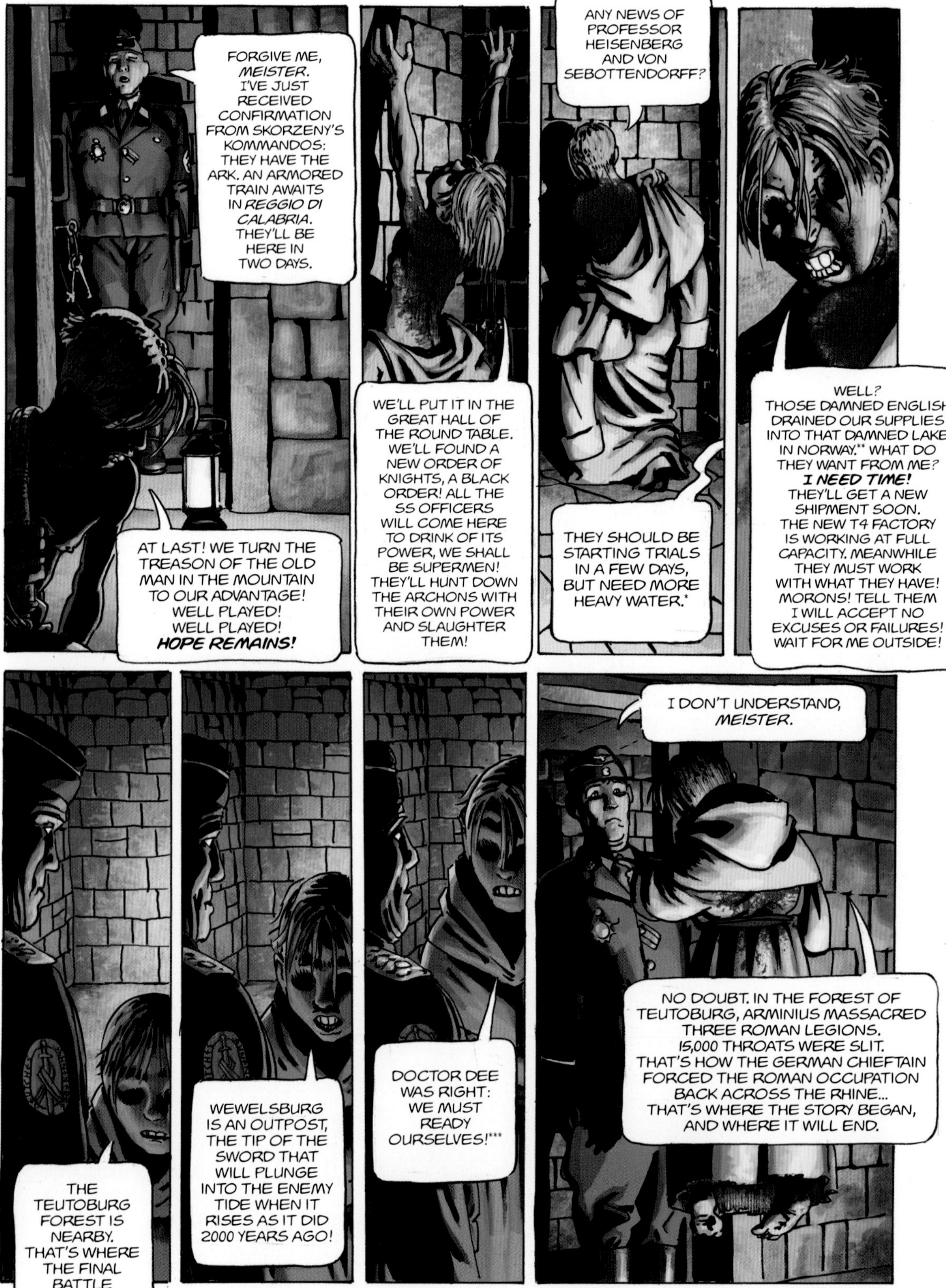
FORGIVE ME, *MEISTER*. I'VE JUST RECEIVED CONFIRMATION FROM SKORZENY'S KOMMANDOS: THEY HAVE THE ARK. AN ARMORED TRAIN AWAITS IN *REGGIO DI CALABRIA*. THEY'LL BE HERE IN TWO DAYS.
AT LAST! WE TURN THE TREASON OF THE OLD MAN IN THE MOUNTAIN TO OUR ADVANTAGE! WELL PLAYED! WELL PLAYED! ***HOPE REMAINS!***
WE'LL PUT IT IN THE GREAT HALL OF THE ROUND TABLE. WE'LL FOUND A NEW ORDER OF KNIGHTS, A BLACK ORDER! ALL THE SS OFFICERS WILL COME HERE TO DRINK OF ITS POWER, WE SHALL BE SUPERMEN! THEY'LL HUNT DOWN THE ARCHONS WITH THEIR OWN POWER AND SLAUGHTER THEM!
ANY NEWS OF PROFESSOR HEISENBERG AND VON SEBOTTENDORFF?
THEY SHOULD BE STARTING TRIALS IN A FEW DAYS, BUT NEED MORE HEAVY WATER.*
WELL? THOSE DAMNED ENGLISH DRAINED OUR SUPPLIES INTO THAT DAMNED LAKE IN NORWAY.** WHAT DO THEY WANT FROM ME? ***I NEED TIME!*** THEY'LL GET A NEW SHIPMENT SOON. THE NEW T4 FACTORY IS WORKING AT FULL CAPACITY. MEANWHILE THEY MUST WORK WITH WHAT THEY HAVE! MORONS! TELL THEM I WILL ACCEPT NO EXCUSES OR FAILURES! WAIT FOR ME OUTSIDE!
THE TEUTOBURG FOREST IS NEARBY. THAT'S WHERE THE FINAL BATTLE WILL BE.
WEWELSBURG IS AN OUTPOST, THE TIP OF THE SWORD THAT WILL PLUNGE INTO THE ENEMY TIDE WHEN IT RISES AS IT DID 2000 YEARS AGO!
DOCTOR DEE WAS RIGHT: WE MUST READY OURSELVES!***
I DON'T UNDERSTAND, *MEISTER*.
NO DOUBT. IN THE FOREST OF TEUTOBURG, ARMINIUS MASSACRED THREE ROMAN LEGIONS. 15,000 THROATS WERE SLIT. THAT'S HOW THE GERMAN CHIEFTAIN FORCED THE ROMAN OCCUPATION BACK ACROSS THE RHINE... THAT'S WHERE THE STORY BEGAN, AND WHERE IT WILL END.

* HEAVY WATER: DEUTERIUM OXIDE, CHEMICALLY IDENTICAL TO NORMAL WATER EXCEPT THAT ITS HYDROGEN ATOMS ARE HEAVY ISOTOPES. USED IN NUCLEAR RESEARCH TO SLOW CHAIN REACTIONS.

** ALLIED MILITARY OPERATIONS AIMED AT DESTROYING A HEAVY WATER-PRODUCING FACILITY IN NORWAY, DURING THE RACE FOR THE NUCLEAR BOMB: SEE THE MOVIE *HEROES OF TELEMARK*.

*** SEE *THE SECRET HISTORY*, BOOK 5: *1666*

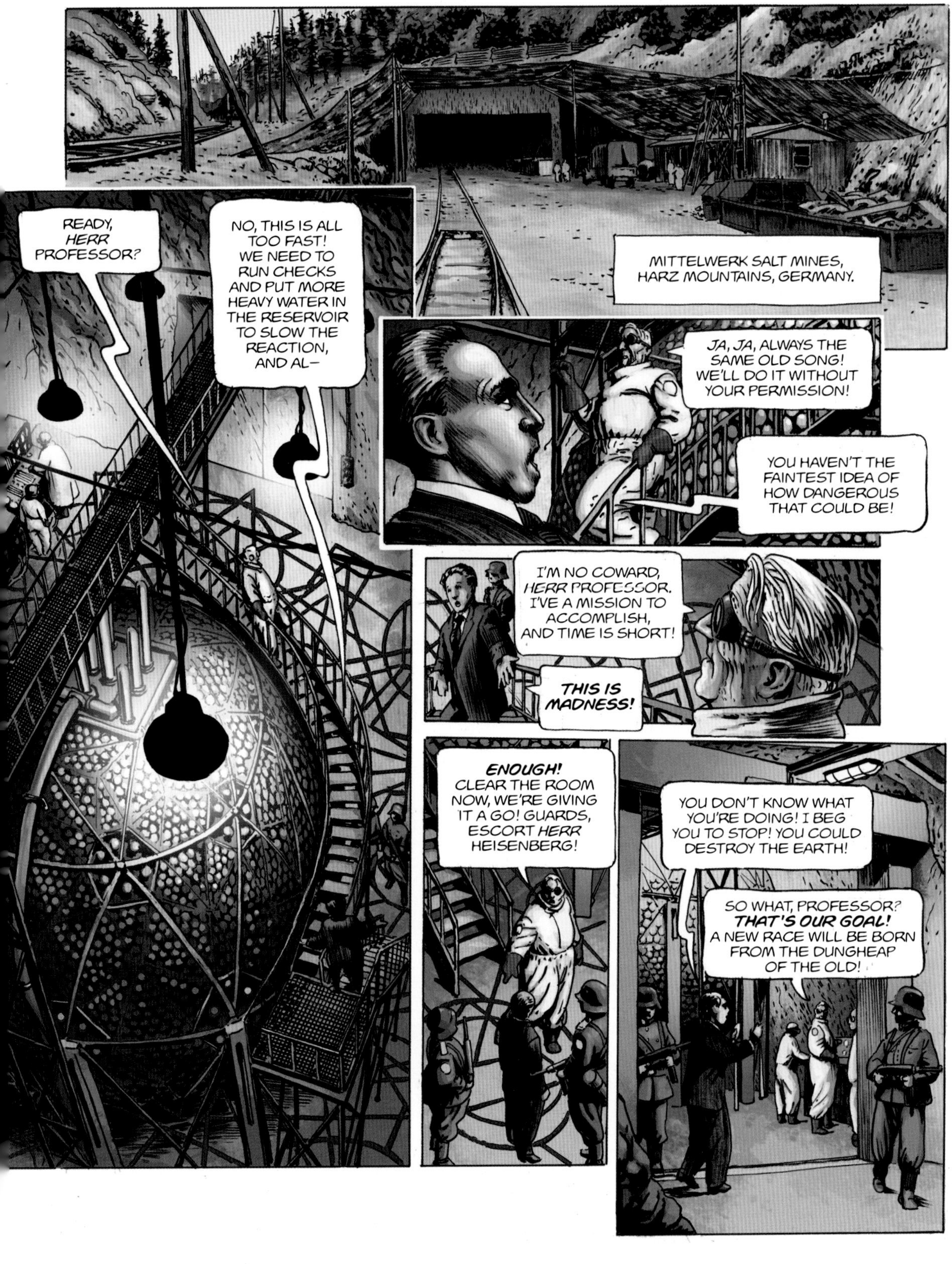
MITTELWERK SALT MINES, HARZ MOUNTAINS, GERMANY.
READY, *HERR* PROFESSOR?
NO, THIS IS ALL TOO FAST! WE NEED TO RUN CHECKS AND PUT MORE HEAVY WATER IN THE RESERVOIR TO SLOW THE REACTION, AND AL—
JA, JA, ALWAYS THE SAME OLD SONG! WE'LL DO IT WITHOUT YOUR PERMISSION!
YOU HAVEN'T THE FAINTEST IDEA OF HOW DANGEROUS THAT COULD BE!
I'M NO COWARD, *HERR* PROFESSOR. I'VE A MISSION TO ACCOMPLISH, AND TIME IS SHORT!
THIS IS MADNESS!
ENOUGH! CLEAR THE ROOM NOW, WE'RE GIVING IT A GO! GUARDS, ESCORT *HERR* HEISENBERG!
YOU DON'T KNOW WHAT YOU'RE DOING! I BEG YOU TO STOP! YOU COULD DESTROY THE EARTH!
SO WHAT, PROFESSOR? ***THAT'S OUR GOAL!*** A NEW RACE WILL BE BORN FROM THE DUNGHEAP OF THE OLD!

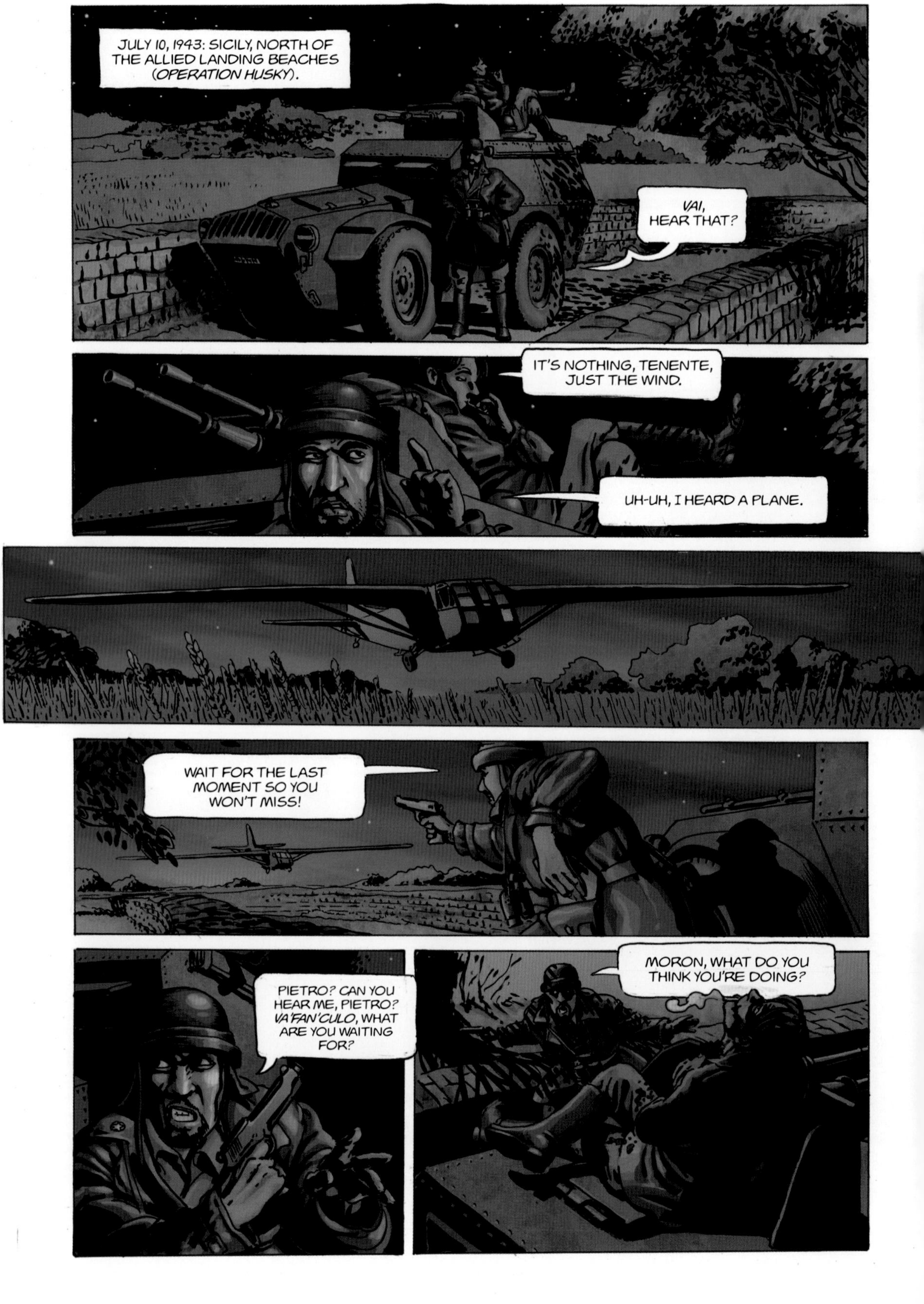
JULY 10, 1943: SICILY, NORTH OF THE ALLIED LANDING BEACHES (OPERATION HUSKY).
VAI, HEAR THAT?
IT'S NOTHING, TENENTE, JUST THE WIND.
UH-UH, I HEARD A PLANE.
WAIT FOR THE LAST MOMENT SO YOU WON'T MISS!
PIETRO? CAN YOU HEAR ME, PIETRO? VA'FAN'CULO, WHAT ARE YOU WAITING FOR?
MORON, WHAT DO YOU THINK YOU'RE DOING?

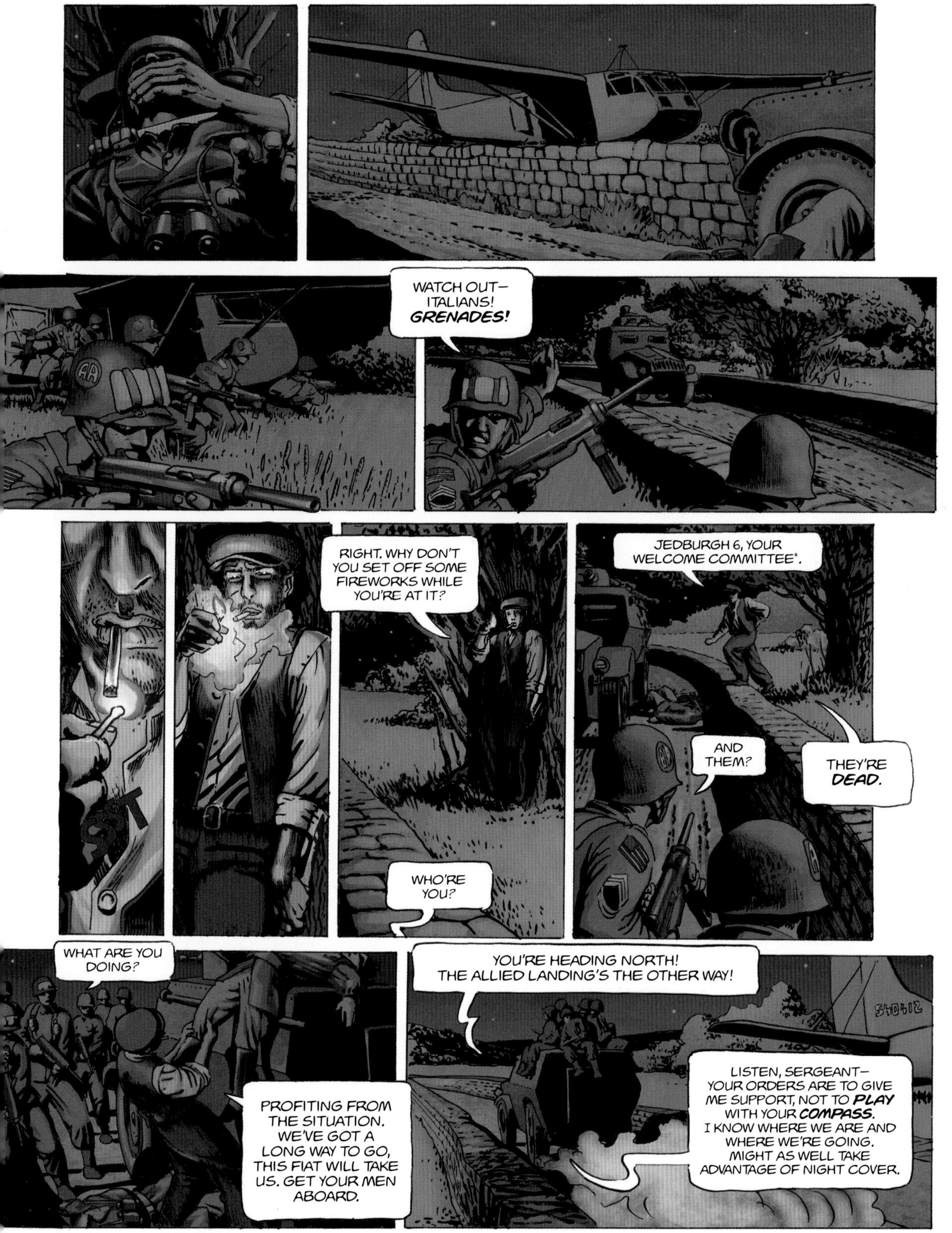
WATCH OUT—
ITALIANS!
GRENADES!
RIGHT. WHY DON'T YOU SET OFF SOME FIREWORKS WHILE YOU'RE AT IT?
WHO'RE YOU?
JEDBURGH 6, YOUR WELCOME COMMITTEE*.
AND THEM?
THEY'RE DEAD.
WHAT ARE YOU DOING?
PROFITING FROM THE SITUATION. WE'VE GOT A LONG WAY TO GO, THIS FIAT WILL TAKE US. GET YOUR MEN ABOARD.
YOU'RE HEADING NORTH! THE ALLIED LANDING'S THE OTHER WAY!
LISTEN, SERGEANT— YOUR ORDERS ARE TO GIVE ME SUPPORT, NOT TO PLAY WITH YOUR COMPASS. I KNOW WHERE WE ARE AND WHERE WE'RE GOING. MIGHT AS WELL TAKE ADVANTAGE OF NIGHT COVER.

* THE JEDBURGH TEAMS WERE OSS COMMANDOS (US SECRET SERVICE) WHO'D INFILTRATED OCCUPIED EUROPE.

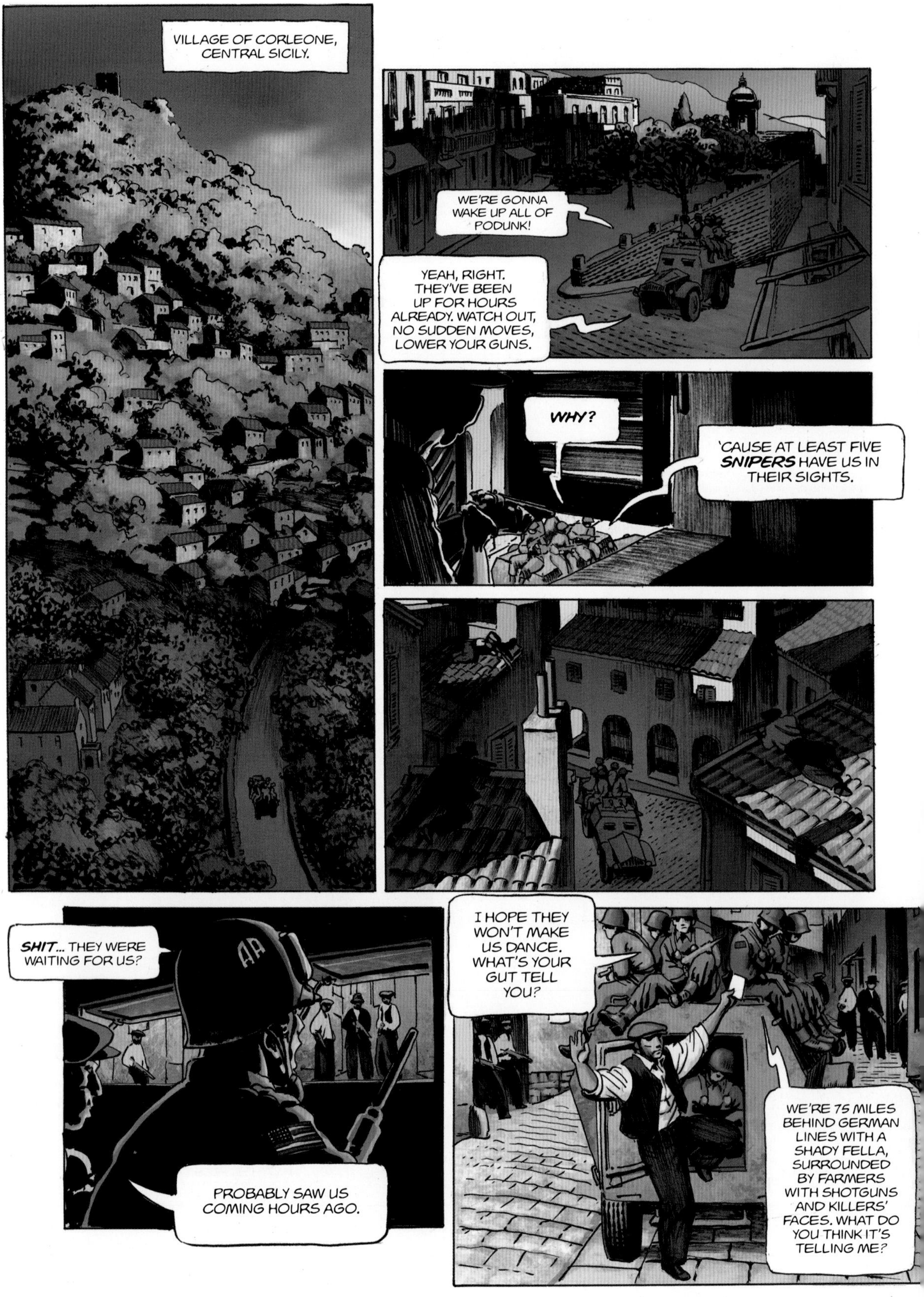
VILLAGE OF CORLEONE, CENTRAL SICILY.
WE'RE GONNA WAKE UP ALL OF PODUNK!
YEAH, RIGHT. THEY'VE BEEN UP FOR HOURS ALREADY. WATCH OUT, NO SUDDEN MOVES, LOWER YOUR GUNS.
WHY?
'CAUSE AT LEAST FIVE SNIPERS HAVE US IN THEIR SIGHTS.
SHIT... THEY WERE WAITING FOR US?
PROBABLY SAW US COMING HOURS AGO.
I HOPE THEY WON'T MAKE US DANCE. WHAT'S YOUR GUT TELL YOU?
WE'RE 75 MILES BEHIND GERMAN LINES WITH A SHADY FELLA, SURROUNDED BY FARMERS WITH SHOTGUNS AND KILLERS' FACES. WHAT DO YOU THINK IT'S TELLING ME?

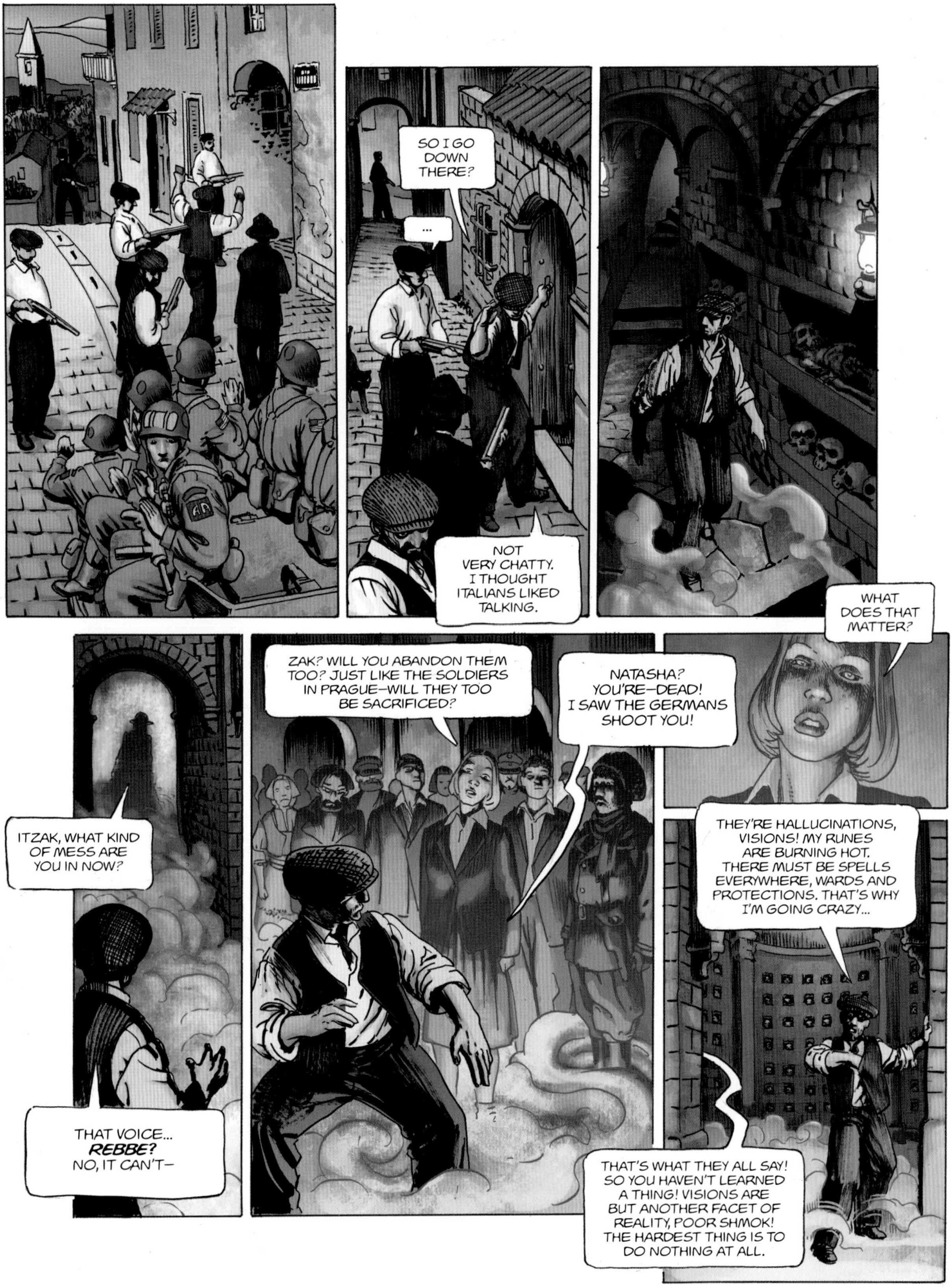
SO I GO DOWN THERE?
...
NOT VERY CHATTY. I THOUGHT ITALIANS LIKED TALKING.
ITZAK, WHAT KIND OF MESS ARE YOU IN NOW?
THAT VOICE... **REBBE?** NO, IT CAN'T—
ZAK? WILL YOU ABANDON THEM TOO? JUST LIKE THE SOLDIERS IN PRAGUE—WILL THEY TOO BE SACRIFICED?
NATASHA? YOU'RE—DEAD! I SAW THE GERMANS SHOOT YOU!
WHAT DOES THAT MATTER?
THEY'RE HALLUCINATIONS, VISIONS! MY RUNES ARE BURNING HOT. THERE MUST BE SPELLS EVERYWHERE, WARDS AND PROTECTIONS. THAT'S WHY I'M GOING CRAZY...
THAT'S WHAT THEY ALL SAY! SO YOU HAVEN'T LEARNED A THING! VISIONS ARE BUT ANOTHER FACET OF REALITY, POOR SHMOK! THE HARDEST THING IS TO DO NOTHING AT ALL.

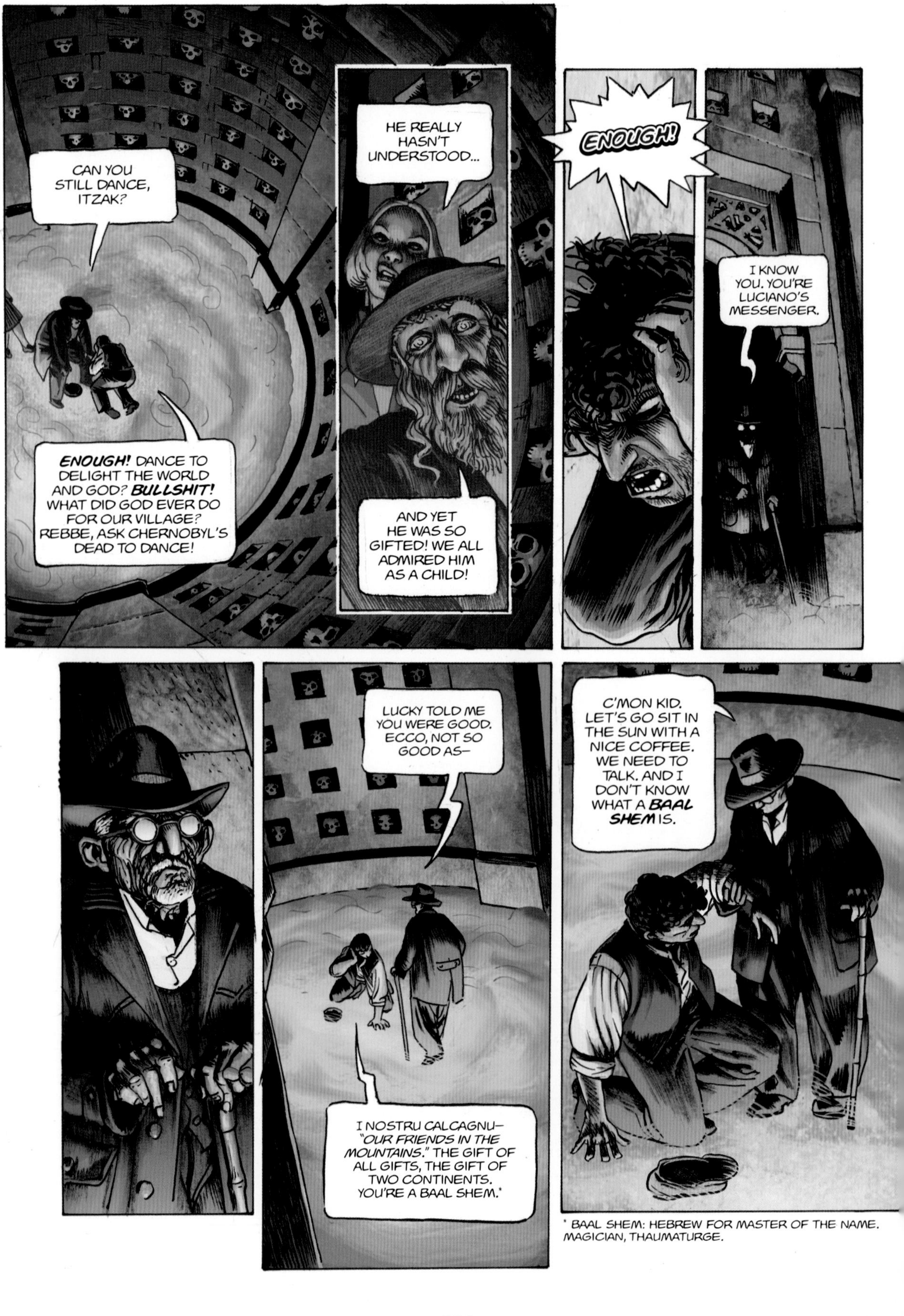
CAN YOU STILL DANCE, ITZAK?
ENOUGH! DANCE TO DELIGHT THE WORLD AND GOD? BULLSHIT! WHAT DID GOD EVER DO FOR OUR VILLAGE? REBBE, ASK CHERNOBYL'S DEAD TO DANCE!
HE REALLY HASN'T UNDERSTOOD...
AND YET HE WAS SO GIFTED! WE ALL ADMIRED HIM AS A CHILD!
ENOUGH!
I KNOW YOU. YOU'RE LUCIANO'S MESSENGER.
LUCKY TOLD ME YOU WERE GOOD. ECCO, NOT SO GOOD AS—
I NOSTRU CALCAGNU— "OUR FRIENDS IN THE MOUNTAINS." THE GIFT OF ALL GIFTS, THE GIFT OF TWO CONTINENTS. YOU'RE A BAAL SHEM.*
C'MON KID. LET'S GO SIT IN THE SUN WITH A NICE COFFEE. WE NEED TO TALK. AND I DON'T KNOW WHAT A BAAL SHEM IS.

* BAAL SHEM: HEBREW FOR MASTER OF THE NAME. MAGICIAN, THAUMATURGE.

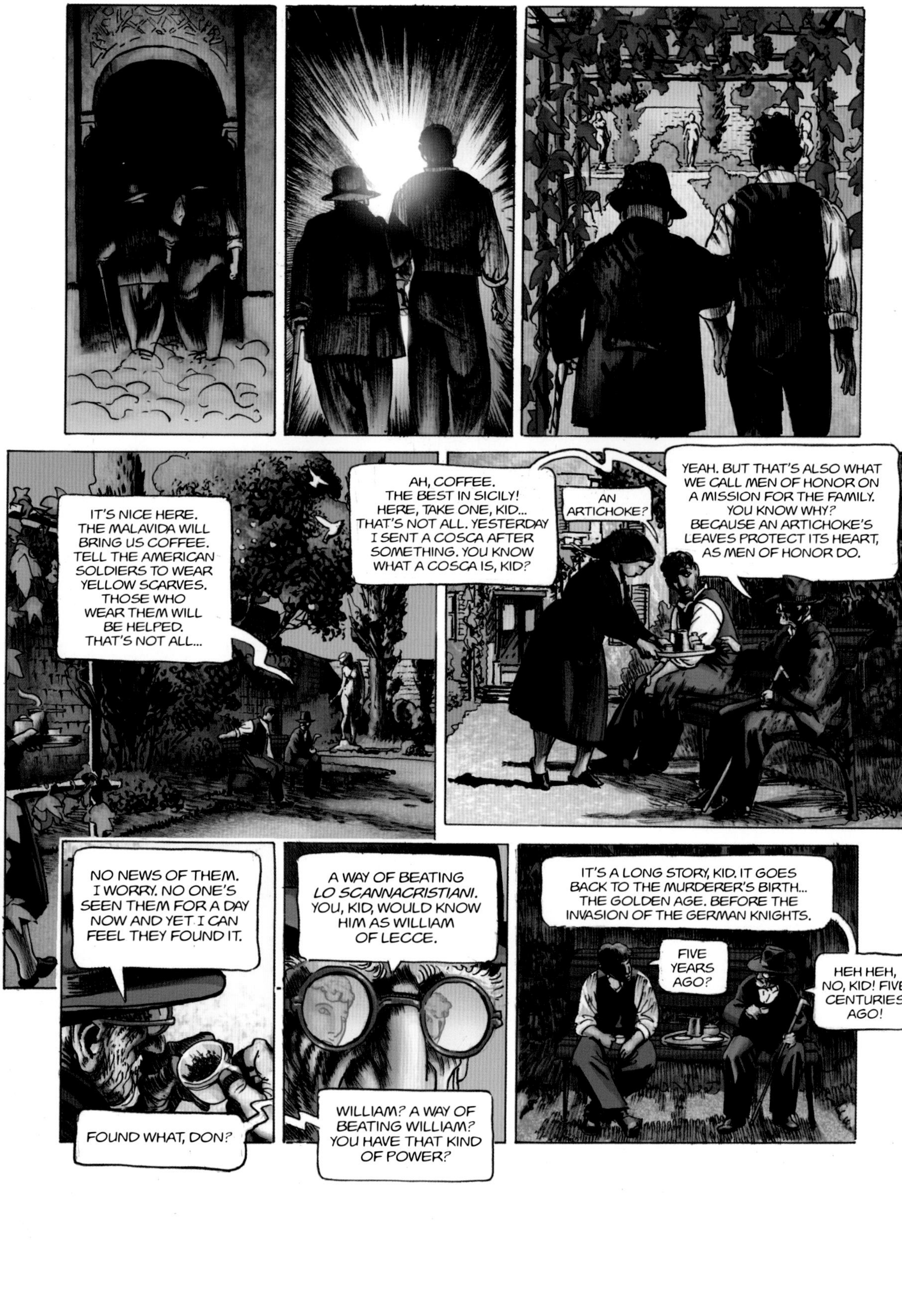
IT'S NICE HERE. THE MALAVIDA WILL BRING US COFFEE. TELL THE AMERICAN SOLDIERS TO WEAR YELLOW SCARVES. THOSE WHO WEAR THEM WILL BE HELPED. THAT'S NOT ALL...
AH, COFFEE. THE BEST IN SICILY! HERE, TAKE ONE, KID... THAT'S NOT ALL. YESTERDAY I SENT A COSCA AFTER SOMETHING. YOU KNOW WHAT A COSCA IS, KID?
AN ARTICHOKE?
YEAH. BUT THAT'S ALSO WHAT WE CALL MEN OF HONOR ON A MISSION FOR THE FAMILY. YOU KNOW WHY? BECAUSE AN ARTICHOKE'S LEAVES PROTECT ITS HEART, AS MEN OF HONOR DO.
NO NEWS OF THEM. I WORRY. NO ONE'S SEEN THEM FOR A DAY NOW AND YET I CAN FEEL THEY FOUND IT.
FOUND WHAT, DON?
A WAY OF BEATING *LO SCANNACRISTIANI*. YOU, KID, WOULD KNOW HIM AS WILLIAM OF LECCE.
WILLIAM? A WAY OF BEATING WILLIAM? YOU HAVE THAT KIND OF POWER?
IT'S A LONG STORY, KID. IT GOES BACK TO THE MURDERER'S BIRTH... THE GOLDEN AGE. BEFORE THE INVASION OF THE GERMAN KNIGHTS.
FIVE YEARS AGO?
HEH HEH, NO, KID! FIVE CENTURIES AGO!

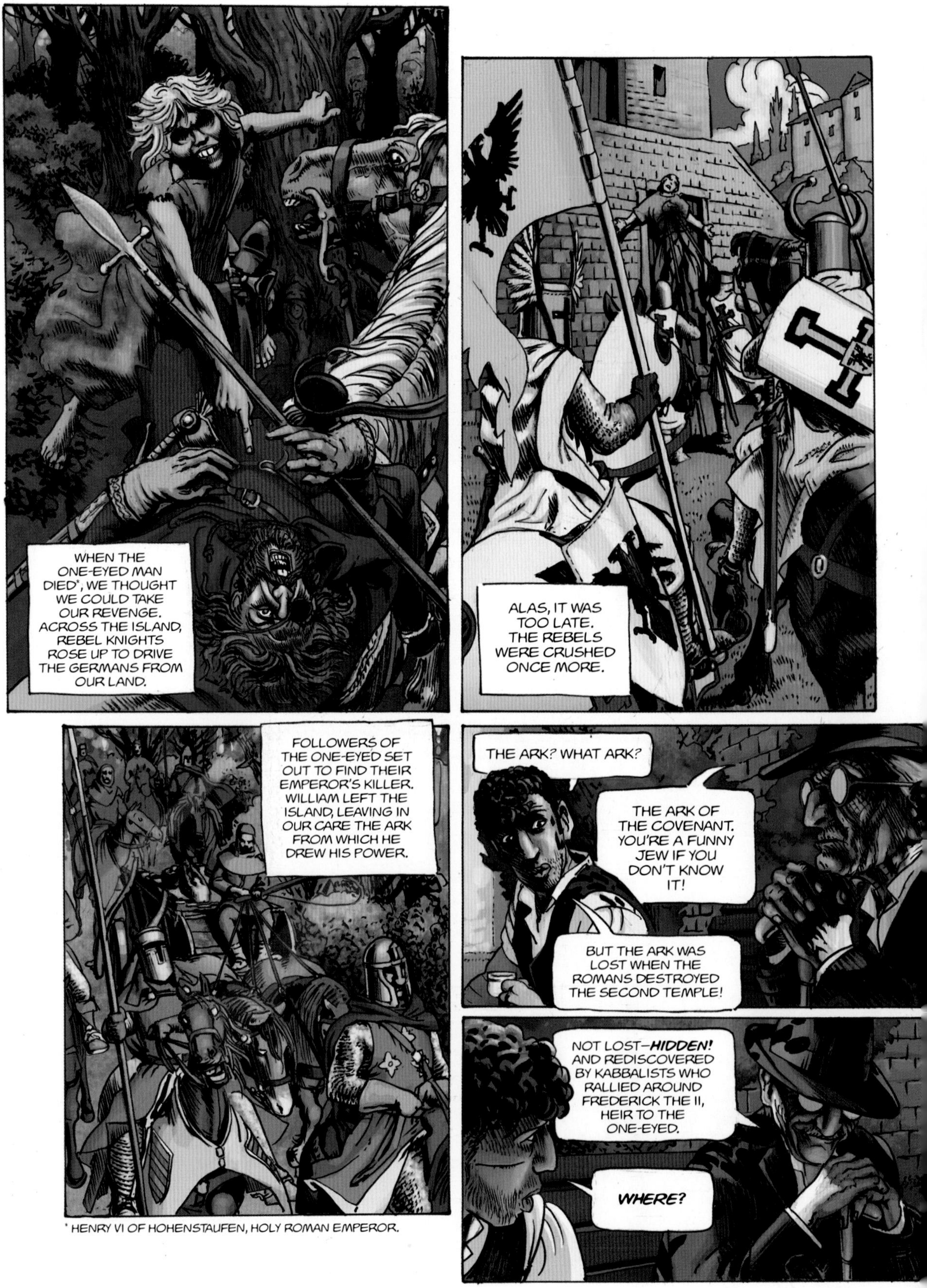
WHEN THE ONE-EYED MAN DIED*, WE THOUGHT WE COULD TAKE OUR REVENGE. ACROSS THE ISLAND, REBEL KNIGHTS ROSE UP TO DRIVE THE GERMANS FROM OUR LAND.
ALAS, IT WAS TOO LATE. THE REBELS WERE CRUSHED ONCE MORE.
FOLLOWERS OF THE ONE-EYED SET OUT TO FIND THEIR EMPEROR'S KILLER. WILLIAM LEFT THE ISLAND, LEAVING IN OUR CARE THE ARK FROM WHICH HE DREW HIS POWER.
THE ARK? WHAT ARK?
THE ARK OF THE COVENANT. YOU'RE A FUNNY JEW IF YOU DON'T KNOW IT!
BUT THE ARK WAS LOST WHEN THE ROMANS DESTROYED THE SECOND TEMPLE!
NOT LOST—**HIDDEN!** AND REDISCOVERED BY KABBALISTS WHO RALLIED AROUND FREDERICK THE II, HEIR TO THE ONE-EYED.
WHERE?

* HENRY VI OF HOHENSTAUFEN, HOLY ROMAN EMPEROR.

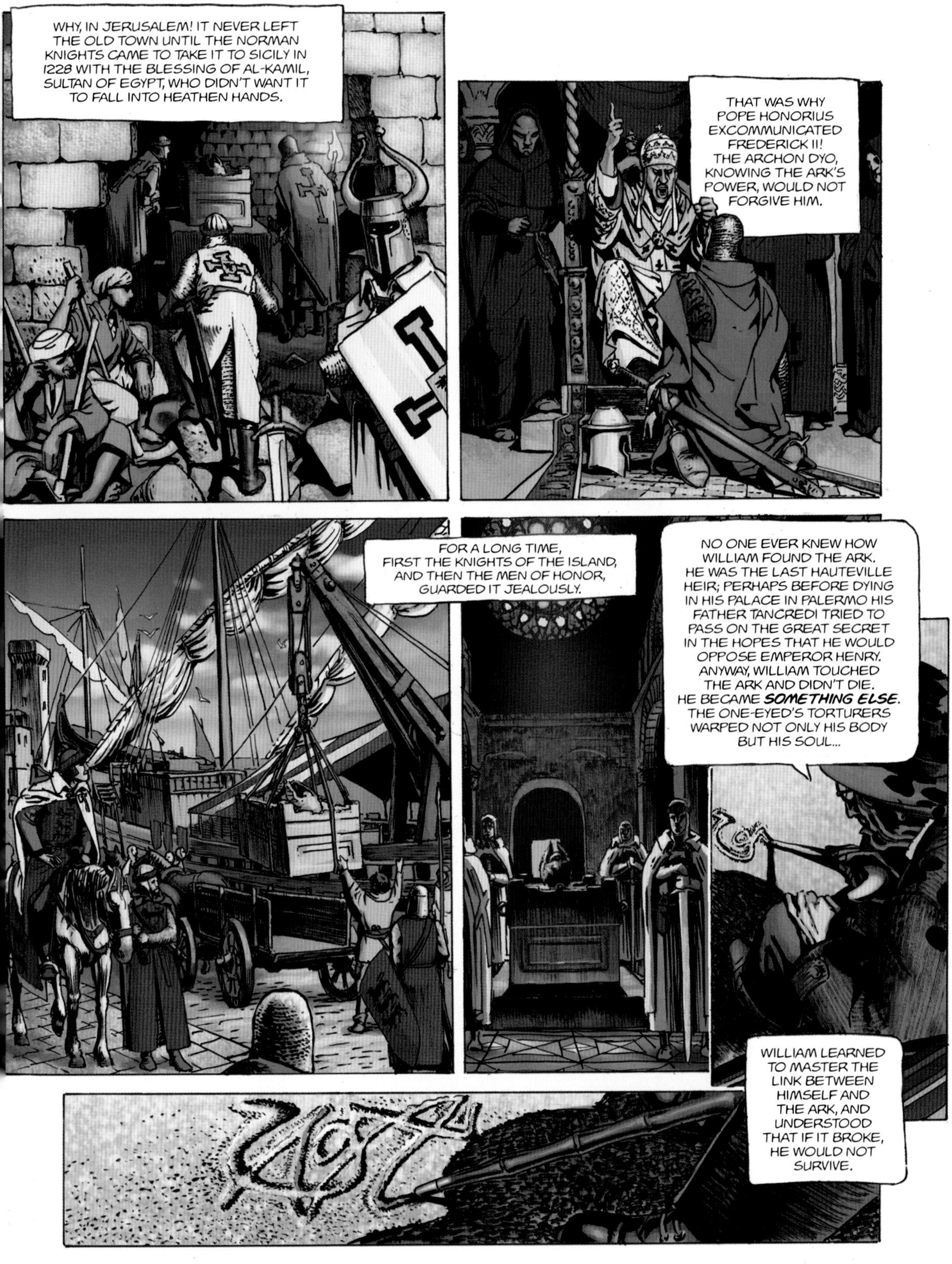
WHY, IN JERUSALEM! IT NEVER LEFT THE OLD TOWN UNTIL THE NORMAN KNIGHTS CAME TO TAKE IT TO SICILY IN 1228 WITH THE BLESSING OF AL-KAMIL, SULTAN OF EGYPT, WHO DIDN'T WANT IT TO FALL INTO HEATHEN HANDS.
THAT WAS WHY POPE HONORIUS EXCOMMUNICATED FREDERICK II! THE ARCHON DYO, KNOWING THE ARK'S POWER, WOULD NOT FORGIVE HIM.
FOR A LONG TIME, FIRST THE KNIGHTS OF THE ISLAND, AND THEN THE MEN OF HONOR, GUARDED IT JEALOUSLY.
NO ONE EVER KNEW HOW WILLIAM FOUND THE ARK. HE WAS THE LAST HAUTEVILLE HEIR; PERHAPS BEFORE DYING IN HIS PALACE IN PALERMO HIS FATHER TANCREDI TRIED TO PASS ON THE GREAT SECRET IN THE HOPES THAT HE WOULD OPPOSE EMPEROR HENRY. ANYWAY, WILLIAM TOUCHED THE ARK AND DIDN'T DIE. HE BECAME **SOMETHING ELSE**. THE ONE-EYED'S TORTURERS WARPED NOT ONLY HIS BODY BUT HIS SOUL...
WILLIAM LEARNED TO MASTER THE LINK BETWEEN HIMSELF AND THE ARK, AND UNDERSTOOD THAT IF IT BROKE, HE WOULD NOT SURVIVE.

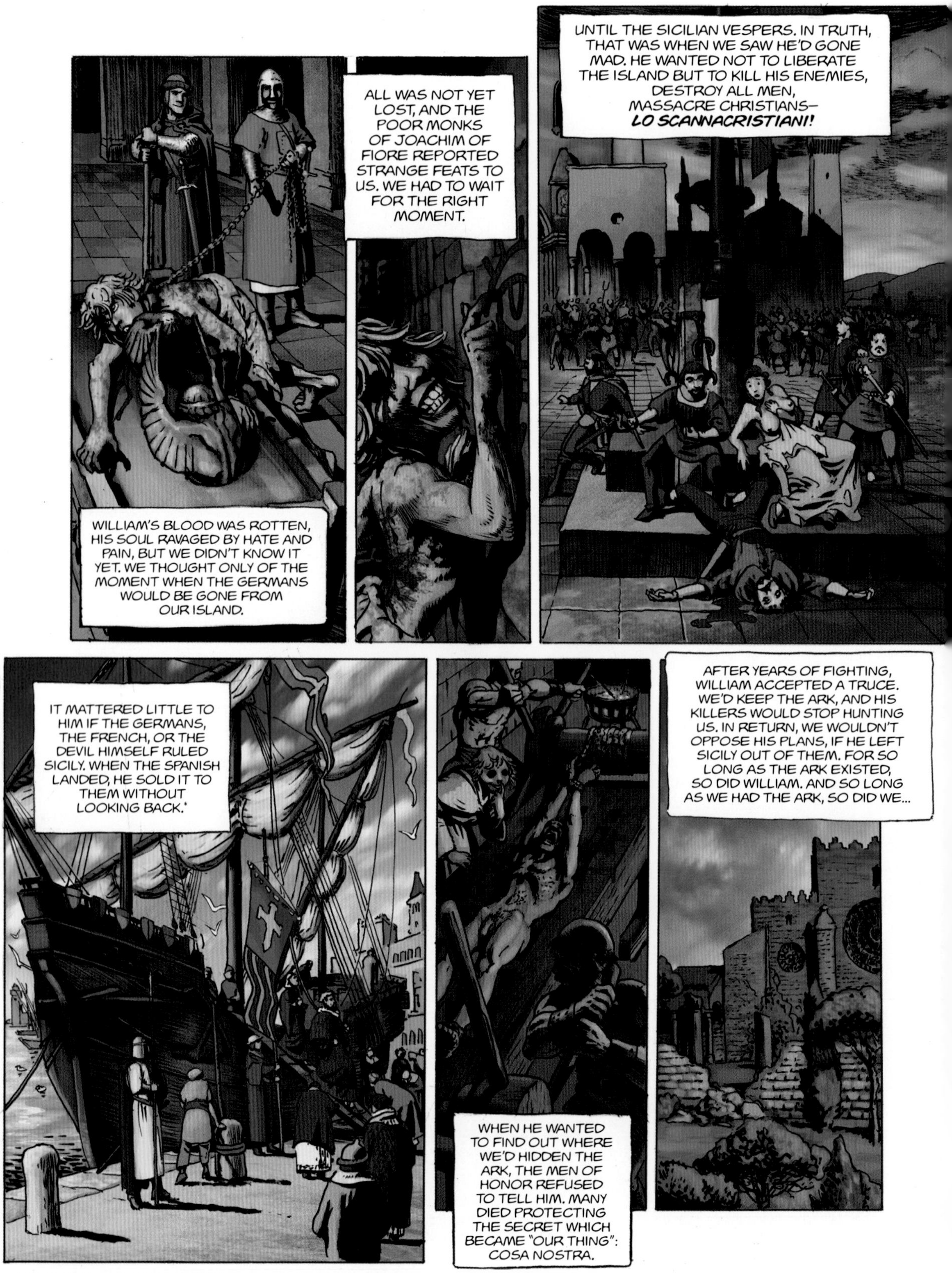
WILLIAM'S BLOOD WAS ROTTEN, HIS SOUL RAVAGED BY HATE AND PAIN, BUT WE DIDN'T KNOW IT YET. WE THOUGHT ONLY OF THE MOMENT WHEN THE GERMANS WOULD BE GONE FROM OUR ISLAND.
ALL WAS NOT YET LOST, AND THE POOR MONKS OF JOACHIM OF FIORE REPORTED STRANGE FEATS TO US. WE HAD TO WAIT FOR THE RIGHT MOMENT.
UNTIL THE SICILIAN VESPERS. IN TRUTH, THAT WAS WHEN WE SAW HE'D GONE MAD. HE WANTED NOT TO LIBERATE THE ISLAND BUT TO KILL HIS ENEMIES, DESTROY ALL MEN, MASSACRE CHRISTIANS— ***LO SCANNACRISTIANI!***
IT MATTERED LITTLE TO HIM IF THE GERMANS, THE FRENCH, OR THE DEVIL HIMSELF RULED SICILY. WHEN THE SPANISH LANDED, HE SOLD IT TO THEM WITHOUT LOOKING BACK.*
WHEN HE WANTED TO FIND OUT WHERE WE'D HIDDEN THE ARK, THE MEN OF HONOR REFUSED TO TELL HIM. MANY DIED PROTECTING THE SECRET WHICH BECAME "OUR THING": COSA NOSTRA.
AFTER YEARS OF FIGHTING, WILLIAM ACCEPTED A TRUCE. WE'D KEEP THE ARK, AND HIS KILLERS WOULD STOP HUNTING US. IN RETURN, WE WOULDN'T OPPOSE HIS PLANS, IF HE LEFT SICILY OUT OF THEM. FOR SO LONG AS THE ARK EXISTED, SO DID WILLIAM. AND SO LONG AS WE HAD THE ARK, SO DID WE...

* SEE *THE SECRET HISTORY*, BOOK 3: *THE GRAIL OF MONTSEGUR*.

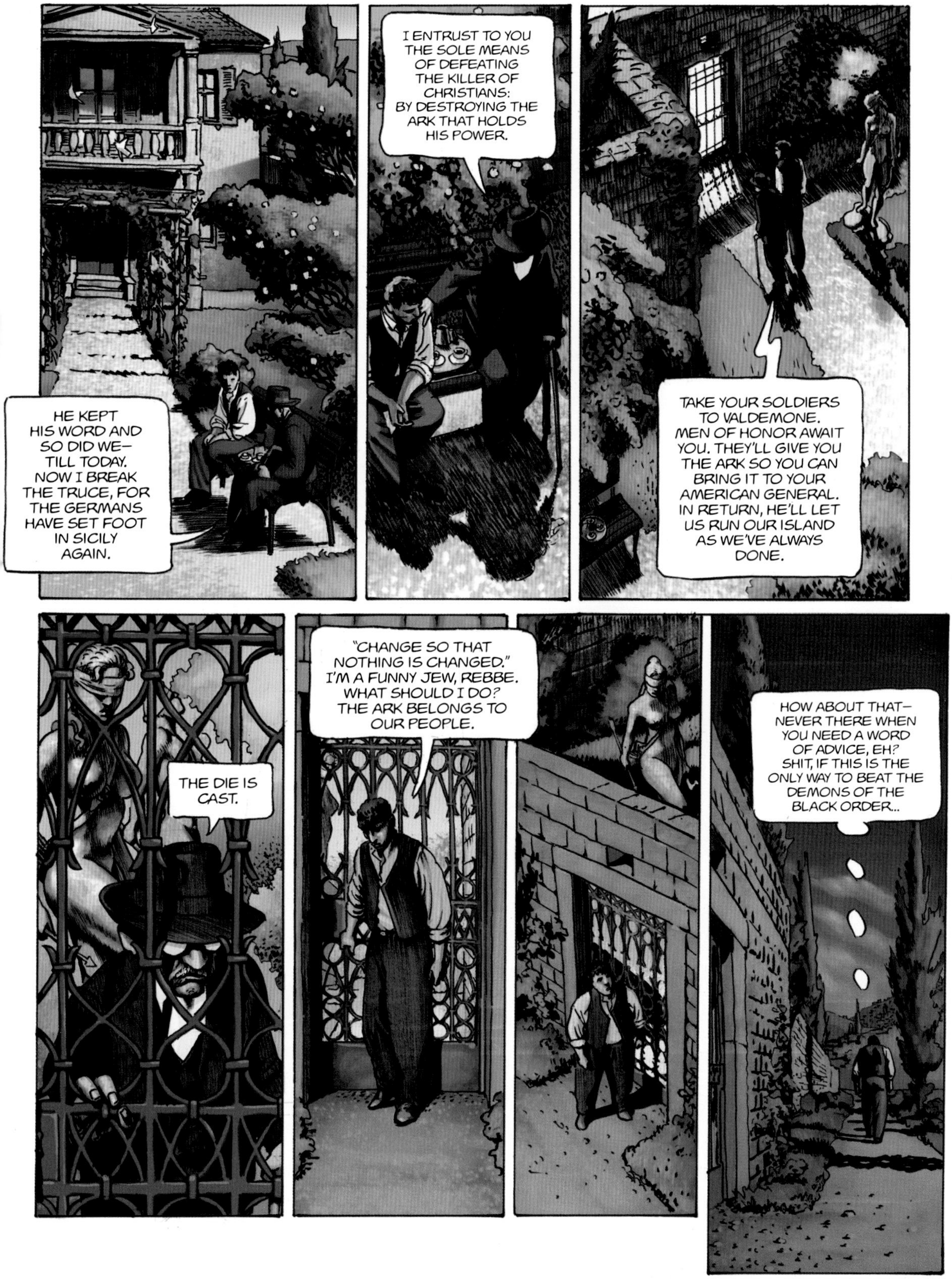
HE KEPT HIS WORD AND SO DID WE— TILL TODAY. NOW I BREAK THE TRUCE, FOR THE GERMANS HAVE SET FOOT IN SICILY AGAIN.
I ENTRUST TO YOU THE SOLE MEANS OF DEFEATING THE KILLER OF CHRISTIANS: BY DESTROYING THE ARK THAT HOLDS HIS POWER.
TAKE YOUR SOLDIERS TO VALDEMONE. MEN OF HONOR AWAIT YOU. THEY'LL GIVE YOU THE ARK SO YOU CAN BRING IT TO YOUR AMERICAN GENERAL. IN RETURN, HE'LL LET US RUN OUR ISLAND AS WE'VE ALWAYS DONE.
THE DIE IS CAST.
"CHANGE SO THAT NOTHING IS CHANGED." I'M A FUNNY JEW, REBBE. WHAT SHOULD I DO? THE ARK BELONGS TO OUR PEOPLE.
HOW ABOUT THAT— NEVER THERE WHEN YOU NEED A WORD OF ADVICE, EH? SHIT, IF THIS IS THE ONLY WAY TO BEAT THE DEMONS OF THE BLACK ORDER...

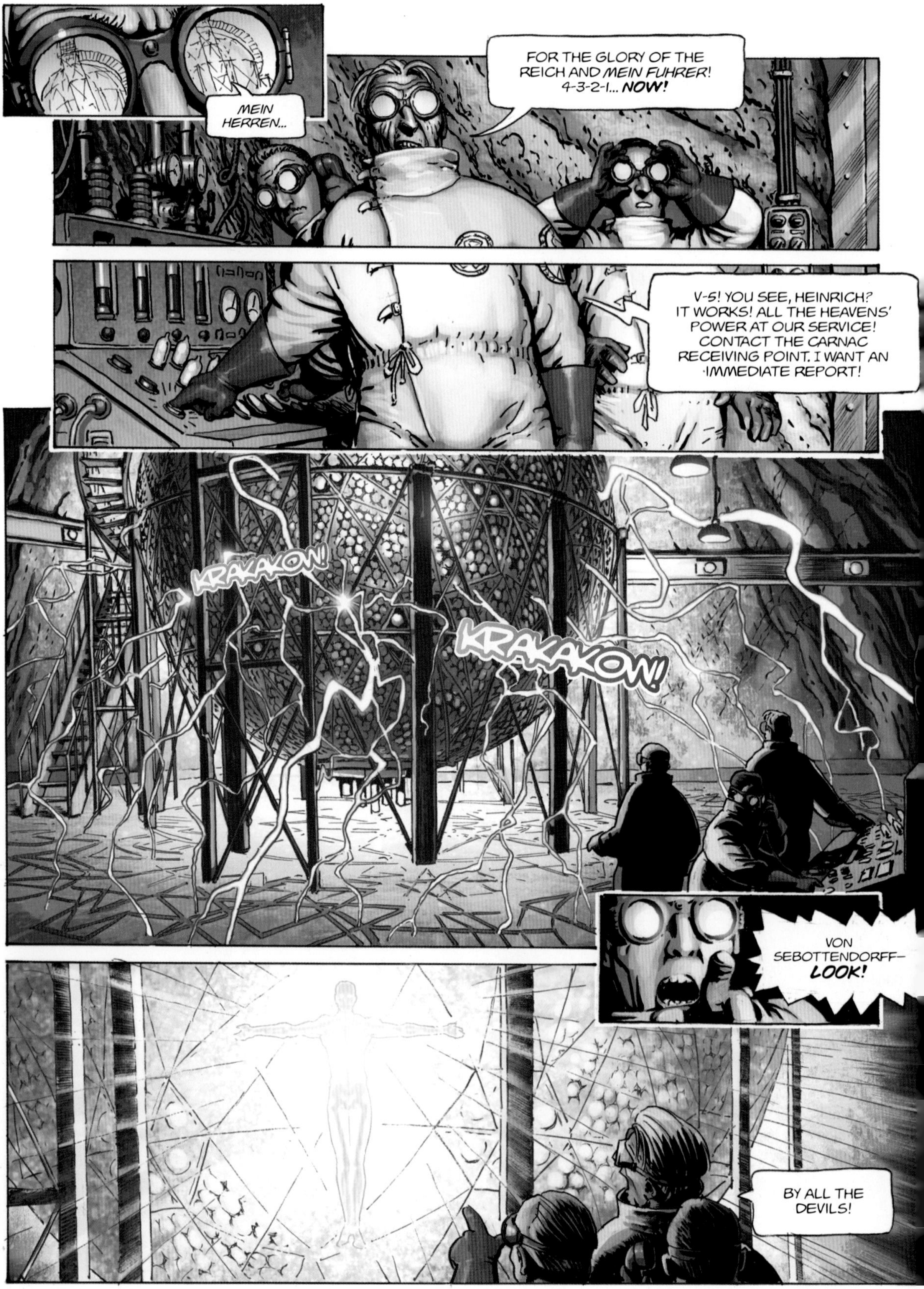
MEIN HERREN...
FOR THE GLORY OF THE REICH AND MEIN FUHRER! 4-3-2-1... NOW!
V-5! YOU SEE, HEINRICH? IT WORKS! ALL THE HEAVENS' POWER AT OUR SERVICE! CONTACT THE CARNAC RECEIVING POINT. I WANT AN IMMEDIATE REPORT!
KRAKAKOW!
KRAKAKOW!
VON SEBOTTENDORFF— LOOK!
BY ALL THE DEVILS!

AT THAT MOMENT:
THE CARNAC
RECEIVING POINT,
BRITTANY.

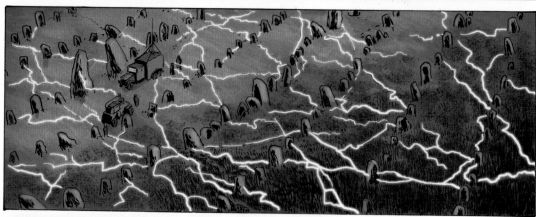

HERNTZ,
CALL
SEBOTTENDORFF.
*THE VORTEX IS
OPERATIONAL!*

KRAKAKON!

WHAT ARE THE
KRAUTS DOING
OVER THERE,
FATHER BEDU?

NO IDEA.
THEY WON'T LET
US NEAR THE
STONES.

HAVE YOU
SEEN THE RAIN!
OUT OF SEASON!
A STORM
AT THIS HOUR,
WHAT BAD LUCK!
YOU STAYING,
FATHER BEDU?

JUST A
BIT LONGER.
GO TELL RENE
I'LL STOP BY
TONIGHT.

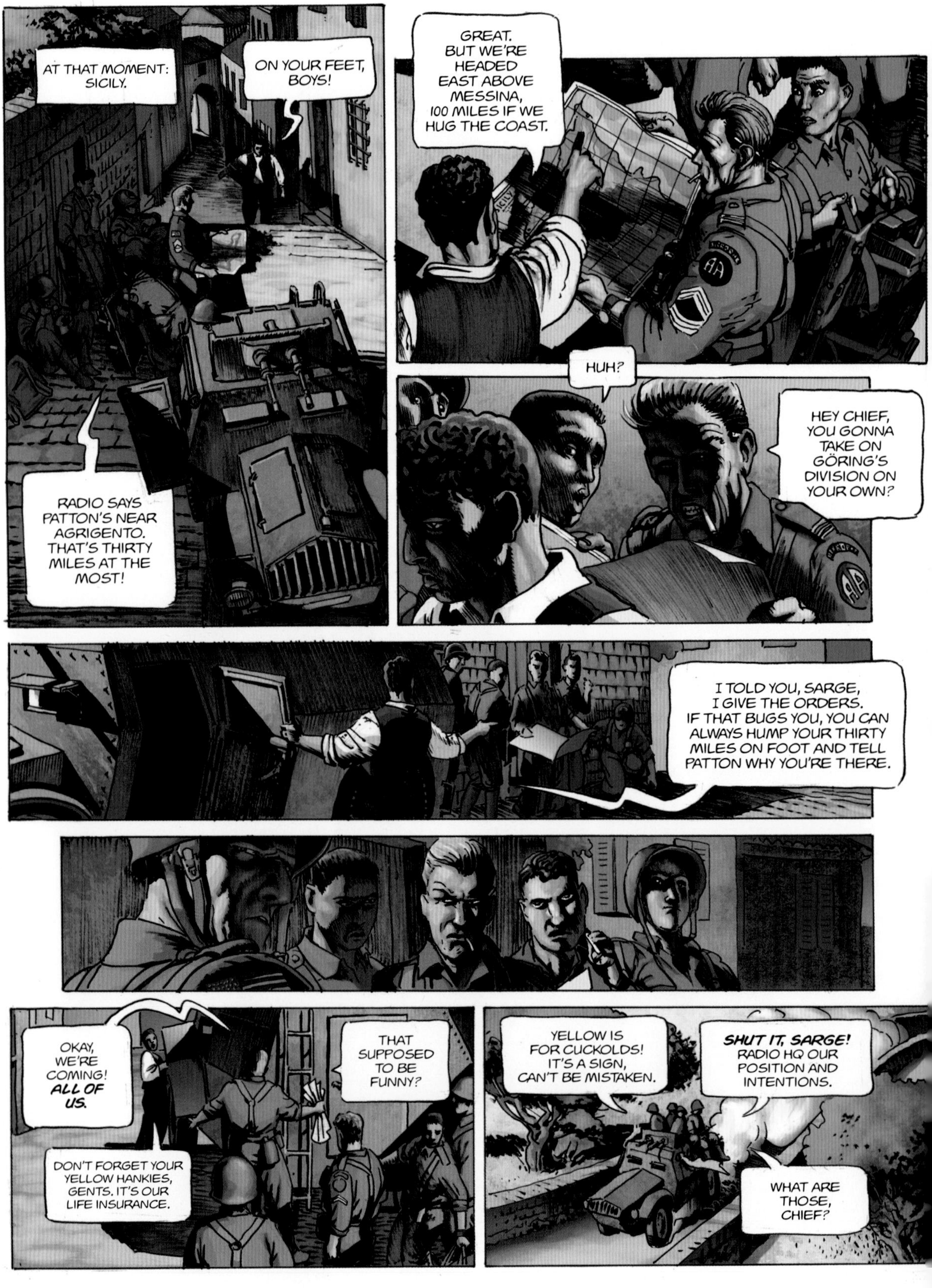
AT THAT MOMENT: SICILY.
ON YOUR FEET, BOYS!
RADIO SAYS PATTON'S NEAR AGRIGENTO. THAT'S THIRTY MILES AT THE MOST!
GREAT. BUT WE'RE HEADED EAST ABOVE MESSINA, 100 MILES IF WE HUG THE COAST.
HUH?
HEY CHIEF, YOU GONNA TAKE ON GÖRING'S DIVISION ON YOUR OWN?
I TOLD YOU, SARGE, I GIVE THE ORDERS. IF THAT BUGS YOU, YOU CAN ALWAYS HUMP YOUR THIRTY MILES ON FOOT AND TELL PATTON WHY YOU'RE THERE.
OKAY, WE'RE COMING! ALL OF US.
DON'T FORGET YOUR YELLOW HANKIES, GENTS. IT'S OUR LIFE INSURANCE.
THAT SUPPOSED TO BE FUNNY?
YELLOW IS FOR CUCKOLDS! IT'S A SIGN, CAN'T BE MISTAKEN.
SHUT IT, SARGE! RADIO HQ OUR POSITION AND INTENTIONS.
WHAT ARE THOSE, CHIEF?

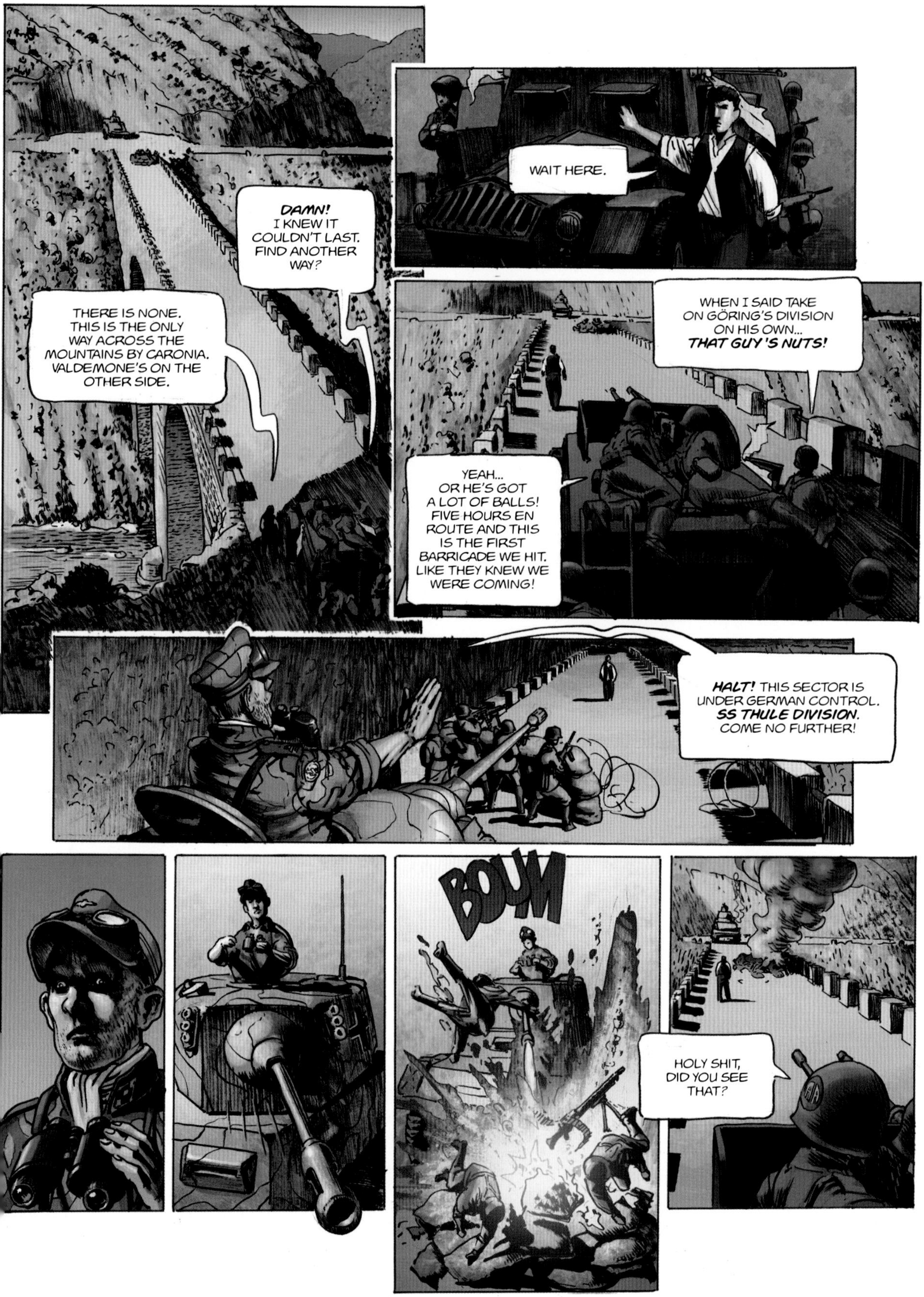
DAMN! I KNEW IT COULDN'T LAST. FIND ANOTHER WAY?
THERE IS NONE. THIS IS THE ONLY WAY ACROSS THE MOUNTAINS BY CARONIA. VALDEMONE'S ON THE OTHER SIDE.
WAIT HERE.
WHEN I SAID TAKE ON GÖRING'S DIVISION ON HIS OWN... THAT GUY'S NUTS!
YEAH... OR HE'S GOT A LOT OF BALLS! FIVE HOURS EN ROUTE AND THIS IS THE FIRST BARRICADE WE HIT. LIKE THEY KNEW WE WERE COMING!
HALT! THIS SECTOR IS UNDER GERMAN CONTROL. SS THULE DIVISION. COME NO FURTHER!
BOUM
HOLY SHIT, DID YOU SEE THAT?

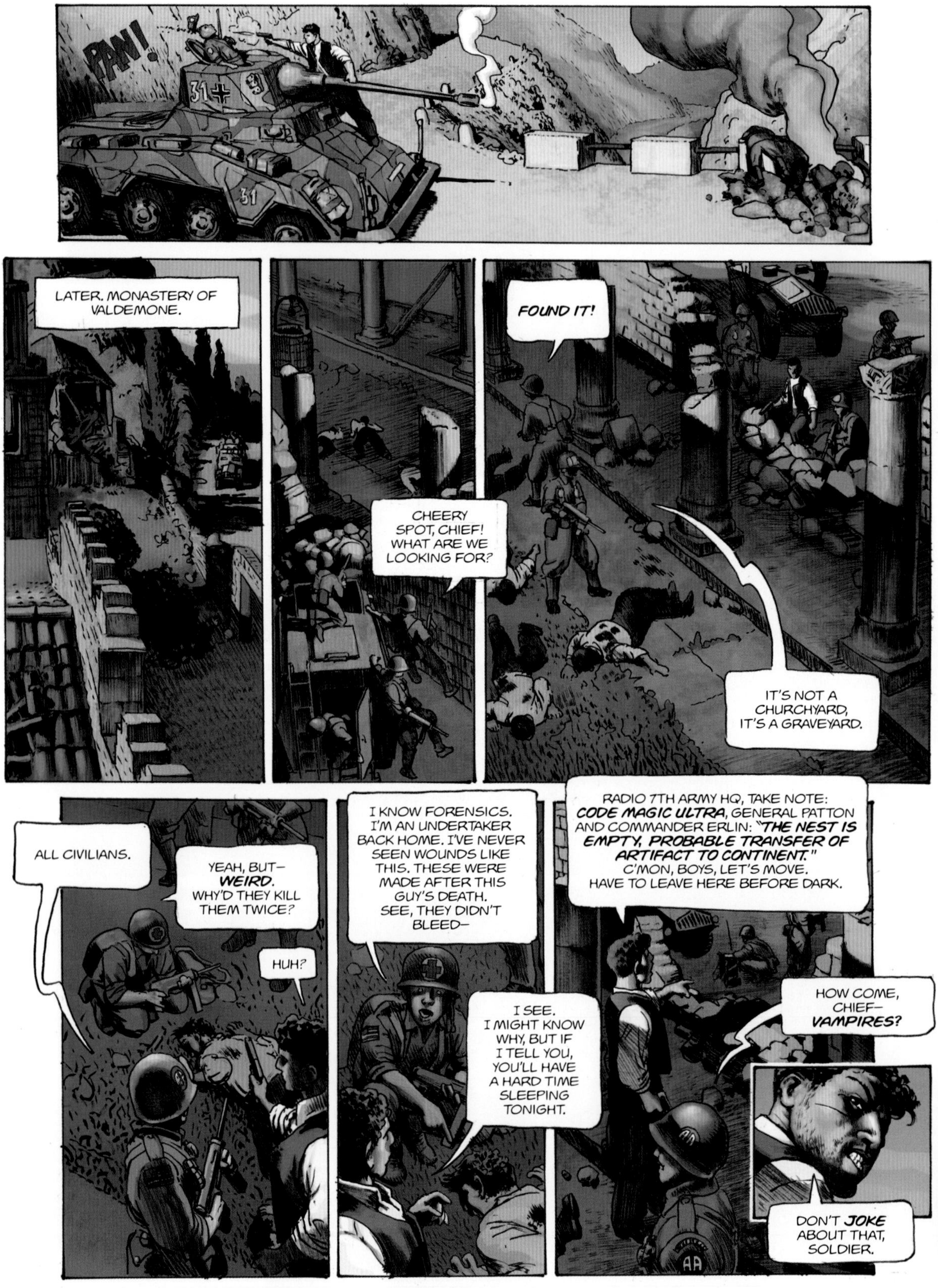
PAN!
31
LATER. MONASTERY OF VALDEMONE.
CHEERY SPOT, CHIEF! WHAT ARE WE LOOKING FOR?
FOUND IT!
IT'S NOT A CHURCHYARD, IT'S A GRAVEYARD.
ALL CIVILIANS.
YEAH, BUT— WEIRD. WHY'D THEY KILL THEM TWICE?
HUH?
I KNOW FORENSICS. I'M AN UNDERTAKER BACK HOME. I'VE NEVER SEEN WOUNDS LIKE THIS. THESE WERE MADE AFTER THIS GUY'S DEATH. SEE, THEY DIDN'T BLEED—
I SEE. I MIGHT KNOW WHY, BUT IF I TELL YOU, YOU'LL HAVE A HARD TIME SLEEPING TONIGHT.
RADIO 7TH ARMY HQ, TAKE NOTE: CODE MAGIC ULTRA, GENERAL PATTON AND COMMANDER ERLIN: "THE NEST IS EMPTY, PROBABLE TRANSFER OF ARTIFACT TO CONTINENT." C'MON, BOYS, LET'S MOVE. HAVE TO LEAVE HERE BEFORE DARK.
HOW COME, CHIEF— VAMPIRES?
DON'T JOKE ABOUT THAT, SOLDIER.

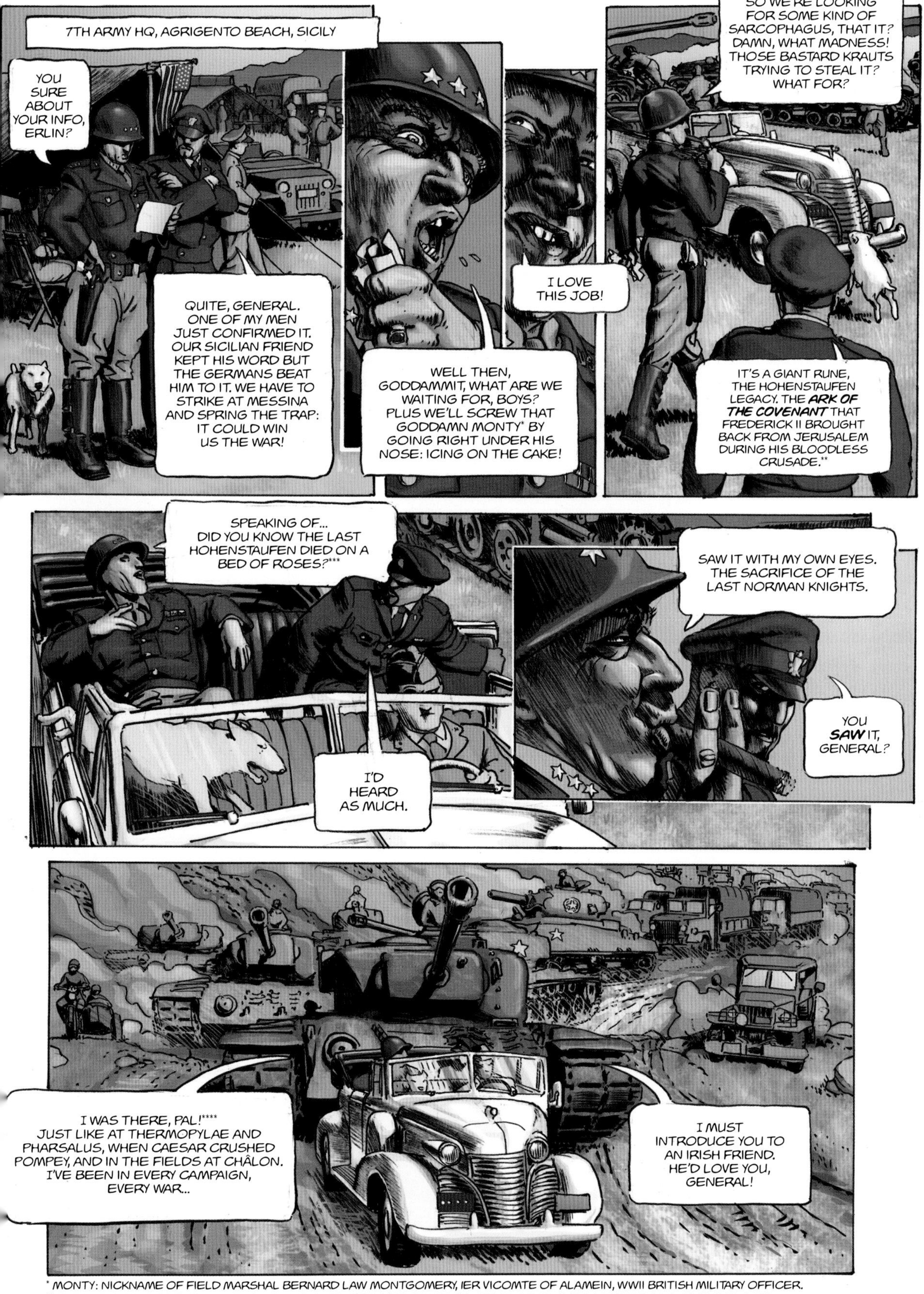
7TH ARMY HQ, AGRIGENTO BEACH, SICILY
YOU SURE ABOUT YOUR INFO, ERLIN?
QUITE, GENERAL. ONE OF MY MEN JUST CONFIRMED IT. OUR SICILIAN FRIEND KEPT HIS WORD BUT THE GERMANS BEAT HIM TO IT. WE HAVE TO STRIKE AT MESSINA AND SPRING THE TRAP: IT COULD WIN US THE WAR!
I LOVE THIS JOB!
WELL THEN, GODDAMMIT, WHAT ARE WE WAITING FOR, BOYS? PLUS WE'LL SCREW THAT GODDAMN MONTY* BY GOING RIGHT UNDER HIS NOSE: ICING ON THE CAKE!
SO WE'RE LOOKING FOR SOME KIND OF SARCOPHAGUS, THAT IT? DAMN, WHAT MADNESS! THOSE BASTARD KRAUTS TRYING TO STEAL IT? WHAT FOR?
IT'S A GIANT RUNE, THE HOHENSTAUFEN LEGACY. THE ***ARK OF THE COVENANT*** THAT FREDERICK II BROUGHT BACK FROM JERUSALEM DURING HIS BLOODLESS CRUSADE.**
SPEAKING OF... DID YOU KNOW THE LAST HOHENSTAUFEN DIED ON A BED OF ROSES?***
I'D HEARD AS MUCH.
SAW IT WITH MY OWN EYES. THE SACRIFICE OF THE LAST NORMAN KNIGHTS.
YOU ***SAW*** IT, GENERAL?
I WAS THERE, PAL!**** JUST LIKE AT THERMOPYLAE AND PHARSALUS, WHEN CAESAR CRUSHED POMPEY, AND IN THE FIELDS AT CHÂLON. I'VE BEEN IN EVERY CAMPAIGN, EVERY WAR...
I MUST INTRODUCE YOU TO AN IRISH FRIEND. HE'D LOVE YOU, GENERAL!

* MONTY: NICKNAME OF FIELD MARSHAL BERNARD LAW MONTGOMERY, 1ER VICOMTE OF ALAMEIN, WWII BRITISH MILITARY OFFICER.
** FREDERICK II NEGOTIATED WITH SULTAN AL-KAMIL OF EGYPT, SALADIN'S NEPHEW. THE SIXTH CRUSADE SAW NO BLOODSHED.
*** SEE *THE SECRET HISTORY, BOOK 4: THE KEYS OF SAINT PETER*.
**** PATTON BELIEVED IN REINCARNATION AND METEMPSYCHOSIS: IN HIS CASE, ALWAYS IN THE BODY OF A SOLDIER OR WARRIOR.

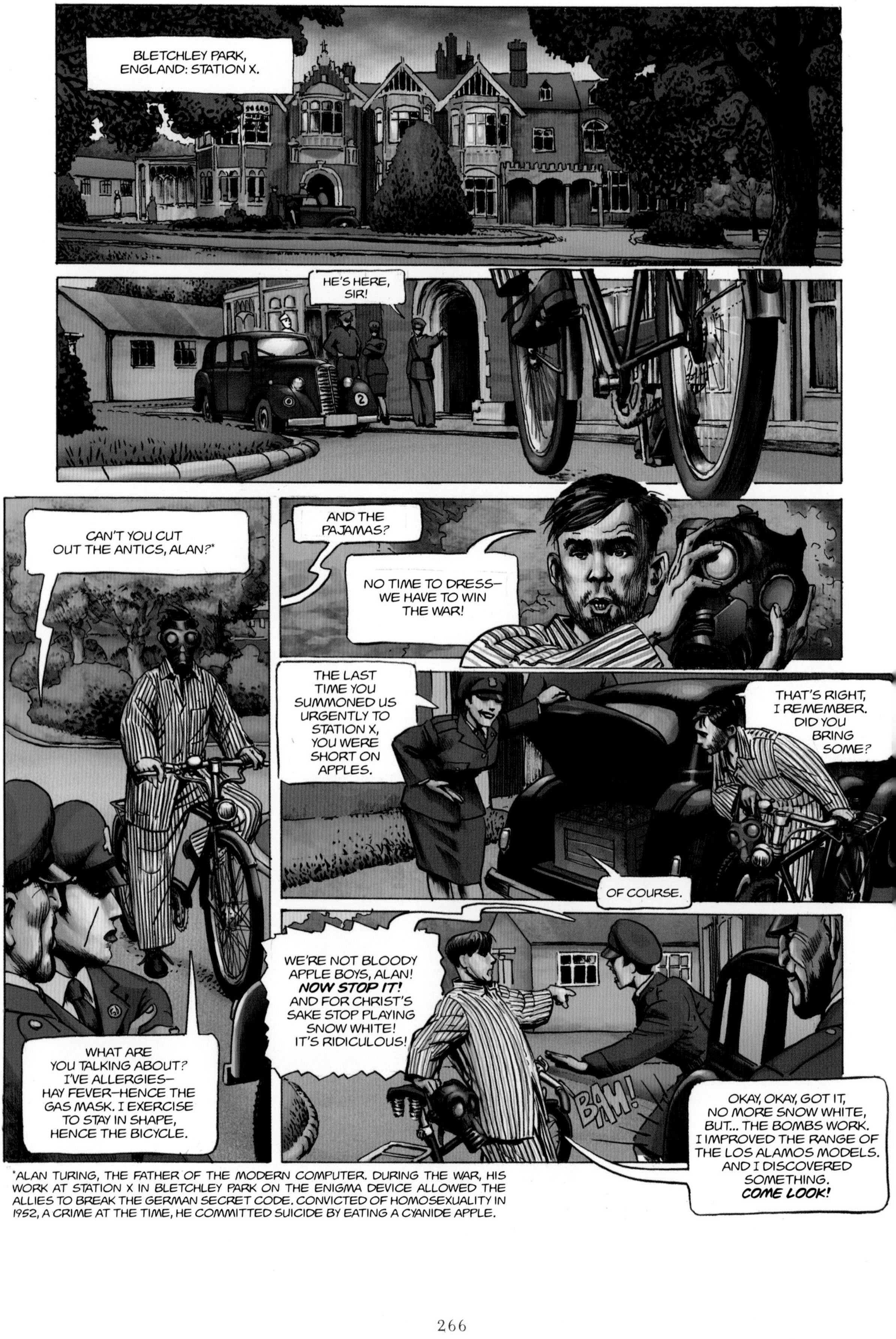
BLETCHLEY PARK, ENGLAND: STATION X.
HE'S HERE, SIR!
CAN'T YOU CUT OUT THE ANTICS, ALAN?*
AND THE PAJAMAS?
NO TIME TO DRESS— WE HAVE TO WIN THE WAR!
THE LAST TIME YOU SUMMONED US URGENTLY TO STATION X, YOU WERE SHORT ON APPLES.
THAT'S RIGHT, I REMEMBER. DID YOU BRING SOME?
OF COURSE.
WHAT ARE YOU TALKING ABOUT? I'VE ALLERGIES— HAY FEVER—HENCE THE GAS MASK. I EXERCISE TO STAY IN SHAPE, HENCE THE BICYCLE.
WE'RE NOT BLOODY APPLE BOYS, ALAN! NOW STOP IT! AND FOR CHRIST'S SAKE STOP PLAYING SNOW WHITE! IT'S RIDICULOUS!
BAM!
OKAY, OKAY, GOT IT, NO MORE SNOW WHITE, BUT... THE BOMBS WORK. I IMPROVED THE RANGE OF THE LOS ALAMOS MODELS. AND I DISCOVERED SOMETHING. COME LOOK!

*ALAN TURING, THE FATHER OF THE MODERN COMPUTER. DURING THE WAR, HIS WORK AT STATION X IN BLETCHLEY PARK ON THE ENIGMA DEVICE ALLOWED THE ALLIES TO BREAK THE GERMAN SECRET CODE. CONVICTED OF HOMOSEXUALITY IN 1952, A CRIME AT THE TIME, HE COMMITTED SUICIDE BY EATING A CYANIDE APPLE.

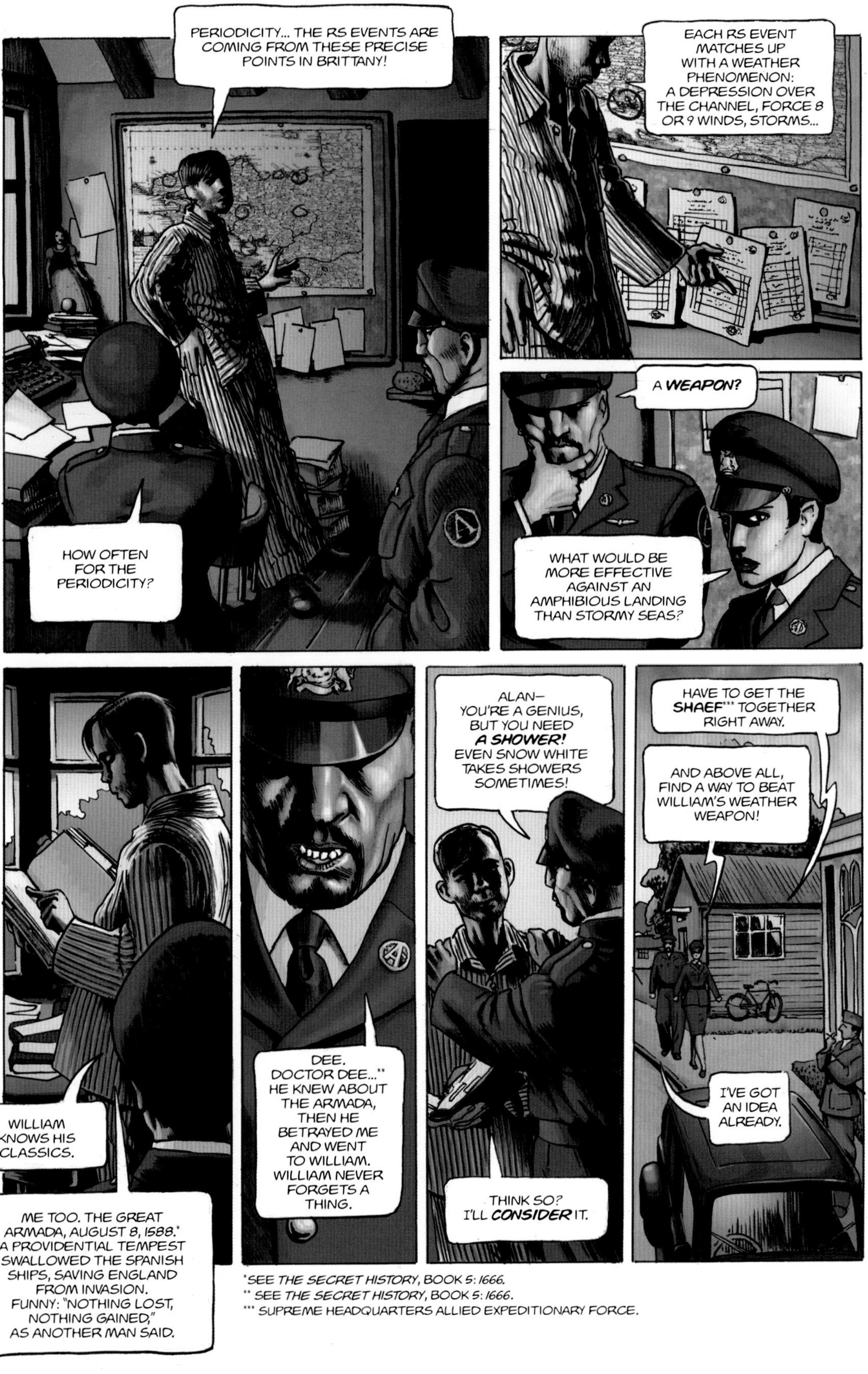
PERIODICITY... THE RS EVENTS ARE COMING FROM THESE PRECISE POINTS IN BRITTANY!
HOW OFTEN FOR THE PERIODICITY?
EACH RS EVENT MATCHES UP WITH A WEATHER PHENOMENON: A DEPRESSION OVER THE CHANNEL, FORCE 8 OR 9 WINDS, STORMS...
A WEAPON?
WHAT WOULD BE MORE EFFECTIVE AGAINST AN AMPHIBIOUS LANDING THAN STORMY SEAS?
WILLIAM KNOWS HIS CLASSICS.
ME TOO. THE GREAT ARMADA, AUGUST 8, 1588.* A PROVIDENTIAL TEMPEST SWALLOWED THE SPANISH SHIPS, SAVING ENGLAND FROM INVASION. FUNNY: "NOTHING LOST, NOTHING GAINED," AS ANOTHER MAN SAID.
DEE. DOCTOR DEE...** HE KNEW ABOUT THE ARMADA, THEN HE BETRAYED ME AND WENT TO WILLIAM. WILLIAM NEVER FORGETS A THING.
ALAN— YOU'RE A GENIUS, BUT YOU NEED **A SHOWER!** EVEN SNOW WHITE TAKES SHOWERS SOMETIMES!
THINK SO? I'LL **CONSIDER** IT.
HAVE TO GET THE **SHAEF***** TOGETHER RIGHT AWAY.
AND ABOVE ALL, FIND A WAY TO BEAT WILLIAM'S WEATHER WEAPON!
I'VE GOT AN IDEA ALREADY.

*SEE *THE SECRET HISTORY*, BOOK 5: 1666.
** SEE *THE SECRET HISTORY*, BOOK 5: 1666.
*** SUPREME HEADQUARTERS ALLIED EXPEDITIONARY FORCE.

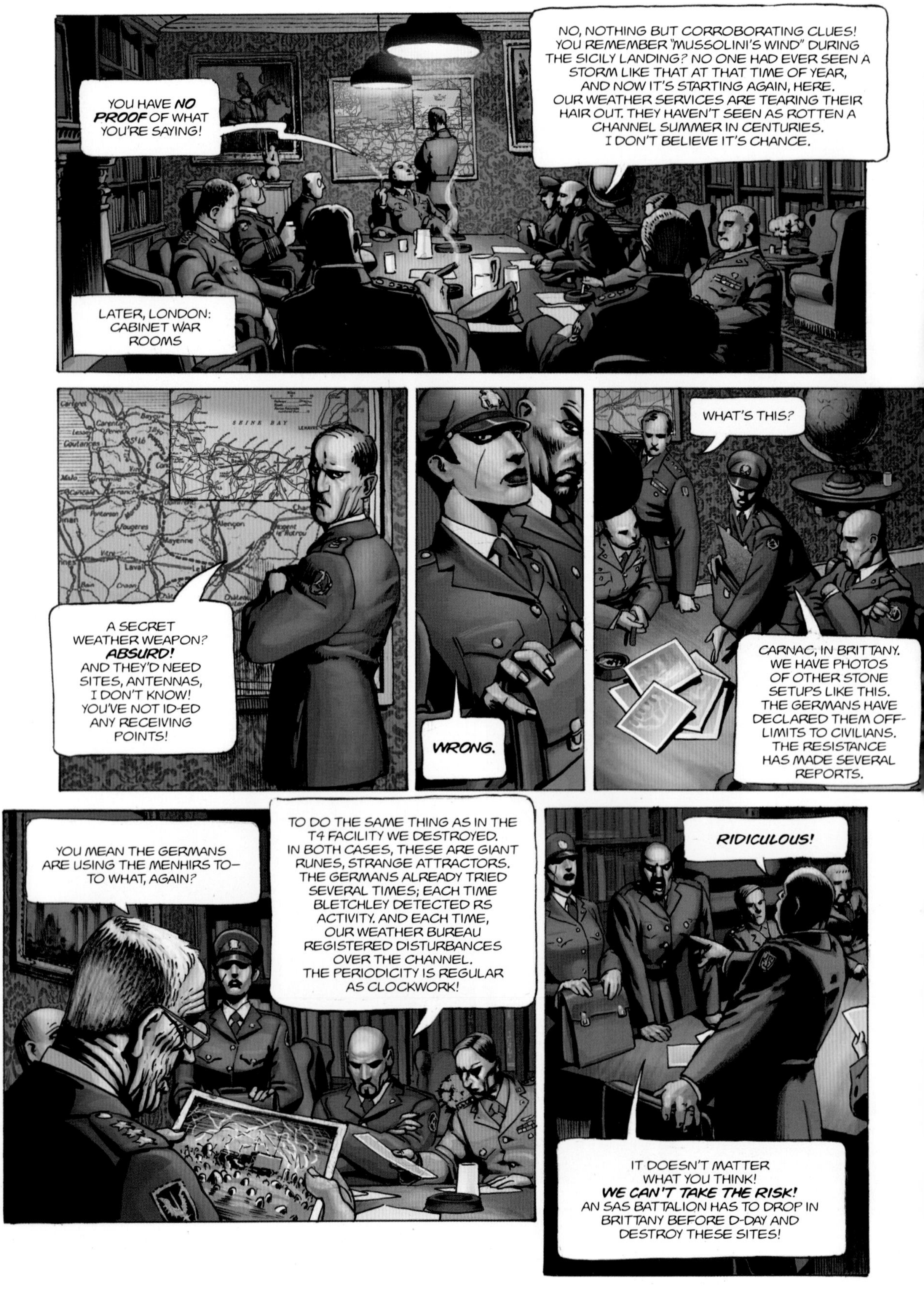

LATER, LONDON: CABINET WAR ROOMS
YOU HAVE **NO PROOF** OF WHAT YOU'RE SAYING!
NO, NOTHING BUT CORROBORATING CLUES! YOU REMEMBER "MUSSOLINI'S WIND" DURING THE SICILY LANDING? NO ONE HAD EVER SEEN A STORM LIKE THAT AT THAT TIME OF YEAR, AND NOW IT'S STARTING AGAIN, HERE. OUR WEATHER SERVICES ARE TEARING THEIR HAIR OUT. THEY HAVEN'T SEEN AS ROTTEN A CHANNEL SUMMER IN CENTURIES. I DON'T BELIEVE IT'S CHANCE.
SEINE BAY
A SECRET WEATHER WEAPON? **ABSURD!** AND THEY'D NEED SITES, ANTENNAS, I DON'T KNOW! YOU'VE NOT ID-ED ANY RECEIVING POINTS!
WRONG.
WHAT'S THIS?
CARNAC, IN BRITTANY. WE HAVE PHOTOS OF OTHER STONE SETUPS LIKE THIS. THE GERMANS HAVE DECLARED THEM OFF-LIMITS TO CIVILIANS. THE RESISTANCE HAS MADE SEVERAL REPORTS.
YOU MEAN THE GERMANS ARE USING THE MENHIRS TO— TO WHAT, AGAIN?
TO DO THE SAME THING AS IN THE T4 FACILITY WE DESTROYED. IN BOTH CASES, THESE ARE GIANT RUNES, STRANGE ATTRACTORS. THE GERMANS ALREADY TRIED SEVERAL TIMES; EACH TIME BLETCHLEY DETECTED RS ACTIVITY. AND EACH TIME, OUR WEATHER BUREAU REGISTERED DISTURBANCES OVER THE CHANNEL. THE PERIODICITY IS REGULAR AS CLOCKWORK!
RIDICULOUS!
IT DOESN'T MATTER WHAT YOU THINK! **WE CAN'T TAKE THE RISK!** AN SAS BATTALION HAS TO DROP IN BRITTANY BEFORE D-DAY AND DESTROY THESE SITES!

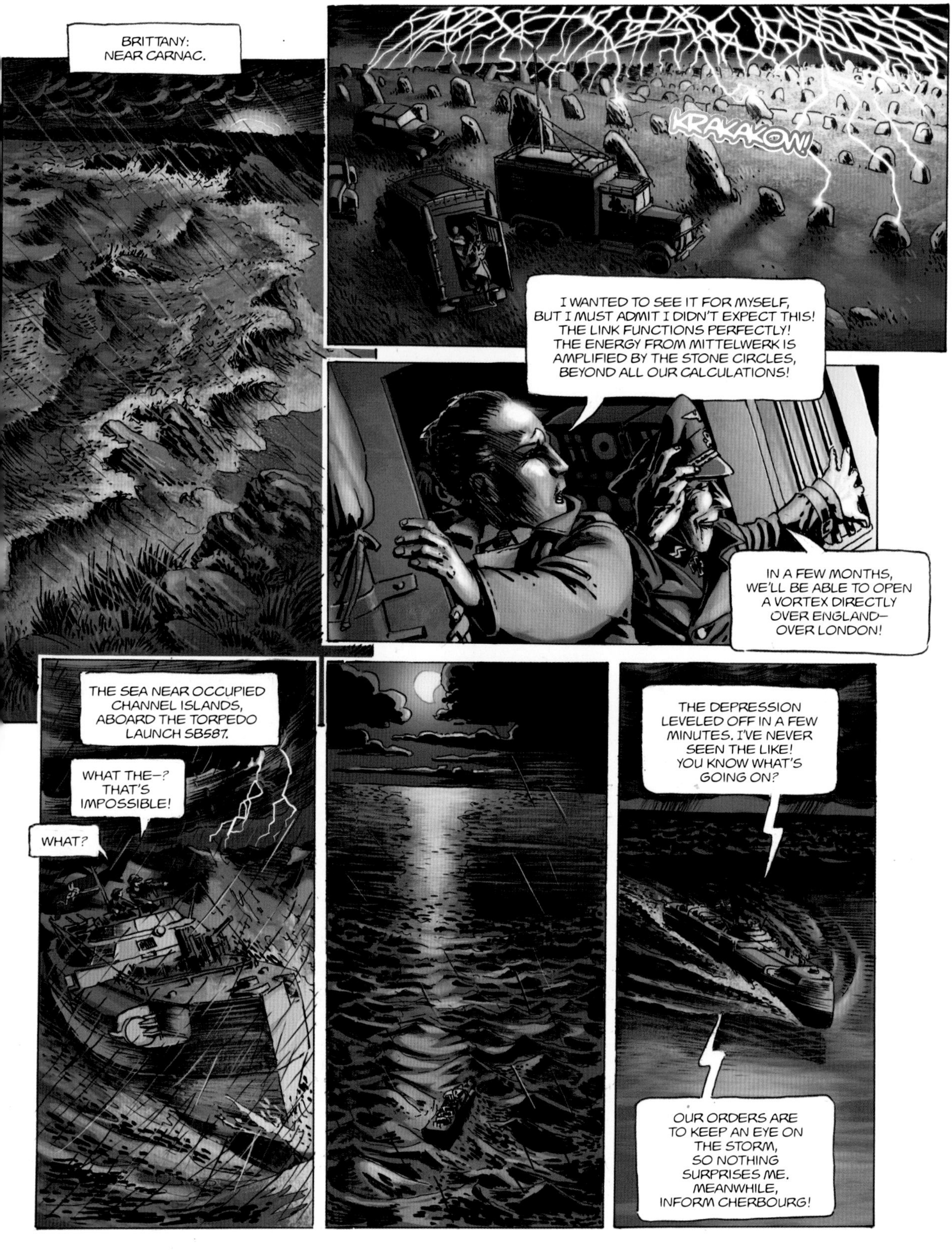
BRITTANY: NEAR CARNAC.
KRAKAKOW!
I WANTED TO SEE IT FOR MYSELF, BUT I MUST ADMIT I DIDN'T EXPECT THIS! THE LINK FUNCTIONS PERFECTLY! THE ENERGY FROM MITTELWERK IS AMPLIFIED BY THE STONE CIRCLES, BEYOND ALL OUR CALCULATIONS!
IN A FEW MONTHS, WE'LL BE ABLE TO OPEN A VORTEX DIRECTLY OVER ENGLAND— OVER LONDON!
THE SEA NEAR OCCUPIED CHANNEL ISLANDS, ABOARD THE TORPEDO LAUNCH SB587.
WHAT THE—? THAT'S IMPOSSIBLE!
WHAT?
THE DEPRESSION LEVELED OFF IN A FEW MINUTES. I'VE NEVER SEEN THE LIKE! YOU KNOW WHAT'S GOING ON?
OUR ORDERS ARE TO KEEP AN EYE ON THE STORM, SO NOTHING SURPRISES ME. MEANWHILE, INFORM CHERBOURG!

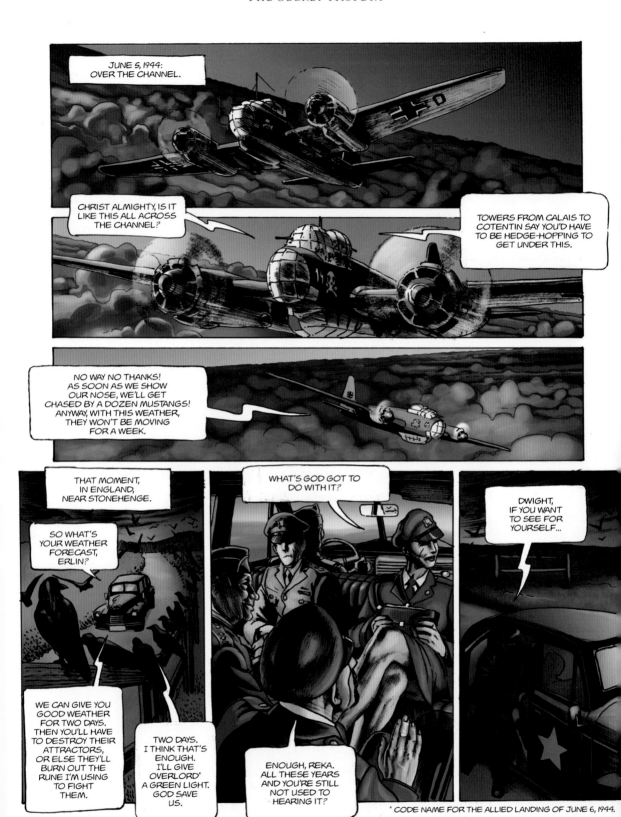

JUNE 5, 1944: OVER THE CHANNEL.

CHRIST ALMIGHTY, IS IT LIKE THIS ALL ACROSS THE CHANNEL?

TOWERS FROM CALAIS TO COTENTIN SAY YOU'D HAVE TO BE HEDGE-HOPPING TO GET UNDER THIS.

NO WAY NO THANKS! AS SOON AS WE SHOW OUR NOSE, WE'LL GET CHASED BY A DOZEN MUSTANGS! ANYWAY, WITH THIS WEATHER, THEY WON'T BE MOVING FOR A WEEK.

THAT MOMENT, IN ENGLAND, NEAR STONEHENGE.

WHAT'S GOD GOT TO DO WITH IT?

DWIGHT, IF YOU WANT TO SEE FOR YOURSELF...

SO WHAT'S YOUR WEATHER FORECAST, ERLIN?

WE CAN GIVE YOU GOOD WEATHER FOR TWO DAYS. THEN YOU'LL HAVE TO DESTROY THEIR ATTRACTORS, OR ELSE THEY'LL BURN OUT THE RUNE I'M USING TO FIGHT THEM.

TWO DAYS. I THINK THAT'S ENOUGH. I'LL GIVE OVERLORD* A GREEN LIGHT. GOD SAVE US.

ENOUGH, REKA. ALL THESE YEARS AND YOU'RE STILL NOT USED TO HEARING IT?

* CODE NAME FOR THE ALLIED LANDING OF JUNE 6, 1944.

270

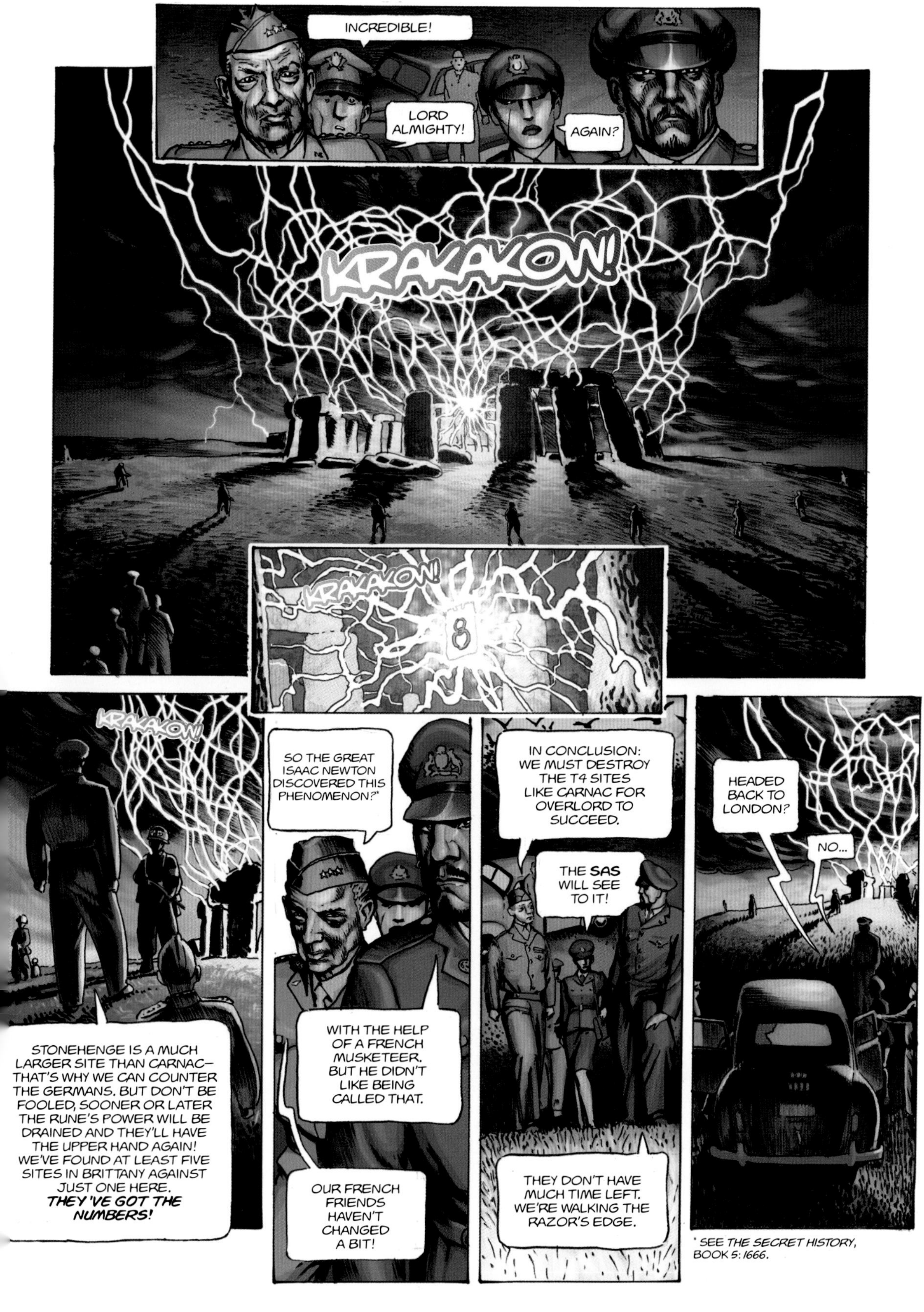
INCREDIBLE!
LORD ALMIGHTY!
AGAIN?
KRAKAKON!
KRAKAKON!
8
KRAKAKON!
STONEHENGE IS A MUCH LARGER SITE THAN CARNAC— THAT'S WHY WE CAN COUNTER THE GERMANS. BUT DON'T BE FOOLED, SOONER OR LATER THE RUNE'S POWER WILL BE DRAINED AND THEY'LL HAVE THE UPPER HAND AGAIN! WE'VE FOUND AT LEAST FIVE SITES IN BRITTANY AGAINST JUST ONE HERE. ***THEY'VE GOT THE NUMBERS!***
SO THE GREAT ISAAC NEWTON DISCOVERED THIS PHENOMENON?*
WITH THE HELP OF A FRENCH MUSKETEER. BUT HE DIDN'T LIKE BEING CALLED THAT.
OUR FRENCH FRIENDS HAVEN'T CHANGED A BIT!
IN CONCLUSION: WE MUST DESTROY THE T4 SITES LIKE CARNAC FOR OVERLORD TO SUCCEED.
THE **SAS** WILL SEE TO IT!
THEY DON'T HAVE MUCH TIME LEFT. WE'RE WALKING THE RAZOR'S EDGE.
HEADED BACK TO LONDON?
NO...

* SEE *THE SECRET HISTORY, BOOK 5: 1666*.

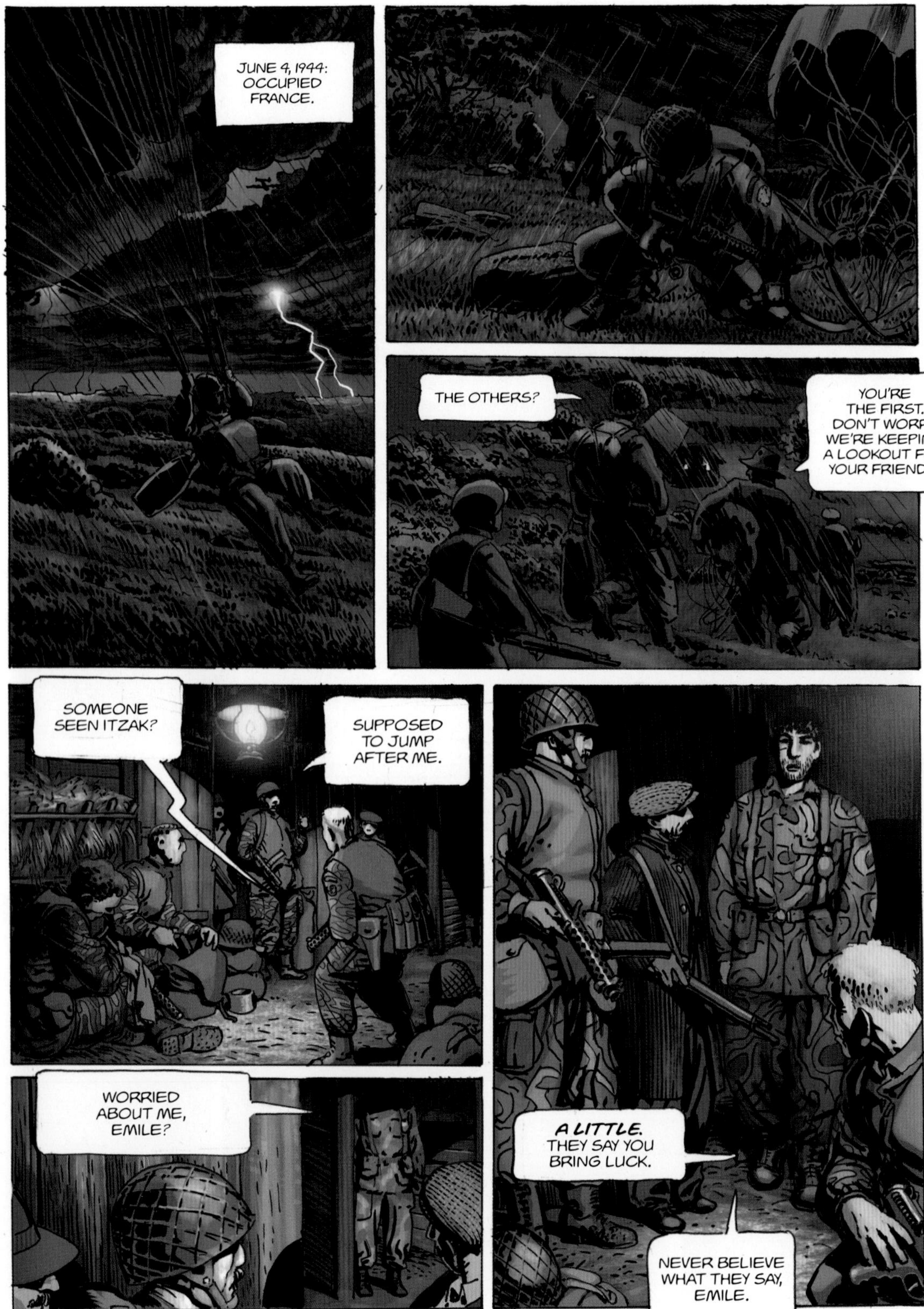
JUNE 4, 1944: OCCUPIED FRANCE.
THE OTHERS?
YOU'RE THE FIRST. DON'T WORRY. WE'RE KEEPING A LOOKOUT FOR YOUR FRIENDS.
SOMEONE SEEN ITZAK?
SUPPOSED TO JUMP AFTER ME.
WORRIED ABOUT ME, EMILE?
A LITTLE. THEY SAY YOU BRING LUCK.
NEVER BELIEVE WHAT THEY SAY, EMILE.

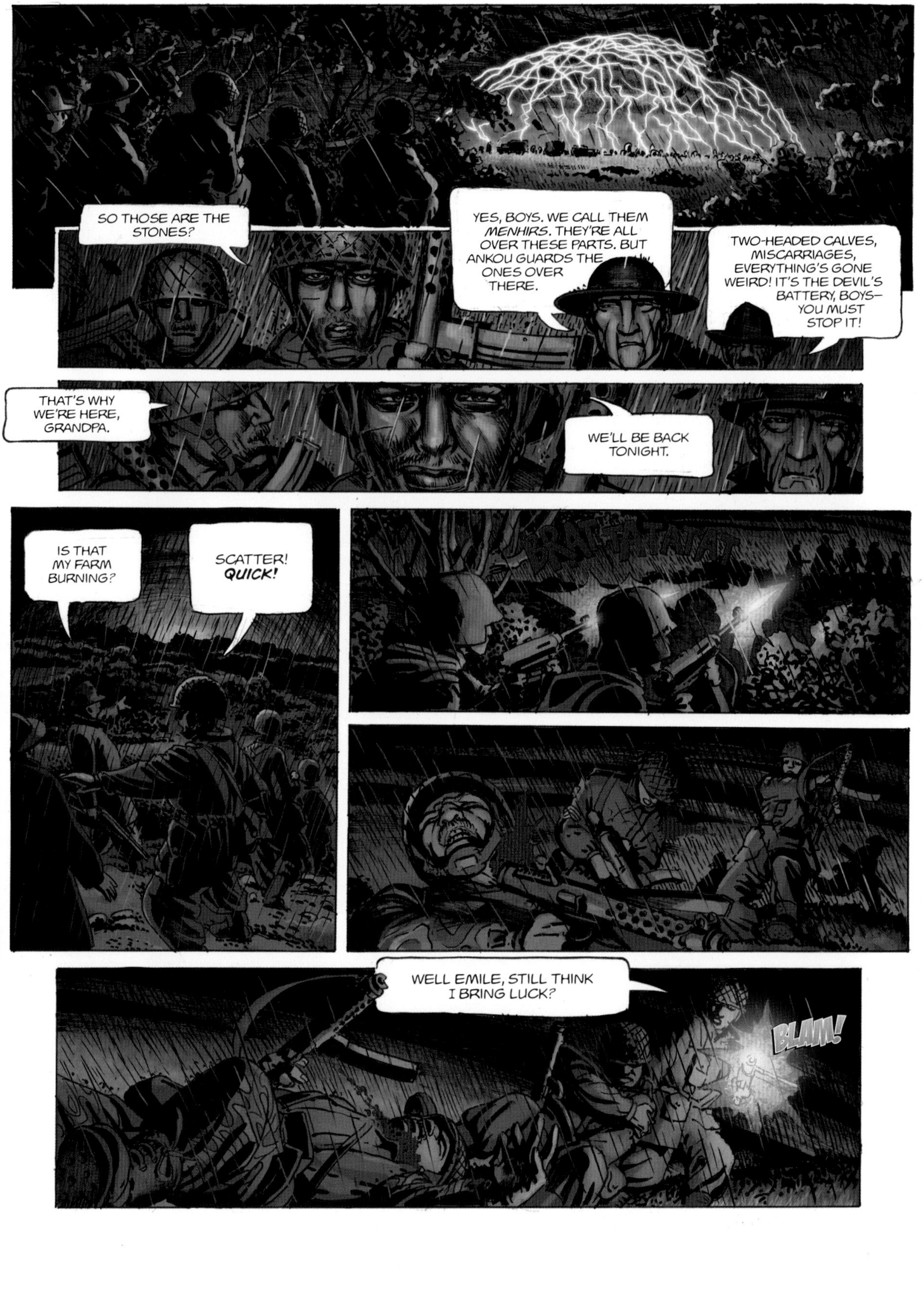
SO THOSE ARE THE STONES?
YES, BOYS. WE CALL THEM *MENHIRS*. THEY'RE ALL OVER THESE PARTS. BUT ANKOU GUARDS THE ONES OVER THERE.
TWO-HEADED CALVES, MISCARRIAGES, EVERYTHING'S GONE WEIRD! IT'S THE DEVIL'S BATTERY, BOYS— YOU MUST STOP IT!
THAT'S WHY WE'RE HERE, GRANDPA.
WE'LL BE BACK TONIGHT.
IS THAT MY FARM BURNING?
SCATTER! **QUICK!**
WELL EMILE, STILL THINK I BRING LUCK?
BLAM!

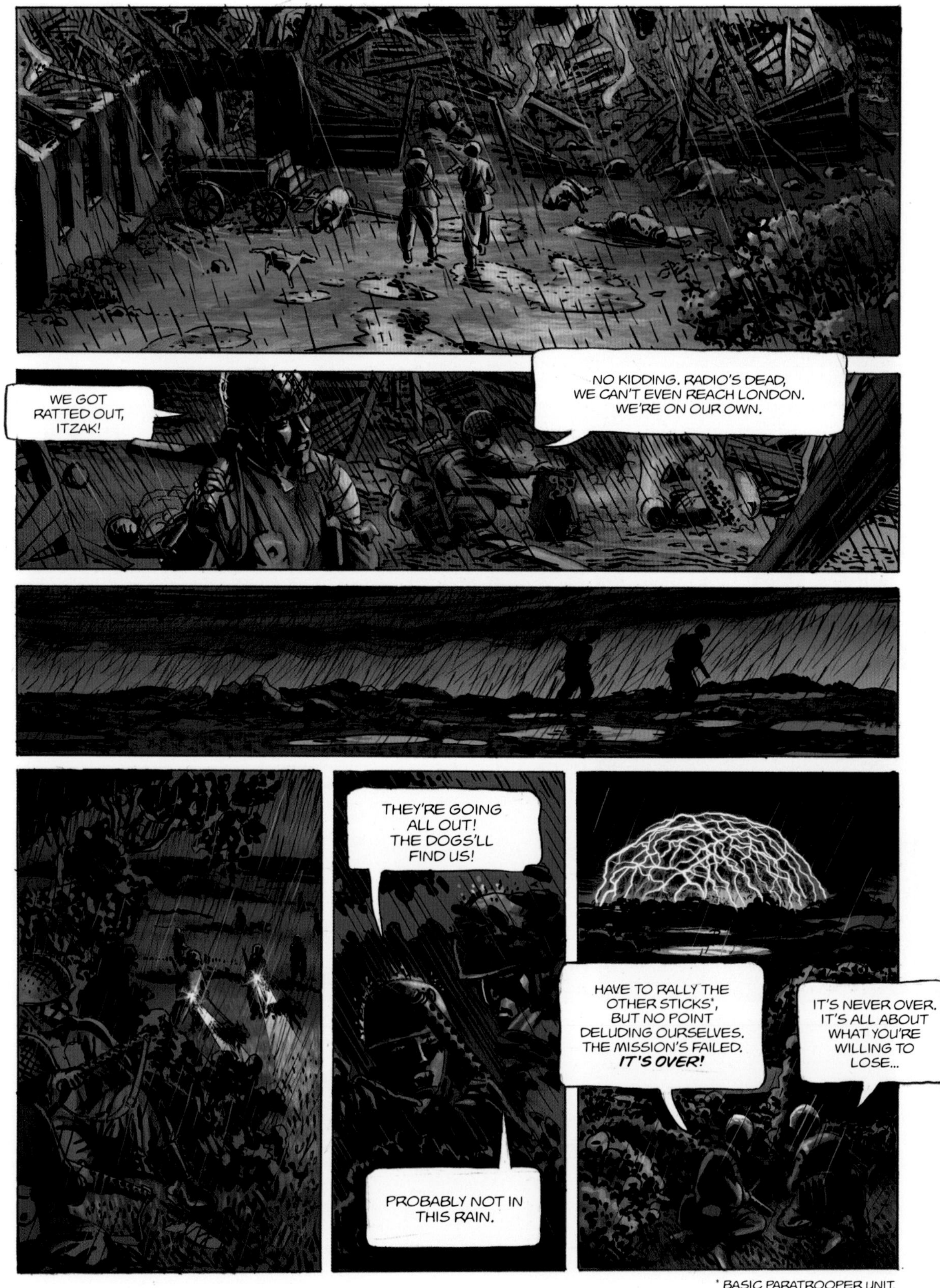
WE GOT RATTED OUT, ITZAK!
NO KIDDING. RADIO'S DEAD, WE CAN'T EVEN REACH LONDON. WE'RE ON OUR OWN.
THEY'RE GOING ALL OUT! THE DOGS'LL FIND US!
PROBABLY NOT IN THIS RAIN.
HAVE TO RALLY THE OTHER STICKS*, BUT NO POINT DELUDING OURSELVES. THE MISSION'S FAILED. *IT'S OVER!*
IT'S NEVER OVER. IT'S ALL ABOUT WHAT YOU'RE WILLING TO LOSE...

* BASIC PARATROOPER UNIT.

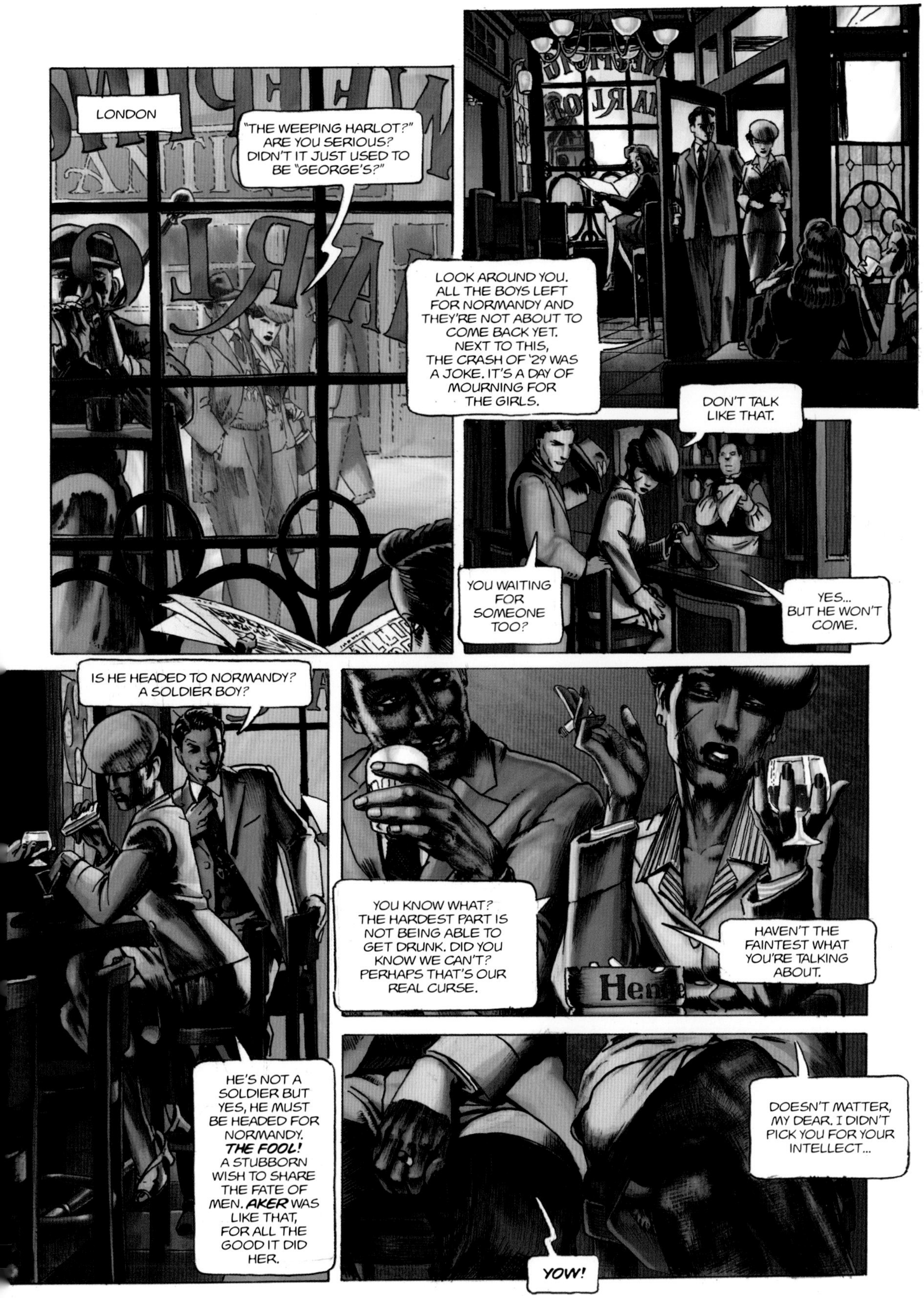
LONDON
"THE WEEPING HARLOT?" ARE YOU SERIOUS? DIDN'T IT JUST USED TO BE "GEORGE'S?"
LOOK AROUND YOU. ALL THE BOYS LEFT FOR NORMANDY AND THEY'RE NOT ABOUT TO COME BACK YET. NEXT TO THIS, THE CRASH OF '29 WAS A JOKE. IT'S A DAY OF MOURNING FOR THE GIRLS.
DON'T TALK LIKE THAT.
YOU WAITING FOR SOMEONE TOO?
YES... BUT HE WON'T COME.
IS HE HEADED TO NORMANDY? A SOLDIER BOY?
HE'S NOT A SOLDIER BUT YES, HE MUST BE HEADED FOR NORMANDY. THE FOOL! A STUBBORN WISH TO SHARE THE FATE OF MEN. AKER WAS LIKE THAT, FOR ALL THE GOOD IT DID HER.
YOU KNOW WHAT? THE HARDEST PART IS NOT BEING ABLE TO GET DRUNK. DID YOU KNOW WE CAN'T? PERHAPS THAT'S OUR REAL CURSE.
HAVEN'T THE FAINTEST WHAT YOU'RE TALKING ABOUT.
DOESN'T MATTER, MY DEAR. I DIDN'T PICK YOU FOR YOUR INTELLECT...
YOW!

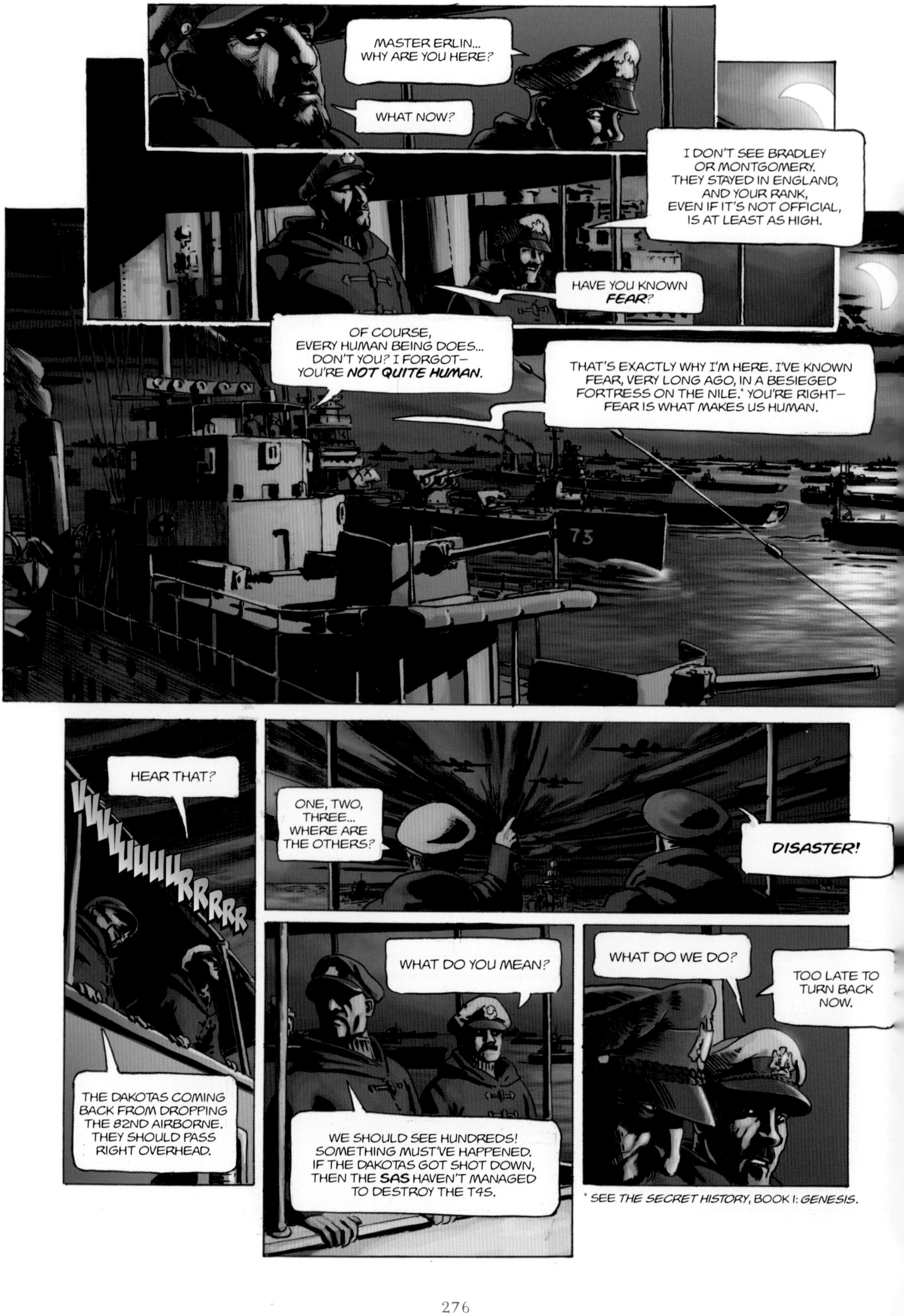
MASTER ERLIN... WHY ARE YOU HERE?
WHAT NOW?
I DON'T SEE BRADLEY OR MONTGOMERY. THEY STAYED IN ENGLAND, AND YOUR RANK, EVEN IF IT'S NOT OFFICIAL, IS AT LEAST AS HIGH.
HAVE YOU KNOWN FEAR?
OF COURSE, EVERY HUMAN BEING DOES... DON'T YOU? I FORGOT— YOU'RE NOT QUITE HUMAN.
THAT'S EXACTLY WHY I'M HERE. I'VE KNOWN FEAR, VERY LONG AGO, IN A BESIEGED FORTRESS ON THE NILE.* YOU'RE RIGHT— FEAR IS WHAT MAKES US HUMAN.
73
HEAR THAT?
VVVUUUUURRRRR
THE DAKOTAS COMING BACK FROM DROPPING THE 82ND AIRBORNE. THEY SHOULD PASS RIGHT OVERHEAD.
ONE, TWO, THREE... WHERE ARE THE OTHERS?
DISASTER!
WHAT DO YOU MEAN?
WE SHOULD SEE HUNDREDS! SOMETHING MUST'VE HAPPENED. IF THE DAKOTAS GOT SHOT DOWN, THEN THE SAS HAVEN'T MANAGED TO DESTROY THE T4S.
WHAT DO WE DO?
TOO LATE TO TURN BACK NOW.
* SEE THE SECRET HISTORY, BOOK I: GENESIS.

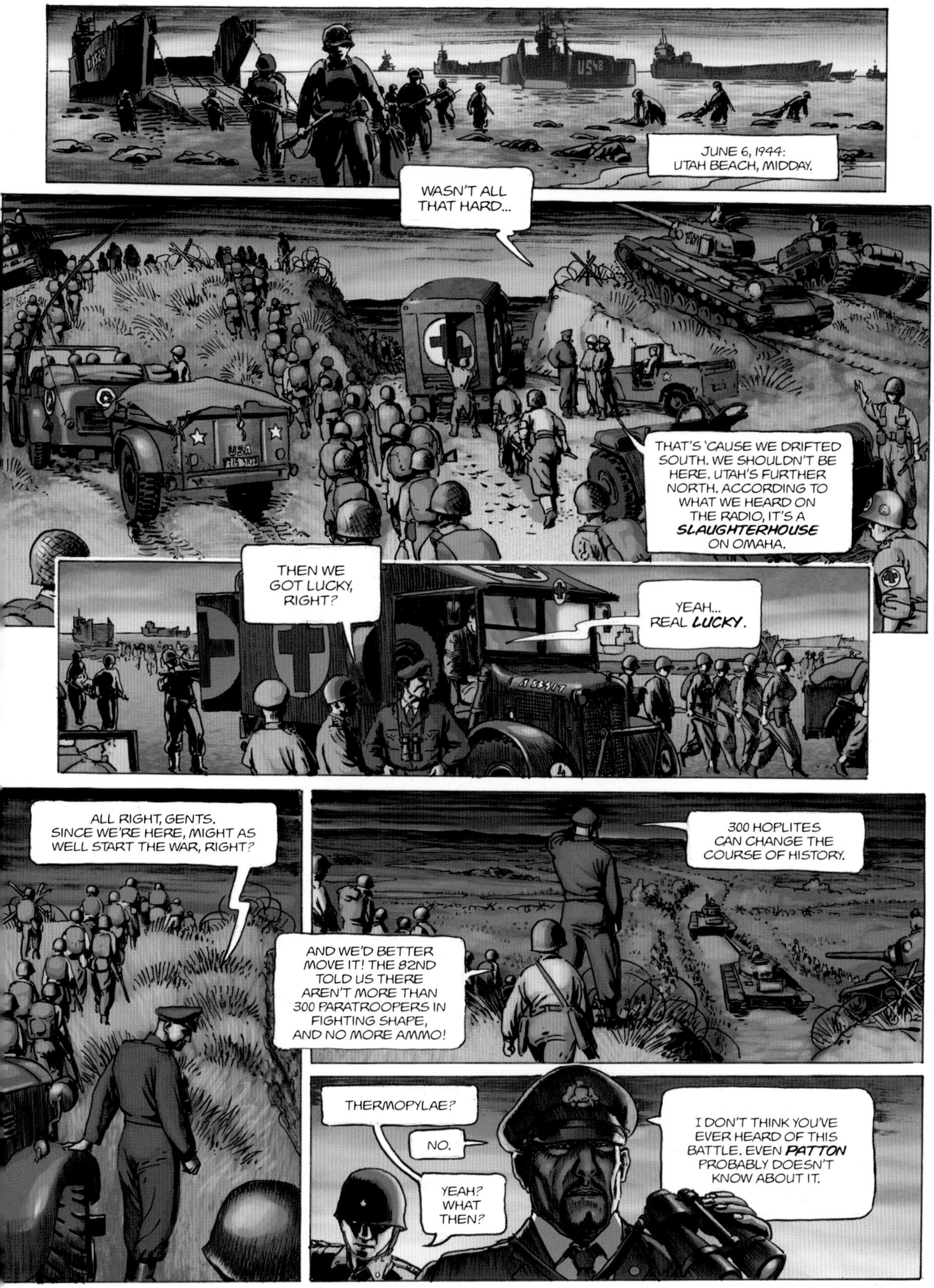
JUNE 6, 1944:
UTAH BEACH, MIDDAY.
WASN'T ALL THAT HARD...
THAT'S 'CAUSE WE DRIFTED SOUTH. WE SHOULDN'T BE HERE. UTAH'S FURTHER NORTH. ACCORDING TO WHAT WE HEARD ON THE RADIO, IT'S A **SLAUGHTERHOUSE** ON OMAHA.
THEN WE GOT LUCKY, RIGHT?
YEAH... REAL **LUCKY**.
ALL RIGHT, GENTS. SINCE WE'RE HERE, MIGHT AS WELL START THE WAR, RIGHT?
AND WE'D BETTER MOVE IT! THE 82ND TOLD US THERE AREN'T MORE THAN 300 PARATROOPERS IN FIGHTING SHAPE, AND NO MORE AMMO!
300 HOPLITES CAN CHANGE THE COURSE OF HISTORY.
THERMOPYLAE?
NO.
YEAH? WHAT THEN?
I DON'T THINK YOU'VE EVER HEARD OF THIS BATTLE. EVEN **PATTON** PROBABLY DOESN'T KNOW ABOUT IT.

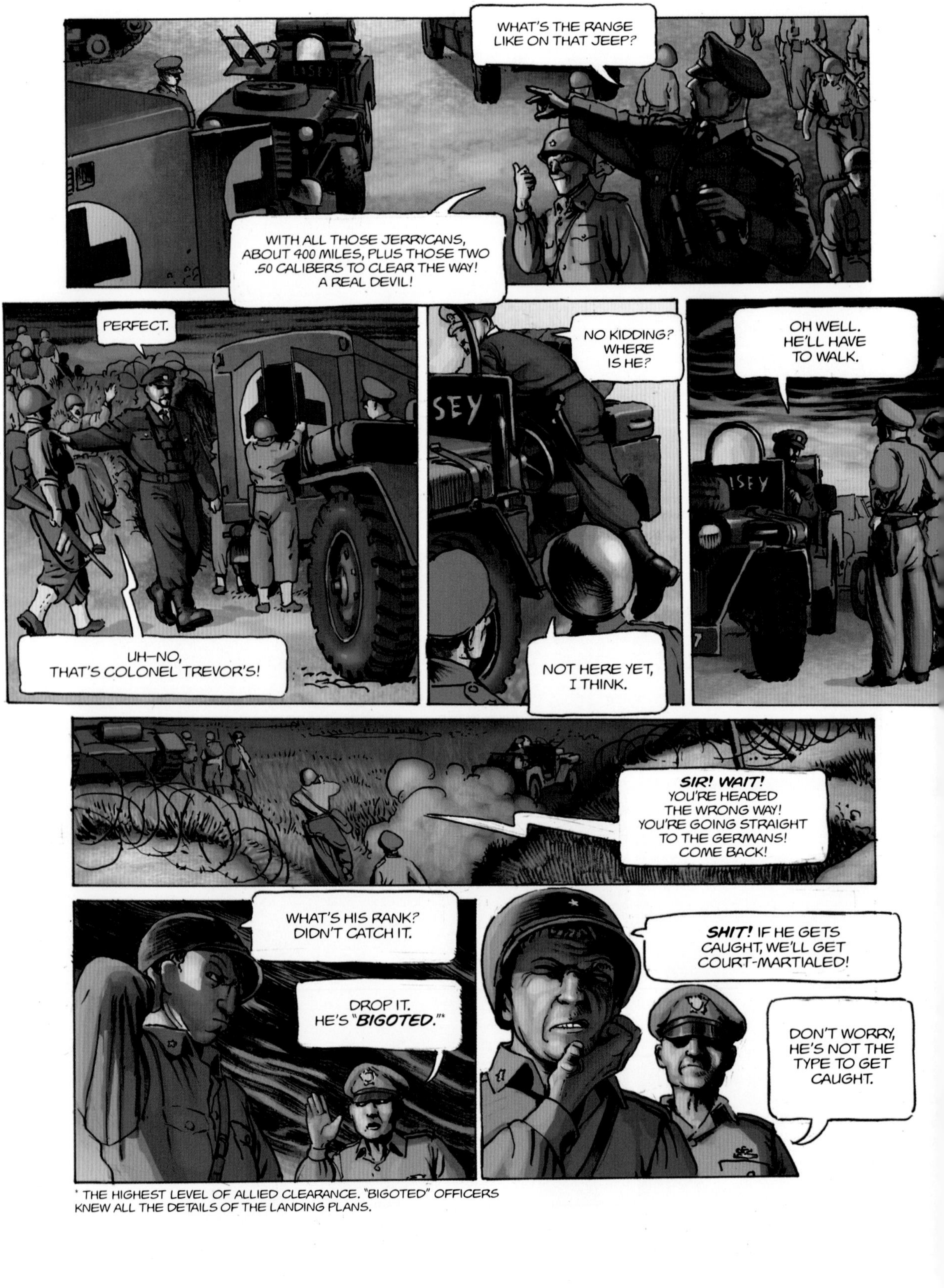
WHAT'S THE RANGE LIKE ON THAT JEEP?
WITH ALL THOSE JERRYCANS, ABOUT 400 MILES, PLUS THOSE TWO .50 CALIBERS TO CLEAR THE WAY! A REAL DEVIL!
PERFECT.
UH—NO, THAT'S COLONEL TREVOR'S!
NO KIDDING? WHERE IS HE?
NOT HERE YET, I THINK.
OH WELL. HE'LL HAVE TO WALK.
SIR! WAIT! YOU'RE HEADED THE WRONG WAY! YOU'RE GOING STRAIGHT TO THE GERMANS! COME BACK!
WHAT'S HIS RANK? DIDN'T CATCH IT.
DROP IT. HE'S "BIGOTED."*
SHIT! IF HE GETS CAUGHT, WE'LL GET COURT-MARTIALED!
DON'T WORRY, HE'S NOT THE TYPE TO GET CAUGHT.

* THE HIGHEST LEVEL OF ALLIED CLEARANCE. "BIGOTED" OFFICERS KNEW ALL THE DETAILS OF THE LANDING PLANS.

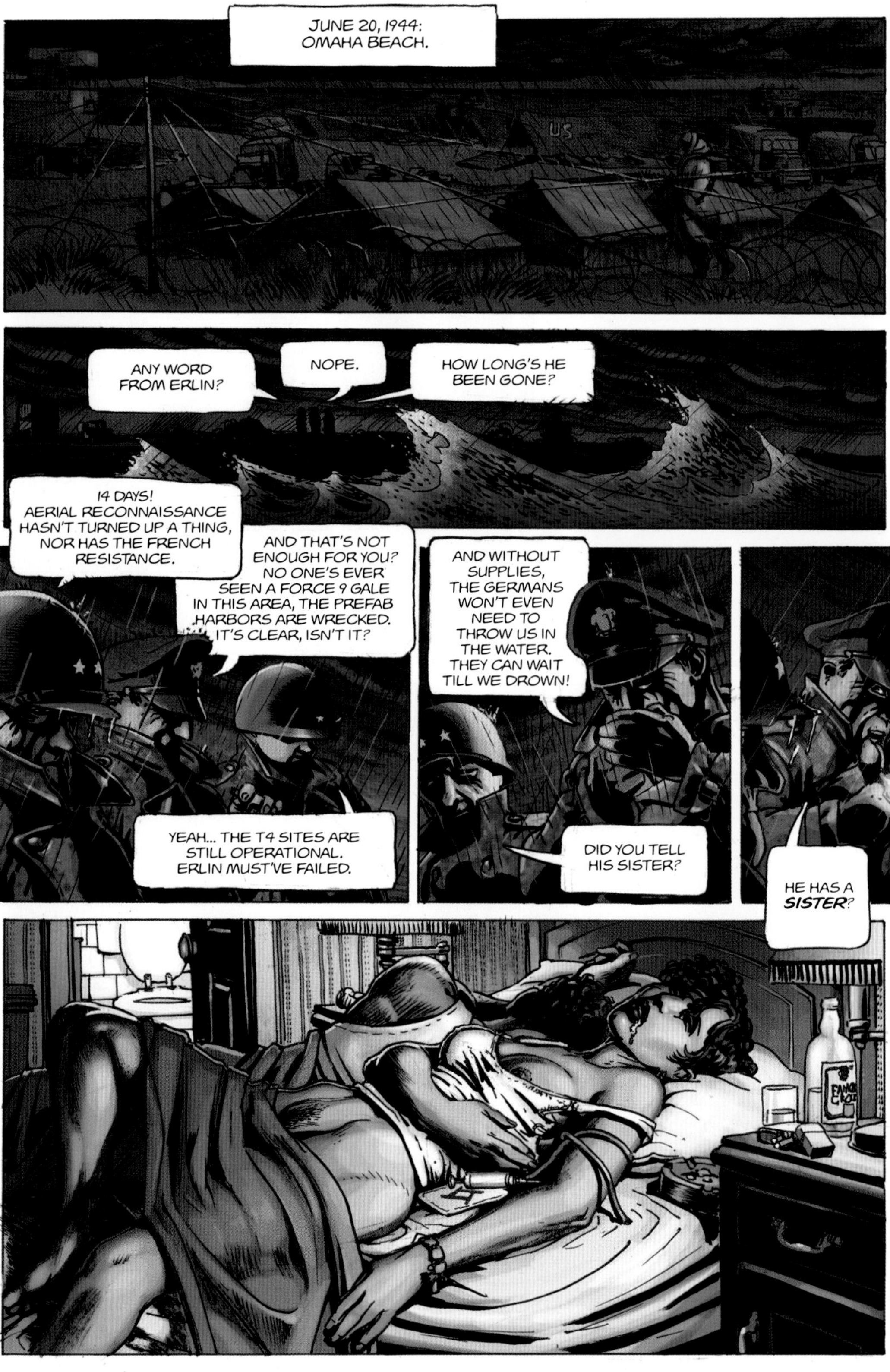
JUNE 20, 1944:
OMAHA BEACH.
ANY WORD FROM ERLIN?
NOPE.
HOW LONG'S HE BEEN GONE?
14 DAYS! AERIAL RECONNAISSANCE HASN'T TURNED UP A THING, NOR HAS THE FRENCH RESISTANCE.
AND THAT'S NOT ENOUGH FOR YOU? NO ONE'S EVER SEEN A FORCE 9 GALE IN THIS AREA, THE PREFAB HARBORS ARE WRECKED. IT'S CLEAR, ISN'T IT?
YEAH... THE T4 SITES ARE STILL OPERATIONAL. ERLIN MUST'VE FAILED.
AND WITHOUT SUPPLIES, THE GERMANS WON'T EVEN NEED TO THROW US IN THE WATER. THEY CAN WAIT TILL WE DROWN!
DID YOU TELL HIS SISTER?
HE HAS A SISTER?

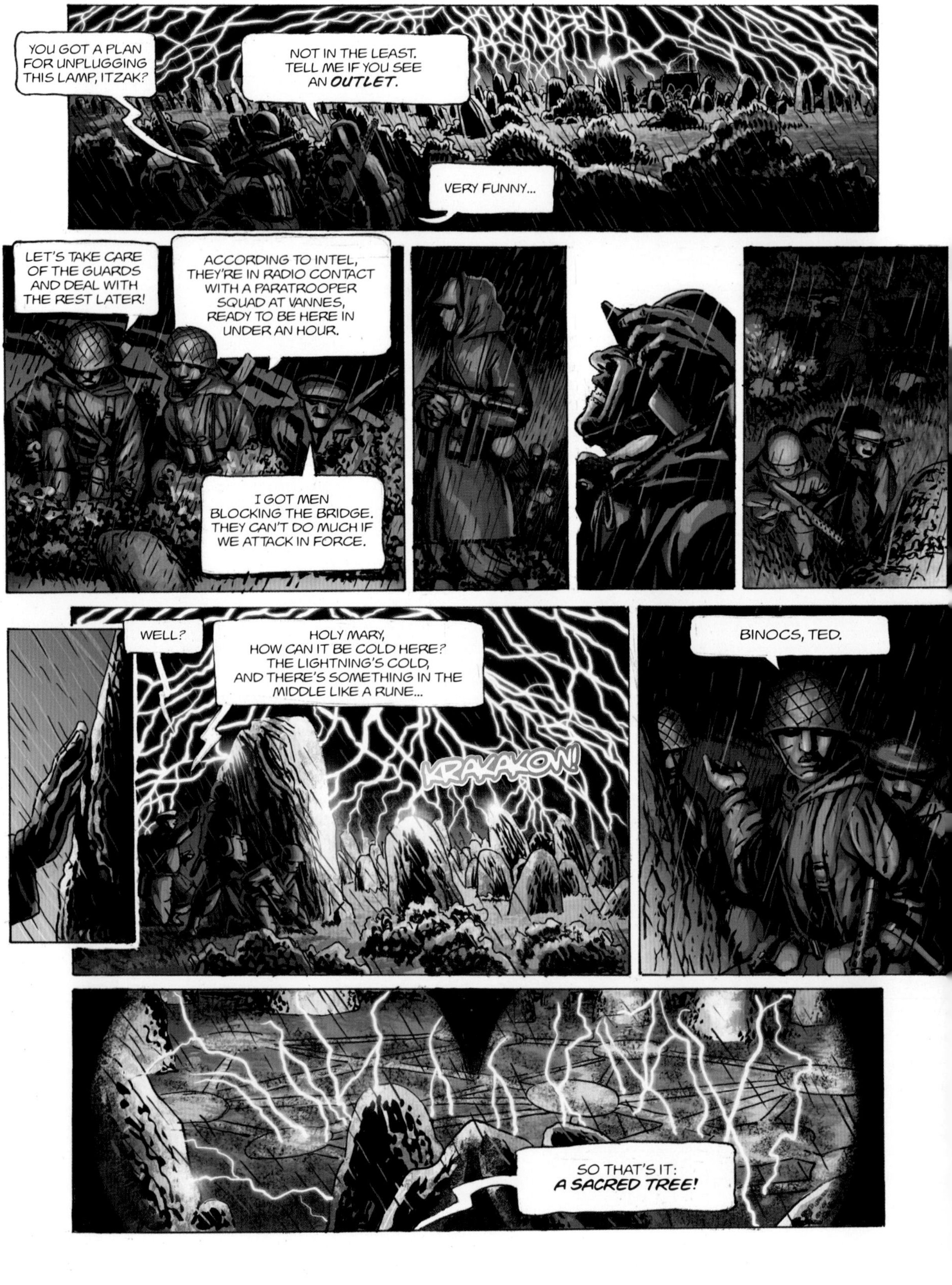
YOU GOT A PLAN FOR UNPLUGGING THIS LAMP, ITZAK?
NOT IN THE LEAST. TELL ME IF YOU SEE AN OUTLET.
VERY FUNNY...
LET'S TAKE CARE OF THE GUARDS AND DEAL WITH THE REST LATER!
ACCORDING TO INTEL, THEY'RE IN RADIO CONTACT WITH A PARATROOPER SQUAD AT VANNES, READY TO BE HERE IN UNDER AN HOUR.
I GOT MEN BLOCKING THE BRIDGE. THEY CAN'T DO MUCH IF WE ATTACK IN FORCE.
WELL?
HOLY MARY, HOW CAN IT BE COLD HERE? THE LIGHTNING'S COLD, AND THERE'S SOMETHING IN THE MIDDLE LIKE A RUNE...
KRAKAKOW!
BINOCS, TED.
SO THAT'S IT: A SACRED TREE!

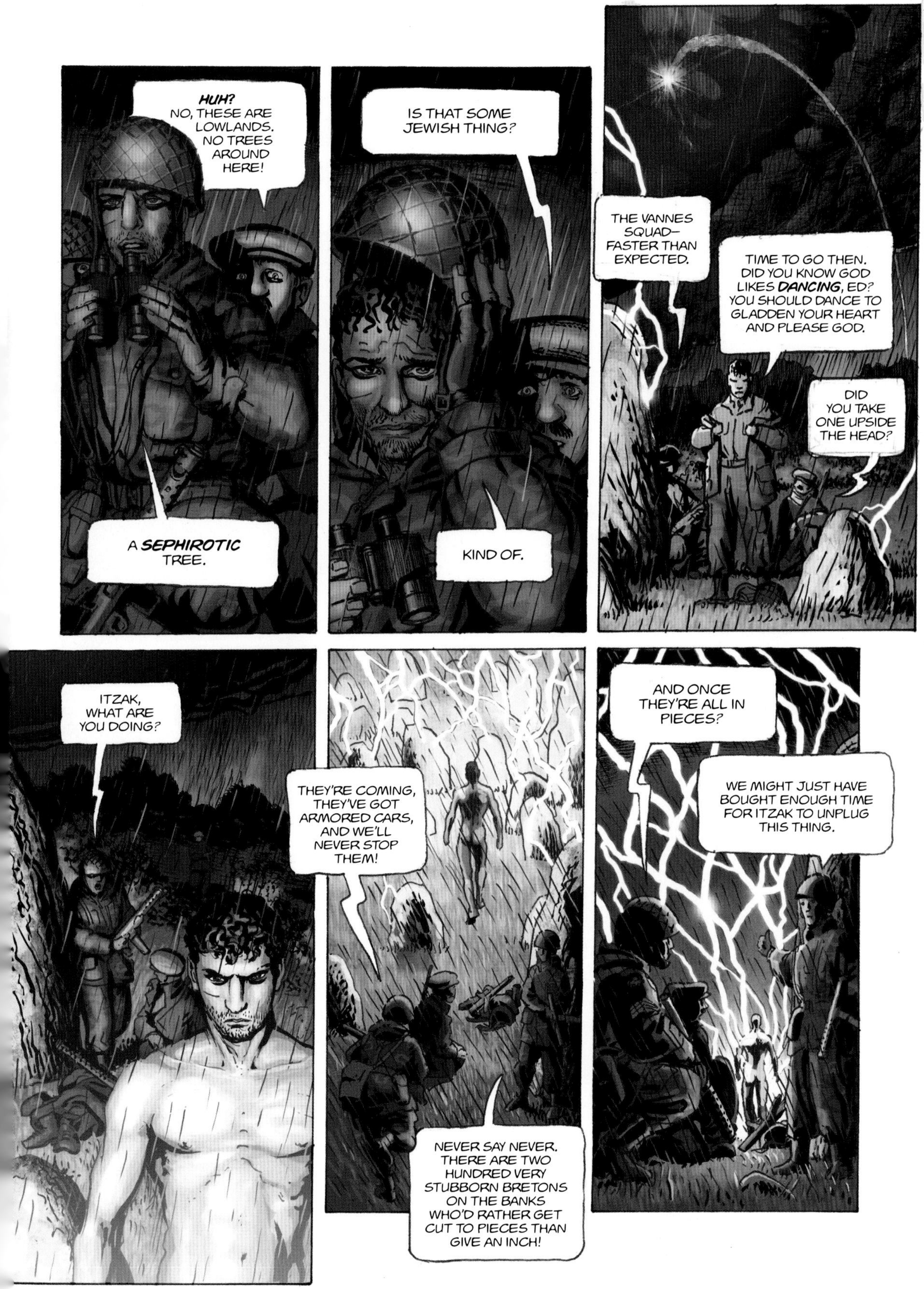
HUH? NO, THESE ARE LOWLANDS. NO TREES AROUND HERE!
A SEPHIROTIC TREE.
IS THAT SOME JEWISH THING?
KIND OF.
THE VANNES SQUAD— FASTER THAN EXPECTED.
TIME TO GO THEN. DID YOU KNOW GOD LIKES DANCING, ED? YOU SHOULD DANCE TO GLADDEN YOUR HEART AND PLEASE GOD.
DID YOU TAKE ONE UPSIDE THE HEAD?
ITZAK, WHAT ARE YOU DOING?
THEY'RE COMING, THEY'VE GOT ARMORED CARS, AND WE'LL NEVER STOP THEM!
NEVER SAY NEVER. THERE ARE TWO HUNDRED VERY STUBBORN BRETONS ON THE BANKS WHO'D RATHER GET CUT TO PIECES THAN GIVE AN INCH!
AND ONCE THEY'RE ALL IN PIECES?
WE MIGHT JUST HAVE BOUGHT ENOUGH TIME FOR ITZAK TO UNPLUG THIS THING.

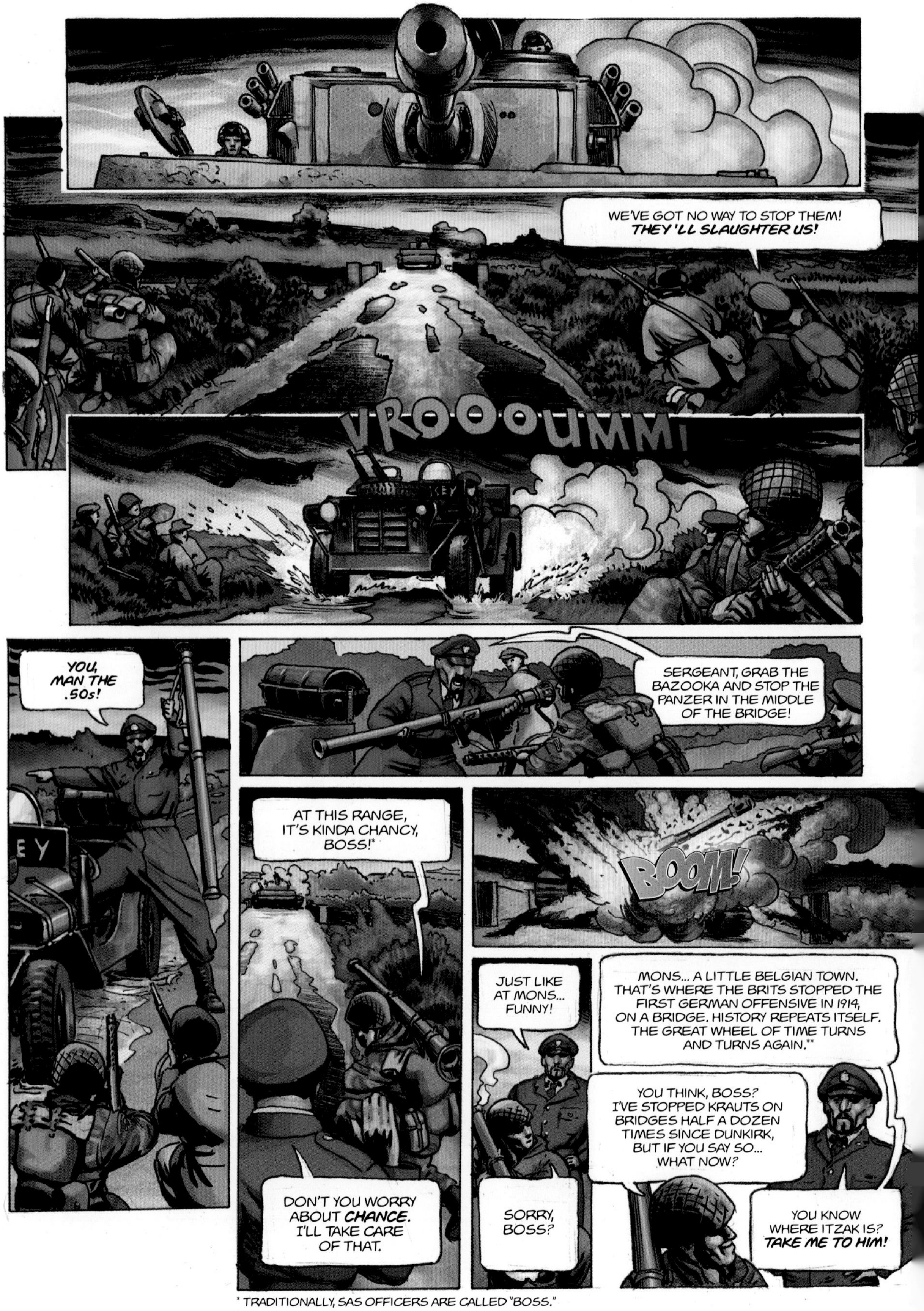
WE'VE GOT NO WAY TO STOP THEM! THEY'LL SLAUGHTER US!
VROOOUMM!
YOU, MAN THE .50s!
SERGEANT, GRAB THE BAZOOKA AND STOP THE PANZER IN THE MIDDLE OF THE BRIDGE!
AT THIS RANGE, IT'S KINDA CHANCY, BOSS!*
DON'T YOU WORRY ABOUT CHANCE. I'LL TAKE CARE OF THAT.
BOOM!
JUST LIKE AT MONS... FUNNY!
SORRY, BOSS?
MONS... A LITTLE BELGIAN TOWN. THAT'S WHERE THE BRITS STOPPED THE FIRST GERMAN OFFENSIVE IN 1914, ON A BRIDGE. HISTORY REPEATS ITSELF. THE GREAT WHEEL OF TIME TURNS AND TURNS AGAIN.**
YOU THINK, BOSS? I'VE STOPPED KRAUTS ON BRIDGES HALF A DOZEN TIMES SINCE DUNKIRK, BUT IF YOU SAY SO... WHAT NOW?
YOU KNOW WHERE ITZAK IS? TAKE ME TO HIM!

* TRADITIONALLY, SAS OFFICERS ARE CALLED "BOSS."
** SEE *THE SECRET HISTORY*, BOOK 7: *OUR LADY OF SHADOWS*.

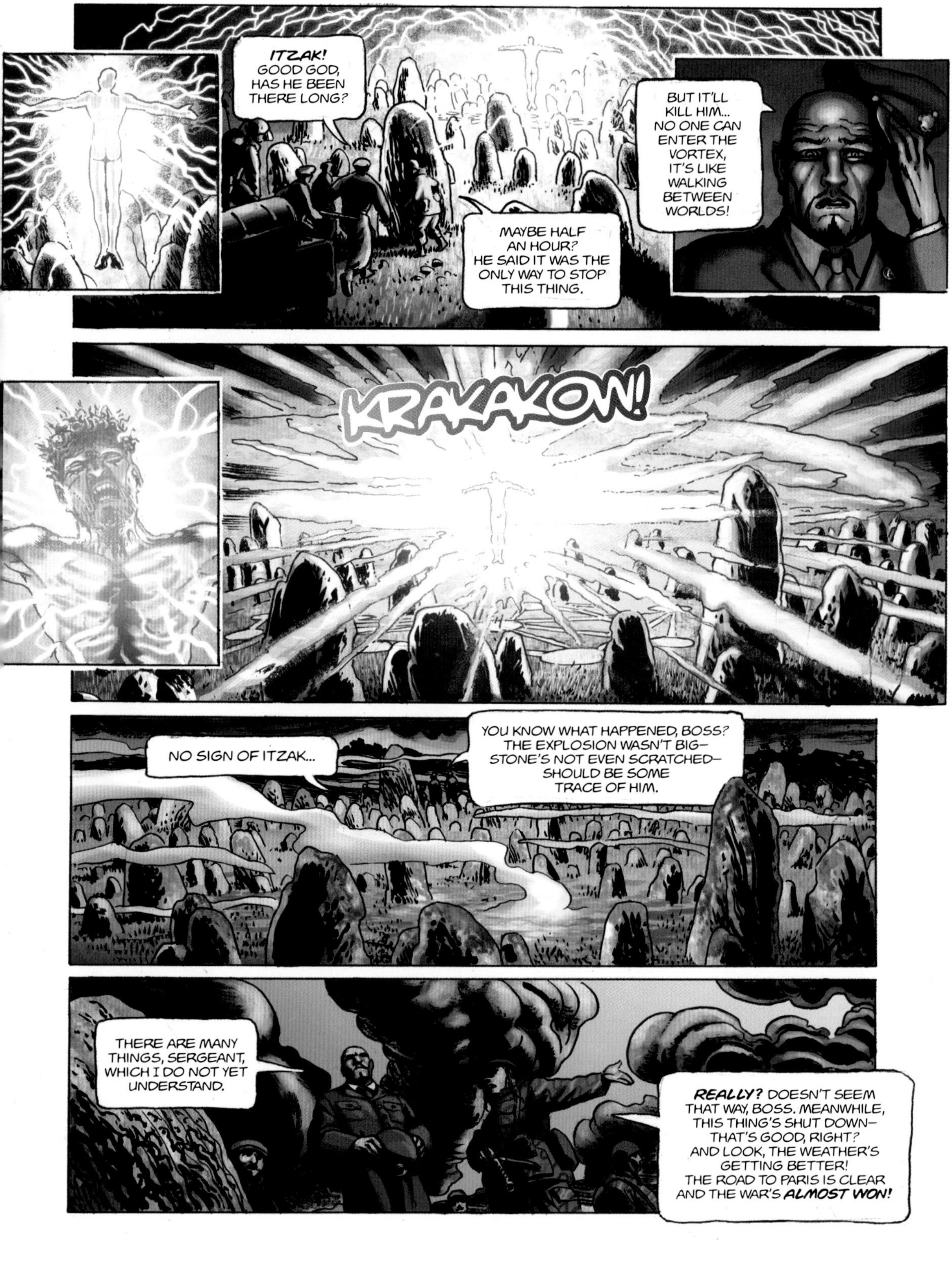
ITZAK! GOOD GOD, HAS HE BEEN THERE LONG?
MAYBE HALF AN HOUR? HE SAID IT WAS THE ONLY WAY TO STOP THIS THING.
BUT IT'LL KILL HIM... NO ONE CAN ENTER THE VORTEX, IT'S LIKE WALKING BETWEEN WORLDS!
KRAKAKOW!
NO SIGN OF ITZAK...
YOU KNOW WHAT HAPPENED, BOSS? THE EXPLOSION WASN'T BIG–STONE'S NOT EVEN SCRATCHED–SHOULD BE SOME TRACE OF HIM.
THERE ARE MANY THINGS, SERGEANT, WHICH I DO NOT YET UNDERSTAND.
REALLY? DOESN'T SEEM THAT WAY, BOSS. MEANWHILE, THIS THING'S SHUT DOWN–THAT'S GOOD, RIGHT? AND LOOK, THE WEATHER'S GETTING BETTER! THE ROAD TO PARIS IS CLEAR AND THE WAR'S ALMOST WON!

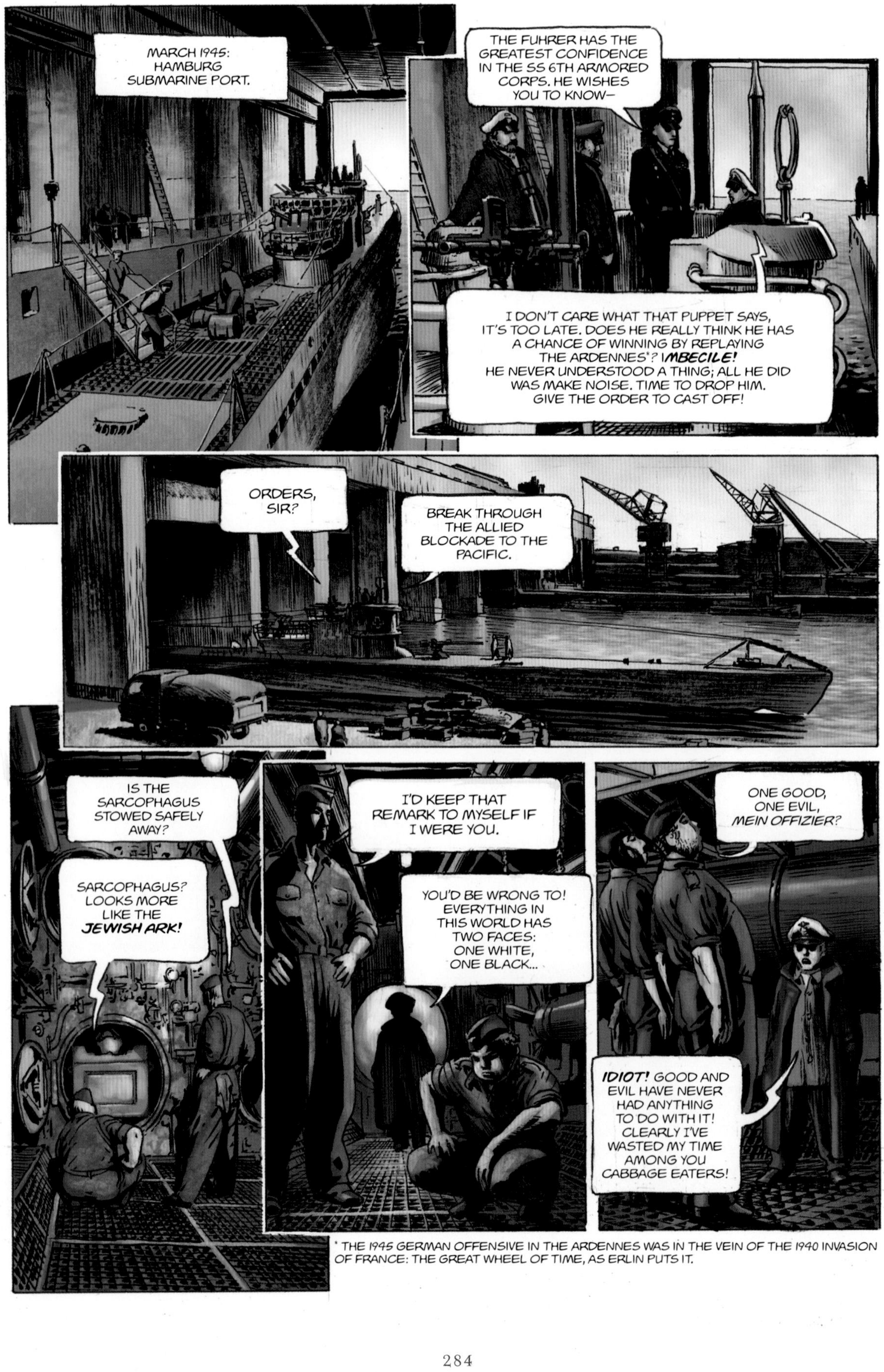
MARCH 1945: HAMBURG SUBMARINE PORT.
THE FUHRER HAS THE GREATEST CONFIDENCE IN THE SS 6TH ARMORED CORPS. HE WISHES YOU TO KNOW—
I DON'T CARE WHAT THAT PUPPET SAYS, IT'S TOO LATE. DOES HE REALLY THINK HE HAS A CHANCE OF WINNING BY REPLAYING THE ARDENNES*? IMBECILE! HE NEVER UNDERSTOOD A THING; ALL HE DID WAS MAKE NOISE. TIME TO DROP HIM. GIVE THE ORDER TO CAST OFF!
ORDERS, SIR?
BREAK THROUGH THE ALLIED BLOCKADE TO THE PACIFIC.
IS THE SARCOPHAGUS STOWED SAFELY AWAY?
SARCOPHAGUS? LOOKS MORE LIKE THE JEWISH ARK!
I'D KEEP THAT REMARK TO MYSELF IF I WERE YOU.
YOU'D BE WRONG TO! EVERYTHING IN THIS WORLD HAS TWO FACES: ONE WHITE, ONE BLACK...
ONE GOOD, ONE EVIL, MEIN OFFIZIER?
IDIOT! GOOD AND EVIL HAVE NEVER HAD ANYTHING TO DO WITH IT! CLEARLY I'VE WASTED MY TIME AMONG YOU CABBAGE EATERS!

* THE 1945 GERMAN OFFENSIVE IN THE ARDENNES WAS IN THE VEIN OF THE 1940 INVASION OF FRANCE: THE GREAT WHEEL OF TIME, AS ERLIN PUTS IT.

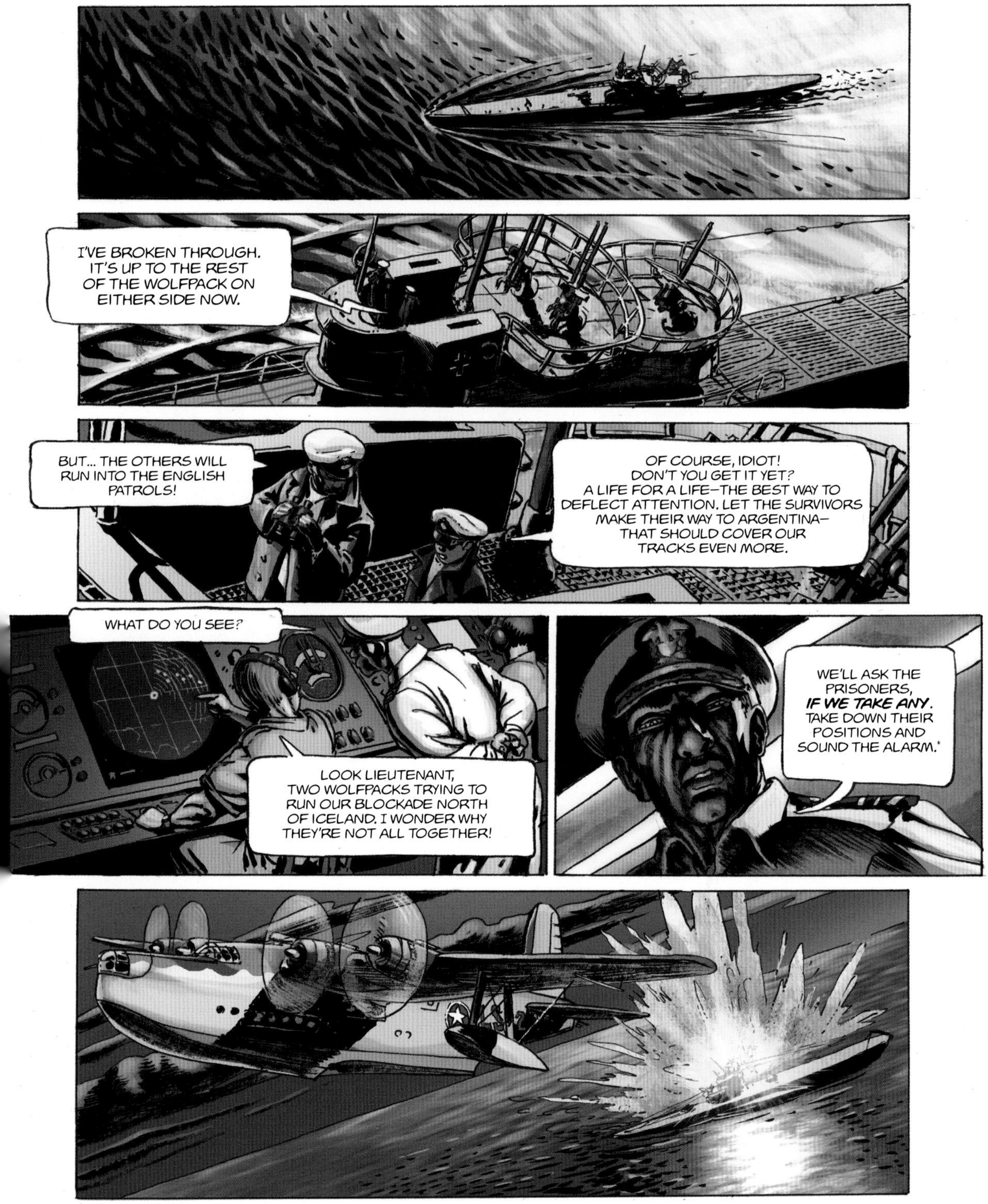
I'VE BROKEN THROUGH. IT'S UP TO THE REST OF THE WOLFPACK ON EITHER SIDE NOW.
BUT... THE OTHERS WILL RUN INTO THE ENGLISH PATROLS!
OF COURSE, IDIOT! DON'T YOU GET IT YET? A LIFE FOR A LIFE—THE BEST WAY TO DEFLECT ATTENTION. LET THE SURVIVORS MAKE THEIR WAY TO ARGENTINA—THAT SHOULD COVER OUR TRACKS EVEN MORE.
WHAT DO YOU SEE?
LOOK LIEUTENANT, TWO WOLFPACKS TRYING TO RUN OUR BLOCKADE NORTH OF ICELAND. I WONDER WHY THEY'RE NOT ALL TOGETHER!
WE'LL ASK THE PRISONERS, **IF WE TAKE ANY.** TAKE DOWN THEIR POSITIONS AND SOUND THE ALARM.*

* TO THIS DAY, NO EXPLANATION EXISTS AS TO WHY 95% OF THE FINAL U-BOAT FORAYS ON THE EVE OF THE ARMISTICE WERE SUNK IN THE NORTH SEA.

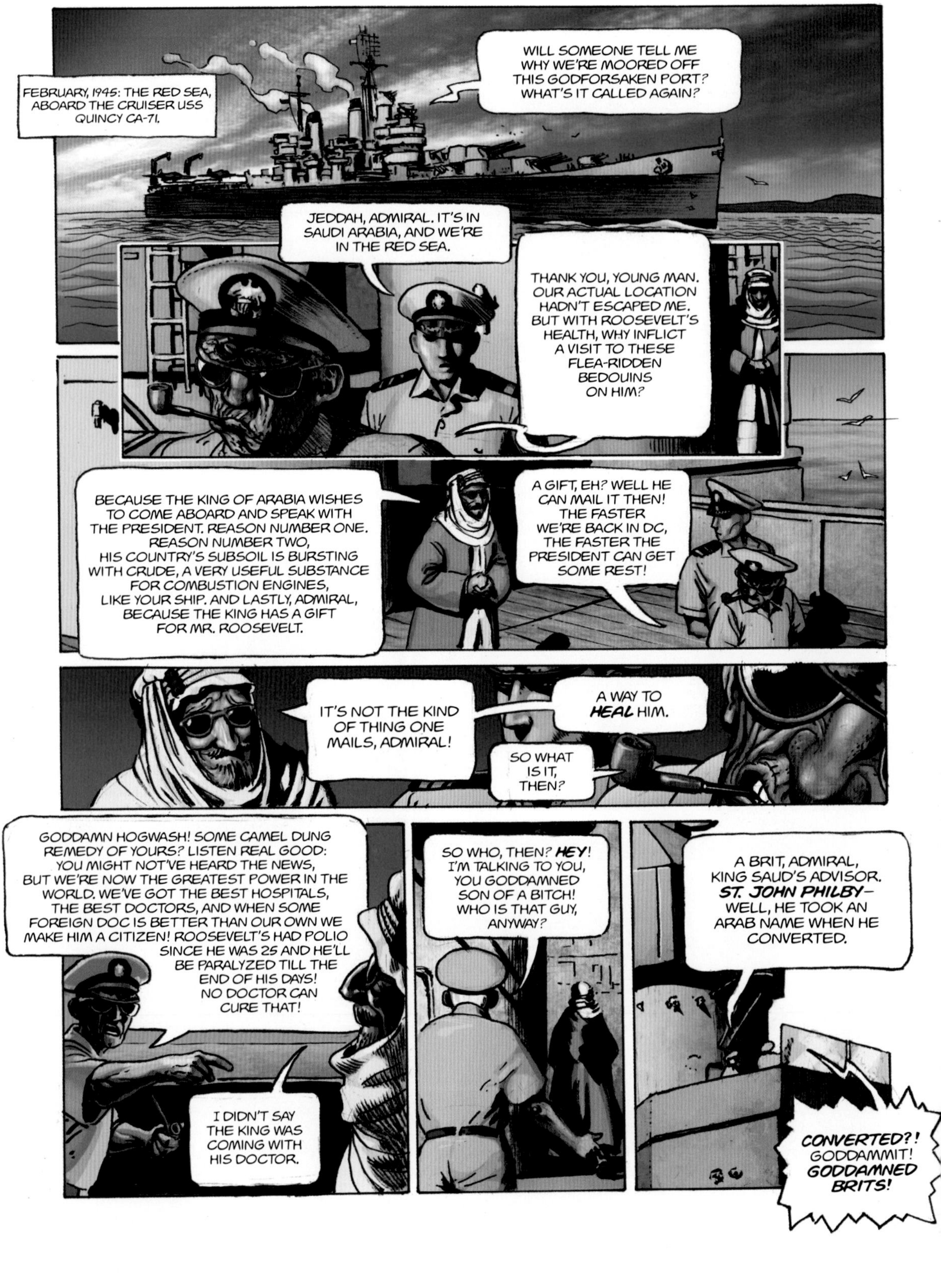
FEBRUARY, 1945: THE RED SEA, ABOARD THE CRUISER USS QUINCY CA-71.
WILL SOMEONE TELL ME WHY WE'RE MOORED OFF THIS GODFORSAKEN PORT? WHAT'S IT CALLED AGAIN?
JEDDAH, ADMIRAL. IT'S IN SAUDI ARABIA, AND WE'RE IN THE RED SEA.
THANK YOU, YOUNG MAN. OUR ACTUAL LOCATION HADN'T ESCAPED ME. BUT WITH ROOSEVELT'S HEALTH, WHY INFLICT A VISIT TO THESE FLEA-RIDDEN BEDOUINS ON HIM?
BECAUSE THE KING OF ARABIA WISHES TO COME ABOARD AND SPEAK WITH THE PRESIDENT. REASON NUMBER ONE. REASON NUMBER TWO, HIS COUNTRY'S SUBSOIL IS BURSTING WITH CRUDE, A VERY USEFUL SUBSTANCE FOR COMBUSTION ENGINES, LIKE YOUR SHIP. AND LASTLY, ADMIRAL, BECAUSE THE KING HAS A GIFT FOR MR. ROOSEVELT.
A GIFT, EH? WELL HE CAN MAIL IT THEN! THE FASTER WE'RE BACK IN DC, THE FASTER THE PRESIDENT CAN GET SOME REST!
IT'S NOT THE KIND OF THING ONE MAILS, ADMIRAL!
SO WHAT IS IT, THEN?
A WAY TO **HEAL** HIM.
GODDAMN HOGWASH! SOME CAMEL DUNG REMEDY OF YOURS? LISTEN REAL GOOD: YOU MIGHT NOT'VE HEARD THE NEWS, BUT WE'RE NOW THE GREATEST POWER IN THE WORLD. WE'VE GOT THE BEST HOSPITALS, THE BEST DOCTORS, AND WHEN SOME FOREIGN DOC IS BETTER THAN OUR OWN WE MAKE HIM A CITIZEN! ROOSEVELT'S HAD POLIO SINCE HE WAS 25 AND HE'LL BE PARALYZED TILL THE END OF HIS DAYS! NO DOCTOR CAN CURE THAT!
I DIDN'T SAY THE KING WAS COMING WITH HIS DOCTOR.
SO WHO, THEN? **HEY**! I'M TALKING TO YOU, YOU GODDAMNED SON OF A BITCH! WHO IS THAT GUY, ANYWAY?
A BRIT, ADMIRAL, KING SAUD'S ADVISOR. **ST. JOHN PHILBY**– WELL, HE TOOK AN ARAB NAME WHEN HE CONVERTED.
CONVERTED?! GODDAMMIT! **GODDAMNED BRITS!**

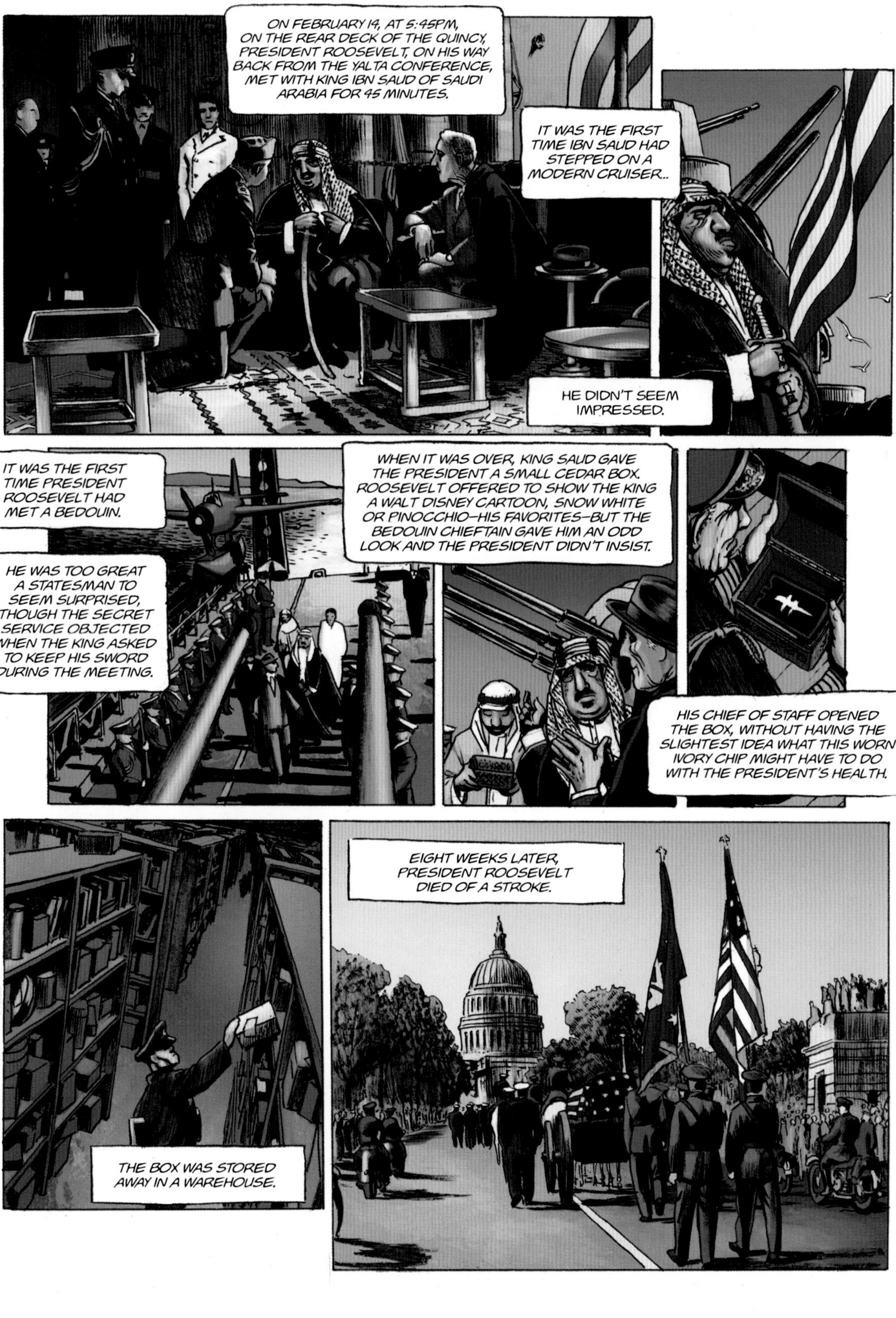
ON FEBRUARY 14, AT 5:45PM, ON THE REAR DECK OF THE QUINCY, PRESIDENT ROOSEVELT, ON HIS WAY BACK FROM THE YALTA CONFERENCE, MET WITH KING IBN SAUD OF SAUDI ARABIA FOR 45 MINUTES.
IT WAS THE FIRST TIME IBN SAUD HAD STEPPED ON A MODERN CRUISER...
HE DIDN'T SEEM IMPRESSED.
IT WAS THE FIRST TIME PRESIDENT ROOSEVELT HAD MET A BEDOUIN.
HE WAS TOO GREAT A STATESMAN TO SEEM SURPRISED, THOUGH THE SECRET SERVICE OBJECTED WHEN THE KING ASKED TO KEEP HIS SWORD DURING THE MEETING.
WHEN IT WAS OVER, KING SAUD GAVE THE PRESIDENT A SMALL CEDAR BOX. ROOSEVELT OFFERED TO SHOW THE KING A WALT DISNEY CARTOON, SNOW WHITE OR PINOCCHIO—HIS FAVORITES—BUT THE BEDOUIN CHIEFTAIN GAVE HIM AN ODD LOOK AND THE PRESIDENT DIDN'T INSIST.
HIS CHIEF OF STAFF OPENED THE BOX, WITHOUT HAVING THE SLIGHTEST IDEA WHAT THIS WORN IVORY CHIP MIGHT HAVE TO DO WITH THE PRESIDENT'S HEALTH.
THE BOX WAS STORED AWAY IN A WAREHOUSE.
EIGHT WEEKS LATER, PRESIDENT ROOSEVELT DIED OF A STROKE.

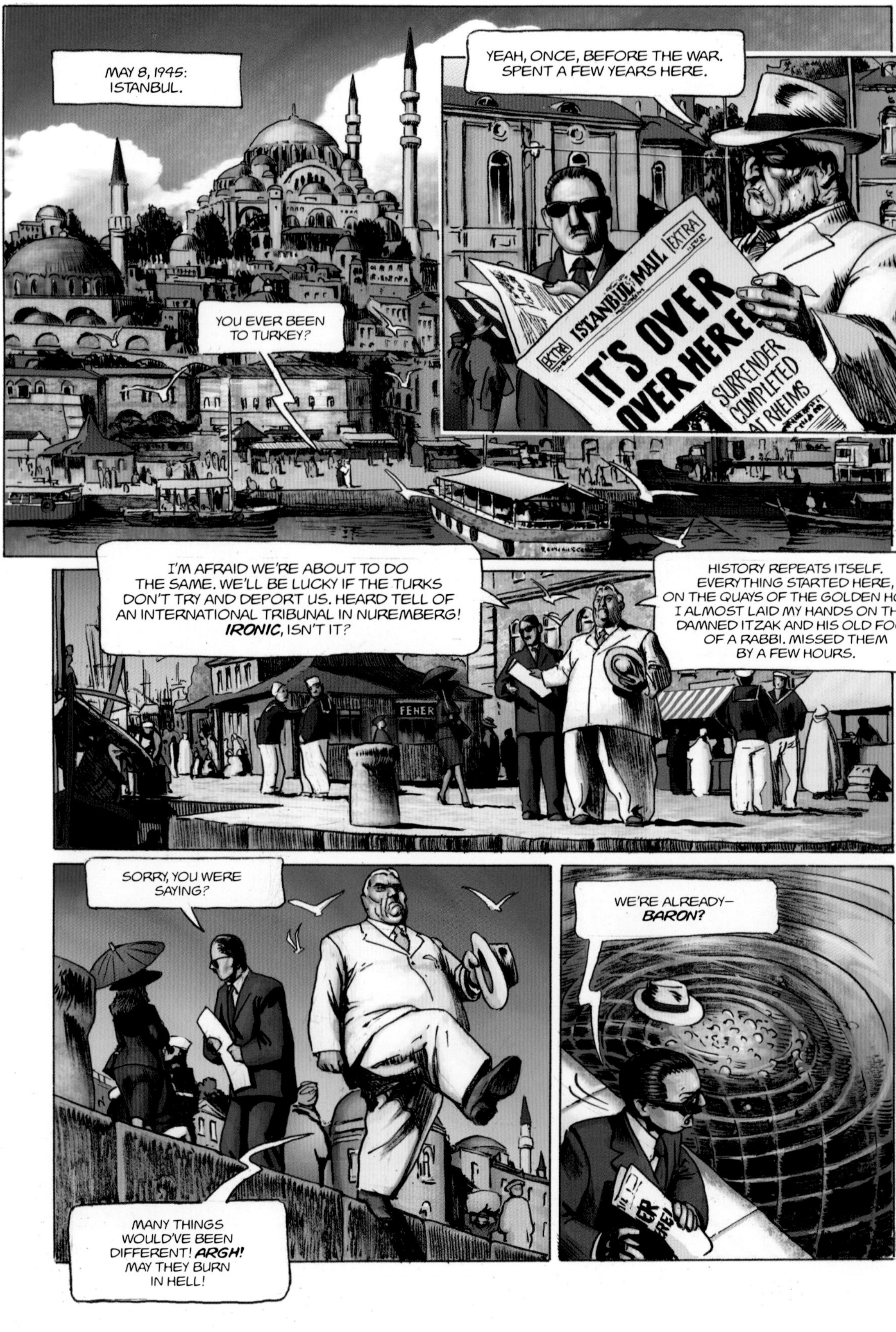
MAY 8, 1945: ISTANBUL.
YOU EVER BEEN TO TURKEY?
YEAH, ONCE, BEFORE THE WAR. SPENT A FEW YEARS HERE.
ISTANBUL MAIL
EXTRA
IT'S OVER OVER HERE!
SURRENDER COMPLETED AT RHEIMS
I'M AFRAID WE'RE ABOUT TO DO THE SAME. WE'LL BE LUCKY IF THE TURKS DON'T TRY AND DEPORT US. HEARD TELL OF AN INTERNATIONAL TRIBUNAL IN NUREMBERG! IRONIC, ISN'T IT?
HISTORY REPEATS ITSELF. EVERYTHING STARTED HERE, ON THE QUAYS OF THE GOLDEN HORN. I ALMOST LAID MY HANDS ON THAT DAMNED ITZAK AND HIS OLD FOOL OF A RABBI. MISSED THEM BY A FEW HOURS.
FENER
SORRY, YOU WERE SAYING?
MANY THINGS WOULD'VE BEEN DIFFERENT! ARGH! MAY THEY BURN IN HELL!
WE'RE ALREADY— BARON?

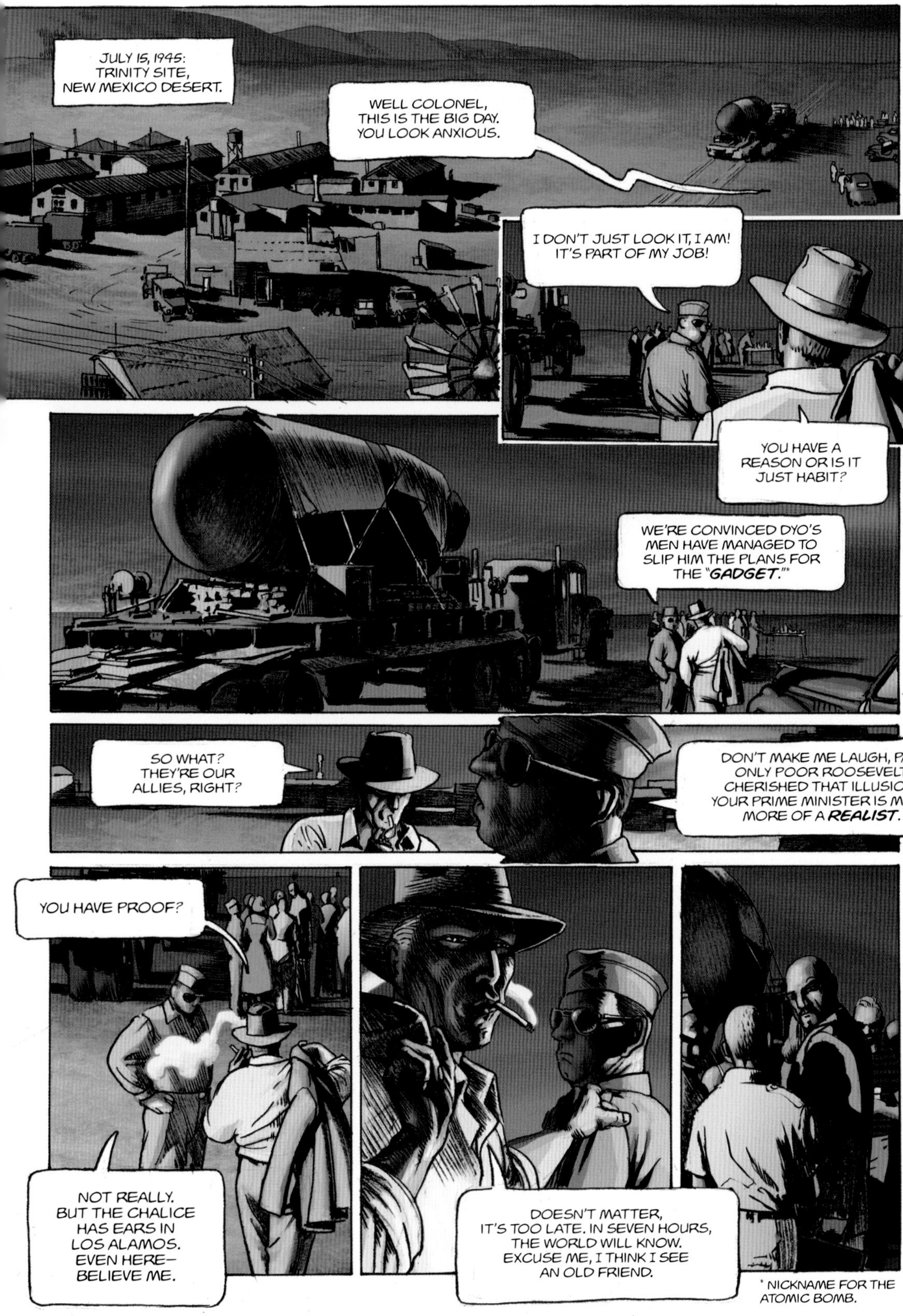
JULY 15, 1945: TRINITY SITE, NEW MEXICO DESERT.
WELL COLONEL, THIS IS THE BIG DAY. YOU LOOK ANXIOUS.
I DON'T JUST LOOK IT, I AM! IT'S PART OF MY JOB!
YOU HAVE A REASON OR IS IT JUST HABIT?
WE'RE CONVINCED DYO'S MEN HAVE MANAGED TO SLIP HIM THE PLANS FOR THE "GADGET."*
SO WHAT? THEY'RE OUR ALLIES, RIGHT?
DON'T MAKE ME LAUGH, PAL. ONLY POOR ROOSEVELT CHERISHED THAT ILLUSION. YOUR PRIME MINISTER IS MUCH MORE OF A REALIST.
YOU HAVE PROOF?
NOT REALLY. BUT THE CHALICE HAS EARS IN LOS ALAMOS. EVEN HERE— BELIEVE ME.
DOESN'T MATTER, IT'S TOO LATE. IN SEVEN HOURS, THE WORLD WILL KNOW. EXCUSE ME, I THINK I SEE AN OLD FRIEND.

* NICKNAME FOR THE ATOMIC BOMB.

YOU COME FOR THE FIREWORKS?

PRECISELY. EVEN BROUGHT A FEW OF MY OWN.

TWO RUNESTONES? NO EXPENSE SPARED, EH!

ONE FROM EACH HOUSE. IF THE GADGET CAN REALLY ACTIVATE THEM, OPPENHEIMER WILL HAVE WON HIS BET.

THAT'S RIGHT. ONLY AN ARCHON CAN ACTIVATE A RUNESTONE. REMEMBER PRAGUE? THAT'S WHY IF THIS EXPERIMENT WORKS, WE'LL HAVE WON THE WAR!

NO ONE'S EVER ACTIVATED TWO AT ONCE, ESPECIALLY WITHOUT AN ARCHON AROUND.

HELLO ROBERT*. EVERYTHING IN PLACE?

EVERYTHING WE WERE ABLE TO CALCULATE IS. THE REST REMAINS A *MYSTERY*.

* ROBERT OPPENHEIMER (1904-1967), AMERICAN PHYSICIST, CONSIDERED THE FATHER OF THE ATOMIC BOMB.

ARE YOU THE SCIENTIST WHO'S SUPPOSED TO EXPLAIN IT ALL?

MY FRIEND, NO SCIENTIST IN THE WORLD HAS THE FAINTEST IDEA WHAT PHENOMENON THE EXPLOSION OF THE GADGET ON THE TWO RUNESTONES WILL UNLEASH. SOME OF MY COLLEAGUES THINK SO MUCH ENERGY WILL BE RELEASED THAT THE *AIR WILL BURST INTO FLAMES* AND NO ONE WILL BE ABLE TO CONTROL IT.

OTHERS THINK THE WHOLE THING WILL DRIVE INTO THE GROUND AND MAKE A HOLE ALL THE WAY TO OUR GOOD OLD EARTH'S CORE. STILL OTHERS THINK NOTHING WILL HAPPEN AT ALL!

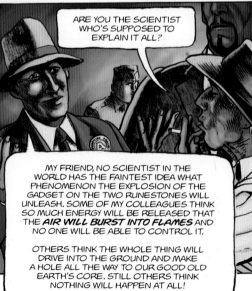

BUNCH OF *PHONIES!*

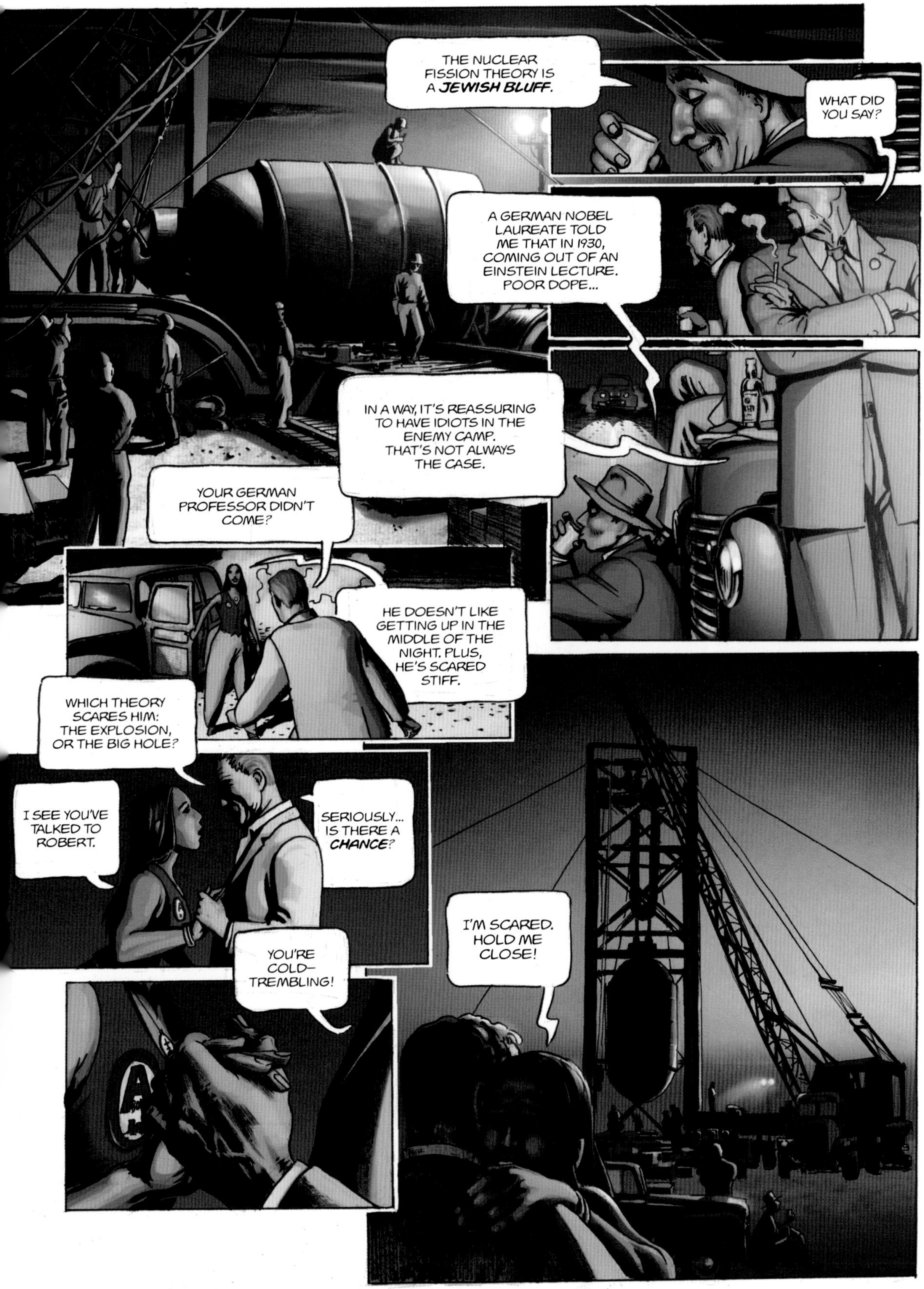
THE NUCLEAR FISSION THEORY IS A JEWISH BLUFF.
WHAT DID YOU SAY?
A GERMAN NOBEL LAUREATE TOLD ME THAT IN 1930, COMING OUT OF AN EINSTEIN LECTURE. POOR DOPE...
IN A WAY, IT'S REASSURING TO HAVE IDIOTS IN THE ENEMY CAMP. THAT'S NOT ALWAYS THE CASE.
YOUR GERMAN PROFESSOR DIDN'T COME?
HE DOESN'T LIKE GETTING UP IN THE MIDDLE OF THE NIGHT. PLUS, HE'S SCARED STIFF.
WHICH THEORY SCARES HIM: THE EXPLOSION, OR THE BIG HOLE?
I SEE YOU'VE TALKED TO ROBERT.
SERIOUSLY... IS THERE A CHANCE?
YOU'RE COLD— TREMBLING!
I'M SCARED. HOLD ME CLOSE!

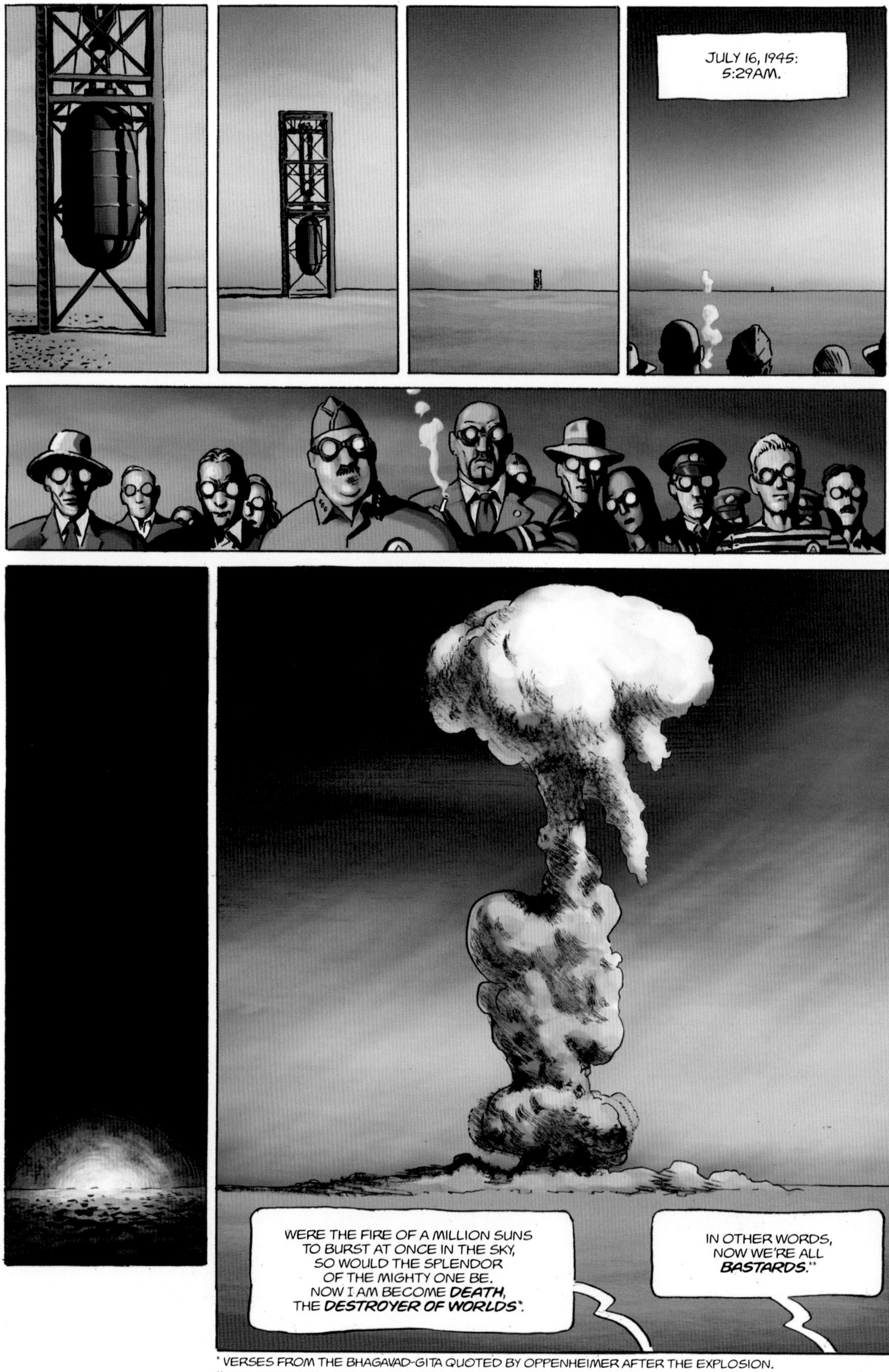
JULY 16, 1945:
5:29AM.
WERE THE FIRE OF A MILLION SUNS TO BURST AT ONCE IN THE SKY, SO WOULD THE SPLENDOR OF THE MIGHTY ONE BE. NOW I AM BECOME DEATH, THE DESTROYER OF WORLDS*.
IN OTHER WORDS, NOW WE'RE ALL BASTARDS.**

* VERSES FROM THE BHAGAVAD-GITA QUOTED BY OPPENHEIMER AFTER THE EXPLOSION.

** ATTRIBUTED TO KENNETH BAINBRIDGE, DIRECTOR OF THE TRINITY TEST.

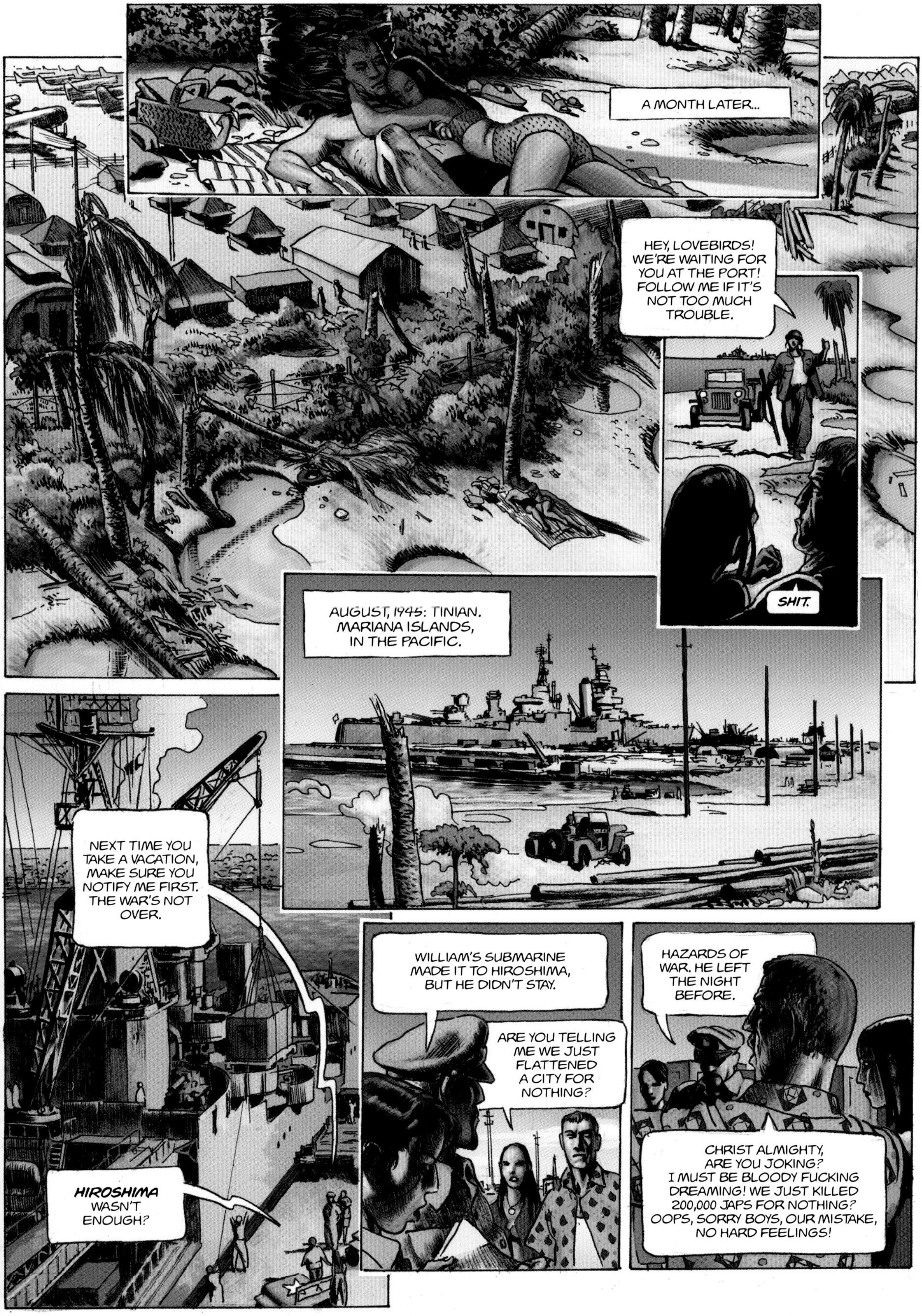
A MONTH LATER...
HEY, LOVEBIRDS! WE'RE WAITING FOR YOU AT THE PORT! FOLLOW ME IF IT'S NOT TOO MUCH TROUBLE.
SHIT.
AUGUST, 1945: TINIAN. MARIANA ISLANDS, IN THE PACIFIC.
NEXT TIME YOU TAKE A VACATION, MAKE SURE YOU NOTIFY ME FIRST. THE WAR'S NOT OVER.
HIROSHIMA WASN'T ENOUGH?
WILLIAM'S SUBMARINE MADE IT TO HIROSHIMA, BUT HE DIDN'T STAY.
ARE YOU TELLING ME WE JUST FLATTENED A CITY FOR NOTHING?
HAZARDS OF WAR. HE LEFT THE NIGHT BEFORE.
CHRIST ALMIGHTY, ARE YOU JOKING? I MUST BE BLOODY FUCKING DREAMING! WE JUST KILLED 200,000 JAPS FOR NOTHING? OOPS, SORRY BOYS, OUR MISTAKE, NO HARD FEELINGS!

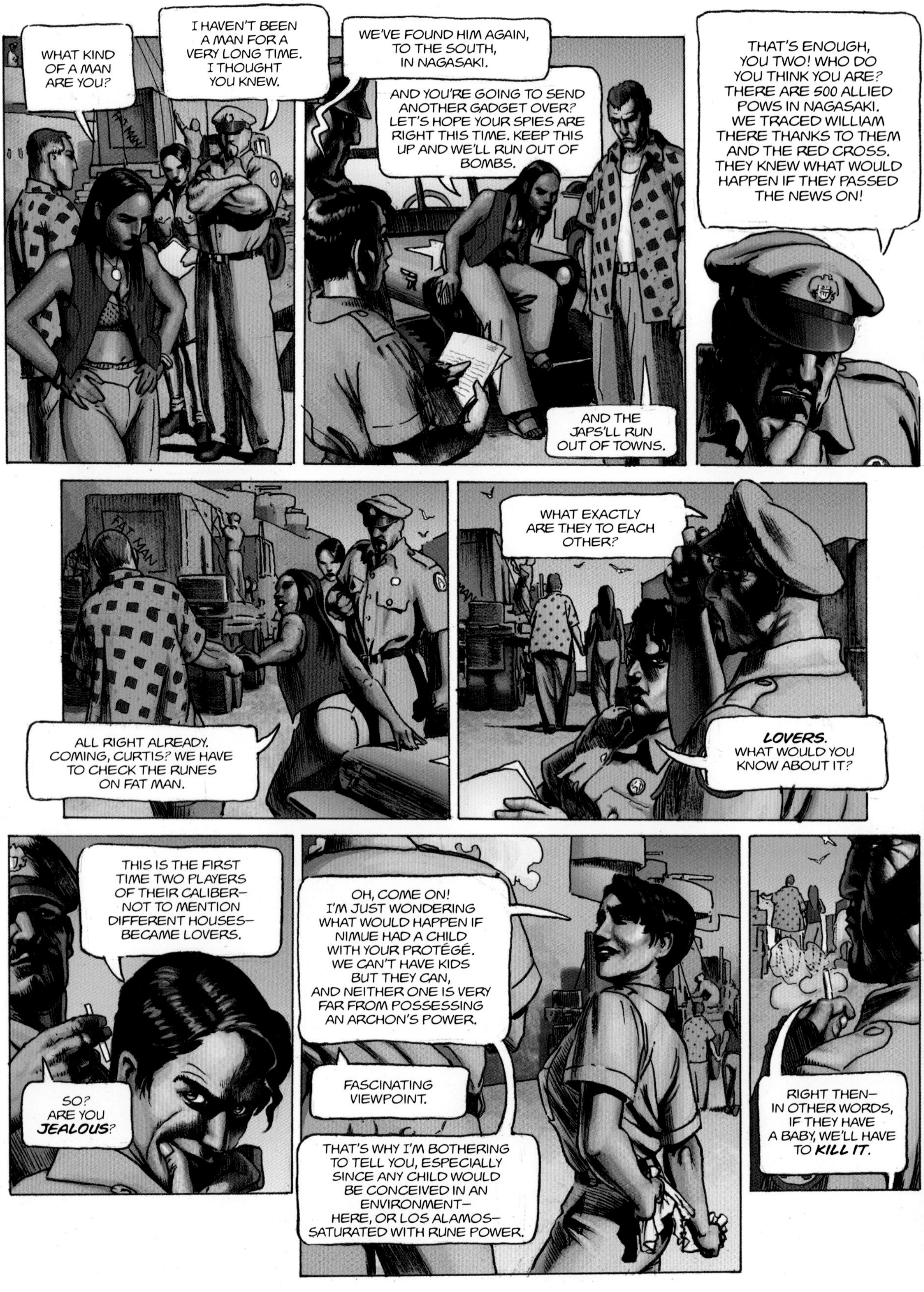
WHAT KIND OF A MAN ARE YOU?
I HAVEN'T BEEN A MAN FOR A VERY LONG TIME. I THOUGHT YOU KNEW.
FAT MAN
WE'VE FOUND HIM AGAIN, TO THE SOUTH, IN NAGASAKI.
AND YOU'RE GOING TO SEND ANOTHER GADGET OVER? LET'S HOPE YOUR SPIES ARE RIGHT THIS TIME. KEEP THIS UP AND WE'LL RUN OUT OF BOMBS.
AND THE JAPS'LL RUN OUT OF TOWNS.
THAT'S ENOUGH, YOU TWO! WHO DO YOU THINK YOU ARE? THERE ARE 500 ALLIED POWS IN NAGASAKI. WE TRACED WILLIAM THERE THANKS TO THEM AND THE RED CROSS. THEY KNEW WHAT WOULD HAPPEN IF THEY PASSED THE NEWS ON!
FAT MAN
ALL RIGHT ALREADY. COMING, CURTIS? WE HAVE TO CHECK THE RUNES ON FAT MAN.
WHAT EXACTLY ARE THEY TO EACH OTHER?
LOVERS. WHAT WOULD YOU KNOW ABOUT IT?
THIS IS THE FIRST TIME TWO PLAYERS OF THEIR CALIBER— NOT TO MENTION DIFFERENT HOUSES— BECAME LOVERS.
SO? ARE YOU **JEALOUS**?
OH, COME ON! I'M JUST WONDERING WHAT WOULD HAPPEN IF NIMUE HAD A CHILD WITH YOUR PROTÉGÉ. WE CAN'T HAVE KIDS BUT THEY CAN, AND NEITHER ONE IS VERY FAR FROM POSSESSING AN ARCHON'S POWER.
FASCINATING VIEWPOINT.
THAT'S WHY I'M BOTHERING TO TELL YOU, ESPECIALLY SINCE ANY CHILD WOULD BE CONCEIVED IN AN ENVIRONMENT— HERE, OR LOS ALAMOS— SATURATED WITH RUNE POWER.
RIGHT THEN— IN OTHER WORDS, IF THEY HAVE A BABY, WE'LL HAVE TO **KILL IT**.

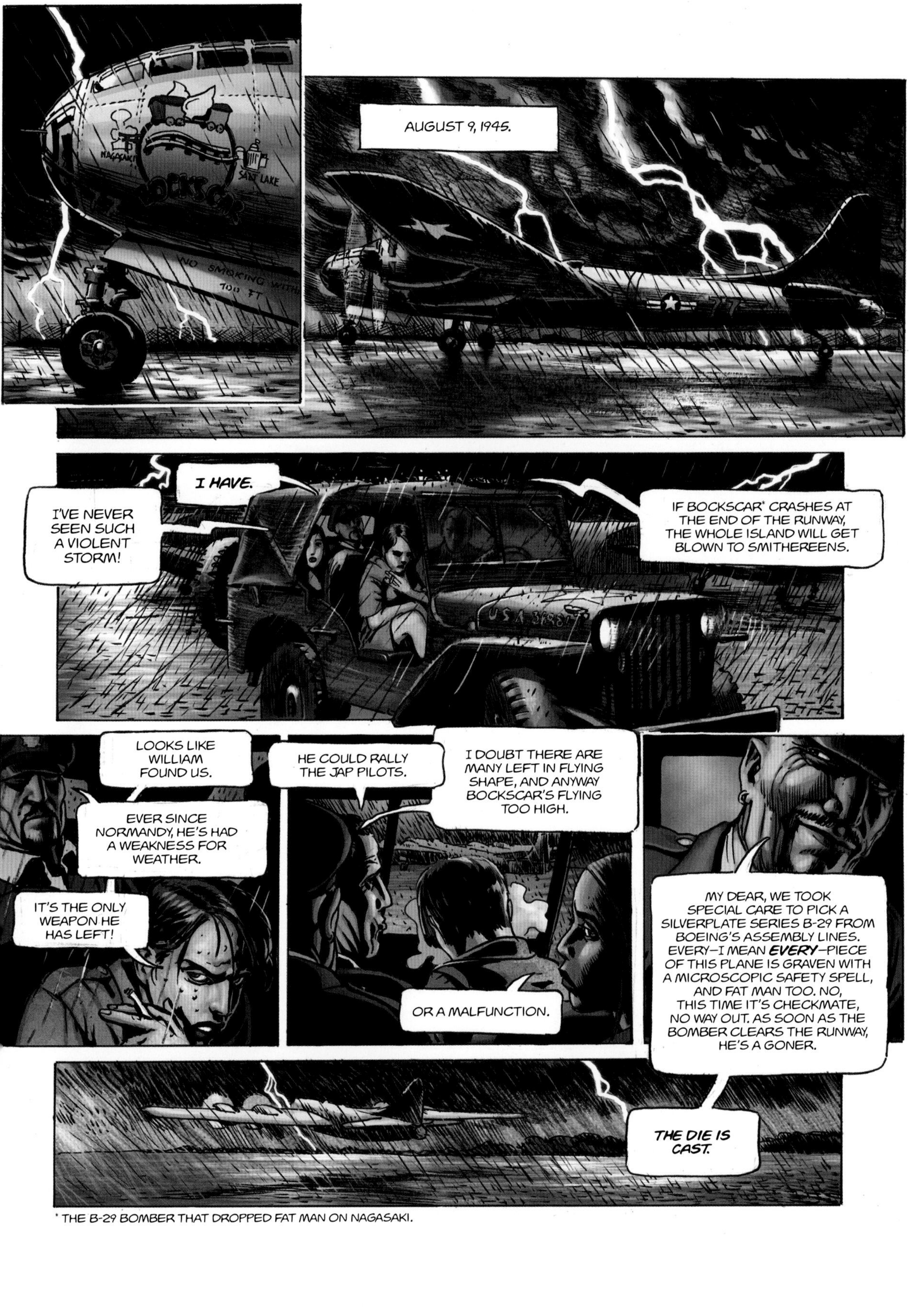
AUGUST 9, 1945.
I'VE NEVER SEEN SUCH A VIOLENT STORM!
I HAVE.
IF BOCKSCAR* CRASHES AT THE END OF THE RUNWAY, THE WHOLE ISLAND WILL GET BLOWN TO SMITHEREENS.
LOOKS LIKE WILLIAM FOUND US.
EVER SINCE NORMANDY, HE'S HAD A WEAKNESS FOR WEATHER.
IT'S THE ONLY WEAPON HE HAS LEFT!
HE COULD RALLY THE JAP PILOTS.
I DOUBT THERE ARE MANY LEFT IN FLYING SHAPE, AND ANYWAY BOCKSCAR'S FLYING TOO HIGH.
OR A MALFUNCTION.
MY DEAR, WE TOOK SPECIAL CARE TO PICK A SILVERPLATE SERIES B-29 FROM BOEING'S ASSEMBLY LINES. EVERY—I MEAN EVERY—PIECE OF THIS PLANE IS GRAVEN WITH A MICROSCOPIC SAFETY SPELL, AND FAT MAN TOO. NO, THIS TIME IT'S CHECKMATE, NO WAY OUT. AS SOON AS THE BOMBER CLEARS THE RUNWAY, HE'S A GONER.
THE DIE IS CAST.

* THE B-29 BOMBER THAT DROPPED FAT MAN ON NAGASAKI.

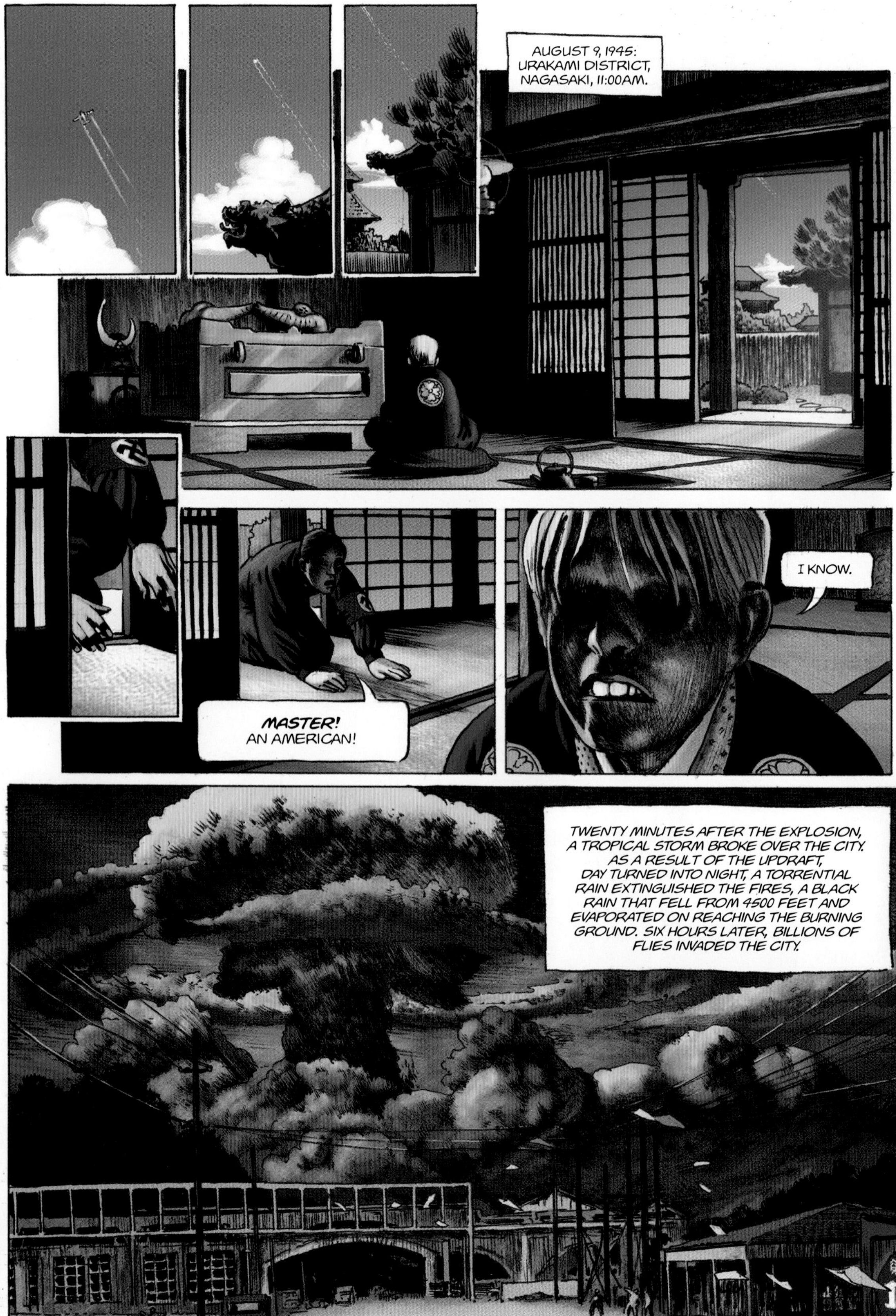
AUGUST 9, 1945: URAKAMI DISTRICT, NAGASAKI, 11:00AM.
MASTER! AN AMERICAN!
I KNOW.
TWENTY MINUTES AFTER THE EXPLOSION, A TROPICAL STORM BROKE OVER THE CITY. AS A RESULT OF THE UPDRAFT, DAY TURNED INTO NIGHT, A TORRENTIAL RAIN EXTINGUISHED THE FIRES, A BLACK RAIN THAT FELL FROM 4500 FEET AND EVAPORATED ON REACHING THE BURNING GROUND. SIX HOURS LATER, BILLIONS OF FLIES INVADED THE CITY.

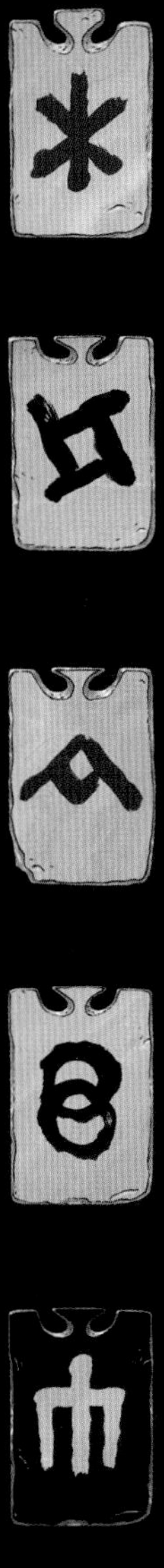

1926 A.D. 1940 A.D. 1942 A.D. 1943 A.D.

1945 A.D.

Book Fourteen
The Watchers
1945 a.d.

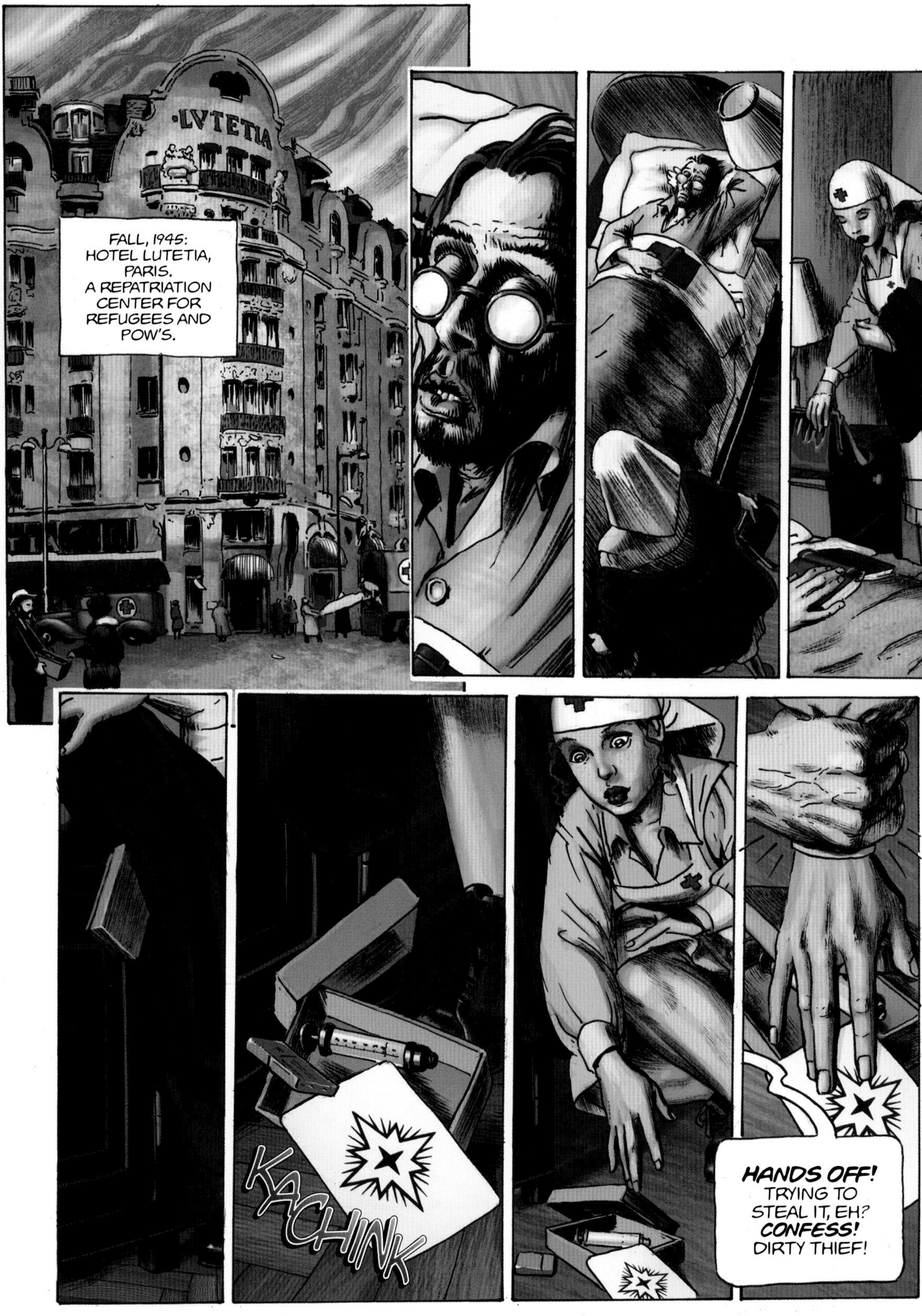
FALL, 1945: HOTEL LUTETIA, PARIS. A REPATRIATION CENTER FOR REFUGEES AND POW'S.
LVTETIA
KACHINK
HANDS OFF! TRYING TO STEAL IT, EH? CONFESS! DIRTY THIEF!

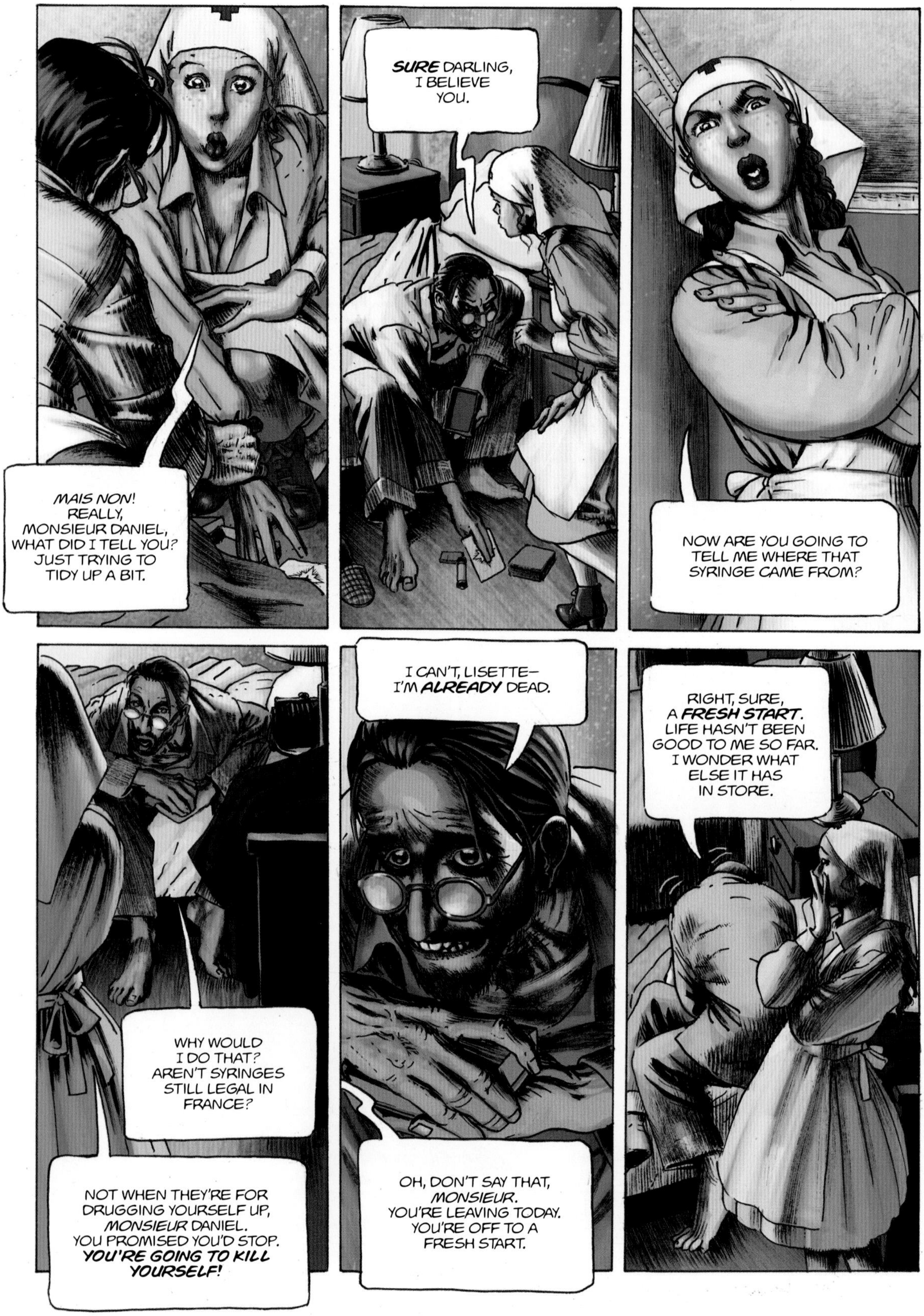
MAIS NON! REALLY, MONSIEUR DANIEL, WHAT DID I TELL YOU? JUST TRYING TO TIDY UP A BIT.
SURE DARLING, I BELIEVE YOU.
NOW ARE YOU GOING TO TELL ME WHERE THAT SYRINGE CAME FROM?
WHY WOULD I DO THAT? AREN'T SYRINGES STILL LEGAL IN FRANCE?
NOT WHEN THEY'RE FOR DRUGGING YOURSELF UP, MONSIEUR DANIEL. YOU PROMISED YOU'D STOP. YOU'RE GOING TO KILL YOURSELF!
I CAN'T, LISETTE— I'M ALREADY DEAD.
OH, DON'T SAY THAT, MONSIEUR. YOU'RE LEAVING TODAY. YOU'RE OFF TO A FRESH START.
RIGHT, SURE, A FRESH START. LIFE HASN'T BEEN GOOD TO ME SO FAR. I WONDER WHAT ELSE IT HAS IN STORE.

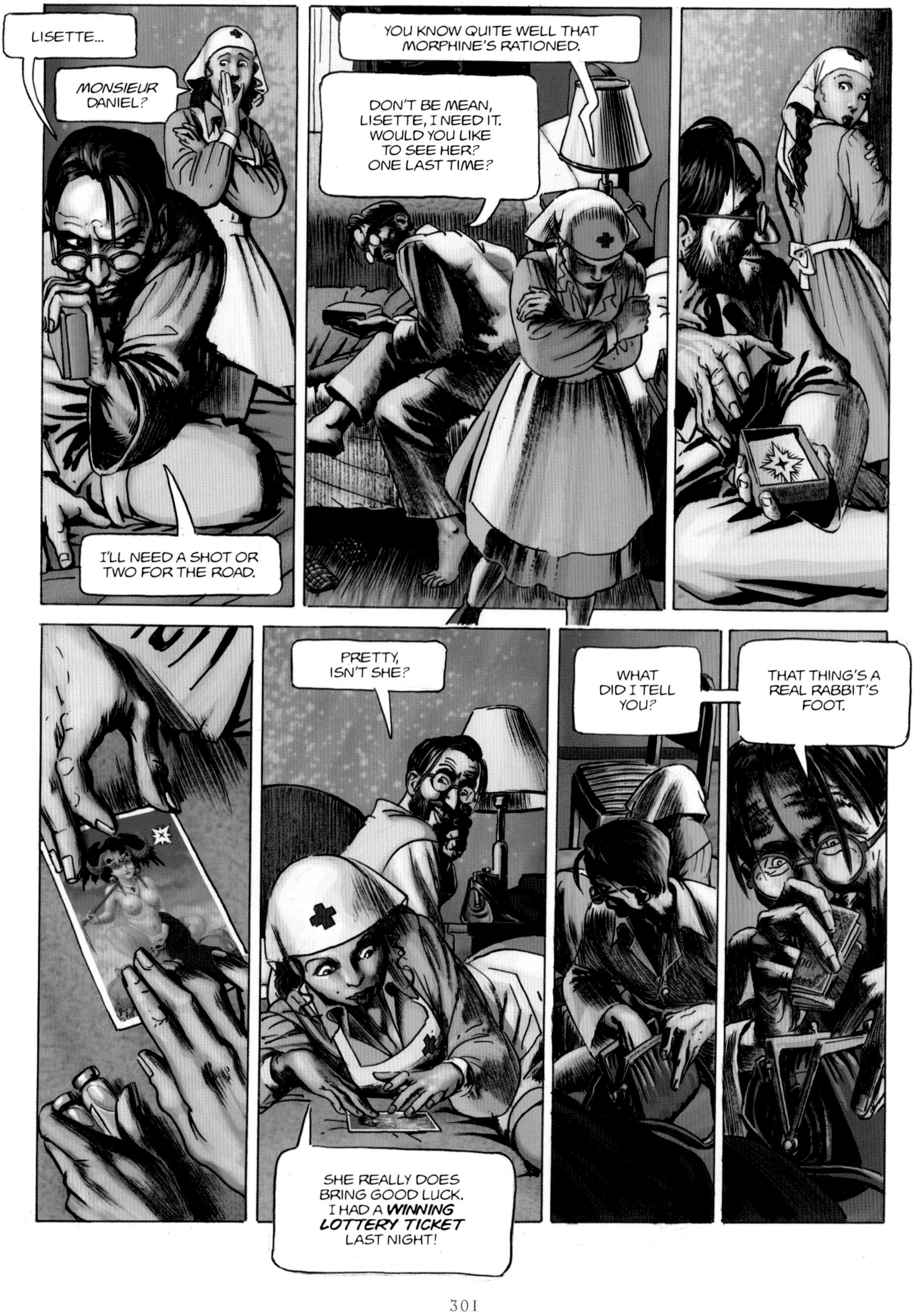
LISETTE...
MONSIEUR DANIEL?
I'LL NEED A SHOT OR TWO FOR THE ROAD.
YOU KNOW QUITE WELL THAT MORPHINE'S RATIONED.
DON'T BE MEAN, LISETTE, I NEED IT. WOULD YOU LIKE TO SEE HER? ONE LAST TIME?
PRETTY, ISN'T SHE?
SHE REALLY DOES BRING GOOD LUCK. I HAD A WINNING LOTTERY TICKET LAST NIGHT!
WHAT DID I TELL YOU?
THAT THING'S A REAL RABBIT'S FOOT.

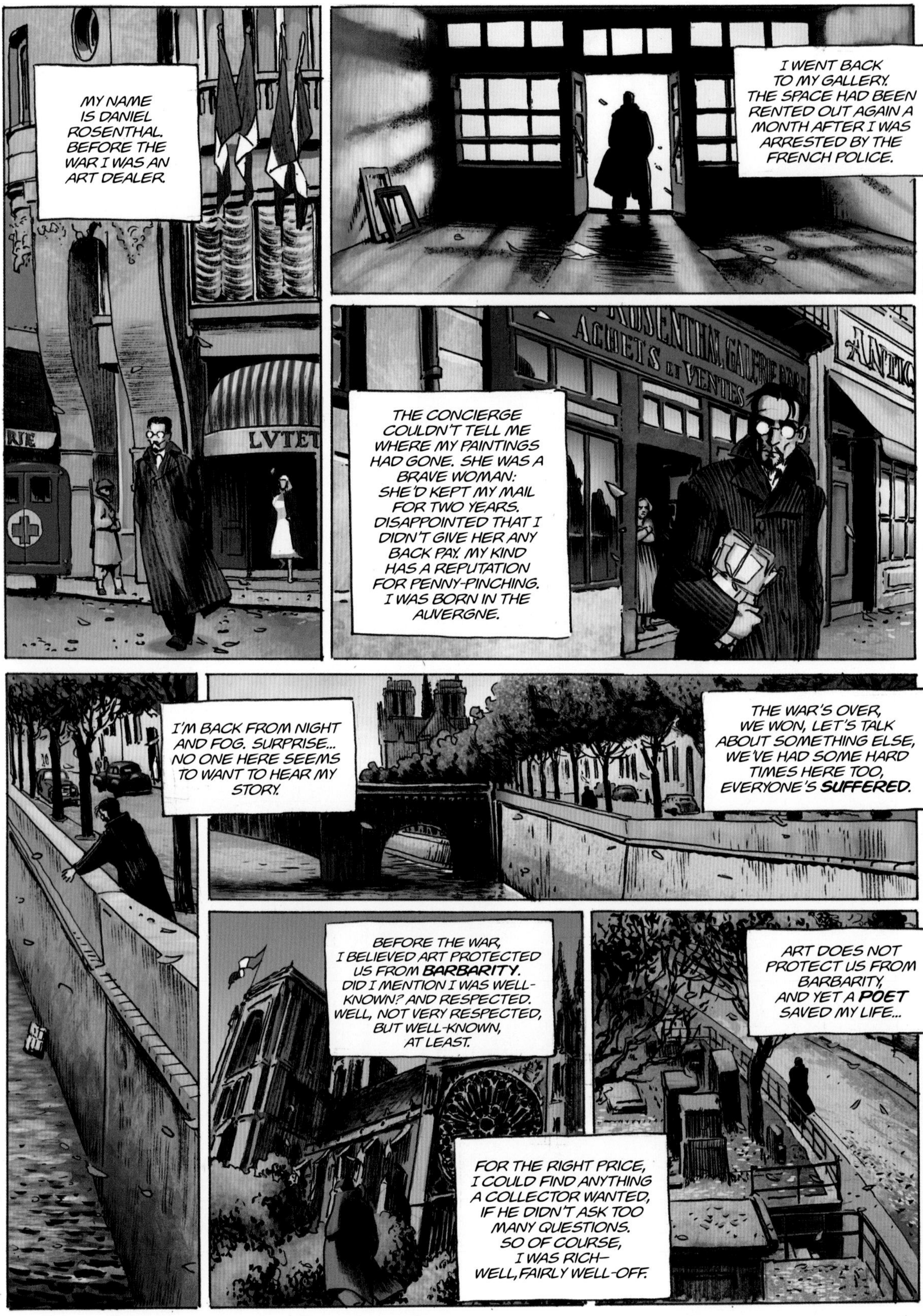
MY NAME IS DANIEL ROSENTHAL. BEFORE THE WAR I WAS AN ART DEALER.
LVTET
I WENT BACK TO MY GALLERY. THE SPACE HAD BEEN RENTED OUT AGAIN A MONTH AFTER I WAS ARRESTED BY THE FRENCH POLICE.
ACHETS ET VENTES
THE CONCIERGE COULDN'T TELL ME WHERE MY PAINTINGS HAD GONE. SHE WAS A BRAVE WOMAN: SHE'D KEPT MY MAIL FOR TWO YEARS. DISAPPOINTED THAT I DIDN'T GIVE HER ANY BACK PAY. MY KIND HAS A REPUTATION FOR PENNY-PINCHING. I WAS BORN IN THE AUVERGNE.
I'M BACK FROM NIGHT AND FOG. SURPRISE... NO ONE HERE SEEMS TO WANT TO HEAR MY STORY.
THE WAR'S OVER, WE WON, LET'S TALK ABOUT SOMETHING ELSE, WE'VE HAD SOME HARD TIMES HERE TOO, EVERYONE'S **SUFFERED**.
BEFORE THE WAR, I BELIEVED ART PROTECTED US FROM **BARBARITY**. DID I MENTION I WAS WELL-KNOWN? AND RESPECTED. WELL, NOT VERY RESPECTED, BUT WELL-KNOWN, AT LEAST.
FOR THE RIGHT PRICE, I COULD FIND ANYTHING A COLLECTOR WANTED, IF HE DIDN'T ASK TOO MANY QUESTIONS. SO OF COURSE, I WAS RICH— WELL, FAIRLY WELL-OFF.
ART DOES NOT PROTECT US FROM BARBARITY, AND YET A **POET** SAVED MY LIFE...

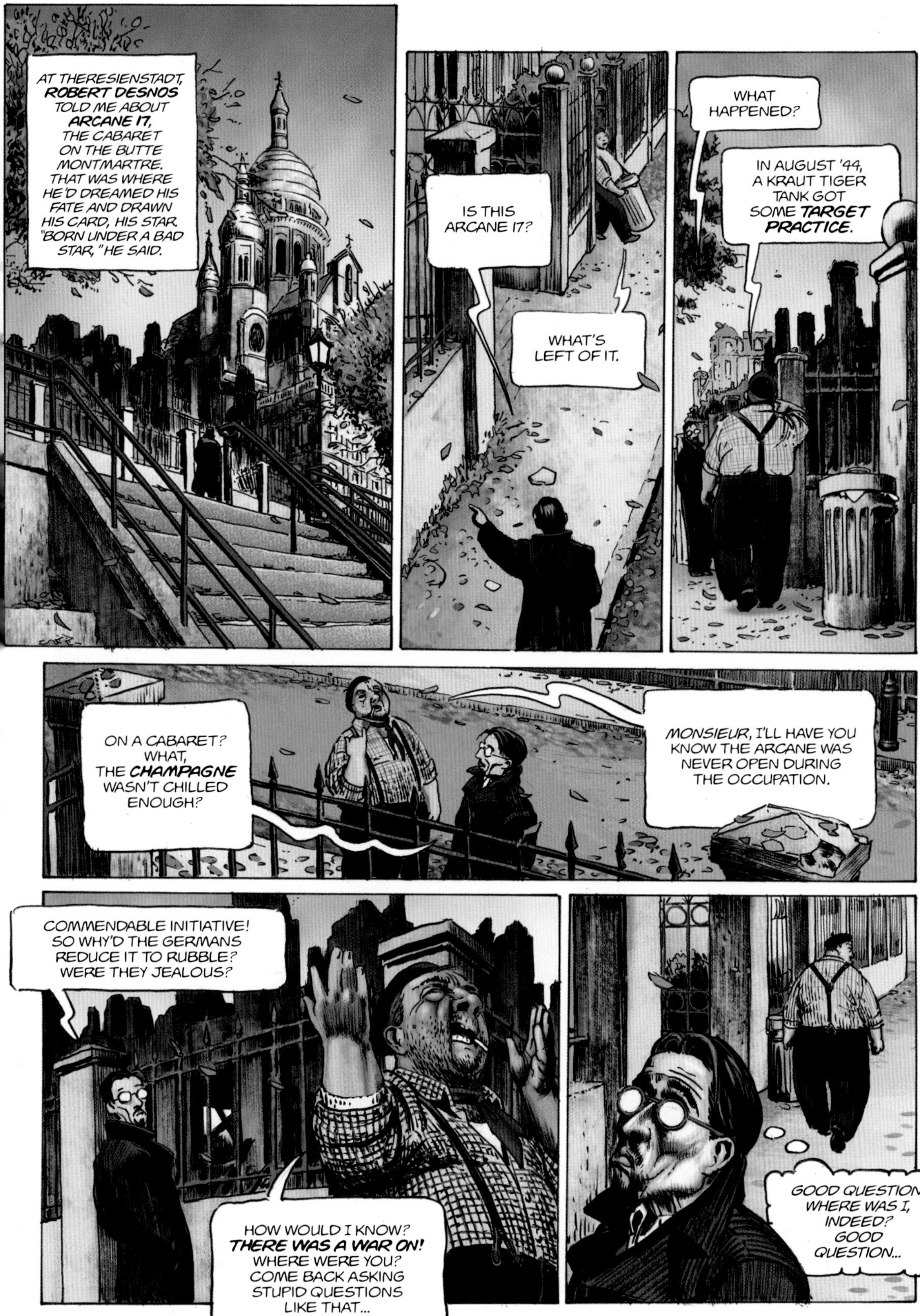
AT THERESIENSTADT, ROBERT DESNOS TOLD ME ABOUT ARCANE 17, THE CABARET ON THE BUTTE MONTMARTRE. THAT WAS WHERE HE'D DREAMED HIS FATE AND DRAWN HIS CARD, HIS STAR. "BORN UNDER A BAD STAR," HE SAID.
IS THIS ARCANE 17?
WHAT'S LEFT OF IT.
WHAT HAPPENED?
IN AUGUST '44, A KRAUT TIGER TANK GOT SOME TARGET PRACTICE.
ON A CABARET? WHAT, THE CHAMPAGNE WASN'T CHILLED ENOUGH?
MONSIEUR, I'LL HAVE YOU KNOW THE ARCANE WAS NEVER OPEN DURING THE OCCUPATION.
COMMENDABLE INITIATIVE! SO WHY'D THE GERMANS REDUCE IT TO RUBBLE? WERE THEY JEALOUS?
HOW WOULD I KNOW? THERE WAS A WAR ON! WHERE WERE YOU? COME BACK ASKING STUPID QUESTIONS LIKE THAT...
GOOD QUESTION. WHERE WAS I, INDEED? GOOD QUESTION...

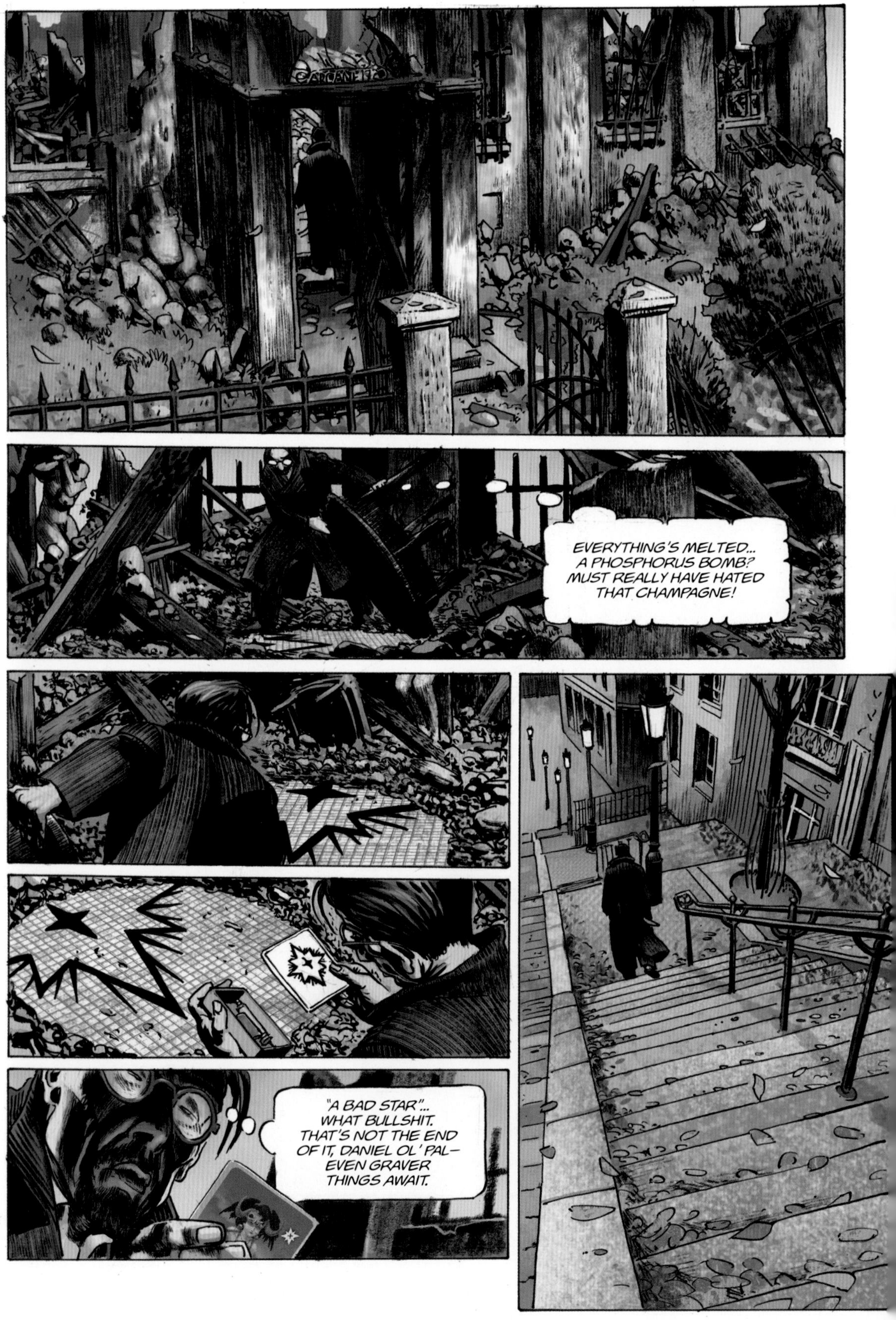
EVERYTHING'S MELTED... A PHOSPHORUS BOMB? MUST REALLY HAVE HATED THAT CHAMPAGNE!
"A BAD STAR"... WHAT BULLSHIT. THAT'S NOT THE END OF IT, DANIEL OL' PAL– EVEN GRAVER THINGS AWAIT.

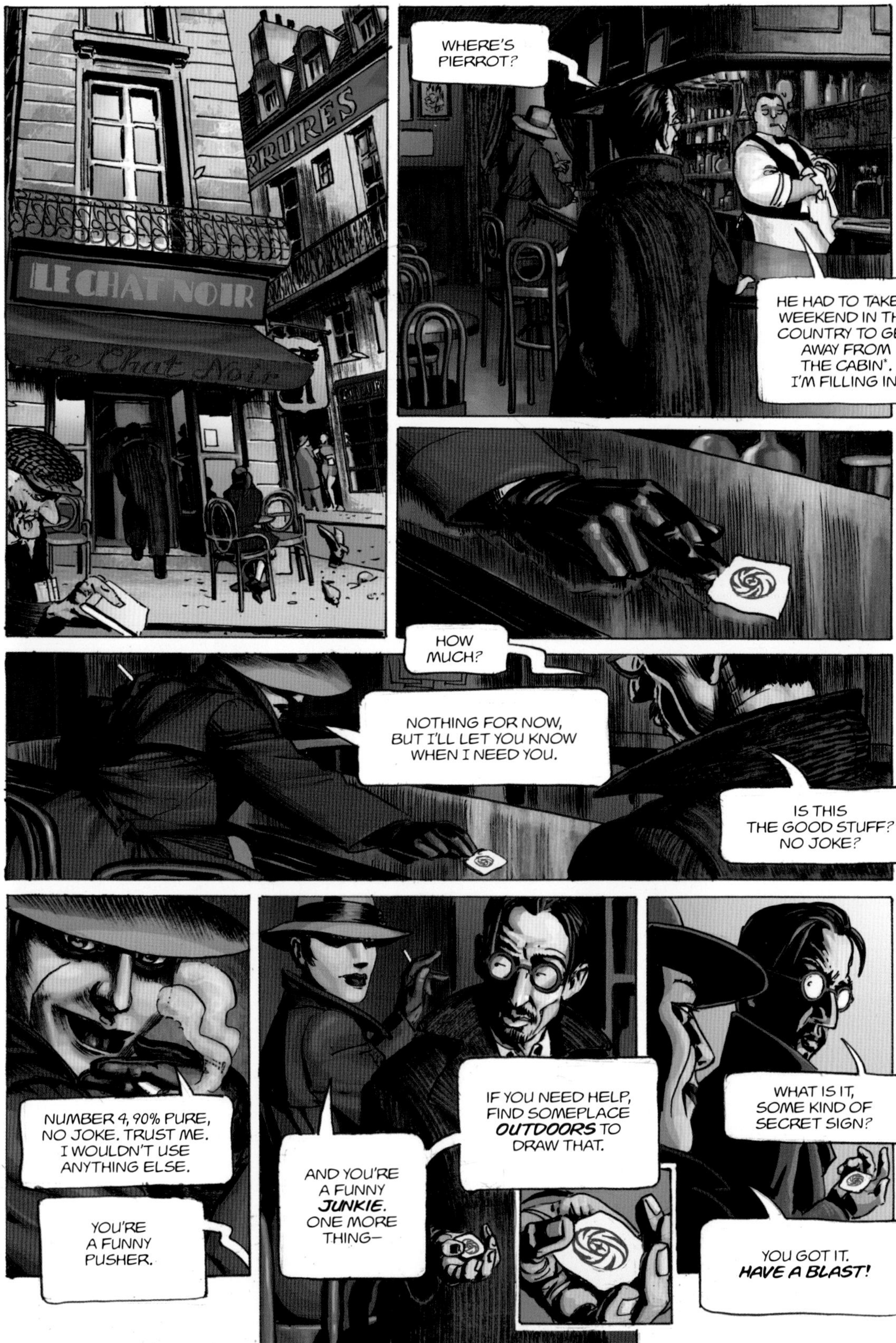
LE CHAT NOIR
Le Chat Noir
RRURES
WHERE'S PIERROT?
HE HAD TO TAKE A WEEKEND IN THE COUNTRY TO GET AWAY FROM THE CABIN*. I'M FILLING IN.
HOW MUCH?
NOTHING FOR NOW, BUT I'LL LET YOU KNOW WHEN I NEED YOU.
IS THIS THE GOOD STUFF? NO JOKE?
NUMBER 4, 90% PURE, NO JOKE. TRUST ME. I WOULDN'T USE ANYTHING ELSE.
YOU'RE A FUNNY PUSHER.
AND YOU'RE A FUNNY ***JUNKIE***. ONE MORE THING—
IF YOU NEED HELP, FIND SOMEPLACE ***OUTDOORS*** TO DRAW THAT.
WHAT IS IT, SOME KIND OF SECRET SIGN?
YOU GOT IT. ***HAVE A BLAST!***

* NICKNAME FOR THE FRENCH GESTAPO.

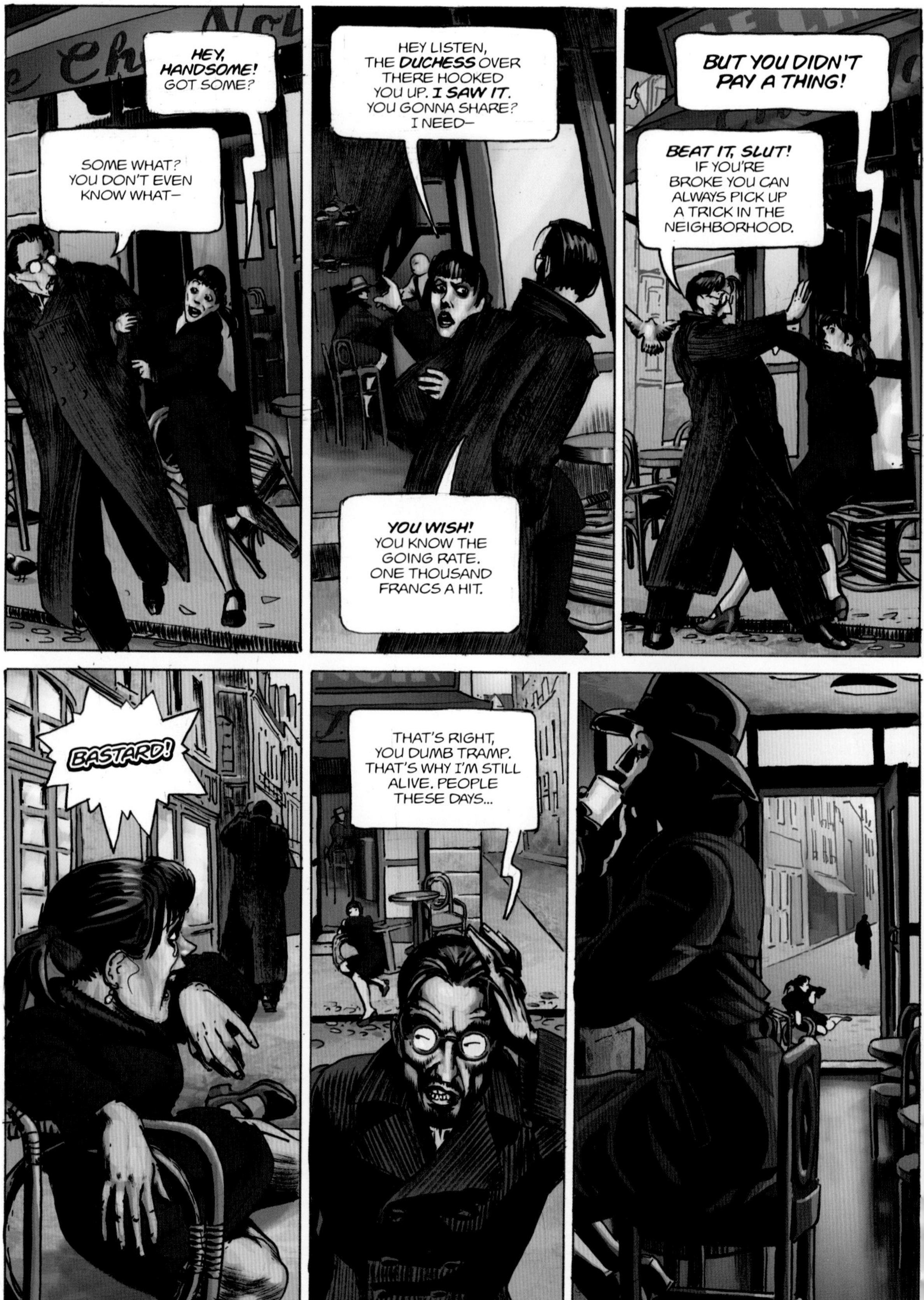
HEY, HANDSOME! GOT SOME?
SOME WHAT? YOU DON'T EVEN KNOW WHAT–
HEY LISTEN, THE DUCHESS OVER THERE HOOKED YOU UP. I SAW IT. YOU GONNA SHARE? I NEED–
YOU WISH! YOU KNOW THE GOING RATE. ONE THOUSAND FRANCS A HIT.
BUT YOU DIDN'T PAY A THING!
BEAT IT, SLUT! IF YOU'RE BROKE YOU CAN ALWAYS PICK UP A TRICK IN THE NEIGHBORHOOD.
BASTARD!
THAT'S RIGHT, YOU DUMB TRAMP. THAT'S WHY I'M STILL ALIVE. PEOPLE THESE DAYS...

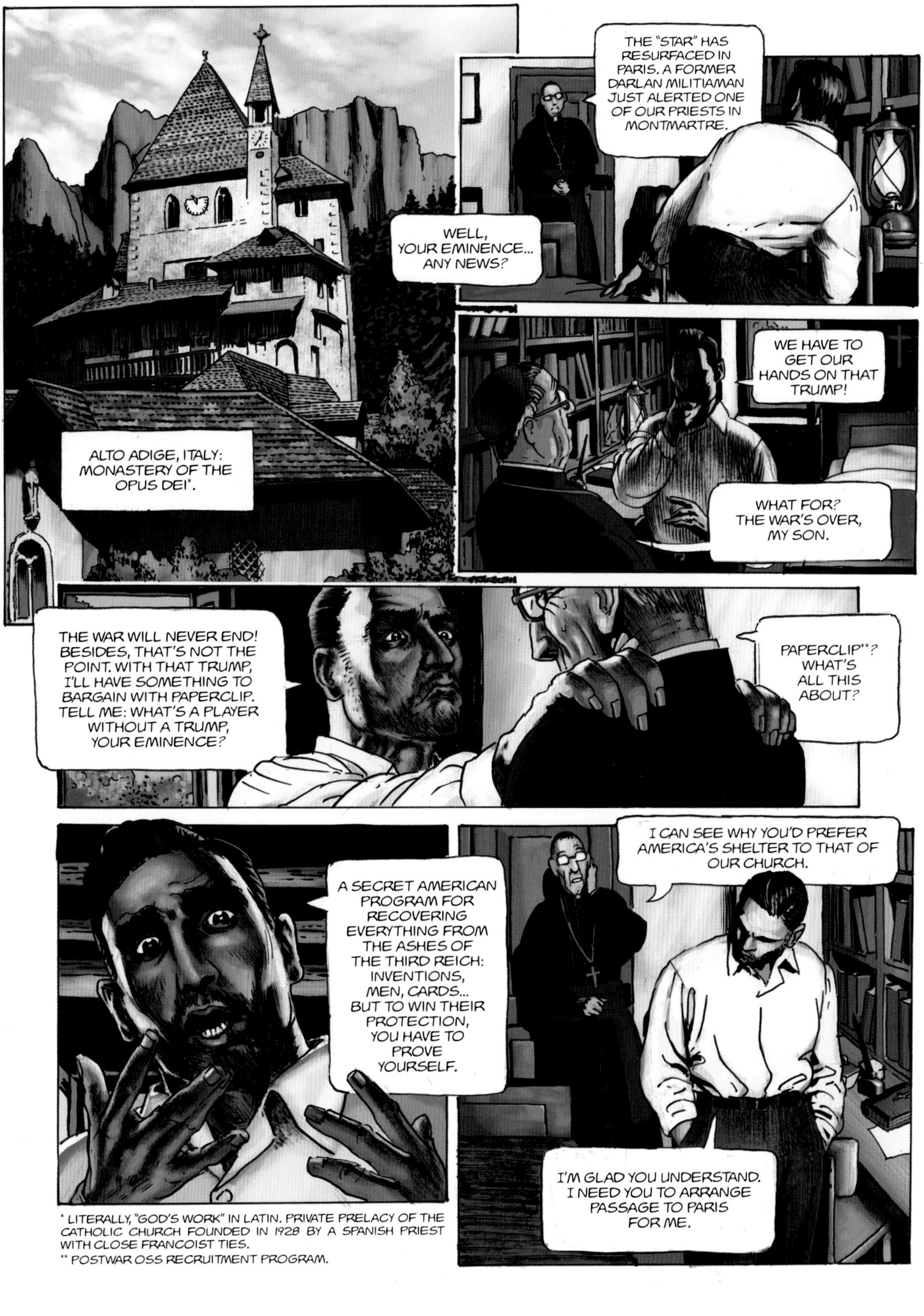
ALTO ADIGE, ITALY: MONASTERY OF THE OPUS DEI*.
WELL, YOUR EMINENCE... ANY NEWS?
THE "STAR" HAS RESURFACED IN PARIS. A FORMER DARLAN MILITIAMAN JUST ALERTED ONE OF OUR PRIESTS IN MONTMARTRE.
WE HAVE TO GET OUR HANDS ON THAT TRUMP!
WHAT FOR? THE WAR'S OVER, MY SON.
THE WAR WILL NEVER END! BESIDES, THAT'S NOT THE POINT. WITH THAT TRUMP, I'LL HAVE SOMETHING TO BARGAIN WITH PAPERCLIP. TELL ME: WHAT'S A PLAYER WITHOUT A TRUMP, YOUR EMINENCE?
PAPERCLIP**? WHAT'S ALL THIS ABOUT?
A SECRET AMERICAN PROGRAM FOR RECOVERING EVERYTHING FROM THE ASHES OF THE THIRD REICH: INVENTIONS, MEN, CARDS... BUT TO WIN THEIR PROTECTION, YOU HAVE TO PROVE YOURSELF.
I CAN SEE WHY YOU'D PREFER AMERICA'S SHELTER TO THAT OF OUR CHURCH.
I'M GLAD YOU UNDERSTAND. I NEED YOU TO ARRANGE PASSAGE TO PARIS FOR ME.

* LITERALLY, "GOD'S WORK" IN LATIN. PRIVATE PRELACY OF THE CATHOLIC CHURCH FOUNDED IN 1928 BY A SPANISH PRIEST WITH CLOSE FRANCOIST TIES.

** POSTWAR OSS RECRUITMENT PROGRAM.

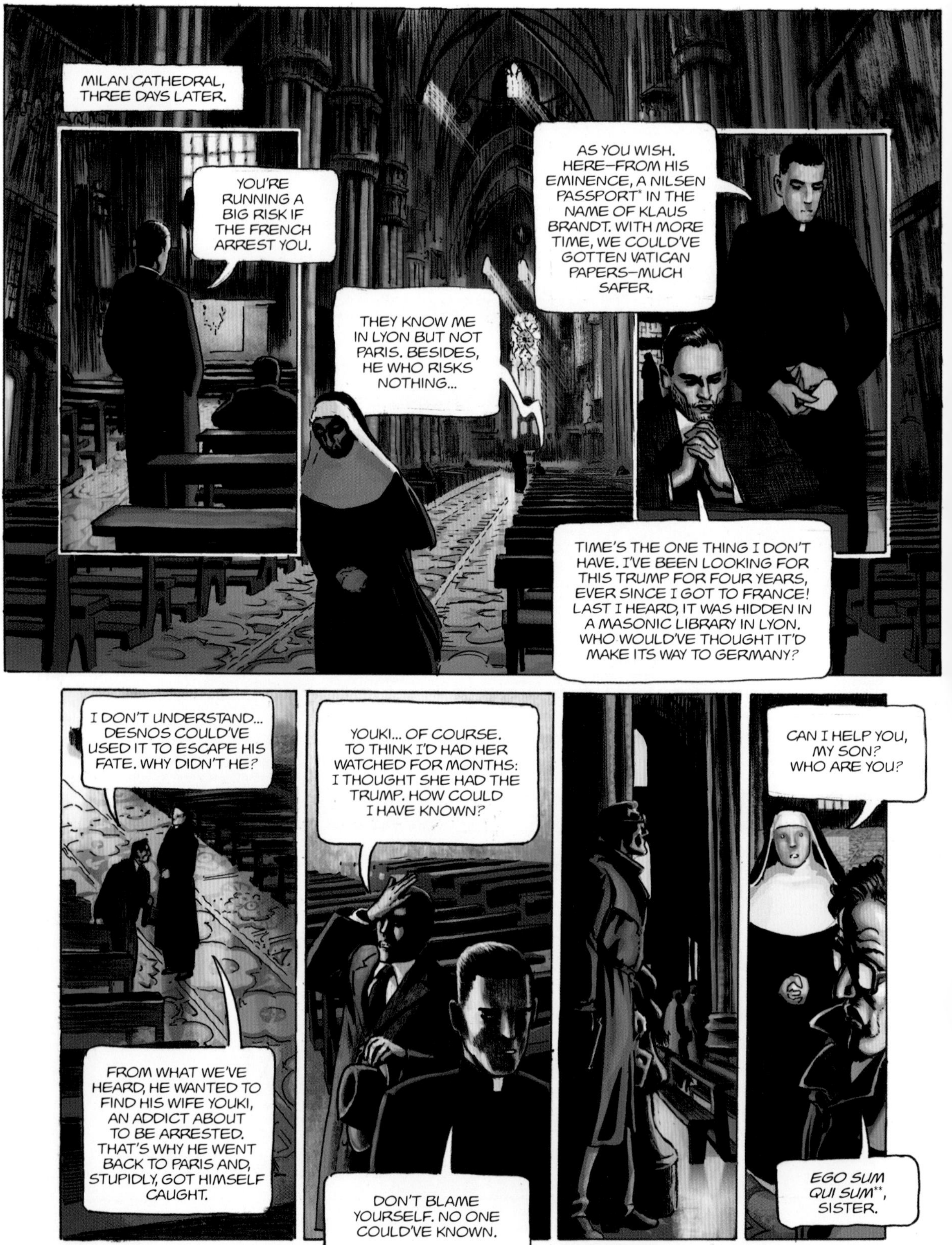
MILAN CATHEDRAL, THREE DAYS LATER.
YOU'RE RUNNING A BIG RISK IF THE FRENCH ARREST YOU.
THEY KNOW ME IN LYON BUT NOT PARIS. BESIDES, HE WHO RISKS NOTHING...
AS YOU WISH. HERE—FROM HIS EMINENCE, A NILSEN PASSPORT* IN THE NAME OF KLAUS BRANDT. WITH MORE TIME, WE COULD'VE GOTTEN VATICAN PAPERS—MUCH SAFER.
TIME'S THE ONE THING I DON'T HAVE. I'VE BEEN LOOKING FOR THIS TRUMP FOR FOUR YEARS, EVER SINCE I GOT TO FRANCE! LAST I HEARD, IT WAS HIDDEN IN A MASONIC LIBRARY IN LYON. WHO WOULD'VE THOUGHT IT'D MAKE ITS WAY TO GERMANY?
I DON'T UNDERSTAND... DESNOS COULD'VE USED IT TO ESCAPE HIS FATE. WHY DIDN'T HE?
FROM WHAT WE'VE HEARD, HE WANTED TO FIND HIS WIFE YOUKI, AN ADDICT ABOUT TO BE ARRESTED. THAT'S WHY HE WENT BACK TO PARIS AND, STUPIDLY, GOT HIMSELF CAUGHT.
YOUKI... OF COURSE. TO THINK I'D HAD HER WATCHED FOR MONTHS: I THOUGHT SHE HAD THE TRUMP. HOW COULD I HAVE KNOWN?
DON'T BLAME YOURSELF. NO ONE COULD'VE KNOWN.
CAN I HELP YOU, MY SON? WHO ARE YOU?
EGO SUM QUI SUM**, SISTER.

* PASSPORT ISSUED BY THE RED CROSS TO STATELESS AND DISPLACED PEOPLE AFTER THE WAR.

** "I AM THAT I AM".

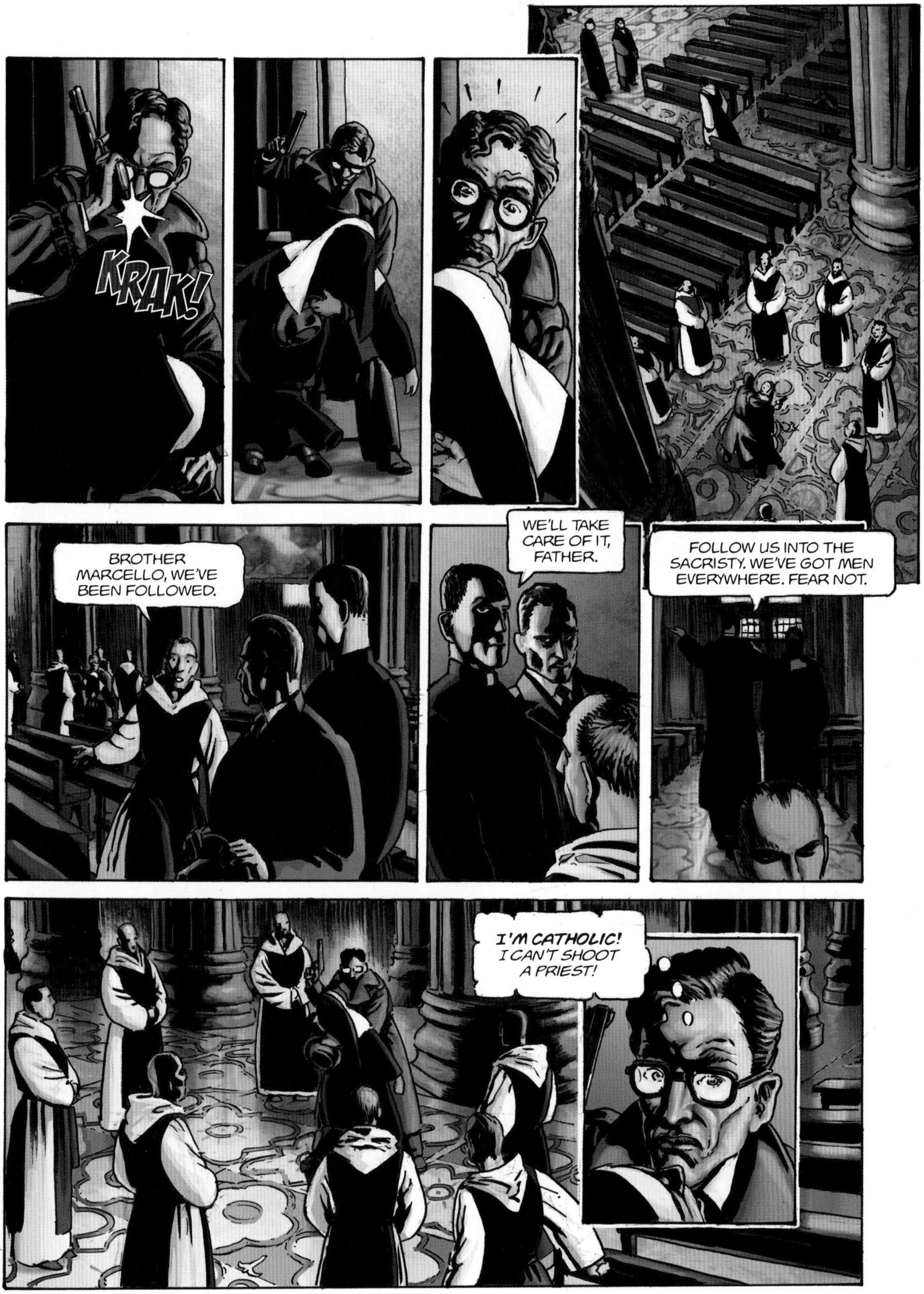
KRAK!
BROTHER MARCELLO, WE'VE BEEN FOLLOWED.
WE'LL TAKE CARE OF IT, FATHER.
FOLLOW US INTO THE SACRISTY. WE'VE GOT MEN EVERYWHERE. FEAR NOT.
I'M CATHOLIC! I CAN'T SHOOT A PRIEST!

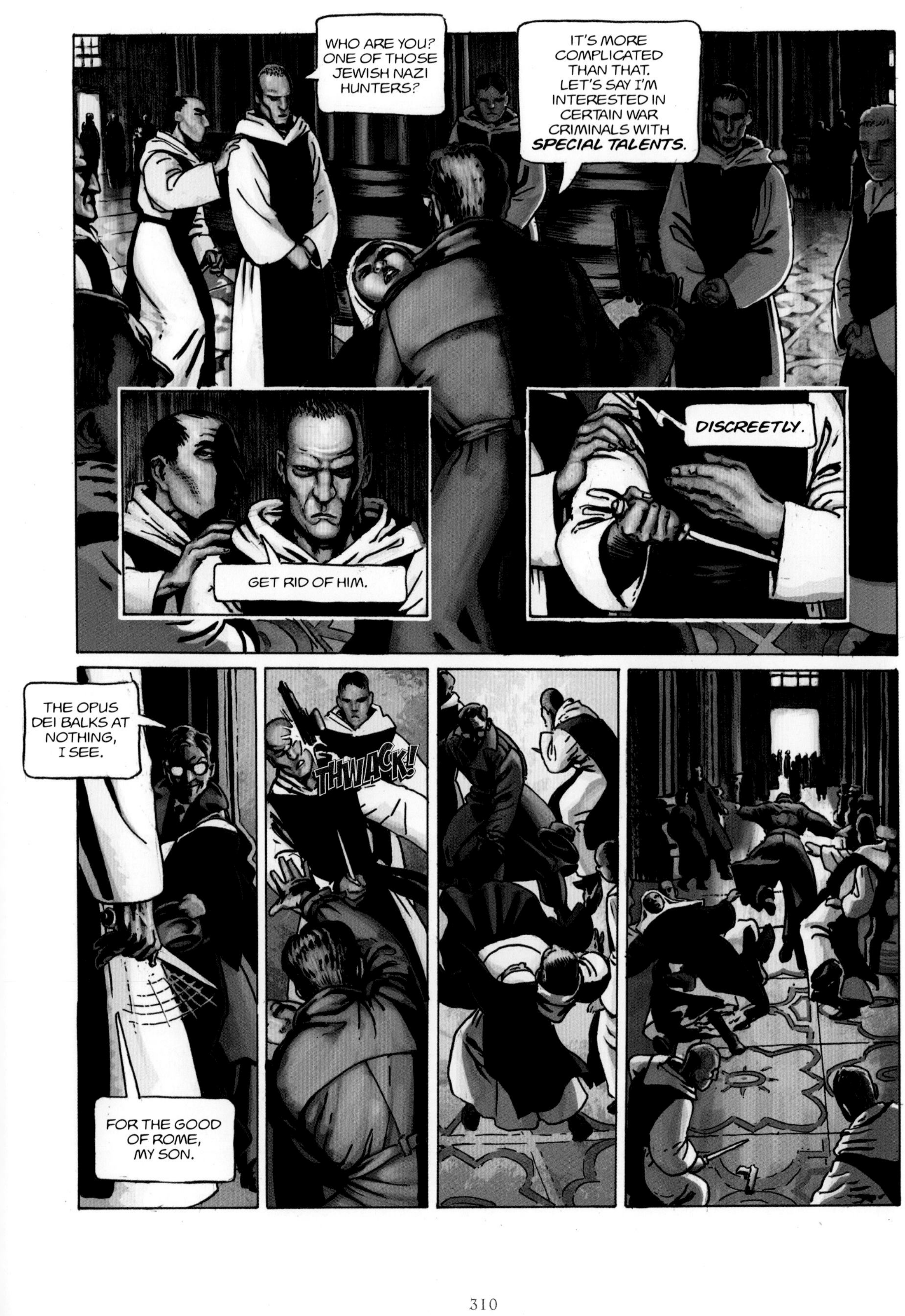
WHO ARE YOU? ONE OF THOSE JEWISH NAZI HUNTERS?
IT'S MORE COMPLICATED THAN THAT. LET'S SAY I'M INTERESTED IN CERTAIN WAR CRIMINALS WITH SPECIAL TALENTS.
GET RID OF HIM.
DISCREETLY.
THE OPUS DEI BALKS AT NOTHING, I SEE.
FOR THE GOOD OF ROME, MY SON.
THWACK!

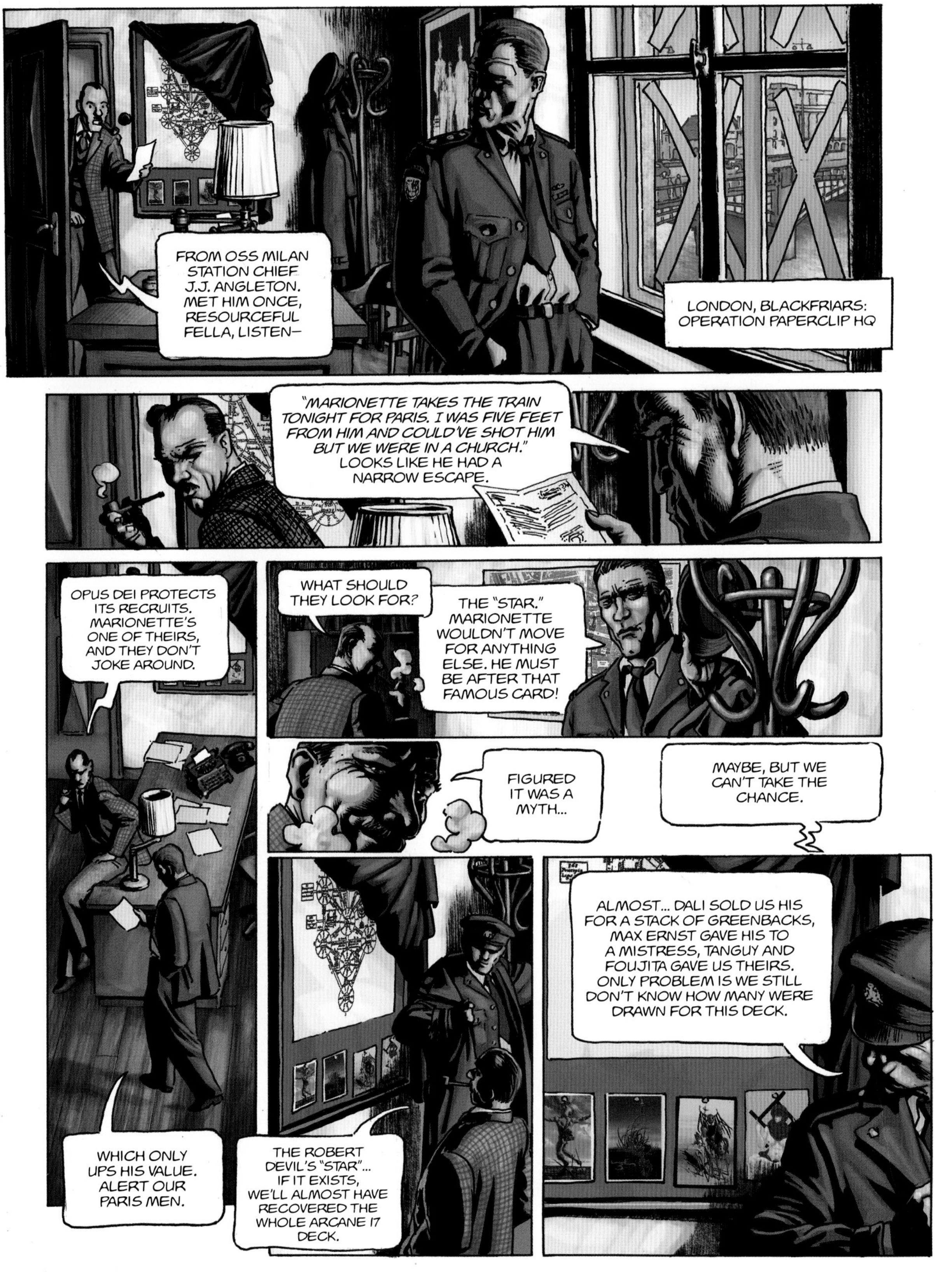
FROM OSS MILAN STATION CHIEF J.J. ANGLETON. MET HIM ONCE, RESOURCEFUL FELLA, LISTEN–
LONDON, BLACKFRIARS: OPERATION PAPERCLIP HQ
"MARIONETTE TAKES THE TRAIN TONIGHT FOR PARIS. I WAS FIVE FEET FROM HIM AND COULD'VE SHOT HIM BUT WE WERE IN A CHURCH." LOOKS LIKE HE HAD A NARROW ESCAPE.
OPUS DEI PROTECTS ITS RECRUITS. MARIONETTE'S ONE OF THEIRS, AND THEY DON'T JOKE AROUND.
WHAT SHOULD THEY LOOK FOR?
THE "STAR." MARIONETTE WOULDN'T MOVE FOR ANYTHING ELSE. HE MUST BE AFTER THAT FAMOUS CARD!
FIGURED IT WAS A MYTH...
MAYBE, BUT WE CAN'T TAKE THE CHANCE.
WHICH ONLY UPS HIS VALUE. ALERT OUR PARIS MEN.
THE ROBERT DEVIL'S "STAR"... IF IT EXISTS, WE'LL ALMOST HAVE RECOVERED THE WHOLE ARCANE 17 DECK.
ALMOST... DALI SOLD US HIS FOR A STACK OF GREENBACKS, MAX ERNST GAVE HIS TO A MISTRESS, TANGUY AND FOUJITA GAVE US THEIRS. ONLY PROBLEM IS WE STILL DON'T KNOW HOW MANY WERE DRAWN FOR THIS DECK.

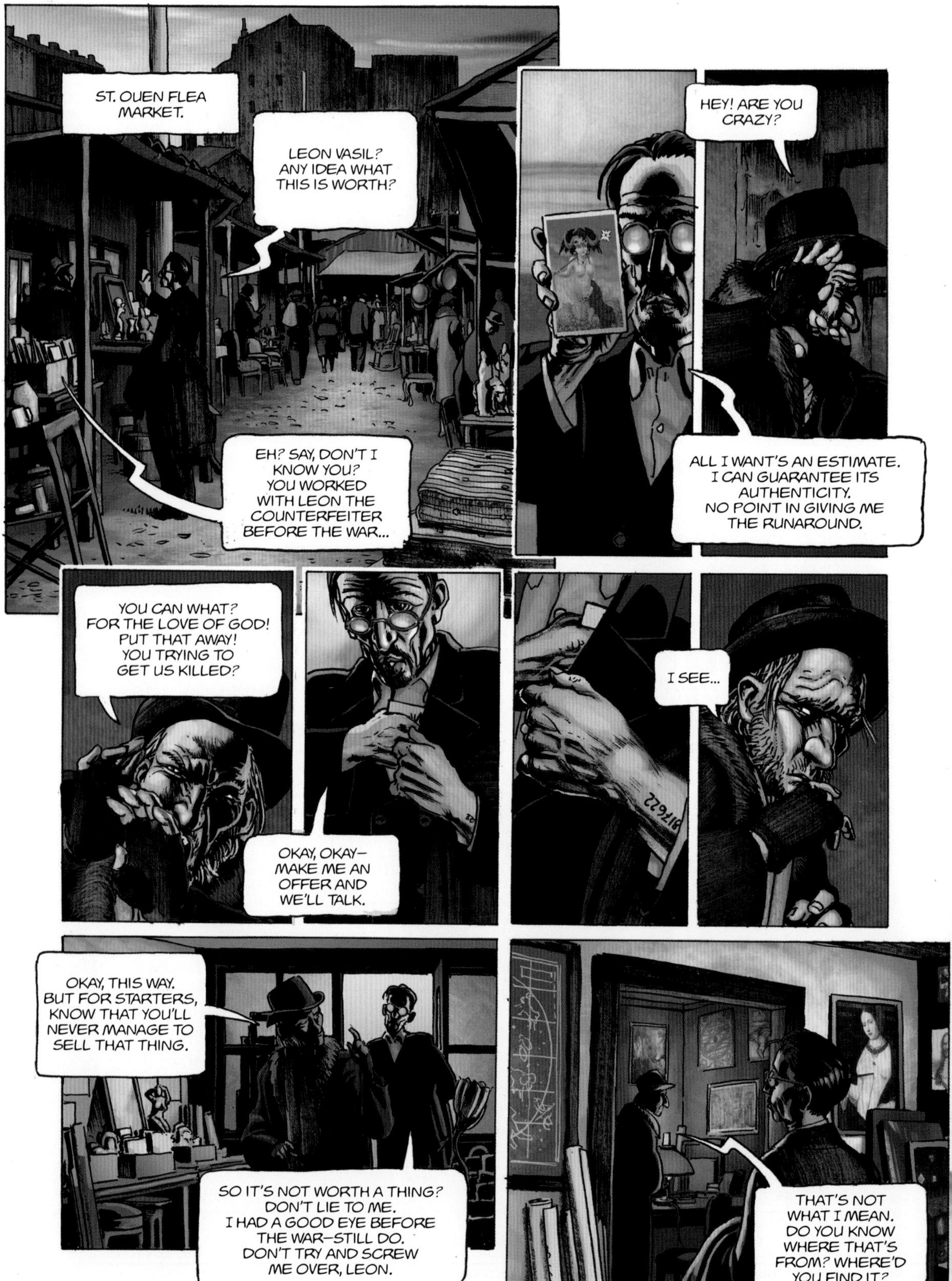
ST. OUEN FLEA MARKET.
LEON VASIL? ANY IDEA WHAT THIS IS WORTH?
EH? SAY, DON'T I KNOW YOU? YOU WORKED WITH LEON THE COUNTERFEITER BEFORE THE WAR...
HEY! ARE YOU CRAZY?
ALL I WANT'S AN ESTIMATE. I CAN GUARANTEE ITS AUTHENTICITY. NO POINT IN GIVING ME THE RUNAROUND.
YOU CAN WHAT? FOR THE LOVE OF GOD! PUT THAT AWAY! YOU TRYING TO GET US KILLED?
OKAY, OKAY— MAKE ME AN OFFER AND WE'LL TALK.
I SEE...
OKAY, THIS WAY. BUT FOR STARTERS, KNOW THAT YOU'LL NEVER MANAGE TO SELL THAT THING.
SO IT'S NOT WORTH A THING? DON'T LIE TO ME. I HAD A GOOD EYE BEFORE THE WAR—STILL DO. DON'T TRY AND SCREW ME OVER, LEON.
THAT'S NOT WHAT I MEAN. DO YOU KNOW WHERE THAT'S FROM? WHERE'D YOU FIND IT?

FIND IT? WHAT IF I BOUGHT IT?

THAT'S NOT HOW IT WORKS. IF YOU'D BOUGHT IT YOU'D BE DEAD. IT TAKES AN EXCHANGE OF *GIFTS*.

ALL RIGHT. I WAS GIVEN IT IN A CONCENTRATION CAMP. BY A POET NAMED ROBERT DESNOS, ROBERT THE DEVIL.

OF COURSE! I WAS SURE THE SURREALISTS HAD BEEN RECRUITED! MAKES SENSE!

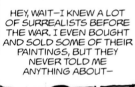

HEY, WAIT—I KNEW A LOT OF SURREALISTS BEFORE THE WAR. I EVEN BOUGHT AND SOLD SOME OF THEIR PAINTINGS, BUT THEY NEVER TOLD ME ANYTHING ABOUT—

BUYING, SELLING— YOUR MONEY KEPT YOU OUT OF THE CIRCLE. IT'S NOT THE KIND OF THING YOU CAN BUY.

DON'T MAKE ME LAUGH— EVERYTHING'S FOR SALE. AREN'T YOU IN BUSINESS?

SINCE YOU'RE AN ART DEALER, HAVE YOU EVER WONDERED WHAT PAINTINGS OF CARD GAMES ARE REALLY ABOUT? THERE ARE SO MANY, A MOTIF USED AS OFTEN AS THE VANITAS SKULL, AND YET THE CHURCH FORBADE GAMES OF CHANCE!

AHA, HERE IT IS! *LOOK!*

THE FIRST MENTION OF A DECK OF CARDS WAS AT THE COUNCIL OF CONSTANCE. ACCORDING TO HISTORY, CARDINAL BORGIA SPENT HIS TIME PLAYING WITH "CARTAS." NO ONE SEEMED TO KNOW YET WHAT THEY WERE, BUT A FEW YEARS LATER, THE CHURCH BANNED THEIR USE UNDER PAIN OF EXCOMMUNICATION.

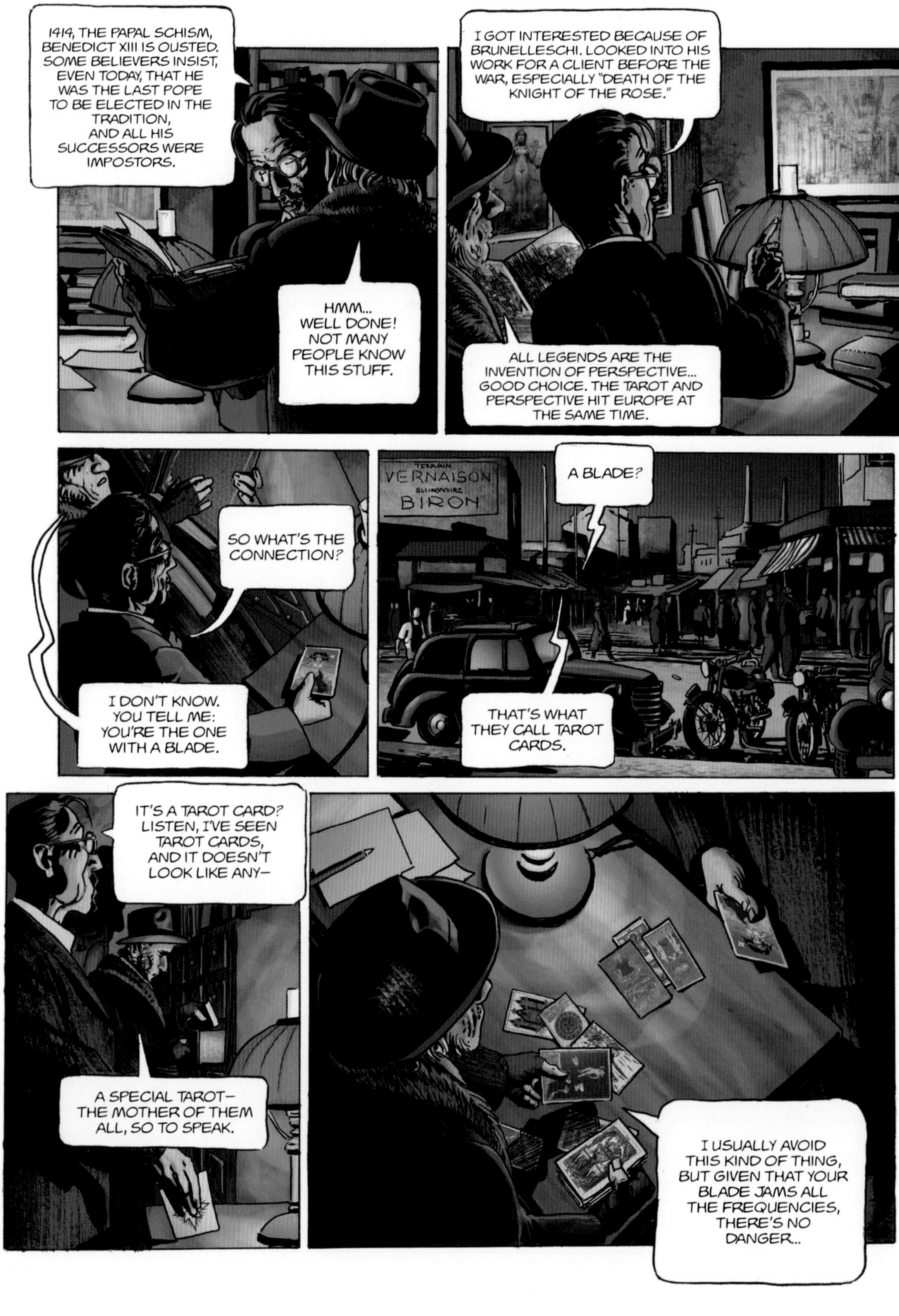
1414, THE PAPAL SCHISM, BENEDICT XIII IS OUSTED. SOME BELIEVERS INSIST, EVEN TODAY, THAT HE WAS THE LAST POPE TO BE ELECTED IN THE TRADITION, AND ALL HIS SUCCESSORS WERE IMPOSTORS.
HMM... WELL DONE! NOT MANY PEOPLE KNOW THIS STUFF.
I GOT INTERESTED BECAUSE OF BRUNELLESCHI. LOOKED INTO HIS WORK FOR A CLIENT BEFORE THE WAR, ESPECIALLY "DEATH OF THE KNIGHT OF THE ROSE."
ALL LEGENDS ARE THE INVENTION OF PERSPECTIVE... GOOD CHOICE. THE TAROT AND PERSPECTIVE HIT EUROPE AT THE SAME TIME.
SO WHAT'S THE CONNECTION?
I DON'T KNOW. YOU TELL ME: YOU'RE THE ONE WITH A BLADE.
VERNAISON
BIRON
A BLADE?
THAT'S WHAT THEY CALL TAROT CARDS.
IT'S A TAROT CARD? LISTEN, I'VE SEEN TAROT CARDS, AND IT DOESN'T LOOK LIKE ANY—
A SPECIAL TAROT— THE MOTHER OF THEM ALL, SO TO SPEAK.
I USUALLY AVOID THIS KIND OF THING, BUT GIVEN THAT YOUR BLADE JAMS ALL THE FREQUENCIES, THERE'S NO DANGER...

THE EMPEROR, THE EMPRESS, THE POPE, THE PAPESS.

ALL THE TAROTS ALLUDE TO FOUR PRINCIPLES, FOUR POWERS: TWO MALE AND TWO FEMALE.

TWO POSITIVE, TWO NEGATIVE, I'VE HEARD IT BEFORE. YIN AND YANG.

THAT'S WHAT I USED TO THINK TOO, BUT IT'S NOT THAT SIMPLE. AS WE GO THROUGH THE CENTURIES, THE PRINCIPLES SEEM TO BLUR, AS IF EVOLVING OR CHANGING ROLES.

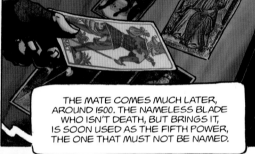

THE MATE COMES MUCH LATER, AROUND 1500. THE NAMELESS BLADE WHO ISN'T DEATH, BUT BRINGS IT, IS SOON USED AS THE FIFTH POWER, THE ONE THAT MUST NOT BE NAMED.

PASS ME YOUR BLADE?

THE STAR IS ARCANE 17. IN THE VISCONTI-SFORZA DECK, IT'S ALSO CALLED HOPE, AND IN OTHERS THE BLACK MOON. IT IS THE NIGREDO, WHICH IN ALCHEMY PRECEDES THE ALBEDO AND THE RUBEDO. THAT'S WHY THE STAR COMES BEFORE THE MOON—ARCANE 18 (WHITE)— AND THE SUN—ARCANE 19 (RED).

THE MOON REFERS TO LILITH, GODDESS OF SENSUALITY, ALSO IDENTIFIED WITH THE PAPESS.

FUNNY, I REMEMBER DESNOS SAYING: "BORN UNDER A BAD STAR." I NEVER KNEW WHAT HE MEANT. I THOUGHT HE MEANT HIS FATE.

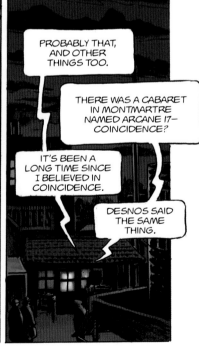

PROBABLY THAT, AND OTHER THINGS TOO.

THERE WAS A CABARET IN MONTMARTRE NAMED ARCANE 17— COINCIDENCE?

IT'S BEEN A LONG TIME SINCE I BELIEVED IN COINCIDENCE.

DESNOS SAID THE SAME THING.

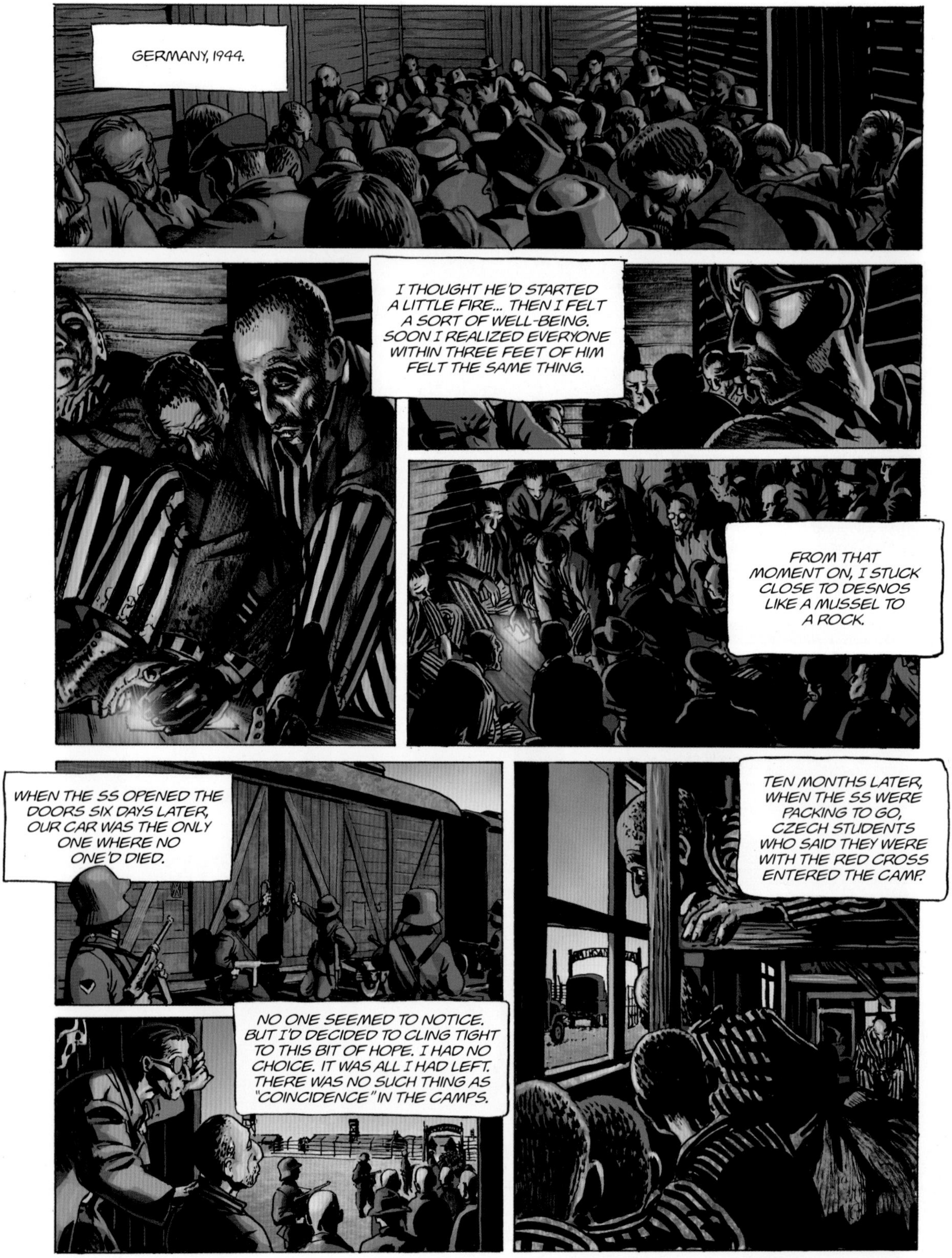
GERMANY, 1944.
I THOUGHT HE'D STARTED A LITTLE FIRE... THEN I FELT A SORT OF WELL-BEING. SOON I REALIZED EVERYONE WITHIN THREE FEET OF HIM FELT THE SAME THING.
FROM THAT MOMENT ON, I STUCK CLOSE TO DESNOS LIKE A MUSSEL TO A ROCK.
WHEN THE SS OPENED THE DOORS SIX DAYS LATER, OUR CAR WAS THE ONLY ONE WHERE NO ONE'D DIED.
NO ONE SEEMED TO NOTICE. BUT I'D DECIDED TO CLING TIGHT TO THIS BIT OF HOPE. I HAD NO CHOICE. IT WAS ALL I HAD LEFT. THERE WAS NO SUCH THING AS "COINCIDENCE" IN THE CAMPS.
TEN MONTHS LATER, WHEN THE SS WERE PACKING TO GO, CZECH STUDENTS WHO SAID THEY WERE WITH THE RED CROSS ENTERED THE CAMP.

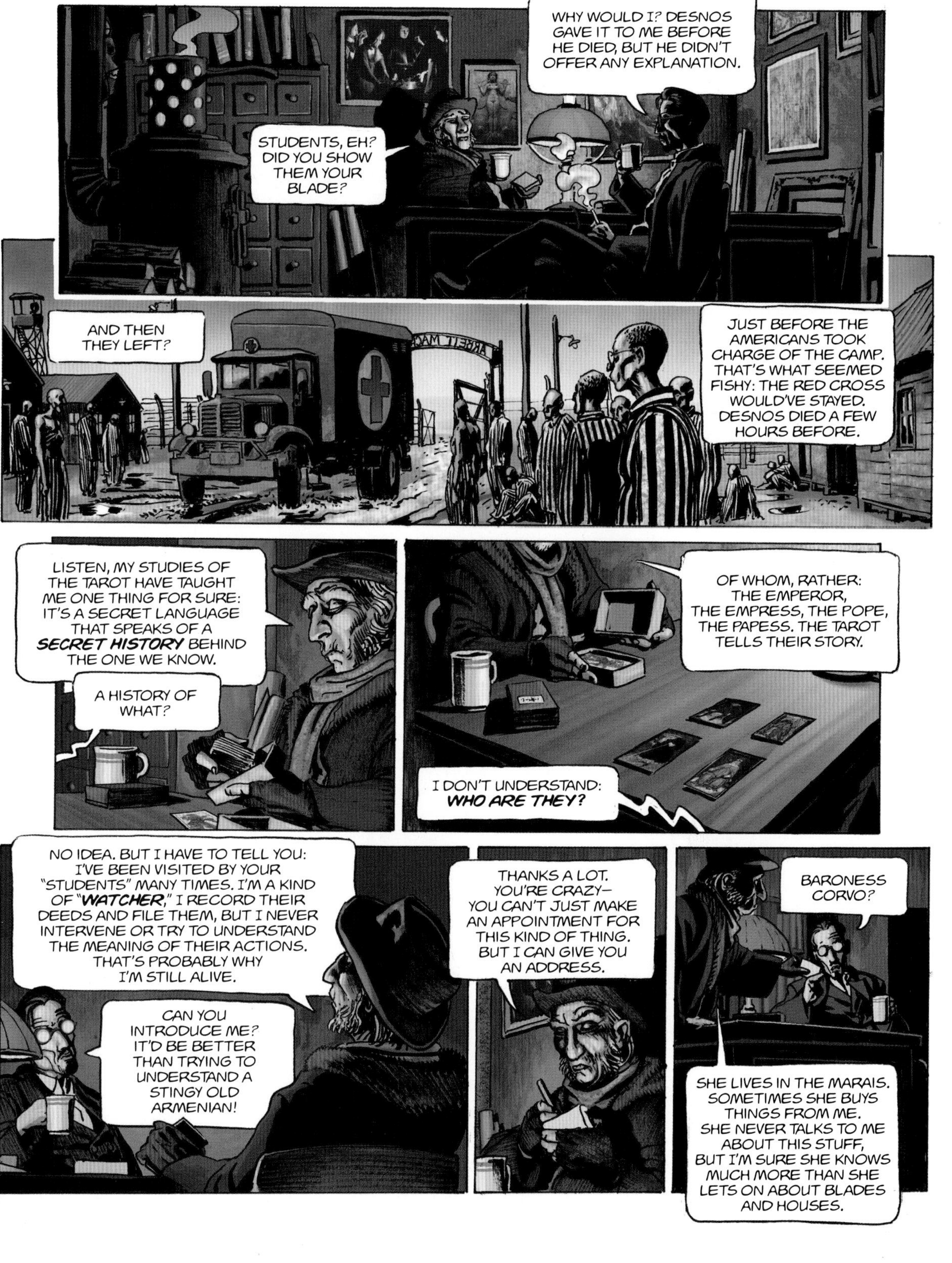
STUDENTS, EH? DID YOU SHOW THEM YOUR BLADE?
WHY WOULD I? DESNOS GAVE IT TO ME BEFORE HE DIED, BUT HE DIDN'T OFFER ANY EXPLANATION.
AND THEN THEY LEFT?
JUST BEFORE THE AMERICANS TOOK CHARGE OF THE CAMP. THAT'S WHAT SEEMED FISHY: THE RED CROSS WOULD'VE STAYED. DESNOS DIED A FEW HOURS BEFORE.
LISTEN, MY STUDIES OF THE TAROT HAVE TAUGHT ME ONE THING FOR SURE: IT'S A SECRET LANGUAGE THAT SPEAKS OF A **SECRET HISTORY** BEHIND THE ONE WE KNOW.
A HISTORY OF WHAT?
OF WHOM, RATHER: THE EMPEROR, THE EMPRESS, THE POPE, THE PAPESS. THE TAROT TELLS THEIR STORY.
I DON'T UNDERSTAND: **WHO ARE THEY?**
NO IDEA. BUT I HAVE TO TELL YOU: I'VE BEEN VISITED BY YOUR "STUDENTS" MANY TIMES. I'M A KIND OF "**WATCHER**," I RECORD THEIR DEEDS AND FILE THEM, BUT I NEVER INTERVENE OR TRY TO UNDERSTAND THE MEANING OF THEIR ACTIONS. THAT'S PROBABLY WHY I'M STILL ALIVE.
CAN YOU INTRODUCE ME? IT'D BE BETTER THAN TRYING TO UNDERSTAND A STINGY OLD ARMENIAN!
THANKS A LOT. YOU'RE CRAZY– YOU CAN'T JUST MAKE AN APPOINTMENT FOR THIS KIND OF THING. BUT I CAN GIVE YOU AN ADDRESS.
BARONESS CORVO?
SHE LIVES IN THE MARAIS. SOMETIMES SHE BUYS THINGS FROM ME. SHE NEVER TALKS TO ME ABOUT THIS STUFF, BUT I'M SURE SHE KNOWS MUCH MORE THAN SHE LETS ON ABOUT BLADES AND HOUSES.

MY FAMILY HAS ALWAYS BEEN INTERESTED IN CARDS, AS FAR BACK AS I CAN TRACE IT.

THE FIRST VASIL— VASIL THE VALIANT— WAS AN ARMENIAN KNIGHT DURING THE CRUSADES. IT ALL STARTS WITH HIM.

AND DID HE LEAVE AN EXPLANATION?

HE'D FOUND A BOOK OR TALISMAN WHEN WARRING WITH THE MASONS OF OULTRE-JOURDAIN, THAT'S ALL HE KNEW. MY FAMILY POSSESSED HUNDREDS OF MANUSCRIPTS WE LEFT IN THE CARE OF MONKS AT THE ARMENIAN MONASTERY IN VENICE. SADLY, THE MONASTERY WAS BOMBED BY THE AUSTRIANS IN 1918 AND ALMOST ALL THE ARCHIVES BURNED.

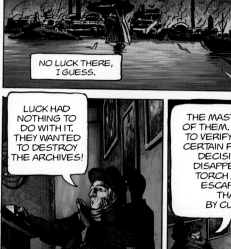

ALMOST ALL! MY GRANDFATHER MOVED THE REST TO IZMIR, BUT TWO YEARS LATER TURKS SACKED THE CITY AND IT WAS NEVER SEEN AGAIN.

NO LUCK THERE, I GUESS.

ALL, OR ALMOST ALL?

LUCK HAD NOTHING TO DO WITH IT. THEY WANTED TO DESTROY THE ARCHIVES!

"THEY"?

THE MASTERS OF THE HOUSES—OR SOME OF THEM. THEY DIDN'T WANT US TO BE ABLE TO VERIFY CERTAIN FACTS, THE ORIGINS OF CERTAIN FORTUNES, OR CERTAIN POLITICAL DECISIONS. AFTER MY GRANDFATHER DISAPPEARED, MY FATHER TOOK UP THE TORCH AND HID THE FEW PAPERS THAT ESCAPED FIRE AND BOMBARDMENT. THAT'S WHY WE WERE VISITED BY CURIOUS STUDENTS... LEAVING?

THANKS FOR THE FAIRY TALE, BUT YOU'D BETTER GET SOME SLEEP, YOU OLD LOON!

YOU'RE ABSOLUTELY RIGHT, *MON AMI.*

IT ALL BEGINS WITH FOUR SIGNS.

I'VE DETERMINED THAT THESE FOUR SIGNS ARE AT THE BASE OF ALL WESTERN GAMES: CLUB, SPADE, HEART, AND DIAMOND. TAKE THE TWO CIRCLES ON THE LEFT, FOR INSTANCE. THEY'RE AMONG THE OLDEST PICTORIAL REPRESENTATIONS.

WE FIND MANY EXAMPLES IN NEOLITHIC CAVES. THEN THE SYMBOL EVOLVES, TURNS INTO THREE CIRCLES. WE FIND THEM GRAVEN EVERYWHERE THROUGHOUT THE IRON AGE. FINALLY THEY BECOME THE THREE BLACK CIRCLES OF DENARIUS COINS, THE ANCIENT NAME FOR THE CLUB AS WE KNOW IT TODAY. I COULD DO THIS FOR THE OTHER HOUSES TOO.

I BELIEVE YOU.

BUT THERE'S MORE: I FOUND THAT THE CARDS INTERACT WITH EACH OTHER. THE SIREN WITH THE LION, THE DOORWAY WITH THE KRAKEN. A BIT LIKE POKER HANDS: A PAIR, THREE OF A KIND— YOU SEE?

I SEE THAT YOU'RE NUTS, PAL.

UNFORTUNATELY, I DON'T THINK ANYONE IN THE WORLD CAN MAKE A LIST OF THESE COMBINATIONS, OR THESE CARDS, EVEN. THERE ARE HUNDREDS, PERHAPS MORE.

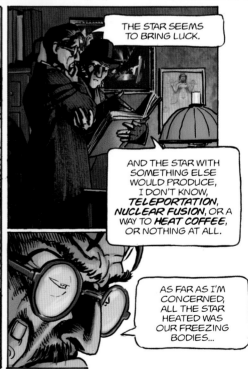

THE STAR SEEMS TO BRING LUCK.

AND THE STAR WITH SOMETHING ELSE WOULD PRODUCE, I DON'T KNOW, *TELEPORTATION, NUCLEAR FUSION,* OR A WAY TO *HEAT COFFEE,* OR NOTHING AT ALL.

AS FAR AS I'M CONCERNED, ALL THE STAR HEATED WAS OUR FREEZING BODIES...

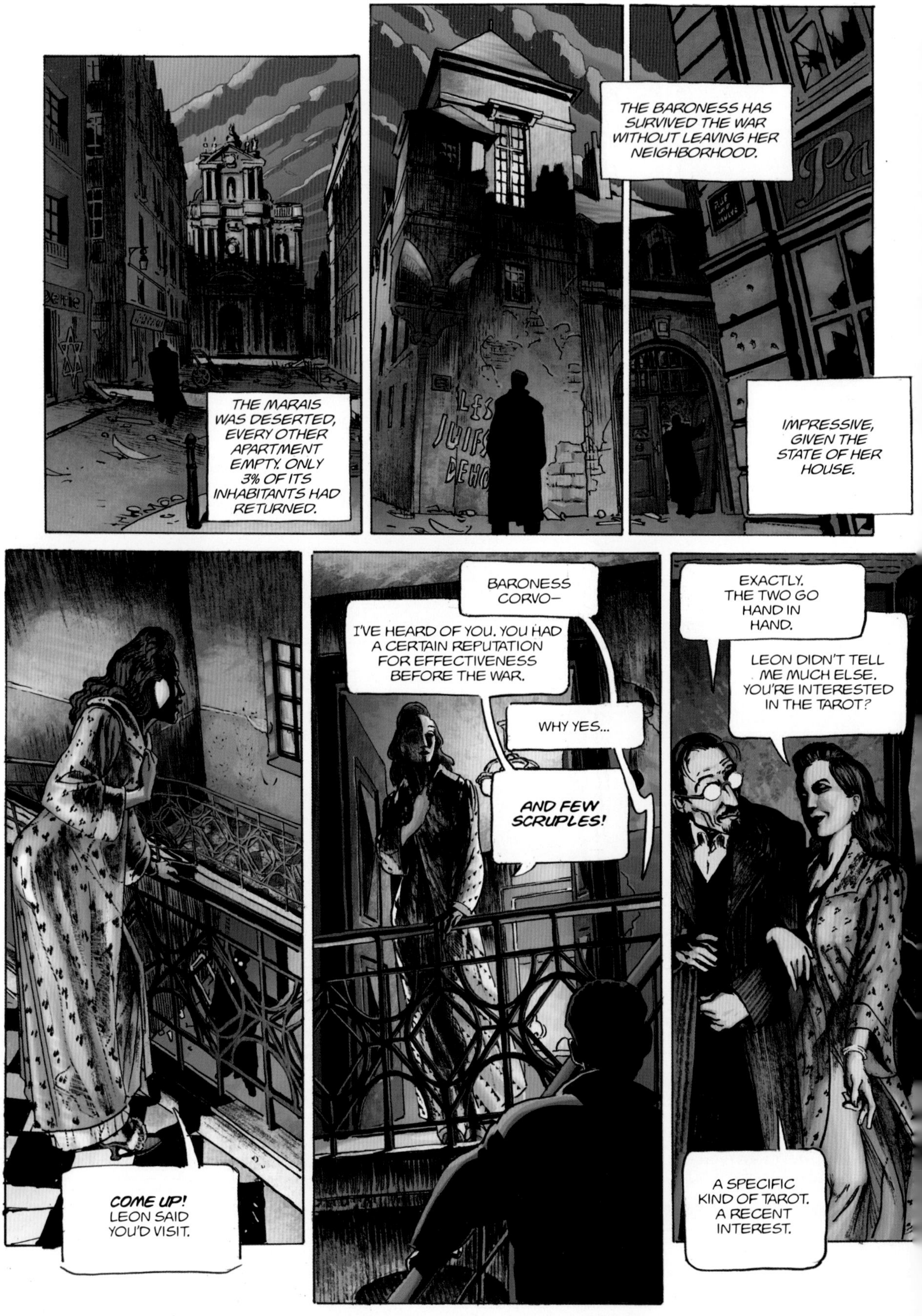
THE MARAIS WAS DESERTED, EVERY OTHER APARTMENT EMPTY. ONLY 3% OF ITS INHABITANTS HAD RETURNED.
THE BARONESS HAS SURVIVED THE WAR WITHOUT LEAVING HER NEIGHBORHOOD.
IMPRESSIVE, GIVEN THE STATE OF HER HOUSE.
COME UP! LEON SAID YOU'D VISIT.
BARONESS CORVO—
I'VE HEARD OF YOU. YOU HAD A CERTAIN REPUTATION FOR EFFECTIVENESS BEFORE THE WAR.
WHY YES...
AND FEW SCRUPLES!
EXACTLY. THE TWO GO HAND IN HAND.
LEON DIDN'T TELL ME MUCH ELSE. YOU'RE INTERESTED IN THE TAROT?
A SPECIFIC KIND OF TAROT. A RECENT INTEREST.

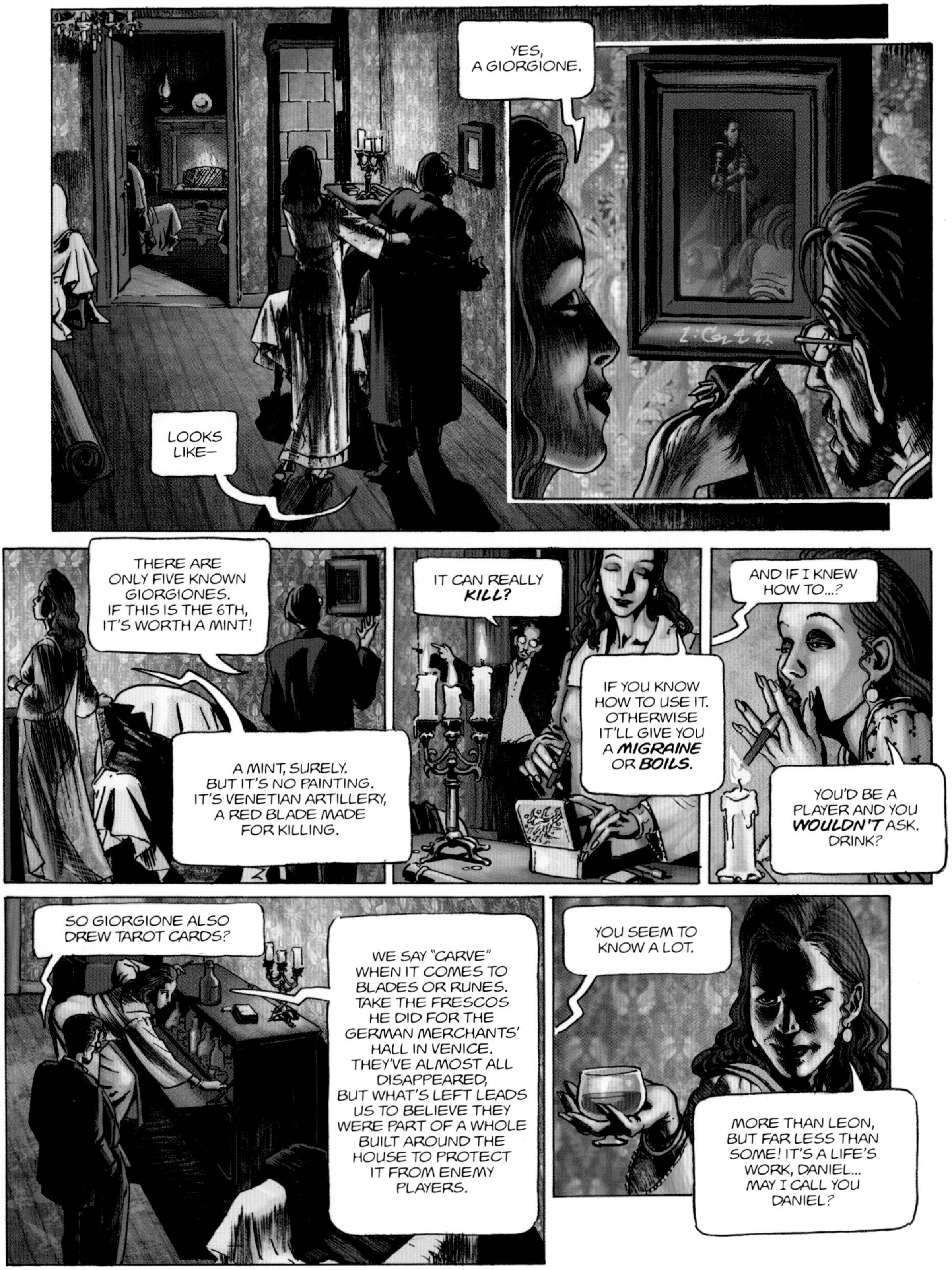
LOOKS LIKE–
YES, A GIORGIONE.
THERE ARE ONLY FIVE KNOWN GIORGIONES. IF THIS IS THE 6TH, IT'S WORTH A MINT!
A MINT, SURELY. BUT IT'S NO PAINTING. IT'S VENETIAN ARTILLERY, A RED BLADE MADE FOR KILLING.
IT CAN REALLY KILL?
IF YOU KNOW HOW TO USE IT. OTHERWISE IT'LL GIVE YOU A MIGRAINE OR BOILS.
AND IF I KNEW HOW TO...?
YOU'D BE A PLAYER AND YOU WOULDN'T ASK. DRINK?
SO GIORGIONE ALSO DREW TAROT CARDS?
WE SAY "CARVE" WHEN IT COMES TO BLADES OR RUNES. TAKE THE FRESCOS HE DID FOR THE GERMAN MERCHANTS' HALL IN VENICE. THEY'VE ALMOST ALL DISAPPEARED, BUT WHAT'S LEFT LEADS US TO BELIEVE THEY WERE PART OF A WHOLE BUILT AROUND THE HOUSE TO PROTECT IT FROM ENEMY PLAYERS.
YOU SEEM TO KNOW A LOT.
MORE THAN LEON, BUT FAR LESS THAN SOME! IT'S A LIFE'S WORK, DANIEL... MAY I CALL YOU DANIEL?

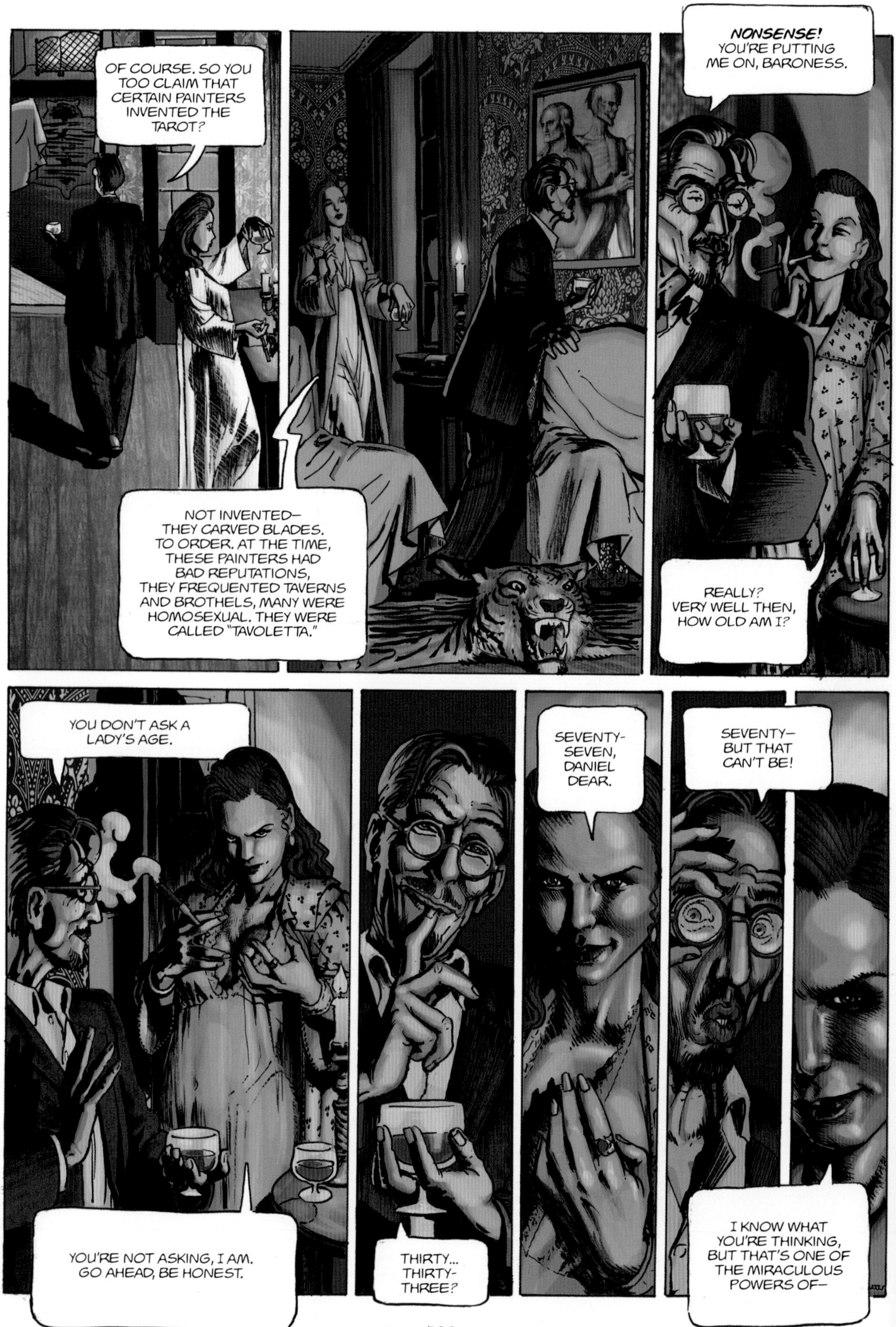
OF COURSE. SO YOU TOO CLAIM THAT CERTAIN PAINTERS INVENTED THE TAROT?
NOT INVENTED— THEY CARVED BLADES. TO ORDER. AT THE TIME, THESE PAINTERS HAD BAD REPUTATIONS, THEY FREQUENTED TAVERNS AND BROTHELS, MANY WERE HOMOSEXUAL. THEY WERE CALLED "TAVOLETTA."
NONSENSE! YOU'RE PUTTING ME ON, BARONESS.
REALLY? VERY WELL THEN, HOW OLD AM I?
YOU DON'T ASK A LADY'S AGE.
YOU'RE NOT ASKING, I AM. GO AHEAD, BE HONEST.
THIRTY... THIRTY-THREE?
SEVENTY-SEVEN, DANIEL DEAR.
SEVENTY— BUT THAT CAN'T BE!
I KNOW WHAT YOU'RE THINKING, BUT THAT'S ONE OF THE MIRACULOUS POWERS OF—

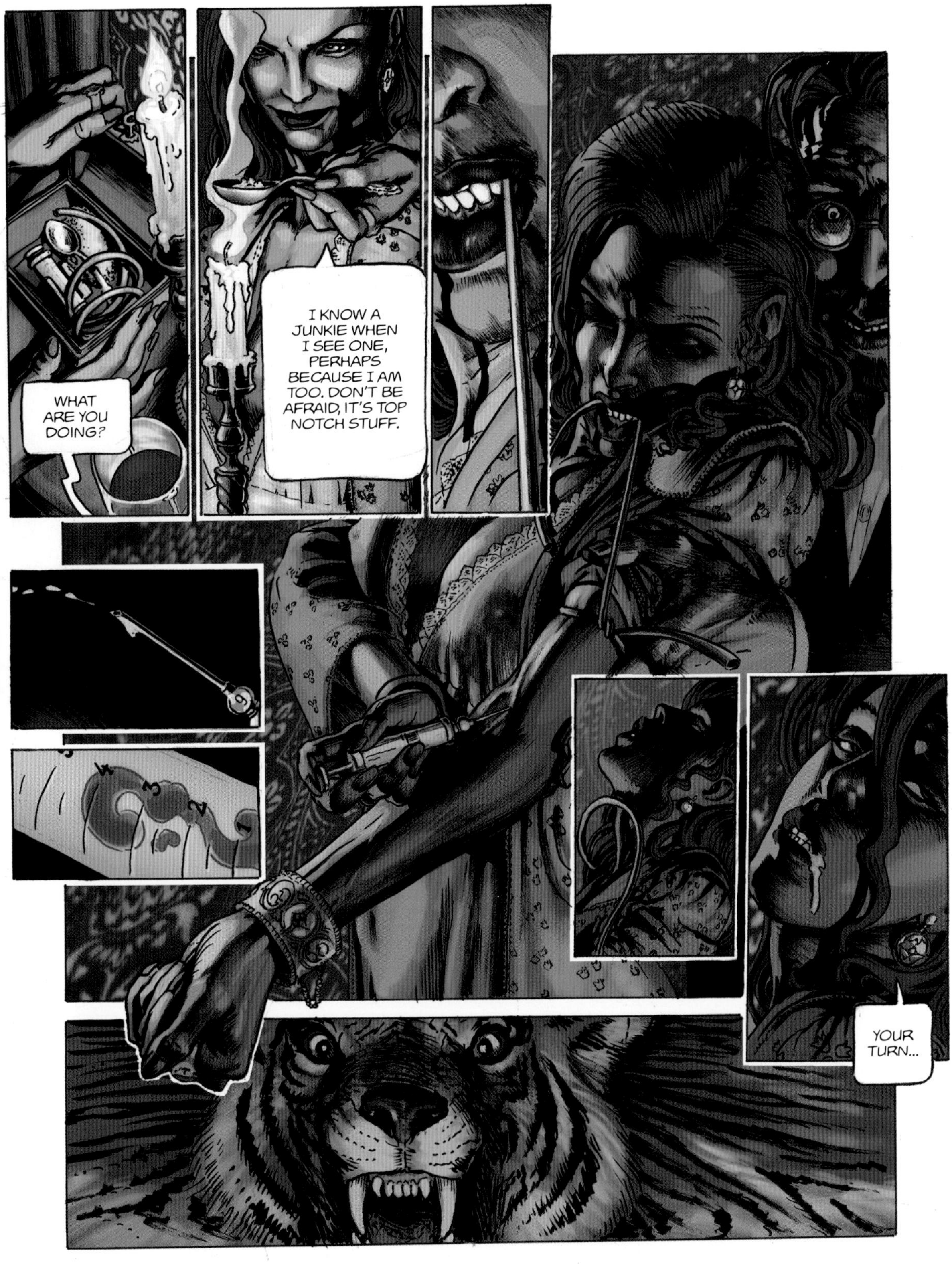
WHAT ARE YOU DOING?
I KNOW A JUNKIE WHEN I SEE ONE, PERHAPS BECAUSE I AM TOO. DON'T BE AFRAID, IT'S TOP NOTCH STUFF.
YOUR TURN...

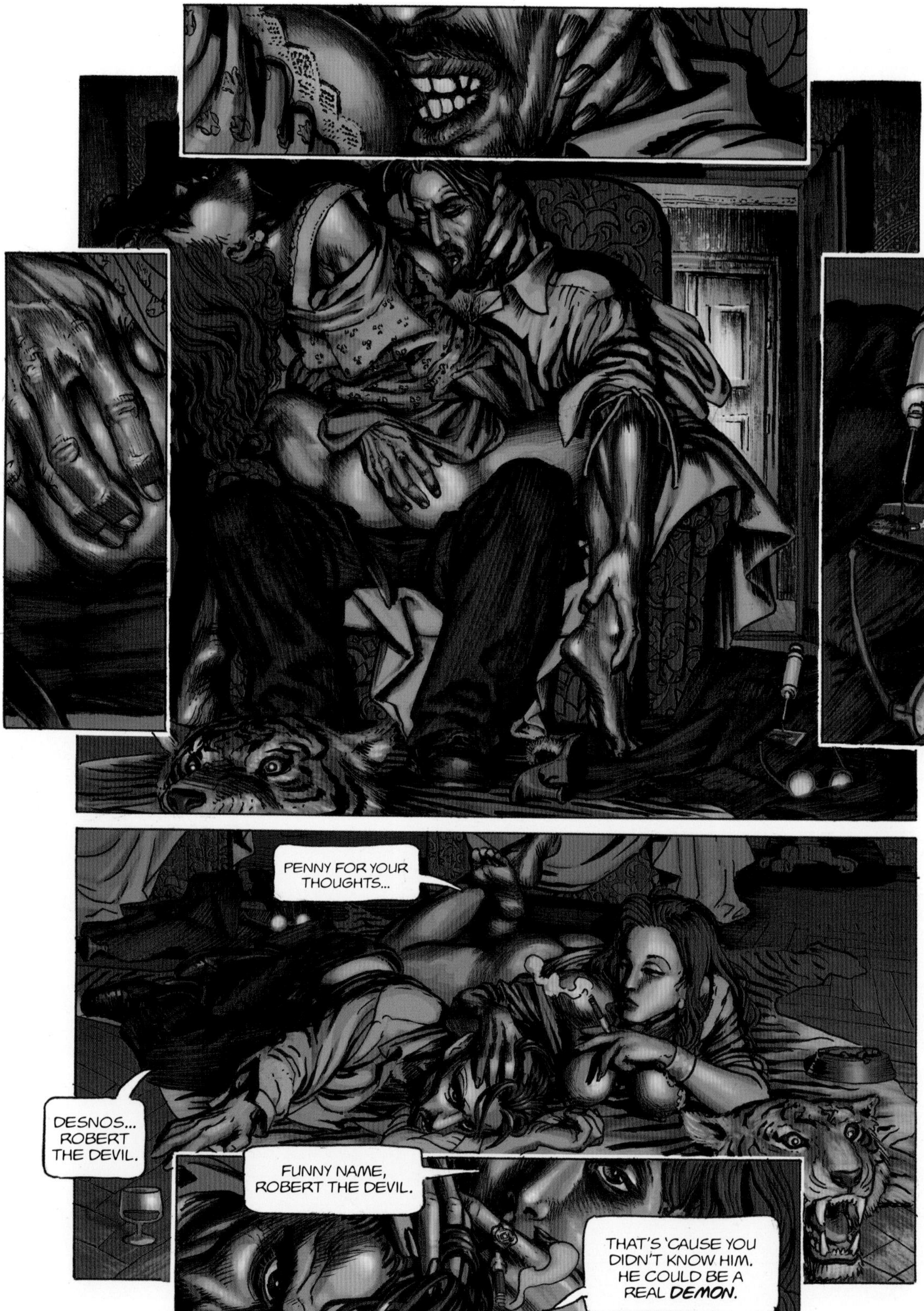
PENNY FOR YOUR THOUGHTS...
DESNOS... ROBERT THE DEVIL.
FUNNY NAME, ROBERT THE DEVIL.
THAT'S 'CAUSE YOU DIDN'T KNOW HIM. HE COULD BE A REAL DEMON.

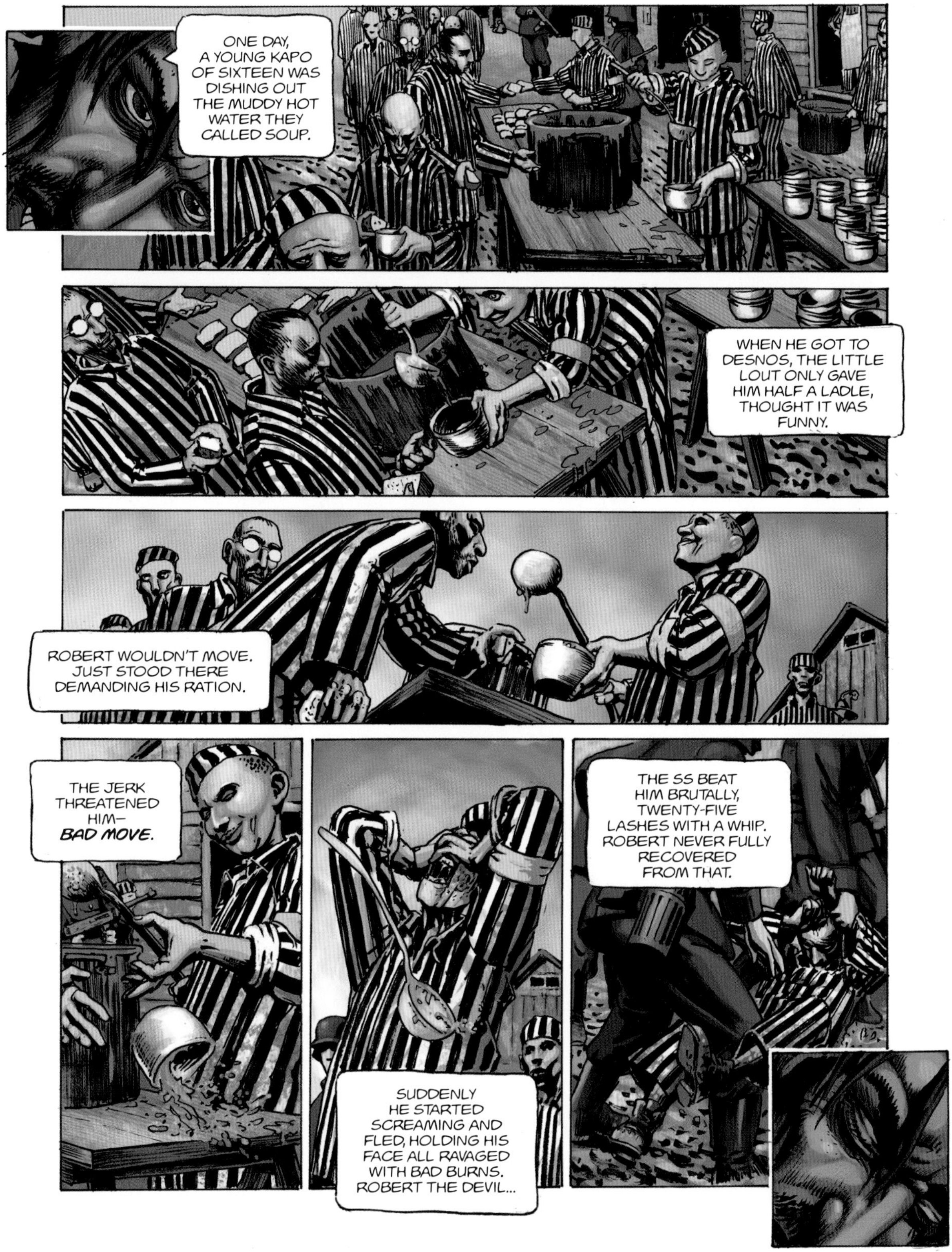
ONE DAY, A YOUNG KAPO OF SIXTEEN WAS DISHING OUT THE MUDDY HOT WATER THEY CALLED SOUP.
WHEN HE GOT TO DESNOS, THE LITTLE LOUT ONLY GAVE HIM HALF A LADLE, THOUGHT IT WAS FUNNY.
ROBERT WOULDN'T MOVE. JUST STOOD THERE DEMANDING HIS RATION.
THE JERK THREATENED HIM— *BAD MOVE*.
SUDDENLY HE STARTED SCREAMING AND FLED, HOLDING HIS FACE ALL RAVAGED WITH BAD BURNS. ROBERT THE DEVIL...
THE SS BEAT HIM BRUTALLY, TWENTY-FIVE LASHES WITH A WHIP. ROBERT NEVER FULLY RECOVERED FROM THAT.

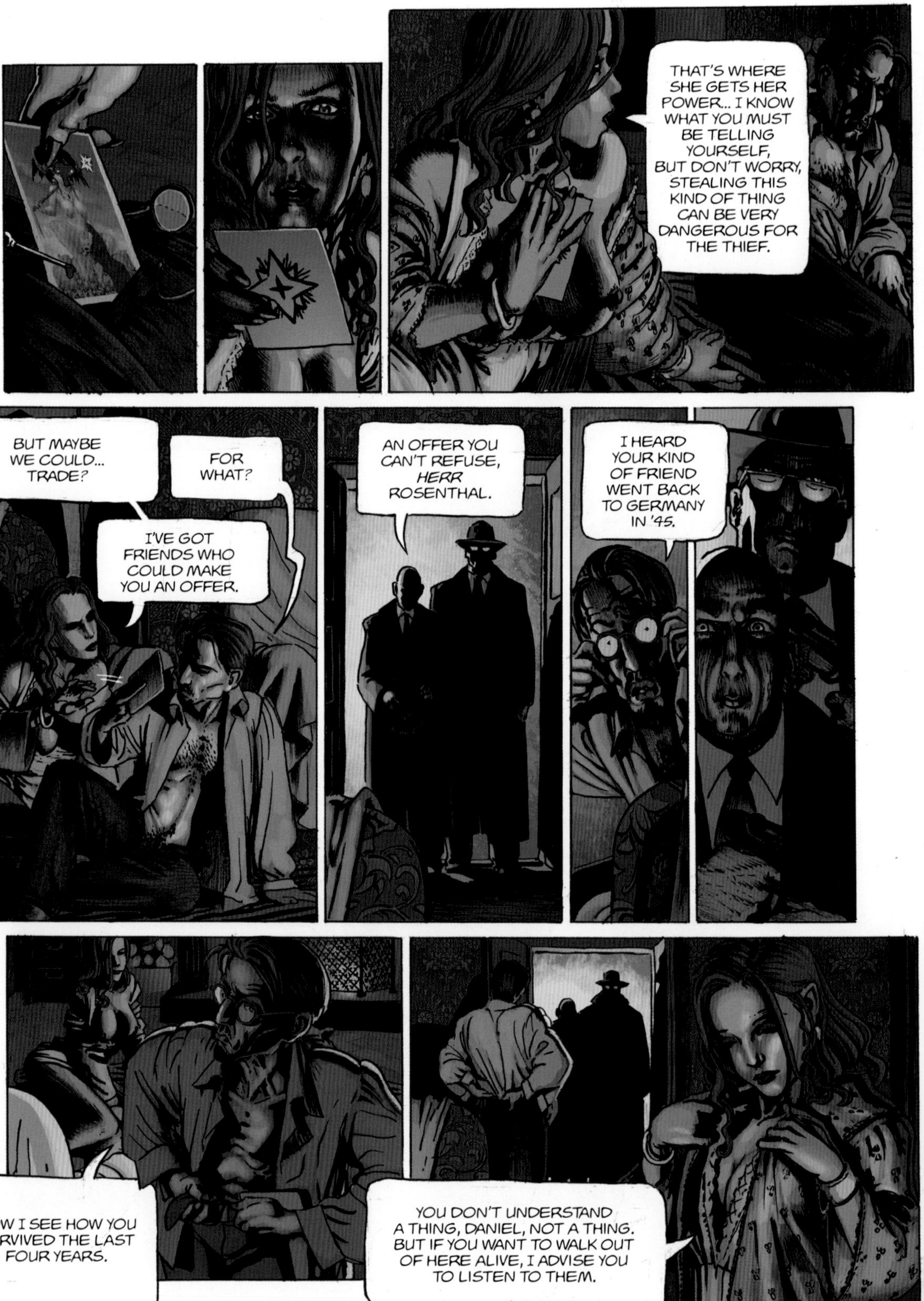

THAT'S WHERE SHE GETS HER POWER... I KNOW WHAT YOU MUST BE TELLING YOURSELF, BUT DON'T WORRY, STEALING THIS KIND OF THING CAN BE VERY DANGEROUS FOR THE THIEF.
BUT MAYBE WE COULD... TRADE?
FOR WHAT?
I'VE GOT FRIENDS WHO COULD MAKE YOU AN OFFER.
AN OFFER YOU CAN'T REFUSE, HERR ROSENTHAL.
I HEARD YOUR KIND OF FRIEND WENT BACK TO GERMANY IN '45.
NOW I SEE HOW YOU SURVIVED THE LAST FOUR YEARS.
YOU DON'T UNDERSTAND A THING, DANIEL, NOT A THING. BUT IF YOU WANT TO WALK OUT OF HERE ALIVE, I ADVISE YOU TO LISTEN TO THEM.

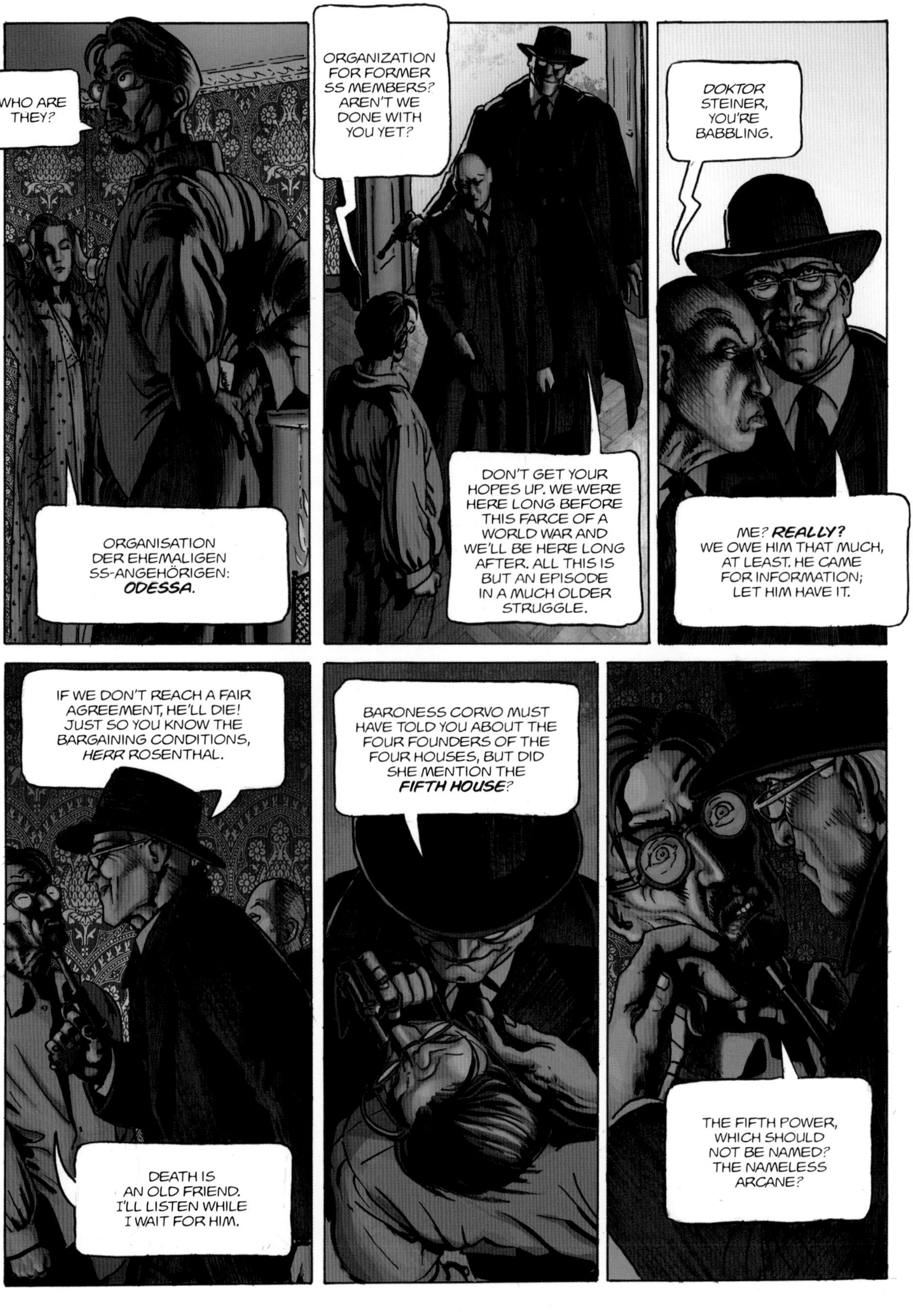
WHO ARE THEY?
ORGANISATION DER EHEMALIGEN SS-ANGEHÖRIGEN: **ODESSA**.
ORGANIZATION FOR FORMER SS MEMBERS? AREN'T WE DONE WITH YOU YET?
DON'T GET YOUR HOPES UP. WE WERE HERE LONG BEFORE THIS FARCE OF A WORLD WAR AND WE'LL BE HERE LONG AFTER. ALL THIS IS BUT AN EPISODE IN A MUCH OLDER STRUGGLE.
DOKTOR STEINER, YOU'RE BABBLING.
ME? ***REALLY?*** WE OWE HIM THAT MUCH, AT LEAST. HE CAME FOR INFORMATION; LET HIM HAVE IT.
IF WE DON'T REACH A FAIR AGREEMENT, HE'LL DIE! JUST SO YOU KNOW THE BARGAINING CONDITIONS, *HERR* ROSENTHAL.
DEATH IS AN OLD FRIEND. I'LL LISTEN WHILE I WAIT FOR HIM.
BARONESS CORVO MUST HAVE TOLD YOU ABOUT THE FOUR FOUNDERS OF THE FOUR HOUSES, BUT DID SHE MENTION THE ***FIFTH HOUSE***?
THE FIFTH POWER, WHICH SHOULD NOT BE NAMED? THE NAMELESS ARCANE?

BRAVO, YOU LEARN FAST. OR PERHAPS OUR BARONESS CAN'T KEEP HER MOUTH SHUT?

I DIDN'T SAY ANYTHING!

SO THAT'S HOW IT IS. SORRY, BUT WE CAN'T TAKE RISKS. NONE MUST KNOW THE RED MONKS STILL EXIST.

BAM!

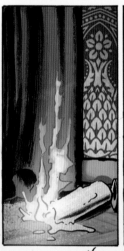

BAM!

BAM! BAM!

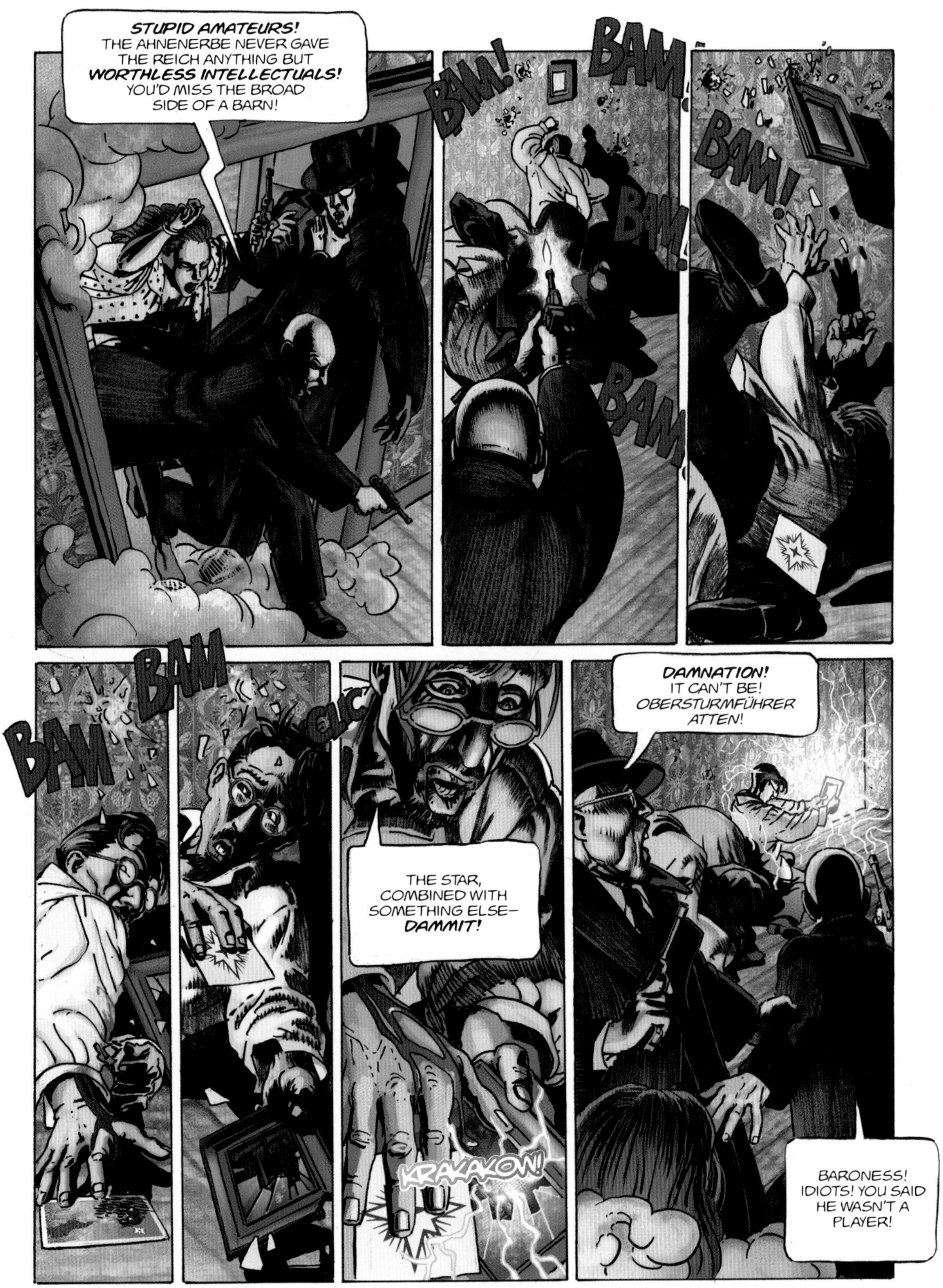
STUPID AMATEURS! THE AHNENERBE NEVER GAVE THE REICH ANYTHING BUT WORTHLESS INTELLECTUALS! YOU'D MISS THE BROAD SIDE OF A BARN!
BAM!
BAM
BAM!
BAM!
BAM
BAM
BAM
BAM
CLIC
THE STAR, COMBINED WITH SOMETHING ELSE— DAMMIT!
KRAKAKOM!
DAMNATION! IT CAN'T BE! OBERSTURMFÜHRER ATTEN!
BARONESS! IDIOTS! YOU SAID HE WASN'T A PLAYER!

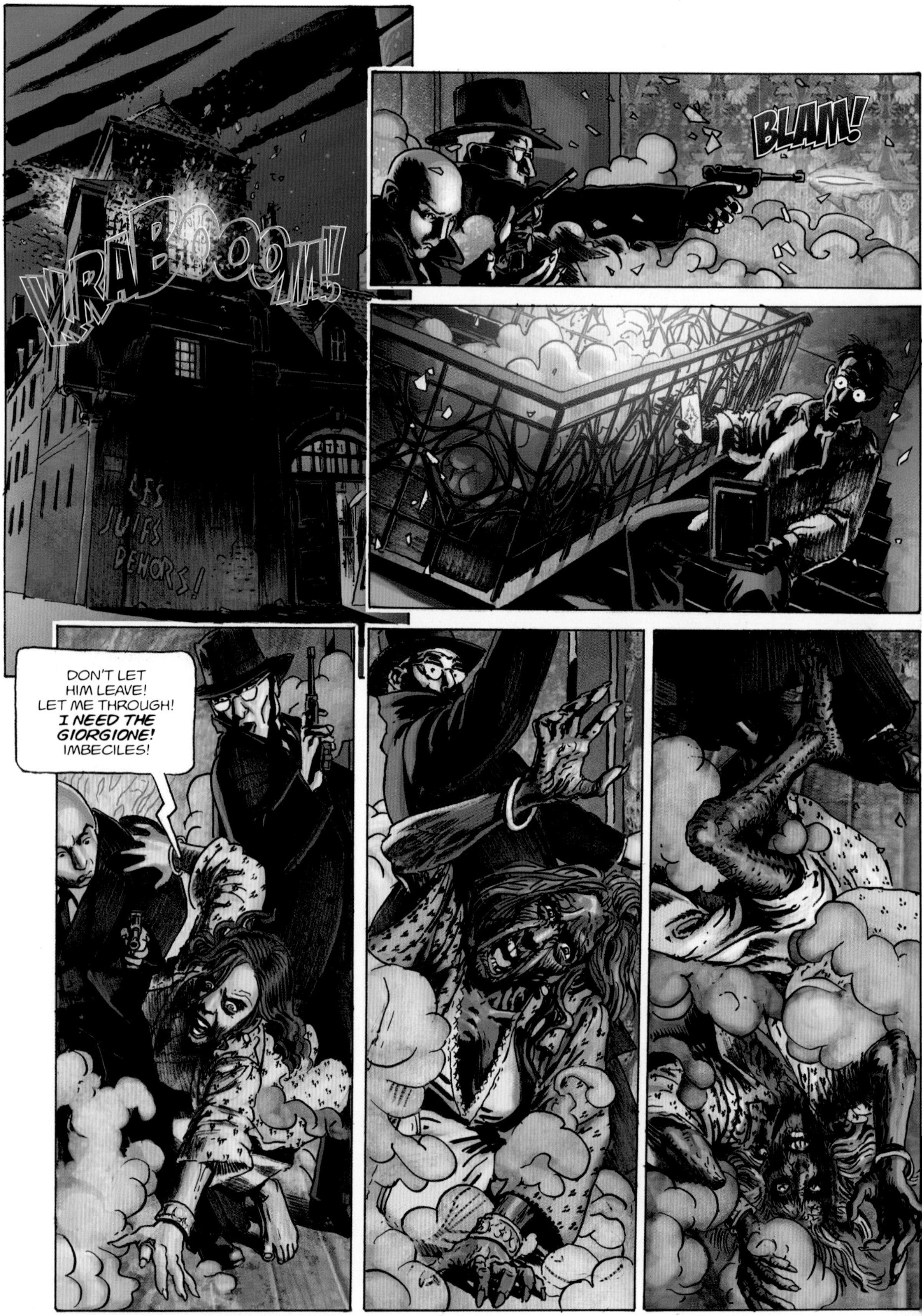
KRABOOOM!!
LES JUIFS DEHORS!
BLAM!
DON'T LET HIM LEAVE! LET ME THROUGH! **I NEED THE GIORGIONE!** IMBECILES!

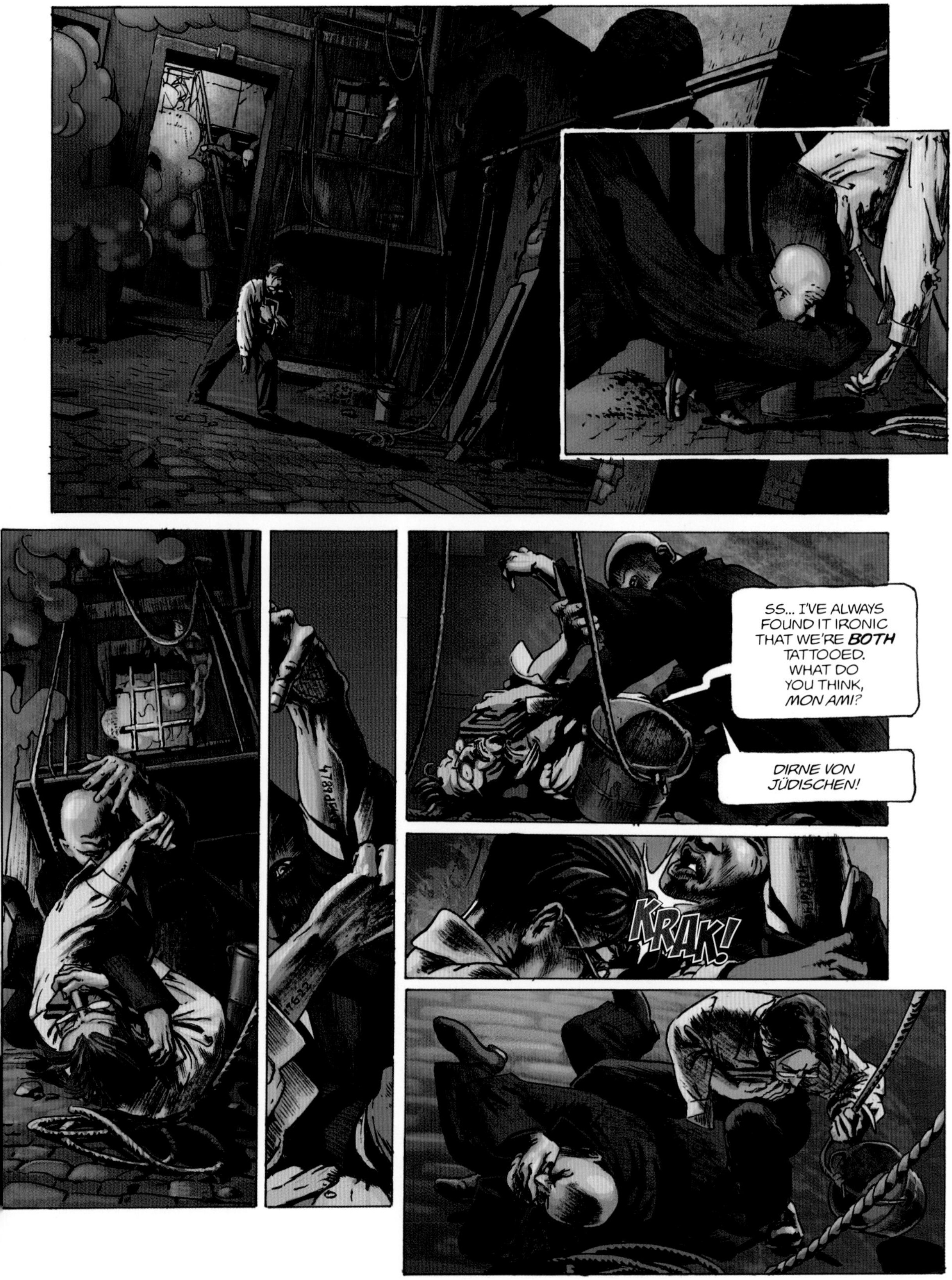
SS... I'VE ALWAYS FOUND IT IRONIC THAT WE'RE **BOTH** TATTOOED. WHAT DO YOU THINK, *MON AMI?*
DIRNE VON JÜDISCHEN!
KRAK!

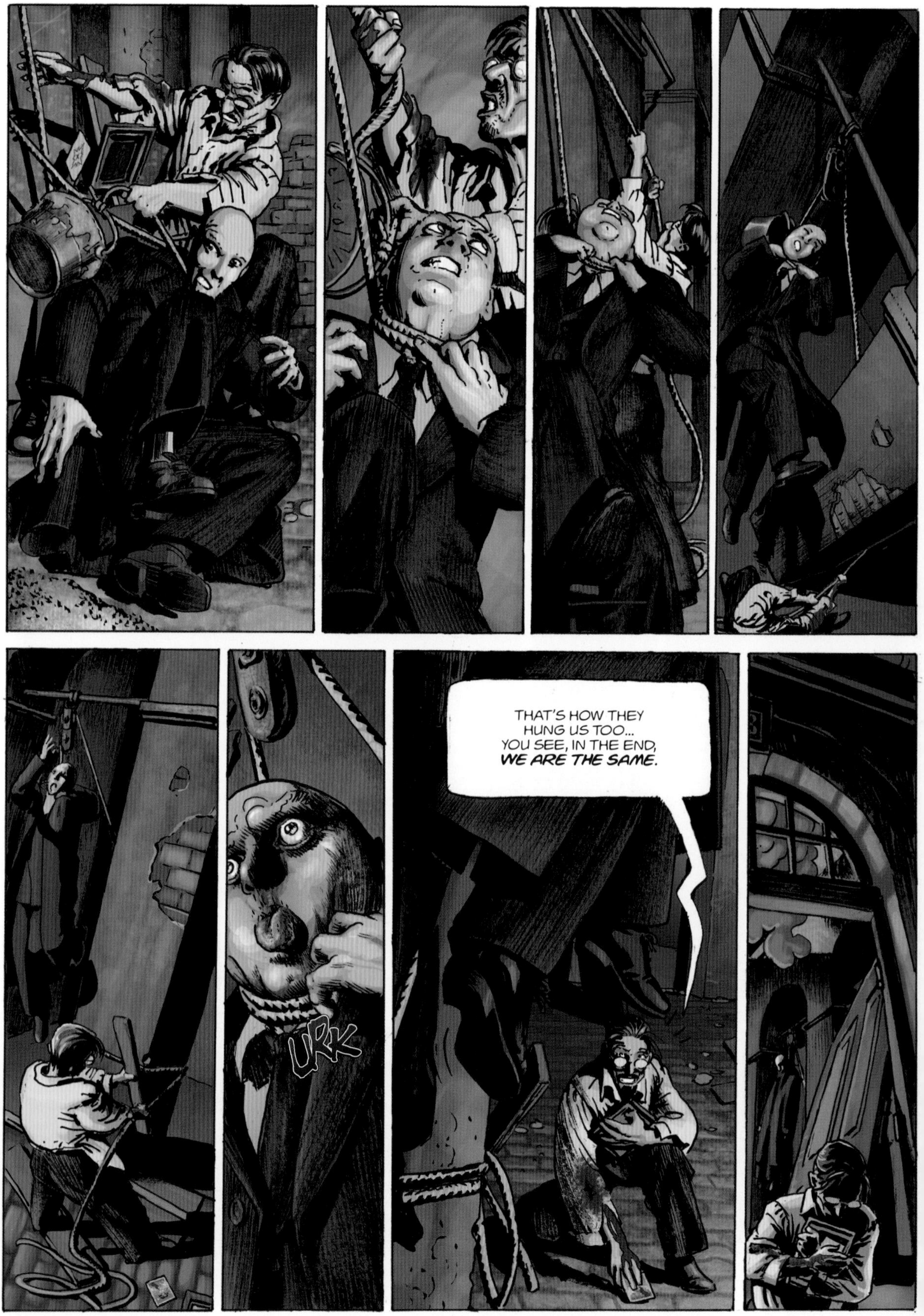
THAT'S HOW THEY
HUNG US TOO...
YOU SEE, IN THE END,
WE ARE THE SAME.
URK

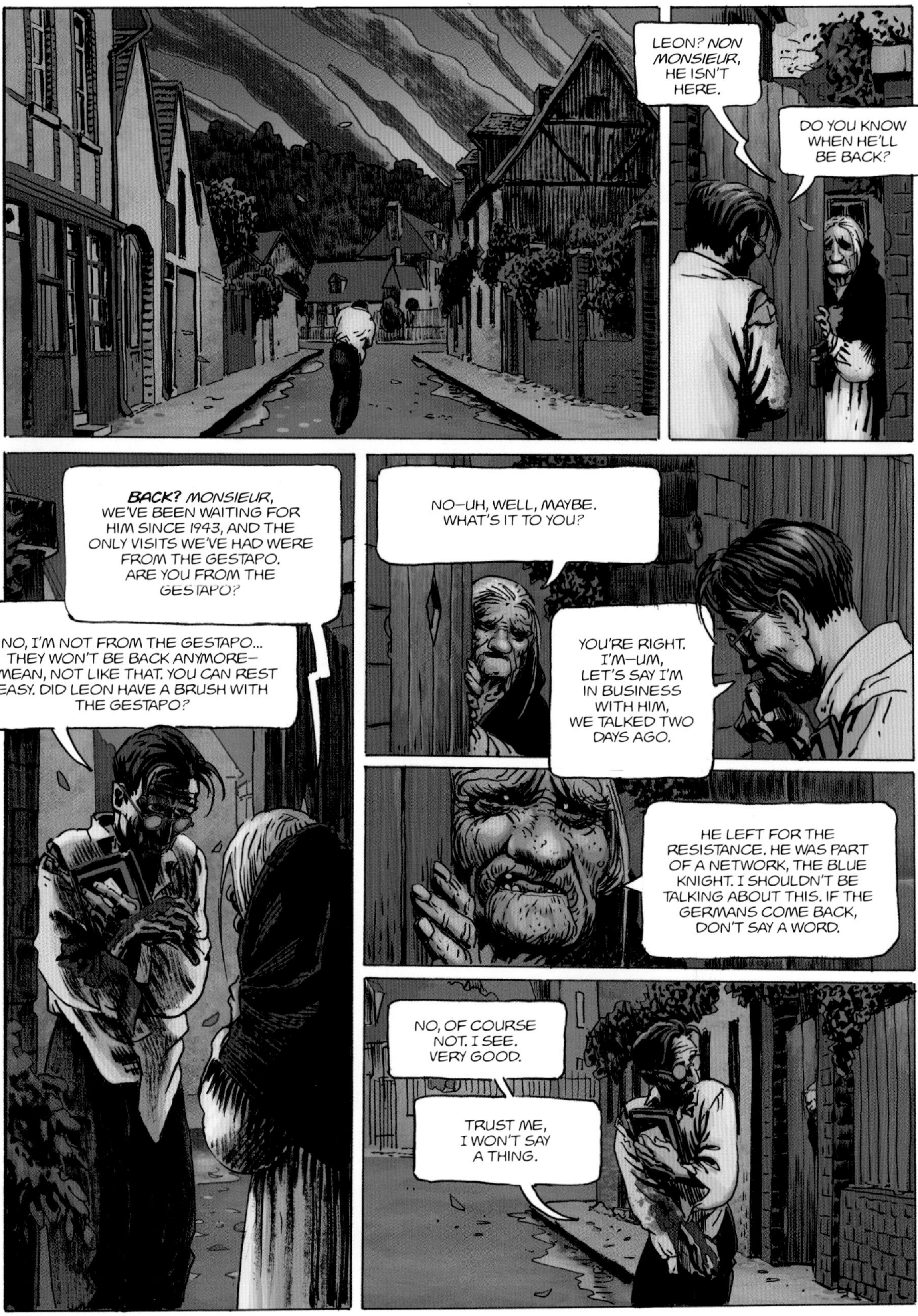
LEON? *NON MONSIEUR*, HE ISN'T HERE.
DO YOU KNOW WHEN HE'LL BE BACK?
BACK? *MONSIEUR*, WE'VE BEEN WAITING FOR HIM SINCE 1943, AND THE ONLY VISITS WE'VE HAD WERE FROM THE GESTAPO. ARE YOU FROM THE GESTAPO?
NO, I'M NOT FROM THE GESTAPO... THEY WON'T BE BACK ANYMORE—I MEAN, NOT LIKE THAT. YOU CAN REST EASY. DID LEON HAVE A BRUSH WITH THE GESTAPO?
NO—UH, WELL, MAYBE. WHAT'S IT TO YOU?
YOU'RE RIGHT. I'M—UM, LET'S SAY I'M IN BUSINESS WITH HIM, WE TALKED TWO DAYS AGO.
HE LEFT FOR THE RESISTANCE. HE WAS PART OF A NETWORK, THE BLUE KNIGHT. I SHOULDN'T BE TALKING ABOUT THIS. IF THE GERMANS COME BACK, DON'T SAY A WORD.
NO, OF COURSE NOT. I SEE. VERY GOOD.
TRUST ME, I WON'T SAY A THING.

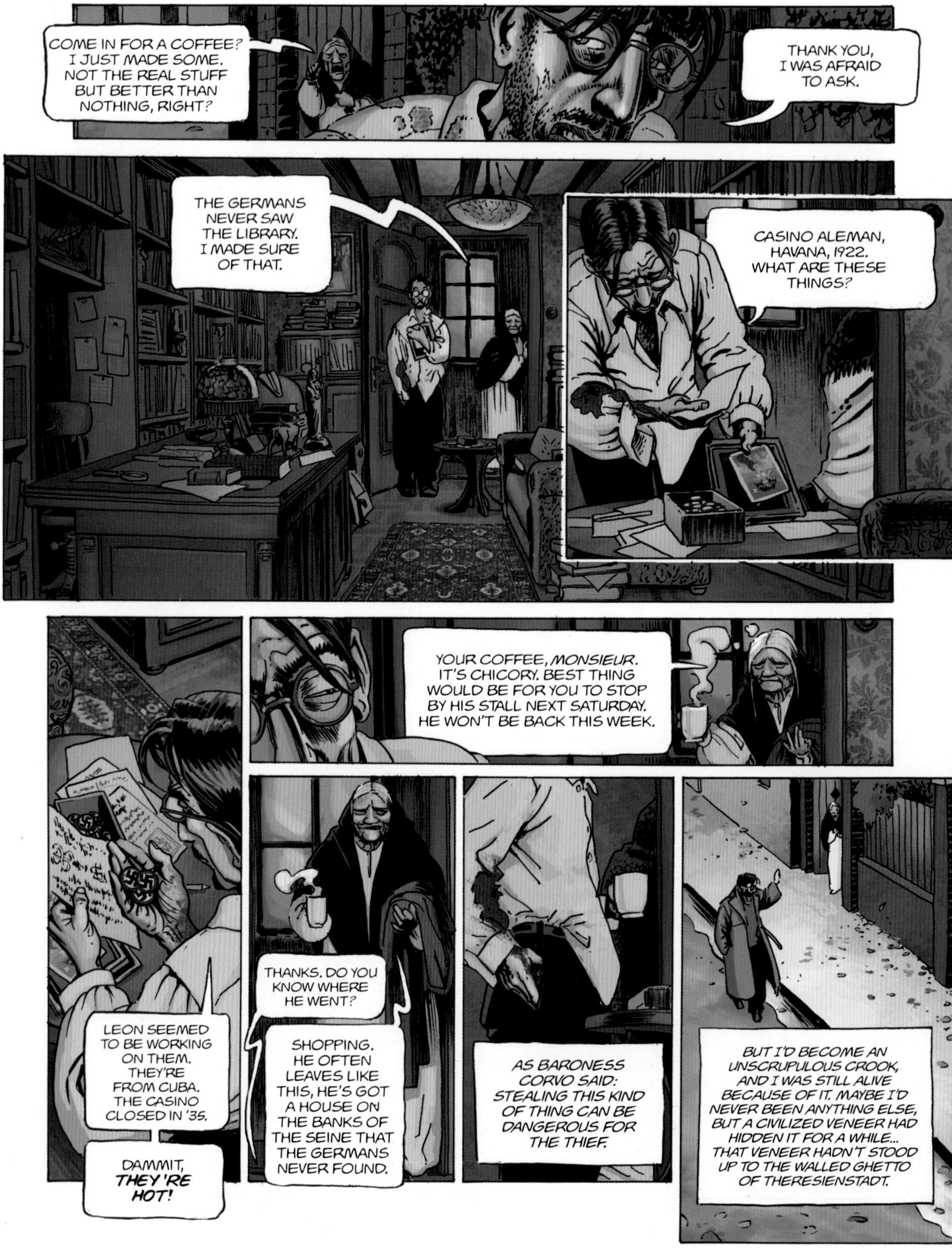
COME IN FOR A COFFEE? I JUST MADE SOME. NOT THE REAL STUFF BUT BETTER THAN NOTHING, RIGHT?
THANK YOU, I WAS AFRAID TO ASK.
THE GERMANS NEVER SAW THE LIBRARY. I MADE SURE OF THAT.
CASINO ALEMAN, HAVANA, 1922. WHAT ARE THESE THINGS?
LEON SEEMED TO BE WORKING ON THEM. THEY'RE FROM CUBA. THE CASINO CLOSED IN '35.
DAMMIT, ***THEY'RE HOT!***
YOUR COFFEE, *MONSIEUR*. IT'S CHICORY. BEST THING WOULD BE FOR YOU TO STOP BY HIS STALL NEXT SATURDAY. HE WON'T BE BACK THIS WEEK.
THANKS. DO YOU KNOW WHERE HE WENT?
SHOPPING. HE OFTEN LEAVES LIKE THIS, HE'S GOT A HOUSE ON THE BANKS OF THE SEINE THAT THE GERMANS NEVER FOUND.
AS BARONESS CORVO SAID: STEALING THIS KIND OF THING CAN BE DANGEROUS FOR THE THIEF.
BUT I'D BECOME AN UNSCRUPULOUS CROOK, AND I WAS STILL ALIVE BECAUSE OF IT. MAYBE I'D NEVER BEEN ANYTHING ELSE, BUT A CIVILIZED VENEER HAD HIDDEN IT FOR A WHILE... THAT VENEER HADN'T STOOD UP TO THE WALLED GHETTO OF THERESIENSTADT.

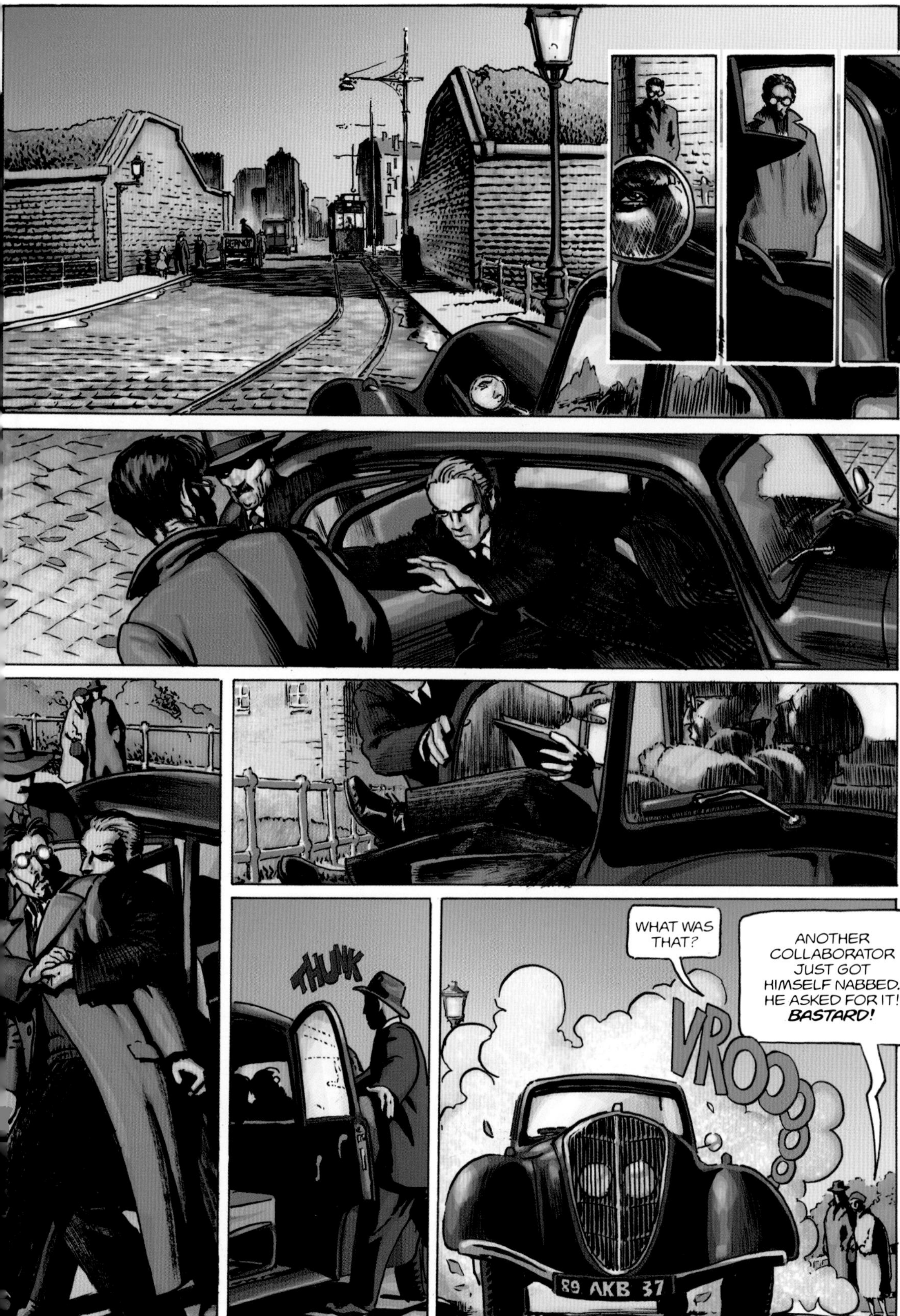
THUNK
WHAT WAS THAT?
VROOOOOO
ANOTHER COLLABORATOR JUST GOT HIMSELF NABBED. HE ASKED FOR IT! ***BASTARD!***
89 AKB 37

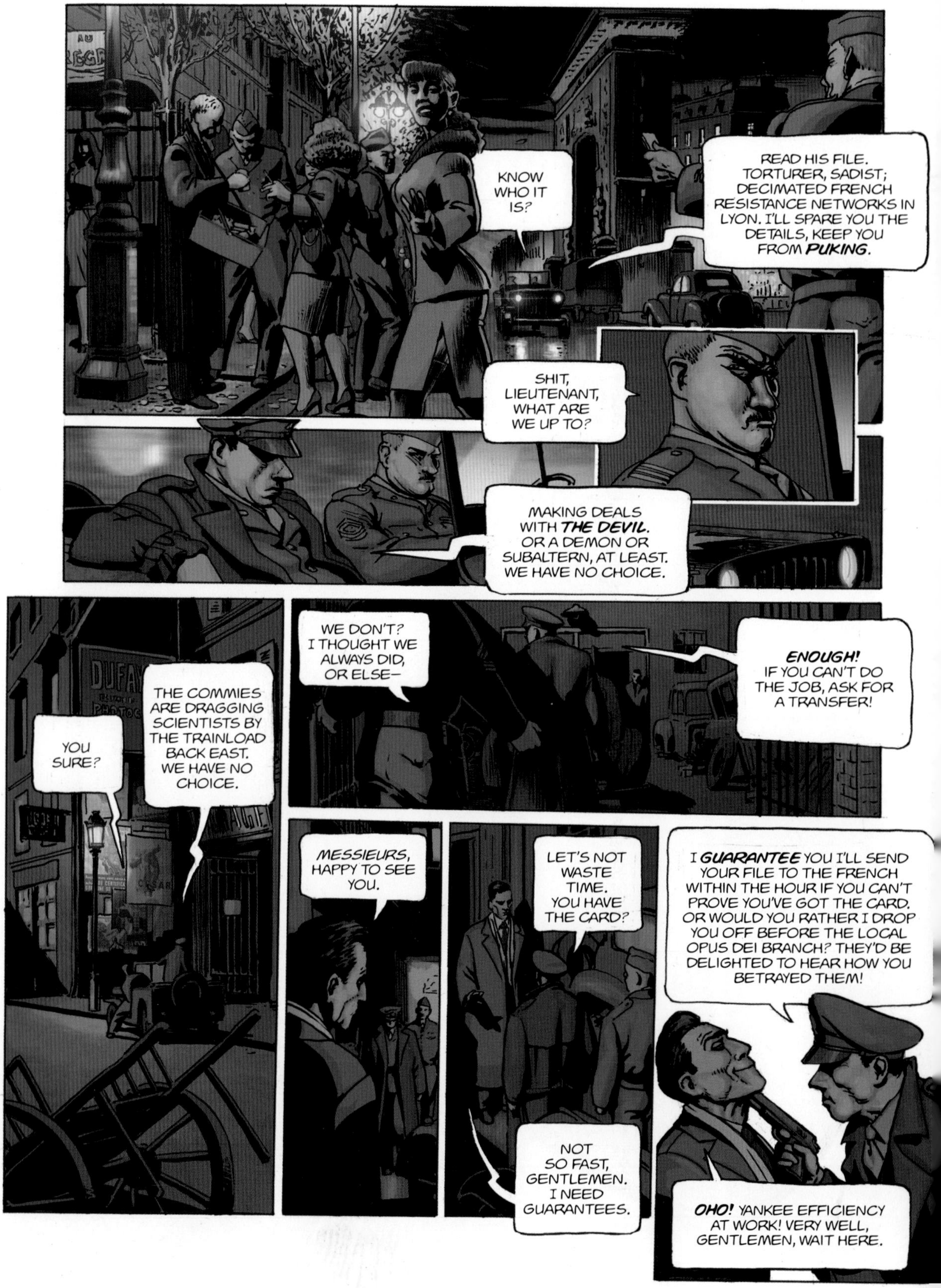
KNOW WHO IT IS?
READ HIS FILE. TORTURER, SADIST; DECIMATED FRENCH RESISTANCE NETWORKS IN LYON. I'LL SPARE YOU THE DETAILS, KEEP YOU FROM PUKING.
SHIT, LIEUTENANT, WHAT ARE WE UP TO?
MAKING DEALS WITH THE DEVIL. OR A DEMON OR SUBALTERN, AT LEAST. WE HAVE NO CHOICE.
YOU SURE?
THE COMMIES ARE DRAGGING SCIENTISTS BY THE TRAINLOAD BACK EAST. WE HAVE NO CHOICE.
WE DON'T? I THOUGHT WE ALWAYS DID, OR ELSE–
ENOUGH! IF YOU CAN'T DO THE JOB, ASK FOR A TRANSFER!
MESSIEURS, HAPPY TO SEE YOU.
LET'S NOT WASTE TIME. YOU HAVE THE CARD?
NOT SO FAST, GENTLEMEN. I NEED GUARANTEES.
I GUARANTEE YOU I'LL SEND YOUR FILE TO THE FRENCH WITHIN THE HOUR IF YOU CAN'T PROVE YOU'VE GOT THE CARD. OR WOULD YOU RATHER I DROP YOU OFF BEFORE THE LOCAL OPUS DEI BRANCH? THEY'D BE DELIGHTED TO HEAR HOW YOU BETRAYED THEM!
OHO! YANKEE EFFICIENCY AT WORK! VERY WELL, GENTLEMEN, WAIT HERE.

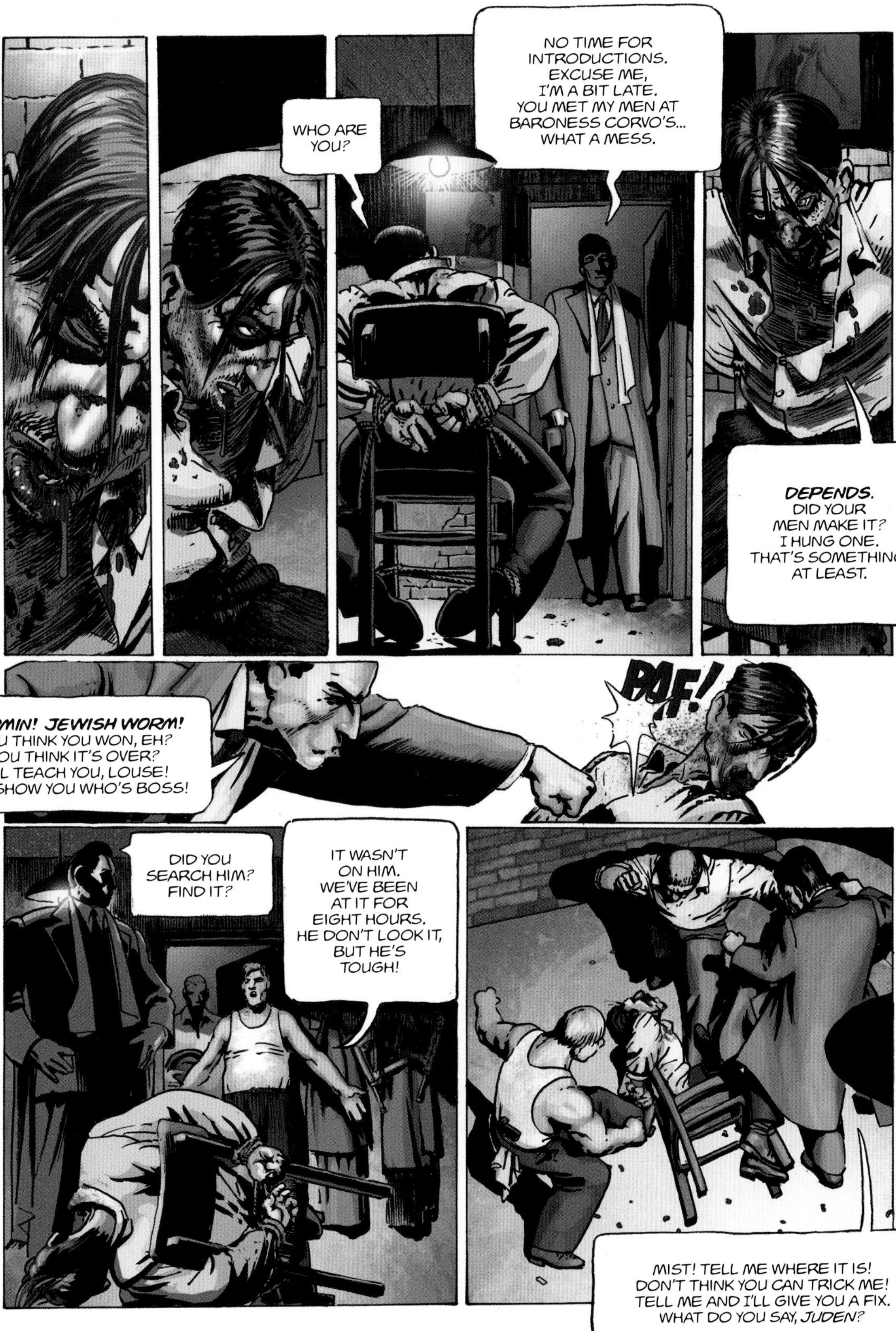
WHO ARE YOU?
NO TIME FOR INTRODUCTIONS. EXCUSE ME, I'M A BIT LATE. YOU MET MY MEN AT BARONESS CORVO'S... WHAT A MESS.
DEPENDS. DID YOUR MEN MAKE IT? I HUNG ONE. THAT'S SOMETHING, AT LEAST.
VERMIN! JEWISH WORM! YOU THINK YOU WON, EH? YOU THINK IT'S OVER? I'LL TEACH YOU, LOUSE! I'LL SHOW YOU WHO'S BOSS!
BAF!
DID YOU SEARCH HIM? FIND IT?
IT WASN'T ON HIM. WE'VE BEEN AT IT FOR EIGHT HOURS. HE DON'T LOOK IT, BUT HE'S TOUGH!
MIST! TELL ME WHERE IT IS! DON'T THINK YOU CAN TRICK ME! TELL ME AND I'LL GIVE YOU A FIX. WHAT DO YOU SAY, JUDEN?

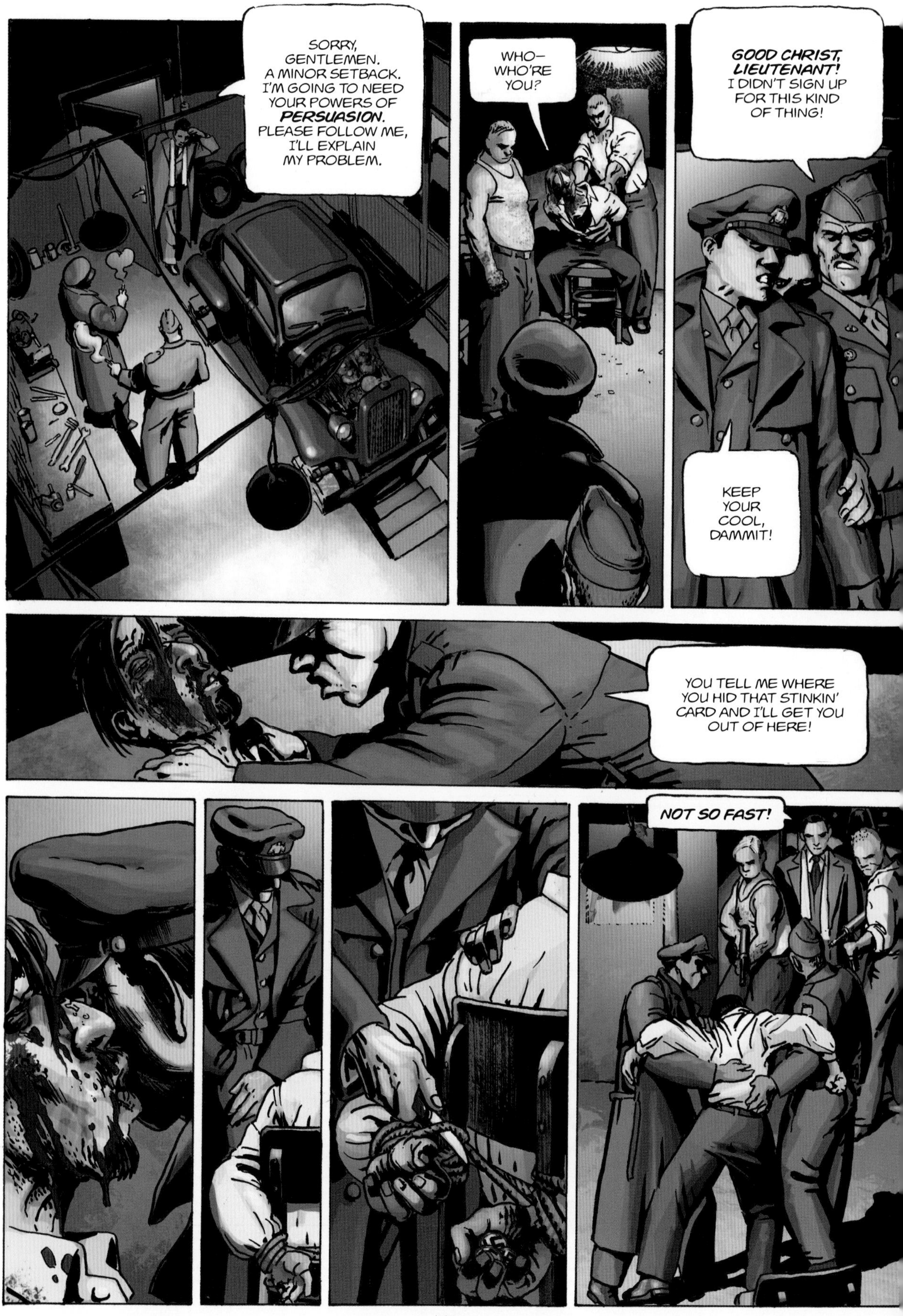
SORRY, GENTLEMEN. A MINOR SETBACK. I'M GOING TO NEED YOUR POWERS OF **PERSUASION.** PLEASE FOLLOW ME, I'LL EXPLAIN MY PROBLEM.
WHO— WHO'RE YOU?
GOOD CHRIST, LIEUTENANT! I DIDN'T SIGN UP FOR THIS KIND OF THING!
KEEP YOUR COOL, DAMMIT!
YOU TELL ME WHERE YOU HID THAT STINKIN' CARD AND I'LL GET YOU OUT OF HERE!
NOT SO FAST!

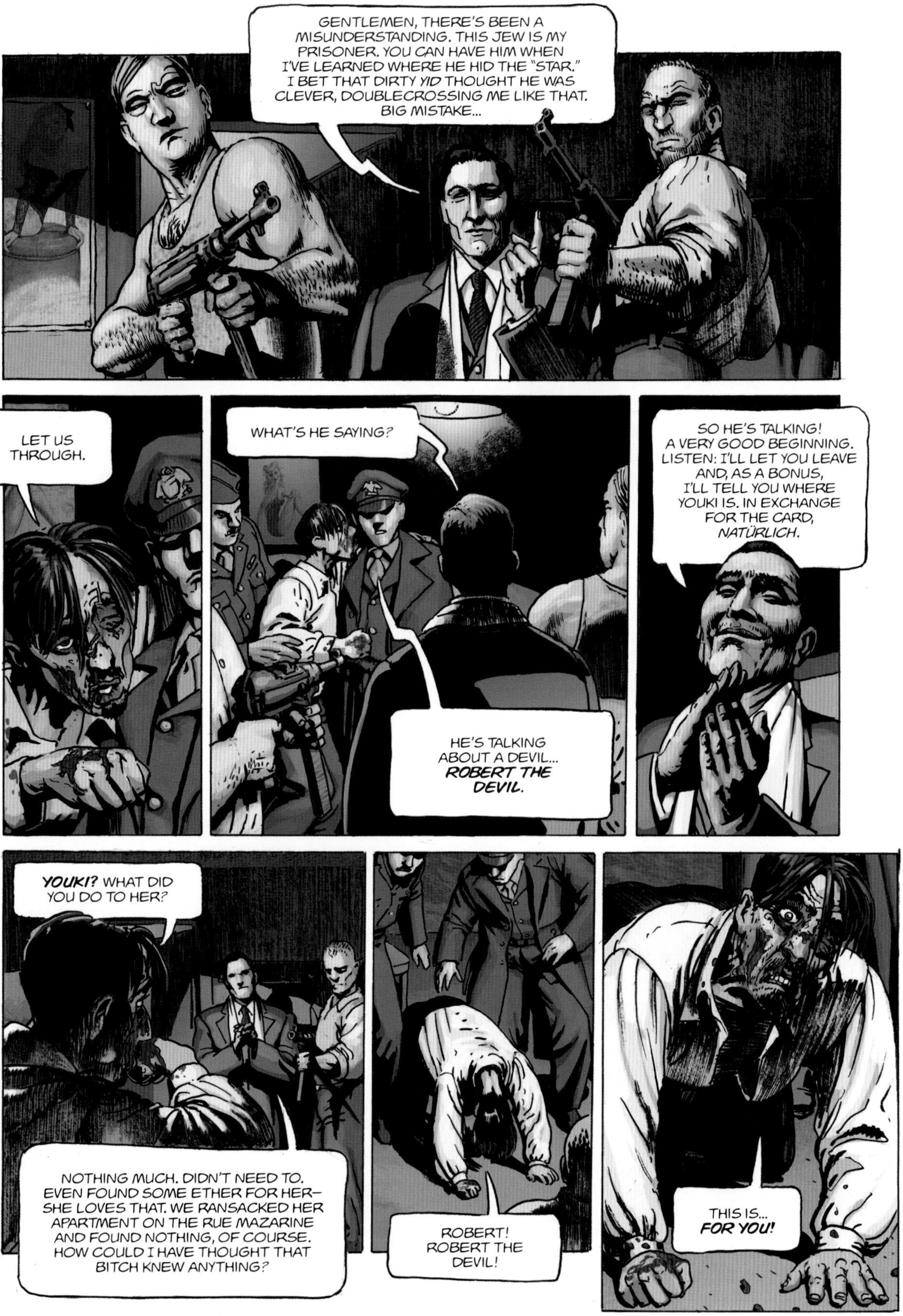
GENTLEMEN, THERE'S BEEN A MISUNDERSTANDING. THIS JEW IS MY PRISONER. YOU CAN HAVE HIM WHEN I'VE LEARNED WHERE HE HID THE "STAR." I BET THAT DIRTY *YID* THOUGHT HE WAS CLEVER, DOUBLECROSSING ME LIKE THAT. BIG MISTAKE...
LET US THROUGH.
WHAT'S HE SAYING?
HE'S TALKING ABOUT A DEVIL... ***ROBERT THE DEVIL.***
SO HE'S TALKING! A VERY GOOD BEGINNING. LISTEN: I'LL LET YOU LEAVE AND, AS A BONUS, I'LL TELL YOU WHERE YOUKI IS. IN EXCHANGE FOR THE CARD, *NATÜRLICH.*
YOUKI? WHAT DID YOU DO TO HER?
NOTHING MUCH. DIDN'T NEED TO. EVEN FOUND SOME ETHER FOR HER— SHE LOVES THAT. WE RANSACKED HER APARTMENT ON THE RUE MAZARINE AND FOUND NOTHING, OF COURSE. HOW COULD I HAVE THOUGHT THAT BITCH KNEW ANYTHING?
ROBERT! ROBERT THE DEVIL!
THIS IS... ***FOR YOU!***

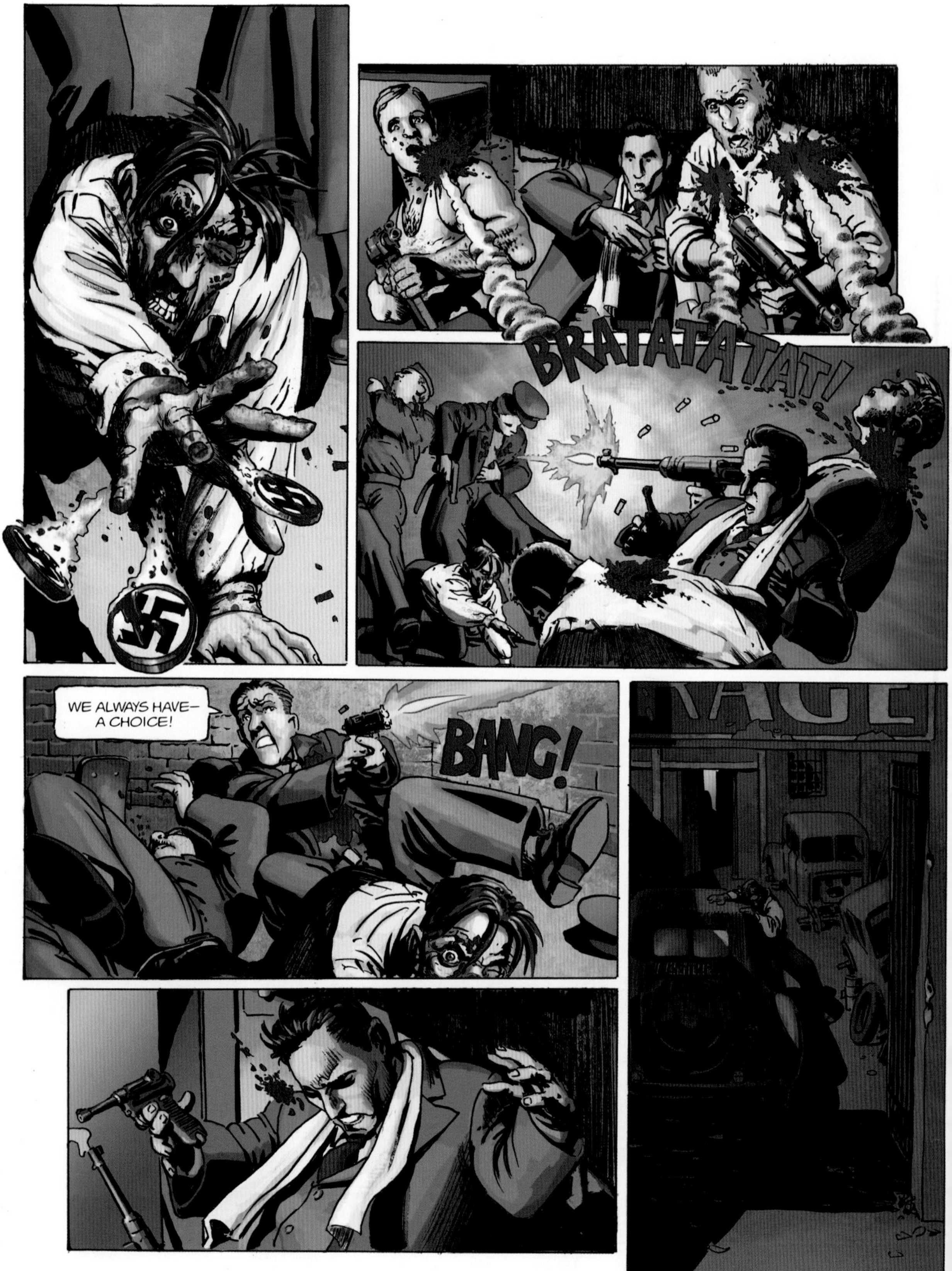
BRATATATAT!
WE ALWAYS HAVE—
A CHOICE!
BANG!

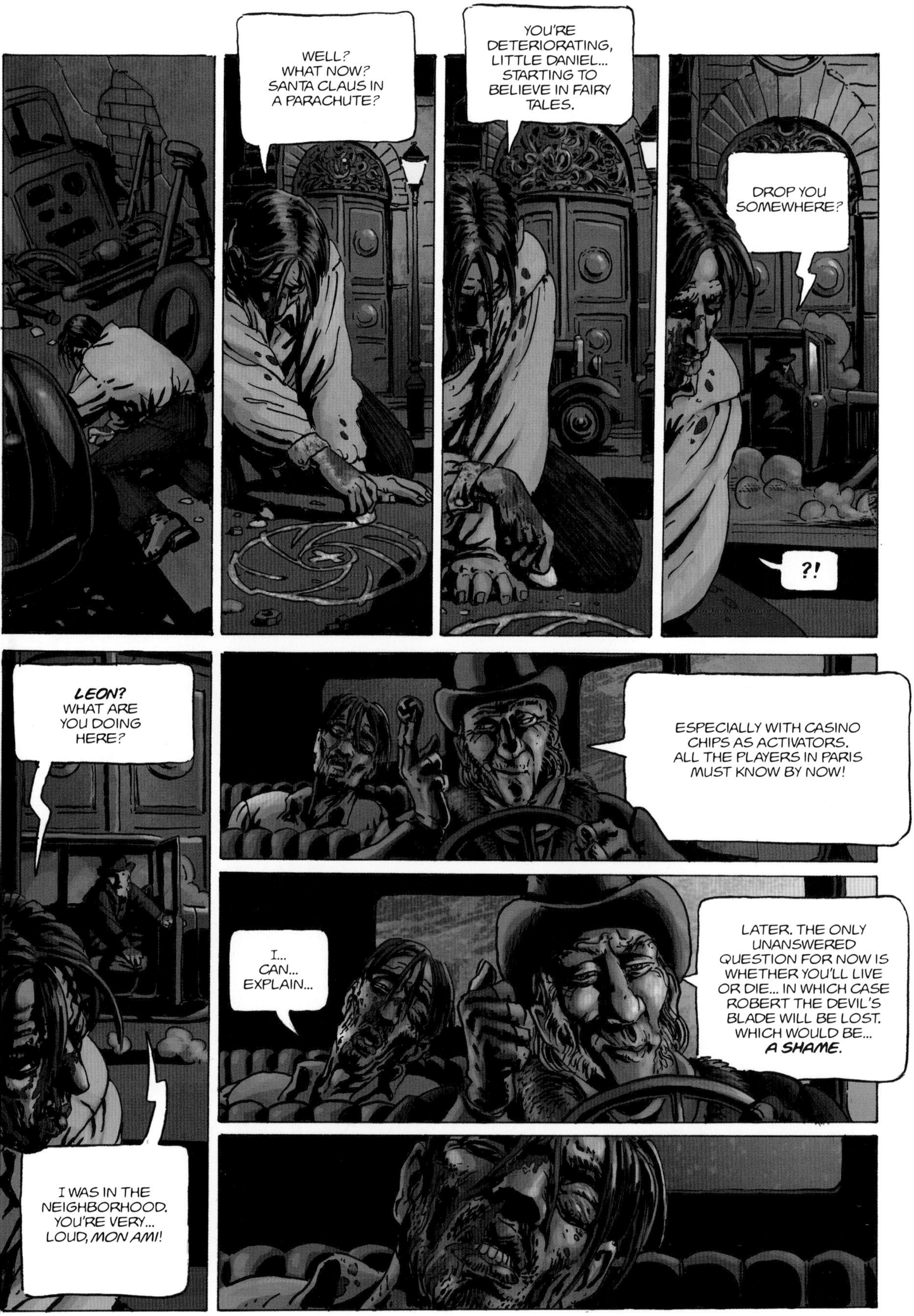
WELL? WHAT NOW? SANTA CLAUS IN A PARACHUTE?
YOU'RE DETERIORATING, LITTLE DANIEL... STARTING TO BELIEVE IN FAIRY TALES.
DROP YOU SOMEWHERE?
?!
LEON? WHAT ARE YOU DOING HERE?
I WAS IN THE NEIGHBORHOOD. YOU'RE VERY... LOUD, *MON AMI*!
ESPECIALLY WITH CASINO CHIPS AS ACTIVATORS. ALL THE PLAYERS IN PARIS MUST KNOW BY NOW!
I... CAN... EXPLAIN...
LATER. THE ONLY UNANSWERED QUESTION FOR NOW IS WHETHER YOU'LL LIVE OR DIE... IN WHICH CASE ROBERT THE DEVIL'S BLADE WILL BE LOST. WHICH WOULD BE... ***A SHAME.***

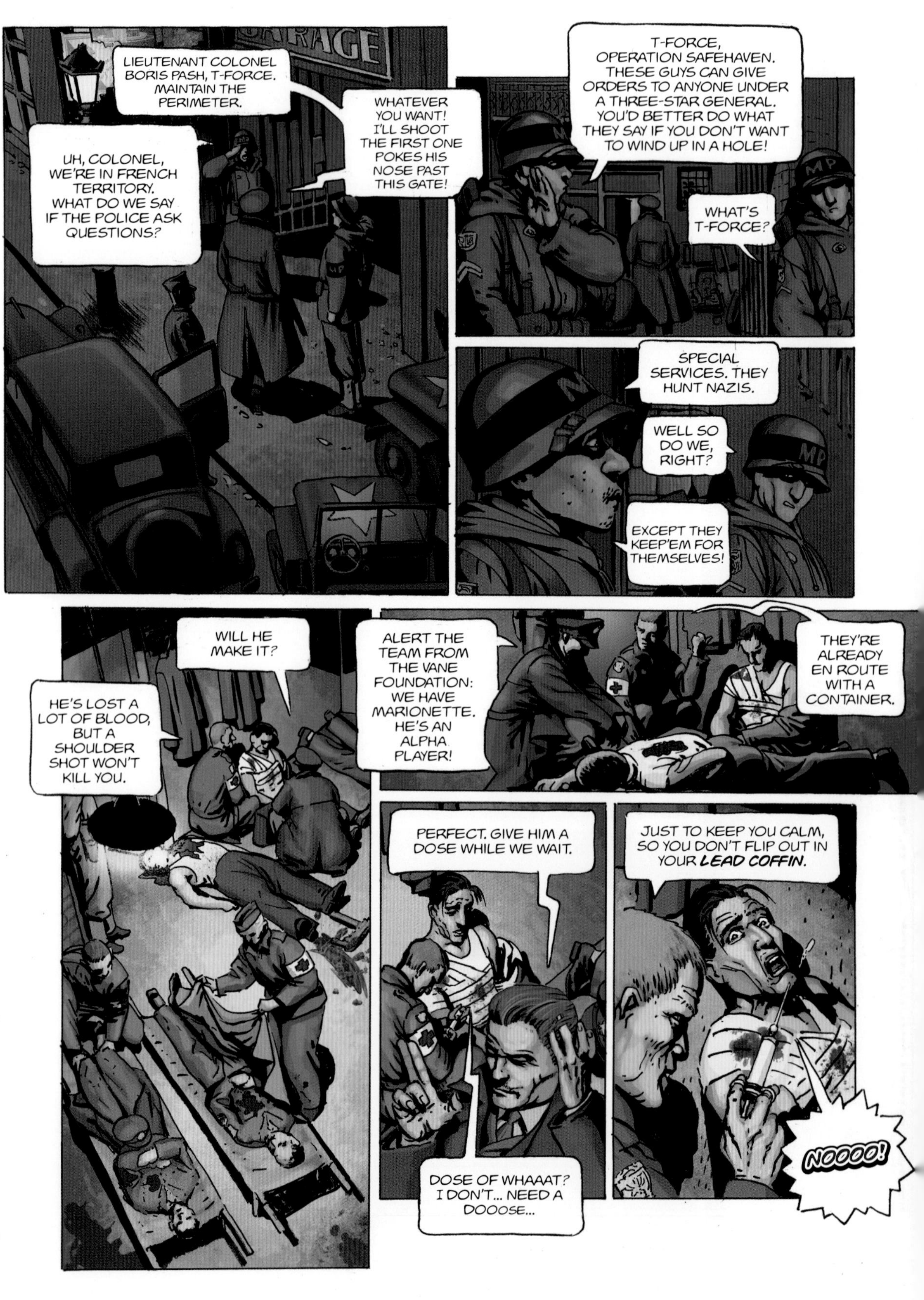
GARAGE
LIEUTENANT COLONEL BORIS PASH, T-FORCE. MAINTAIN THE PERIMETER.
WHATEVER YOU WANT! I'LL SHOOT THE FIRST ONE POKES HIS NOSE PAST THIS GATE!
UH, COLONEL, WE'RE IN FRENCH TERRITORY. WHAT DO WE SAY IF THE POLICE ASK QUESTIONS?
T-FORCE, OPERATION SAFEHAVEN. THESE GUYS CAN GIVE ORDERS TO ANYONE UNDER A THREE-STAR GENERAL. YOU'D BETTER DO WHAT THEY SAY IF YOU DON'T WANT TO WIND UP IN A HOLE!
WHAT'S T-FORCE?
SPECIAL SERVICES. THEY HUNT NAZIS.
WELL SO DO WE, RIGHT?
EXCEPT THEY KEEP'EM FOR THEMSELVES!
WILL HE MAKE IT?
HE'S LOST A LOT OF BLOOD, BUT A SHOULDER SHOT WON'T KILL YOU.
ALERT THE TEAM FROM THE VANE FOUNDATION: WE HAVE MARIONETTE. HE'S AN ALPHA PLAYER!
THEY'RE ALREADY EN ROUTE WITH A CONTAINER.
PERFECT. GIVE HIM A DOSE WHILE WE WAIT.
DOSE OF WHAAAT? I DON'T... NEED A DOOOSE...
JUST TO KEEP YOU CALM, SO YOU DON'T FLIP OUT IN YOUR LEAD COFFIN.
NOOOO!

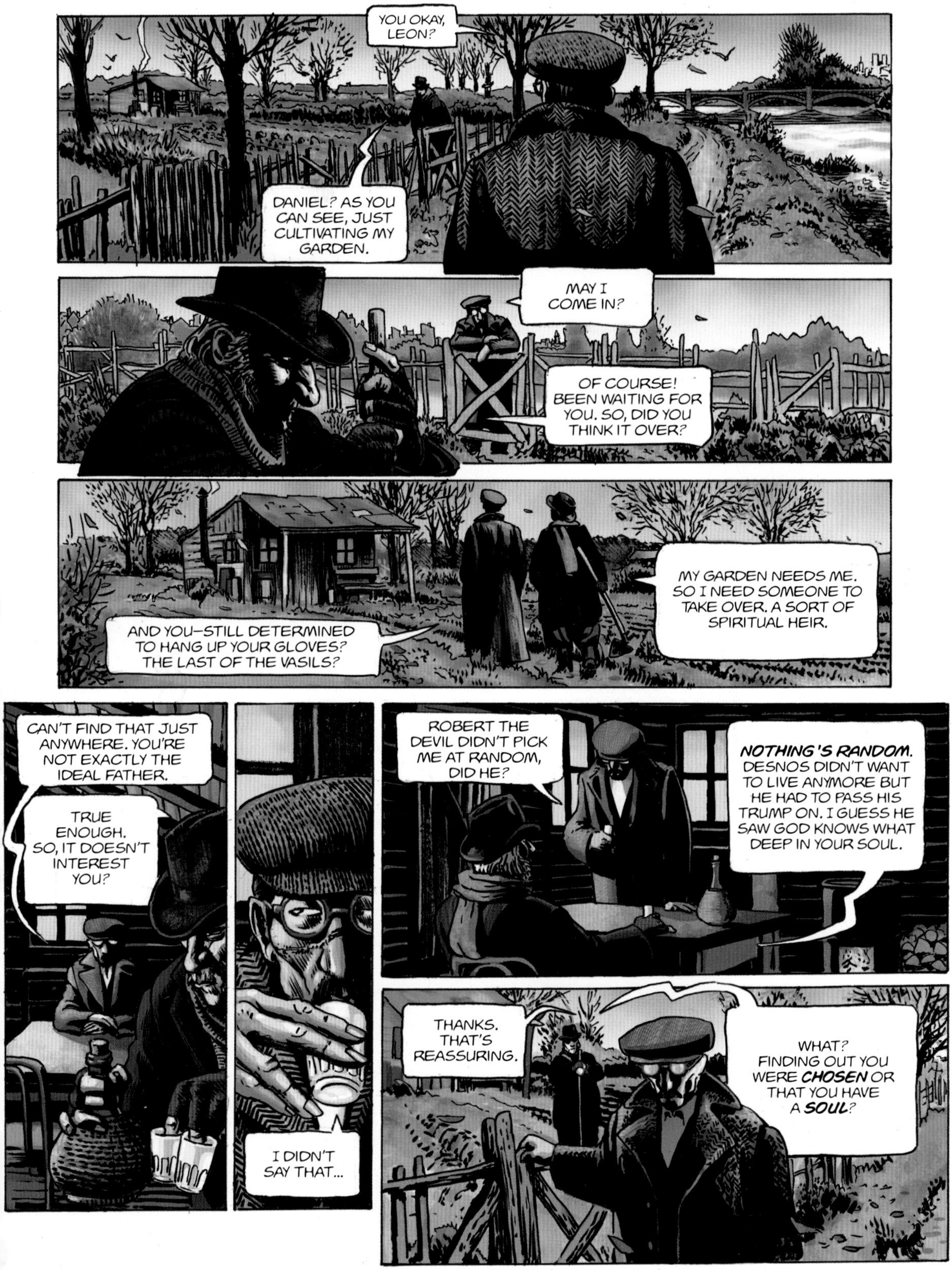
YOU OKAY, LEON?
DANIEL? AS YOU CAN SEE, JUST CULTIVATING MY GARDEN.
MAY I COME IN?
OF COURSE! BEEN WAITING FOR YOU. SO, DID YOU THINK IT OVER?
MY GARDEN NEEDS ME. SO I NEED SOMEONE TO TAKE OVER. A SORT OF SPIRITUAL HEIR.
AND YOU—STILL DETERMINED TO HANG UP YOUR GLOVES? THE LAST OF THE VASILS?
CAN'T FIND THAT JUST ANYWHERE. YOU'RE NOT EXACTLY THE IDEAL FATHER.
TRUE ENOUGH. SO, IT DOESN'T INTEREST YOU?
I DIDN'T SAY THAT...
ROBERT THE DEVIL DIDN'T PICK ME AT RANDOM, DID HE?
NOTHING'S RANDOM. DESNOS DIDN'T WANT TO LIVE ANYMORE BUT HE HAD TO PASS HIS TRUMP ON. I GUESS HE SAW GOD KNOWS WHAT DEEP IN YOUR SOUL.
THANKS. THAT'S REASSURING.
WHAT? FINDING OUT YOU WERE CHOSEN OR THAT YOU HAVE A SOUL?

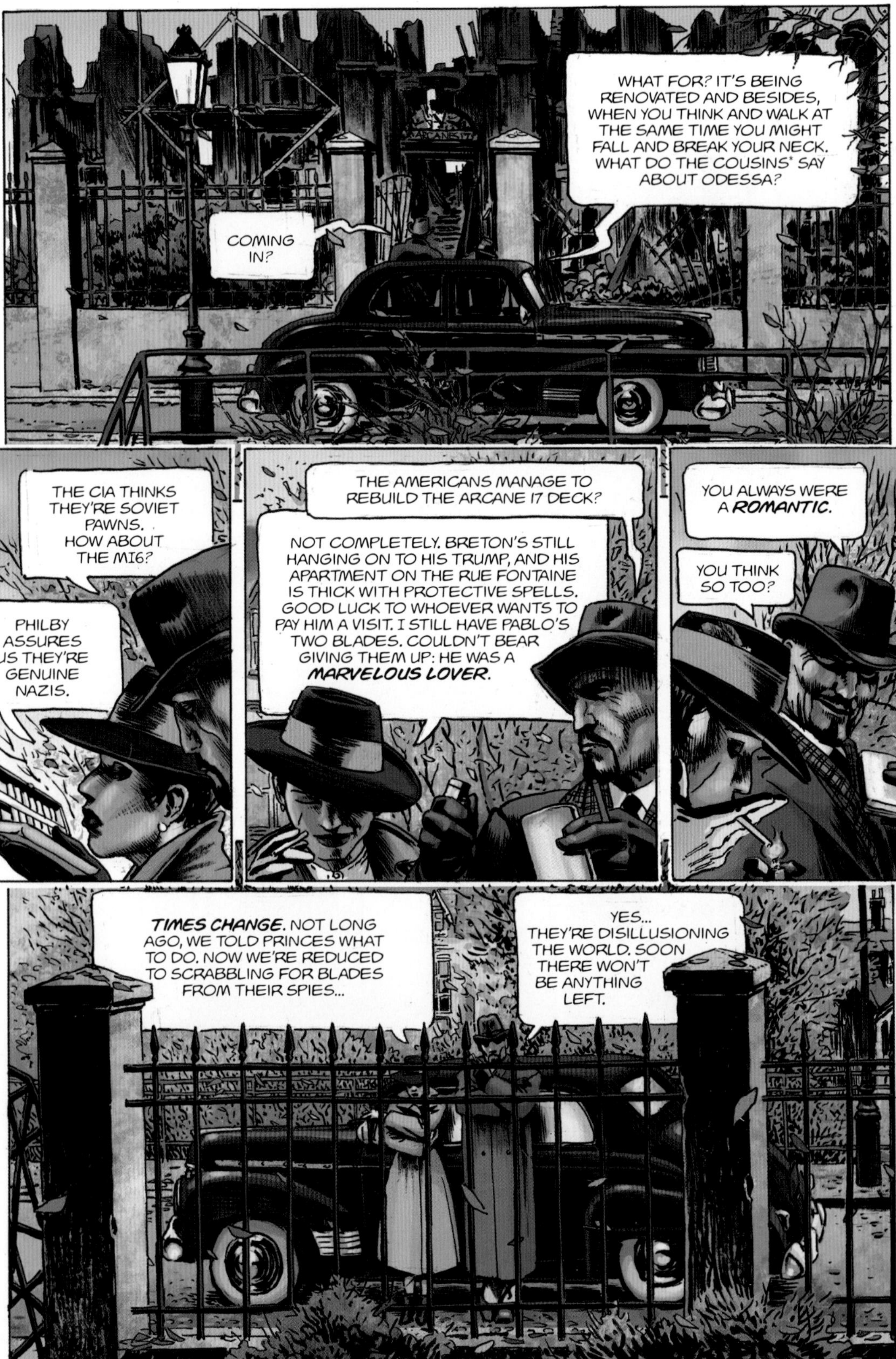
COMING IN?
WHAT FOR? IT'S BEING RENOVATED AND BESIDES, WHEN YOU THINK AND WALK AT THE SAME TIME YOU MIGHT FALL AND BREAK YOUR NECK. WHAT DO THE COUSINS* SAY ABOUT ODESSA?
THE CIA THINKS THEY'RE SOVIET PAWNS. HOW ABOUT THE MI6?
PHILBY ASSURES US THEY'RE GENUINE NAZIS.
THE AMERICANS MANAGE TO REBUILD THE ARCANE 17 DECK?
NOT COMPLETELY. BRETON'S STILL HANGING ON TO HIS TRUMP, AND HIS APARTMENT ON THE RUE FONTAINE IS THICK WITH PROTECTIVE SPELLS. GOOD LUCK TO WHOEVER WANTS TO PAY HIM A VISIT. I STILL HAVE PABLO'S TWO BLADES. COULDN'T BEAR GIVING THEM UP: HE WAS A MARVELOUS LOVER.
YOU ALWAYS WERE A ROMANTIC.
YOU THINK SO TOO?
TIMES CHANGE. NOT LONG AGO, WE TOLD PRINCES WHAT TO DO. NOW WE'RE REDUCED TO SCRABBLING FOR BLADES FROM THEIR SPIES...
YES... THEY'RE DISILLUSIONING THE WORLD. SOON THERE WON'T BE ANYTHING LEFT.

* THE CIA.

END OF THE SECOND CYCLE